Lecture Notes in Computer Science 1512
Edited by G. Goos, J. Hartmanis and J. van Leeuwen

Springer
Berlin
Heidelberg
New York
Barcelona
Budapest
Hong Kong
London
Milan
Paris
Singapore
Tokyo

Eduardo Giménez
Christine Paulin-Mohring (Eds.)

Types for Proofs and Programs

International Workshop TYPES '96
Aussois, France, December 15-19, 1996
Selected Papers

Springer

Volume Editors

Eduardo Giménez
INRIA
Rocquencourt, Domaine de Voluceau
BP 105, F-78153 Le Chesnay Cedex, France
E-mail: Eduardo.Gimenez@inria.fr

Christine Paulin-Mohring
LRI-Bat. 490, Université Paris-Sud
F-91405 Orsay Cedex, France
E-mail: Christine.Paulin@lri.fr

Cataloging-in-Publication data applied for

Die Deutsche Bibliothek - CIP-Einheitsaufnahme

Types for proofs and programs : selected papers / International Workshop TYPES '96, Aussois, France, December 15 - 19, 1996. Eduardo Giménez ; Christine Paulin-Mohring (ed.). - Berlin ; Heidelberg ; New York ; Barcelona ; Budapest ; Hong Kong ; London ; Milan ; Paris ; Singapore ; Tokyo : Springer, 1998
(Lecture notes in computer science ; Vol. 1512)
ISBN 3-540-65137-3

CR Subject Classification (1991): F.3.1, F.4.1, D.3.1, G.4, I.2.3

ISSN 0302-9743
ISBN 3-540-65137-3 Springer-Verlag Berlin Heidelberg New York

Typesetting: Camera-ready by author
SPIN 10692689 06/3142 – 5 4 3 2 1 0 Printed on acid-free paper

Preface

This book is made up of a selection of papers presented at the first annual workshop held under the auspices of the Esprit Working Group 21900 TYPES. It took place in Aussois, France, December 15-19, 1996. The workshop was attended by 89 people.

This volume is a follow-up to the proceedings of the workshops organised in 1993, 1994, and 1995 under the auspices of the Esprit Basic Research Action 6453 *Types for Proofs and Programs*. These proceedings were also published in the LNCS series, edited by Henk Barendregt and Tobias Nipkow (number 806, 1993), by Peter Dybjer, Bengt Nordström, and Jan Smith (number 996, 1994), and by Stefano Berardi and Mario Coppo (number 1158, 1995). The Esprit BRA 6453 was a continuation of the former Esprit Action 3245 *Logical Frameworks: Design, Implementation and Experiments*. The articles from the annual workshops organised under that action were edited by Gérard Huet and Gordon Plotkin in the books *Logical Frameworks* and *Logical Environments*, both published by Cambridge University Press.

Acknowledgments

We thank the following institutions for the funding that made the workshop possible: European Community, *Institut National de Recherche en Informatique et Automatique*, *Ministères de la Recherche et des Affaires Etrangères de France* and *Laboratoire de l'Informatique du Parallélisme de l'Ecole Normale Supérieure de Lyon*. We also thank Valérie Roger-Ubeda and Sylvie Boyer, who both took care of the local arrangements.

Selection

30 papers were submitted and fully reviewed. The final choice was made by the editors. We thank the following people who acted as referees.

Thorsten Altenkirch
Philippe Audebaud
Henk Barendregt
Antony Bailey
Stefano Berardi
Gustavo Betarte
Mark Bezem
Jan Cederquist
Yann Coscoy
Judicaël Courant
Thierry Coquand
Pierre Crégut
René David
Joëlle Despeyroux

Gilles Dowek
Catherine Dubois
Peter Dybjer
Daniel Fridlender
Veronica Gaspes
Herman Geuvers
Eduardo Giménez
Jean Goubault
Thomas Hallgren
John Harrison
Hugo Herbelin
Martin Hoffman
Furio Honsell
Delphine Kaplan-Terrasse
Alain Lecomte
Zhaohui Luo
Petri Mäenpää
Maria Emilia Maietti
James McKinna
Valérie Ménissier-Morain
Dale Miller
César Muñoz
Tobias Nipkow
Christine Paulin
Erik Poll
Randy Pollack
Frédéric Prost
David Pym
Amokrane Saïbi
Anne Salvesen
Carsten Schürmann
Sergei Soloviev
Makoto Takeyama
Jan von Plato
Benjamin Werner

July 1998

Eduardo Giménez and Christine Paulin
Editors

Table of Contents

Introduction

Type theory was introduced at the beginning of this century by philosophers and mathematicians, who originally conceived it as a tool for avoiding antinomies in mathematical language [36, 4]. Several decades after, in the early seventies, type theory knows a renewal based on the correspondence between proofs in natural deduction and typed functional terms [28, 13]. Computer scientists became interested in it, and they have been kept on developing it until nowadays [6, 26, 20, 35]. The interest of this new scientific community in type theory is motivated by several reasons. We may cite at least the following ones:

- Type theory appears as a possible foundation for Computer Science, providing a precise explanation of some of its basic concepts, like *program*, *computation* and *specification* [26, 20].
- In the context of an increasing use of software in critical applications, it has revealed as a very interesting logical framework for carrying out program verification [29, 25, 16, 11].
- It opens the way to a new approach of doing Mathematics, where computers may play an active role in the development of proofs [3, 10].
- It can be also used as a *logical framework* for developing and testing other theories that could be used as a foundation of Computer Science [19, 30, 32].

Type Theory, Logic and Proofs

The application of type theory in computer science is strongly connected to a constructive explanation of Logic called the *proposition-as-types paradigm* [18, 7]. In this explanation of Logic, the notion of *truth* is identified with the existence of proof, and the judgment "the proposition A is true" is just seen as a shorthand for "we know how to construct a proof a of A". Hence, to explain the meaning of a proposition amounts to describe the collection of its proofs [17]. For example, the proofs of the proposition $(A \Rightarrow B)$ are defined as the collection of effective methods which allow to *compute* a proof of B from a proof of A. If such proofs are described in a natural deduction style, then it is possible to encode them as a lambda term [7], i.e as a functional program. In this way, this vision of logic enables to identify the notions of set, proposition and type on the one hand, and the notions of element, proof and functional program on the other. The specification of a program may be hence seen as a proposition describing a mathematical formula, while the program is nothing but (an optimization of) the constructive proof of such formula. Then programming and proving becomes the same, and type checking serves both as proof checking and as program verification.

From a foundational point of view, this simultaneous explanation of programming and logic is quite interesting for several reasons. One of them is the central role that the notion of *computation* plays in their semantics. This enables an operational understanding of logic which is simple to grasp for those people familiar with computing systems. The contrast between their conceptual simplicity and their expressive power is also remarkable. Built up from a few basic notions (type of an object, value of a computation) and a very simple language (basically, a lambda calculus extended with constants), they can be actually used as very expressive programming languages, in which it is possible to specify and program real computing systems [16].

Type theory has also important features from the point of view of program verification and the design of proof environments. We would like to mention at least three of them.

First, in type theory proofs are also considered as mathematical objects, as well as function or sets. This enables to stock a trace of the reasoning done for proving a theorem, which can be easily explained or mechanically re-verified. Yet more important, there exists a method for mechanically generating an efficient functional program from this trace. The program obtained by this method can be considered as an optimization of the proof, which erases those parts which are not necessary for computing the program, and only serve to ensure the correctness of its result.

Second, it is possible to mechanically check if a given program (proof) a actually satisfies a given specification (proposition) A. Since propositions and types are identified, the same techniques used in programming languages for verifying the type of a program can also be used to check the correctness of a proof.

Third, any expression that can be typed can be computed in finite time into a value of the same type. This enables to mechanize an important part of reasoning, in particular that concerning equations which can be checked by computation, like for example $2 + 5 = 7$.

Type Theory and Proof Environments

Several proof environments based on type theories are currently developed around the world. They can be distinguished by the variant of type theory they implement, and also by their architecture, i.e, the tools they provide for building and checking proofs.

Architectures and Tools. HOL [15], Isabelle [31], Nuprl [5] and PVS [27] are all based on the architecture of the early proof-checker LCF [14] developed by R. Milner and his team. The implementation contains an abstract datatype of *theorems* which only contains provable theorems of the logic. The user interactively builds proofs using special programs called *tactics*, that are intended to construct a value of the abstract datatype of theorems. Tactics may be sophisticated proof procedures, and the correctness of the theorems depends on the correct implementation of tactics.

Automath [24] or ALF [21] adopt a different point of view: in order to justify a theorem A, the user has to provide a term a of type A, and the task of the system is to check if such term is correctly typed. The advantage of this approach lays on the fact that the correctness of theorems only relies on the small set of deduction rules that the typechecker implements. In Automath, it was necessary to completely write down the term before it was checked. The system ALF introduced the notion of *partial term* —i.e., a term containing holes that can be instantiated later on— which gives a way to build proofs incrementally.

Lego and Coq use a mixed approach, where proofs can be explicitly given as typed terms, but are usually developed interactively using tactics. Tactics are used to build a concrete term that is then type-checked. In this way, the user can apply arbitrary complex proof strategies, but the correctness of the theorems ultimately relies on the typechecker.

The Underlying Type Theories. Let us now give an overview of the logical formalism behind each of the previously mentioned proof environments. HOL is built on Church's Higher-Order Logic. The objects of this logic are simply typed lambda-terms. Deductions are performed in an higher-order predicate calculus, where it is possible to quantify over predicates variables. PVS extends this logic by introducing dependent types for objects, like the type of lists of a given length n. These systems are based on classical logic, where properties are identified with boolean values and functions are represented extensionally by relations.

Isabelle is a logical framework which does not implement a particular logic but can support many different deduction systems. It is mainly used as a support for Higher Order Logic and ZF Set theory. Mizar [34] is also a proof environment based on Set theory which is used for the development of large piece of mathematics.

Automath and ALF are built on languages where proofs and objects are identified. Automath uses a weak logic (first-order predicate calculus) which provides a minimal logical framework where more powerful proof principles like induction can be introduced as axioms. On the other hand, ALF is based on Martin-Löf's type theory, where the logic principles are built-in. In these theories, recursive types like natural numbers or well-founded trees are taken as primitive notions, and the corresponding induction principles are part of the deduction rules of the logic. This logic at least contains the full Peano arithmetic and should support the development of usual mathematical results. Nuprl is based on the same principles but extends the original theory. In particular, it allows the introduction of partial objects and extensional equality, leading to a theory where typecheking it is no longer decidable.

The previous approach can be extended to higher-order quantifications by introducing dependent types in Girard's F_ω functional calculus [12]. Such system is called the Calculus of Constructions, and was introduced by Coquand and Huet [8]. It has been later extended with universes and primitive definitions of recursive types, and it is now the logical basis of the Coq and Lego proof environments.

In Martin-Löf's type theory and in the Calculus of Constructions there is a powerful intensional notion of functions represented as algorithms rather than relations. These logics are also constructive, which means that they do not accept a priori the excluded middle principle. Actually, given a property P, a proof of $\forall x.P(x) \vee \neg P(x)$ ensures that the predicate P is decidable and gives the opportunity to exhibit an algorithm implementing a decision procedure for $P(x)$. It is consequently possible in these formalisms to specify and prove decidability without introducing a specific notion of computability.

The Articles in this Volume

We have chosen to classify the articles selected for these proceeding into three main lines of research. Of course, we do not claim this classification to be a complete or detailed overview of all the active research areas concerning type theory, but representative of some of the challenges that our research community is presently facing.

The underlying calculus and its basic properties. One challenge concerns the precise formulation of the language and the typing calculus of type theory. Of course, the problem of designing such calculus also involves the basic meta-theoretical properties that we expect it to satisfy. For example, in most of the traditional formulations of type theory, the substitution of free variables is described as a meta-theoretical operation, external to the calculus. During the last years there has been several attempts to make precise the rules for dealing with substitution, leading to new formulations of type theories where substitutions are also syntactical constructions of the language. However, it has been shown that some calculus with explicit substitutions may fail to satisfy some of the properties we expect from them [23]. In this volume we present two complementary works concerning typing calculus with explicit substitutions and its properties: Cesar Muñoz focuses in a calculus with dependent types, while Jean Goubault studies the normalization property in a calculus with second order types.

Proving the normalization property may be difficult even for the usual formulations of a typing calculus. Thus, it is important to gain in the understanding of their structure and to formulate proofs as general as possible, so that they can be reused for different calculus. In their article, Paul-André Mellis and Benjamin Werner present a generic normalization proof valid for a large class of typing systems, the so-called "pure type systems" [2].

A different approach to the study of type theory is to compare it with other known mathematical structures, like those studied in category theory [22]. The article of Maria Emilia Maietti goes in this direction, showing that type theories containing dependent types are equivalent to the category of Heyting pretoposes.

Finally, an open question concerning the basic properties of type theory is its exact connection with other theories that could be used as a foundation for mathematics, like for example set theory. Gilles Dowek offers a contribution to this open problem, describing a theory closer to set theory, but having some of the interesting properties of type theory –say, that proofs are objects in the sense of the Heyting-Kolmogorov interpretation [17].

Proof transformation. A second line of research has to do with different methods of proof transformation, for example to present a proof in a more readable form, or to obtain an efficient functional program from it.

In some sense, part of this second line of research goes in the opposite direction of the first one. While it is important to make explicit some of the basic operations of the typing calculus, we also would like to keep the notation as lighter as possible, introducing a certain number of ambiguities and *abus de langage* which are of common use in mathematics. The motivation for this is to get as close as possible of the proofs style used in mathematical books. The article by John Harrison offers a general overview of this problem, comparing the proof styles proposed by different proof assistants.

From a more technical point of view, one way of introducing such *abus de langage* is by means of the notion of coercive sub-typing, introduced by Peter Aczel and Gilles Barthe in the Types'94 meeting [1]. Two articles concerning coercive sub-typing are presented in these proceedings. On one hand, Anthony Bailey surveys the problems posed by the implementation of coercion mechanisms for (dependent) type theories, and describes a concrete implementation in LEGO that can be easily extended to other environments. On the other, Alex Jones, Zhaohui Luo and Sergei Soloviev report the basic development of some metatheoretic properties of coercive sub-typing, and present a sound type-checking algorithm dealing with this sub-typing method.

Another way to get lighter and easier proofs is to implement some frequently used proof techniques as tactics provided by the proof system. A typical case is what is known as the "inversion proof principle" for inductive predicates. The article [9] presented in Types'95 described how to generate an inversion lemma. In this volume, Conor McBride extends that work, describing how first-order unification can be used to solve the equations generated by such lemma.

We have already mentioned that an important characteristic of the type theoretical explanation of Logic is the possibility of extracting functional programs from the proof of its specification. In this case, proofs are transformed with optimization purposes. Current implementations of such procedure are based on a realisability method, consisting in splitting the universe of propositions in those that have a computational contents and those that have not. The articles by Frédéric Prost, and by Damiani Ferruccio and Frédéric Prost propose two completely new techniques for proof extraction. The former is based on an unexpected use of the traditional ML typing algorithm, which enables to detect and erase dead code; the latter presents an extension of the method based on intersection types proposed by Coppo, Ferruccio and Giannini.

A long term goal concerning program extraction is to verify the correctness of the proof assistant itself, i.e. to extract its type-checker from a proof of the decidability of the typing relation. The article form Bruno Barras describes a step towards this ultimate goal, showing how to specify and extract the top level loop of a proof editor, and focusing on the treatment of errors and names done by the editor.

Applications of type theory to mathematics and programming. Another important branch of research concerns carrying on constructions in type theory, in most of the cases with the assistance of proof environments. Presently, the use of proof environments involves two principal domains of application. One concerns the formalization of mathematical concepts and theories, as part of the constructive mathematics programme. The other involve the certification of programming systems. Such developments are not only interesting in themselves, as part of a new form of doing mathematics or programming, but also because they provide an invaluable feedback for the research groups that work in the implementation of proof environments. We would like to remark the important leapt forward in problem complexity that has been done from the pioneering developments at the beginning of the nineties to some of the most recent machine-checked proofs, like for example [16].

In what respects the formalization of mathematical concepts, four articles are presented. The papers from Jan Cederquist and Sara Negri study the development of formal topology in type theory, an area of growing interest in the Types community. Daniel Fridlender analyses the formalization of several theorems and logical principles needed for machine-checking Valdman's proof of Higman's lemma. All these works has been developed with the assistance of the proof editor ALF.

Concerning program verification, Jean-Francois Monin describes an interesting case study in Coq, formalizing a correctness proof of an algorithm for real time devices in ATM networks. Wolfgang Naraschewski and Tobias Nipkow prove in Isabelle/HOL the soundness and the completeness of the type inference algorithm of ML. Alvaro Tasistro illustrates the use of dependent record types in type theory proving the correctness of an abstract insertion sort algorithm in an extension of the system ALF.

Finally, Petri Mäenpää explains an original application of dependent types to the domain of language recognition. This work is connected not only with Computer Science, but also with the type-theoretical foundations of Linguistics, another raising domain of application of type theory [33].

References

1. P. Aczel. A notion of class for theory development in algebra in a predicative type theory. Talk presented at the Workshop on Types for Proofs and Programs, June 1994.
2. H. Barendregt. Lambda calculi with types. In S. Abramsky, D. M. Gabbay, and T.S.E. Maibaum, editors, *Handbook of Logic in Computer Science*, volume 3. Oxford science publications, 1994.
3. Henk Barendregt. The quest of correctness. Images of SMC research, Stichting Mathematisch Centrum, P.O. Box 94079, 1090 GB Amsterdam, 39-58.
4. A. Church. A formulation of the simple theory of types. *Journal of Symbolic Logic*, 5:56–68, 1940.

5. R.L. Constable et al. *Implementing Mathematics with the Nuprl Proof Development System*. Prentice-Hall, 1986.
6. T. Coquand. Metamathematical Investigations of a Calculus of Constructions. In P. Odifreddi, editor, *Logic and Computer Science*, volume 31 of *The APIC series*, pages 91–122. Academic Press, 1990.
7. T. Coquand. On the analogy between propositions and types. In G. Huet, editor, *Logical Foundations of Functional Programming*, pages 399–417. Addison-Wesley, 1990.
8. Th. Coquand and G. Huet. Constructions: A higher order proof system for mechanizing mathematics. In *EUROCAL'85*, volume 203 of *LNCS*, Linz, 1985. Springer-Verlag.
9. C. Cornes and D. Terrasse. Automatizing Inversion Predicates in Coq. In *Workshop on Types for Proofs on Programs*, number 1152 in LNCS. Springer-Verlag, 1995.
10. EC Types Working Group. *First Workshop on Formal Topology*, Padova, October 1997.
11. E. Giménez. An application of co-Inductive types in Coq: verification of the Alternating Bit Protocol. In *Workshop on Types for Proofs and Programs*, number 1158 in LNCS, pages 135–152. Springer-Verlag, 1995.
12. J.-Y. Girard. Proceedings of the 2nd scandinavian logic symposium. In J.E. Fenstad, editor, *Une extension de l'interprétation de Gödel à l'analyse, et son application à l'élimination des coupures dans l'analyse et la téorie des types*, pages 63–92. North-Holland, 1971.
13. J.-Y. Girard, Y. Lafont, and P. Taylor. *Proofs and Types*. Cambridge Tracts in Theoretical Computer Science 7. Cambridge University Press, 1989.
14. M.J. Gordon, R. Milner, and C. Wadsworth. *Edinburgh LCF*, volume 78 of *LNCS*. Springer-Verlag, 1979.
15. M.J.C. Gordon and T. F. Melham. *Introduction to HOL. A theorem proving environment for higher order logic*. University of Cambridge, 1993.
16. L. Helmink, M.P.A. Sellink, and F.W. Vaandrager. Proof-Checking a Data Link Protocol. In Henk Barendregt, Tobias Nipkow, editor, *Workshop on Types for Proofs and Programs*, volume 806 of *LNCS*, pages 127–165. Springer-Verlag, 1993.
17. A. Heyting. *Intuitionism: An Introduction*. North-Holland, 1971.
18. W.A. Howard. The formulae-as-types notion of constructions. In J.P. Seldin and J.R. Hindley, editors, *to H.B. Curry : Essays on Combinatory Logic, Lambda Calculus and Formalism*. Academic Press, 1980. Unpublished 1969 Manuscript.
19. G. Huet and G. Plotkin, editors. *Logical Frameworks*. Cambridge University Press, May 1991.
20. Z. Luo. *Computation and Reasoning: A Type Theory for Computer Science*, volume 11 of *International Series of Monographs on Computer Science*. Oxford Science Publications, 1994.
21. L. Magnusson. *The implementation of ALF– a Proof Editor based on Martin-Löf's Monomorphic Type Theory with Explicit Substitution*. PhD thesis, Chalmers University of Göteborg, 1994.
22. C. McLarty. *Elementary Categories, Elementary Toposes*. Oxford University Press, 1992.
23. P.-A. Melliès. Typed λ-calculi with explicit substitutions may not terminate. In *Typed Lambda Calculi and Applications*, number 902 in LNCS. Second International Conference TLCA'95, Springer-Verlag, 1995.
24. P. Nederpelt, J.H. Geuvers, and R.C. de Vrijer, editors. *Selected Papers on Automath*. North-Holland, 1994.

25. T. Nipkow, , and K. Slind. IO Automata in Isabelle/HOL. In P Dybjer, B. Nordström, and J. Smith, editors, *Workshop on Types for Proofs and Programs*, number 996 in LNCS, pages 101–119. Springer-Verlag, 1994.
26. B. Nordström, K. Petersson, and J. Smith. *Programming in Martin-Löf's Type Theory: An Introduction*, volume 7 of *International Series of Monographs on Computer Science*. Oxford Science Publications, 1990.
27. S. Owre, S. Rajan, J.M. Rushby, N. Shankar, and M.K. Srivas. PVS: Combining specification, proof checking, and model checking. In Rajeev Alur and Thomas A. Henzinger, editors, *Computer-Aided Verification, CAV '96*, volume 1102 of *Lecture Notes in Computer Science*, pages 411–414, New Brunswick, NJ, July/August 1996. Springer-Verlag.
28. P. Martin-Löf. *Intuitionistic Type Theory*. Studies in Proof Theory. Bibliopolis, 1984.
29. C. Paulin-Mohring and B. Werner. Synthesis of ML programs in the system Coq. *Journal of Symbolic Computation*, 15:607–640, 1993.
30. L. Paulson. Set theory for verification: from foundations to functions. *Journal of Automatic Reasoning*, 11(2):353–389, 1993.
31. L. Paulson. The Isabelle reference manual. Technical Report 283, Computer Laboratory, University of Cambridge, 1993.
32. L. Paulson. Set theory for verification: induction and recursion. *Journal of Automatic Reasoning*, 15(3), 1995.
33. A. Ranta. *Type-theoretical grammar*. Oxford : Clarendon, 1994.
34. P. Rudnicki. An overview of the Mizar project, 1992.
35. G. Sambin and J. Smith, editors. *Twenty-Five Years of Constructive Type Theory*. Oxford University Press, 1998.
36. A. Whitehead and B. Russel. *Principia Mathematica*. Cambridge University Press, 1910.

Coercion Synthesis in Computer Implementations of Type-Theoretic Frameworks

Anthony Bailey

Department of Computer Science, University of Manchester, UK
<URL:mailto:BaileyA@CS.Man.ac.UK>
<URL:http://WWW.CS.Man.ac.UK/~baileya/>

Abstract. A coercion is a function that acts on a representation of some object in order to alter its type. The idea is that although applying a coercion to an object changes its type, the result still represents the "same" object in some sense; perhaps it is some essential underlying part of the original object, or a different representation of that object.
This paper examines some of the issues involved in the computer implementation of systems that allow a user to define coercions that may then be left implicit in the syntax of expressions and synthesised automatically. From a type-theoretic perspective, coercions are often left implicit in mathematical texts, so they can be used to improve the readability of a formalisation, and to implement other tricks of syntax if so desired.

1 Introduction

Traditionally, mathematicians have used a set-theoretic framework for formalisation. However, over the past few decades the type-theoretic paradigm has been seen to have many nice features. One of the things that it lacks is that whilst an element may belong to many distinguishable sets within set theory, in type theory a term tends to have only one unique type (up to some notion of convertibility.) This has led type-theorists to examine various notions of *subtyping*, in an attempt to extend type theories with some of the facilities and idioms of set theory without compromising their agreeable meta-theoretic properties.

The basic principle of subtyping is that if S is a subtype of T, then terms of type S may be considered to have type T as well. This allows a term with a subterm of type T to remain well-typed when a second subterm which has type S is used in place of the original.

One form of subtyping that has received a fair amount of investigation is subtyping based on records[BetTas]. In this approach, objects are tuples (or records) whose components correspond to named fields. One record type, S, is a subtype of another, T, if S contains all the fields of T (and possibly some additional ones too.) Whenever a term with type S is used, one can simply forget the components in the extra fields to retrieve a term with the record type T. There is thus some computational way in which to give a meaning to this form of subtyping.

Coercions extend the idea that subtyping and other forms of inheritance can be justified computationally[BCGS] by allowing functions of a more general nature than "forgetful" ones that simply get rid of information held in extraneous fields of a record. The concept can be considered at the level of logical frameworks; this yields systems of coercive subkinding that have been studied by Zhaohui Luo[Luo96] amongst others.

As well as providing a theoretical framework for subtyping, coercions can also be thought of as providing an implicit syntax[Pol90] for expressions in an existing type theory. In an implicit syntax, some information (in this case, coercions) that may be reconstructed from the context can be omitted. The idea is that having defined a coercion $\kappa : S \to T$ one may use $x : S$ to represent the term $\kappa(x) : T$ in certain circumstances. For example, if f is a function which expects its argument to have type T, then $f(x)$ may be thought of as an abbreviation for the term $f(\kappa(x))$.

I note that a mechanism known as argument synthesis is already implemented in many proof-checkers. This mechanism allows certain functions to be used as if they had a polymorphic type, and it has a concrete implementation as an implicit syntax that allows the omission in expressions of implicit arguments, which are later reconstructed through unification. In this paper I examine methods for the implementation of a corresponding mechanism of coercion synthesis.

As an addition to the standard subtyping paradigm, coercions provide a means of making subtyping into a more general relation than a partial ordering. Each of two distinct types S and S' may be considered to be a subtype of the other by defining coercions $\kappa : S \to S'$ and $\kappa' : S' \to S$ between them. This allows the sharing operations defined on either of S or S' so that they work on both of these types. The idea here is that S and S' may be considered to be equivalent representations of the same abstract concept.

Finally, coercions also give one a mechanism within a formal framework by which to implement and understand some of the other useful *abus de notation* that make more informal mathematics easy to read. For example, one might use a coercion to write a natural number n as an abbreviation for an indexing set with n elements.

2 Coercions in informal mathematics

Although the mathematicians who use them may not consciously be aware of coercions, if one approaches the language of informal mathematics from a type-theoretic perspective, one can make the case that they are one of the most powerful and useful features of this language.

If one applies the type-theoretic perspective, within which terms have particular types, to an average piece of informal mathematics, then at first sight the mathematics may simply seem to be ill-typed. Take, as an example, the number 5. In different circumstances it may be considered to be a natural number, an integer, a rational, a real, or even a complex number. However, if these types of number are specified in a formal framework, then the representations of 5 that have these types will be different objects. There seem to be at least five different representation of the number.

One can just take the view that one is *overloading* the particular name "5"; that there are indeed many different objects with that name, and the same name is being used to refer to each of them. Which particular object is being referenced in any given circumstance can be discovered by examining the context in which the name is used.

I argue that the above view doesn't tell the whole story as it makes the connection between these different things named "5" seem arbitrary, when it seems clear that they are supposed to be differently typed instances of the *same* underlying object. One way to persuade oneself of this is to observe the general relationships that exist between the differently typed representations.

One might conclude that *any* natural number, such as the one denoted by "5", can be made into an element of one of the other types mentioned by means of a canonical construction. Of course, the exact details of the construction will depend on the choice of representation used for these types of numbers. To give an example, if an integer is to be represented as the difference $a - b$ between a pair of naturals (a, b) then one might turn the natural n into the integer $(n, 0)$.

This is the process of *coercing* the natural number to be an integer. The canonical function that is applied to move between these types is called a *coercion.*

As another example, consider the construction of the set of binary mappings over some given set. There seems to be a constructor that takes a set as an argument and returns the set of binary mappings over that set as a result. However, if one has some group, then it would be quite acceptable to a mathematician to talk about binary mappings over it, even though it is a group and not a set. Similarly one may talk about elements of the group, even though a type-theorist might object that it is sets, not groups, that have elements. I claim one reason that these idioms do not seem unreasonable is that any group can be coerced to be a set by means of a canonical operation that extracts its underlying carrier. Inserting this coercion into the formal expressions would recover the well-typedness of the idioms.

3 Coercions as an implicit syntax

As mentioned at the start of this paper, coercions may be used as a means with which to formalise a subtyping relation. Luo considers using coercions at the level of a logical framework. (Alex Jones presented this work at the *Types '96* conference[Jon].) Within such a framework the more specialised theories such as some of the common extensions to Martin-Löf Type Theory[MLöf] or the Calculus of Constructions[CoqHue] can be defined; this would extend those theories with coercive subtyping.

Another way to use coercions is to produce from them an *implicit syntax*[Pol90] for an existing type theory. The user defines a collection of coercions which may then be left implicit in an extended syntax of expressions, both in input and output. On input, the implicit coercions may be automatically synthesised using information in the context of the expression to recover a term of the original type theory. This term of the official syntax that exists inside the machine is said to *explain* the original term of the implicit syntax. On output, the parts of terms that were synthesised coercions are suppressed again.

From the viewpoint of the user, the implicit syntax thus acts as an alternative grammar for the type theory which *improves* the expressiveness of the theory (more terms have types), making it more succinct or intuitive, but without *increasing* this expressiveness (no additional types are inhabited) or introducing ambiguities (a unique official term explains each piece of implicit syntax.) Such syntax can be seen as a step in bridging the gap between formalisations, which have the advantage of being essentially unambiguous and machine-checkable, and informal accounts, which have the advantage of being easy to read and understand.

In this paper I look at ways to implement such an implicit syntax via coercion synthesis in existing computer implementations of type theory. In particular, I have made some changes to LEGO[LuoPol] to incorporate coercion synthesis and hence implement an implicit syntax within the flavours of type theory used by LEGO. I start by reviewing this the resultant system, which I call LEGO with coercion synthesis, or LEGOwcs. A knowledge of the specifics of LEGO or its type theory will be helpful in understanding all the details, but a familiarity with any flavour of dependent type theory should suffice for the essentials. Other existing systems can be extended in very similar ways; Coq[COQ] has also been extended with coercion synthesis by Amokrane Saïbi[Saï] to provide an implicit syntax for its underlying Calculus of Inductive Constructions[Wer].

4 The specific system LEGOwcs

4.1 Overview

I shall summarise the basics of the traditional LEGO system, introduce the idea of a coercive graph, then note some of its properties and how it may be maintained. I should make it clear what this section is not; it is not a description of the implementation of LEGOwcs at an algorithmic level. Rather, it is a description of how the system works at a conceptual level. Also, this paper does not seek to illustrate how coercions add to the readability of a development or provide an introduction to ways in which to use them[Bai].

LEGO implements variants of the Unified Theory of Types (UTT)[Luo94]. The main flavour is a dependent type theory with strong sum-types, inductive types with rewriting, and a hierarchy of universes with subsumption. The convertibility relation within UTT is quite generous; in addition to standard $\alpha\beta$-convertibility, it contains conversions following from the expansion of definitions, rewriting, and projection from sums.

A user of LEGO works with a *context*. This is a list of identified terms or expressions that are either *defined* or else *declared* without giving a definition;

they are entered into the context one at a time. Once an identifier has entered the context it can be used in future expressions.

In LEGOwcs, some context entries may also be tagged as *coercion definitions* when they are first entered. The list of coercion definitions represents a set of edges in a directed *coercive graph.* Paths through this graph constitute the *coercions* that may be *synthesised* within expressions and left implicit by the system in input and output. I use "coercion" and "path" interchangeably in the remainder of this paper.

The nodes between which a path runs are types; they are the domain and codomain of the functional type of the coercion it constitutes. I refer to these as the *source* and *target* types of the coercion, respectively. The source is the type a term needs to have for a coercion to be synthesised for it and applied to it, and the target is the type it will have after the application of the coercion. Each node of the graph is a specific type and each path represents a specific function between its source and target types.

Limitations on the properties that the coercive graph is permitted to have force restrictions on the combinations of coercion definitions that will be accepted by the system. The main limitation is a requirement of coherency, explained in the next subsection.

Coercion definitions may be parameterised, and therefore one definition may introduce arbitrary numbers of nodes and edges into the graph. However, although infinite, the graph has a finite description; the list of coercion definitions gives rise to a finite collection of parameterised paths, built from the finite composition of the parameterised coercion definitions. This description may be used by deterministic algorithms to check that a graph has the required properties, and to synthesise the coercions left implicit in expressions.

Although the coercive graph may be thought of as being regenerated in its entirety every time the list of coercion definitions is changed, it is maintained incrementally in practice, since in LEGO context entries (and hence coercion definitions) are introduced, and removed, one at a time.

There are some other general features of the LEGOwcs system, the reasons for which will be explained in section 5. Paths through the graph are constructed statically at the time that coercions are defined, not dynamically at the time of synthesis. Coercions are considered applicable in some situation only if the types involved match at a syntactical level; the weaker requirement of convertibility is not sufficient. Finally, in all circumstances, if more than one coercion could be synthesised by the system, then the possibilities must be coherent is the sense defined in the next subsection. This allows a non-ambiguous form of "multiple inheritance."

4.2 Coercion definition

To enter a coercion definition into the context, the user needs to provide an identifier and a term. This term must be a function. It may take a number of initial arguments that can be reconstructed by LEGO's argument synthesis algorithm when the function is applied; these parameterise the coercion definition. The type of the first non-synthesised argument is the source type (or the parameterised class of source types) of the coercion definition. The type of the remaining function body is the target type (or the parameterised class of target types); this may depend on the source if so desired, and can be explicitly specified by the user through LEGO's type-casting mechanism if desired. Thus the most general type for a coercion definition is

$$\Pi x_1 : p_1 . \Pi x_2 : p_2(x_1). \ldots \Pi x_n : p_n(x_1, \ldots, x_{n-1}).$$
$$\Pi x : S(x_1, \ldots, x_n). T(x_1, \ldots, x_n, x)$$

where $p_1 \ldots p_n$ are the (parameterised) types of the parameters, S is the (parameterised) source type, and T is the (parameterised) target type.

When a new coercion definition enters the context, new coercions (paths through the coercive graph) are generated from it. The simplest new paths are all of the single edges which result from the arbitrary instantiation of the parameters of the new definition. Also, existing paths to the source types of these new edges, and from their target types, are composed with these edges, to make new paths.

If competing paths are produced (ones that run between the same source and target types), then these paths are allowed only if they are extensionally equal on the source type. By this I mean that their applications to an arbitrary argument of this type should be convertible. I call the competing paths *coherent* in such a circumstance. A coercive graph is coherent if all competing coercions within it are. New paths which do not compromise the coherency of the coercive graph are allowed to be added. However, if a new path competes with an old one and they are not coherent, then the coercion definition which resulted in the competing path being generated is disallowed. This generation of paths and checking for coherence is performed statically, at the moment that a new coercion definition is made.

In practice, one cannot generate (and check the coherence of) all the new paths individually, since the definitions may be parameterised over arbitrary types. Instead, the implementation works at the most general level of parameterisation of paths and definitions that it can. Since there are only a finite number of definitions, and each can be used only once in each path, only a finite number of combinations of these into parameterised paths is ever necessary. It is thus feasible to implement the system using suitable algorithms. The reader need not know the details of the algorithms used; the process is most clearly understood through the preceding explanation at the level of the possibly infinite collection of individual non-parameterised paths.

4.3 Special flavours of coercion

Normally, coercions run between nodes that are particular source and target types. This is because generally when it comes to doing synthesis, the proof-checker knows that it has a term with the source type where one with the target type is required. However, sometimes the precise target type that the term must have after it has been coerced may not be known. One may just know that one wishes it to have one of a general class of types.

One such class is the class of kind types. In the terminology of LEGO, a kind is any term which may appear on the right-hand side of a typing judgement. The types of kinds are thus Prop (the type of propositions), Type_i (the hierarchy of type universes), and Type (the ambiguous type universe.)

I thus introduce a special node into the coercive graph representing the class of kind types. Coercions with this node as a target are of a special flavour called ***kind-coercions***. They are the paths which end with an edge formed from a coercion definition that has been explicitly specified to be of this flavour. It is these coercions which allow the treatment of composite objects, such as instances of groups or sets, as types over which one can quantify and range; if G is a group, we may also write G to represent its carrier type, projecting this by a kind-coercion. Competing coercions from a source type to the special node of all kind types must be coherent, just as is the case for other targets.

The other special node in the graph represents the class of functional types or Π-types. Functions are terms which may be applied to other terms. ***Π-coercions*** are the flavour of paths with this node as a target, and they end with an edge formed from a coercion definition explicitly specified to have this flavour. This flavour of coercion is useful in formalising mathematics in type theory because proof information is often bundled up with functions (for example, to prove that a function is a set mapping, or an isomorphism), but often one still wishes to apply the composite object directly to arguments.

Π-coercions must also cohere when they compete. A less strong coherency requirement that allowed the existence of more then one Π-coercion from an individual type would be possible, but I did not attempt to implement this since I have never wanted a term to represent more than one function in my own work.

4.4 Coercion synthesis

Whenever the system attempts to synthesise a coercion, it is always the case that there is an expression that requires some subterm to have a different type in order for the expression as a whole to be well-formed or well-typed. Therefore the proof-checker will need to decide whether or not the type of some term matches the source or target type of some coercion, and I must explain what I mean by matching.

In UTT, every term may have many different types. However, the LEGO system provides each term with a ***principal type***. This type follows from the structure of the expression and from the principal types of its subterms. The principal type of a term can be changed by the user by means of an explicit ***type-casting*** if desired. When talking about ***the*** type of some term as if it is uniquely defined, I will mean the principal type.

Two types will then be said to match only if they have the same syntactic form, rather than the weaker condition of the types being convertible. The syntax in question is the well-typed explicit syntax that underlies the system; thus other implicit coercions and arguments may be synthesised in the types themselves before the comparison is made.

If any of the following expressions involving the subterm X with principal type S fail to be well-formed or well-typed within the standard grammar, then the system attempts to synthesise a coercion $\kappa : S \to T$, and then replaces X with $\kappa(X)$ in order to produce a well-typed expression.

The first sort of expression is very common and is the canonical case in which a coercion is synthesised. These are the sort of syntheses that will allow one to talk about binary mappings over a group rather than a set. The second allows the invocation of a coercion through an explicit type-casting.

- An application, $f\ X$ where f has principal type $\Pi x : T.\ t$
- A type-casting, $(X : T)$

A Π-coercion from S is synthesised in the circumstance when X is not a function, but it is being applied to another term as if it were.

- An application, $X\ a$

Kind-coercions from S are synthesised in many circumstances when X is not a kind, but a kind is nonetheless expected in order to provide a well-formed expression:

- An abstraction, $\lambda x : X.\ t$, $\Pi x : X.\ t$, $\Pi x : s.\ X$, $\Sigma x : X.\ t$ or $\Sigma x : s.\ X$
- A type-casting, $(x : X)$

There are some additional occasions in which coercions are synthesised; these involve the UTT's specific formulation of dependent strong sums. Within the LEGO formulation coercions are also allowed to be synthesised in other circumstances where interactive proof commands expect an expression to have a certain type or one of a certain class of types. These syntheses are those that one might intuitively expect. The details of these and of how coercions are handled with respect to LEGO's notion of locality and discharge will be relegated to Appendix B as they would distract from the main discussion.

5 The design decisions taken

The decisions that were taken in formulating the LEGOwcs system are interrelated in a complicated way, and were influenced by both theoretical and pragmatic motivations. The remainder of the paper will look at these decisions and their motivation, exploring the reasoning behind them and looking at the alternatives that could be (or have been) used in principle (or in practice.) This was the topic of my talk at TYPES'96 and I consider it to be the most interesting issue addressed in this paper.

5.1 Motivations

Gilles Barthes has examined the meta-theoretic consequences of introducing various systems of coercions into existing type theories[Bar]. Zhaohui Luo has taken a similarly meta-theoretic look at coercions and their use in subkinding for logical frameworks[Luo96]. My motivations were more immediate and short-term. I started this project because I wished to undertake the literate and large-scale formalisation of some algebra. I thus wanted to produce a working implementation that was feasible to use in practice and that was as well-suited as possible to the demands of such a project.

The system therefore had to run relatively efficiently and not slow the operation of the existing machinery inordinately. Especially when dealing with large terms, the existing generation of proof-checkers are fairly expensive in terms of compute time and resources. Modifications which caused too much of a further slowdown would not be feasible to use for a large-scale development. This influenced the sort of matching I used and had a bearing on the decision to generate the coercive graph statically.

The implicit syntax that results from the implemented features had to be as flexible as possible and have the ability to express as many useful notations and to synthesise as many convenient coercions as possible. This influenced my decision to allow coercions to be parameterised, and for paths between nodes to compete if necessary.

If a final formal development is to be usefully read, then it is important that the reader can parse the formal expressions and understand what they mean. This is the reason for using coercions in the first place - to provide an implicit syntax that eliminates some unnecessary clutter in order to allow some informal idioms. However, it is important that succinctness of expressions is not achieved at the cost of introducing ambiguity. Potential ambiguities are dangerous, for even if the writer of a development is able to avoid mistakes in their own understanding, a reader who is not as familiar with the material may be misled if the syntax reads in an ambiguous manner. This influenced the enforcing of coherency between competing coercions.

Finally, since such a change involved tinkering with the proof-checker itself and risks introducing bugs, it is important that a proof produced by the extended system should be easy to translate back into a form that can be checked by the original version or by other trusted proof-checkers; it must be believable[Pol96]. Since the system only implements an implicit syntax for an existing type theory, the translation is not difficult; one just makes all the coercions synthesised by the extended system explicit. This produces terms of the original type theory.

However, I note that making these coercions explicit may clutter the expressions that need to be read to understand what has been proved, because these expressions were originally formulated in the cleaner, kinder, implicit syntax. It might well be worthwhile, therefore, to include in any trusted system the ability to suppress upon output those functions understood to be coercions. Thus while coercions need play no special role in formal checking, the fact that they do in informal understanding may mean that they are too important to ignore when a reader is trying to believe a proof.

5.2 Parameterisation

Parameterisation allows the simultaneous introduction of large classes of coercions into the graph. Although this does not affect the underlying rationale of the system, it has consequences for any implementation on a machine, as it produces a potentially infinite number of individual coercions.

Without parameterisation, a finite number of coercion definitions results in a finite number of paths, each of which can be considered individually and in sequence when coherency is checked, or when deciding whether something can be synthesised. With parameterisation, one can no longer act in so simple a manner. An algorithmic process is necessary to decide which instantiations of parameters will yield the coercions that are relevant to the given situation. The need to make the process feasible will influence the other decisions taken later. Therefore, it is important to justify the decision to make use of parameterisation.

The motivation for making the decision to allow parameterisation was my desire for flexibility and expressiveness. The importance of such things is clearly difficult to quantify. I have found parameterised coercions to very greatly increase the usability of the system. However, I am wary of giving examples in great detail since these details are arbitrary, complicated, and thus non-trivial to understand. Instead I will attempt a more general explanation.

The coercions that are left implicit to improve the readability of an expression act on objects of certain types. Parameterisation of coercions is necessary if these types are drawn from a parameterised class. For example, coercions from sets or groups do not need to be parameterised since these types are unparameterised. However, many interesting objects in algebra do have such parameterised types. One example is the type of vectorspaces parameterised over arbitrary fields. A second is subgroups of arbitrary groups. A third would be mappings over arbitrary sets; almost all Π-coercions tend to be parameterised. Lastly, some coercions act on elements of models of particular algebras; these thus need to be parameterised over instances of the models in question. In fact, within the development I have undertaken, more than half of all coercion definitions are parameterised.

Parameterisation also offers a simple method for dealing with dependent coercions, where the target type depends on the source argument. An example of this would be to coerce a field into a vectorspace over itself. Such dependencies can be dealt with by treating the source argument as an additional parameter in the target type. Thus an implementation of parameterisation is sufficient to handle such dependent coercions.

Since my system was built with the particular piece of mathematics that I am formalising in mind, I should make the disclaimer that what I have found in practice may not concord with other experiences. For example, it may be that algebra is unusual in its demand for parameterised coercions. However, I would guess that parameterisation is similarly useful in other domains. It also features in another practical implementation of coercions, that of Saïbi in Coq.

5.3 Graph generation

LEGOwcs statically generates a representation of all paths through the coercive graph whenever the set of coercion definitions is changed. An alternative to static generation would be to perform some path-searching in the graph dynamically when a coercion needs to be synthesised.

A dynamic approach requires a different approach to coherency (see subsections 5.5 and 5.6.) However, this is not necessarily a bad thing in itself. In some ways, a dynamic search allows more expressiveness and flexibility since there is more information to hand when synthesising a specific path than when generating a general parameterised one. It also allows the easy extension of existing coercions on base types to ones on inductive types and Π-types over these bases. This is not performed by LEGOwcs because I found it complicated static coherency-checking and have not found a need for it in my own developments.

Static generation is used in LEGOwcs (and in the Coq implementation) because the amount of computation involved in the dynamic graph-searching that would be required to trace paths and synthesise coercions on-the-fly is very large. Each expression of average size contains several implicit coercions. In the interests of efficiency, it is preferable to do as much of the computation as possible once only, at the moment the coercion definitions are made, rather than repeating the same work every time an expression is type-checked. This is the same sort of reasoning as that which implies that compilation is usually preferable to interpretation when trying to implement an efficient programming language.

Faster machines and better algorithms might change things, but for the moment any pragmatic implementation would seem to need to do most of the work involving coercions statically at "compile-time" rather than dynamically at "run-time."

5.4 Matching

Coercions run between nodes in the coercive graph. These nodes represent particular types. Thus when synthesising a coercion for a subterm one needs to have some way of matching types to decide which coercions might be applicable. In LEGOwcs, types must have the same syntactic form to match. A similar requirement of syntactic matching is also enforced in the Coq implementation. However, other sameness relations on types exist which may seem more natural to use. An obvious one is the more generous one of convertibility; the theoretical presentations of coercions by Barthes and Luo both use the convertibility relation. I should therefore explain why a different approach is used in LEGOwcs. There are four main reasons.

Firstly, there is an immediate efficiency concern. A comparison of syntax is quicker to perform than a check for convertibility. Although algorithmic tricks can be used to speed up convertibility checks, in the worst case one is required to reduce the types being compared to their normal forms. Since two matches are necessary for each coercion in the graph, a single coercion synthesis involves a large number of matches. In turn, as previously mentioned, an average expression may require a number of such syntheses.

Secondly, although a statement of convertibility

$$s \simeq t$$

is decidable in UTT for simple types, it is no longer decidable when one or both types involve unknown term-variables

$$\exists x_1, \ldots, x_m.\ s(x_1, \ldots, x_m) \simeq t$$

since in general this requires higher-order unification, which is undecidable[Gol]. When parameterisation is used, this sort of unification is necessary, since parameters might be assigned to arbitrary terms. Most matches will require only first-order unification, and there are tactics that can be used to solve the higher-order unification problem in certain cases[Nip], but it can be seen that there are some fundamental problems here, and that even an incomplete implementation will have to do some complex unification computations.

Since I have decided that parameterisation is essential in a flexible and expressive system of coercions, and that a practical implementation must be reasonably efficient, convertibility seems to be unsuitable. Syntax-based matching does not present these problems, as parameter assignments can be calculated without difficulty for such a stricter matching of types.

Thirdly, although a generous matching relation means it will be possible to synthesise coercions without further work in more cases, there is a related drawback in that the generosity makes it easier for coercions to compete. Therefore more combinations of coercions will be incoherent. When using a syntax-based matching, if one wants a particular pair of convertible (but syntactically different) types to be matched, then this can be achieved with a little extra work by defining a coercion between the two types that has no computational effect other than to change the type of its argument. This gives the user a finer degree of control, but they have to put in extra effort to achieve it. For example, a definition is convertible with its definiens, but is not a syntactic match for it. To allow this match requires the user to define a coercion explicitly. One might wonder why this match could not be accepted by default.

The reason is that it happens in practice that one wishes to define combinations of coercions that would be coherent using syntax-based matching, but that become incoherent when using a more generous matching relation. This occurs since one may wish to use representations of distinct abstract concepts that are nevertheless convertible within the framework of type theory. An example might be using lists to represent both polynomials and finite sets. One would then have the ability to use an existing library of list operations and results to define further constructions over these types.

However, one would not want the coercions defined on polynomials to be synthesised for finite sets, and vice versa. Under a syntax-based form of matching, such syntheses can be prevented by giving the representations different names. Ignoring the representation of some abstract type in some circumstances but accessing it in others can be seen as an information hiding problem. This probably has a more general solution borrowed from the realm of object-oriented programming, but that is not my concern in the current implementations I consider here.

A fourth reason for the different approaches is that in the case of the LEGO system there is already a specific algorithm available for computing the principal types necessary to perform a syntactic match, and its operation is familiar to the user. In the more theory-based presentations of Luo and Barthes, formalising the notion of principal types required for syntax-based matching would add extra baggage to the existing elegant theories.

For the above reasons, syntax-based matching seems preferable to conversion in present implementations. However, I do note that my decision on this was reached in tandem with other decisions (e.g. the wish to allow parameterisation.) Also, there may be arguments for using some relation less generous than full convertibility, but more so than syntax-based matching; for example, perhaps β-reduction might be allowed.

5.5 Graph shape

The simplest restriction that might be placed on the shape of the coercive graph is that there should be only one path between any pair of types. Forests and some other graphs would satisfy this restriction. As well as avoiding any difficult decisions about resolving competition between paths, it would make any dynamic graph-searching algorithm much simpler to implement.

However, once again a simple approach has the disadvantage of reducing flexibility and expressiveness. It would prevent two kinds of coercion combinations which have been found to be common and useful in practice. These are depicted below, in figures 2 and 3.

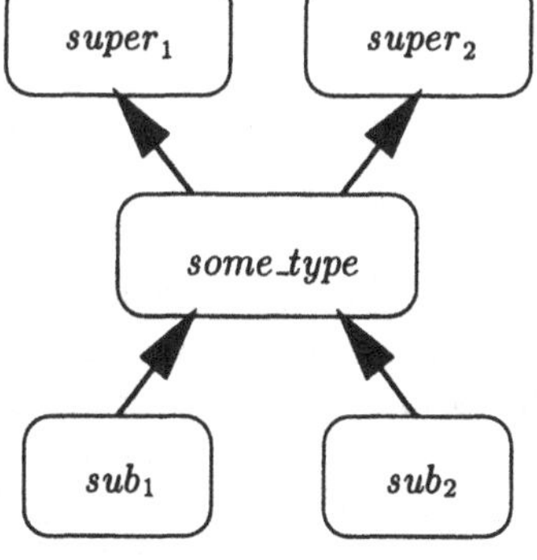

Fig. 1. Graph without sharing

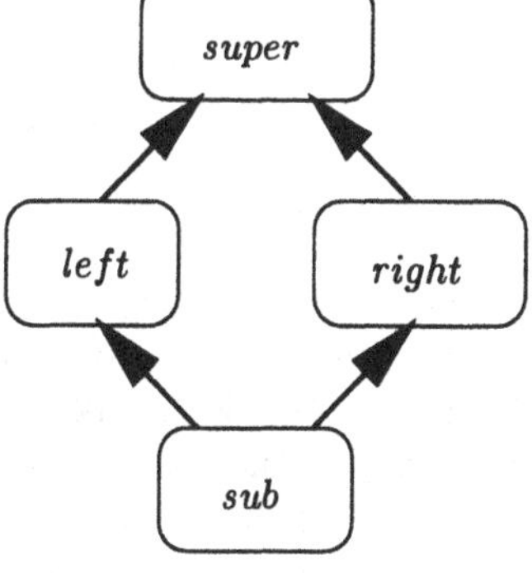

Fig. 2. Graph with sharing

The restriction does not force a forest structure on the graph; some non-treelike pieces of connected graph have no competing paths, as can be seen by Figure 1. The type *some_type* can be coerced to both $super_1$ and $super_2$, and both sub_1 and sub_2 can be coerced to *some_type*. However, it does prevent what might be described as supertypes with sharing. This occurs when two types $left$ and *right* to which some subtype *sub* can be coerced themselves have a common supertype *super*, as shown in Figure 2. In such a case there are two competing paths in the graph between the types *sub* and *super*; one via the type $left$ and the other via the type *right*.

I should give an example of supertypes with sharing in practice. *super* might be the type of maps. Let $left$ be the type of injections and *right* be the type of surjections. It is clear that coercions from these two types to maps would be useful. Now if *sub* is the type of bijections it would seem useful to be able to coerce a bijection to be either an injection or a surjection. These coercions would produce the competing paths to the shared map supertype shown in the diagram.

Another example might concern flavours of algebras. For example, suppose that *super* is the type of sets, $left$ that of discrete sets, *right* that of groups, and *sub* that of discrete groups. Again, all the coercions in the graph would be useful in practice but there are competing coercions from discrete groups to their underlying carrier sets.

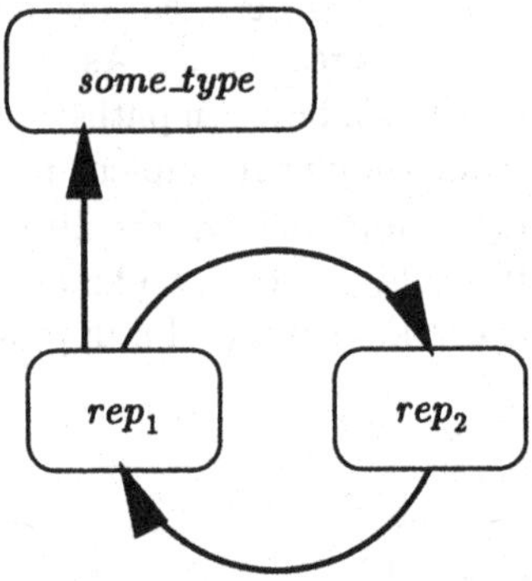

Fig. 3. Graph with cycle

The second circumstance occurs when one wishes to use coercions to move between two alternative representations of the same concept so that functions can be applied to such objects without having to take into account on which representation the functions were originally defined. Such coercions introduce a cycle into the graph, as can be seen in Figure 3. Even if coercion definitions are not allowed to be used more than once within a path, cycles still cause competing coercions; for example, there are two paths from rep_1 to *some_type*;

one involving the single edge between them, and another which first loops around the cycle via rep_2.

This is the circumstance that occurs when one has two different but essentially isomorphic concrete representations within the type theory of the same abstract concept. For example, a finite sequence could be represented as a list (rep_1) or as a tuple (rep_2.) In some circumstances the list representation might be the most convenient to use; in others the alternative tuple representation might be preferable. A coercive graph like that of Figure 3 would allow the use of both these representations interchangeably.

The approach taken within LEGOwcs is to allow sharing, but to insist that all competing paths are coherent. As explained previously, coherence means that their applications to an arbitrary argument should be convertible. The different possible syntheses thus produce the same result after the coercion is applied. In the case of a graph with a cycle, the graph will remain coherent so long as the application of any cyclic path has no net effect. This concurs with the intuition that rep_1 and rep_2 are isomorphic representations. The LEGOwcs system insists on coherence because, for me, a very important motivation was that there should be no ambiguity in an expression in which a coercion is left implicit. If the graph is coherent, then any apparent ambiguities concerning which coercion might be synthesised are inconsequential, since the same result follows whichever is used.

Instead, a different approach could be taken; to allow incoherent competing paths, but to have some deterministic means by which to decide which should be synthesised. In the Coq implementation, if two different paths could be synthesised, then the path that was generated first is the one that is used. This means that they must consider the latest coercion definitions that contributed to each competing path, and then choose the path for which the latest definition is the older. Thus the coercive graph is determined by an ordered sequence of coercion definitions, rather than by an unordered set.

Resolving incoherencies gives the user more freedom, since, when writing a formal development, they can decide to define coercions which compete in ways that are not necessarily coherent, so long as they can keep track of which will actually be synthesised in a given circumstance. For someone familiar with the system this may not be an unreasonable responsibility. However, it was not an acceptable compromise for my own system of coercions, since I am intending to use it to write mathematics in a way that is as close as possible to informal practice without introducing any ambiguities. The exact formal structure of a coercive graph would be difficult for someone without experience of the particular type theory in question to keep in mind whilst they read a formalisation. It seemed preferable to prevent any dangerous ambiguities by insisting on coherency, and thus allowing the user to rely on their intuitions as to the meaning of the implicit syntax.

5.6 Other approaches

An alternative to insisting on coherency would be to allow any combination of coercion definitions, but to consider a term to be ill-typed if incoherent competing coercions could be synthesised within it. This would act as a reasonable compromise between the two approaches outlined previously. It would allow the user to define coercions that generated potential incoherent competitors, but would prevent them from actually introducing any such ambiguities into the expressions they write. Alternatively, perhaps the system should only allow incoherent coercions to be defined if the user gives some explicit indication as to how to resolve the ambiguities that could arise as part of the definition. The important motivation for me is to ensure that the reader of a formal presentation cannot be misled into assuming that one coercion is being synthesised when in actuality a different incoherent coercion is synthesised by the system.

It was pointed out to the author by Zhaohui Luo that although the coercive graph may contain an infinite number of paths, only finitely many are ever synthesised within the course of a given formalisation. Since synthesised coercions are simple, unparameterised terms of the type theory, this reintroduces the possibility of checking the coherency of individual paths directly rather than working with parameterised paths. However such an approach would mean that type-checking would become slower and slower as the length of the development, and hence the number of coercions synthesised, increased. Still, in an efficient enough implementation, this approach would remove the need to statically check the coherency of the graph. (The paths themselves might still be statically generated, in order to maximise the run-time efficiency of the system.)

Another ambitious change would be to attempt to allow types to be matched by some kind of conversion rather than a syntax-based comparison, although as previously noted, synthesis within such a system would still necessarily be incomplete. Still, the argument synthesis used in existing proof-checkers is incomplete, as in its full generality it requires higher-order unification; nonetheless it has been found to be very useful even in its restricted form. If the additional problems of checking coherency requirements and resolving ambiguities were dealt with by some other means (such as those outlined in the previous two paragraphs) then an incomplete but more extensive system of coercion synthesis might also be found to be useful in practice.

6 Summary

Coercion synthesis can provide an expressive implicit syntax for type-theoretic expressions, which can be made safe and unambiguous if this is desired by placing restrictions of coherency on the graph of coercions that is defined. The system is most useful when parameterised definitions of coercions are allowed, and is best implemented by statically generating the paths through the coercive graph when definitions are made, to make the more common synthesis process as efficient as possible. To implement the system within an existing proof-checker in a feasible way currently seems to require a syntax-based form of matching between types to be used in the coercion synthesis algorithm. Syntax-based matching is more strict than using the relation of full convertibility that might be intuitively expected, but there are other reasons why syntax-based matching might be preferred.

References

[Acz] P. Aczel. *Galois: a theory development project.* Representation of Mathematics in Logical Frameworks, Turin, 1993.

[Bai] A. Bailey. *LEGO with implicit coercions.* Draft documenting an earlier version of LEGOwcs.
`<URL:http://www.cs.man.ac.uk/~baileya/LAG/>`

[Bar] G. Barthe. *Implicit coercions in type systems.* Proceedings of TYPES'95, Springer-Verlag, 1996.

[BetTas] G. Betarte, A. Tasistro. *Extension of Martin-Löf 's theory of types with record types and subtyping.* Two manuscripts, 1995.

[BCGS] V. Breazu-Tannen, T. Coquand, C. Gunter, A. Scedrov. *Inheritance as Implicit Coercion.* Information and Computation 93, July 1991.

[COQ] B. Barras, S. Boutin, C. Cornes, J. Courant, J. Fillâtre, E. Giménez, H. Herbelin, G. Huet, C. Muñoz, C. Murthy, C. Parent, C. Paulin-Mohring, A. Saïbi, B. Werner. *The Coq proof assistant reference manual.* INRIA-Rocquencourt and CNRS-ENS Lyon, 1996.

[CoqHue] Th. Coquand, G. Huet. *The calculus of constructions.* Information and Computation 76, 1988.

[Gol] W. Goldfarb. *The undecidability of the second-order unification problem.* Theoretical Computer Science 13, 1981.

[Jon] A. Jones. *Some algorithmic and proof-theoretical aspects of coercive subtyping.* Informal Proceedings of TYPES'96 (Aussois), 1997.

[Luo94] Z. Luo. *Computation and reasoning: a type theory for computer science.* Oxford University Press, 1994.

[Luo96] Z. Luo. *Coercive subtyping in type theory.* Annual Conference of the European Association for Computer Science Logic, Utrecht, 1996.

[LuoPol] Z. Luo, R. Pollack. *The LEGO proof development system: user's manual.* Technical Report ECS-LFCS-92-211, LFCS, University of Edinburgh, 1992.

[MLöf] P. Martin-Löf. *Intuitionistic type theory.* Bibliopolis, 1984.

[Nip] T. Nipkow. *Higher-order unification, polymorphism, and subsorts.* Proceedings of the Second International Workshop on Conditional and Typed Rewriting Systems, LNCS 516, 1990.

[Pol90] R. Pollack. *Implicit syntax.* Informal Proceedings of the First Workshop on Logical Frameworks (Antibes), 1990.

[Pol96] R. Pollack. *How to believe a machine-checked proof.* submitted to Twenty-Five Years of Constructive Type Theory: Proceedings of the Venice Meeting
`<URL:ftp://ftp.dcs.ed.ac.uk/pub/lego/pollack-belief.ps.gz>`.

[Saï] A. Saïbi. *Typing algorithm in type theory with inheritance.* 24th Annual SIGPLAN-SIGACT Symposium on Principles of Programming Languages, Paris, 1997.

[Wer] B. Werner. *Une théorie des constructions inductives.* Doctoral thesis, Université Paris 7, 1994.

A History

This appendix seeks to place the paper in a recent historical context and to note some of the relationships between subtyping and object-orientedness.

My own work on coercions developed out of previous research by Gilles Barthes and Peter Aczel. It took some inspiration from an implementation of classes in LEGO started by Randy Pollack as a result of their work, and also benefited greatly from collaboration with Amokrane Saïbi, who helped with the first implementation of coercions in LEGO, and went on to implement coercions in the Coq proof-checker.

Aczel and Barthes started looking at notions of classes and inheritance between classes borrowed from object-oriented programming whilst working on GALOIS, a long-term project[Acz] to formalise and machine-check the main results of Galois theory in a type-theoretic framework. Galois theory draws together many pieces of abstract algebra. As a result, it involves a dense hierarchy of algebraic objects such as sets, groups, fields, and vectorspaces. There are various functions that can plausibly act on more than one of these types of object; these include operators, theories, proofs, and the construction of other structures. In the object-oriented terminology, such functions would be called *methods*. Having separate versions of these methods for many different types of object seems ungainly, and is out of step with informal mathematical convention.

As a result, Aczel and Barthes became interested in inheriting particular methods defined on a class of objects for other objects in subclasses built from the original class. The approach taken involved setting up a forest of class definitions where objects in a subclass could be coerced into being in a superclass by forgetting some extraneous information. As the connection with subtyping became evident, it began to seem preferable to concentrate on the coercions themselves and to consider all types to be classes. Thus the object-oriented terminology has been suppressed in this account, but the connections outlined above may still be of interest; hence this appendix.

B Technicalities

Here I outline three of the technical aspects of the system that are specific to the precise workings of LEGO and so seemed best left out of the main account.

Firstly, the type theory UTT draws a distinction between dependent and non-dependent sum types. If a has type T' and b has type $T[a/x]$ (that is, T with a substituted for x) then the pair (a, b) has a non-dependent type $T' \times T[a/x]$ by default, and it must be explicitly specified if it is to have dependent type $\Sigma x : T'.T$. This is indicated by writing $\mathsf{pair}_{\Sigma x:T'.T}(a, b)$.

This distinction yields three more occasions when it is useful to use a coercion between S and T on a subterm X of type S when the expression will not otherwise type-check:

- A casting within a dependent Σ-type, $\mathsf{pair}_{\Sigma x:T.\ t}(X, b)$
- A casting within a dependent Σ-type, $\mathsf{pair}_{\Sigma x:s.\ T[x/a]}(a, X)$
- A kind-coercion in a casting within a dependent Σ-type, $(a, b : X)$

Secondly, there are various commands in LEGO which expect their arguments to be terms with certain types. In these cases also, coercions may be synthesised in order to give the argument the correct type. One example is that a coercion from S to T can be used on $X : S$ in a refinement "`Refine` X", where the end of the current goal is T. Other commands require an argument which is a type, and so kind-coercions could be synthesised for X in the following:

- A goal command, "`Goal` X".
- A subclaim command, "`Claim` X".
- A command to use an equivalent goal, "`Equiv` X".

Thirdly, in LEGO some forms of entries (called *local* entries, as opposed to the other *global* ones) may be *discharged* from the context. The discharge of an identifier removes it from the context and generalises any context entries that followed it and had some dependency on it by prefixing them with an appropriate abstraction.

Coercion definitions may be made local. When they are discharged, then all paths that were generated from them are removed from the coercive graph, and all synthesised instances of these paths become local definitions within the body of the expressions in which they occur.

Coercions may also rely on local declarations; when such declarations are discharged then they are thereafter treated as extra implicit parameters to the coercion, as one might expect.

If a discharge command affects the set of coercion definitions, then the graph is regenerated and coherency rechecked from the point of the earliest of the coercion definition that is affected. If a problem concerning coherency results, then the discharge command that caused the problem is not allowed.

Verification of the Interface of a Small Proof System in Coq

Bruno Barras

INRIA-Rocquencourt
Domaine de Voluceau, B.P. 105,
78153 Le Chesnay Cedex, France

Abstract. This article describes the formalization of the interface of a proof-checker. The latter is based on a kernel consisting of type-checking functions for the Calculus of Constructions, but it seems the ideas can generalize to other type systems, as far as they are based on the proofs-as-terms principle. We suppose that the metatheory of the corresponding type system is proved (up to type decidability). We specify and certify the toplevel loop, the system invariant, and the error messages.

1 Introduction

Our ultimate goal is to verify a whole proof system. This would improve the reliability of the tool, but it would also be a good benchmark for the methodology of formally certified software design Coq [4] recommends. Applying this to the proof system itself would eventually lead to a *bootstrapped* version of Coq.

One of the major contributions of the LCF system [12], is that it implements a reliable proof-checker with a very small part of critical code: the *kernel.* Around this kernel stands an interface, in charge of translating the high-level directives of the user (such as tactics), into a proof-term that the kernel is able to check. The interface does not need to be certified because the kernel re-checks everything and would refuse a wrong proof. This approach makes it easier to formally check the program.

Following the presentation of cross-checking in [5], a proof-checker for the Calculus of Construction was certified [2, 3], requiring the formalization of the metatheory of this type system. This work has to be related to previous ones, such as [18, 19]. The extraction (some details on the extraction in Coq may be found in [16]) of the type-checking functions was performed, and a hand-written interface allowed to use it like a stand-alone proof system.

It appeared to be efficient, but unable to help the user when developing a proof, since it supports no error messages. Another drawback is that it allows only a linear presentation, proving one lemma after another. As a motivation, an interesting feature of a proof assistant the above system cannot provide, is to allow a modular and parameterized style. When implementing a proof system, there are two ways to have this kind of feature supported:

- By extending the type system: adding a module system with functors would allow parametric developments. This solution surely is the best in the long

term, but it requires the extension to be fully understood and formalized, which is not the case for many advanced features. It is not considered in the present article, but some recent works [14, 9] develop a metatheory of module systems.
- A preprocessing function may compile the higher-level language into the basic operations, given to the kernel. This approach is illustrated by the section mechanism of Coq (see example below).

The latter solution is easier to implement, but may jeopardize the soundness of the system, because it does not only affect the way to produce proof-terms, but also the way the theorems are stated. The problem is not that we may prove absurd propositions (this is guaranteed by the typing rules). It is that we are not sure that what the kernel actually checked is what we meant. The user has to check that the statements were processed as he expected. Indeed, if we compare this preprocessing function to a compiler, it is not very satisfying to ask the user to check the compiled code.

The following example illustrates this idea that soundness is not just a matter of typing. In Coq, the status of axioms inside a section is very sensitive: depending on the keyword that introduced it, it is either considered as a local hypothesis to be discharged at the end of the section, or an axiom that should survive the section closure.

```
Section VariableOrParameter.
  Variable absurd: False.

  Lemma false_impl_0_equal_1: O=(S O).
  Proof (False_ind O=(S O) absurd).
End VariableOrParameter.
```

When exiting the section, the axiom `absurd` is discharged: `absurd` disappears from the context, and the lemma `false_impl_0_equal_1` has the type `False->O=(S O)`. If we replace the word "`Variable`" by "`Parameter`", the script has radically different semantics: the two absurd statements `False` and `O=(S O)` are left unchanged after the section `S` is closed, which is undoubtedly not what the user expects. If he does not check the exact state of the environment, he may believe he proved `O=(S O)`. This is, of course, not the case.

The fact that the semantics rely on the choice of one word may be confusing for the user. From the the implementation point of view, this may lead to numerous subtle mistakes. We are thus urged to urged to formalize a command language. In this article, we consider three different components in a proof-checker:

- the parser and pretty-printer, reading commands on the keyboard and displaying messages on the screen,
- the interface with the user, the link between the command language and the typing operations to be performed,
- the kernel which provides the type-checking functions.

We describe the formalization[1] of the last two parts for a proof system based on the Calculus of Constructions: a basic command language with error messages, but without section mechanism. This language being defined and explained in the user manual, we feel that a good idea is to follow the style of this document, i.e. describing the commands by giving their effect on the system state, the list of errors they may raise, and what these errors mean.

2 Kernel

This section gives a quick description of the Calculus of Constructions (introduced by Coquand and Huet in [7]), and the metatheoretic results upon which we have built the proof system. The following can be read as a kind of interface specification for the kernel.

The internal representation of sorts, terms and contexts in de Bruijn notations uses the following syntax (terms and types share the same syntactic class):

$$\begin{aligned} \text{SRT} &:= \star \mid \square \\ \text{TRM} &:= s \mid n \mid \lambda T_1.T_2 \mid (T_1\ T_2) \mid \Pi T_1.T_2 \\ \text{CTX} &:= [] \mid \Gamma; T \end{aligned}$$

where $s \in \text{SRT}$, $T, T_1, T_2 \in \text{TRM}$, $\Gamma \in \text{CTX}$ and $n \in \mathbb{N}$. We write $|t|$ for the highest free de Bruijn variable of t.

Contexts are lists of terms. The list notations used in this article are $|\Gamma|$ for the length of lists, and $\Gamma(n)$ for the n-th item (the rightmost item has rank 0).

The one step β-reduction is written $\triangleright_\beta$. Its reflexive transitive closure is $\triangleright_\beta^*$, and $\approx_\beta$ stands for the β-conversion.

Then we define two forms of judgements:

- a context validity judgement, noted $\Gamma \vdash$, which expresses that the assumptions in Γ are well-formed,
- a typing judgement, noted $\Gamma \vdash m : t$, expressing that the term m has type t in the context Γ.

The precise inference rules (Fig. 1) for these judgements are not really relevant to understand the discussion: this could be adapted to the case of Pure Type Systems (PTS) [1]. Let us just stress that they are mutually recursive: terms are typed only in valid contexts, and the validity of a context requires that all its components are typed by sorts.

We prove the usual metatheoretic properties of type systems as in [11]. A detailed description of the proofs formalized in Coq can be found in [2, 3]. We only list the main properties:

- Confluence of β-reduction: the main corollary is the unicity of normal forms

$$a \triangleright_\beta^* b \wedge a \triangleright_\beta^* c \Rightarrow \exists d.\ b \triangleright_\beta^* d \wedge c \triangleright_\beta^* d$$

[1] The whole proof script is available at the following address: `http://pauillac.inria.fr/~barras/typechecker/`

$$\text{(WF-[])}\ \frac{}{[\,]\vdash} \qquad \text{(WF-VAR)}\ \frac{\Gamma\vdash T : s}{\Gamma;T\vdash}(s\in \mathrm{SRT})$$

$$\text{(PROP)}\ \frac{\Gamma\vdash}{\Gamma\vdash \star : \Box} \qquad \text{(VAR)}\ \frac{\Gamma\vdash \qquad \uparrow^{n+1}\Gamma(n)=T}{\Gamma\vdash n : T}$$

$$\text{(ABS)}\ \frac{\Gamma\vdash T : s_1 \qquad \Gamma;T\vdash M : U \qquad \Gamma;T\vdash U : s_2}{\Gamma\vdash \lambda T.M : \Pi T.U}(s_1, s_2\in \mathrm{SRT})$$

$$\text{(APP)}\ \frac{\Gamma\vdash v : V \qquad \Gamma\vdash u : \Pi V.T}{\Gamma\vdash (u\ v) : T[0 := v]}$$

$$\text{(PROD)}\ \frac{\Gamma\vdash T : s_1 \qquad \Gamma;T\vdash U : s_2}{\Gamma\vdash (\Pi T.U) : s_2}\ (s_1, s_2\in \mathrm{SRT})$$

$$\text{(CONV)}\ \frac{\Gamma\vdash M : U \qquad \Gamma\vdash V : s \qquad U\approx_\beta V}{\Gamma\vdash M : V}\ (s\in \mathrm{SRT})$$

Fig. 1. Typing Rules for the Calculus of Constructions

- Subject reduction: a term keeps its type by reduction

$$\Gamma\vdash m : t\ \wedge\ m \rhd_\beta^* m' \ \Rightarrow\ \Gamma\vdash m' : t$$

- Type uniqueness modulo β-conversion: all the types of a given term are convertible

$$\Gamma\vdash m : u\ \wedge\ \Gamma\vdash m : v\ \Rightarrow\ u\approx_\beta v$$

- Strong normalization ($\mathcal{SN}$ is the set of terms from which no infinite reduction path starts): all the well-typed terms are strongly normalizing

$$\Gamma\vdash m : t\ \Rightarrow\ m\in \mathcal{SN}$$

- Decidability of typing judgements:

$$(\Gamma\vdash) + \neg(\Gamma\vdash)$$
$$(\Gamma\vdash m : t) + \neg(\Gamma\vdash m : t)$$

The + denotes the constructive OR connective; this means we can produce by extraction a program that answers `true` when the judgement is derivable, and `false` otherwise. We will also write $\exists^* x.\ P(x)$ for the constructive existential, which gives, by extraction, a program computing a witness x satisfying the predicate P.

We could have proved simultaneously the decidability results by a mutual recursion, but this would yield a very inefficient program, which would re-check the validity of the context a huge number of times[2]. The resulting exponential complexity factor is avoided, by distinguishing three typing operations:

- type-inference in a valid context

$$\Gamma \vdash \Rightarrow \exists^* t.\ (\Gamma \vdash m : t)\ +\ \forall t.\ \neg(\Gamma \vdash m : t) \tag{1}$$

- type-checking in a valid context

$$\Gamma \vdash \Rightarrow (\Gamma \vdash m : t) + \neg(\Gamma \vdash m : t) \tag{2}$$

- checking the extension of a valid context

$$\Gamma \vdash \Rightarrow (\Gamma ; t \vdash) + \neg(\Gamma ; t \vdash) \tag{3}$$

The decidability results can easily be proved: $(\Gamma \vdash) + \neg(\Gamma \vdash)$, by repeating (3) on the successive terms of Γ, and $(\Gamma \vdash m : t) + \neg(\Gamma \vdash m : t)$, by checking Γ, then typechecking m with (2).

We give no details on the type-checking algorithm. It should not be necessary, because we describe a general method we want to apply to many type systems. The question of finding algorithms for type systems is a major concern in type theory, and has been answered for various systems by [15, 13, 18, 2] and many others. The above functions may take advantage of all these works. As an example, we could consider the type-checking function as a strategy for the Constructive Engine of Huet [13].

Since a proof may be reduced to a derivable typing judgement $\Gamma \vdash m : t$ stating that under the assumptions Γ, m is a proof of the proposition t, this may be already considered as a proof-checker. But it cannot be considered as a proof system, because it provides no help in error recovery, and the judgement has to be given in a whole. In the following sections, we describe and formalize the interface, that transforms a mere type-checker into an executable proof system.

3 Certified Error Messages

The first feature we add is the possibility to return error messages instead of an uninformative failure. These messages should help understanding what is wrong, and should give the location of the error. In our approach, it is not just a comment that is printed when one of the typing operations fails; it should carry a piece of *checked* information that explains why the typing operation cannot succeed.

Error messages are usually directly displayed as strings. But it would be obviously tedious and awkward to have the main type-checking loop handle actual

[2] This is similar to the naive way of computing the terms of Fibonacci's sequence, with a double recursive call. We use the same trick, keeping track of the context validity proofs. Note that, by extraction, these proofs are not actually computed.

messages in string format. Instead, we define an abstract notation, corresponding to the different possible failures of the typing process:

$$
\begin{aligned}
\textsc{TypErr} := \;& \mathrm{Under}(T, e) \mid \mathrm{DbError}(n) \mid \mathrm{Topsort(s)} \\
& \mid \mathrm{LambdaTopsort}(T, s) \mid \mathrm{ExpectType}(T_1, T_2, T_3) \\
& \mid \mathrm{NotAType}(T_1, T_2) \mid \mathrm{NotAFun}(T_1, T_2) \\
& \mid \mathrm{ApplyErr}(T_1, T_2, T_3, T_4)
\end{aligned}
$$

where $T, T_1, T_2, T_3, T_4 \in \textsc{Trm}$, $e \in \textsc{TypErr}$, $s \in \textsc{Srt}$ and $n \in \mathbb{N}$.

These abstract syntax trees have a concrete representation as strings. This translation is straightforward. As an example, Fig. 2 shows how they would be mapped in an English language-tuned implementation.

Under($t_1, \ldots$ Under(t_n, e))	"In the local context $t_1, \ldots, t_n$, e"
DbError(n)	"The de Bruijn variable n is unbound"
Topsort(s)	"The sort s is ill-typed"
LambdaTopsort(t, s)	"The term t is a λ-abstraction over a type of sort s"
ExpectType(m, t, t_e)	"The term m of type t, is expected to have the type t_e"
NotAType(m, t)	"The term m of type t cannot be typed by a sort"
NotAFun(m, t)	"The term m of type t is non-functional"
ApplyErr(u, a, v, b)	"The term u of type a cannot be applied to v of type b"

Fig. 2. Concrete syntax of error messages

Note that Under(T, e) is the only recursive constructor. It contains the type of the variables of the local context the error occurred in. It could be chosen more verbose and keep track of the exact path in the term, and not only the successive local variables.

Error messages depend on the type system: for the general case of PTS, we would need an error message for forbidden product formations; for those not satisfying type uniqueness, we may want to infer the principal type, etc. But we claim that the method remains general enough to be applied in other cases. Adapting the error messages to the type system is not the main point here.

The messages must use a language the user can understand, regardless of the actual type-checking algorithm. All we require is the knowledge of the typing rules and the basic metatheoretic results[3] such as subject-reduction, the fact that objects of type $\Box$ cannot be abstracted, etc.

We define Expln_Γ, the set of meaningful errors in context Γ, given as Prolog-like clauses in Fig. 3. In Coq, we use an inductive predicate, well adapted to this

[3] The knowledge necessary for PTS is not so important. For ML, understanding error messages requires some notions of unification, which is much more difficult.

kind of definition. This predicate is meant to encode the meaning of the error messages by a logical proposition. We are ensured that if the error e belongs to Expln_Γ, then there is a proof of what the error message intuitively means (compare Fig. 2 and 3). Let us explain two of these clauses:

- In order to be typed, a de Bruijn variable n must be defined in (or bound by) the context, i.e. n must be less than the length of the context. Thus, the error DbError(n) may be raised when n is greater than or equal to the length of the context, and the variable is said unbound.
- The error message ExpectType($m, t_{\mathrm{act}}, t_{\mathrm{exp}}$) is said consistent only when we have a proof that $\Gamma \vdash m : t_{\mathrm{act}}$ is derivable but not $\Gamma \vdash m : t_{\mathrm{exp}}$, which is the formal equivalent of the associated sentence in natural language. t_{exp} may be ill-typed, but all its variables must be bound in the context, or else it could not be printed.

$$\frac{\Gamma;t \vdash \quad e \in \mathrm{Expln}_{\Gamma;t}}{\mathrm{Under}(t,e) \in \mathrm{Expln}_\Gamma} \qquad \frac{n \geq |\Gamma|}{\mathrm{DbError}(n) \in \mathrm{Expln}_\Gamma}$$

$$\frac{\forall t.\ \neg(\Gamma \vdash s : t)}{\mathrm{Topsort}(s) \in \mathrm{Expln}_\Gamma} \qquad \frac{\Gamma;t \vdash m : s \qquad \forall t.\ \neg(\Gamma \vdash s : t)}{\mathrm{LambdaTopsort}(\lambda t.m, s) \in \mathrm{Expln}_\Gamma}$$

$$\frac{\Gamma \vdash m : t_{\mathrm{act}} \qquad \neg(\Gamma \vdash m : t_{\mathrm{exp}}) \qquad |t_{exp}| < |\Gamma|}{\mathrm{ExpectType}(m, t_{\mathrm{act}}, t_{\mathrm{exp}}) \in \mathrm{Expln}_\Gamma}$$

$$\frac{\Gamma \vdash m : t \qquad \forall s \in \mathrm{SRT}.\ \neg(\Gamma \vdash m : s)}{\mathrm{NotAType}(m,t) \in \mathrm{Expln}_\Gamma}$$

$$\frac{\Gamma \vdash m : t \qquad \forall a,b.\ \neg(\Gamma \vdash m : \Pi a.b)}{\mathrm{NotAFun}(m,t) \in \mathrm{Expln}_\Gamma}$$

$$\frac{\Gamma \vdash u : \Pi a.b \qquad \Gamma \vdash v : c \qquad \neg(\Gamma \vdash v : a)}{\mathrm{ApplyErr}(u, \Pi a.b, v, c) \in \mathrm{Expln}_\Gamma}$$

Fig. 3. Meaning of errors

This notion discards inconsistent error messages such as "$\star$ isn't typed by a sort" (its type is the sort $\Box$), or the very annoying "m has type t, but is expected to have type t", sometimes yielded by bogus compilers.

Being more precise, only a subset of all possible errors can be raised for each of the three possible typing operations:

- The set InfErr_t gives the allowed errors when inferring the type of t. It is recursively defined:

$$\mathrm{InfErr}_s = \{\mathrm{Topsort(s)}\}$$

$$\begin{aligned}
\mathrm{InfErr}_n &= \{\mathrm{DbError}(n)\} \\
\mathrm{InfErr}_{\lambda t.m} &= \mathrm{InfErr}_t \cup \mathrm{NotAType}(t, \mathrm{TRM}) \cup \mathrm{Under}(t, \mathrm{InfErr}_m) \\
&\quad \cup \{\mathrm{LambdaTopsort}(\lambda t.m, s)\} \\
\mathrm{InfErr}_{(u\ v)} &= \mathrm{InfErr}_u \cup \mathrm{NotAFun}(u, \mathrm{TRM}) \cup \mathrm{InfErr}_v \\
&\quad \cup \mathrm{ApplyErr}(u, \mathrm{TRM}, v, \mathrm{TRM}) \\
\mathrm{InfErr}_{\Pi t.u} &= \mathrm{InfErr}_t \cup \mathrm{NotAType}(t, \mathrm{TRM}) \cup \mathrm{Under}(t, \mathrm{InfErr}_u) \\
&\quad \cup \mathrm{Under}(t, \mathrm{NotAType}(u, \mathrm{TRM}))
\end{aligned}$$

We prove that any meaningful error of InfErr_t witnesses that t is an ill-typed term (i.e. the inference operation fails):

$$e \in \mathrm{Expln}_\Gamma \cap \mathrm{InfErr}_m \Rightarrow \forall t.\ \neg(\Gamma \vdash m : t) \tag{4}$$

- Checking whether m has type t fails when m is ill-typed, t is ill-typed (but not equal to $\Box$) or when the inferred type of m is not convertible with t:

$$\begin{aligned}
\mathrm{ChkErr}_{(m:t)} = \mathrm{InfErr}_m &\cup \{e \mid e \in \mathrm{InfErr}_t \wedge t \neq \Box\} \\
&\cup \mathrm{ExpectType}(m, \mathrm{TRM}, t)
\end{aligned}$$

  Here again, the restriction to the set $\mathrm{ChkErr}_{(m:t)}$ allows to prove that m has not the type t:

$$e \in \mathrm{Expln}_\Gamma \cap \mathrm{ChkErr}_{(m:t)} \Rightarrow \neg(\Gamma \vdash m : t) \tag{5}$$

- Adding a variable of type t is forbidden when t is ill-typed or when it is not typed by a sort:

$$\mathrm{DeclErr}_t = \mathrm{InfErr}_t \cup \mathrm{NotAType}(t, \mathrm{TRM})$$

  The meaningful errors of $\mathrm{DeclErr}_t$ implies that $\Gamma; t$ is not valid:

$$e \in \mathrm{Expln}_\Gamma \cap \mathrm{DeclErr}_t \Rightarrow \neg(\Gamma; t \vdash) \tag{6}$$

The following examples illustrate the necessity of these subsets: when trying to infer the type of $\lambda\star.\lambda 0.0$[4], we do not allow any error to be raised because this term is well-formed: its type is $\Pi\star.\Pi 0.1$[5]. We avoid completely unrelated error messages such as DbError(42657) (the de Bruijn 42657 does not occur in the term), but also the irrelevant, though consistent, errors such as $\mathrm{NotAType}(\lambda\star.\lambda 0.0, \Pi\star.\Pi 0.1)$, because pointing out that a term is not typed by a sort does not imply that it has no type.

In the present work, error messages reflect the steps of the type-checking function. We propose a variation on the above definition, to show that this similarity is not necessary even though it makes the proofs easier. We could define InfErr_m and $\mathrm{ChkErr}_{(m:t)}$ as mutually dependent sets: type-checking involves

[4] This term would be written $\lambda A{:}\star.\lambda x{:}A.x$ in named variable notation

[5] stands for $\Pi A{:}\star.\Pi x{:}A.A$

type-inference and type-inference involves type-checking in the case of the application. When inferring the type of $(u\ v)$ with u of type $\Pi a.b$, we check that v has type a. The type-checking function could return the error ExpectType(v, t, a), but it is more appropriate to return the error ApplyErr$(u, \Pi a.b, v, t)$ of our specification, because it gives more details on the context of the error.

These error messages are incorporated in the typing functions (i.e. in the kernel). This gives raise to the following redesigned specifications:

$$\Gamma \vdash \Rightarrow\ \exists^* t.\ (\Gamma \vdash m : t) + \exists^* e \in \mathrm{Expln}_\Gamma \cap \mathrm{InfErr}_m$$
$$\Gamma \vdash \Rightarrow\ (\Gamma \vdash m : t) + \exists^* e \in \mathrm{Expln}_\Gamma \cap \mathrm{ChkErr}_{(m:t)}$$
$$\Gamma \vdash \Rightarrow\ (\Gamma; t \vdash) + \exists^* e \in \mathrm{Expln}_\Gamma \cap \mathrm{DeclErr}_t$$

The algorithms used are the same, but instead of just proving derivability or not of a given judgement, we give a certified error message with its justification when typing fails. Remark that these specifications are a refinement of the original ones, thanks to the results (4, 5, 6).

The error messages appear as an extension of the kernel, but now, it is possible to have an algorithm without error messages. If we consider that errors are indeed a kind of debugging facility, we are not very concerned by reporting errors efficiently. In that case, we can use any algorithm returning uninformative failure, and if it fails, call our algorithm that will also fail, but with informative failure.

4 Specification of the Machine

We would like to integrate the kernel in a proof system allowing the development of proofs in a more natural way for the user (i.e. closer to the usual mathematical style). In this section, we show how the incremental style of the mathematical language may be reflected.

To any point of a theory script, we can associate the list of assumptions made. Every sentence of the script refers implicitly to this list, and can modify it. This incremental style recalls the notion of state. Therefore, we model the proof system as an automaton whose state is mainly a list of axioms. The state of the system may change by transitions, enabled by reading commands in an input stream. There are two kinds of transitions:

- successful transitions, producing an acknowledgment message and the new state of the system,
- error transitions, yielding an error message.

The state of the proof-checker is a well-formed context, with the list of print names associated to these axioms. The print names should be unique and the two lists have the same length. This is formalized by a structure $S = (\Gamma, \Sigma, \pi_1, \pi_2, \pi_3)$

composed of two computational objects and three proofs (the latter are sometimes omitted and a state may be noted (Γ, Σ)), such that:

$$\begin{aligned} &\Gamma \in \text{CTX} \\ &\Sigma \in \text{NAME}^* \\ &\pi_1 \ : \Gamma \vdash \\ &\pi_2 \ : |\Gamma| = |\Sigma| \\ &\pi_3 \ : \text{AllDiff}(\Sigma) \end{aligned}$$

The set of names (NAME) is abstract. For the moment, we only require the equality of it to be decidable. NAME* is the set of lists of names, and the proposition AllDiff(Σ) means that all the components of Σ are distinct:

$$\text{AllDiff}(\Sigma) \ := \ \forall i, j.\ \Sigma(i) = \Sigma(j) \Rightarrow i = j$$

The fields π_1, π_2, π_3 are the proofs of the invariant of the system. Since the proofs are part of the structure, the invariant is guaranteed by typing. The proof π_2 ensures that every axiom has a name, and π_3 avoids hiding a variable by declaring another one with the same name.

The operations of that machine are similar to the ones the user will enter. As a consequence, a machine like the Constructive Engine is not what we need, because it can be used only to type-check terms. We are enclosing the type-checking machines (or functions) inside a new one. The set of commands defines the mathematical language of the proof system. We consider a very simple one, consisting of six commands:

$$\begin{aligned} \text{COMMAND} := \ & \text{INFER}(T) \mid \text{CHECK}(T_1, T_2) \mid \text{AXIOM}(x, T) \\ & \mid \text{DELETE} \mid \text{LIST} \mid \text{QUIT} \end{aligned}$$

performing, respectively, type inference of a term, checking that a term has a given type, adding an assumption to the current state, removing the latest introduced axiom, printing the list of current assumption names, and exiting.

For each successful command, the proof system answers with one of the following messages (like for error messages, there is in each case, a corresponding natural language sentence):

$$\begin{aligned} \text{MESSAGE} := \ & \text{Inferred}(T) \mid \text{Correct} \mid \text{Assumed}(x) \mid \text{Deleted}(x) \\ & \mid \text{DisplayNames}(\Sigma) \mid \text{Exiting} \end{aligned}$$

A predicate defines the correct transitions: the rules in Fig. 4 define the proposition $(S_{\text{i}}, c) \stackrel{\text{exec}}{\longrightarrow} (S_{\text{f}}, m)$, meaning that in the state S_{i}, the command c allows to reach the state S_{f}, and the acknowledgment message m is displayed.

Note that in the axiom rule, we do not have to specify that $\Gamma; T$ is a valid context and x is fresh, because this is ensured by the invariant. This allows concise (and more readable) specifications. The premises of the first two rules represent calls to auxiliary machines beside those required to maintain the invariant. They would not be necessary if any derivable judgement (context validity or typing

$$\frac{\Gamma \vdash m : t}{((\Gamma, \Sigma), \text{INFER}(m)) \xrightarrow{\text{exec}} ((\Gamma, \Sigma), \text{Inferred}(t))}$$

$$\frac{\Gamma \vdash m : t}{((\Gamma, \Sigma), \text{CHECK}(m, t)) \xrightarrow{\text{exec}} ((\Gamma, \Sigma), \text{Correct})}$$

$$\frac{}{((\Gamma, \Sigma), \text{AXIOM}(x, t)) \xrightarrow{\text{exec}} (((\Gamma; t), (\Sigma; x)), \text{Assumed}(x))}$$

$$\frac{}{(((\Gamma; t), (\Sigma; x)), \text{DELETE}) \xrightarrow{\text{exec}} ((\Gamma, \Sigma), \text{Deleted}(x))}$$

$$\frac{}{((\Gamma, \Sigma), \text{LIST}) \xrightarrow{\text{exec}} ((\Gamma, \Sigma), \text{DisplayNames}(\Sigma))}$$

$$\frac{}{((\Gamma, \Sigma), \text{QUIT}) \xrightarrow{\text{exec}} ((\Gamma, \Sigma), \text{Exiting})}$$

Fig. 4. Successful transitions

judgement) could be the state of the proof-checker. But it would split commands like INFER and CHECK in two subcommands: one building the judgement, and the other one displaying and discarding the judgement, thus restoring the initial state. Also, we consider these two commands as queries about the current state. Therefore, they should not change the state. Only AXIOM and DELETE should.

When no successful transition can occur, the system may return an error message. The latter are not only the type error messages introduced in the previous section: some errors may result from a bad usage of commands that would break the invariant. The set of errors is the following:

$$\text{ERROR} := \text{NameClash}(x) \mid \text{TypeError}(e) \mid \text{CantDelete}$$

where $x \in \text{NAME}$ and $e \in \text{TYPERR}$.

The error NameClash(x) is raised when a command tries to add an axiom under the already used name x. The command DELETE raises CantDelete when the current context is empty. These error transitions are formally defined in Fig. 5.

The main result is that for any command in any state, we can either reach a new state printing an acknowledgment message, or find an error consistent with the initial state:

$$\forall S_i, c.\ \exists^*(S_f, m).\ (S_i, c) \xrightarrow{\text{exec}} (S_f, m)\ +\ \exists^* e.\ (S_i, c) \xrightarrow{\text{error}} e$$

This ensures that the extracted program **interp_command** (the command interpreter) is sound, i.e. it allows only valid transitions.

$$\frac{e \in \mathrm{Expln}_{\Gamma} \cap \mathrm{InfErr}_m}{((\Gamma, \Sigma), \mathrm{INFER}(m)) \xrightarrow{\text{error}} \mathrm{TypeError}(e)}$$

$$\frac{e \in \mathrm{Expln}_{\Gamma} \cap \mathrm{ChkErr}_{(m:t)}}{((\Gamma, \Sigma), \mathrm{CHECK}(m, t)) \xrightarrow{\text{error}} \mathrm{TypeError}(e)}$$

$$\frac{e \in \mathrm{Expln}_{\Gamma} \cap \mathrm{DeclErr}_t}{((\Gamma, \Sigma), \mathrm{AXIOM}(x, t)) \xrightarrow{\text{error}} \mathrm{TypeError}(e)}$$

$$\frac{x \in \Sigma}{((\Gamma, \Sigma), \mathrm{AXIOM}(x, t)) \xrightarrow{\text{error}} \mathrm{NameClash}(x)}$$

$$\frac{}{(([\,], \Sigma), \mathrm{DELETE}) \xrightarrow{\text{error}} \mathrm{CantDelete}}$$

Fig. 5. Error transitions

The following lemma is a kind of completeness result:

$$\neg(\ (S_{\mathrm{i}}, c) \xrightarrow{\text{exec}} (S_{\mathrm{f}}, m) \ \wedge\ (S_{\mathrm{i}}, c) \xrightarrow{\text{error}} e\ )$$

It proves that in a given state, an error may be raised only when there is no transition towards a new state. Therefore the system will never reject well-formed commands.

5 De Bruijn vs Named Variables Notations

Type systems are generally easier to formalize in de Bruijn notation [6] because it avoids the renaming problems, and gives better intuition on the scope of variables. But this notation isn't user-friendly and the human wants to handle names.

This section describes how this translation between named variables and de Bruijn notation can be made, by adding a layer on top of the proof system of the previous section.

The abstract type of names of the previous section may be instantiated by any type fulfilling some basic conditions. The equality of names should be decidable, as already required, but we also require the existence of an injection of naturals to names:

$$\exists^* f \in \mathbb{N} \to \textsc{Name}.\ \forall n, m \in \mathbb{N}.\ f(n) = f(m) \Rightarrow n = m$$

If we choose the type `string` of Objective Caml to implement the set of names, the function `(fun n -> "x"^(string_of_int n))` fits (ignoring overflow problems). It would be equivalent to assume that the set of names is infinite:

$$\forall \Sigma \in \textsc{Name}^*.\ \exists^* x \notin \Sigma$$

Indeed, the above statement specifies a function that, given a list of names, returns a fresh name.

The parser returns expressions with names:

$$\text{EXPR} := s \mid x \mid \lambda x\!:\!E_1.E_2 \mid (E_1\ E_2) \mid \Pi x\!:\!E_1.E_2$$

where $s \in \text{SRT}$, $x \in \text{NAME}$ and $E_1, E_2 \in \text{EXPR}$. We define $\text{FV}(E)$, the set of free variables of an expression E, in the usual way.

Given a list of print names Σ, we define the translation predicate, Fig. 6. The n-th item of the list is the name of the de Bruijn variable n. We cannot assume all the elements of Σ to be distinct, because we must allow the hiding of variables, as in $\lambda x\!:\!A.\lambda x\!:\!B.x$. Instead, we can translate a de Bruijn variable n into x only when the latest occurrence of x in Σ is at rank n.

$$\frac{}{\Sigma \vdash s \overset{\text{dB}}{\longleftrightarrow} s}\ (s \in \text{SRT})$$

$$\frac{\Sigma(n) = x \qquad \forall k < n.\Sigma(k) \neq x}{\Sigma \vdash x \overset{\text{dB}}{\longleftrightarrow} n}$$

$$\frac{\Sigma \vdash E_1 \overset{\text{dB}}{\longleftrightarrow} A \qquad \Sigma; x \vdash E_2 \overset{\text{dB}}{\longleftrightarrow} M}{\Sigma \vdash \lambda x\!:\!E_1.E_2 \overset{\text{dB}}{\longleftrightarrow} \lambda A.M}$$

$$\frac{\Sigma \vdash E_1 \overset{\text{dB}}{\longleftrightarrow} u \qquad \Sigma \vdash E_2 \overset{\text{dB}}{\longleftrightarrow} v}{\Sigma \vdash (E_1\ E_2) \overset{\text{dB}}{\longleftrightarrow} (u\ v)}$$

$$\frac{\Sigma \vdash E_1 \overset{\text{dB}}{\longleftrightarrow} A \qquad \Sigma; x \vdash E_2 \overset{\text{dB}}{\longleftrightarrow} M}{\Sigma \vdash \Pi x\!:\!E_1.E_2 \overset{\text{dB}}{\longleftrightarrow} \Pi A.M}$$

Fig. 6. De Bruijn and named variables translation

An expression e may be translated into a term, unless some of its free variables are not members of Σ. This specifies the translation function from expressions to terms:

$$\forall(\Sigma, E).\ (\exists^* t \in \text{TRM}.\ \Sigma \vdash E \overset{\text{dB}}{\longleftrightarrow} t)\ +\ (\exists^* l \neq [\,].\ l \subset \text{FV}(E)\backslash\Sigma)$$

The opposite translation is not supposed to fail because it will be used only on terms of the (well-formed) messages generated by the system, and are therefore defined in the current context:

$$\forall(\Sigma, t).\ \text{AllDiff}(\Sigma)\ \wedge\ |t| < |\Sigma|\ \Rightarrow\ \exists^* E \in \text{EXPR}.\ \Sigma \vdash E \overset{\text{dB}}{\longleftrightarrow} t$$

where $|t|$ denotes the highest free de Bruijn variable in term t. This is a bit restrictive: the translation is possible without $\text{AllDiff}(\Sigma)$, as far as t does not refer to hidden variables.

We can prove that it defines a bijection between the domain quotiented by α-conversion and the range:

- two terms equivalent to the same expression are equal:

$$\Sigma \vdash E \stackrel{\mathrm{dB}}{\longleftrightarrow} t \wedge \Sigma \vdash E \stackrel{\mathrm{dB}}{\longleftrightarrow} u \Rightarrow t = u$$

- two expressions equivalent to the same term are α-convertible:

$$\Sigma \vdash E_1 \stackrel{\mathrm{dB}}{\longleftrightarrow} t \wedge \Sigma \vdash E_2 \stackrel{\mathrm{dB}}{\longleftrightarrow} t \Rightarrow E_1 \stackrel{\alpha}{\equiv} E_2$$

Every structure described in the previous section (commands, messages and errors) is duplicated by changing terms into expressions. The commands are called abstract syntax trees (AST), messages and errors are said printable. The translation predicate is extended to these pairs of sets.

Only the error messages change, because new errors may appear during this translation. Instead of having De Bruijn errors, we may have unbound variable names. The Under constructor also changes: it introduces not only a type expression but also the print name of the variable.

The behavior of the machine is the following: the read AST is processed to build a command. It only consists of translating the expressions into terms. In the future, it could include other syntactic processes (e.g. macro expansions), and this phase would rather be called command synthesis. This operation may fail, and a printable error message is emitted. If it succeeds, the command is given to the internal machine, and the output of the machine (message or error) is translated to make it printable.

The correct behavior is defined by one clause, calling the machine of the previous section:

$$\frac{S_{\mathrm{i}} \vdash a \stackrel{\mathrm{dB}}{\longleftrightarrow} c \qquad (S_{\mathrm{i}}, c) \stackrel{\mathrm{exec}}{\longrightarrow} (S_{\mathrm{f}}, m) \qquad S_{\mathrm{i}} \vdash m' \stackrel{\mathrm{dB}}{\longleftrightarrow} m}{(S_{\mathrm{i}}, a) \stackrel{\mathrm{step}}{\longrightarrow} (S_{\mathrm{f}}, m')}$$

Note that the message is translated in the initial state S_{i}, because we feel that the output message should be understood without knowing exactly the effect of the command.

The failure behavior needs two rules, because errors may be raised either during synthesis, or during the execution of the command:

$$\frac{l \neq [\,] \qquad l \subset \mathrm{FV}(a) \backslash \Sigma}{((\Gamma, \Sigma), a) \stackrel{\mathrm{fail}}{\longrightarrow} \mathrm{UnboundVars}(l)}$$

$$\frac{S_{\mathrm{i}} \vdash a \stackrel{\mathrm{dB}}{\longleftrightarrow} c \qquad (S_{\mathrm{i}}, c) \stackrel{\mathrm{error}}{\longrightarrow} e \qquad S_{\mathrm{i}} \vdash e' \stackrel{\mathrm{dB}}{\longleftrightarrow} e}{(S_{\mathrm{i}}, a) \stackrel{\mathrm{fail}}{\longrightarrow} e'}$$

The machine is now fully specified, and we can prove that any AST in any state may be answered either by a message or an error:

$$\forall S_i, a.\ \exists^*(S_f, m).\ (S_i, a) \xrightarrow{\text{step}} (S_f, m)\ +\ \exists^* e.\ (S_i, a) \xrightarrow{\text{fail}} e$$

This theorem gives, by extraction, the AST interpreter. The difficulty is to ensure that no de Bruijn translation error occurs in the generated messages. This holds because the members of the messages are well-typed (the constructor ExpectType requires an extra hypothesis for that).

Finally, we check that the steps are not ambiguous:

$$\neg(\ (S_i, a) \xrightarrow{\text{step}} (S_f, m)\ \ \wedge\ \ (S_i, a) \xrightarrow{\text{fail}} e\ )$$

This requires the synthesis step to be deterministic. Or else we could imagine that an AST could be translated into two commands, one succeeding, and the other one failing.

6 Building the System

We performed the extraction of the AST interpreter. The output is an Objective Caml program that takes the current state and an AST and returns either the new state, with an acknowledgment message, or an error message. This function is used to make a single step.

The effective system iterates this function on an input stream of commands and yields a stream of messages. Having acknowledgment and error messages in different types distinguishes two behaviors w.r.t the errors:

- The usual behavior of a compiler would be to abort when an error occurs.
- A toplevel would just print the error message, and resume with the same state, displaying a prompt.

We write a toplevel loop by hand. Since such a loop may potentially not terminate, it must be specified in Coq using co-inductive types, but during the extraction, they cannot be easily mapped to Objective Caml, which is a strict language.

The input stream is not a command stream, but a character one. We have to write a parser. In the same way, the output stream should also be a character stream. We also write a pretty-printer for the messages. Since the concrete syntax is close to the abstract syntax, these functions are very easy to write, and are assumed correct.

These programs may be pasted together and make up a stand-alone system, and the previous sections form its user manual. As an example, we can define the set of naturals and check a few terms:

```
Coc < Axiom nat:Prop.
nat is assumed.
Coc < Axiom O:nat.
```

```
O is assumed.
Coc < Axiom S:nat->nat.
S is assumed.
Coc < Infer (S (S O)).
Inferred type: nat
Coc < Check [x:nat](S (S x)) : nat->nat.
Correct.
```

The examples below show how the system reacts when entering a command that would violate the invariant:

```
Coc < Axiom S:Prop.
Error: Name clash with S.
Coc < Infer (S S).
Error: The term S of type nat->nat cannot be applied
 to S of type nat->nat.
```

These messages are, as expected, relevant and suggest precisely the nature of the error. But there is a problem with local contexts:

```
Coc < Infer [A:Prop][x:A](x x).
Error: In the local context
 x0 : Prop
 x1 : x0
The term x1 of type x0 is non-functional.
```

The message is very difficult to read because the names given by the user are changed. This happens because the internal representation of terms does not handle names. The latter are simply forgotten during the synthesis process. Only the objects introduced at toplevel have a name.

We may consider two ways to fix this problem, by changing the structure of terms. First, adopting a named-based presentation, like in [17, 18]. This makes the metatheory more difficult to prove, because we do not use the usual structural induction scheme, but a scheme taking the α-conversion into account.

We would suggest keeping the de Bruijn notation, and annotating the binding constructions λ and Π with names. The latter are seen as basenames for the names actually printed. These annotations would simply be ignored in all kernel operations (typing, reduction, substitution, etc.). The name capture problem would be dealt with at printing, by adding a suffix to discriminate the binders with the same basename.

Formally, this is not as trivial as it may seem, because we have to reason modulo a pseudo-α-conversion rule, instead of the handy Leibniz equality. The problem may be serious when proving the confluence property. For example, if we consider the η-reduction, the Calculus of Constructions without names is confluent, but the system with names is not (w.r.t. Leibniz equality): $\lambda x.((\lambda y.y)\ x)$ β-reduces to $\lambda x.x$, but η-reduces to $\lambda y.y$. This issue also occurs in the name-based presentation.

7 Conclusion

All the results about the interface are rather easy to prove: the main difficulty is to find a presentation which is both intuitive and concise. The formalization of the translation between de Bruijn and named variables notations is sometimes a bit tedious. This is due to the initial choice of using de Bruijn variables, and then building a thin layer of names on top of it.

The command language we proved is still a very low-level one. The natural extension of this work would be to include more elaborate mathematical concepts, e.g. the section mechanism that initially motivated this approach.

Another direction to explore would be to prove the parser and the pretty-printer. This is not our concern for the moment: one can always want to go further in the formalization. But, if we do, we will have to go on and prove the file system, and then, the operating system, and so on. We would better try to find a limit to what we prove in Coq. Our choice of assuming the parser and the printer to be correct is pragmatic: such functions are easy to write, and tools such as Yacc may help.

Since this development was inspired from the reference manual, we may think that it can in fact become the documentation itself. Of course, it would ask the user to be able to read a Coq script before he reads the Coq documentation, which seems contradictory. But, extrapolating Yann Coscoy's work on the extraction of textual explanations from proof-terms [8], we can imagine that the user manual in natural language could be an extracted version from this formal manual.

Acknowledgments

I would like to thank Benjamin Werner for urging me on writing this article, and I owe him a lot for his precious comments on what error messages should look like. Some aspects that needed more explanation and the references to related works have been improved thanks to the (anonymous) referees.

References

1. Barendregt, H.: Lambda Calculi with Types. In *Handbook of Logic in Computer Science*, Vol II, Elsevier, 1992.
2. Barras, B.: Coq en Coq. Rapport de Recherche INRIA 3026. Octobre 1996.
3. Barras, B., Werner, B.: Coq in Coq. *Submitted to publication.* `http://pauillac.inria.fr/~barras/coqincoq.ps.gz`
4. Barras, B., Boutin, S., Cornes, C., Courant, J., Filliâtre, J.-C., Giménez, E., Herbelin, H., Huet, G., Muñoz, C., Murthy, C., Parent, C., Paulin-Mohring, C., Saïbi, A., Werner, B.: The Coq Proof Assistant Reference Manual Version 6.1. Technical Report 0203. Coq Project-INRIA Rocquencourt-ENS Lyon. May 97.
5. Boyer, R.S., Dowek, G.: Towards Checking Proof-Checkers. In Herman Geuvers, editor, *Informal Proceedings of the Nijmegen Workshop on Types for Proofs and Programs*, May 1993.

6. De Bruijn, N.J.: Lambda-Calculus Notation with Nameless Dummies, a Tool for Automatic Formula Manipulation, with Application to the Church-Rosser Theorem. *Indag. Math. Vol. 34 (5), pp. 381–392*, 1972.
7. Coquand, T., Huet, G.: The Calculus of Constructions. In: *Information and Computation Vol. 76, February/March 1988* (ed. A.R.Meyer), Academic Press, London, 95-120.
8. Coscoy, Y., Khan, G., Théry, L.: Extracting text from proofs. INRIA Research Report 2459. January 1995.
9. Courant, J.: A Module Calculus for Pure Type Systems. In: *Proceedings of the Third International Conference on Typed Lambda Calculi and Applications, TLCA'97, Nancy* (ed. Ph. de Groote and J. R. Hindley), Springer-Verlag, LNCS 1210, April 1997.
10. Girard, J.-Y., Lafont, Y., Taylor, P.: Proofs and Types. *Cambridge Tracts in Theoretical Computer Science 7.* Cambridge University Press.
11. Geuvers, H., Nederhof, M.-J.: A Modular Proof of Strong Normalization for the Calculus of Constructions. *Journal of Functional Programming*, 1(2):155-189, April 1991.
12. Gordon, M., Milner, R., Wadsworth, C.: Edinburgh LCF: A Mechanized Logic of Computation. *Springer-Verlag*, LNCS 78, 1979.
13. Huet, G.: The Constructive Engine. In R. Narasimhan, editor, *A Perspective in Theoretical Computer Science.* WorldScientific Publishing, 1989. Commemorative Volume for Gift Siromoney.
14. Leroy, X.: Applicative Functors and Fully Transparent Higher-Order Modules. In: *22nd Symposium on Principles of Programming Languages*, pp. 142-153. ACM Press, 1995.
15. Martin-Löf, P.: A Theory of Types. Technical Report 71-3, University of Stockholm, 1971.
16. Paulin-Mohring, C., Werner, B.: Synthesis of ML programs in Coq. *Journal of Symbolic Computation–special issue on automated programming*,1993.
17. Pollack, R.: Closure Under Alpha-Conversion. In: *Types for Proofs and Programs: International Workshop TYPES'93, Nijmegen, May 1993, Selected Papers*, `file://ftp.dcs.ed.ac.uk/pub/lego/alpha_closure.ps.gz`, (ed. H. Barendregt and T. Nipkow), Springer-Verlag, pp. 313–332, LNCS 806, 1994.
18. Pollack, R.: A Proof Checker for the Extended Calculus of Constructions. Ph. D. Thesis, `ftp://ftp.dcs.ed.ac.uk/pub/lego/thesis-pollack.ps.Z`, University of Edinburgh, 1994.
19. Pollack, R.: A Verified Typechecker. In: *Proceedings of the Second International Conference on Typed Lambda Calculi and Applications, TLCA'95, Edinburgh*, (ed. M. Dezani-Ciancaglini and G. Plotkin), Springer-Verlag, LNCS 902, April 1995.

An Implementation of the Heine-Borel Covering Theorem in Type Theory

Jan Cederquist

Department of Computing Science
University of Göteborg
S-412 96 Göteborg, Sweden
e-mail: ceder@cs.chalmers.se

Abstract. We describe an implementation, in type theory, of a proof of a pointfree formulation of the Heine-Borel covering theorem for intervals with rational endpoints.

1 Introduction

The proof presented here is a complete formalisation of the proof presented in "*A constructive proof of the Heine-Borel covering theorem for formal reals*" [CN]. We describe an implementation, in type theory, of a proof of a pointfree formulation of the Heine-Borel covering theorem for intervals with rational endpoints. The implementations also contain a definition of formal spaces as a type, and definitions of the continuum and the closed rational interval as instances of that type.

The paper is organised as follows: in section 2 we describe the proof-checker Half, in which the implementation has been done, and the type theory it is based on. The rest of the paper is devoted to formal definitions and the proof of the Heine-Borel covering theorem. In section 3 some general definitions are given. In section 4 we define a general formal topology, we also define the notion of compact space and Stone space. Then the rational numbers are defined as an object of an abstract data type. In section 6 the continuum is defined as a formal space and some of its properties are proved. Then the closed rational interval [a,b] is defined as a formal space and compactness of this space is proved.

In order to make this paper readable, we concentrate on the definitions and many proofs (or lemmas and definitions used in these proofs) are left out. In the code these omitted proofs are replaced by the ellipsis ....[1] However, all identifiers used in the proofs presented are defined and the main theorem is given with all details.

2 Description of the Proof-Checker Half

The implementation has been done in the proof-checker Half, developed by

[1] The complete proofs are obtainable from the URL: `ftp://ftp.cs.chalmers.se/pub/users/ceder/heineb/hb.tar`.

Thierry Coquand, using a type-checker and an **emacs**-interface implemented by Dan Synek.

The Half system is a successor to ALF [M]. It is a logical framework based on Martin-Löf's polymorphic type theory with one universe [ML], extended by a *theory* mechanism (similar to the theory mechanism in PVS [OSR]) and *let-expressions* (cf. [C, Br, Ba]).

The system has three levels; **Set**, **Type** and **Kind**. **Set** is an element and a subset of **Type**. Elements can be formed in both **Set** and **Type**; both **Set** and **Type** are closed under function types (Π-types) and disjoint union (Σ-types) and allow recursive definitions. There is also a type **Theory** for theories. **Kind** consists of the types **Set**, **Type** and **Theory**, and function types.

A proof (program) in Half consists of a list of definitions and lemmas, having the form $f(x_1 : T_1, \ldots, x_n : T_n) = e : T$, where the type T_i may depend on the parameters $x_1, \ldots, x_{i-1}$ and e is an expression of type T.

The Π-type is used for expressing dependent function spaces. Given two types A and B, the Π-type of functions from A to B is written $(x : A) \to B$. Elements of $(x : A) \to B$ are functions $\lambda x \to e$, where the abstracted variable x has type A and e is an expression of type B. The elimination form for elements of Π-types is application.

A recursive data type is defined using the reserved word **data**:

$$\begin{array}{l} \mathbf{data}\{ \\ \quad c_1(a_{11} : A_{11}, \ldots, a_{1m} : A_{1m}), \\ \qquad\qquad \vdots \\ \quad c_n(a_{n1} : A_{n1}, \ldots, a_{nk} : A_{nk})\}, \end{array}$$

where A_{ij} is an arbitrary type. Elements are introduced using the constructors c_i

$$c_i\ a_{i1} \cdots a_{ij}$$

and the elimination form, for objects of a recursively defined data type, is the *case-expression*

$$\begin{array}{l} \mathbf{case}\ x\ \mathbf{of}\ \{ \\ \quad c_1\ a_{11} \cdots a_{1m} \to e_1, \\ \qquad\qquad \vdots \\ \quad c_n\ a_{n1} \cdots a_{nk} \to e_n\}, \end{array}$$

where $e_1, \ldots, e_n$ are expressions of the same type (the type of the case-expression). For example, the set of finite lists may be defined by

$$list(A : \mathbf{Set}) = \mathbf{data}\{Nil, Cons(x : A,\ xs : list\ A)\} : \mathbf{Set}$$

and a list can then be analysed using a case-expression as in the following definition of append:

$$\begin{array}{l} append(A : \mathbf{Set},\ l_1 : list\ A,\ l_2 : list\ A) = \\ \quad \mathbf{case}\ l_1\ of\ \{ \\ \quad\quad Nil \to l_2, \\ \quad\quad Cons\ x\ xs \to Cons\ x\ (append\ A\ xs\ l_2)\} : list\ A. \end{array}$$

Note that, using these recursive definitions on functional form, non-linear inductive types cannot be defined, i.e. dependencies between the parameters cannot be introduced. It turned out that pattern matching together with non-linear inductive definitions is a non-conservative extension of Martin-Löf's type theory (see [H]). The approach taken in Half is to allow only linear inductive definitions. As a consequense, the *Id*-type

$$\frac{a \in A}{id(A,a) \in Id(A,a,a)}$$

is not definable: without dependencies between the parameters there is no way of saying that the two elements are the same. Therefore, for abstract sets, instead of working with sets and the *Id*-type, we work in a more general setting using *setoids*, i.e. sets with equivalence relations. For concrete sets, equalities are explicitly defined. This is also closer to the usual mathematical approach where a set comes together with an equality relation.

A Σ-type is a dependent record $\mathbf{sig}\{t_1 : T_1, \ldots, t_n : T_n\}$, where the type T_i may depend on $t_1, \ldots, t_{i-1}$. An object of a Σ-type is formed by constructing objects of the types T_i, $\mathbf{struct}\{t_1 = e_1, \ldots, t_n = e_n\}$, where e_i is an expression of type T_i. The elimination rule for Σ-types is projection; if M is of type $\mathbf{sig}\{t_1 : T_1, \ldots, t_n : T_n\}$, the value of its i'th component is accessed by $M.t_i$.

Adding Σ-types to the system is a conservative extension of the system; it does not affect the strength of the theory, equivalent definitions can always be obtained using recursive definitions with one constructor. However, to analyse objects of a recursively defined set, case-analysis is required, even if there is only one case to consider.

Theories are lists of definitions and proofs:

$$\begin{aligned} th = \mathbf{theory}\{ & \\ & f_1(a_{11} : A_{11}, \ldots, a_{1m} : A_{1m}) = e_1 : T_1, \\ & \quad \vdots \\ & f_n(a_{n1} : A_{n1}, \ldots, a_{nk} : A_{nk}) = e_n : T_n\} \\ : \mathbf{Theory} & \end{aligned}$$

Theories are used to collect definitions and lemmas that logically belong together. Identifiers defined in a theory can be accessed from outside: if th is a theory and f_i an identifier defined in th, then the value of f_i is reached by $th.f_i$.

By defining functions giving theories as result, a notion of parametrised theory is obtained. Identifiers defined in a parametrised theory can then be accessed from outside, provided they are given proper parameters. Also the notion of (parametrised) theory is a conservative extension of the system: functions occuring in a parametrised theory can always be parametrised themselves and defined outside the theory.

The *let-expressions* are used for local lemmas and abbreviations:

$$\mathbf{let}\ x = e_1 : T\ \mathbf{in}\ e_2$$

In the environment ρ, the expression above computes to $e_2(\rho, x = e_1\rho)$, i.e. the value of e_2 in the environment ρ extended with $x = e_1\rho$.

Expressions of this language are thus formed by

sorts	**Set**, **Type** and **Theory**
Π-types	$(x : A) \to B$
abstractions	$\lambda x \to e$
applications	$a\ b$
Σ-types	$\mathbf{sig}\{a_1 : A_1, \ldots, a_n : A_n\}$
structures	$\mathbf{struct}\{a_1 = e_1, \ldots, a_n = e_n\}$
projections	$b.a_i$
rec. def. types	$\mathbf{data}\{ c_1(a_{11} : A_{11}, \ldots, a_{1m} : A_{1m}), \ \vdots \ c_n(a_{n1} : A_{n1}, \ldots, a_{nk} : A_{nk})\}$
constructors	c_i
case expressions	$\mathbf{case}\ x\ \mathbf{of}\ \{ c_1\ a_{11} \cdots a_{1m} \to e_1, \ \vdots \ c_n\ a_{n1} \cdots a_{nk} \to e_n\}$
let expressions	$\mathbf{let}\ x = e_1 : T\ \mathbf{in}\ e_2$
theories	$\mathbf{theory}\{ f_1(a_{11} : A_{11}, \ldots, a_{1m} : A_{1m}) = e_1 : T_1, \ \vdots \ f_n(a_{n1} : A_{n1}, \ldots, a_{nk} : A_{nk}) = e_n : T_n\}$
projections	$th.f_i$
variables	x

The system also allows mutual recursive definitions. But this has not been used in the proofs in this paper, and we have also avoided mutual recursion between a function f and functions locally defined in f.

There is a "size check" for inductively defined types. The type

$$\begin{array}{l}\textbf{data}\{\\ \quad c_1(a_{11}:A_{11},\ldots,a_{1m}:A_{1m}),\\ \qquad\qquad\vdots\\ \quad c_n(a_{n1}:A_{n1},\ldots,a_{nk}:A_{nk})\}\end{array}$$

lives in **Set** or **Type** if all A_{ij}'s live in **Set** or **Type**, respectively.

The definitional equality is a combination of structural equality and equal by name; for checking equality of "complex" structures, i.e. **data, sig, struct** and **case**, comparision "by name" is used. This means for instance that in

$$\begin{array}{l}Bool = \textbf{data}\{False, True\} : \textbf{Set},\\ Bool' = \textbf{data}\{False, True\} : \textbf{Set},\\ Bool'' = Bool : \textbf{Set}\end{array}$$

Bool and *Bool'* are not equal, but *Bool* and *Bool"* are. This is the approach taken for several strongly typed languages.

The presence of both **Set** and **Type** in Half, where **Set** corresponds to a universe, allows a more abstract reasoning than is possible in a system without a universe. We show this by a small example with subsets of a set represented as propositional functions. First we give a name for the type of predicates over a type A:

$$pred(A:\textbf{Type}) = (x:A) \to \textbf{Set} : \textbf{Type}.$$

The predicates over A are objects in the function space from A to **Set**. This function space does not form a set in predicative type theory (it has the type **Type**). In the same way, given a type A, we form the type for relations on A:

$$rel(A:\textbf{Type}) = (x:A,\ y:A) \to \textbf{Set} : \textbf{Type}.$$

Now we represent subsets of a set A as predicates over A. We say that U is a subset of A if U is a propositional function ranging over A and that an element a of A is a member of U iff $U(a)$ holds. A propositional function U is then a subset of another propositional function V provided that Ux implies Vx for all x of type A:

$$subset(A:\textbf{Set}) = \lambda U\ V \to (x:A,\ h:Ux) \to Vx : rel\ (pred\ A).$$

Note that in the type we can see that, given a set A, *subset* A is a relation on predicates of A. Also note that, in the last definition, A must be a set, since by the definition of *rel*, $(x:A,\ h:Ux) \to Vx$ has to be a set. The system checks this for us.

3 Preliminary Definitions

From now on, Half-code in `typewriter font` is mixed with comments, motivations and less formal definitions and proofs.

First some definitions about relations, predicates and operations:

```
rel(A:Type) = (x:A,y:A) -> Set : Type,
pred(A:Type) = (x:A) -> Set : Type,
bin(A:Type) = (x:A,y:A) -> A : Type,
op(A:Type) = (x:A) -> A : Type,
ref(A:Set,R:rel A) = (x:A) -> R x x : Set,
sym(A:Set,R:rel A) = (x:A,y:A,p:R x y) -> R y x : Set,
trans(A:Set,R:rel A) = (x:A,y:A,z:A,p:R x y,q:R y z) -> R x z : Set,
```

Note that `rel`, `pred`, `bin` and `op` also are applicable to elements of type `Set`.

The propositions *false* and *true* are defined as the empty set and a singleton set, respectively:

```
n0 = data{} : Set,
n1 = data{$True} : Set,
```

(In Half-code the constructors start with `$`). The connectives are defined by

```
not (A:Set) = (x:A) -> n0 : Set,
and (A:Set,B:Set) = sig{fst:A,snd:B} : Set,
or (A:Set,B:Set) = data{$Inl (x:A),$Inr (y:B)} : Set,
```

The definition of `and` should be compared to the equivalent definition using a *pair-constructor*,

```
and2(A:Set,B:Set) = data{$pair(a:A,b:B)} : Set.
```

However, a case-expression is required in order to analyse an object of type `and2 A B`, whereas for `and`, the proofs of `A` and `B` are obtained directly using the names `fst` and `snd`, respectively.

The existential quantifier is here defined using a *Σ-set* and, as was the case with `and`, the elimination rules are first and second projection:

```
exists(A:Set,B:pred A) = sig{fst:A,snd:B fst} : Set,
```

A set A is dense with respect to a relation R, if for all related x and y in A, there exists a z in A such that $R\ x\ z$ and $R\ z\ y$. (If `e` is an expression then `\x -> e` is the notation for a lambda abstraction.)

```
dense(A:Set,R:rel A) =
  (x:A,y:A,h:R x y) -> exists A (\z -> and (R x z) (R z y)) : Set,
```

A set A is decidable if $A \vee \neg A$ holds, and a relation R on A is decidable, if for all x and y, $R\ x\ y$ is decidable:

```
dec(A:Set) = or A (not A) : Set,
dec_rel(A:Set,R:rel A) = (x:A,y:A) -> dec (R x y) : Set,
```

A setoid is a set with an equivalence relation:

```
setoid(A:Set,R:rel A) =
  sig{isref:ref A R,issym:sym A R,istrans:trans A R} : Set,
```

A monoid is a setoid with a binary operation satisfying congruence, commutativity and associativity:

```
monoid(A:Set,eq:rel A,add:bin A) =
  sig{issetoid:setoid A eq,
      iscong:(x:A,y:A,z:A,t:A,h1:eq x z,h2:eq y t) ->
               eq (add x y) (add z t),
      iscom:(x:A,y:A) -> eq (add x y) (add y x),
      isassoc:(x:A,y:A,z:A) -> eq (add x (add y z)) (add (add x y) z)}
  : Set,
```

In the definition of formal space (section 4), propositional functions are used as subsets. Below we define what it means for a propositional function to be a subset of another propositional function. In general predicates do not respect equivalence relations, therefore the second (weaker) definition, that takes the equality relation as parameter, is used at some places. To justify the second subset relation, consider the following example: let $=$ be an equality defined on a set containing the elements x and y, and let U and V be predicates over that set; then using the first definition we do not in general have $x = y \ \& \ Ux \ \& \ U \subseteq V \Rightarrow Vy$. Moreover, in a formal topology the cover relation respects the equality relation. So, the second definition below is just as strong as it needs to be.

```
Subset(A:Set) = \U V -> (x:A,h:U x) -> V x : rel (pred A),

Subset2(A:Set,eq:rel A) =
  \U V -> (x:A,h:U x) -> exists A (\y -> and (eq x y) (V y))
  : rel (pred A),
```

Binary union for subsets as predicates is defined using disjunction:

```
Union(A:Set) = \U V -> \x -> or (U x) (V x) : bin (pred A),
```

We now define finite lists and use the concept of parametrised theory to collect some definitions and lemmas for lists.

```
list(A:Set) = data{$Nil,$Cons (x:A,xs:list A)} : Set,

theory_fin_list(A:Set,R:rel A) = theory{
  mem_list(x:A) = \xs -> case xs of {
                            $Nil -> n0,
                            $Cons y xs1 -> or (R x y) (mem_list x xs1)}
                  : pred (list A),
  ...
```

(Just observe here that several definitions and lemmas are left out. We take the liberty of freely writing text inside theories like this.)

```
} : Theory {- end of theory_fin_list -}
```

An easy way to handle finite subsets is to use lists. But since lists of a type A and predicates over A have different types, a method for converting lists into predicates is needed when mixing the two notions. To transform a list into a predicate we simply abstract a variable belonging to the list (see **finset** below). The meaning of **finsubset l U** is "l is a finite subset of U". Finally, **findpart** takes a list X and a proof that X is a subset of a union, and finds the sublist Y of X belonging to the first subset in the union.

```
theory_subsets(A:Set,eq:rel A,issetoid:setoid A eq) = theory {
  th_fin_list = theory_fin_list A eq : Theory,

  finset(l:list A) = \x -> th_fin_list.mem_list x l : pred A,

  finsubset(l:list A,U:pred A) =
    case l of {
     $Nil -> nl,
     $Cons x xs -> and (U x) (finsubset xs U)} : Set,

  subset2 = Subset2 A eq:rel (pred A),

  findpart(X:list A,U:pred A,V:pred A,h:finsubset X (union U V)) = ...
    :exists
     (list A)
     (\Y->and (finsubset Y U) (subset2 (finset X) (union (finset Y) V)))
   ...
} : Theory,
```

We conclude this section by giving a type for intervals and a theory for intervals. Given a set, an interval is simply the pair of its endpoints:

```
interval(A:Set) = sig{lp:A,rp:A} : Set,
```

Given a set A and a relation R on A, we define the corresponding relation S, for intervals of A. This is used in the definition of the continuum (section 6), where $=$, $<$ and $\leq$ for rational intervals are defined from the corresponding relations on the rational numbers.

```
theory_interval(A:Set,R:rel A) = theory{
  B = interval A : Set,
  S = \I J -> and (R J.lp I.lp) (R I.rp J.rp) : rel B,
   ...
} : Theory
```

4 Formal Spaces

We recall the definition of *formal topology* given by Giovanni Sambin [S]. A formal topology over a set A is a structure

$$\langle A, =, \cdot, \lhd \rangle$$

where $\langle A, =, \cdot\rangle$ is a commutative monoid, $\lhd$ is a relation, called *cover*, between elements and subsets of A such that, for any $x, y \in A$ and $U, V \subseteq A$, the following conditions hold:

$$\text{(substitutivity)} \quad \frac{x = y \qquad y \lhd U}{x \lhd U}$$

$$\text{(reflexivity)} \quad \frac{x \in U}{x \lhd U}$$

$$\text{(transitivity)} \quad \frac{x \lhd U \qquad U \lhd V}{x \lhd V} \quad \text{where} \quad U \lhd V \equiv (\forall u \in U)(u \lhd V)$$

$$\text{(dot - left)} \quad \frac{x \lhd U}{x \cdot y \lhd U}$$

$$\text{(dot - right)} \quad \frac{x \lhd U \qquad x \lhd V}{x \lhd U \cdot V} \quad \text{where} \quad U \cdot V \equiv \{u \cdot v \mid u \in U, v \in V\}.$$

Subsets of the base A are represented by propositional functions ranging over A (see the previous sections).

We point out that, in contrast to the definition of formal topology given in [S], we do not require the base monoid to have a unit, nor do we have the positivity predicate used in [S]. The equality relation on the base set is also explicit here.

The formal topologies are here defined as a *Σ-type*: The set A with the relation $=$, the binary operation $\cdot$ and the relation $\lhd$ form a formal space, if A, $=$, $\cdot$ form a monoid and the rules of a formal topology (substitutivity, reflexivity, transitivity, dot-left, dot-right) are satisfied. In the implementation **eq**, **dot** and **cov** are used for $=$, $\cdot$ and $\lhd$, respectively. **DOT** and **COV** are used for the generalisations of $\cdot$ and $\lhd$, respectively, to subsets. Since **DOT** and **COV** are used both in the definition of the formal space and in the theory for formal spaces, they are defined globally; and, since $\cdot$ and $\lhd$ for subsets, depend on $\cdot$ and $\lhd$ for elements, **DOT** and **COV** have **A**, **eq**, **dot** and **cov** as parameters.

```
COV(A:Set,cov:(x:A,U:pred A)->Set)=
  \U V -> (x:A,p:U x) -> cov x V:rel (pred A),
DOT(A:Set,eq:rel A,dot:bin A)=
  \U V z -> sig{x:A,y:A,px:U x,py:V y,iseq:eq z (dot x y)}
  :bin (pred A),
```

If x and y are elements in U and V, respectively, then, immediate by the definition of $\cdot$ for subsets, $x \cdot y$ is an element in $U \cdot V$.

```
lemDOT(A:Set,eq:rel A,isref:ref A eq,dot:bin A,
       x:A,y:A,U:pred A,V:pred A,p:U x,q:V y)=
  struct{x=x,y=y,px=p,py=q,iseq=isref (dot x y)}
  :DOT A eq dot U V (dot x y),

space(A:Set,eq:rel A,dot:bin A,cov:(x:A,U:pred A)->Set)=
  sig{ismonoid:monoid A eq dot,
```

```
        ax0:(x:A,y:A,h2:eq x y,U:pred A,h3:cov y U)->cov x U,
        ax1:(x:A,U:pred A,h2:U x)->cov x U,
        ax2:(x:A,U:pred A,V:pred A,h2:cov x U,h3:COV A cov U V)->cov x V,
        ax3:(x:A,y:A,U:pred A,h2:cov x U)->cov (dot x y) U,
        ax4:(x:A,U:pred A,V:pred A,h2:cov x U,h3:cov x V)->
              cov x (DOT A eq dot U V)} : Type,
```

In the theory below some general facts of formal spaces are proved and some definitions are given. Later on we will define concrete formal spaces as instances of this theory.

```
  theory_space (A:Set,eq:rel A,dot:bin A,cov:(x:A,U:pred A)->Set,
                s:space A eq dot cov) =
  theory{
    union=Union A:bin (pred A),
    subset2=Subset2 A eq:rel (pred A),
    Cov=COV A cov:rel (pred A),
    Dot=DOT A eq dot:bin (pred A),

    lemDot=lemDOT A eq isref dot
          :(x:A,y:A,U:pred A,V:pred A,p:U x,q:V y)->Dot U V (dot x y),
```

The following lemmas say that $U \subseteq V \Rightarrow U \lhd V$ and $(U \cup V) \cdot (W \cup V) \lhd (U \cdot W) \cup V$, respectively.

```
    lem12(U:pred A,V:pred A)=
      \h->\x p->let {h1=h x p:exists A (\y ->and (eq x y) (V y))}
                in s.ax0 x h1.fst V h1.snd.fst (s.ax1 h1.fst V h1.snd.snd)
      :(h:subset2 U V)->Cov U V,

    lem7(U:pred A,V:pred A,W:pred A)=
      \x p->s.ax0
            x
            (dot p.x p.y)
            (union (Dot U W) V)
            p.iseq
            (case p.px of {
              $Inl x1->
                case p.py of {
                 $Inl x2->
                   s.ax1 (dot p.x p.y) (union (Dot U W) V)
                     ($Inl (lemDot p.x p.y U W x1 x2)),
                 $Inr y->
                   ax31 p.x p.y (union (Dot U W) V)
                     (s.ax1 p.y (union (Dot U W) V) ($Inr y))},
              $Inr y->
                s.ax3 p.x p.y (union (Dot U W) V)
                   (s.ax1 p.x (union (Dot U W) V) ($Inr y))})
      :Cov (Dot (union U V) (union W V)) (union (Dot U W) V),
```

Given a formal space (note that we still are inside the theory **theory_space**), we now define the space induced by a subset. In our implementation that is achieved by a nested theory, in which the induced cover is defined and the cover-rules are proved.

```
theory_indspace(V:pred A) = theory{
```

Let $\lhd$ be a cover. The cover induced by the subset V is defined by $a \lhd_V U \equiv a \lhd U \cup V$:

```
    covind=\x U->cov x (union U V):(x:A,U:pred A)->Set,
```

In order to prove that the space induced by V really is a formal space, an object of `space A eq dot covind` is constructed:

```
    indspace=
      struct{
       ismonoid=s.ismonoid,
       ax0=\x y h2 U h3->s.ax0 x y h2 (union U V) h3,
       ax1=\x U h2->s.ax1 x (union U V) ($Inl h2),
       ax2=\x U V1 h2 h3->
              s.ax2
              x
              (union U V)
              (union V1 V)
              h2
              (\x1 p->case p of {
                        $Inl x2->h3 x1 x2,
                        $Inr y->s.ax1 x1 (union V1 V) ($Inr y)}),
       ax3=\x y U h2->s.ax3 x y (union U V) h2,
       ax4=\x U V1 h2 h3->
              s.ax2
              x
              (Dot (union U V) (union V1 V))
              (union (Dot U V1) V)
              (s.ax4 x (union U V) (union V1 V) h2 h3)
              (lem7 U V V1)}
      :space A eq dot covind
  }:Theory,  {- end of theory_indspace -}
```

In order to define compactness and Stone spaces, a notion of finite subset is needed. For that purpose finite lists are used. Given a list, the function `finset` returns the corresponding subset, and the meaning of `finsubset l U` is "`l` is a finite subset of `U`".

```
th_subs=theory_subsets A eq issetoid:Theory,
finset=th_subs.finset:(l:list A)->pred A,
finsubset=th_subs.finsubset:(l:list A,U:pred A)->Set,
```

The following predicate says that, given a subset `U` and predicate `P` for subsets, there exists a finite subset of `U` for which `P` holds.

```
existsFin(U:pred A,P:pred (pred A))=
  exists (list A) (\l->and (finsubset l U) (P (finset l))):Set,
```

isCover U is an abbreviation for "U covers the whole space":

```
isCover=\U->(x:A)->cov x U:pred (pred A),
```

Now compactness, saying that if a subset U covers the whole space then there exists a finite subset of U that covers the whole space, and Stone cover (see [S]), saying that if the element x is covered by U then there exists a finite subset of U that covers x, are easily defined:

```
  compact=(U:pred A)->(h:isCover U)->existsFin U isCover:Type,
  stone=(x:A,U:pred A,h:cov x U)->existsFin U (\U0->cov x U0):Type
}:Theory,  {- end of theory_space -}
```

We conclude this section by "covering" the definitions above with one more level of abstraction.

```
SPACE = sig{A:Set,eq:rel A,dot:bin A,cov:(x:A,U:pred A)->Set,
            is_a_space:space A eq dot cov} : Type,
```

Given a space s, **Token** s returns the base of s

```
Token(s:SPACE) = s.A : Set,
```

and **Open** s returns the subsets of the space s.

```
Open(s:SPACE) = pred (Token s) : Type,
```

Given a space s and a subset U in s, **indSpace** U s forms the space where the cover in s is induced by U.

```
indSpace(s:SPACE,U:Open s) =
  let {th1=theory_space s.A s.eq s.dot s.cov s.is_a_space:Theory,
       th2=th1.theory_indspace U:Theory}
  in struct{
      A=s.A,
      eq=s.eq,
      dot=s.dot,
      cov=th2.covind,
      is_a_space=th2.indspace}:SPACE,
```

CompactSPACE is a predicate of over all spaces (SPACE), saying that the space is compact.

```
CompactSPACE(s:SPACE)=
  let {th=theory_space s.A s.eq s.dot s.cov s.is_a_space:Theory}
  in th.compact:Type,
```

Using a Σ-type, a compact space is a space which is compact.

```
COMPACTSPACE=sig{s:SPACE,iscompact:CompactSPACE s}:Type,
```

We also define the corresponding for Stone spaces:

```
StoneSPACE(s:SPACE)=
  let {th=theory_space s.A s.eq s.dot s.cov s.is_a_space:Theory}
  in th.stone:Type,

STONESPACE=sig{s:SPACE,isstone:StoneSPACE s}:Type
```

5 Linear Ordering

The rational numbers are formed abstractly as an unbounded, dense, decidable linear ordering. Following von Plato [vP], we start with the order relation $<$ satisfying the axioms $\neg(x < y \ \& \ y < x)$ and $x < y \Rightarrow (x < z \vee z < y)$.

```
islinear(A:Set,lt:rel A) =
 sig{LO1:(x:A,y:A,p:lt x y,q:lt y x) -> n0,
     LO2:(x:A,y:A,z:A,p:lt x y) -> or (lt x z) (lt z y)}
 : Set,
```

Less-then-or-equal (or rather *not-greater-than*) is defined as $x \leq y \equiv \neg(y < x)$. The equality $x = y \equiv x \leq y \ \& \ y \leq x$ then satisfying reflexivity, symmetry and transitivity.

```
leq = \x y -> not (lt y x) : rel A,
eq = \x y -> and (leq x y) (leq y x) : rel A,
```

To this ordering decidability $(x < y \vee y \leq x)$ is added:

```
isdeclinear(A:Set,lt:rel A)=sig{DLO1:islinear A lt,
                                DLO2:dec_rel A lt}:Set,
```

Then `max` and `min` can be defined by analysing the proof of $x < y \vee y \leq x$.

The rationals also form an unbounded $((\forall a)(\exists x)(x < a)$ and $(\forall a)(\exists x)(a < x))$ and dense $(x < y \Rightarrow (\exists z)(x < z < y))$ set.

```
isdenseunbdeclinear(A:Set,lt:rel A)=
  sig{isdeclin:isdeclinear A lt,
      nolb:(a:A)->exists A (\x->lt x a),
      noub:(a:A)->exists A (\x->lt a x),
      isdense:dense A lt}:Set,
```

Now we collect the definitions above in the following theory:

```
theoryUnboundedDenseDecidableLinear(
    A:Set,lt:rel A,isdudl:isdenseunbdeclinear A lt)=theory{
  leq=...:rel A,
  eq=...:rel A,
  min=...:bin A,
  max=...bin A,
   ...
} : Theory
```

6 The Continuum as a Formal Space

The *topology of formal reals* is the structure

$$\langle Q \times Q, =_{Q\times Q}, \cdot, \lhd \rangle ,$$

where Q is the set of rational numbers. The monoid operation is defined by $(p, q) \cdot (r, s) \equiv (max(p, r), min(q, s))$; the cover $\lhd$ is defined by

$$(p, q) \lhd U \equiv (\forall p', q')(p < p' \ \& \ q' < q \Rightarrow (p', q') \lhd_f U) ,$$

where the relation $\lhd_f$ is inductively defined by

1. $\dfrac{q \leq p}{(p,q) \lhd_f U}$

2. $\dfrac{(p,q) \in U}{(p,q) \lhd_f U}$

3. $\dfrac{r < s \quad (p,s) \lhd_f U \quad (r,q) \lhd_f U}{(p,q) \lhd_f U}$

4. $\dfrac{(p',q') \lhd_f U \quad p' \leq p \quad q \leq q'}{(p,q) \lhd_f U}$.

For properties of this formal space we refer to [CN, NS].

Starting from the linear ordering of the previous section, the continuum is here to be defined as a formal space. In the following theory, $\cdot$, $\lhd_f$ and $\lhd$ are defined (having the names **dot**, **covf** and **cov**, respectively). We also prove that $\lhd_f$ is a Stone cover and that $\lhd$ is a cover relation.

```
theory_continuum(Q:Set,ltQ:rel Q,
                 isdudl:isdenseunbdeclinear Q ltQ)=theory{
  th_dudl=theoryUnboundedDenseDecidableLinear Q ltQ isdudl
        :Theory,
  leqQ=th_dudl.leq:rel Q,
  max=th_dudl.max:bin Q,
  min=th_dudl.min:bin Q,
  eqQ=th_dudl.eq:rel Q,
  eqQsym=...:sym Q eqQ,
```

The base consists of the rational intervals:

```
  QxQ=interval Q:Set,
  int(p:Q,q:Q)=struct{lp=p,rp=q}:QxQ,
```

By instantiating the theory `theory_interval` with `Q` and a relation on `Q`, the corresponding relation on intervals is obtained.

```
  th_int_eqQ=theory_interval Q eqQ:Theory,
  eqQxQ=th_int_eqQ.S:rel QxQ,
  th_int_ltQ=theory_interval Q ltQ:Theory,
  ltQxQ=th_int_ltQ.S:rel QxQ,
  th_int_leqQ=theory_interval Q leqQ:Theory,
  leqQxQ=th_int_leqQ.S:rel QxQ,
  eqQxQref=...:ref QxQ eqQxQ,
```

The dot-operation is defined as intersection:

```
  dot=\x y -> int (max x.lp y.lp) (min x.rp y.rp):bin QxQ,
```

The formalised version of $\lhd_f$ is recursively defined by the following:

```
  covf(I:QxQ,U:pred QxQ)=
    data{$C1(h:leqQ I.rp I.lp),
         $C2(h:U I),
         $C3(J:QxQ,h1:ltQ J.lp J.rp,
```

```
            h2:covf (int I.lp J.rp) U,
            h3:covf (int J.lp I.rp) U),
        $C4(J:QxQ,h1:leqQxQ I J,h2:covf J U)}:Set,
```

`(QxQ,eqQxQ,dot)` forms a commutative monoid:

```
ismonoid=struct{
          issetoid=struct{
                    isref=...,
                    issym=...,
                    istrans=...},
          iscong=...,
          iscom=...,
          isassoc=...}:monoid QxQ eqQxQ dot,
```

`(QxQ,eqQxQ,dot,covf)` is a formal space:

```
Rf=struct{
    ismonoid=ismonoid,
    ax0=...,
    ax1=\x U h2->$C2 h2,
    ax2=...,
    ax3=...,
    ax4=...}:space QxQ eqQxQ dot covf,
th_Rf=theory_space QxQ eqQxQ dot covf Rf:Theory,
```

The formalised version of $\lhd$ is explicitly defined by the following:

```
cov(I:QxQ,U:pred QxQ)=(J:QxQ,h:ltQxQ J I)->covf J U:Set,
```

`(QxQ,eqQxQ,dot,cov)` forms a formal space:

```
R=struct{
   ismonoid=ismonoid,
   ax0=...,
   ax1=...,
   ax2=...,
   ax3=...,
   ax4=...}
  :space QxQ eqQxQ dot cov,
th_R=theory_space QxQ eqQxQ dot cov R:Theory,

th_subs=theory_subsets QxQ eqQxQ (ismonoid.issetoid):Theory,
finset=th_subs.finset:(l:list QxQ) -> pred QxQ,
finsubset=th_subs.finsubset:(l:list QxQ,U:pred QxQ)->Set,
```

`covf` is a Stone cover:

```
covfSc(I:QxQ,U:pred QxQ)=...
  :(h:covf I U)->
     exists
     (list QxQ)
     (\U0->and (finsubset U0 U) (covf I (finset U0))),

isstone=covfSc:th_Rf.stone,
```

and (QxQ,eqQxQ,dot,covf) form a Stone space:

```
    isStoneSpace=struct{
                 s=struct{
                    A=QxQ,
                    eq=eqQxQ,
                    dot=dot,
                    cov=covf,
                    is_a_space=Rf},
                 isstone=covfSc}:STONESPACE
  } :Theory  {- end of theory_continuum -}
```

7 The Heine-Borel Covering Theorem

We now define the closed rational interval $[a, b]$ as a formal space and prove the Heine-Borel covering theorem, saying that if U is a subset that covers $[a, b]$ then there exists a finite subset of U that covers $[a, b]$.

Let $\mathcal{R} \equiv \langle Q \times Q, =_{Q\times Q}, \cdot, \lhd_{\mathcal{R}} \rangle$ be the formal topology of formal reals and let

$$[a, b] \equiv \langle Q \times Q, =_{Q\times Q}, \cdot, \lhd_{[a,b]} \rangle$$

where the relation $\lhd_{[a,b]}$ is defined by

$$(p, q) \lhd_{[a,b]} U \equiv (p, q) \lhd_{\mathcal{R}} U \cup \{(r, a) \mid r \in Q\} \cup \{(b, s) \mid s \in Q\}.$$

Intuitively, the interval (p, q) is covered by U in the space $[a, b]$, if (p, q) intersected with *the closed interval* $[a, b]$ is covered by U in the space $\mathcal{R}$. In the sequel we will use the notation $\mathcal{C}[a, b]$ for $\{(r, a) \mid r \in Q\} \cup \{(b, s) \mid s \in Q\}$ and we understand $\mathcal{C}[a, b]$ as the complement of $[a, b]$.

```
  theory_heineborel(Q:Set,ltQ:rel Q,
                    isdudl:isdenseunbdeclinear Q ltQ,a:Q,b:Q)=
  theory{
    th_c=theory_continuum Q ltQ isdudl:Theory,
    th_R=th_c.th_R:Theory,
    th_Rf=th_c.th_Rf:Theory,
    th_subs=th_c.th_subs:Theory,

    eqQ=th_c.eqQ:rel Q,

    QxQ=th_c.QxQ:Set,
    eqQxQ=th_c.eqQxQ:rel QxQ,
    int=th_c.int:(p:Q,q:Q)->QxQ,
    dot=th_c.dot:bin QxQ,
    covR=th_c.cov:(I:QxQ,U:pred QxQ)->Set,
    covRf=th_c.covf:(I:QxQ,U:pred QxQ)->Set,

    Rf=th_c.Rf:space QxQ eqQxQ dot (th_c.covf),
```

```
union=th_R.union:bin (pred QxQ),
finset=th_subs.finset:(l:list QxQ)->pred QxQ,

ltQxQ=th_c.ltQxQ:rel QxQ,
```

The cover on $[a,b]$ is defined in the following way: I is covered by U in $[a,b]$ if I is covered by the union of U and the the complement of $[a,b]$ in $\mathcal{R}$. The fact that $[a,b]$ really is a formal space is immediate, since the cover is an instance of a cover induced by a subset.

```
Cab=union (\x->(eqQ a x.rp)) (\x->(eqQ b x.lp)):pred QxQ,

covab(I:QxQ,U:pred QxQ)=covR I (union U Cab):Set,

th_ind=th_R.theory_indspace Cab:Theory,
ab=th_ind.indspace:space QxQ eqQxQ dot covab,
th_ab=theory_space QxQ eqQxQ dot covab ab:Theory,
```

`hblem1,2` below prove the equivalence

$$(\forall I)(I \lhd_{[a,b]} U) \Leftrightarrow (\exists r,s)(r < a \;\&\; b < s \;\&\; (r,s) \lhd_{\mathcal{R}_f} U \cup C[a,b]).$$

$\Rightarrow$: By the axiomatisation of the rational numbers, there exist p and q such that $p < a$ and $b < q$. So given $(\forall I)(I \lhd_{[a,b]} U) \equiv (\forall I)(I \lhd_{\mathcal{R}} U \cup C[a,b])$, then in particular $(p,q) \lhd_{\mathcal{R}} U \cup C[a,b]$. Again by the axioms, there exists r and s such that $p < r < a$ and $b < s < q$. Then by the definition of $\lhd_{\mathcal{R}}$, $(r,s) \lhd_{\mathcal{R}_f} U \cup C[a,b]$.

```
hblem1(U: pred QxQ)=
  \h->let {p=isdudl.no_lb a:exists Q (\x->ltQ x a),
           q=isdudl.no_ub b:exists Q (\x->ltQ b x),
           r=isdudl.isdense p.fst a p.snd
            :exists Q (\x->and (ltQ p.fst x) (ltQ x a)),
           s=isdudl.isdense b q.fst q.snd
            :exists Q (\x->and (ltQ b x) (ltQ x q.fst))}
      in struct{
          fst=int r.fst s.fst,
          snd=struct{
               fst=struct{
                    fst=r.snd.snd,
                    snd=s.snd.fst},
               snd=h (int p.fst q.fst) (int r.fst s.fst)
                    (struct{
                      fst=r.snd.fst,
                      snd=s.snd.snd})}}
  :(h:(I:QxQ)->covab I U)->
     exists QxQ (\x->and (ltQxQ (int a b) x) (covRf x (union U Cab))),
```

$\Leftarrow$: It is enough to prove $(p,q) \lhd_{\mathcal{R}_f} U \cup C[a,b]$, for arbitrary p and q. Since $r < a$ and $b < s$, $(p,q) \lhd_{\mathcal{R}_f} \{(p,a),(r,s),(b,q)\}$. Since $(p,a) \in C[a,b]$, $(r,s) \lhd_{\mathcal{R}_f} U \cup C[a,b]$ and $(b,q) \in C[a,b]$, $\{(p,a),(r,s),(b,q)\} \lhd_{\mathcal{R}_f} U \cup C[a,b]$. The claim now follows by transitivity.

```
hblem2(U:pred QxQ)=
  \h->\I->\J->\h1->
    let {rs=h.fst:QxQ,
         U1=finset
            ($Cons rs ($Cons (int J.lp a) ($Cons (int b J.rp) $Nil)))
           :pred QxQ,
         h1=$C3
            (int rs.lp a)
            h.snd.fst.fst
            (Rf.ax1 (int J.lp a) U1
               ($Inr ($Inl (th_c.eqQxQref (int J.lp a)))))
            ($C3
             (int b rs.rp)
             h.snd.fst.snd
             (Rf.ax1 (int h.fst.lp h.fst.rp) U1
                ($Inl (th_c.eqQxQref rs)))
             (Rf.ax1 (int b J.rp) U1
                ($Inr ($Inr ($Inl (th_c.eqQxQref (int b J.rp)))))))
           :th_c.covf J U1,
         h2=\J1->\p->
              case p of {
               $Inl x -> Rf.ax0 J1 rs (union U Cab) x h.snd.snd,
               $Inr y ->
                 case y of {
                  $Inl x ->Rf.ax1
                           J1
                           (union U Cab)
                           ($Inr ($Inl (th_c.eqQsym J1.rp a x.snd))),
                  $Inr y ->
                    case y of {
                     $Inl x -> Rf.ax1 J1 (union U Cab)
                                 ($Inr ($Inr x.fst)),
                     $Inr y -> case y of {}}}}
           :th_c.Covf U1 (union U Cab)}
    in (Rf.ax2 J U1 (union U Cab) h1 h2)
  :(h:exists QxQ (\rs->and
                       (ltQxQ (int a b) rs)
                       (covRf rs (union U Cab))))->
     (I:QxQ)->covab I U,
```

The Heine-Borel covering theorem: $[a,b]$ is compact, i.e.

$$(\forall I)(I \lhd_{[a,b]} U) \Rightarrow (\exists U_0 \subseteq_f U)(\forall I)(I \lhd_{[a,b]} U_0),$$

where $U_0 \subseteq_f U$ means that U_0 is a finite subset of U.

The proof goes as follows. Given $(\forall I)(I \lhd_{[a,b]} U)$, by **hblem1**, $(\exists r,s)(r < a \;\&\; b < s \;\&\; (r,s) \lhd_{\mathcal{R}_f} U \cup \mathcal{C}[a,b])$. Since $\lhd_{\mathcal{R}_f}$ is a Stone cover, there exists $W_0 \subseteq_f U \cup \mathcal{C}[a,b]$ such that $(r,s) \lhd_{\mathcal{R}_f} W_0$. By **findpart**, in **theory_subsets**, the part of W_0 belonging to U can be extracted, thus $(\exists U_0 \subseteq_f U)(\exists r,s)(r < a \;\&\; b < s \;\&\; (r,s) \lhd_{\mathcal{R}_f} U_0 \cup \mathcal{C}[a,b])$. The claim then follows by **hblem2**.

```
  subset2=Subset2 QxQ eqQxQ:rel (pred QxQ),

  heine_borel=\U h->
    let {rs=hblem1 U h
           :exists
            QxQ
            (\rs->and (ltQxQ (int a b) rs) (covRf rs (union U Cab))),
         W0=th_c.covfSc (rs.fst) (union U Cab) rs.snd.snd
           :exists (list QxQ) (\W0->and
                                      (th_subs.finsubset W0 (union U Cab))
                                      (covRf rs.fst (finset W0))),
         U0=th_subs.findpart W0.fst U Cab W0.snd.fst
           :exists
            (list QxQ)
            (\U0->and
                  (th_subs.finsubset U0 U)
                  (subset2 (finset W0.fst) (union (finset U0) Cab))),
         h1=Rf.ax2
            rs.fst
            (finset W0.fst)
            (union (finset U0.fst) Cab)
            W0.snd.snd
            (th_Rf.lem12
             (finset W0.fst)
             (union (finset U0.fst) Cab)
             U0.snd.snd)
           :covRf rs.fst (union (finset U0.fst) Cab)}
    in struct{
        fst=U0.fst,
        snd=struct{
             fst=U0.snd.fst,
             snd=hblem2 (finset U0.fst) (struct{
                                          fst=rs.fst,
                                          snd=struct{
                                               fst=rs.snd.fst,
                                               snd=h1}})}}
    :th_ab.compact
}:Theory  {- end of theory_heineborel -}
```

8 Acknowledgement

Parts of the formalisation in section 4 are due to Thierry Coquand. Sara Negri, Jan von Plato and Jan Smith have also contributed with useful remarks to this paper.

References

[Ba] H. Barendregt. *Lambda calculi with types*, In S. Abramsky, D.M. Gabbay and T.S.E. Maibaum eds., "Handbook of Logic in Computer Science, Vol. 2", Oxford University Press, Oxford, 1992.

[Br] N.G. de Bruijn. *A plea for weaker frameworks*, In G. Huet and G. Plotkin eds., "Logical Frameworks", pp. 40-68, Cambridge University Press, Cambridge, 1991.

[CN] J. Cederquist, S. Negri. *A constructive proof of the Heine-Borel covering theorem for formal reals*, In S. Berardi and M. Coppo eds., "Types for Proofs and Programs", Lecture Notes in Computer Science 1158, pp. 62–75, Springer-Verlag, 1996.

[C] T. Coquand. *An algorithm for type-checking dependent types*, Science of Computer Programming 26, pp. 167-177, Elsevier, 1996.

[H] M. Hofmann. *A model of intensional Martin-Löf type theory in which unicity of identity proofs does not hold*, Technical report, Dept. of Computer Science, University of Edinburgh, 1993.

[M] L. Magnusson. "The Implementation of ALF - a Proof Editor based on Martin-Löf's Monomorphic Type Theory with Explicit Substitution", Chalmers University of Technology and University of Göteborg, PhD Thesis, 1995.

[ML] P. Martin-Löf. *An Intuitionistic Theory of Types* (1972), To be published in the proceedings of Twenty-five years of Constructive Type Theory, G. Sambin and J. Smith eds., Oxford University Press.

[NS] S. Negri, D. Soravia. *The continuum as a formal space*, Archive for Mathematical Logic, to appear.

[OSR] S. Owre, N. Shankar, J. M. Rushby. *The PVS Specification Language (Beta Release)*, Computer Science Laboratory, SRI International, Menlo Park, CA 94025, USA, 1993.

[vP] J. von Plato. *A memorandum on the constructive axioms of linear order*, Dept. of Philosophy, University of Helsinki, 1995.

[S] G. Sambin. *Intuitionistic formal spaces – a first communication*, In D. Skordev ed., "Mathematical logic and its applications", pp. 187-204, Plenum Press, 1987.

Detecting and Removing Dead-Code Using Rank 2 Intersection

Ferruccio Damiani[1] and Frédéric Prost[2]

[1] Dipartimento di Informatica, Università di Torino, Corso Svizzera 185, 10149 Torino (Italy)
[2] Laboratoire de l'Informatique du Parallélisme, Ecole Normale Supérieure de Lyon, 46 Allée d'Italie, 69364 Lyon Cedex 07 (France)

Abstract. In this paper we extend, by allowing the use of rank 2 intersection, the *non-standard* type assignment system for the detection and elimination of dead-code in typed functional programs presented by Coppo et al in the *Static Analysis Symposium '96*. The main application of this method is the optimization of programs extracted from proofs in logical frameworks, but it could be used as well in the elimination of dead-code determined by program specialization. The use of non-standard types (also called *annotated* types) allows to exploit the type structure of the language for investigating program properties. Dead-code is detected via annotated type inference, which can be performed in a complete way, by reducing it to the solution of a system of inequalities between annotation variables. Even though the language considered in the paper is the simply typed λ-calculus with cartesian product, if-then-else, fixpoint, and arithmetic constants we can generalize our approach to polymorphic languages like Miranda, Haskell, and CAML.

Introduction

Types have been recognized as useful in programming languages because they provide a semantical (context dependent) analysis of programs. Such analysis can be incorporated in the compiling process. It is used on one side to check the consistency of programs and on the other to improve the efficiency of the code produced.

Many static programs analyses, such as strictness, totality, binding-time etc., have been specified as *non-standard* type inferences, see [20, 18, 3, 16, 17, 27, 30, 13]. In this perspective non-standard types (also called *annotated* types) represent program properties, and their inference systems are systems for reasoning formally about them.

Types are also used in the area of program extraction from formal proofs, see [24, 23, 28, 5, 7, 26], to detect and remove useless parts from the the extracted programs. In fact, programs extracted from proofs usually contain parts that are useless for the computation of the final result (i.e., dead-code); they therefore require some sort of simplification. One of the more effective simplification techniques is the "pruning", and it has been developed by Berardi in [4] (journal version in [5]). In this technique dead-code is discovered by analyzing the type of terms. The method was improved in [6] (see also [7] Chap. 4) with the use of type inclusion. The optimization algorithm proposed in [6] is rather difficult to understand and this makes its correctness proof even more difficult to follow.

In [10] a dead-code analysis based on the technique of [6] is specified as a non-standard type inference. Both the non-standard type inference system and the simplification algorithm presented in [10] are based on the technique of [6], but the dead-code detecting algorithm is much more self-evident than the original one. In [10], in fact, it is made a clear distinction between the type structure of the language (types in the usual sense) and the non-standard types (there called *refinement* types) which represent, inside the type structure of the language, particular properties. This distinction has been showed very useful from a theoretical point of view, see [18, 3, 27, 11], as well as in the design of both checking algorithms, see [16, 27], and inference algorithms, see [13, 15].

Type based analyzers rely on an implicit representation of types, either via type inequalities, see [22], or via lazy (implicit) types, see [16]. In [10] it is pursued the first approach, reducing the annotated type inference problem to the solution of a system of inequalities between annotations on types.

The language considered in [10] is a typed (à la Church) λ-calculus with a primitive recursor over natural numbers, pairs and arithmetic constants. The idea is to start from a typed term and to decorate it by annotated types that indicate whether or not a subterm is dead-code. To this aim two annotations for the basic type nat (the type of natural numbers) are introduced:

- δ^{nat}, corresponding to the idea that the value may be used, and so could only be replaced with a term with the same behavior (observationally equivalent), and
- ω^{nat}, corresponding to the fact that the value is not used, and so it does not matter what the term is (it could be any closed term of the same type).

These properties are propagated to higher types using the standard type constructors. For instance, if a function of type $\mathsf{nat} \to \mathsf{nat}$ has the properties $\delta^{\mathsf{nat}} \to \omega^{\mathsf{nat}}$ or $\omega^{\mathsf{nat}} \to \omega^{\mathsf{nat}}$ then the whole term will not be used. The property $\omega^{\mathsf{nat}} \to \delta^{\mathsf{nat}}$, instead, is satisfied by all the terms of type $\mathsf{nat} \to \mathsf{nat}$ which yield a useful output whenever applied to an argument which is not used for the computation of this output (like $\lambda x^{\mathsf{nat}}.Q$ where x does not occur in Q). In other words, $\omega^{\mathsf{nat}} \to \delta^{\mathsf{nat}}$ characterizes all the (necessary constant) functions of type $\mathsf{nat} \to \mathsf{nat}$ not using their argument. Finally, the property $\delta^{\mathsf{nat}} \to \delta^{\mathsf{nat}}$ does not contain any information about dead-code.

Let us consider a simple example. Let $M = (\lambda x^{\mathsf{nat}}.3)P$ where P is a term of type nat. Since x is not used in the body of the λ-abstraction $F = \lambda x^{\mathsf{nat}}.3$, we have that F has the property $\omega^{\mathsf{nat}} \to \delta^{\mathsf{nat}}$. This implies that P is not used in the computation of the value of M and could be replaced by any term of the same type. I.e., in a call-by-name language, M behaves like the simplified term $M' = (\lambda x^{\mathsf{nat}}.3)\mathsf{d}$, where d is a placeholder for the dead-code removed.

In [10] the soundness of the annotated type inference system and of the optimizing transformation induced is proved via a partial equivalence relation semantics (p.e.r. for short) of the annotated types, showing that the optimized programs are observationally equivalent to the original ones. Annotated types are equipped with an inclusion relation (the logical implication between properties) which models the set-theoretic inclusion between their interpretations in the p.e.r. model. According to this semantics we have that δ^{nat} is included in ω^{nat}. The inclusion between annotated higher types (i.e., types involving the arrow constructor) follows the standard inclusion rule for the arrow constructor, which is contravariant in the left argument and covariant in the right one. For instance: $\omega^{\mathsf{nat}} \to \delta^{\mathsf{nat}}$ is included in $\delta^{\mathsf{nat}} \to \delta^{\mathsf{nat}}$ (note that the reverse inclusion does not hold), while the annotated types $\phi_1 = (\omega^{\mathsf{nat}} \to \delta^{\mathsf{nat}}) \to \omega^{\mathsf{nat}} \to \delta^{\mathsf{nat}}$ and $\phi_2 = (\delta^{\mathsf{nat}} \to \delta^{\mathsf{nat}}) \to \delta^{\mathsf{nat}} \to \delta^{\mathsf{nat}}$ are not comparable.

In this paper, we extend the annotated type inference system of [10] by allowing rank 2 intersection (see [29]) of annotated types. In other words, given two different annotated types (like ϕ_1 and ϕ_2 above), we allow to assign both them (i.e., $\phi_1 \wedge \phi_2$) to the same function f. As a first example (for a more perspicacious example we refer to Sect. 4) of use for this extension consider the term:

$$N = (\lambda f^{(\mathsf{nat}\to\mathsf{nat})\to\mathsf{nat}\to\mathsf{nat}}.f(\lambda x^{\mathsf{nat}}.3)P + f(\lambda y^{\mathsf{nat}}.y)Q)\,(\lambda h^{\mathsf{nat}\to\mathsf{nat}}.\lambda z^{\mathsf{nat}}.hz)\ ,$$

where the application map $\lambda h^{\mathsf{nat}\to\mathsf{nat}}.\lambda z^{\mathsf{nat}}.hz$ is assigned to the formal parameter f. It is easy to see that the subterm P is dead-code, i.e., in a call-by-name language, N is observational equivalent to the simplified term

$$N' = (\lambda f^{(\mathsf{nat}\to\mathsf{nat})\to\mathsf{nat}\to\mathsf{nat}}.f(\lambda x^{\mathsf{nat}}.3)\mathsf{d} + f(\lambda y^{\mathsf{nat}}.y)Q)\,(\lambda h^{\mathsf{nat}\to\mathsf{nat}}.\lambda z^{\mathsf{nat}}.hz)\ ,$$

where the subterm P has been replaced by the placeholder d. To prove this by the annotated type assignment system we need to assign annotated type $\phi_1 = (\omega^{\mathsf{nat}} \to \delta^{\mathsf{nat}}) \to \omega^{\mathsf{nat}} \to \delta^{\mathsf{nat}}$ to the first occurrence of f in the body of the λ-abstraction. On the other hand, since Q is useful to the computation of the final value of N, we are forced to assign the annotated type: $\phi_2 = (\delta^{\mathsf{nat}} \to \delta^{\mathsf{nat}}) \to \delta^{\mathsf{nat}} \to \delta^{\mathsf{nat}}$ to the the second occurrence of f in the body of the λ-abstraction. Both the annotated types ϕ_1 (function to function) and ϕ_2 (constant function to constant function) can be assigned to $\lambda h^{\mathsf{nat}\to\mathsf{nat}}.\lambda z^{\mathsf{nat}}.hz$ by using the system in [10], but they are not comparable using the type inclusion relation of [10] (see the previous discussion on the inclusion relation), moreover, in the language of properties considered in [10] there is no property ϕ of $\lambda h^{\mathsf{nat}\to\mathsf{nat}}.\lambda z^{\mathsf{nat}}.hz$ that implies both them. So with the system of [10] it is not possible to prove that P is dead-code, since for doing this it is necessary to assume such a property ϕ for the λ-abstracted variable f. As we will see, the system proposed in the present paper allows to assume the intersection (or conjunction) $\phi_1 \wedge \phi_2$ for f, and so allows to prove that P is dead-code.

In general, the use of rank 2 intersection types allows to handle the situation in which (as in the example above) the argument of a function $\lambda f^{\rho}.M$ can be assigned different (non comparable) annotated types that are both needed to discover some dead-code in the body M of the function.

The first section of this paper introduces the language we are dealing with and its semantics. Section 2 presents the rank 2 annotated type assignment system. In Sect. 3 we introduce a code simplification based on annotated type information, in particular we show that a term and its simplified version are observationally equivalent. In Sect. 4 we propose a more perspicacious example of optimization of a program extracted from proof. In Sect. 5 we briefly describe the design of a complete algorithm for inferring annotated typings of terms, i.e., an algorithm that, by using the same technique of [10], takes a term and finds all the dead-code that can be detected by using the annotated type assignment system.

1 A Typed Functional Language and its Semantics

In this section we introduce a typed functional language (basically the simply typed λ-calculus with cartesian product, if-then-else, fixpoint, and arithmetic constants) and its operational semantics. The set of types is defined assuming as basic types nat and bool: the set of naturals and the set of booleans. Types are ranged over by ρ, σ, ...

Definition 1 (Types). The language of *types* (**T**) is defined by the following grammar: $\rho ::= \iota \mid \rho \to \rho \mid \rho \times \rho$, where $\iota \in \{\mathsf{nat}, \mathsf{bool}\}$.

Typed terms are defined from a set of typed *term constants*

$$\begin{aligned}\mathcal{K} = \{\, & 0^{\mathsf{nat}},\ 1^{\mathsf{nat}},\ \ldots\ \mathsf{succ}^{\mathsf{nat}\to\mathsf{nat}},\ \mathsf{pred}^{\mathsf{nat}\to\mathsf{nat}},\ +^{\mathsf{nat}\times\mathsf{nat}\to\mathsf{nat}},\ *^{\mathsf{nat}\times\mathsf{nat}\to\mathsf{nat}},\ \ldots\\ & \mathsf{true}^{\mathsf{bool}},\ \mathsf{false}^{\mathsf{bool}},\ \mathsf{not}^{\mathsf{bool}\to\mathsf{bool}},\ =^{\mathsf{bool}\times\mathsf{bool}\to\mathsf{bool}},\ \mathsf{and}^{\mathsf{bool}\times\mathsf{bool}\to\mathsf{bool}},\ \ldots\\ & =^{\mathsf{nat}\times\mathsf{nat}\to\mathsf{bool}},\ <^{\mathsf{nat}\times\mathsf{nat}\to\mathsf{bool}},\ \ldots \qquad \}\,,\end{aligned}$$

(ranged over by C), and a set $\mathcal{V}$ of typed *term variables* (ranged over by $x^\rho, y^\sigma, \ldots$). The type of a constant C is denoted by $\mathbf{T}(C)$. Typed terms, ranged over by M, N, ..., are defined as follows.

Definition 2 (Typed terms). We write $\vdash_{\mathbf{T}} M : \rho$, and say that M is a typed term of type ρ, if $\vdash M : \rho$ is derivable by the rules in Fig. 1.

The program constructors case, it and rec have been included in view of an application to the optimization of terms extracted from proofs. Note that with this notation we explicitly mention in M the types of all its variables and constants. In the following we often omit to write types which are clear from the context.

The set of *free variables* of a term M, denoted by $\mathrm{FV}(M)$, is defined in the standard way. In the following we take terms to be α-equivalences classes of syntax trees, i.e., we will identify terms modulo the renaming of bound variables.

As usual a substitution is a finite function mapping term variables to terms, denoted by $[x_1 := N_1, \ldots, x_n := N_n]$, which respects the types, i.e., each $x_i^{\rho_i}$ is

(Var) $\vdash x^\rho : \rho$ (Con) $\vdash C^\rho : \rho$

$$(\to \text{I})\ \frac{\vdash M : \sigma}{\vdash \lambda x^\rho.M : \rho \to \sigma} \qquad (\to \text{E})\ \frac{\vdash M : \rho \to \sigma \quad \vdash N : \rho}{\vdash MN : \sigma}$$

$$(\times \text{I})\ \frac{\vdash M_1 : \rho_1 \quad \vdash M_2 : \rho_2}{\vdash \langle M_1, M_2 \rangle : \rho_1 \times \rho_2} \qquad (\times \text{E}_i)\ \frac{\vdash M : \rho_1 \times \rho_2}{\vdash \pi_i M : \rho_i}\ i \in \{1,2\}$$

$$(\text{Fix})\ \frac{\vdash M : \rho}{\vdash \mathsf{fix}\, x^\rho.M : \rho} \qquad (\text{If})\ \frac{\vdash N : \mathsf{bool} \quad \vdash M_1 : \rho \quad \vdash M_2 : \rho}{\vdash \mathsf{if}\ N\ \mathsf{then}\ M_1\ \mathsf{else}\ M_2 : \rho}$$

$$(\text{Case})\ \frac{\vdash N : \mathsf{nat} \quad \vdash M : \rho \quad \vdash F : \mathsf{nat} \to \rho}{\vdash \mathsf{case}(N, M, F) : \rho}$$

$$(\text{It})\ \frac{\vdash N : \mathsf{nat} \quad \vdash M : \rho \quad \vdash F : \rho \to \rho}{\vdash \mathsf{it}(N, M, F) : \rho}$$

$$(\text{Rec})\ \frac{\vdash N : \mathsf{nat} \quad \vdash M : \rho \quad \vdash F : \mathsf{nat} \to \rho \to \rho}{\vdash \mathsf{rec}(N, M, F) : \rho}$$

Fig. 1. Rules for term formation

substituted by a term N_i of the same type. Substitution acts on free variables, the renaming of the bound variables is implicitly supposed.

Let $\Lambda_\mathbf{T}$ be the set of the terms, i.e., $\Lambda_\mathbf{T} = \{M \mid \vdash_\mathbf{T} M : \rho \text{ for some type } \rho\}$, and $\Lambda^\mathsf{c}_\mathbf{T}$ be the set of the *closed* terms, i.e., $\Lambda^\mathsf{c}_\mathbf{T} = \{M \mid M \in \Lambda_\mathbf{T} \text{ and } \mathrm{FV}(M) = \emptyset\}$. Following Kahn, see [19], we define the values of terms in $\Lambda^\mathsf{c}_\mathbf{T}$ via a standard operational semantics described by judgments of the form $M \Downarrow K$, where M is a closed term and K is a closed canonical term, i.e., $K \in \mathcal{K} \cup \{\lambda x^\rho.N \mid \lambda x^\rho.N \in \Lambda^\mathsf{c}_\mathbf{T}\} \cup \{\langle M_1, M_2\rangle \mid \langle M_1, M_2\rangle \in \Lambda^\mathsf{c}_\mathbf{T}\}$. Assume that any functional constant has a type of the shape $\iota_1 \to \iota_2$ or $\iota_1 \times \iota_2 \to \iota_3$, for some $\iota_1, \iota_2, \iota_3 \in \{\mathsf{nat}, \mathsf{bool}\}$. The meaning of a functional constant C is given by a set $\mathbf{mean}(C)$ of pairs, i.e., if $(C_1, C_2) \in \mathbf{mean}(C)$ then CC_1 evaluates to C_2. For example $(5, 6) \in \mathbf{mean}(\mathsf{succ})$ and $(\langle 1, 3\rangle, 4) \in \mathbf{mean}(+)$.

Definition 3 (Value of a term). We write $M \Downarrow K$ if this statement is derivable by using the rules in Fig. 2.

Let $M \Downarrow$, to be read "M is convergent", mean that for some K, $M \Downarrow K$. We are interested in observing the behavior of terms at the ground level, so, as in Pitts [25], we consider the congruence on terms induced by the contextual preorder that compares the behavior of terms just at the ground type nat. Let $(\mathcal{C}[\ ]^\rho)^\sigma$ denote a typed context of type σ with a hole of type ρ in it. Let M and N be terms of type ρ. Define $M \preceq_{\mathsf{obs}} N$ whenever, for all closed contexts $(\mathcal{C}[\ ]^\rho)^{\mathsf{nat}}$, if $\mathcal{C}[M]$ and $\mathcal{C}[N]$ are closed terms, then $\mathcal{C}[M] \Downarrow$ implies $\mathcal{C}[N] \Downarrow$. Let $\simeq_{\mathsf{obs}}$ be the equivalence induced by $\preceq_{\mathsf{obs}}$. (As shown in [25] such equivalence can also be defined directly as a bisimilarity.)

The *closed term model* $\mathcal{M}$ of $\Lambda_\mathbf{T}$ is defined by interpreting each type ρ as the set of the equivalence classes of the relation $\simeq_{\mathsf{obs}}$ on the closed terms of type ρ.

$$\text{(CAN)}\ K \Downarrow K \qquad \text{(FIX)}\ \frac{M[x := \mathsf{fix}\, x.M] \Downarrow K}{\mathsf{fix}\, x.M \Downarrow K}$$

$$\text{(APP)}\ \frac{M \Downarrow \lambda x.P \quad P[x := N] \Downarrow K}{MN \Downarrow K} \qquad \text{(PROJ}_i\text{)}\ \frac{P \Downarrow \langle M_1, M_2\rangle \quad M_i \Downarrow K}{\pi_i P \Downarrow K}\ i \in \{1,2\}$$

$$\text{(IF}_1\text{)}\ \frac{N \Downarrow \mathsf{true} \quad M_1 \Downarrow K}{\mathsf{if}\ N\ \mathsf{then}\ M_1\ \mathsf{else}\ M_2 \Downarrow K} \qquad \text{(IF}_2\text{)}\ \frac{N \Downarrow \mathsf{false} \quad M_2 \Downarrow K}{\mathsf{if}\ N\ \mathsf{then}\ M_1\ \mathsf{else}\ M_2 \Downarrow K}$$

$$\text{(CASE}_1\text{)}\ \frac{N \Downarrow \mathsf{0} \quad M \Downarrow K}{\mathsf{case}(N, M, F) \Downarrow K} \qquad \text{(CASE}_2\text{)}\ \frac{N \Downarrow \mathsf{n} \quad F\,\mathsf{n} \Downarrow K}{\mathsf{case}(N, M, F) \Downarrow K}\ \mathsf{n} \neq \mathsf{0}$$

$$\text{(IT}_1\text{)}\ \frac{N \Downarrow \mathsf{0} \quad M \Downarrow K}{\mathsf{it}(N, M, F) \Downarrow K} \qquad \text{(IT}_2\text{)}\ \frac{N \Downarrow \mathsf{n} \quad F(\mathsf{it}(\mathsf{pred}\,\mathsf{n}, M, F)) \Downarrow K}{\mathsf{it}(N, M, F) \Downarrow K}\ \mathsf{n} \neq \mathsf{0}$$

$$\text{(REC}_1\text{)}\ \frac{N \Downarrow \mathsf{0} \quad M \Downarrow K}{\mathsf{rec}(N, M, F) \Downarrow K} \qquad \text{(REC}_2\text{)}\ \frac{N \Downarrow \mathsf{n} \quad F\,\mathsf{n}\,(\mathsf{rec}(\mathsf{pred}\,\mathsf{n}, M, F)) \Downarrow K}{\mathsf{rec}(N, M, F) \Downarrow K}\ \mathsf{n} \neq \mathsf{0}$$

$$\text{(APP}_1\text{)}\ \frac{M \Downarrow C \quad N \Downarrow C_1}{MN \Downarrow C_2}\ (C_1, C_2) \in \mathbf{mean}(C)$$

$$\text{(APP}_2\text{)}\ \frac{M \Downarrow C \quad N \Downarrow \langle N_1, N_2\rangle \quad N_1 \Downarrow C_1 \quad N_2 \Downarrow C_2}{MN \Downarrow C_3}\ (\langle C_1, C_2\rangle, C_3) \in \mathbf{mean}(C)$$

Fig. 2. "Natural semantics" evaluation rules

Let $\mathbf{I}(\rho)$ denote the interpretation of type ρ in this model, and $[M]$ denote the equivalence class of term M. For each type ρ, $[\mathsf{fix}\, x^\rho.x]$ (the equivalence class of the canonical divergent element) is the least element, w.r.t. $\preceq_{\mathbf{obs}}$, of $\mathbf{I}(\rho)$. An *environment* is a mapping $e : \mathcal{V} \to \bigcup_{\rho \in \mathbf{T}} \mathbf{I}(\rho)$ which respects types, i.e., such that, for each x^ρ, $e(x^\rho) \in \mathbf{I}(\rho)$. The interpretation of a term M in an environment e is defined in a standard way by: $[\![M]\!]_e = [M[x_1 := N_1, \ldots, x_n := N_n]]$, where $\{x_1, \ldots, x_n\} = \mathrm{FV}(M)$ and $[N_l] = e(x_l)$ $(1 \le l \le n)$.

2 A Type Assignment for Detecting Dead-Code

In this section we introduce a non-standard type assignment system for detecting dead-code in $\Lambda_{\mathbf{T}}$ terms. Starting from a typed term we want to be able to represent dead-code information about this term. To this aim we define two *annotations* of the basic types: δ^ι and ω^ι ($\iota \in \{\mathsf{nat}, \mathsf{bool}\}$), which represent, respectively, the notion of values of type ι which are (possibly) necessary or (certainly) useless for the determination of the final value of a computation. I.e., we identify δ^ι with *(possibly) live* and ω^ι with *dead.* Annotated types are defined from $\{a^\iota \mid a \in \{\delta, \omega\}$ and $\iota \in \{\mathsf{nat}, \mathsf{bool}\}\}$ following the type construction rules. Moreover, to get more expressivity, we allow the use of intersection at rank 2.

2.1 Annotated Types

Definition 4 (Rank 0 annotated types). The language $\mathbf{L}^0$ of *annotated rank 0 intersection types* (*a-0-types* for short), ranged over by ϕ, is defined by the following grammar: $\phi ::= a^\iota \mid \phi \to \phi \mid \phi \times \phi$, where $a \in \{\delta, \omega\}$ and $\iota \in \{\mathsf{nat}, \mathsf{bool}\}$.

Let $\epsilon(\phi)$ denote the $\mathbf{T}$ type obtained from the annotated type ϕ by removing all the annotations $a \in \{\delta, \omega\}$, i.e., by replacing each occurrence of δ^ι and ω^ι with ι. Moreover, if ρ is a type and $a \in \{\delta, \omega\}$, let $a(\rho)$ denote the annotated type obtained from ρ by replacing each occurrence of any basic type ι by a^ι. For instance:

$$\delta(((\mathsf{nat} \to \mathsf{nat}) \to \mathsf{nat} \to \mathsf{nat}) \to \mathsf{nat}) = ((\delta^{\mathsf{nat}} \to \delta^{\mathsf{nat}}) \to \delta^{\mathsf{nat}} \to \delta^{\mathsf{nat}}) \to \delta^{\mathsf{nat}} \ .$$

Definition 5 (Rank 1 and rank 2 annotated types). 1. The language $\mathbf{L}^1$ of *annotated rank 1 intersection types* (*a-1-types* for short), ranged over by ξ, is defined by:
   - $\phi_1 \wedge \cdots \wedge \phi_n \in \mathbf{L}^1$, if $n \geq 1$, $\phi_1, \ldots, \phi_n \in \mathbf{L}^0$, and $\epsilon(\phi_1) = \cdots = \epsilon(\phi_n)$.

2. The language $\mathbf{L}^2$ of *annotated rank 2 intersection types* (*a-2-types* for short), ranged over by ψ, is inductively defined by:
   - $\phi \in \mathbf{L}^2$, if $\phi \in \mathbf{L}^0$.
   - $\xi \to \psi \in \mathbf{L}^2$, if $\xi \in \mathbf{L}^1$ and and $\psi \in \mathbf{L}^2$.
   - $\psi_1 \times \psi_2 \in \mathbf{L}^2$, if $\psi_1, \psi_2 \in \mathbf{L}^2$.

Notice that $\mathbf{L}^0 \subseteq \mathbf{L}^1$, $\mathbf{L}^0 \subseteq \mathbf{L}^2$, and $\mathbf{L}^1 \cap \mathbf{L}^2 = \mathbf{L}^0$.

Since a-types are properties of terms, in the following we will use the words a-type and property interchangeably. The notation $\epsilon(\cdot)$ introduced above naturally extends to a-1-types and a-2-types: $\epsilon(\xi)$ and $\epsilon(\psi)$ denote respectively the (standard) type obtained from the a-1-type ξ and the a-2-type ψ by removing all the annotations $a \in \{\delta, \omega\}$ and by keeping just the first component of each intersection. For instance:

$$\epsilon((((\delta^{\mathsf{nat}} \to \delta^{\mathsf{nat}}) \to \delta^{\mathsf{nat}} \to \delta^{\mathsf{nat}}) \wedge ((\omega^{\mathsf{nat}} \to \delta^{\mathsf{nat}}) \to \omega^{\mathsf{nat}} \to \delta^{\mathsf{nat}})) \to \delta^{\mathsf{nat}}) = \\ ((\mathsf{nat} \to \mathsf{nat}) \to \mathsf{nat} \to \mathsf{nat}) \to \mathsf{nat} \ .$$

Intuitively, an a-2-type $\psi = \phi_1 \wedge \cdots \wedge \phi_n \to \psi' \in \mathbf{L}^2$ such that $\epsilon(\psi) = \rho \to \rho'$ represents the set of all functional terms of type $\rho \to \rho'$ sending an input satisfying $\phi_1 \wedge \cdots \wedge \phi_n$ into an output satisfying ψ'. One can note the restriction $\epsilon(\phi_1) = \cdots = \epsilon(\phi_n)$, which is not usual for standard intersection types (see [12, 1]). It intuitively corresponds to the fact that each ϕ_i represents a property of a same term. For example, the term $\lambda h^{\mathsf{nat} \to \mathsf{nat}}.\lambda z^{\mathsf{nat}}.hz$, of type $(\mathsf{nat} \to \mathsf{nat}) \to \mathsf{nat} \to \mathsf{nat}$, can be assigned both the a-0-types $\phi_1 = (\omega^{\mathsf{nat}} \to \delta^{\mathsf{nat}}) \to \omega^{\mathsf{nat}} \to \delta^{\mathsf{nat}}$ and $\phi_2 = (\delta^{\mathsf{nat}} \to \delta^{\mathsf{nat}}) \to \delta^{\mathsf{nat}} \to \delta^{\mathsf{nat}}$. So it can be passed as argument to a function requiring an input satisfying the property $\phi_1 \wedge \phi_2$.

The meaning of a-types is formalized by interpreting each a-type ψ as a partial equivalence relation (p.e.r. for short) over the interpretation of the type $\epsilon(\psi)$, i.e., the set of equivalence classes of closed terms of type $\epsilon(\psi)$ with respect to $\simeq_{\mathsf{obs}}$. In the following definition let $[M]$ denote the equivalence class of M in $\simeq_{\mathsf{obs}}$, and (in the second clause of point 1) $\times$ denote the cartesian product of sets.

Definition 6 (Semantics of annotated types). 1. The interpretation $[\![\psi]\!]$ of an a-2-type is defined by:

$$[\![\delta^{\iota}]\!] = \{\langle [N],[N]\rangle \mid [N] \in \mathbf{I}(\iota)\} \qquad [\![\omega^{\iota}]\!] = \mathbf{I}(\iota) \times \mathbf{I}(\iota)$$

$$[\![\psi_1 \times \psi_2]\!] = \{\langle [M],[N]\rangle \mid \forall i \in \{1,2\}.\langle [\pi_i M],[\pi_i N]\rangle \in [\![\phi_i]\!]\}$$

$$[\![\xi \to \psi]\!] = \{\langle [M],[N]\rangle \mid \forall \langle [P],[Q]\rangle \in [\![\xi]\!].\langle [MP],[NQ]\rangle \in [\![\psi]\!]\}\ ,$$

where the interpretation $[\![\xi]\!]$ of an a-1-type $\xi = \phi_1 \wedge \cdots \wedge \phi_n$ is defined by:

$$[\![\xi]\!] = \bigcap\nolimits_{1\leq i\leq n} [\![\phi_i]\!]\ .$$

2. By $\sim_{\psi}$ (for $\psi \in \mathbf{L}^2$) we denote the relation between closed terms defined by: $M \sim_{\psi} N$ if and only if $\langle [M],[N]\rangle \in [\![\psi]\!]$. The relation $\sim_{\xi}$ (for $\xi \in \mathbf{L}^1$) is defined analogously.

As explained in [6], the intuition behind this p.e.r. semantics of a-types is that

- the interpretation of ω^{nat}, which is the property of being a useless term of type nat, brings just the information of being a term of type nat (to reflect the fact that the value of the term is not used in the computation), and expresses the fact that an occurrence of a term having the property ω^{nat} can be replaced by any term of type nat, while
- the interpretation of δ^{nat}, which is the property of being a useful term of type nat, brings the information of being a term of type nat with a precise value (to reflect the fact that the value of the term is used in the computation), and expresses the fact that an occurrence a term having the property δ^{nat} can be replaced only with an observational equivalent term.

I.e., the p.e.r. semantics captures the informal meaning of ω^{nat} by interpreting it as the trivial p.e.r. over $\mathbf{I}(\mathsf{nat})$ (the one that equates all the elements in $\mathbf{I}(\mathsf{nat})$), and captures the informal meaning of δ^{nat} by interpreting it as the diagonal p.e.r. over $\mathbf{I}(\mathsf{nat})$ (which equates each element in $\mathbf{I}(\mathsf{nat})$ only with itself).

We now introduce two subclasses of a-types, the *ω-annotated types* (*ω-a-types* for short) and the *δ-annotated types* (*δ-a-types*), which collect all the a-types expressing the notion of not being and of (possibly) being relevant to the computation, i.e., of being or (possibly) not being dead-code, respectively. For each set of a-types $\mathbf{L}^i$ ($i \in \{0,1,2\}$, see Definitions 4 and 5) we define the subset of ω-a-i-types and the subset of δ-a-i-types. As we will see (Proposition 8) the informal meaning of such a-types is reflected by their interpretation in the p.e.r. model. I.e., if ψ is an ω-a-2-type, then $[\![\psi]\!] = \mathbf{I}(\epsilon(\psi)) \times \mathbf{I}(\epsilon(\psi))$, i.e., $[\![\psi]\!]$ is the p.e.r. which relates all pairs of elements of $\mathbf{I}(\epsilon(\psi))$, and, if ψ is an δ-a-2-type, then $[\![\psi]\!] = \{\langle [M],[M]\rangle \mid [M] \in \mathbf{I}(\epsilon(\psi))\}$, i.e., $[\![\psi]\!]$ is the p.e.r. which relates each element of $\mathbf{I}(\epsilon(\psi))$ with itself. The same holds for ω-1-types and δ-1-types.

Definition 7 (δ-a-types and ω-a-types). 1. For $i \in \{0,1,2\}$, the set $\mathbf{L}^i_{\delta}$ of δ-a-i-types is the subset of $\mathbf{L}^i$ containing only δ annotations.

2. The set $\mathbf{L}^2_{\omega}$ of ω-a-2-types is inductively defined by:

- $\omega^\iota \in \mathbf{L}^2_\omega$, if $\iota \in \{\mathsf{nat}, \mathsf{bool}\}$,
- $\xi \to \psi \in \mathbf{L}^2_\omega$, if $\xi \in \mathbf{L}^1$ and $\psi \in \mathbf{L}^2_\omega$,
- $\psi_1 \times \psi_2 \in \mathbf{L}^2_\omega$, if $\psi_1, \psi_2 \in \mathbf{L}^2_\omega$.

The sets $\mathbf{L}^0_\omega$ of ω-a-0-types is defined by $\mathbf{L}^0_\omega = \mathbf{L}^2_\omega \cap \mathbf{L}^0$, and the set $\mathbf{L}^1_\omega$ of ω-a-1-types is defined by:

- $\phi_1 \wedge \cdots \wedge \phi_n \in \mathbf{L}^1_\omega$, if $n \geq 1$, $\phi_1, \ldots, \phi_n \in \mathbf{L}^0_\omega$, and $\epsilon(\phi_1) = \cdots = \epsilon(\phi_n)$.

For instance ω^{bool}, $\delta^{\mathsf{nat}} \to \omega^{\mathsf{nat}}$, $\omega^{\mathsf{nat}} \to \omega^{\mathsf{nat}}$, and $(\delta^{\mathsf{nat}} \times \delta^{\mathsf{nat}}) \to (\omega^{\mathsf{nat}} \times (\delta^{\mathsf{nat}} \to \omega^{\mathsf{nat}}))$, are ω-a-types. While $\omega^{\mathsf{nat}} \times \delta^{\mathsf{nat}}$ and $(\omega^{\mathsf{nat}} \times \omega^{\mathsf{nat}}) \to (\omega^{\mathsf{nat}} \times (\omega^{\mathsf{nat}} \to \delta^{\mathsf{nat}}))$ are not ω-a-types.

Proposition 8. *For every closed terms M, N of type ρ:*

- *$M \sim_{\omega(\rho)} N$, and*
- *$M \sim_{\delta(\rho)} N$ if and only if $M \simeq_{\mathrm{obs}} N$.* □

We now introduce a notion of inclusion between a-2-types, denoted $\leq_2$; $\psi_1 \leq_2 \psi_2$ means that ψ_1 is less informative then ψ_2, i.e., that $[\![\psi_1]\!] \subseteq [\![\psi_2]\!]$. The $\leq_2$ inclusion relation is defined on the top of the inclusion relation for a-0-types, $\leq_0$ (which is the inclusion relation of [10]).

Definition 9 (Inclusion relations $\leq_0$ and $\leq_2$). 1. Let $\phi_1, \phi_2 \in \mathbf{L}^0$. We write $\phi_1 \leq_0 \phi_2$ to mean that $\phi_1 \leq_0 \phi_2$ is derivable by the rules in Fig. 3, and we write $\phi_1 \cong_0 \phi_2$ if both $\phi_1 \leq_0 \phi_2$ and $\phi_2 \leq_0 \phi_1$ hold.
2. Let $\psi_1, \psi_2 \in \mathbf{L}^2$. We write $\psi_1 \leq_2 \psi_2$ to mean that $\psi_1 \leq_2 \psi_2$ is derivable by the rules in Fig. 4, and we write $\psi_1 \cong_2 \psi_2$ if both $\psi_1 \leq_2 \psi_2$ and $\psi_2 \leq_2 \psi_1$ hold.

$$(\mathrm{Ref}_0)\ \phi \leq_0 \phi \qquad\qquad (\omega_0)\ \frac{\phi_2 \in \mathbf{L}^0_\omega \quad \epsilon(\phi_1) = \epsilon(\phi_2)}{\phi_1 \leq_0 \phi_2}$$

$$(\to_0)\ \frac{\phi_2 \leq_0 \phi_2' \quad \phi_1' \leq_0 \phi_1}{\phi_1 \to \phi_2 \leq_0 \phi_1' \to \phi_2'} \qquad\qquad (\times_0)\ \frac{\phi_1 \leq_0 \phi_1' \quad \phi_2 \leq_0 \phi_2'}{\phi_1 \times \phi_2 \leq_0 \phi_1' \times \phi_2'}$$

Fig. 3. Inclusion rules for a-0-types

The intuition behind the inclusion $\leq_0$ is that it corresponds to loss of information, i.e., it represents a logical implication between properties: $\phi_1 \leq_0 \phi_2$ means that ϕ_2 is implied by ϕ_1, so it cannot contain more information than ϕ_1. For instance, consider the inclusion $\delta^{\mathsf{nat}} \leq_0 \omega^{\mathsf{nat}}$, which is straightforwardly derivable from rule (ω_0). The intuitive meaning of this inclusion is the following: we have that (as explained after Definition 6) δ^{nat} express the fact of being a term of type nat with a precise value, while ω^{nat} express just the fact of being a term of type nat (its precise value does not matter), so ω^{nat} brings less information than δ^{nat}. Let us consider a couple of examples involving the arrow constructor.

$$(\mathrm{Ref}_2)\ \psi \leq_2 \psi \qquad (\omega_2)\ \frac{\psi_2 \in \mathbf{L}^2_\omega \quad \epsilon(\psi_1) = \epsilon(\psi_2)}{\psi_1 \leq_2 \psi_2}$$

$$(\rightarrow_2)\ \frac{\psi \leq_2 \psi' \quad \forall i \in \{1,\ldots,m\}.\exists j \in \{1,\ldots,n\}.\phi'_j \leq_0 \phi_i}{\phi_1 \wedge \cdots \wedge \phi_m \rightarrow \psi \leq_2 \phi'_1 \wedge \cdots \wedge \phi'_n \rightarrow \psi'} \qquad (\times_2)\ \frac{\psi_1 \leq_2 \psi'_1 \quad \psi_2 \leq_2 \psi'_2}{\psi_1 \times \psi_2 \leq_2 \psi'_1 \times \psi'_2}$$

Fig. 4. Inclusion rules for a-2-types

- If a function has a-type $\delta^{\mathsf{nat}} \rightarrow \delta^{\mathsf{nat}}$, then it maps a precise value of type nat to a precise value of type nat. From rule (ω_0) we can derive $\delta^{\mathsf{nat}} \rightarrow \delta^{\mathsf{nat}} \leq_0 \delta^{\mathsf{nat}} \rightarrow \omega^{\mathsf{nat}}$ and $\delta^{\mathsf{nat}} \rightarrow \delta^{\mathsf{nat}} \leq_0 \omega^{\mathsf{nat}} \rightarrow \omega^{\mathsf{nat}}$. Both these inclusions fits well with the intuition given above, since being a function which gives back a precise value of type nat is more informative that being a function returning any value of type nat.
- If a function has a-type $\omega^{\mathsf{nat}} \rightarrow \delta^{\mathsf{nat}}$, then it maps any value of type nat to a precise value of type nat. From rule $(\rightarrow_0)$ we can derive $\omega^{\mathsf{nat}} \rightarrow \delta^{\mathsf{nat}} \leq_0 \delta^{\mathsf{nat}} \rightarrow \delta^{\mathsf{nat}}$. Also this inclusion fits with the given intuition, since it is clear that a function mapping any value to a precise value also maps a precise value to a precise value.

The rules for the $\leq_2$ inclusion are the straightforward extension of the ones for $\leq_0$. The only non trivial case is rule $(\rightarrow_2)$, which takes in account the fact that an intersection $\xi' = \phi'_1 \wedge \cdots \wedge \phi'_n$ is included into another intersection $\xi = \phi_1 \wedge \cdots \wedge \phi_m$ if for each ϕ_i in ξ $(1 \leq i \leq m)$ there is a ϕ'_j in ξ' $(1 \leq j \leq n)$ which is included in ϕ_i.

It is immediate to show that both $\leq_0$ and $\leq_2$ are reflexive and transitive, and that they behave in the same way on $\mathbf{L}^0$, i.e., for all $\phi, \phi' \in \mathbf{L}^0$, $\phi \leq_0 \phi'$ if and only if $\phi \leq_2 \phi'$. Notice that, if ψ_1 and ψ_2 are ω-a-2-types such that $\epsilon(\psi_1) = \epsilon(\psi_2)$, then $\psi_1 \cong_2 \psi_2$. Moreover, for all $\psi_1, \psi_2 \in \mathbf{L}^2$, $\psi_1 \leq_2 \psi_2$ implies $\epsilon(\psi_1) = \epsilon(\psi_2)$.

The $\leq_2$ relation between annotated types is sound w.r.t. the interpretation, indeed, the following theorem holds.

Theorem 10 (Soundness of $\leq_2$). *$\psi_1 \leq_2 \psi_2$ implies $[\![\psi_1]\!] \subseteq [\![\psi_2]\!]$.* □

2.2 Annotated Type Assignment System

Annotated types are assigned to $\Lambda_{\mathbf{T}}$ terms by a set of annotated type inference rules.

If x^ρ is a term variable of type ρ, an assumption for x^ρ is an expression of the shape $x^\rho : \xi$, or $x : \xi$ for short, where $\xi \in \mathbf{L}^1$, and $\epsilon(\xi) = \rho$. A basis is a set Σ of a-types assumptions for term variables. The functions $\epsilon(\cdot)$, $\delta(\cdot)$ and $\omega(\cdot)$ defined above are extended to bases. More precisely: $\epsilon(\Sigma) = \{x^\rho \mid x^\rho : \xi \in \Sigma \text{ for some } \xi\}$ is the set of term variables which occur in Σ and, for any finite set Γ of term variables, $\delta(\Gamma)$ and $\omega(\Gamma)$ denote respectively the basis $\{x^\sigma : \delta(\sigma) \mid x^\sigma \in \Gamma\}$ and $\{x^\sigma : \omega(\sigma) \mid x^\sigma \in \Gamma\}$.

We will prove judgments of the form $\Sigma \vdash_{\mathbf{L}} M^{\psi}$ where $\epsilon(M^{\psi})$ is a typed term of type $\epsilon(\psi)$ whose free variables are in Σ, i.e., such that $\vdash_{\mathbf{T}} \epsilon(M^{\psi}) : \epsilon(\psi)$ and $\epsilon(\Sigma) \supseteq \mathrm{FV}(M)$. We use this notation since it allows to attach an a-type to all subterms of M. Note the difference with the more usual notation $\Sigma \vdash_{\mathbf{L}} M : \psi$ in which this is not possible.

For each constant C an a-0-type $\mathbf{L}(C)$, such that $\epsilon(\mathbf{L}(C)) = \mathbf{T}(C)$, is specified. For example, for all integers n, $\mathbf{L}(\mathsf{n}) = \delta^{\mathsf{nat}}$ and $\mathbf{L}(+) = \delta^{\mathsf{nat}} \times \delta^{\mathsf{nat}} \to \delta^{\mathsf{nat}}$. The idea is that every a-0-type that includes ($\geq_0$) the a-0-type $\mathbf{L}(C)$ can be assigned to C.

Definition 11 (A-type assignment system $\vdash_{\mathbf{L}}$). An a-typing statement is an expression $\Sigma \vdash_{\mathbf{L}} M^{\psi}$ where Σ is a basis containing an assumption for each free variable of M. $\Sigma, x : \phi_1 \wedge \cdots \wedge \phi_n$ denotes the basis $\Sigma \cup \{x : \phi_1 \wedge \cdots \wedge \phi_n\}$ where it is assumed that x does not appear in Σ. We write $\Sigma \vdash_{\mathbf{L}} M^{\psi}$ to mean that $\Sigma \vdash M^{\psi}$ can be derived by the rules in Fig. 5.

Remark. 1. Due to the $\Lambda_{\mathbf{T}}$ evaluation rules, for any constant C of type ρ of the language, the δ-a-type $\delta(\rho)$ is indeed the smallest (w.r.t. $\leq_0$) a-type of C. So we can assume that, for every $\Lambda_{\mathbf{T}}$ constant C, $\mathbf{L}(C) = \delta(\mathbf{T}(C))$. Moreover since, for every $\Lambda_{\mathbf{T}}$ constant C,

$$\mathbf{T}(C) \in \{\iota_1, \iota_1 \to \iota_2, \iota_1 \times \iota_2 \to \iota_3 \mid \iota_1, \iota_2, \iota_3 \in \{\mathsf{nat}, \mathsf{bool}\}\},$$

we have that, for every a-type ϕ, $\mathbf{L}(C) \leq_2 \phi$ implies either $\phi \cong_2 \mathbf{L}(C)$ or $\phi \in \mathbf{L}^2_{\omega}$.

2. It is worth mentioning that, in the rule ($\to$ E), the conditions
   - $\epsilon(\phi'_1 \wedge \cdots \wedge \phi'_n) = \epsilon(\phi_1 \wedge \cdots \wedge \phi_n)$, and
   - $\psi \notin \mathbf{L}^2_{\omega}$ implies $\forall i \in \{1, \ldots, n\}.\phi'_i \leq_0 \phi_i$,

   are used instead of

   $$\forall i \in \{1, \ldots, n\}.\phi'_i \leq_0 \phi_i \ .$$

   This is done to take into account the fact that: if $\phi_1 \wedge \cdots \wedge \phi_n \to \psi$ is an ω-a-type then $\phi_1, \ldots, \phi_n$ can be any a-0-types such that $\epsilon(\phi_1) = \cdots \epsilon(\phi_n) = \epsilon(\phi'_1) = \cdots = \epsilon(\phi'_n)$.
3. The $\bullet$-sequence $N^{\phi'_1} \bullet \cdots \bullet N^{\phi'_n}$, in the rule ($\to$ E), is just a way of storing n decorations of the argument of an application. These decorations correspond to different uses of the argument in the body of function. Indeed this space-consuming code duplication is not necessary and can easily be avoided in the implementation of the a-type inference algorithm sketched in Sect. 5. □

If $\Sigma \vdash_{\mathbf{L}} M^{\psi}$ then M^{ψ} has written in it the a-types assigned to its subterms. We say that M^{ψ} is a *decorated* term. Note that, being $\vdash_{\mathbf{L}}$ an inference system, the same terms can have different decorations. Let $\Lambda_{\mathbf{L}}$ be the set of decorated terms, i.e.,

$$\Lambda_{\mathbf{L}} = \{M^{\psi} \mid \Sigma \vdash_{\mathbf{L}} M^{\psi} \text{ for some a-2-type } \psi \text{ and basis } \Sigma\}.$$

$$\text{(Var)}\ \frac{\phi_i \leq_0 \phi'_i}{\Sigma, x : \phi_1 \wedge \cdots \wedge \phi_n \vdash x^{\phi'_i}}\ 1 \leq i \leq n \qquad \text{(Con)}\ \frac{\mathbf{L}(C) \leq_0 \phi}{\Sigma \vdash C^{\phi}}$$

$$(\rightarrow \mathrm{I})\ \frac{\Sigma, x : \phi_1 \wedge \cdots \wedge \phi_n \vdash M^{\psi}}{\Sigma \vdash (\lambda x^{\phi_1 \wedge \cdots \wedge \phi_n}.M^{\psi})^{\phi_1 \wedge \cdots \wedge \phi_n \rightarrow \psi}}$$

$$(\rightarrow \mathrm{E})\ \frac{\begin{array}{c}\Sigma \vdash M^{\phi_1 \wedge \cdots \wedge \phi_n \rightarrow \psi} \quad \Sigma \vdash N^{\phi'_1} \ \ldots\ \Sigma \vdash N^{\phi'_n} \\ \epsilon(\phi'_1 \wedge \cdots \wedge \phi'_n) = \epsilon(\phi_1 \wedge \cdots \wedge \phi_n) \\ \psi \notin \mathbf{L}^2_\omega \text{ implies } \forall i \in \{1, \ldots, n\}.\phi'_i \leq_0 \phi_i\end{array}}{\Sigma \vdash (M^{\phi_1 \wedge \cdots \wedge \phi_n \rightarrow \psi}(N^{\phi'_1} \bullet \cdots \bullet N^{\phi'_n}))^{\psi}}$$

$$(\times \mathrm{I})\ \frac{\Sigma \vdash M_1{}^{\psi_1} \quad \Sigma \vdash M_2{}^{\psi_2}}{\Sigma \vdash \langle M_1{}^{\psi_1}, M_2{}^{\psi_2}\rangle^{\psi_1 \times \psi_2}} \qquad (\times \mathrm{E}_i)\ \frac{\Sigma \vdash M^{\psi_1 \times \psi_2}}{\Sigma \vdash (\pi_i M^{\psi_1 \times \psi_2})^{\psi_i}}\ i \in \{1, 2\}$$

$$\text{(Fix)}\ \frac{\Sigma, x : \phi \vdash M^{\phi}}{\Sigma \vdash (\mathsf{fix}\, x^{\phi}.M^{\phi})^{\phi}} \qquad \text{(If)}\ \frac{\begin{array}{c}\Sigma \vdash N^{\delta^{\mathsf{bool}}} \quad \Sigma \vdash M_1{}^{\psi_1} \quad \Sigma \vdash M_2{}^{\psi_2} \\ \psi_1 \leq_2 \psi \quad \psi_2 \leq_2 \psi\end{array}}{\Sigma \vdash (\mathsf{if}\ N^{\delta^{\mathsf{bool}}}\ \mathsf{then}\ M_1{}^{\psi_1}\ \mathsf{else}\ M_2{}^{\psi_2})^{\psi}}$$

$$\text{(Case)}\ \frac{\begin{array}{c}\Sigma \vdash N^{\delta^{\mathsf{nat}}} \quad \Sigma \vdash M^{\psi_1} \quad \Sigma \vdash F^{a^{\mathsf{nat}} \rightarrow \psi_2} \\ \psi_1 \leq_2 \psi \quad \psi_2 \leq_2 \psi\end{array}}{\Sigma \vdash \mathsf{case}(N^{\delta^{\mathsf{nat}}}, M^{\psi_1}, F^{a^{\mathsf{nat}} \rightarrow \psi_2})^{\psi}}$$

$$\text{(It)}\ \frac{\begin{array}{c}\Sigma \vdash N^{\delta^{\mathsf{nat}}} \quad \Sigma \vdash M^{\phi_1} \quad \Sigma \vdash F^{\phi_2 \rightarrow \phi_3} \\ \phi_1 \leq_0 \phi \quad \phi_2 \rightarrow \phi_3 \leq_0 \phi \rightarrow \phi\end{array}}{\Sigma \vdash \mathsf{it}(N^{\delta^{\mathsf{nat}}}, M^{\phi_1}, F^{\phi_2 \rightarrow \phi_3})^{\phi}}$$

$$\text{(Rec)}\ \frac{\begin{array}{c}\Sigma \vdash N^{\delta^{\mathsf{nat}}} \quad \Sigma \vdash M^{\phi_1} \quad \Sigma \vdash F^{a^{\mathsf{nat}} \rightarrow \phi_2 \rightarrow \phi_3} \\ \phi_1 \leq_0 \phi \quad a^{\mathsf{nat}} \rightarrow \phi_2 \rightarrow \phi_3 \leq_0 \delta^{\mathsf{nat}} \rightarrow \phi \rightarrow \phi\end{array}}{\Sigma \vdash \mathsf{rec}(N^{\delta^{\mathsf{nat}}}, M^{\phi_1}, F^{a^{\mathsf{nat}} \rightarrow \phi_2 \rightarrow \phi_3})^{\phi}}$$

Fig. 5. Rules for a-type assignment

The functions $\epsilon(\cdot)$, $\delta(\cdot)$, and $\omega(\cdot)$, defined for annotated types in Sect. 2.1, can naturally be extended to decorated terms. $\epsilon(M^{\psi})$ in particular is simply the term M^{ψ} in which each $\bullet$-sequence has been replaced by its first component and all the a-type annotations have been erased. The proof of the following fact is immediate.

Fact 12. *1.* $\Sigma \vdash_{\mathbf{L}} M^{\psi}$ *implies* $\vdash_{\mathbf{T}} \epsilon(M^{\psi}) : \epsilon(\psi)$ *and* $\epsilon(\Sigma) \supseteq \mathrm{FV}(M)$.
2. $\vdash_{\mathbf{T}} M : \rho$ *implies, for* $a \in \{\delta, \omega\}$, $a(\mathrm{FV}(M)) \vdash_{\mathbf{L}} a(M)$. □

Example 1. Take the term $M = (\lambda x^{\mathsf{nat}}.3)P$, considered in the introduction. Let $y_1^{\sigma_1}, \ldots, y_n^{\sigma_n}$ $(n \geq 0)$ be the free variables of M. It is easy to check that the following a-typing of M holds

$$\{y_1^{\sigma_1} : \omega(\sigma_1), \ldots, y_n^{\sigma_n} : \omega(\sigma_n)\} \vdash_{\mathbf{L}} ((\lambda x^{\omega^{\mathsf{nat}}}.3^{\delta^{\mathsf{nat}}})^{\omega^{\mathsf{nat}} \rightarrow \delta^{\mathsf{nat}}} P^{\omega^{\mathsf{nat}}})^{\delta^{\mathsf{nat}}}\ .$$

To state the soundness of the a-type assignment system w.r.t. the semantics we introduce the following definition.

Definition 13. 1. Two environments e_1, e_2 are Σ-related if and only if, for all $x : \phi_1 \wedge \cdots \wedge \phi_n \in \Sigma$, $\langle e_1(x), e_2(x) \rangle \in [\![\phi_1 \wedge \cdots \wedge \phi_n]\!]$.
2. Let $\Sigma \vdash_{\mathbf{L}} M^{\psi}$ and $\Sigma \vdash_{\mathbf{L}} N^{\psi}$. We write $\epsilon(M^{\psi}) \sim_{\psi}^{\Sigma} \epsilon(N^{\psi})$ to mean that for all e_1, e_2, if e_1 and e_2 are Σ-related, then $\langle [\![\epsilon(M^{\psi})]\!]_{e_1}, [\![\epsilon(N^{\psi})]\!]_{e_2} \rangle \in [\![\psi]\!]$.

Now we can state the main theorem for p.e.r. interpretation, which is standard (in various forms) in the literature. The proof of the following theorem is by induction on terms.

Theorem 14 (Soundness of $\vdash_{\mathbf{L}}$). *Let $\Sigma \vdash_{\mathbf{L}} M^{\psi}$. Then $\epsilon(M^{\psi}) \sim_{\psi}^{\Sigma} \epsilon(M^{\psi})$.* □

3 Dead-Code Elimination

In this section we introduce a dead-code elimination mapping **O** that, given a decorated term M^{ψ}, returns an optimized version of $\epsilon(M^{\psi})$.

To define the optimization mapping we introduce, following [5], a notion of pruning on the set of terms $\Lambda_{\mathbf{T}}$.

3.1 Dummy Variables and Pruning Relation

For each type ρ, define d^{ρ} be a *dummy variable* of type ρ. Dummy variables are not present in the original programs, but they are introduced by the dead-code elimination mapping in Sect. 3.2, that replaces all the maximal subterms that are proved to be dead-code by (free) dummy variables of the same type.

Dummy variables are simply placeholders for some dead-code removed, therefore each occurrence of a dummy variable in a program is dead-code. According to this fact, the annotated type assignment system $\vdash_{\mathbf{L}}$ must handle dummy variables in a special way, i.e., only ω-a-types should be assigned to dummy variables. This can be ensured by:

- forbidding dummy variables to occur in bases, and
- adding to the rules in Fig. 5 the following rule

$$(\mathsf{d})\ \frac{\vdash_{\mathbf{T}} \mathsf{d}^{\rho} : \rho}{\vdash \mathsf{d}^{\omega(\rho)}}\ .$$

For every term M, define $\mathrm{FV}^{\bullet}(M)$ be the set of the free non dummy variables in M.

We can now introduce the pruning relation on terms.

Definition 15 (Pruning relation). Let $\vdash_{\mathbf{T}} M : \rho$. We say that a term N is a *pruning* of M, and write $N \preceq_{\mathrm{prune}} M$, if N can be obtained from M by replacing some subterms by dummy variables of the corresponding type.

Fact 16. *Let* $\vdash_{\mathrm{T}} M : \rho$ *and* $N \preceq_{\mathrm{prune}} M$. *Then* $\vdash_{\mathrm{T}} N : \rho$ *and* $\mathrm{FV}^{\bullet}(N) \subseteq \mathrm{FV}^{\bullet}(M)$. □

Example 2. Consider the terms $M = (\lambda x^{\mathsf{nat}}.3)P$ and $M' = (\lambda x^{\mathsf{nat}}.3)\mathsf{d}^{\mathsf{nat}}$. It is easy to check that $M' \preceq_{\mathrm{prune}} M$. □

Definition 17 (Operation sup). 1. **Let** $\vdash_{\mathrm{T}} M : \rho$, $M_1 \preceq_{\mathrm{prune}} M$, **and** $M_2 \preceq_{\mathrm{prune}} M$. **Then** $\mathbf{sup}(M_1, M_2)$ **is the term defined by the clauses in Fig. 6 (note that** this definition is exhaustive, i.e., all the possible cases are considered).
2. Let $\vdash_{\mathrm{T}} M : \rho$, $M_1 \preceq_{\mathrm{prune}} M, \ldots, M_n \preceq_{\mathrm{prune}} M$, $(n \geq 1)$ Define $\mathbf{sup}(M_1)$ be M_1 and, for $n \geq 2$, define $\mathbf{sup}(M_1, \ldots, M_n)$ be

$$\mathbf{sup}(\cdots \mathbf{sup}(\mathbf{sup}(M_1, M_2), M_3) \cdots, M_n) \ .$$

Theorem 18. *Let* $\vdash_{\mathrm{T}} M : \rho$. *The set*

$$\{M' \mid M' \preceq_{\mathrm{prune}} M\} \ ,$$

with the order relation $\preceq_{\mathrm{prune}}$ *is a finite lattice with bottom* d^{ρ} *and top* M. *The operation* **sup** *of Definition 17 is the join of the lattice.* □

$\mathbf{sup}(M, \mathsf{d}^{\rho}) = \mathbf{sup}(\mathsf{d}^{\rho}, M) = M$, for every term M of type ρ

$\mathbf{sup}(C^{\rho}, C^{\rho}) = C^{\rho}$
$\mathbf{sup}(x^{\rho}, x^{\rho}) = x^{\rho}$
$\mathbf{sup}(\langle M_1, M_2\rangle, \langle N_1, N_2\rangle) = \langle \mathbf{sup}(M_1, N_1), \mathbf{sup}(M_2, N_2)\rangle$
$\mathbf{sup}(\pi_i M, \pi_i N) = \pi_i \mathbf{sup}(M, N)$, where $i \in \{1, 2\}$
$\mathbf{sup}(M_1 M_2, N_1 N_2) = \mathbf{sup}(M_1, N_1)\mathbf{sup}(M_2, N_2)$
$\mathbf{sup}(\lambda x^{\rho}.M, \lambda x^{\rho}.N) = \lambda x^{\rho}.\mathbf{sup}(M, N)$
$\mathbf{sup}(\mathsf{fix}\, x^{\rho}.M, \mathsf{fix}\, x^{\rho}.N) = \mathsf{fix}\, x^{\rho}.\mathbf{sup}(M, N)$
$\mathbf{sup}(\mathsf{if}\ M\ \mathsf{then}\ M_1\ \mathsf{else}\ M_2,\ \mathsf{if}\ N\ \mathsf{then}\ N_1\ \mathsf{else}\ N_2) =$
$\quad \mathsf{if}\ \mathbf{sup}(M, N)\ \mathsf{then}\ \mathbf{sup}(M_1, N_1)\ \mathsf{else}\ \mathbf{sup}(M_2, N_2)$
$\mathbf{sup}(\mathsf{case}(M, P, F), \mathsf{case}(N, Q, G)) = \mathsf{case}(\mathbf{sup}(M, N), \mathbf{sup}(P, Q), \mathbf{sup}(F, G))$
$\mathbf{sup}(\mathsf{it}(M, P, F), \mathsf{it}(N, Q, G)) = \mathsf{it}(\mathbf{sup}(M, N), \mathbf{sup}(P, Q), \mathbf{sup}(F, G))$
$\mathbf{sup}(\mathsf{rec}(M, P, F), \mathsf{rec}(N, Q, G)) = \mathsf{rec}(\mathbf{sup}(M, N), \mathbf{sup}(P, Q), \mathbf{sup}(F, G))$

Fig. 6. Operation sup

3.2 The Optimization Mapping

Let Λ_{L} be the set of all decorated terms which are defined according to Definition 11, i.e., $\Lambda_{\mathrm{L}} = \{M^{\psi} \mid \Sigma \vdash_{\mathrm{L}} M^{\psi}$ for some a-2-type ψ and basis $\Sigma\}$.

Definition 19 (Optimization mapping O on terms). 1. The function

$$\mathbf{O} : \Lambda_{\mathbf{L}} \to \Lambda_{\mathbf{T}}$$

is defined by the clauses in Fig. 7.
2. If Σ is a basis then

$$\mathbf{O}(\Sigma) = \{x^{\epsilon(\phi_1)} \mid x : \phi_1 \wedge \cdots \wedge \phi_n \in \Sigma,\ n \geq 1 \text{ and } \exists i \in \{1, \ldots, n\}.\phi_i \notin \mathbf{L}^0_\omega\}.$$

$\mathbf{O}(M^\psi) = \mathsf{d}^{\epsilon(\psi)}, \quad \text{if } \psi \in \mathbf{L}^2_\omega$

otherwise:

$$\mathbf{O}(C^\psi) = C^{\epsilon(\psi)}$$
$$\mathbf{O}(x^\psi) = x^{\epsilon(\psi)}$$
$$\mathbf{O}(\langle {M_1}^{\psi_1}, {M_2}^{\psi_2}\rangle^{\psi_1 \times \psi_2}) = \langle \mathbf{O}({M_1}^{\psi_1}), \mathbf{O}({M_2}^{\psi_2})\rangle$$
$$\mathbf{O}((\pi_i M^{\psi_1 \times \psi_2})^{\psi_i}) = \pi_i \mathbf{O}(M^{\psi_1 \times \psi_2}), \quad \text{where } i \in \{1, 2\}$$
$$\mathbf{O}((M^{\phi_1 \wedge \cdots \wedge \phi_n \to \psi}(N^{\phi'_1} \bullet \cdots \bullet N^{\phi'_n}))^\psi) = \mathbf{O}(M^{\phi_1 \wedge \cdots \wedge \phi_n \to \psi})\mathbf{sup}(\mathbf{O}(N^{\phi'_1}), \ldots, \mathbf{O}(N^{\phi'_n}))$$
$$\mathbf{O}((\lambda x^{\phi_1 \wedge \cdots \wedge \phi_n}.M^\psi)^{\phi_1 \wedge \cdots \wedge \phi_n \to \psi}) = \lambda x^{\epsilon(\phi_1)}.\mathbf{O}(M^\psi)$$
$$\mathbf{O}((\mathsf{fix}\, x^\phi.M^\phi)^\phi) = \mathsf{fix}\, x^{\epsilon(\phi)}.\mathbf{O}(M^\phi)$$
$$\mathbf{O}((\mathsf{if}\ N^{\delta^{\mathsf{bool}}}\ \mathsf{then}\ {M_1}^{\psi_1}\ \mathsf{else}\ {M_2}^{\psi_2})^\psi) = \mathsf{if}\ \mathbf{O}(N^{\delta^{\mathsf{bool}}})\ \mathsf{then}\ \mathbf{O}({M_1}^{\psi_1})\ \mathsf{else}\ \mathbf{O}({M_2}^{\psi_2})$$
$$\mathbf{O}(\mathsf{case}(N^{\delta^{\mathsf{nat}}}, M^{\psi_1}, F^{a^{\mathsf{nat}} \to \psi_2})^\psi) = \mathsf{case}(\mathbf{O}(N^{\delta^{\mathsf{nat}}}), \mathbf{O}(M^{\psi_1}), \mathbf{O}(F^{a^{\mathsf{nat}} \to \psi_2}))$$
$$\mathbf{O}(\mathsf{it}(N^{\delta^{\mathsf{nat}}}, M^{\phi_1}, F^{\phi_2 \to \phi_3})^\phi) = \mathsf{it}(\mathbf{O}(N^{\delta^{\mathsf{nat}}}), \mathbf{O}(M^{\phi_1}), \mathbf{O}(F^{\phi_2 \to \phi_3}))$$
$$\mathbf{O}(\mathsf{rec}(N^{\delta^{\mathsf{nat}}}, M^{\phi_1}, F^{a^{\mathsf{nat}} \to \phi_2 \to \phi_3})^\phi) = \mathsf{rec}(\mathbf{O}(N^{\delta^{\mathsf{nat}}}), \mathbf{O}(M^{\phi_1}), \mathbf{O}(F^{a^{\mathsf{nat}} \to \phi_2 \to \phi_3}))$$

Fig. 7. Mapping **O** on terms

The fact that the optimization mapping produces well typed terms is stated by the following proposition.

Proposition 20. *If* $\Sigma \vdash_{\mathbf{L}} M^\psi$ *then*

1. $\mathbf{O}(M^\psi) \preceq_{\mathsf{prune}} \epsilon(M^\psi)$,
2. $\vdash_{\mathbf{T}} \mathbf{O}(M^\psi) : \epsilon(\psi)$, *and*
3. $\mathbf{O}(\Sigma) \supseteq \mathrm{FV}^\bullet(\mathbf{O}(M^\psi))$. □

Example 3. Take the term M and the a-typing of M presented in Example 1: $M = (\lambda x^{\mathsf{nat}}.3)P$ and $\{y_1^{\sigma_1} : \omega(\sigma_1), \ldots, y_n^{\sigma_n} : \omega(\sigma_n)\} \vdash_{\mathbf{L}} M'^{\delta^{\mathsf{nat}}}$ where

$$M'^{\delta^{\mathsf{nat}}} = ((\lambda x^{\omega^{\mathsf{nat}}}.3^{\delta^{\mathsf{nat}}})^{\omega^{\mathsf{nat}} \to \delta^{\mathsf{nat}}} P^{\omega^{\mathsf{nat}}})^{\delta^{\mathsf{nat}}} ,$$

By applying the optimization mapping **O** on $M'^{\delta^{\mathsf{nat}}}$ we get the following simplified version of M: $\mathbf{O}(M'^{\delta^{\mathsf{nat}}}) = (\lambda x^{\mathsf{nat}}.3)\mathsf{d}^{\mathsf{nat}}$. □

To prove the correctness of the optimization mapping $\mathbf{O}$ we identify a subset of a-typings for which the $\sim_{\psi}^{\Sigma}$ relation implies the $\simeq_{\mathsf{obs}}$ relation.

Definition 21 (Faithful a-type assignment). $\Sigma \vdash_{\mathbf{L}} M^{\phi}$ is a *faithful* a-type assignment statement if $\phi \in \mathbf{L}_{\delta}^{0}$, and for all $x : \phi_1 \wedge \cdots \wedge \phi_n \in \Sigma$, $n = 1$ and $\phi_1 \in \mathbf{L}_{\omega}^{0} \cup \mathbf{L}_{\delta}^{0}$.

Example 4. The a-typing statement considered in Example 3 is faithful. □

Theorem 22. *Let $\Sigma \vdash_{\mathbf{L}} M^{\phi}$ and $\Sigma \vdash_{\mathbf{L}} N^{\phi}$ be faithful a-typings. Then $\epsilon(M^{\phi}) \sim_{\phi}^{\Sigma} \epsilon(N^{\phi})$ implies $\epsilon(M^{\phi}) \simeq_{\mathsf{obs}} \epsilon(N^{\phi})$.* □

Remark. The condition of being a faithful a-type assignment is simply the translation in our framework of the condition introduced by Berardi in [5] to find dead-code. Namely, in the Berardi's type assignment system a subterm is dead-code if once removed (replaced by a dummy constant having a special type, corresponding to our ω-a-types) the global type of the term is unchanged. More precisely, in a faithful a-type assignment, the fact that the global a-type of the term is in $\mathbf{L}_{\delta}^{0}$, reflects the Berardi's requirement that all the types that occurs in the global type are useful. □

The following result can be proved using the a-type semantics.

Theorem 23. *If $\Sigma \vdash_{\mathbf{L}} M^{\psi}$ then, for each term N of type ρ, $\mathbf{O}(M^{\psi}) \preceq_{\mathsf{prune}} N$ implies $\epsilon(M^{\psi}) \sim_{\psi}^{\Sigma} N$.* □

Note that, since the $\preceq_{\mathsf{prune}}$ relation is reflexive, we have in particular that $\epsilon(M^{\psi}) \sim_{\psi}^{\Sigma} \mathbf{O}(M^{\psi})$. This result is especially interesting when the typing of M is faithful since, from the above theorem and Theorem 22, we get that if $\Sigma \vdash_{\mathbf{L}} M^{\psi}$ is a faithful a-typing statement then $\epsilon(M^{\psi})$ and $\mathbf{O}(M^{\psi})$ are observationally equivalent.

Theorem 24. *Let $\Sigma \vdash_{\mathbf{L}} M^{\psi}$ be a faithful typing. Then $\epsilon(M^{\psi}) \simeq_{\mathsf{obs}} \mathbf{O}(M^{\psi})$.* □

Example 5. Let $\vdash_{\mathbf{T}} M : \mathsf{nat}$ where $\mathrm{FV}(M) = \{u_1{}^{\mathsf{nat}}, u_2{}^{\mathsf{nat}}\}$ and $M =$

$$
\begin{array}{l}
(\lambda f^{(\mathsf{nat}\to\mathsf{nat})\to\mathsf{nat}\to\mathsf{nat}}. \\
\qquad +\langle f\,(\lambda x^{\mathsf{nat}}.3)\,u_1,\ f\,(\lambda y^{\mathsf{nat}}.y)\,u_2\rangle) \\
\qquad\qquad (\lambda h^{\mathsf{nat}\to\mathsf{nat}}.\lambda z^{\mathsf{nat}}.hz)\ .
\end{array}
$$

Note that M is very similar to the term N considered in the Introduction, the only differences are the use of the prefix notation for the operator $+$ and the replacement of the subterms P and Q by the free variables u_1 and u_2, respectively.

Let $\phi_1 = (\omega^{\mathsf{nat}} \to \delta^{\mathsf{nat}}) \to \omega^{\mathsf{nat}} \to \delta^{\mathsf{nat}}$ and $\phi_2 = (\delta^{\mathsf{nat}} \to \delta^{\mathsf{nat}}) \to \delta^{\mathsf{nat}} \to \delta^{\mathsf{nat}}$. It is easy to check that $\Sigma \vdash_{\mathbf{L}} M'^{\delta^{\mathsf{nat}}}$ is a faithful a-typing, where (writing, for short, δ and ω instead of δ^{nat} and ω^{nat}): $\Sigma = \{u_1^{\mathsf{nat}} : \omega, u_2^{\mathsf{nat}} : \delta\}$ and $M'^{\delta} =$

$$
\begin{array}{l}
((\lambda f^{\phi_1 \wedge \phi_2}. \\
\quad (+^{\delta\times\delta\to\delta}\langle(((f^{\phi_1}(\lambda x^{\omega}.3^{\delta})^{\omega\to\delta})^{\omega\to\delta}u_1^{\omega})^{\delta}, (((f^{\phi_2}(\lambda y^{\omega}.y^{\delta})^{\delta\to\delta})^{\delta\to\delta}u_2^{\delta})^{\delta}\rangle^{\delta\times\delta})^{\delta})^{\phi_1\wedge\phi_2\to\delta} \\
\qquad\qquad ((\lambda h^{\omega\to\delta}.(\lambda z^{\omega}.(h^{\omega\to\delta}z^{\omega})^{\delta})^{\omega\to\delta})^{\phi_1} \\
\qquad\qquad\quad \bullet \\
\qquad\qquad (\lambda h^{\delta\to\delta}.(\lambda z^{\delta}.(h^{\delta\to\delta}z^{\delta})^{\delta})^{\delta\to\delta})^{\phi_2}))^{\delta} \ .
\end{array}
$$

Applying the $\mathbf{O}$ optimization mapping we get $\mathbf{O}(M'^{\delta}) =$

$$
\begin{array}{l}
(\lambda f^{(\mathsf{nat}\to\mathsf{nat})\to\mathsf{nat}\to\mathsf{nat}}. \\
\qquad +\langle f\,(\lambda x^{\mathsf{nat}}.3)\,\mathsf{d}^{\mathsf{nat}},\ f\,(\lambda y^{\mathsf{nat}}.y)\,u_2\rangle) \\
\qquad\qquad (\lambda h^{\mathsf{nat}\to\mathsf{nat}}.\lambda z^{\mathsf{nat}}.hz)\ ,
\end{array}
$$

where $\vdash_{\mathbf{T}} \mathbf{O}(M'^{\delta}) : \mathsf{nat}$, and $\mathrm{FV}^{\bullet}(\epsilon(\mathbf{O}(M'^{\delta}))) = \mathbf{O}(\Sigma) = \{u_2^{\mathsf{nat}}\}$. □

4 A Paradigmatic Example

In the previous section we have showed a first example of use of rank 2 intersection a-types handling a situation in which the argument of a function $\lambda f^{\rho}.M$ can be assigned different (non comparable) annotated types that are both needed to discover some dead-code in the body M of the function.

We believe that situations requiring the use of rank 2 annotated types rise quite naturally in the case of the optimization of programs obtained by extraction from constructive proof of their specification. In fact, when proving theorems in a given theory using systems like Coq [2] and Lego [21] (which are proof assistants handling the extraction of programs), it is quite common to use lemmas not in their full generality, but in a weaker way. Usually, lemmas are proved by showing that, under some hypotheses (say, three hypothesis $x : \alpha$, $y : \beta$ and $z : \gamma$), there exists a tuple of elements (say a pair $\langle S, T\rangle : \sigma \times \tau$) satisfying a predicate. Consider now a situation in which

- S and T can computed independently, and S depends just from x, y, and
- in some use of the lemma only S is needed, while in some other T is needed.

This is a situation in which intersection is useful. In fact we may assign to the lemma both $\phi_1 = \delta(\alpha) \to \delta(\beta) \to \omega(\gamma) \to (\delta(\sigma) \times \omega(\tau))$ and $\phi_2 = \delta(\alpha) \to \delta(\beta) \to \delta(\gamma) \to (\delta(\sigma) \times \delta(\tau))$, hence $\phi_1 \wedge \phi_2$.

We have found some (quite complex) examples of the situation described above in the framework of computational geometry. For sake of readability we prefer to illustrate the kind of situation we have in mind by a sketchy example.

Example 6. Take a function

$$F = \lambda x^{\mathsf{nat}}.\lambda y^{\mathsf{nat}}.\lambda z^{\mathsf{nat}}.\langle S, T\rangle$$

of type $\rho = \mathsf{nat} \to \mathsf{nat} \to \mathsf{nat} \to (\mathsf{nat} \times \mathsf{nat})$, with $S = x + y$ and $T = x + y + z$. The function F takes 3 arguments an returns a pair. Note that S and T can be computed independently, moreover S does not depend from z.

Consider now

$$M = \lambda f^{\rho}.\langle \pi_1(fPQR), \pi_2(fUVW)\rangle$$

of type $\rho \to (\mathsf{nat} \times \mathsf{nat})$, for some terms P, Q, R, U, V, W of type nat. In the left-hand side of MF we only use S, while in the right-hand side we use only T.

It is easy to see that in the application

$$MF$$

the subterm R of M is dead-code. It is also easy to check that this can be proved with the system $\vdash_{\mathbf{L}}$ by assuming the a-1-type $\xi = \phi_1 \wedge \phi_2$, where

$$\phi_1 = \delta \to \delta \to \omega \to (\delta \times \omega) \text{ and}$$
$$\phi_2 = \delta \to \delta \to \delta \to (\delta \times \delta),$$

for the λ-abstracted variable f in M, and by assigning a-types ϕ_1 and ϕ_2 to the first and to the second occurrence of f in the body of M, respectively (in such a way that R is decorated by ω). In fact both the a-0-types ϕ_1 and ϕ_2 can be assigned to F.

Note that, since there is no a-0-type of F which implies both ϕ_1 and ϕ_2, this dead-code cannot be found with the system in [10]. □

5 An Algorithm for Annotated Type Inference

In this section we deal with the problem of defining a complete inference algorithm for the annotated type assignment system $\vdash_{\mathbf{L}}$. To this aim the main problem is to use the inference rules to detect a faithful decoration showing the maximum amount of dead code, i.e., assigning an ω-a-type to all the maximal subterms that can be proved to be dead code by the system. The application of the optimization mapping $\mathbf{O}$ is then trivial.

Due to space limitation we do not present here the inference algorithm. It will be found in the forthcoming first author's PhD thesis [14].

The annotated type assignment system $\vdash_{\mathbf{L}}$ presented in Section 2 is not immediately suggestive of an algorithm. The main problems are the possibility of assuming intersections of arbitrary length for the free variables and the fact that there are rules that make an explicit use of the $\leq_2$ inclusion.

So the first step to design an inference algorithm is the definition of a syntax directed version of the a-type assignment system $\vdash_{\mathbf{L}}$ which enforces some discipline in the use of the assumptions and uses only the $\leq_0$ inclusion relation. To definition of the syntax directed annotated type assignment system require the introduction of a stratification on the set of the a-2-types.

Definition 25 (Sets $\mathbf{L}[p]$). For every natural number p, let $\mathbf{L}[p]$ denote the set of the a-2-types inductively defined by:

- $\phi \in \mathbf{L}[p]$, if $\phi \in \mathbf{L}^0$
- $\xi \to \psi \in \mathbf{L}[p+1]$, if $\xi \in \mathbf{L}^1$ and $\psi \in \mathbf{L}[p]$
- $\psi_1 \times \psi_2 \in \mathbf{L}[p]$, if $\psi_1, \psi_2 \in \mathbf{L}[p]$.

To have an intuition of the meaning of such a stratification on $\mathbf{L}^2$ observe that, for every natural number p, if $\psi \in \mathbf{L}[p]$ and ψ does not contain occurrences of the constructor $\times$, then ψ is of the shape

$$\xi_1 \to \cdots \to \xi_q \to \phi \ ,$$

where $0 \leq q \leq p$, $\xi_1, \ldots, \xi_q \in \mathbf{L}^1$, and $\phi \in \mathbf{L}^0$. I.e., at most the first p antecedents of ψ are allowed to be intersections. For instance: $\phi_1 \to (\phi_2 \wedge \phi_2') \to \phi_3 \in \mathbf{L}[2]$, but $\phi_1 \to (\phi_2 \wedge \phi_2') \to (\phi_3 \wedge \phi_3') \to \phi_4 \notin \mathbf{L}[2]$.

In the judgments of the syntax directed a-type assignment system there are two basis: the first contains a set of variables for which it is allowed to assume only a-0-types (and not a-1-types), while the second contains exactly the free variables of the term that does not occur in the first one. Moreover each judgment is parameterized by a natural number p. The idea is that,

- if the judgment $\Upsilon; \Sigma \vdash^{[p]} M^{\psi}$ holds, then $\psi \in \mathbf{L}[p]$, and
- for every $x^{\rho} : \phi_1 \wedge \cdots \wedge \phi_n \in \Sigma$, we have that $n \geq 1$ and each ϕ_i $(1 \leq i \leq n)$ corresponds to a free occurrence of x^{ρ} in the decorated term M^{ψ}.

All the dead-code that can be detected by using the annotated type assignment system $\vdash_{\mathbf{L}}$ can also be detected by using its syntax directed version, and vice versa. In particular for every faithful a-typing $\Upsilon \vdash_{\mathbf{L}} M'^{\phi}$, there is a $\vdash^{[0]}$ typing $\Upsilon; \emptyset \vdash^{[0]} M''^{\phi}$, such that $\mathbf{O}(M'^{\phi}) = \mathbf{O}(M''^{\phi})$.

Using the technique described in [10], we have developed an algorithm that, given a $\Lambda_{\mathbf{T}}$ term, returns a decoration of the term containing annotation variables and a set of constraints involving annotation variables. The output of the algorithm characterizes all the possible faithful $\vdash^{[0]}$-typings of the term, i.e., any solution of the set of constraints corresponds to a faithful $\vdash^{[0]}$-typing, and vice versa. Moreover, the set of constraints has a maximal solution, i.e., a solution corresponding to a $\vdash^{[0]}$-typing showing all the dead-code that can be proved using the type assignment system $\vdash^{[0]}$. Since the language of constraints is the same of [10], the maximal solution can be found in an effective way by using the same constraints solving algorithm described in [10].

Conclusions and Further Work

In this paper we have presented an extension of the annotated type assignment system for detecting dead-code introduced in [10]. The main achievement over that system is the extension of the language of annotated types with rank 2 intersection. We have showed through examples that the new system, $\vdash_{\mathbf{L}}$, is strictly more powerful then the one of [10] (which is in turn as powerful as the one presented in [6]). Moreover we also know that $\vdash_{\mathbf{L}}$ allows to prove dead-code that cannot be proved by the *polymorphic* type system proposed in [7] Chap. 5.

This fact is not a surprise, since the fact that intersection and polymorphism are in some sense orthogonal has been already pointed out in literature.

In this paper we have considered a limited use of intersection in the language of annotated types, namely the restriction at rank 2, since the general case is quite difficult to handle. In particular we have no idea of how it is possible to extend the inference algorithm to the general case.

The use of rank 2 intersection that we have proposed in this paper brings us to consider another kind of program transformation: the idea of *specializing* the argument of an application according to its different uses in the body of the function to which that argument is passed. Take for instance the term $(\lambda f.M)\,N$. If we look at the different occurrences of the bound variable f in M (let us denote them by f_i), then it may happen that each f_i has a different annotated type. By using rank 2 intersection it is possible to deal with *covariance* in the left part of the arrow operator, and this use of covariance is what it is needed to specialize a term (see [8]).

To illustrate this idea of specializing terms, let us consider a slight variation of Example 6.

Example 7. Take the term

$$F = \lambda x^{\mathsf{nat}}.\lambda y^{\mathsf{nat}}.\lambda z^{\mathsf{nat}}.\langle S, T\rangle$$

of type $\rho = \mathsf{nat} \to \mathsf{nat} \to \mathsf{nat} \to (\mathsf{nat} \times \mathsf{nat})$, with $S = x + y$ and $T = x * y$. The function F takes 3 arguments an returns a pair. Both S and T can be computed independently, moreover the S does not depend from z and T does not depend from the x. Take then the term

$$M = \lambda f^{\rho}.\langle \pi_1(fPQR), \pi_2(fUVW)\rangle$$

of type $\rho \to (\mathsf{nat} \times \mathsf{nat})$, for some terms P, Q, R, U, V, W of type nat.

Then consider the problem of optimizing the application MF. It is not difficult to see that by using the system $\vdash_{\mathrm{L}}$ we can prove that both the subterm R and U of M are dead-code in the application MF. This can be done by assuming the a-1-type $\xi = \phi_1 \wedge \phi_2$, where

$$\phi_1 = \delta \to \delta \to \omega \to (\delta \times \omega) \text{ and}$$
$$\phi_2 = \omega \to \delta \to \delta \to (\omega \times \delta),$$

for the λ-abstracted variable f in M, and by assigning a-types ϕ_1 and ϕ_2 to the first and to the second occurrence of f in the body of M, respectively. In fact both the a-0-types ϕ_1 and ϕ_2 can be assigned to F. So by applying the optimization mapping $\mathbf{O}$ we can replace MF by $M'F$ when

$$M' = \lambda f^{\rho}.\langle \pi_1(fPQ\mathsf{d}^{\mathsf{nat}}), \pi_2(f\mathsf{d}^{\mathsf{nat}}VW)\rangle$$

is the term M in which the dead-code has been replaced by dummy variables.

However we could proceed in a different way, i.e., we can introduce two specialization of the function F:

$$F_1 = \lambda x^{\mathsf{nat}}.\lambda y^{\mathsf{nat}}.x + y \text{ and}$$
$$F_2 = \lambda y^{\mathsf{nat}}.\lambda z^{\mathsf{nat}}.y * z \ ,$$

and consider the following optimized version of the application MF:

$$(\lambda f^{\rho}.\langle fPQ, fVW\rangle)\ (F_1 \bullet F_2)$$

where the λ-abstracted variable f is an *overloaded function*. I.e., f is bound to two different branches and, when it is used in the body of the λ-abstraction, we have to choose the corresponding branch. This can be done at compile time when doing the optimization. The $\lambda\&$ calculus of Castagna, see [9], seems a good candidate to explore further this idea. □

Acknowledgment

During the preparations of the paper we have benefited greatly from discussions with Stefano Berardi and Mario Coppo. We also thank the anonymous referees for their suggestions to improve the presentation of the paper.

References

1. H. P. Barendregt, M. Coppo, and M. Dezani-Ciancaglini. A filter lambda model and the completeness of type assignment. *Journal of Symbolic Logic*, 48:931–940, 1983.
2. B. Barras, S. Boutin, C. Cornes, J. Courant, J.-C. Filliâtre, H. Herbelin, G. Huet, P. Manoury, C. Muñoz, C. Murthy, C. Parent, C. Paulin-Mohring, A. Saïbi, and B. Werner. *The Coq Proof Assistant Reference Manual Version 6.1.* INRIA-Rocquencourt-CNRS-ENS Lyon, December 1996.
3. P. N. Benton. *Strictness Analysis of Lazy Functional Programs.* PhD thesis, University of Cambridge, Pembroke College, 1992.
4. S. Berardi. Pruning Simply Typed Lambda Terms, 1993. Internal report. Dipartimento di Informatica, Universitá di Torino.
5. S. Berardi. Pruning Simply Typed Lambda Terms. *Journal of Logic and Computation*, 6(5):663–681, 1996.
6. S. Berardi and L. Boerio. Using Subtyping in Program Optimization. In *Typed Lambda Calculus and Applications*, 1995.
7. L. Boerio. *Optimizing Programs Extracted from Proofs.* PhD thesis, Universitá di Torino, 1995.
8. G. Castagna. Covariance and contravariance: conflict without a cause. *ACM Transactions on Programming Languages and Systems*, 17(3):431–447, 1995.
9. G. Castagna. *Object-Oriented Programming: A Unified Foudation.* Progress in Theoretical Computer Science Series. Birkhauser, Boston, December 1996.
10. M. Coppo, F. Damiani, and P. Giannini. Refinement Types for Program Analysis. In *SAS'96*, LNCS 1145, pages 143–158. Springer, 1996.

11. M. Coppo, F. Damiani, and P. Giannini. On Strictness and Totality. In *TACS'97*, LNCS 1281, pages 138–164. Springer, 1997.
12. M. Coppo and M. Dezani-Ciancaglini. An extension of basic functional theory for lambda-calculus. *Notre Dame Journal of Formal Logic*, 21(4):685–693, 1980.
13. D. Dussart and F. Henglein and C. Mossin. Polymorphic Recursion and Subtype Qualifications: Polymorphic Binding-Time Analysis in Polynomial Time. In *SAS'95*, LNCS 983, pages 118–135. Springer, 1995.
14. F. Damiani. *Non-standard type inference for the static analysis of lazy functional programs*. PhD thesis, Universitá di Torino. In preparation.
15. F. Damiani and P. Giannini. An Inference Algorithm for Strictness. In *TLCA'97*, LNCS 1210, pages 129–146. Springer, 1997.
16. C. Hankin and D. Le Métayer. Deriving algorithms for type inference systems: Applications to strictness analysis. In *POPL'94*, pages 202–212. ACM, 1994.
17. C. Hankin and D. Le Métayer. Lazy type inference and program analysis. *Science of Computer Programming*, 25:219–249, 1995.
18. T. P. Jensen. *Abstract Interpretation in Logical Form*. PhD thesis, University of London, Imperial College, 1992.
19. G. Kahn. Natural semantics. In K. Fuchi and M. Nivat, editors, *Programming Of Future Generation Computer*. Elsevier Sciences B.V. (North-Holland), 1988.
20. T. M. Kuo and P. Mishra. Strictness analysis: a new perspective based on type inference. In *Functional Programming Languages and Computer Architecture*, pages 260–272. ACM, 1989.
21. Z. Luo and R. Pollack. Lego proof development system : User's manual. Technical Report ECS-LFCS-92-211, University of Edinburgh., 1992.
22. J. Palsberg and P. O'Keefe. A Type System Equivalent to Flow Analysis. In *POPL'95*, pages 367–378. ACM, 1995.
23. C. Paulin-Mohring. Extracting F_ω's Programs from Proofs in the Calculus of Constructions. In *POPL'89*. ACM, 1989.
24. C. Paulin-Mohring. *Extraction des Programmes dans le Calcul des Constructions*. PhD thesis, Université Paris VII, 1989.
25. A. M. Pitts. Operationally-based theories of program equivalence. In A. M. Pitts and P. Dybjer, editors, *Semantics and Logics of Computation*, pages 241–298. Cambridge University Press, 1997.
26. F. Prost. Marking techniques for extraction. Technical Report RR95-47, Ecole Normale Supérieure de Lyon, Lyon, December 1995.
27. K. L. Solberg. *Annotated Type Systems for Program Analysis*. PhD thesis, Aarhus University, Denmark, 1995. Revised version.
28. Y. Takayama. Extraction of Redundancy-free Programs from Constructive Natural Deduction Proofs. *Journal of Symbolic Computation*, 12:29–69, 1991.
29. S. van Bakel. *Intersection Type Disciplines in Lambda Calculus and Applicative Term Rewriting Systems*. PhD thesis, Katholieke Universiteit Nijmegen, 1993.
30. D. A. Wright. *Reduction Types and Intensionality in the Lambda-Calculus*. PhD thesis, University of Tasmania, 1992.

A Type-Free Formalization of Mathematics Where Proofs Are Objects

Gilles Dowek

INRIA-Rocquencourt, B.P. 105, 78153 Le Chesnay Cedex, France.
Gilles.Dowek@inria.fr, http://pauillac.inria.fr/~dowek

Abstract. We present a first-order type-free axiomatization of mathematics where proofs are objects in the sense of Heyting-Kolmogorov functional interpretation. The consistency of this theory is open.

Introduction

As mathematical truth is not decidable, mathematical statements need to be proved. In the usual formalizations of the language of mathematics, proofs are sequences of propositions produced by some deduction rules. Such proofs are not terms of the language i.e. not elements of the universe of the discourse. Without going back to ancient Greeks for whom the universe of the mathematical discourse contained only natural numbers, this situation can be compared to that of functions that were used, but not considered as objects before the seventeenth century or sets that were not considered as objects before the nineteenth century.

In contrast, in natural languages, the truth of a proposition can be justified by a complement. For example, the truth of the proposition "there are natural numbers such that $x^2 + y^2 = z^2$" can be justified by adding a complement "there are natural numbers such that $x^2 + y^2 = z^2$, e.g. $3, 4, 5$". In contrast, the truth of this proposition must be decided by some algorithm to avoid endless justifications of justifications. It must be decided also by an algorithm that the first proposition is true as the second is.

To do the same thing in a formal way, we want to define a language with a symbol *pr* such that if P is a provable proposition, then there is a term t such that $t \in pr(P)$ is also a provable proposition and moreover the truth of this proposition can be established by a proof-checking algorithm. We do not need every provable proposition of the form $t \in pr(P)$ to be established by the algorithm, but we need that for each provable proposition P there is at least one term t such that the proposition $t \in pr(P)$ is established by the algorithm. Such a term t is called a *checkable proof-term*.

Having such proof-terms can be useful. For instance, if we skolemize the proposition

$$\forall x\ \forall y\ (y \neq 0) \Rightarrow \exists z\ x = y * z$$

we introduce a binary function symbol / and the proposition

$$\forall x\ \forall y\ (y \neq 0) \Rightarrow x = y * (x/y)$$

Although we cannot prove the proposition $1 = 0 * (1/0)$ we can form the term $1/0$. This term is usually considered as meaningless. But the meaningfulness of such a term may be difficult to establish in particular, as we cannot decide if a real number is 0 or not. If, in contrast, we skolemize the proposition

$$\forall x \; \forall y \; \forall p \; (p \in pr(y \neq 0)) \Rightarrow \exists z \; x = y * z$$

then we get a ternary function symbol and the proposition

$$\forall x \; \forall y \; \forall p \; (p \in pr(y \neq 0)) \Rightarrow x = y * /(x, y, p)$$

Again, we can form the meaningless term $/(1, 0, t)$ but now we can easily check that t is not a checkable proof of $0 \neq 0$ and thus that this term is meaningless [20].

Deciding if a term $/(x, y, p)$ is meaningful or not permits to decide if we get back x or not when we multiply it by y.

The same holds when we want to define a function on a quotient set. If f is a function from a set A to a set B and R is an equivalence relation on A, we can define a function $g = Quo(f, A, B, R)$ from A/R to B if the proposition

$$\forall x \in A \; \forall y \in A \; R(x, y) \Rightarrow f(x) = f(y)$$

is provable. Again, this term is meaningless when this proposition is not provable. Meaningfulness is decidable if we include the proof of this proposition in the term g, $g = Quo(f, A, B, R, p)$.

A last example is the choice operator (resp. descriptions operator). The term $C(A)$ is meaningful only when A is a non empty set (resp. a singleton). Providing a proof that A is nonempty (resp. a singleton), $C(A, p)$ permits to decide if such an expression is meaningful.

Giving such an existence proof permits also to define this choice operator. A proof of the existence of an object in A is a pair consisting in an object and a proof that this object is in A. Thus the chosen object $C(A, < a, p >)$ can be a. This way, the choice operator can be defined as the function projecting a pair on its first component. Thus, there is no need to extend the language with a new operator because the choice operator can be defined in the language [24].

Having a choice operator taking a proof in argument is needed to program computers in the language of mathematics [23, 21, 26]. In this case, we want to have, as usual, the possibility to define a function using the choice operator. For instance, as we know that there exists a function f such that

$$(f \; 0 \; m) = m$$

$$(f \; (S \; n) \; m) = (S \; (f \; n \; m))$$

we want to express it by the term

$$+ = C(\{f \in N \rightarrow N \rightarrow N \mid \forall m \in N \; (f \; 0 \; m) = m$$
$$\wedge \forall n \in N \; \forall m \in N \; (f \; (S \; n) \; m) = (S \; (f \; n \; m))\})$$

But, we want also to be able to execute this program, i.e. for instance to compute the term $(S\ (S\ (S\ 0)))$ from the term $(+\ (S\ (S\ 0))\ (S\ 0))$. This computation cannot be done when the choice operator takes only a set in argument, but it can when this operator takes also a (constructive) proof of the existence of an element in this set.

Such proof-terms are also useful in automated theorem proving. Trying to prove the proposition P can be reduced to searching a term t such that $t \in pr(P)$ is decided by the algorithm.

Having proofs as objects is also a natural way to construct truth predicates (see, for instance, [15]) taking $\exists y\ (y \in pr(x))$ for $\mathcal{T}(x)$ and thus to formalize indirect arguments through reflection. For instance, we may want to state an axiom expressing that an undecided statement asserting the existence of some natural number verifying some decidable property is false.

At last, we could hope that some metamathematical results, like Gödel's incompleteness theorem, showing the existence of a true but unprovable proposition would be theorems in such a theory

$$\exists P\ (P \wedge \neg \exists x\ (x \in pr(P)))$$

(however, this is still not the case in the the simple approach suggested below, see the discussion in section 3.5).

1 State of the art

This idea of having proofs as genuine mathematical objects has already been developed in several ways.

1.1 Proof theory

An early occurrence of proofs considered as mathematical objects is the notion of proof as defined in Frege-Hilbert systems, and then in natural deduction and sequent calculus. Since Gentzen's work, such proofs have been extensively studied in *proof theory*. However, the goal of proof theory is to study the proofs of some theories in the usual language of mathematics, not to extend the language of mathematics by internalizing the proofs of the language itself. Thus, goals are differents, but tools can be shared.

1.2 Reflection

Another approach to proofs as objects comes from the proof of Gödel's incompleteness theorems. These proofs require the construction of a proposition *Proof* in arithmetic such that $Proof(n, p)$ expresses that n is the Gödel number of a proposition A and p the Gödel number of a proof of A. Gödel numbers may be avoided if one considers a theory of trees instead as a theory of natural numbers [14]. But, in both cases, the proof terms (numbers or trees) depend on the way proofs are written. Two proofs differing by a renaming of bound variables are different objects, two proofs differing by the permutation of two steps are different objects and two proofs differing by cut elimination are different objects. A proof t of a proposition P containing a free variable x is a closed term, thus to construct a proof of $P[x \leftarrow u]$ we cannot substitute x by u in t, but we must apply a function mimicking substitution at the level of the encoding. The same holds if the proof uses an hypothesis. Thus, although this encoding meets its goal and permits to prove incompleteness theorems, it does not respect proofs structure and it does not provide a simple and direct expression of proofs.

1.3 Proofs according to Heyting and Kolmogorov

Such a simple and direct expression of proofs is provided by Heyting-Kolmogorov interpretation. As opposed to formal proof trees or Gödel numbers of proof trees, this interpretation of proofs as mathematical objects respects proof structure: two proofs differing by a renaming of bound variables are equal objects, two proofs differing by the permutation of two steps are equal objects and two proofs differing by cut elimination are equal objects. A proof of a proposition P containing a free variable x is expressed by a term t containing also this variable x and $t[x \leftarrow u]$ is a proof of $P[x \leftarrow u]$. A proof t using an hypothesis is expressed by a term containing a free variable x standing for a proof of this hypothesis and if u is a proof of this hypothesis, then $t[x \leftarrow u]$ is also a proof of P.

This interpretation is only defined for intuitionistic proofs. This is not as much a restriction as it could seem because classical mathematics can be built within intuitionistic mathematics, for instance taking the excluded middle as an axiom or defining classical connectives by double negation.

Definition (Heyting-Kolmogorov interpretation)

- A proof of a proposition of the form $A \Rightarrow B$ is a function mapping any proof of A to a proof of B.
- A proof of a proposition of the form $\forall x\ A$ is a function mapping any object a to a proof of $A[x \leftarrow a]$.
- A proof of a proposition of the form $A \wedge B$ is a pair formed with a proof of A and a proof of B.
- A proof of a proposition of the form $\exists x\ A$ is a pair formed with an object a and a proof of $A[x \leftarrow a]$.
- A proof of a proposition of the form $A \vee B$ is either a proof of A or a proof of B.
- There is no proof of $\bot$.

The proposition $\neg A$ is an alternative notation for $A \Rightarrow \bot$, the proposition $A \Leftrightarrow B$ for $(A \Rightarrow B) \wedge (B \Rightarrow A)$ and the proposition $\top$ for $\bot \Rightarrow \bot$.

This interpretation has been used in proof theory to express proofs of various logical systems in typed lambda-calculi (Curry [10], Tait [28], Howard [19], Girard [16], Krivine and Parigot [21], etc.). It has also been used to formalize mathematics with proofs as objects (de Bruijn [4], Martin-Löf [24], Coquand and

Huet [8], Paulin [25], etc.). In proof theory, proofs are encoded in a language of functions independent of the logical formalism (even if this formalism provides a language for functions) while in the formalizations of mathematics proofs are encoded in the language of functions of the logical formalism itself.

1.4 Propositions as types v.s. propositions as sets

From Heyting-Kolmogorov interpretation, a proof of a proposition $A \Rightarrow B$ is a function mapping proofs of A to proofs of B. Thus, it is an element of the set of functions from the set of proofs of A to the set of proofs of B.

In proof theory where proofs are encoded in typed lambda-calculi or in typed combinatoric languages, but with no sets available, this has often been stated as the fact that proofs of $A \Rightarrow B$ have type $A' \rightarrow B'$ where A' (resp. B') is the type of proofs of A (resp. B). Thus propositions and types (i.e. propositions of the logical formalism and types of the lambda-calculus) have isomorphic structures. In formalizations of mathematics with proofs as objects, propositions and types (i.e. propositions and types of the logical formalism) also have isomorphic structure. This isomorphism is used to ensure decidability of proof-checking: the decidability of type-checking implies that of proof-checking.

In formalizations of mathematics with proofs as objects, this identification of proposition with types has however some drawbacks. In typed formalizations of mathematics (Whitehead and Russell [29], Church [5], etc.) types are syntactical devices used to restrict the formation of terms and propositions. Thus, because types play this double game, the relation between a proposition and one of its proofs cannot be expressed in the language. Indeed, if we had a symbol *pr* in such a language, the proposition $p \in pr(A)$ would either be well typed and true when p is a proof of A or ill-typed when it is not, thus we cannot express in the language a well-typed proposition expressing that some term is not a proof of a proposition. In such formalisms, the statement $p \in pr(P)$, usually written $p : P$, is expressed in language different of that of propositions. Moreover, using a typed formalization of mathematics introduces a distinction between the notions of type and set, that one may want to avoid [12].

To be able to express such a proposition, we propose in this paper an untyped formalization of mathematics where proofs are objects. Thus, the decidability of proof-checking will not be a property built in the language, but a fact proved *a posteriori*. Although, the language proposed here is untyped, and permits the expression of a symbol *pr*, it takes a lot from the typed languages proposed by de Bruijn [4], Martin-Löf [24], Coquand and Huet [8] and Paulin [25]. More precisely, this language can be seen as an untyped formulation of the Calculus of constructions [8].

1.5 Beeson's theory C

Another source of inspiration of this language is Beeson's theory C [2] that also uses Heyting-Kolmogorov interpretation of proofs in an untyped setting. This theory introduces a modal operator *proof* such that $proof(p, P)$ expresses that p is a proof of the proposition P.

A minor difference is that, in the language proposed here, propositions are objects, thus we do not need to introduce a modal operator, but a predicate symbol or a function symbol is enough.

Another minor difference is that the theory C uses a formalization of mathematics based on a partial combinatory language, i.e. functions have no explicit domain of definition and self application paradoxes are avoided by using a predicate $\downarrow$ for *denoting terms*, while we use a more common notion of function explicitly given with a domain of definition. The theory C also permits quantification over all the universe while our quantifiers are bounded.

A more important difference is that we provide a proof-checking algorithm recognizing the truth of some propositions of the form $t \in pr(P)$ and we show that whenever a proposition P is provable, there is a term t such that the proposition $t \in pr(P)$ is recognized by the algorithm (although not all true propositions of the form $t \in pr(P)$ are). As a consequence we can drop usual proofs rules and use proof-terms to justify, in practice, the truth of propositions.

At last, while in the theory C, a proof of the proposition $A \Rightarrow B$ is a function f from proofs of A to proofs of B *together with a proof that f is a function from proofs of A to proofs of B*, here, a proof of $A \Rightarrow B$ is merely a function f from proofs of A to proofs of B. For checkable proof-terms, the fact that t expresses a function from proofs of A to proofs of B must be recognized by the algorithm. If we want to justify the truth of a proposition P by a non checkable proof-term t justifying the proposition $t \in pr(P)$ by a checkable proof term u. Then we have to use the axiom $\forall x \in pr(P)\ P$. Call c the proof of this axiom, the term $(c\ t\ u)$ is a checkable proof-term of the proposition P.

Thus we can still use indirect arguments by proving that some object is a proof of some proposition, but the use of this axioms forces us to take into account that the justification of justifications must come to an end, where the soundness of the justification must be recognized by an algorithm.

2 A variant of set theory

We want to extend the language of mathematics to include a symbol pr such that $pr(A)$ is the set of proofs of A. The first candidate to such an extension is the most common formalization of mathematics, i.e. set theory formalized with Zermelo's axioms or Zermelo-Fraenkel axioms. However extending set theory with a notion of explicit proofs requires a few minor modifications of set theory itself. This section is devoted to the presentation of such modifications. The language developed here is rather close to the untyped formulation of type theory developed in [12].

2.1 Set theory

Set theory is a first-order theory in a language containing two binary predicate symbols $=$ and $\in$. Deduction rules can be any formulation of deduction, we use a formulation of natural deduction. We start with equality axioms: the identity axiom

$$x = x \tag{1}$$

and Leibniz scheme

$$a = b \Rightarrow P[z \leftarrow a] \Rightarrow P[z \leftarrow b] \tag{2}$$

Then come axioms expressing the existence of some sets. For instance, the power set axiom states that for each set x there is a set X such that the elements of X are the subsets of x

$$\forall x \; \exists X \; \forall y \; ((y \in X) \Leftrightarrow \forall z \; ((z \in y) \Rightarrow (z \in x)))$$

The union axiom and the pairing axiom are formulated in a similar way. The subset scheme (restricted comprehension scheme) expresses that for each set x we can build the subset of x containing the elements verifying the property P. Thus for each proposition P such that $z_1, ..., z_n$ are the free variables of P minus x we have the axiom

$$\forall z_1 \; ... \; \forall z_n \; \forall a \; \exists y \; \forall x \; (x \in y) \Leftrightarrow ((x \in a) \wedge P)$$

Using this scheme we can, for instance, deduce the existence of the empty set

$$\exists y \; \forall x \; \neg(x \in y)$$

2.2 Existential axioms v.s. algebraic axioms

This scheme does not provide any notation for the empty set. This choice is not a very good one when we want to use set theory as a practical language to formalize mathematics. Indeed, we cannot express the proposition $\emptyset = \emptyset$ but only a proposition $\exists x \; ((x = x) \wedge (E \; x))$ where E is a characteristic property of the empty set. Moreover as we want to express proofs as objects, for instance a proof of the proposition $A \Rightarrow A$ as the identity function over proofs of A, we want a term id for this object to be able to express the proposition $id \in pr(A \Rightarrow A)$ and not $\exists y \; (y \in pr(A \Rightarrow A))$. Indeed, to ensure the decidability of proof-checking we want to use the information carried by the term id.

An explicit presentation of set theory is obtained by skolemizing the axioms. For instance, skolemizing the power set axiom introduces a function symbol $\mathcal{P}$ and an axiom

$$\forall x \; \forall y \; ((y \in \mathcal{P}(x)) \Leftrightarrow \forall z \; ((z \in y) \Rightarrow (z \in x)))$$

In this language, the power set of some set x is now written $\mathcal{P}(x)$.

Skolemizing the union axiom introduces a function symbol $\bigcup$ and a notation $\bigcup(a)$ for the union of the elements of a. Skolemizing the pairing axiom introduces a function symbol $\{,\}$ and a notation $\{a, b\}$ for the pair containing the object a and the object b.

Skolemizing the subset scheme introduces an infinite number of function symbols $h_{x,z_1,...,z_n,P}$ and the axioms

$$\forall z_1 \ldots \forall z_n \ \forall a \ \forall x \ (x \in h_{x,z_1,...,z_n,P}(z_1, ..., z_n, a)) \Leftrightarrow ((x \in a) \wedge P)$$

We write $\{x \in a \mid P\}$ for the term $h_{x,z_1,...,z_n,P}(z_1, ..., z_n, a)$. Notice that the free variables of $\{x \in a \mid P\}$ are those of P minus x and those of a. In this language we can form the term $\{x \in a \mid P\}$ only when P contains no Skolem symbols. Nested abstractions can be built by applying the symbol $h_{x,z_1,...,z_n,P}$ to terms $b_1, ..., b_n$ containing Skolem symbols, but the variables free in these terms cannot be bound in this terms. This language is however equivalent to one with the full power of nested abstraction (see, for instance, [11]).

2.3 Functions as primitive objects

The next point concerns functions. In set theory, functions are defined as functional relations and relations as sets of ordered pairs. Thus to express a function, for instance the function square, we need to express first the set of pairs i.e. $G = \{< x, y > \in N \times N \mid x * x = y\}$ and then a proof of the proposition

$$\forall x \in N \ \exists_1 y \in N \ \ < x, y > \in G$$

Thus a function is expressed by a set and a proof. If, following Heyting-Kolmogorov interpretation, we want to express a proof of $A \Rightarrow A$ as a function mapping proofs of A to proofs of A, we express this proof as a function, i.e. as a set $G = \{< x, y > \in pr(A) \times pr(A) \mid x = y\}$ and a proof of the proposition

$$\forall x \in pr(A) \ \exists_1 y \in pr(A) \ \ < x, y > \in G$$

Thus we get a circular definition: a proof is expressed by a set and a proof. This circularity could be avoided if the proof-checking algorithm could establish by itself the functionality of G, but this seems to be rather difficult in the general case. In contrast, if we express the function above by the term $x \mapsto x$, or rather $x \in pr(A) \mapsto x$, then to establish that this term expresses a function of $pr(A) \rightarrow pr(A)$ we only need to prove the proposition

$$\forall x \in pr(A) \ x \in pr(A)$$

and this proposition can be established by the proof-checking algorithm (see section 4 below).

Here, we take a formalization of mathematics where functions are primitive objects, i.e. we axiomatize and not define what functions are. But, the important point its not that $\{< x, y > \in pr(A) \times pr(A) \mid x = y\}$ and $x \in pr(A) \mapsto x$ are different objects, it is that we need also the notation $x \in pr(A) \mapsto x$ for this object.

The idea of axiomatizing mathematics with functions as a primitive notion has already been investigated in combinatory logic [9, 10]. The main difference with this formalism is that our functions are not defined on all the universe but have a domain of definitions. For instance, we do not have a function $x \mapsto x$ but for each set a, we have a function $x \in a \mapsto x$. The axiom $((x \in a \mapsto x)\ t) = t$ is only valid if t belongs to a. This is also the main difference with partial combinatory logic (see, for instance, [2]) that has unrestricted conversion axioms but a predicate $\downarrow$ for *denoting terms*.

We first introduce a new function symbol α (for "apply"). We write $(f\ a)$ for $\alpha(f,a)$ and $(f\ a_1\ ...\ a_n)$ for $(...(f\ a_1)\ ...\ a_n)$. There is a notational difference between the application of a function symbol f to a term a, written $f(a)$, and the "application" of a term a to a term b, written $(a\ b)$, that is an alternative notation for $\alpha(a,b)$.

Then, we take a functional comprehension scheme

$$\exists f\ \forall x_1 \in a_1\ ...\ \forall x_n \in a_n\ (f\ x_1\ ...\ x_n) = t$$

Notice that to build a function, we need to give its domain $a_1, ..., a_n$, but we do not need to give its codomain. In set theory the codomain of such a function can always be constructed with the replacement scheme.

When we skolemize this axiom scheme we introduce function symbols $f_{(a_1,...,a_n),(z_1,...,z_p),(x_1,...,x_n),t}$ where $z_1, ..., z_p$ are the free variables of t minus $x_1, ..., x_n$, and an axiom

$$\forall x_1 \in a_1\ ...\ \forall x_n \in a_n \quad (f_{(a_1,...,a_n),(z_1,...,z_p),(x_1,...,x_n),t}(a_1, ..., a_n, z_1, ..., z_p)\ x_1\ ...\ x_n) = t$$

The term $f_{(a_1,...,a_n),(z_1,...,z_p),(x_1,...,x_n),t}(a_1, ..., a_n, z_1, ..., z_p)$ is also written $x_1 \in a_1 ..., x_n \in a_n \mapsto t$.

Then we need to axiomatize the notion of function space. We introduce a new function symbol $\rightarrow$ to construct such function spaces. We write $a \rightarrow b$ for $\rightarrow (a,b)$ and $a_1 \rightarrow ... \rightarrow a_{n-1} \rightarrow a_n$ for $a_1 \rightarrow (... \rightarrow (a_{n-1} \rightarrow a_n)...)$. We take the axioms

$$(f \in A \rightarrow B) \Rightarrow (a \in A) \Rightarrow (\alpha(f,a) \in B)$$

$$((\forall x_1 \in a_1\ ...\ \forall x_n \in a_n\ t \in b) \Rightarrow f_{(a_1,...,a_n),(z_1,...,z_p),(x_1,...,x_n),t}(a_1, ..., a_n, z_1, ..., z_p) \in a_1 \rightarrow ... \rightarrow a_n \rightarrow b$$

Remark As shown in [11] we cannot iterate the definition of functions of one argument to build function of n arguments.

Remark Let B be the function from N to $\mathcal{P}(N)$ mapping a natural number x to the singleton $\{x\}$ and f be the function $x \in N \mapsto x$. We have

$$\forall x \in N\ (f\ x) \in N$$

From this proposition we can deduce $f \in N \rightarrow N$. But we also have

$$\forall x \in N\ (f\ x) \in (B\ x)$$

and we do not have any notation for the set of functions verifying this property. To express proofs, we want to give a name and a notation for this set. Thus, we extend the function symbol $\rightarrow$ to a function symbol Π and we take the axiom

$$f \in \Pi(A, B) \Rightarrow a \in A \Rightarrow (f\ a) \in (B\ a) \tag{3}$$

and the functional comprehension scheme

$$\exists f\ \forall x_1 \in a_1\ ...\ \forall x_n \in (a_n\ x_1\ ...\ x_{n-1})\ (f\ x_1\ ...\ x_n) = t$$

When we skolemize this scheme, we introduce new function symbols $f_{(a_1,...,a_n),(z_1,...,z_p),(x_1,...,x_n),t}$ and axioms

$$\forall x_1 \in a_1\ ...\ \forall x_n \in (a_n\ x_1\ ...\ x_{n-1})$$
$$(f_{(a_1,...,a_n),(z_1,...,z_p),(x_1,...,x_n),t}(a_1, ..., a_n, z_1, ..., z_p)\ x_1\ ...\ x_n) = t \tag{4}$$

We also take the axiom

$$(\forall x_1 \in a_1\ ...\ \forall x_n \in (a_n\ x_1\ ...\ x_{n-1})\ t \in (b\ x_1\ ...\ x_n)) \Rightarrow$$
$$f_{(a_1,...,a_n),(z_1,...,z_p),(x_1,...,x_n),t}(a_1, ..., a_n, z_1, ..., z_p) \in \Pi(a_1, ..., \Pi(a_n, b)) \tag{5}$$

At last we take a functional extensionality axiom

$$\forall f \in \Pi(A, B)\ \forall g \in \Pi(A, B)\ (\forall x \in A\ (f\ x) = (g\ x)) \Rightarrow f = g \tag{6}$$

Now the symbol $\rightarrow$ is not needed anymore, the term $A \rightarrow B$ is an alternative notation for $\Pi(A, x \in A \mapsto B)$ where x is a variable not occurring in B.

Remark (Lambda-calculus as an abuse of notation) In this language we can form the term $x \in A \mapsto t$ only when t contains no Skolem symbols. Nested abstractions can be built by considering a term t applying the symbol $f_{(a_1,...,a_n),(z_1,...,z_p),(x_1,...,x_n),t}$ to terms $u_1, ..., u_p$ containing Skolem symbols, but the variables free in these terms cannot be bound in this term [11]. This language is however equivalent to one with the full power of nested abstraction. Each time we want to build the function $x \in A \mapsto t$, we first replace every abstractions $y_1 \in B_1, ..., y_n \in B_n \mapsto u$ in t by the term $((x \in A, y_1 \in B_1, ..., y_n \in B_n \mapsto u)\ x)$. This way x in not free in abstractions subterms of t' and the function $x \in A \mapsto t'$ can be constructed with the scheme above.

2.4 Propositions as objects

To form a term $pr(P)$ we need the statement P to be a term. Statements must be both terms and propositions of the language. Thus instead of taking $\in$ and $=$ to be predicate symbols, we take them to be functions symbols. This permits to have atomic propositions as objects. The case of propositions formed with connectors and quantifiers is studied below.

The expression $0 = 0$ is now a term and not a proposition. This term can be seen as the content (*lexis*) of the proposition.

We introduce also an individual symbol O for a set containing contents of propositions.

Then we need a unary predicate symbol ε to assert a proposition-term, i.e. to express that the proposition is indeed true. We take an extensionality axiom expressing that two equivalent propositions have the same content

$$((\varepsilon(x) \Leftrightarrow \varepsilon(y))) \Rightarrow \varepsilon(x = y) \tag{7}$$

Now, in the notation $\{z \in A \mid P\}$, P also is a term.

2.5 Sets as functions

When functions are primitive objects, sets can in turn be defined as their characteristic functions, i.e. sets need not be primitive objects anymore. Thus, the term $a \in B$ is now an alternative notation for $(B\ a)$ and $\{x \in A \mid P\}$ for $x \in A \mapsto P$.

Remark As functions are defined with a domain of definition, when we define a set A by its characteristic function $f \in B \to O$, we cannot say anything of $(f\ x)$ if x is outside of B. Thus we need a special axiom to state that elements outside of B are not in A (i.e. all the elements of A are in B).

$$(\varepsilon(a \in (B \to O)) \wedge \varepsilon(b \in a)) \Rightarrow \varepsilon(b \in B) \tag{8}$$

Remark Now the term $\mathcal{P}(A)$ is an alternative notation for $A \to O$. Notice that if A is an element of $B \to O$ and $A \neq B$ then $A \notin \mathcal{P}(A)$. Indeed, A cannot have both the domain A and B. But the set $|A| = x \in A \mapsto \top$ belongs to $\mathcal{P}(A)$ and with the axiom above we have $(x \in A) \Leftrightarrow (x \in |A|)$.

2.6 Connectors and Quantifiers

Taking $=$ and $\in$ as function symbol permits to have atomic propositions as objects. To have all propositions as objects we take new individual symbols $\dot\wedge$, $\dot\vee$, $\dot\Rightarrow$ and $\dot\bot$. Then we take the axioms

$$\varepsilon(\dot\wedge \in (O \to O \to O)) \tag{9}$$

$$\varepsilon(\dot\vee \in (O \to O \to O)) \tag{10}$$

$$\varepsilon(\dot\Rightarrow \in (O \to O \to O)) \tag{11}$$

$$\varepsilon(\dot\bot \in O) \tag{12}$$

$$\varepsilon(\dot\wedge\ A\ B) \Leftrightarrow (\varepsilon(A) \wedge \varepsilon(B)) \tag{a}$$

$$\varepsilon(\dot\vee\ A\ B) \Leftrightarrow (\varepsilon(A) \vee \varepsilon(B)) \tag{b}$$

$$\varepsilon(\dot\Rightarrow\ A\ B) \Leftrightarrow (\varepsilon(A) \Rightarrow \varepsilon(B)) \tag{c}$$

$$\varepsilon(\dot{\bot}) \Leftrightarrow \bot \qquad (d)$$

Then, we want to take some symbols allowing to build contents of propositions built by quantification. In the languages of propositions quantifiers are unbounded, i.e. we can quantify over all the objects of the universe. But Heyting-Kolmogorov interpretation of proofs restricts the use of quantifiers to bounded ones. Indeed, a proof of the unboundedly quantified proposition $\forall x\ P$ would need to be a function mapping any object of the universe to a proof. The domain of this function would need to be the set of all objects and postulating the existence of such a set leads to known paradoxes. Thus, it seems that if we want to express proofs with Heyting-Kolmogorov interpretation, we have to banish the use of unbounded quantification.

Thus, we introduce a unary function symbol $\dot{\forall}$ and axioms

$$\varepsilon(\dot{\forall}(A) \in ((A \rightarrow O) \rightarrow O)) \qquad (13)$$

$$\varepsilon(\dot{\forall}(A)\ f) \Leftrightarrow \forall x\ (\varepsilon(x \in A) \Rightarrow \varepsilon(f\ x)) \qquad (e)$$

Now the proposition $\dot{\forall} x \in A\ P$ is an alternative notation for $(\dot{\forall}(A)\ (x \in A \mapsto P))$.

In the same way, we introduce a unary function symbols $\dot{\exists}$ and axioms

$$\varepsilon(\dot{\exists}(A) \in ((A \rightarrow O) \rightarrow O)) \qquad (14)$$

$$\varepsilon(\dot{\exists}(A)\ f) \Leftrightarrow \exists x\ (\varepsilon(x \in A) \wedge \varepsilon(f\ x)) \qquad (f)$$

and the proposition $\dot{\exists} x \in A\ P$ is an alternative notation for $(\dot{\exists}(A)\ (x \in A \mapsto P))$.

The proposition $\dot{\exists} x \in A$ is an alternative notation for $\dot{\exists} x \in A\ \top$.

Remark Not all propositions have contents, because the language of proposition uses unbounded quantifiers, while that of contents of propositions bounded ones.

Remark According to the Heyting-Kolmogorov interpretation, a proof of a proposition of the form $(\dot{\forall}(A)\ B)$ would be a function f mapping any object a of A to a proof of $(B\ a)$. But if a is a term, to know if $(f\ a)$ is a proof of $(B\ a)$ we have to decide if a is in A or not. Thus a better choice is to take for proofs of $(\dot{\forall}(A)\ B)$ a function mapping any objet a and any proof b of $a \in A$ to a proof of $(B\ a)$.

This choice is close to that of naïve Heyting-Kolmogorov interpretation. In such an interpretation, a proof of $(\dot{\forall}(A)\ B)$ is a proof of $\forall x\ ((x \in A) \Rightarrow (B\ x))$ and thus a function mapping any object a and proof b of the proposition $a \in A$ to a proof of $(B\ a)$. The only difference is that we use the fact that quantification is bounded to give a domain to this function.

In the same way a proof of a proposition of the form $(\dot{\exists}(A)\ B)$ is a triple $< a, b, c >$ where a is an element of A, b a proof of the proposition $a \in A$ and c a proof of the proposition $(B\ a)$.

Remark The connectors and quantifiers in the axioms (1) to (6) can be read as function symbols puting a dot over each of them. Then, we add the ε predicate symbol in front of these propositions. Axiom (7) and (8) can be rewritten

$$\varepsilon((x \dot{\Leftrightarrow} y) \dot{\Rightarrow} (x = y)) \qquad (7)$$

$$\varepsilon((a \in (B \to O))\dot{\wedge}(b \in a))\dot{\Rightarrow}(b \in B) \quad (8)$$

Remark The axioms above and below contain free variables. What is meant is the universal closure of these propositions with the universal unbounded quantifier (not the function symbol). Axioms seem to be the only place where unbounded quantification is required.

2.7 Pairing, ordered pairs, disjoint unions and numbers

In this theory, if we have a set A, we can build, its definable subsets, its power set $(A \to O)$, and if A is a set of sets (i.e. if it belongs to $(B \to O) \to O$ for some set B) we can define the union of its elements as a subset of B, i.e. as an element of $B \to O$.

If we compare this with Zermelo's set theory, only one construction is missing: the possibility to construct pairs $\{A, B\}$ with any two elements. Of course, if A and B already belong to a common set C then we can construct the subset of C of objects equal to A or to B, but we cannot, for instance, construct the set $\{A, \{A\}\}$.

In the construction of mathematical objects, pairs are used at several places, first they are used to build ordered pairs $< a, b >= \{\{a\}, \{a, b\}\}$. Then, they are used to form unions of any to sets $A \cup B = \bigcup\{A, B\}$ and thus disjoint unions $A \oplus B = (\{0\} \times A) \cup (\{1\} \times B)$. At last they are used to form numbers $0 = \emptyset$, $1 = \{0\}$, $2 = \{0, 1\}$, etc.

Instead of taking this pairing construct, we rather take as primitive ordered pairing and disjoint unions, i.e. we take function symbols $\times$, *pair*, π, $\otimes$, i, j and δ and the axioms expressing the meaning of these symbols. In fact, like for dependent function space, we want dependent cartesian products. An element of $\Sigma(A, B)$ is a pair $pair(A, B, a, b)$ such that a is an element of A and b is an element of $(B\ a)$.

The term $< a, b >_{A,B}$ is an alternative notation for $pair(A, B, a, b)$. The term $A \times B$ is an alternative notation for $\Sigma(A, x \in A \mapsto B)$.

$$\varepsilon(\dot{\forall} x \in A\ \dot{\forall} y \in (B\ x)\ (< x, y >_{A,B} \in \Sigma(A, B))) \quad (15)$$

$$\varepsilon((f \in \Pi x \in A\ ((B\ x) \to C))\dot{\Rightarrow}\pi(A, B, C, < x, y >_{A,B}, f) = (f\ x\ y)) \quad (16)$$

$$\varepsilon((x \in A)\dot{\Rightarrow}(i(A, B, x) \in (A \oplus B))) \quad (17)$$

$$\varepsilon((y \in B)\dot{\Rightarrow}(j(A, B, y) \in (A \oplus B))) \quad (18)$$

$$\varepsilon(\delta(A, B, C, i(A, B, x), f, g) = (f\ x)) \quad (19)$$

$$\varepsilon(\delta(A, B, C, j(A, B, x), f, g) = (g\ x)) \quad (20)$$

Remark The condition $f \in \Pi x \in A\ ((B\ x) \to C)$ in axiom (16) above defines the so-called *weak dependent cartesian product*. Indeed, we can build the function mapping an element of $\Sigma(A, B)$ to its first component by defining $f = x \in$

$A, y \in (B\ x) \mapsto x$, proving $f \in \Pi x \in A\ ((B\ x) \to A)$ and defining the function $\pi_1 = a \in \Sigma(A, B) \mapsto \pi(A, x \in A \mapsto B, A, a, f)$. But we cannot construct the function mapping an element of $\Sigma(A, B)$ to its second component because $g = x \in A, y \in (B\ a) \mapsto y$ fails to be in a set $\Pi x \in A\ ((B\ x) \to C)$. In contrast we can build the function mapping an element of $A \times B$ to its second component by defining $g = x \in A, y \in B \mapsto y$, proving $g \in A \to B \to B$ and defining the function $\pi_2 = a \in A \times B \mapsto \pi(A, x \in A \mapsto B, B, a, g)$.

Remark The expression $\pi_1(A, B, a)$ is an alternative notation for the term

$$a \in \Sigma(A, B) \mapsto \pi(A, (x \in A \mapsto B), A, a, (x \in A, y \in (B\ x) \mapsto x))$$

Remark The term $< a, b, c >_{A,B,C}$ is an alternative notation for

$$< a, < b, c >_{(B\ a), y \in (B\ a) \mapsto (C\ a\ y)} >_{A, x \in A \mapsto \Sigma((B\ x), y \in (B\ x) \mapsto (C\ x\ y))}$$

and the term $\pi'(A, B, C, D, e, f)$ for

$$\pi(A, x \in A \mapsto \Sigma((B\ x), y \in (B\ x) \mapsto (C\ x\ y)), D, e,$$
$$(x \in A, z \in \Sigma((B\ x), y \mapsto (C\ x\ y))$$
$$\mapsto \pi((B\ x), y \in (B\ x) \mapsto (C\ x\ y), D, z, (f\ x))))$$

We have

$$\varepsilon(f \in \Pi x \in A\ \Pi y \in (B\ x)\ ((C\ x\ y) \to D)$$
$$\dot{\Rightarrow} \pi'(A, B, C, D, < a, b, c >, f) = (f\ a\ b\ c))$$

Remark To construct natural numbers, we consider an infinite set I of atoms, i.e. a set having a non surjective injection.

$$\varepsilon(\dot{\exists} z \in I\ \dot{\exists} s \in I \to I\ (\dot{\forall} x \in I\ (\dot{\neg}((s\ x) = z)))$$
$$\dot{\wedge} \dot{\forall} x \in I\ \dot{\forall} y \in I\ ((s\ x) = (s\ y) \dot{\Rightarrow} (x = y)))$$

When we skolemize this axiom we get

$$\varepsilon((\dot{\forall} x \in I\ (\dot{\neg}((s\ x) = z)))) \quad (21)$$

$$\varepsilon(\dot{\forall} x \in I\ \dot{\forall} y \in I\ ((s\ x) = (s\ y) \dot{\Rightarrow} (x = y))) \quad (22)$$

We can then either construct natural numbers as finite cardinals in $(I \to O) \to O$ or take numbers as atoms, defining n as being the object $(s\ ...\ (s\ z)...)$ and thus the set of numbers as the smallest set containing z and closed by s.

2.8 A first-order theory

The axioms (1)-(22) and (a)-(f) above define a first-order theory in the language containing the only predicate symbol ε and the function symbols $=$, O, $\dot{\wedge}$, $\dot{\vee}$, $\dot{\Rightarrow}$, $\dot{\bot}$, $\dot{\forall}$, $\dot{\exists}$, Π, α, $f_{(a_1,...,a_n),(z_1,...,z_p),(x_1,...,x_n),t}$, Σ, $pair$, π, $\oplus$, i, j, δ, I, z, s.

As usual, when functions are primitive and not defined as sets of pairs, the comprehension scheme alone does not provide enough functions to formalize mathematics, the description axioms (or the axiom of choice) needs to be added (see section 3.4).

2.9 Consistency

The relative consistency of the axioms above with respect to Zermelo-Fraenkel set theory seems to be easy to establish. Interpreting the set O by $\{0,1\}$ and following the usual definitions of function spaces, cartesian products, disjoint unions and numbers in set theory.

The differences between this theory and Zermelo-Fraenkel set theory concern three points.

- the axioms are skolemized,
- the predicate symbols $=$ and $\in$ are decomposed into two function symbols $=$ and $\in$ and a predicate symbol ε and consequently a set O is introduced and connectors and quantifiers are replicated as function symbols,
- function spaces, cartesian products, disjoint unions and numbers are axiomatized and not defined thus we can drop the pairing axiom, the replacement scheme and have a slightly weaker union axiom.

The third point is in some sense optional. We could take the Zermelo-Fraenkel axioms instead and define these notions as usual in set theory, provided we extend the language to be allowed to write $x \in N \mapsto x * x$ and not only $\{< x,y >\in N \times N \mid y = x * x\}$ (it is well-known that there is little differences between defining some notions and axiomatizing them first and then proving consistency by constructing a model.) However this permits to formalize mathematics with weaker axioms than Zermelo-Fraenkel and as we shall see to avoid some paradoxes when we add proofs as objects.

3 Proofs as objects

3.1 The symbol pr

We add a function symbol pr that maps the contents of propositions to the sets of their proofs. We extend the comprehension scheme to instances containing the symbol pr. We take the axioms:

$$\varepsilon(pr(P \dot{\Rightarrow} Q) = pr(P) \rightarrow pr(Q)) \tag{23}$$

$$\varepsilon(pr(P \dot{\wedge} Q) = pr(P) \times pr(Q)) \tag{24}$$

$$\varepsilon(pr(P \dot{\vee} Q) = pr(P) \oplus pr(Q)) \tag{25}$$

$$\varepsilon(pr(\dot{\perp}) = \emptyset_I) \tag{26}$$

$$\varepsilon(pr(\dot{\forall}(A)\ f) = (\Pi\ x \in A\ \Pi y \in pr(x \in A)\ pr(f\ x))) \tag{27}$$

$$\varepsilon(pr(\dot{\exists}(A)\ f) = (\Sigma\ x \in A\ \Sigma y \in pr(x \in A)\ pr(f\ x))) \tag{28}$$

Example

$$\varepsilon((x \in O, y \in pr(x) \mapsto y) \in pr(\dot{\forall} X \in O\ (X \dot{\Rightarrow} X)))$$

3.2 Leibniz scheme, equality of denotations and equality of meanings

In contrast with the comprehension scheme, we do not extend Leibniz scheme with instances containing the symbol *pr*. Indeed even if we can prove $a = b$ we do not want $p \in pr(P\ a)$ and $p \in pr(P\ b)$ to be equivalent propositions. We do not want every proof of $(P\ a)$ to be a proof of $(P\ b)$ because we want the proof of $(P\ b)$ to be built from the proof of $(P\ a)$ and the proof of $a = b$. This behavior of equality can be compared with the behavior of equality in some modal logics where from "The murder = Professor Moriarty" and "Sherlock Holmes knows (The murder = The murder)" we cannot deduce "Sherlock Holmes knows (The murder = Professor Moriarty)". This relation between modal logic and the provability operator has already been noticed in many ways [17, 2, 3]. A consequence is that equality cannot be interpreted as equality in a model: even if a and b are two terms provably equal they are not always interpreted as the same object in the model. Equality is just a casual binary predicate symbol.

We may now introduce another symbol $\equiv$ for genuine equality, and axioms

$$\varepsilon(x \equiv x) \tag{29}$$

$$\varepsilon(a \equiv b \dot{\Rightarrow} P[z \leftarrow a] \dot{\Rightarrow} P[z \leftarrow b]) \tag{30}$$

Where P here can be any proposition, i.e. may contain the symbol *pr*.

The proposition $a = b$ expresses that the terms a and b have the same denotation while the proposition $a \equiv b$ expresses that they have the same meaning. Indeed if $a \equiv b$ then any proof of $(P\ a)$ is a proof of $(P\ b)$. In other words, two propositions A and B have the same meaning if what what is needed to be done to prove A is what is needed to be done to prove B and two terms a and b have the same meaning is $P[x \leftarrow a]$ and $P[x \leftarrow b]$ always have the same meaning.

If we only have the two axioms above, we can prove propositions of the form $a \equiv b$ only when a and b are the same term. But, if R is a decidable equivalence relation on terms such that if $a\ R\ b$ then $a = b$ is a provable proposition, then we can extend the equality of meanings by an axiom scheme $a \equiv b$ for each pair of R-equivalent terms keeping decidability of proof-checking (compare with the opposition internal equality/external equality in Martin-Löf type theory [24] or and in the Calculus of constructions [8] and with Plotkin-Andrews program in automated theorem proving [27, 1]).

Consequently, the extensionality axioms do not jeopardize the intentional aspects of terms. The axiom

$$\varepsilon((x \dot{\Leftrightarrow} y) \dot{\Rightarrow} (x = y))$$

only states that if x and y are equivalent propositions, they have the same denotation, not that they have the same meaning.

3.3 Truth as provability

Now, we wish to be able to prove propositions by constructing an object that is a proof of this proposition. Also we wish to prove an implication $A \Rightarrow B$, proving

B using not only the truth, but also the proof of A. Thus, we take the axiom "truth = proof" i.e.

$$\varepsilon(P \dot{\Leftrightarrow} \dot{\exists} x \in pr(P))$$

This axiom can de decomposed in two axioms: the *conecessitation* axiom

$$\varepsilon(\dot{\forall} x \in pr(P)\ P) \tag{31}$$

and the *necessitation* axiom

$$\varepsilon(P \dot{\Rightarrow} (\dot{\exists} x \in pr(P)))$$

When we skolemize this axiom we introduce a new function symbol c and the axiom becomes

$$\varepsilon(P \dot{\Rightarrow} (c(P) \in pr(P))) \tag{32}$$

Remark When proofs are encoded as Gödel numbers, if P is an unprovable proposition valid in the standard model of arithmetic, then the proposition

$$P \Rightarrow \exists x\ proof(x, `P')$$

is false in the standard model. Thus the standard model is not a model of the necessitation axiom. In other words the necessitation axiom implies the existence of non standard numbers for proofs of true but unprovable propositions (McGee [22] shows that even very weak conditions on a truth predicate imply ω-inconsitency and thus the loss of the standard model of arithmetic.) Here, it only implies the existence of non standard functions, i.e. more functions that can be proved to exist with the usual axioms.

Remark The use of dummy proofs $c(P)$ can jeopardize constructivity, i.e. the possibility to compute a value from any term. Thus, from a constructive point of view, we might want to drop this axiom.

3.4 The axiom of choice

The functional comprehension scheme permits to prove the existence of explicitly definable functions. Usually the descriptions axiom or the axiom of choice is added to be able to define, for instance, addition. When proofs are objects, the choice operator can take in argument, a proof of the existence of an element in A and this operator can be the first projection. But we still need an axiom to state that $\pi_1(p)$ has the right property

$$\begin{aligned}\varepsilon(\dot{\forall} p \in pr(\dot{\exists}(A)\ P)\ ((\pi_1(A, x \in A \mapsto pr(x \in A) \times pr(P\ x), p)) \in A \\ \dot{\wedge}(P\ (\pi_1(A, x \in A \mapsto pr(x \in A) \times pr(P\ x), p)))))\end{aligned} \tag{33}$$

To prove this proposition, we would need the second projection [24]

$$p \in pr(\dot{\exists}(A)\ P) \mapsto (\pi_2(A, x \in A \mapsto \Sigma(pr(x \in A) \times pr(P\ x)), p))$$

3.5 Paradoxes

The consistency of this theory is open and can be doubted. We have two kinds of paradoxes that could jeopardize its consistency. First, the proofs as objects principle permits to construct too large sets or functions with a too large domains allowing to reproduce variants of Russell's or Burali-Forti's paradox. Then Gödel's incompleteness theorems and Tarski's undefinability theorem could be turned into paradoxes when we take the axiom "truth = proof".

Russell-like paradoxes **Remark** The language presented in this paper is not polymorphic, because we cannot build, for instance the polymorphic identity, taking as argument a set A and an element x of A and giving back x

$$id = A \in ?, x \in A \mapsto x$$

We can build a function taking as argument a proposition A, a proof x of A and giving it back

$$id = A \in O, x \in pr(A) \mapsto x$$

but sets of the form $pr(A)$ are not all the sets, in particular, the set O in not one of them. This prevents a naïve encoding of the (inconsistent) polymorphic higher-order logic [7].

Like in set theory, we can define $Refl(A, R)$ as an alternative notation for the proposition $\dot{\forall} x \in A\ (R\ x\ x)$, and we can define the set of reflexive relations over a given set $\{R \in A \to A \to O \mid \dot{\forall} x \in A\ (R\ x\ x)\}$ but there is no set of all reflexive relations.

Like in set theory, we can introduce an axiom stating the existence of a set C_0 containing I and O and closed by the usual operations, then a set C_1 containing I, O, C_0, etc. very closely to the predicative polymorphism universe hierarchy of [6].

Remark Above, we have given a presentation where function spaces, cartesian products, disjoint unions and numbers are axiomatized and not defined. We may wonder what could happen if we had kept Zermelo-Fraenkel axioms and defined such notions.

In that case, extending the replacement scheme with instances containing occurrences of the symbol pr permits to construct the set $\Omega = \{pr(x) \mid x \in O\}$.

Then the union axiom permits to form the set of all proofs $\Omega' = \bigcup(\Omega)$. If a is any object of the universe and p a proof of $a \in A$ and t a proof of $\top$, then the set Ω' contains an encapsulation $< a, p, t >$ of a as a proof of $\dot{\exists} x \in A\ \top$ and this is enough to express Russell's paradox:

$$R = \{x \in \Omega' \mid x \notin \pi_1(x)\}$$

we have $R \in \mathcal{P}(\Omega')$, let p be a proof of this proposition. We have

$$\varepsilon(< R, p, t > \in pr(\dot{\exists} y \in \mathcal{P}(\Omega')\ \top) \in \Omega)$$

thus

$$\varepsilon(< R, p, t > \in \bigcup(\Omega))$$
$$\varepsilon(< R, p, t > \in \Omega')$$

thus

$$\varepsilon(< R, p, t > \in R \dot{\Leftrightarrow} < R, p, t > \dot{\notin} \pi_1(< R, p, t >))$$
$$\varepsilon(< R, p, t > \in R) \Leftrightarrow \neg\varepsilon(< R, p, t > \in R)$$

Hence we can prove both $\neg\varepsilon(< R, p, t > \in R)$ and $\varepsilon(< R, p, t > \in R)$.

This justifies the need to weaken Zermelo-Fraenkel set theory, as we did above.

Remark In the language above, we have no way to construct the second projection mapping any ordered pair to its second element. If we could we would get an inconsistent system, because we could express Coquand's strong dependent cartesian product paradox [6].

Indeed consider the proposition

$$A_0 = \dot{\exists} x \in O\ \dot{\exists} R \in pr(x) \rightarrow pr(x) \rightarrow O\ \top$$

A proof of this proposition is a tuple formed with a proposition P an proof that P is a proposition, a binary relation R on proofs of P, a proof that R is a binary relation on proofs of P and a proof of the proposition $\top$. Any binary relation over the proof of any proposition can therefore be encapsulated into a proof of A_0 and with the second projection, from such a proof we can get back the proposition and the relation. This is enough to express Girard's paradox [16, 6].

Thus, if we have the second projection, even if we weaken set theory as we did in section 2, the set of the proofs of the proposition $\dot{\exists} x \in O\ \dot{\exists} R \in pr(x) \rightarrow pr(x) \rightarrow O\ \top$ is large enough to express Coquand's strong dependent cartesian product paradox. There are two ways to avoid this paradox. Either, like in the Calculus of constructions [8] and in this paper, we weaken the cartesian product to avoid the second projection, but this forces us to take the axiom of choice as an axiom, or, as it is done in Martin-Löf type theory [24], we avoid quantification over sets and relations. A less radical position might be to avoid quantifications over sets of proofs but not over all sets.

Gödel-like paradoxes Gödel's first incompleteness theorem is often read "there is a true proposition that is not provable". Thus we may try to reproduce the proof of Gödel's theorem within this theory to prove the inconsistency of the axiom "truth = proof". We would construct a predicate G such that $(G\ P\ x) = \dot{\exists} y \in pr(P\ x)$ and a predicate H such that $(H\ x) = \neg(G\ x\ x)$ and $A = (H\ H)$ yielding

$$A = (H\ H) = \neg(G\ H\ H) = \neg\dot{\exists} y \in pr(H\ H) = \neg\dot{\exists} y \in pr(A)$$

hence with the axiom "truth = proof"

$$\varepsilon(A) \Leftrightarrow \neg\varepsilon(A)$$

which is contradictory.

This contradiction can also be seen as a consequence of Tarski's theorem that there is no predicate $\mathcal{T}$ such that $\varepsilon(P) \Leftrightarrow \varepsilon(\mathcal{T}(P))$. Again, we would construct a predicate G such that $(G\ P\ x) = \mathcal{T}(P\ x)$ and a predicate H such that $(H\ x) = \neg(G\ x\ x)$ and $A = (H\ H)$ yielding

$$A = (H\ H) = \neg(G\ H\ H) = \neg\mathcal{T}(H\ H) = \neg\mathcal{T}(A)$$

hence

$$\varepsilon(A) \Leftrightarrow \neg\varepsilon(A)$$

which is contradictory.

In fact, these proofs do not go through as in the definition of G we need to give a domain to it. If we take, for instance,

$$G = P \in E \rightarrow O, x \in E \mapsto \dot{\exists} y \in pr(P\ x)$$

and

$$H = x \in E \mapsto \neg(G\ x\ x)$$

applying H to H we get $((x \in E \mapsto \neg(G\ x\ x))\ (x \in E \mapsto \neg(G\ x\ x)))$ but to reduce this term to $\neg\exists y \in pr(H\ H)$ we first need to prove that $H \in E$ and this cannot be done.

Gödel's proof and Tarski's proof rely on the existence of a proposition *Subst* such that *Subst*('P', 'x', 't', 'Q') is provable if and only if $Q = P[x \leftarrow t]$ thus the "function" *Subst* permits to apply the "function" P to (the Gödel number of) any object. It is well-known that postulating the existence of functions defined on all the universe leads to paradoxes. In Gödel's proof and Tarski's proof such a function can be defined because all the objects, predicates and propositions are replicated as numbers. Thus the problem is not with the axiom "truth = proof" but with the fact that internalization replicates anything as a number and thus permits to speak about all the expressions (i.e. all the objects) at the same time.

Here, interalization is much weaker. First, objects are not replicated (we do not have one term for the number 0 and another for the Gödel number of the term "0"). Then, propositions are replicated as object in the set O. Thus we have no way to construct a "function" *Subst* applying any function to any object. This seems to permit to state the axiom "truth = proof" without contradiction.

It seems also that there is no contradiction between Gödel's second incompleteness theorem and the fact that, from the conecessitation axiom, we have $(\exists y\ \varepsilon(y \in pr(\dot{\bot}))) \Rightarrow \bot$ and hence that the theory seems to prove its own consistency.

4 Judgements

Now we want to prove that each time a proposition $\varepsilon(P)$ is provable, there is a term t such that $t \in pr(P)$ is provable and moreover we want to build a proof-checking algorithm to recognize that the proposition $t \in pr(P)$ holds.

Definition Let $\mathcal{T}$ be the set of axioms containing the universal closure of the propositions (1) to (33) and (a) to (f) above (the universal quantifier is the unbounded quantifier of the logic, not the function symbol) and $\mathcal{T}^-$ the set of axioms containing the universal closure of the propositions (1) to (33).

4.1 Natural deduction on contents

First, we replace the axioms (a) to (f) by new deduction rules replicating natural deduction rules at the level of contents. e.g.

$$\frac{\Gamma \vdash \varepsilon(A \dot{\wedge} B)}{\Gamma \vdash \varepsilon(A)} \dot{\wedge}\text{-elim}$$

keeping obvioulsy an equivalent theory.

These rules are called *internal rules*. The true natural deduction rules are called *external rules*.

Proposition (External cut elimination) In the system using external rules and internal rules, the elimination of external cuts terminates.
Proof See [13].

Proposition Let Γ be a set of propositions that are either atomic propositions $\varepsilon(P)$ or universal closures of such atomic propositions. If the sequent $\Gamma \vdash \varepsilon(Q)$ has a proof free of external cuts and whose last rule is external, then $\varepsilon(Q)$ is an instance of some axiom $\forall x_1 ... \forall x_n\ \varepsilon(P)$.
Proof See [13].

Corollary For sequents of the form $\mathcal{T}^- \vdash \varepsilon(A)$, the system is equivalent to the system with internal rules only and an axiom rule

$$\frac{}{\Gamma \cup \{\forall x_1 ... \forall x_n\ \varepsilon(P)\} \vdash \varepsilon(P[x_1 \leftarrow t_1, ..., x_n \leftarrow t_n])} \text{axiom}$$

4.2 An algorithm

Call $\mathcal{S}$ the set of propositions A such that $\mathcal{T} \vdash \varepsilon(A)$. In this section we define a subset $\mathcal{S}'$ of $\mathcal{S}$ such that $\mathcal{S}'$ is decidable and whenever a proposition A is in $\mathcal{S}$ there is a term t such that the proposition $t \in pr(A)$ is in $\mathcal{S}'$.

Definition

$$\frac{}{\Gamma \cup \{\forall x_1 \ldots \forall x_n\ \varepsilon(t \in pr(A))\} \rhd (t \in pr(A))[x_1 \leftarrow t_1, ..., x_n \leftarrow t_n]}$$

$$\frac{\Gamma \cup \{x \in pr(A)\} \rhd t \in pr(B)}{\Gamma \rhd (x \in pr(A) \mapsto t)) \in pr(A \dot{\Rightarrow} B)}\ x \text{ fresh variable}$$

$$\frac{\Gamma \rhd f \in pr(A \dot{\Rightarrow} B) \quad \Gamma \rhd a \in pr(A)}{\Gamma \rhd (f\ a) \in pr(B)}$$

$$\frac{\Gamma \cup \{x' \in pr(x \in A)\} \rhd t \in (B\ x)}{\Gamma \rhd (x \in A, x' \in pr(x \in A) \mapsto t) \in pr(\dot{\forall}(A)\ B)}\ x, x' \text{ fresh variables}$$

$$\frac{\Gamma \rhd f \in pr(\dot{\forall}(A)\ B) \quad \Gamma \rhd p \in pr(a \in A)}{\Gamma \rhd (f\ a\ p) \in pr(B\ a)}$$

$$\frac{\Gamma \rhd a \in pr(A) \quad \Gamma \rhd b \in pr(B)}{\Gamma \rhd < a, b >_{pr(A), x \in pr(A) \mapsto pr(B)} \in pr(A \dot{\wedge} B)}$$

$$\frac{\Gamma \rhd t \in pr(A \dot{\wedge} B)}{\Gamma \rhd \pi(pr(A), x \in pr(A) \mapsto pr(B), pr(A), t, (x \in pr(A), y \in pr(B) \mapsto x)) \in pr(A)}$$

$$\frac{\Gamma \rhd t \in pr(A \dot{\wedge} B)}{\Gamma \rhd \pi(pr(A), x \in pr(A) \mapsto pr(B), pr(B), t, (x \in pr(A), y \in pr(B) \mapsto y)) \in pr(B)}$$

$$\frac{\Gamma \rhd p \in pr(a \in A) \quad \Gamma \rhd b \in pr(B\ a)}{\Gamma \rhd < a, p, b >_{A, x \in A \mapsto pr(x \in A), x \in A, q \in pr(x \in A) \mapsto pr(B\ x)} \in pr(\dot{\exists}(A)\ B)}$$

$$\frac{\Gamma \rhd t \in pr(\dot{\exists}(A)\ B) \quad \Gamma \rhd f \in pr(\dot{\forall}(A)\ (x \in A \mapsto (B \dot{\Rightarrow} C)))}{\Gamma \rhd \pi'(A, x \in A \mapsto pr(x \in A), x \in A, y \in pr(x \in A) \mapsto pr(B\ x), pr(C), t, f) \in pr(C)}$$

$$\frac{\Gamma \rhd t \in pr(A)}{\Gamma \rhd i(A, B, t) \in pr(A \dot{\vee} B)}$$

$$\frac{\Gamma \rhd t \in pr(B)}{\Gamma \rhd j(A, B, t) \in pr(A \dot{\vee} B)}$$

$$\frac{\Gamma \rhd t \in pr(A \dot{\vee} B) \quad \Gamma \cup \{x \in pr(A)\} \rhd t \in pr(C) \quad \Gamma \cup \{y \in pr(B)\} \rhd u \in pr(C)}{\Gamma \rhd \delta(pr(A), pr(B), pr(C), t, x \in pr(A) \mapsto t, x \in pr(B) \mapsto u) \in pr(C)}$$

$$\frac{\Gamma \rhd t \in pr(\dot{\bot})}{\Gamma \rhd ((x \in pr(\dot{\bot}) \mapsto c(A))\ t) \in pr(A)}$$

Definition Let $\mathcal{A}$ be the set containing, for each proposition of $\mathcal{T}^-$ $\forall x_1 \ldots \forall x_n\ \varepsilon(P)$, the proposition

$$\forall x_1 \ldots \forall x_n\ \varepsilon(c(P) \in pr(P))$$

A proposition P is said to be provable in the system above if $\mathcal{A} \rhd P$

Proposition If P is provable in the system above (i.e. if $\mathcal{A} \rhd P$) then $\varepsilon(P)$ is provable in the theory $\mathcal{T}$ (i.e. $\mathcal{T} \vdash \varepsilon(P)$).

Remark Some propositions are provable in $\mathcal{T}$ but not in this system.

Proposition The set of sequents provable with the system above is decidable.
Proof See [13].

4.3 From proofs to terms

Definition Let Γ be a set of atomic propositions, we let Γ^+ be the set containing for each proposition $\varepsilon(P)$ of Γ, the proposition $x \in pr(P)$ where x is a fresh variable.

Proposition If $\mathcal{T} \vdash \varepsilon(P)$ is intuitionistically provable then there is a term t such that $\mathcal{A} \rhd t \in pr(P)$.
Proof See [13].

Remark It is not the case that each time a proposition of the form $t \in pr(P)$ is provable, it is decided by the algorithm above (for instance a proposition of the form $c(P) \in pr(P)$ is almost never decided by this algorithm). But for each provable proposition, there is a term such that the proposition $t \in pr(P)$ is decided by this algorithm.

Definition Let $\mathcal{S}'$ be the decidable set of propositions $\varepsilon(P)$ such that $\mathcal{A} \rhd P$.

Theorem A proposition $\varepsilon(P)$ is intuitionistically provable in the theory $\mathcal{T}$ if and only if it is provable in the system having all the propositions of $\mathcal{S}'$ as axioms and the single deduction rule

$$\frac{\varepsilon(t \in pr(P))}{\varepsilon(P)}$$

Conclusion

We have developed a first-order theory that formalizes mathematics in such a way that proofs are objects, as are numbers, functions and sets. In this system proving a proposition can be replaced by providing a proof-term.

Having proofs as objects does not require to formalize mathematics in a typed language. But, it seems to require to formalize mathematics with weaker axioms than Zermelo-Fraenkel set theory, that together with the proofs-as-objects axioms permits to form too large sets and encode paradoxes. Even with a weaker theory, like that presented in section 2, paradoxes may be encoded when we have both the possibility to quantify over any set and the strong cartesian product. Thus we have to drop one or the other.

The truth of a proposition P and of a proposition $t \in pr(P)$ are defined differently as the latter needs to be decided by an algorithm and the former cannot. But these propositions are expressed in the same universal language and the two notions of truth are compatible: if $t \in pr(P)$ is true for the second definition of truth, then it is also true for the first.

When proofs are objects, equality splits into two symbols: equality of denotations and equality of meanings. The latter being the true equality and the former verifying a restricted Leibniz scheme.

In an extension of the theory presented here, we can add a rewriting system, and extend equality of meaning with the relation defined by this system. Proofs are shorter, because some equational reasoning are be droped. If this reduction eliminates cuts when applied to proof-terms, proving its termination may be a way to prove the consistency of the theory.

Waiting for a model, a normalization proof or a paradox, the consistency of this theory is open.

References

1. P.B. Andrews, Resolution in type theory, *The Journal of Symbolic Logic*, 36, 3 (1971) pp. 414-432.
2. M.J. Beeson, *Foundations of Constructive Mathematics*, Springer-Verlag (1985).
3. G. Boolos, The logic of provability, *Cambridge University Press* (1993).
4. N.G. de Bruijn, A Survey of the project automath, *To H.B. Curry: Essays on Combinatory Logic, Lambda Calculus and Formalism*, J.R. Hindley, J.P. Seldin (Eds.), Academic Press (1980).
5. A. Church, A formulation of the simple theory of types, *The Journal of Symbolic Logic*, 5 (1940) pp. 56-68.
6. Th. Coquand, An analysis of Girard's paradox, *Rapport de Recherche 531*, Institut National de Recherche en Informatique et en Automatique (1986).
7. Th. Coquand, A new paradox in type theory, *Logic, Methodology and Philosophy of Science IX*, D. Prawitz, B. Skyrms and D. Westerståhl (Ed.), Elsevier (1994) pp. 555-570.
8. Th. Coquand, G. Huet, The calculus of constructions, *Information and Computation*, 76 (1988) pp. 95-120.
9. H.B. Curry, The combinatory foundations of mathematical logic, *The Journal of Symbolic Logic*, 7, 2, (1942) pp. 49-64.
10. H.B. Curry, R. Feys, Combinatory logic, Vol. 1, *North Holland*, Amsterdam (1958).
11. G. Dowek, Lambda-calculus, combinators and the comprehension scheme, *Typed Lambda Calculi and Applications*, Lecture Notes in Computer Science 902 (1995) pp. 154-170. *Rapport de Recherche* 2565, Institut National de Recherche en Informatique et en Automatique (1995).
12. G. Dowek, Collections, types and sets, *Rapport de Recherche* 2708, Institut National de Recherche en Informatique et en Automatique (1995). *Mathematical Structures in Computer Science* (to appear).
13. G. Dowek, A type-free formalization of mathematics where proofs are objects *Rapport de Recherche* 2915, Institut National de Recherche en Informatique et en Automatique (1996).
14. S. Feferman, Finitary inductively presented logics, *Logic Colloquium '88*, R. Ferro, C. Bonotto, S. Valentini and A. Zanardo (Ed.), North Holland (1989).
15. S. Feferman, Reflecting on incompleteness, *The Journal of Symbolic Logic*, 56, 1, (1991) pp. 1-49.
16. J.Y. Girard, Interprétation fonctionnelle et élimination des coupures dans l'arithmétique d'ordre supérieur, *Thèse de Doctorat d'État*, Université de Paris 7 (1972).
17. K. Gödel, An interpretation of the intuitionistic propositional calculus, 1933, in K. Gödel collected works, S. Feferman, J.W. Dawson Jr., S.C. Kleene G.H. Moore, R.M. Solovay, J. van Heijenoort (Ed.), Oxford University Press (1986).
18. V. Halbach, A system of complete and consistent truth, *Notre Dame Journal of Formal Logic*, 35, 3 (1994) pp. 311-327.
19. W.A. Howard, The Formulæ-as-type notion of construction, 1969, *To H.B. Curry : Essays on Combinatory Logic, Lambda Calculus and Formalism*, J.R. Hindley, J.P. Seldin (Ed.), Academic Press (1980).
20. G. Huet, personal communication.
21. J.L. Krivine, M. Parigot, Programming with proofs, *J. Inf. Process. Cybern. EIK* 26 (1990) pp. 149-167.
22. V. McGee, How truthlike can a predicate be ? A negative result, *Journal of Philosophical Logic* 14 (1985) pp. 399-410.
23. P. Martin-Löf, Constructive mathematics and computer programming, *Logic, Methodology and Philosophy of Science VI*, 1979, L.J. Cohen, J. Łoś, H. Pfeiffer, K.-P. Podewski (Ed.), North-Holland (1982) pp. 153-175.
24. P. Martin-Löf, Intuitionistic type theory, *Bibliopolis*, Napoli (1984).
25. Ch. Paulin-Mohring, Inductive definitions in the system COQ, Rules and properties, *Typed Lambda Calculi and Applications*, Lecture Notes in Computer Science 664 (1993) pp. 328-345.
26. Ch. Paulin-Mohring, B. Werner, Synthesis of ML programs in the system Coq, *Journal of Symbolic Computation*, 15, 5-6 (1993) pp. 607-640.
27. G.Plotkin. Building-in equational theories, *Machine Intelligence*, 7 (1972) pp. 73-90.
28. W. W. Tait, Infinitely long terms of transfinite type, *Formal Systems and Recusrive Functions*, J.N. Crossley, M. Dummett (Ed.), North-Holland (1965).
29. A.N. Whitehead, B. Russell, Principia mathematica, *Cambridge University Press*, (1910-1913, 1925-1927).

Higman's Lemma in Type Theory

Daniel Fridlender

Department of Computing Science
University of Göteborg and Chalmers University of Technology
S 412 96 Göteborg, Sweden
e-mail: `frito@cs.chalmers.se`

Abstract. This paper starts with a brief exploration of the history of Higman's lemma with emphasis on Veldman's recent intuitionistic proof, which established the lemma in its most general form. The rest of the paper is devoted to the description of a type-theoretic proof of such a general form of Higman's lemma. This involves considering type-theoretic formulations of bar induction, fan theorem, Ramsey theorem, and Higman's lemma. The proof was formalized in Martin-Löf's type theory without universes, and edited and checked in the proof editor ALF.

1 Introduction

Higman's lemma is a significant result in combinatorics. It was discovered by Higman [Hig52] and presented a number of times by different authors with some variations, both in the generality of its statement and in the logical principles used to demonstrate it. The main purpose of this paper is to present a proof of a version of the lemma in Martin-Löf's type theory.

Section 2 is a historical survey of Higman's lemma. It describes and compares the various forms in which the lemma appeared in the literature, and motivates our choice of Veldman's formulation [Vel94] as the one to prove in type theory.

Section 3 makes precise the formalism in which we proved Higman's Lemma, by exhibiting the sets defined in Martin-Löf's logical framework for the formalization of the proof. The absence of a definition of a universe of small sets results in a limited formal system. Some examples illustrate the significance of these limitations for the development of the proof.

Section 4 presents the proof itself, which is a type-theoretic interpretation of Veldman's proof. This involves interpreting also bar induction, fan theorem, and Ramsey theorem. Because of the limitations of the formal system mentioned above, finding appropriate formulations is often delicate even when it concerns minor properties.

The proof was edited with ALF, an interactive proof editor based on Martin-Löf's type theory [Mag94]. The presentation of the proof in Section 4 consists of informal arguments together with pieces of code, that is, fragments of the formal proof as they are seen with the interface of ALF. This agrees with the presentation of the definitions in Section 3 which are displayed just as ALF shows them.

2 Higman's lemma: an overview

As mentioned above, Higman's lemma was first presented in [Hig52]. Related results were contemporarily but independently found by Neumann [Neu49] and Erdös and Rado [ER52], in this last case motivated by a problem formulated by Erdös [Erd49]. However, among these first publications the lemma is only clearly expressed in [Hig52]. Since then, the theory of well-quasi-orderings in general, and Higman's lemma in particular has been object of persistent study.

Nash-Williams [Nas63] discovered a diagonalization argument which yields a simple and very elegant proof of Higman's lemma. Jullien [Jul68] sketched an original proof and Haines [Hai69], unaware of all the previous proofs, rediscovered the result with yet a different proof.

Simpson [Sim88] presented a constructive proof of a version of Higman's lemma in terms of ordinals. This proof is a translation to English of the proof of Schütte and Simpson [SS85]. The proofs by Schütte and Simpson would have been inspired by that of Schmidt [Sch79], which in turn refers to [JP77].

Independently of the proofs just mentioned, Stolzenberg noticed that as a consequence of Gödel's double negation translation [Göd33] and Friedman's A-translation [Fri78], Higman's lemma had a constructive proof. Moreover, the translations provided a method to build a constructive proof from a classical one. Murthy [Mur90] applied the method to Nash-Williams' proof, obtaining another constructive proof of the lemma, which was also the first completely formal proof, coded in Nuprl [Con86]. Contemporarily, Murthy and Russell [MR90] found a direct constructive proof, and so did Richman and Stolzenberg [RS93]. In [Fri93], a formalization of Richman and Stolzenberg's proof in ALF was described. Yet another constructive proof was presented in [CFH93], also formalized in ALF.

With the constructive results, the attention given to Higman's lemma increased, since they gave rise to new and interesting questions. Gödel and Friedman translations made it possible to get constructive proofs out of classical proofs. What are the constructions implicit in those proofs? The experience of [Mur90] showed that the size of the proofs obtained by the translations made it difficult to analyze their computational content. Herbelin tried this further using automatic program extraction tools. This resulted in a readable and runnable functional program of which however it has not been possible to make sense yet. In contrast with this both in [MR90] and in [RS93] the algorithms were trivial. Between these two extremes the proof in [CFH93] for a particular case of the lemma was followed by a full description of its computational content.

Another new question which arises in a constructive approach is what the appropriate formulation of the lemma is. A single classical notion usually admits many different constructive interpretations. This applies to Higman's lemma as well. This question originated this work. The motivation was the belief that the statement in [Mur90], [MR90] and [RS93] could be strengthened. This belief was finally confirmed by Veldman who succeeded in proving intuitionistically the so far most general formulation of the lemma [Vel94]. And it is corroborated in this paper, by exhibiting a type-theoretic proof of this formulation.

The rest of the section deals with the concrete formulations of the lemma mentioned in this survey. This involves introducing some terminology (the notions of well-quasi-ordering and finite basis property) and discussing the convenience of the different versions of the lemma.

2.1 Well-quasi-orderings

Most formulations of Higman's lemma are expressed in terms of well-quasi-orderings, whose definition is given below. We use α, β, etc for infinite sequences, and $\alpha(i)$ for the $(i+1)$-th component of α.

Definition 1. Given a (binary) relation S on a set A and an infinite sequence α of elements of A, we say that α is *good* if it is possible to find $\alpha(i)$ preceding $\alpha(j)$ such that $\alpha(i)S\alpha(j)$. Otherwise it is *bad*. These notions apply analogously to finite sequences.

S is a *quasi-order* if it is reflexive and transitive. S has the *finite basis property* (abbreviated fbp) if every infinite sequence α is good. S is a *well-quasi-ordering* (abbreviated wqo) if it is a quasi-order and has the fbp.

The relation $=$ on a finite set is a wqo, since every infinite sequence of elements taken from a finite set must contain repetitions. The relation $\leq$ on natural numbers is a wqo, since given an infinite sequence α of natural numbers, it is always possible to find $\alpha(i)$ preceding $\alpha(j)$ such that $\alpha(i) \leq \alpha(j)$ among the first $\alpha(0)+2$ elements.

Dickson's lemma [Dic13] is a pioneer result in the theory of wqo. It asserts that the relation $\leq^n$ on tuples of natural numbers is a wqo, where $\leq^n$ is the component-wise relation, i.e., $(i_0, \ldots, i_{n-1}) \leq^n (j_0, \ldots, j_{n-1})$ iff for all k, $i_k \leq j_k$.

Given a set A, we denote by A^* the set of words over the alphabet A. Given a relation S on A, the *embedding relation* on the set A^* is the relation S^* such that $a_0 \ldots a_{n-1} S^* b_0 \ldots b_{m-1}$ iff there exist $i_0, \ldots, i_{n-1}$ such that $0 \leq i_0 < i_1 < \ldots < i_{n-1} < m$ and for all k, $a_k S b_{i_k}$. That is to say, if u and v denote arbitrary words, S^* is the relation satisfying uS^*v iff u is S-*majorized* by a subword of v.

For instance, 3.7.5 $\leq^*$ 1.7.0.7.6, since the subword 7.7.6 majorizes 3.7.5, but 3.7.5 $\not\leq^*$ 1.7.6.6.98 (the best we can do is to pick the subword 7.98 which majorizes only 3.7). It is a non-evident fact that $\leq^*$ is a wqo.

The theory of wqo is described by Kruskal [Kru72] as an intriguing and frequently discovered subject. There are applications of it to rewrite systems [DJ90], to computer algebra (for instance, to the theory of Gröbner bases), and also in concurrency [AJ93] and [ACJT96]. In general, wqo can be helpful to prove termination of programs, and therefore, the possible applications are unlimited.

2.2 Classical formulations

Higman's lemma is often considered to be an important result in the theory of well-quasi-orderings.

Theorem 2 ([Hig52]). *For any relation S, if S is a wqo so is S^*.*

This is the original formulation of the lemma, which was presented in [Hig52] as a corollary of a more general result. Observe that the examples listed before ($=$ on a finite set, $\leq$ on natural numbers, $\leq^n$ on tuples of natural numbers, and $\leq^*$ on words of natural numbers) can be proved to be wqo by repeated applications of Theorem 2 to the trivial fact that $=$ on a singleton set is a wqo.

The following statement appears also often under the name of Higman's lemma:

Theorem 3 ([Jul68], [Hai69]). *Let $=$ be the equality relation on a finite alphabet. Then $=^*$ is a wqo.*

By the previous observation that $=$ on finite sets is a wqo, Theorem 3 is an easy consequence of Theorem 2.

2.3 Constructive formulations

Among the first constructive proofs of Higman's lemma ([SS85], [Sim88], [RS93], [Mur90] and [MR90]), probably the clearest formulation is the one in [RS93].

Theorem 4 ([RS93]). *For any* decidable *relation S, if S is a wqo so is S^*.*

With the constructive proofs, a new question arises concerning the formulation of the lemma. Theorem 4 requires S to be decidable. Is it really necessary?

Moreover, given that the decidability of S implies the decidability of S^*; that the reflexivity of S implies that of S^*; that the transitivity of S implies that of S^*; wouldn't it be the case that the fbp of S implies that of S^*?

If this is the case, given that the preservation of decidability, reflexivity and transitivity are all elementary, the essence of Higman's lemma would be that the fbp is preserved. The answer to the question is the following, most general, formulation of Higman's lemma.

Theorem 5 ([Vel94]). *For any relation S on the set of natural numbers, if S has the fbp so does S^*.*

By this being the most general formulation of Higman's lemma we mean that it is the most general version regarding the requirements on S. But words can be generalized to trees, for instance, as stated by Kruskal theorem [Kru60].

The statement we proved in type theory is the following.

Theorem 6 (Higman's lemma). *Given any relation S, if S has the fbp so does S^*.*

Even if the requirement that S is a relation on natural numbers is dropped, this formulation should not be considered to be more general than the one of Theorem 5. The difference is not due to our discovery of a better proof, it is a consequence of allowing ourselves to use generalized inductive definitions. In fact, the type-theoretic proof we will present here is a translation to type theory of the proof by Veldman.

In the rest of the paper, Higman's lemma means Theorem 6.

3 Type theory

By Martin-Löf's type theory one usually refers to a family of formal systems deviced by Martin-Löf for formalizing intuitionistic mathematics. Some of the early formulations are [Mar75] and [Mar84]. In more recent formulations ([NPS90] and [Tas97]), Martin-Löf put forward a framework in which different theories can be implemented. Implementing a theory can be understood as extending the rules of the framework with the rules of the theory.

This section presents the particular theory we implement in the framework for the proof of Higman's lemma. The theory consists of a few inductively defined sets which follow the scheme presented by Dybjer [Dyb94], hereafter called *the scheme.* We restrict ourselves to this scheme rather than making free use of Coquand's pattern matching [Coq92], or appealing to the use of universes, as explained in [NPS90].

The result is a very limited theory, which admits a proof-irrelevant model in the style of Smith [Smi88], and consequently consistency becomes elementary. It is sometimes impossible to prove intuitively true statements but these situations can often be solved by giving the statements appropriate reformulations.

3.1 An extension to type theory

The formal system used to prove Higman's lemma is obtained by putting together the rules of Martin-Löf's logical framework (as presented by Tasistro [Tas97]) and the rules corresponding to the definitions of the sets presented in this section.

Following Curry-Howard interpretation ([CF58] and [How80]) every proposition is represented by the set of its proofs. Every predicate over the elements of a set A is represented by a family of sets indexed by the elements of A. There is a natural identification between predicates, subsets and families of sets.

The proof was edited in ALF [Mag94]. Every definition will be given in its actual ALF notation, according to which $[x_1,\ldots,x_n]\mathrm{t}$ denotes abstraction, $\mathrm{t}(\mathrm{a}_1,\ldots,\mathrm{a}_n)$, denotes application, and $(x \in \mathrm{A})\mathrm{B}$ denotes function types, which may also be written $(\mathrm{A})\mathrm{B}$ when x does not occur in B. Also, $(x_1 \in \mathrm{A}_1)\ldots(x_n \in \mathrm{A}_n)\mathrm{B}$ is written $(x_1 \in \mathrm{A}_1;\ldots;x_n \in \mathrm{A}_n)\mathrm{B}$. Again, "$x_i\in$" may be omitted if x_i does not occur in A_{i+1}, $\ldots$, A_n, B. Finally, $(x,y \in \mathrm{A})\mathrm{B}$ abbreviates $(x \in \mathrm{A};y \in \mathrm{A})\mathrm{B}$.

Logical connectives The definition of disjunction and universal and existential quantification in Fig. 1 are natural. They illustrate already some conventions, like the choice of names A, B and X for sets, U, V and Y for families of sets over a given set. Usually a ranges over elements of the set A, b over elements of B, and x, y and z over functions with values in X or in instances of the family Y. The variable u ranges over functions with values in instances of the family U, and the variable $u.a$, over elements in (or proofs of) $U(a)$. Notice that the dot is not an operator but just one more letter in the name of the variable $u.a$.

We use also argument hiding to improve readability. For instance, the type of *when* is in fact

$$(A, B, X \in \mathbf{Set};\, x \in (A)X;\, y \in (B)X;\, \mathrm{Or}(A, B))\, X$$

$$
\begin{array}{l}
\mathrm{Or} \in (A, B \in \mathbf{Set})\ \mathbf{Set}\\
\quad \mathrm{inl} \in (a \in A)\ \mathrm{Or}(A, B)\\
\quad \mathrm{inr} \in (b \in B)\ \mathrm{Or}(A, B)\\
\mathrm{when} \in (x \in (A)X;\ y \in (B)X;\ \mathrm{Or}(A, B))\ X\\
\quad \mathrm{when}(x, y, \mathrm{inl}(a)) \equiv x(a)\\
\quad \mathrm{when}(x, y, \mathrm{inr}(b)) \equiv y(b)\\
\forall \in (A \in \mathbf{Set};\ U \in (A)\mathbf{Set})\ \mathbf{Set}\\
\quad \lambda \in (u \in (a \in A)\ U(a))\ \forall(A, U)\\
\mathrm{inst} \in (\forall(A, U);\ a \in A)\ U(a)\\
\quad \mathrm{inst}(\lambda(u), a) \equiv u(a)
\end{array}
$$

$$
\begin{array}{l}
\exists \in (A \in \mathbf{Set};\ U \in (A)\mathbf{Set})\ \mathbf{Set}\\
\quad \mathrm{pair} \in (a \in A;\ u.a \in U(a))\ \exists(A, U)\\
\exists\mathrm{elim} \in (Y \in (\exists(A, U))\mathbf{Set};\\
\qquad x \in (a \in A; u.a \in U(a))\ Y(\mathrm{pair}(a, u.a));\\
\qquad p \in \exists(A, U)\\
\qquad)\ Y(p)\\
\quad \exists\mathrm{elim}(Y, x, \mathrm{pair}(a, u.a)) \equiv x(a, u.a)
\end{array}
$$

Fig. 1. Logical connectives.

but we can hide the first three arguments, and write it just like in Fig. 1. Notice that inl and inr each have two arguments hidden, namely A and B, both of type **Set**. The hidden arguments never become visible. For instance, in the equations defining when, both inl and inr appear with one argument each, instead of three. Similarly λ, inst, pair and $\exists$elim have two hidden arguments. For every constant only the first arguments are hidden. In the rest of the presentation we will not make explicit what arguments are hidden since, on the one hand, it will always be possible to infer them from the context and conventions, and on the other, they do not convey useful information.

The induction principles when and inst associated to disjunction and universal quantification are direct consequences of the elimination rules proposed by the scheme, according to which, in the definition of when, for instance, X would be a family of sets over $\mathrm{Or}(A, B)$, rather than a set.

In the definition of universal quantifier, the scheme indicates an induction principle $\forall$elim of type

$$(Y \in (\forall(A, U))\mathbf{Set};\ x \in (u \in (a \in A)U(a))Y(\lambda(u));\ p \in \forall(A, U))\ Y(p)$$

defined by

$$\forall\mathrm{elim}(Y, x, \lambda(u)) \equiv x(u).$$

However, instantiation can be defined directly in terms of $\forall$elim

$$\mathrm{inst}(p, a) \equiv \forall\mathrm{elim}([h]U(a), [u]u(a), p).$$

In spite of being less general than the induction principles determined by the scheme, when and inst are general enough for our proofs.

Lists We use lists with two different purposes: to represent words over a given alphabet, and to represent finite approximations to infinite sequences of elements of a given set. In this second use of lists, going from one approximation $\alpha(0), \ldots, \alpha(n-1)$ of the infinite sequence α to the next approximation $\alpha(0), \ldots, \alpha(n-1), \alpha(n)$, amounts to adding an element, $\alpha(n)$, at the end of the first approximation. For this reason, it is convenient to define snoc lists, as in Fig. 2, rather than the usual lists.

```
List ∈ (A ∈ Set) Set
   [] ∈ List(A)
   snoc ∈ (as ∈ List(A); a ∈ A) List(A)
listind ∈ (Y ∈ (List(A)) Set;
          x ∈ Y([]);
          y ∈ (as ∈ List(A); ih ∈ Y(as); a ∈ A) Y(snoc(as, a));
          as ∈ List(A)
         ) Y(as)
   listind(Y, x, y, []) ≡ x
   listind(Y, x, y, snoc(as, a)) ≡ y(as, listind(Y, x, y, as), a)
All ∈ (U ∈ (A) Set; as ∈ List(A)) Set
   allb ∈ All(U, [])
   alli ∈ (as ∈ List(A); all.U.as ∈ All(U, as); a ∈ A; u.a ∈ U(a)) All(U, snoc(as, a))
allelim ∈ (Y ∈ (List(A)) Set;
          x ∈ Y([]);
          y ∈ (as ∈ List(A); all ∈ All(U, as); ih ∈ Y(as); a ∈ A; u.a ∈ U(a)) Y(snoc(as, a));
          as ∈ List(A);
          All(U, as)
         ) Y(as)
   allelim(Y, x, y, _, allb) ≡ x
   allelim(Y, x, y, _, alli(as, all.U.as, a, u.a)) ≡ y(as, all.U.as, allelim(Y, x, y, as, all.U.as), a, u.a)
Some ∈ (U ∈ (A) Set; as ∈ List(A)) Set
   someb ∈ (as ∈ List(A); a ∈ A; u.a ∈ U(a)) Some(U, snoc(as, a))
   somei ∈ (as ∈ List(A); some.U.as ∈ Some(U, as); a ∈ A) Some(U, snoc(as, a))
someelim ∈ (Y ∈ (List(A)) Set;
            x ∈ (as ∈ List(A); a ∈ A; u.a ∈ U(a)) Y(snoc(as, a));
            y ∈ (as ∈ List(A); some.U.as ∈ Some(U, as); ih ∈ Y(as); a ∈ A) Y(snoc(as, a));
            as ∈ List(A);
            Some(U, as)
           ) Y(as)
   someelim(Y, x, y, _, someb(as, a, u.a)) ≡ x(as, a, u.a)
   someelim(Y, x, y, _, somei(as, some.U.as, a)) ≡
      y(as, some.U.as, someelim(Y, x, y, as, some.U.as), a)
Good ∈ (R ∈ (A; A) Set; as ∈ List(A)) Set
   goodb ∈ (as ∈ List(A); a ∈ A; some.as ∈ Some([a1]R(a1, a), as)) Good(R, snoc(as, a))
   goodi ∈ (as ∈ List(A); good.R.as ∈ Good(R, as); a ∈ A) Good(R, snoc(as, a))
goodelim ∈ (Y ∈ (List(A)) Set;
            x ∈ (as ∈ List(A); a ∈ A; some.as ∈ Some([a1]R(a1, a), as)) Y(snoc(as, a));
            y ∈ (as ∈ List(A); good.R.as ∈ Good(R, as); ih ∈ Y(as); a ∈ A) Y(snoc(as, a));
            as ∈ List(A);
            Good(R, as)
           ) Y(as)
   goodelim(Y, x, y, _, goodb(as, a, some.as)) ≡ x(as, a, some.as)
   goodelim(Y, x, y, _, goodi(as, good.R.as, a)) ≡ y(as, good.R.as, goodelim(Y, x, y, as, good.R.as), a)
```

Fig. 2. Lists

Formally, the difference is just the order of the arguments of the second constructor of lists, which in the case of the usual lists would be

$$\text{cons} \in (a \in A;\ as \in \text{List}(A))\ \text{List}(A)$$

and accordingly the type of the argument y in the definition of listind would be

$$(a \in A;\ as \in \text{List}(A);\ ih \in Y(as))\ Y(\text{cons}(as, a))$$

and the second equation defining listind,

$$\text{listind}(Y, x, y, \text{cons}(a, as)) \equiv y(a, as, \text{listind}(Y, x, y, as)).$$

Because of this change in the order of the arguments, the definition of lists in Fig. 2 does not follow pedantically the scheme, which requires the inductive arguments in the constructors (like *as* in the type of snoc) to be listed last. However, this requirement is not essential, it is merely stipulated in [Dyb94] to simplify the notation for the description of the scheme.

The same remark applies to the definition of the quantifiers over the elements of lists. In addition the induction principles allelim and someelim are again less general than the induction principles established by the scheme.

Intuitively, All(U, *as*) means that all the elements in the list *as* satisfy U, and Some(U, *as*), that some element in *as* satisfies U. The constants allb, alli, someb, and somei are the formal counterpart of, respectively, the rules

$$\frac{}{\text{All}(U, [])} \qquad \frac{\text{All}(U, as) \quad U(a)}{\text{All}(U, \text{snoc}(as, a))} \qquad \frac{U(a)}{\text{Some}(U, \text{snoc}(as, a))} \qquad \frac{\text{Some}(U, as)}{\text{Some}(U, \text{snoc}(as, a))}$$

Recall that the dot is just one more letter in the name of the variables *all.U.as* and *some.U.as*. ALF introduces the symbol _ in patterns with the purpose of avoiding non-linear patterns.

Fig. 2 gives also an inductive definition of the notion of good finite sequence introduced in Definition 1. Intuitively, Good(R, *as*) means that *as* has two elements such that the one which occurs before from left to right is related (by R) to the one which occurs later. The variable R ranges over binary relations. We interpret them by binary predicates, that is, a relation on the set A is of type (A; A)**Set**. The constants goodb, and goodi correspond, respectively, to the informal rules

$$\frac{\text{Some}([a_1]R(a_1, a), as)}{\text{Good}(R, \text{snoc}(as, a))} \qquad \frac{\text{Good}(R, as)}{\text{Good}(R, \text{snoc}(as, a))}$$

Inductive bars In [VB93], a recursion theoretical analysis of the role of the bar theorem in the intuitionistic Ramsey theorem leaves no hope for proving it in intuitionistic analysis without the axiom of bar induction. This applies to Higman's lemma as well, since it elementarily implies the intuitionistic Ramsey theorem. This means that Higman's lemma is not intuitionistically provable if infinite sequences are interpreted as finitely describable functions from natural numbers to the set from where the elements of the sequences are chosen.

On the other hand, as shown by Veldman [Vel94], it is provable if infinite sequences are interpreted as choice sequences, using the axiom of bar induction for natural numbers. This axiom is explained for instance by Dummett [Dum77] and Martino and Giaretta [MG79].

The axiom of bar induction for a set A is expressed by the following rule.

$$\frac{\begin{array}{ll} (as \in \mathrm{List}(A);\ U(as))Y(as) & (U \text{ is included in } Y) \\ (as \in \mathrm{List}(A);\ a \in A;\ U(as))U(\mathrm{snoc}(as, a)) & (U \text{ is monotone}) \\ (as \in \mathrm{List}(A);\ (a \in A)Y(\mathrm{snoc}(as, a)))Y(as) & (Y \text{ is hereditary}) \\ U \text{ is a bar} & (U \text{ is a bar}) \end{array}}{Y([])}\ \mathrm{BI}$$

Being a bar is only written informally since its statement involves choice sequences, which have no direct interpretation in type theory.

Definition 7 (Bar). Given a set A and a predicate U over the set List(A), then U is a *bar* if every infinite sequence of elements of A has an initial segment which satisfies U. Given a list as, *U bars as* if every infinite sequence starting with as has an initial segment which satisfies U. We write it $U|as$.

Clearly, U is a bar iff $U|[]$. To formalize Veldman's proof in type theory we need a principle like BI, and so, we need a type-theoretic interpretation of being a bar. For this purpose, we introduce the notion of inductive bar in Fig. 3. We say that U is an *inductive bar* if Bar(U, []) holds. In Section 4.2 we show that BI can be proved when its last premise is replaced by one expressing that U is an inductive bar.

$$
\begin{array}{l}
\mathrm{Bar} \in (U \in (\mathrm{List}(A))\,\mathbf{Set};\ as \in \mathrm{List}(A))\ \mathbf{Set} \\
\quad \mathrm{barb} \in (as \in \mathrm{List}(A);\ u.as \in U(as))\ \mathrm{Bar}(U, as) \\
\quad \mathrm{barm} \in (as \in \mathrm{List}(A);\ bar.U.as \in \mathrm{Bar}(U, as);\ a \in A)\ \mathrm{Bar}(U, \mathrm{snoc}(as, a)) \\
\quad \mathrm{barh} \in (as \in \mathrm{List}(A);\ bar \in (a \in A)\,\mathrm{Bar}(U, \mathrm{snoc}(as, a)))\ \mathrm{Bar}(U, as) \\
\mathrm{barelim} \in (Y \in (\mathrm{List}(A))\,\mathbf{Set}; \\
\qquad\qquad x \in (as \in \mathrm{List}(A);\ U(as))\ Y(as); \\
\qquad\qquad y \in (as \in \mathrm{List}(A);\ bar.U.as \in \mathrm{Bar}(U, as);\ ih \in Y(as);\ a \in A)\ Y(\mathrm{snoc}(as, a)); \\
\qquad\qquad z \in (as \in \mathrm{List}(A);\ bar \in (a \in A)\mathrm{Bar}(U, \mathrm{snoc}(as, a));\ ih \in (a \in A)Y(\mathrm{snoc}(as, a)))\ Y(as); \\
\qquad\qquad as \in \mathrm{List}(A); \\
\qquad\qquad \mathrm{Bar}(U, as) \\
\qquad\quad)\ Y(as) \\
\quad \mathrm{barelim}(Y, x, y, z, as, \mathrm{barb}(\_, u.as)) \equiv x(as, u.as) \\
\quad \mathrm{barelim}(Y, x, y, z, \_, \mathrm{barm}(as_1, bar.U.as, a)) \equiv y(as_1, bar.U.as, \mathrm{barelim}(Y, x, y, z, as_1, bar.U.as), a) \\
\quad \mathrm{barelim}(Y, x, y, z, as, \mathrm{barh}(\_, bar)) \equiv z(as, bar, [a]\mathrm{barelim}(Y, x, y, z, \mathrm{snoc}(as, a), bar(a)))
\end{array}
$$

Fig. 3. Inductive bars.

It remains to explain why inductive bars are correct representations of bars. The explanation relies on the validity of Brouwer's thesis —also called Brouwer's dogma in [MG79]— a statement which captures the arguments used by Brouwer in his proof of the bar theorem [Bro54].

Brouwer's thesis (for a set A). *Any intuitionistic proof that U is a bar can be transformed into another proof of it which only uses the rules*

$$\frac{U(as)}{U|as} \qquad \frac{U|as}{U|\mathrm{snoc}(as, a)} \qquad \frac{(a \in A)\ U|\mathrm{snoc}(as, a)}{U|as} \tag{1}$$

Brouwer's thesis can be interpreted in the following way. Instead of taking $U|as$ as defined by Definition 7 consider it being inductively defined, the introduction rules of its inductive definition being precisely the rules in (1). Then, Brouwer's thesis would say that U is a bar implies $U|[]$. Since the converse is true as well, Brouwer's thesis means that U is a bar iff $U|[]$, or in other words, that bars are equivalent to inductive bars, since there is a clear correspondence between the rules in (1) and the introduction rules in Fig. 3.

The adoption of the notion of inductive bar as the representation of bar is a variation of the same idea presented in [Mar68], where in addition bars are assumed to be monotone. This assumption would simplify the definition of inductive bars, but the correspondence between inductive bars and bars, would depend on the predicate in question being monotone. Then, the claim that a formal statement has a certain meaning would require proving that some predicates are monotone. With the definition of Fig. 3 instead, the correspondence between inductive bars and bars is direct.

Embedding relation on words We have an inductive definition of the embedding relation informally defined in Section 2.1. The embedding relation is the only notion involved in the statement of Theorem 6 which has not yet been formally defined. This is done in Fig. 4.

We think of Star as an operator, which when applied to a relation S over A yields a relation on words over the alphabet A, namely, the relation denoted informally by S^*. The constants starb, starm and stari correspond to the informal rules

$$\frac{}{S^*([],[])} \qquad \frac{S^*(w_1,w_2)}{S^*(w_1, \mathrm{snoc}(w_2, a_2))} \qquad \frac{S^*(w_1,w_2) \quad S(a_1,a_2)}{S^*(\mathrm{snoc}(w_1, a_1), \mathrm{snoc}(w_2, a_2))}$$

When $S^*(w_1,w_2)$ holds, we say that w_1 is S-majorized by a subword of w_2, or that w_1 is S-embeddable in w_2.

Equality Fig. 4 introduces also the usual definition of propositional equality. In large parts of the proof in Section 4 we avoided using equality. However, eventually its inclusion became necessary.

3.2 Limitations of the formal system

The theory presented in Section 3 admits a proof-irrelevant model like the one given in [Smi88]. This model provides an elementary proof of consistency. It also shows that many intuitively true statements are not provable. Such statements appeared very frequently during the development of the proof of Higman's

```
Star ∈ (S ∈ (A; A) Set; w1, w2 ∈ List(A)) Set
    starb ∈ Star(S, [], [])
    starm ∈ (w1, w2 ∈ List(A); star.S.w's ∈ Star(S, w1, w2); a2 ∈ A) Star(S, w1, snoc(w2, a2))
    stari ∈ (w1, w2 ∈ List(A);
              star.S.w's ∈ Star(S, w1, w2);
              a1, a2 ∈ A;
              s.a's ∈ S(a1, a2)
             ) Star(S, snoc(w1, a1), snoc(w2, a2))
starelim ∈ (Y ∈ (w1, w2 ∈ List(A)) Set;
             x ∈ Y([], []);
             y ∈ (w1, w2 ∈ List(A);
                   star.w's ∈ Star(S, w1, w2);
                   ih ∈ Y(w1, w2);
                   a2 ∈ A
                  ) Y(w1, snoc(w2, a2));
             z ∈ (w1, w2 ∈ List(A);
                   star.w's ∈ Star(S, w1, w2);
                   ih ∈ Y(w1, w2);
                   a1, a2 ∈ A;
                   s.a's ∈ S(a1, a2)
                  ) Y(snoc(w1, a1), snoc(w2, a2));
             w1, w2 ∈ List(A);
             Star(S, w1, w2)
            ) Y(w1, w2)
    starelim(Y, x, y, z, _, _, starb) ≡ x
    starelim(Y, x, y, z, w1, _, starm(_, w2, star.S.w's, a2)) ≡
        y(w1, w2, star.S.w's, starelim(Y, x, y, z, w1, w2, star.S.w's), a2)
    starelim(Y, x, y, z, _, _, stari(w1, w2, star.S.w's, a1, a2, s.a's)) ≡
        z(w1, w2, star.S.w's, starelim(Y, x, y, z, w1, w2, star.S.w's), a1, a2, s.a's)
Eq ∈ (a1, a2 ∈ A) Set
    refl ∈ (a ∈ A) Eq(a, a)
eqpeel ∈ (Y ∈ (a1, a2 ∈ A) Set; x ∈ (a ∈ A) Y(a, a); a1, a2 ∈ A; e ∈ Eq(a1, a2)) Y(a1, a2)
    eqpeel(Y, x, _, a2, refl(_)) ≡ x(a2)
```

Fig. 4. Embedding and equality.

lemma. Mentioning all the cases would require a too detailed exposition. We give a couple of examples to illustrate the general situation.

One such example is the assertion (Some(U, []); $X \in$ **Set**)X expressing that there is no element in the empty list satisfying a given predicate U. This type is false in the proof-irrelevant model, so we cannot hope to prove it to be inhabited. Another example is the statement (All(U, *as*); Some(V, *as*)) Some([a]And($U(a)$, $V(a)$), *as*), saying that if *as* is such that all its elements satisfy U and some of them satisfy V then some of them satisfy the conjunction between U and V. Items *3* and *8* of Proposition 8 propose provable reformulations of them.

In most of the proof we avoid using equality. However, it is still possible to do some equational reasoning. For instance, the fact that [] is a left identity is expressed by the type ($P \in$ (List(A))**Set**; P(append([], *as*))) P(*as*). This can be proved as a corollary of ($bs \in$ List(A); P(dneppa(append([], as), bs))) P(dneppa(as, bs)), where the function dneppa is a variation of append satisfying the equations

$$\text{dneppa}(as_1, []) \equiv as_1$$
$$\text{dneppa}(as_1, \text{snoc}(as_2, a)) \equiv \text{dneppa}(\text{snoc}(as_1, a), as_2)$$

4 Higman's lemma in type theory

The proof of Higman's lemma we present here is a type-theoretic version of Veldman's proof [Vel94]. The translation of this proof to type theory gave rise to type-theoretic formulations of bar induction, fan theorem, Ramsey theorem, and Higman's lemma.

4.1 Preliminaries

Logical Connectives In terms of the logical connectives Or, $\forall$ and $\exists$ defined in Fig. 1, it is straightforward to define the binary (And) and ternary (And_3) Cartesian product, the set of functions (Imply) from one set to another and ternary (Or_3) and 5-ary (Or_5) disjunction.

Lists We easily define standard functions on lists, like head (which takes as an extra argument the default value, that is, the value to return when it is applied to the empty list), tail, map, fold and append. As the lists are snoc lists, head returns in fact the rightmost element, and tail, the rest. We proved, among others properties of Some, the following.

Proposition 8. *Given a set A, predicates U and V over A, and lists as, as_1 and as_2 of elements of A the following hold:*

1. (Some(U, as)) $\exists$(A, U)
2. ($d \in A$; Some(U, as)) Or(U(head(d, as)), Some(U, tail(as)))
3. (Some(U, []); $X \in$ **Set**; $Y \in (X)$ **Set**; $x, y \in X$; $Y(x)$)$Y(y)$
4. (Some(U, []); $x \in A$)$U(x)$
5. (($a \in A$; $U(a)$)$V(a)$; Some(U, as)) Some(V, as)
6. (Some(U, as_1)) Some(U, append(as_1, as_2))
7. (Some(U, as_2)) Some(U, append(as_1, as_2))
8. ($d \in A$; $U(d)$; All(U, as); Some(V, as)) Some([a]And($U(a)$, $V(a)$), as)

The properties *1* (if there is an element in as satisfying U, then U is inhabited), *5* (if U is included in V then Some(U) is included in Some(V)), *6* and *7* are clear. Property *2* says that if some element in as satisfies a predicate, then either it is the head or it is in the tail. A default value d for head is needed but property *1* says that it can always be found.

Property *3* states that Some(U, []) does not hold. It is proved by showing that if Some(U, as) then $Y(\phi(as))$ where $\phi(as)$ evaluates to y when as is [], and x otherwise. With the assumption that Some(U, []), we obtain $Y(\phi([]))$, that is, $Y(y)$. The proof that Some(U, as) implies $Y(\phi(as))$ is by someelim; it amounts to proving $Y(x)$ twice, which is trivial by assumption.

Property *4* follows from *1* and *3*. The latter allows us to conclude that any property which is satisfied by some element is satisfied by any element. The former, that U is satisfied by some element.

One would expect to be able to prove property *8* (if all the elements in as satisfy U and some of them satisfies V, then some of them satisfies the conjunction) without assuming $d \in A$ such that $U(d)$. But it is not provable, since it is false in the proof-irrelevant model. We need $U(d)$ only in the base case, to prove Some([a]And($U(a)$, $V(a)$), []), under the assumption Some(V, []). This is not technically immediate, even if the assumption is intuitively false. By property *3*, it sufficed to prove Some([a]And($U(a)$, $V(a)$), snoc([], d)) instead, for which it is enough to show that $U(d)$ and $V(d)$. The former is by hypothesis, and the latter by property *4*.

Similar properties hold also for Good.

Proposition 9. *Given a set A, relations R and S over A, and lists as, as_1 and as_2 of elements of A the following hold:*

1. (Good(R, as)) $\exists$(A, [a]$\exists$(A, [a_1] $R(a_1,a)$))
2. ($d \in A$; Good(R, as)) Or(Some([a]R(a,head(d, as)), tail(as)), Good(R, tail(as)))
3. (Good(R, []); $X \in$ **Set**; $Y \in$ (X) **Set**; $x, y \in X$; $Y(x)$)$Y(y)$
4. (Good(R, []); $x, y \in A$) $R(x,y)$
5. (($a_1, a_2 \in A$; $R(a_1,a_2)$)$S(a_1,a_2)$; Good(R, as)) Good(S, as)
6. (Good(R, as_1)) Good(R, append(as_1, as_2))
7. (Good(R, as_2)) Good(R, append(as_1, as_2))
8. (Some([a]Some([a_1] $R(a_1,a)$, as_1), as_2)) Good(R, append(as_1, as_2))

According to Definition 1 a relation R has the fbp if every infinite sequence α is good, that is, if every infinite sequence has a finite initial segment which is good. In other words, R has the fbp if Good(R) is a bar.

fbp $\in$ ($R \in$ (A; A) **Set**) **Set**
fbp $\equiv$ [R]Bar(Good(R), [])

Intuitively, if a relation has the fbp, it is reflexive since, in particular, for any a in A the sequence a, a, a, ... is good.

Proposition 10. *Given a set A, and a relation R over A, then* (fbp(R); $a \in A$)$R(a,a)$.

If we avoid using equality, the proof is not as straightforward as the intuition might suggest. We introduce the following definition which will also be helpful for other lemmas and for the proof of the main result.

Ctxt $\in$ ($R \in$ (A; A) **Set**; $as \in$ List(A); $a_1, a_2 \in A$) **Set**
Ctxt $\equiv$ [R, as, a_1, a_2]Or$_3$(Good(R, as), Some([a]$R(a, a_1)$, as), $R(a_1, a_2)$)

Intuitively, given a set A, a relation R over A and a list as of elements of A, Ctxt(R, as) is another relation over A. Two elements a_1 and a_2 are in that relation if as is good, or has an element a such that $R(a,a_1)$, or if $R(a_1,a_2)$. The relation Ctxt(R, as) satisfies the following properties.

Proposition 11. *Given a set A, a relation R over A, a list as of elements of A, and a_1 and a_2 in A, then the following hold:*

1. $(\mathrm{Ctxt}(R, [], a_1, a_2))R(a_1, a_2)$
2. $(d \in A; \mathrm{Ctxt}(R, as, a_1, a_2))\mathrm{Or}(\mathrm{Ctxt}(R, \mathrm{tail}(as), \mathrm{head}(d, as), a_1), \mathrm{Ctxt}(R, \mathrm{tail}(as), a_1, a_2))$

To prove Proposition 10 we use property *1* and prove Ctxt(R, [], a, a) instead of $R(a, a)$. This allows us to use BI, where Y is $[as]\mathrm{Ctxt}(R, as, a, a)$ and U is Good(R). The inclusion of U in Y is trivial, and so is the monotonicity of U. By property *2*, from Ctxt(R, snoc(as, a), a, a) we get Ctxt(R, as, a, a), hence Y is hereditary. Proposition 11 follows from properties *4* and *2* of Propositions 8 and 9.

The following propositions are also necessary. We omit the proofs here.

Proposition 12. *Given a set A, a relation R over A, three words w, w_1 and w_2 over the alphabet A and a in A, then if* $\mathrm{Star}(\mathrm{Ctxt}(R, \mathrm{snoc}(w, a)), w_1, w_2)$ *holds, so does* $\mathrm{Or}(\mathrm{Star}(\mathrm{Ctxt}(R, w), w_1, w_2), \mathrm{Star}(\mathrm{Ctxt}(R, w), \mathrm{snoc}([], a), w_1))$.

Proposition 13. *Given a set A, a relation R over A and two lists as_1 and as_2 of elements of A, then* $\mathrm{Bar}(\mathrm{Good}(R), \mathrm{append}(as_1, as_2))$ *iff* $\mathrm{Bar}(\mathrm{Good}(\mathrm{Ctxt}(R, as_1)), as_2)$.

Proposition 14. *Given two sets A and B, a function f from A to B, a predicate U over* List(A) *and a monotone predicate V over* List(B), *such that for all lists as of elements of A,* $V(\mathrm{map}(f, as))$ *implies* $U(as)$. *Then, for all lists as of elements of A,* $\mathrm{Bar}(V, \mathrm{map}(f, as))$ *implies* $\mathrm{Bar}(U, as)$.

4.2 Bar induction

We use a slightly different formulation of bar induction, in which the premise *U is a bar* is replaced by *U bars as* and accordingly, the conclusion $Y([])$ by $Y(as)$.

Proposition 15 (Bar induction). *Given a set A, a monotone predicate U over* List(A), *an hereditary predicate Y over* List(A) *which contains U and a list as of elements of A such that U bars as, then $Y(as)$.*

This is proved by showing $\Psi(as)$, where $\Psi(as) \equiv \forall(\mathrm{List}(A), [as_1]Y(\mathrm{dneppa}(as, as_1)))$, using barelim from Fig. 3. First, the proof that U is included in Ψ follows by iterated applications of the monotonicity of U and the fact that Y contains U. Second, the proof that Ψ is monotone is straightforward. Just take any as, assume $\Psi(as)$, take any a and any as_1 and prove $Y(\mathrm{dneppa}(\mathrm{snoc}(as, a), as_1))$. This is the same as $Y(\mathrm{dneppa}(as, \mathrm{snoc}(as_1, a)))$ which follows from $\Psi(as)$. Third and last, the proof that Ψ is hereditary is as follows. Take any as, assume $(a \in A)\Psi(\mathrm{snoc}(as, a))$. We must show $\Psi(as)$. We take any as_1 and prove $Y(\mathrm{dneppa}(as, as_1))$. In the case in which as_1 is [], it becomes $Y(as)$. As Y is hereditary, it is enough to prove that for all a, $Y(\mathrm{snoc}(as, a))$ which follows immediately from the assumption. Otherwise, if as_1 is $\mathrm{snoc}(as_2, a_2)$, $Y(\mathrm{dneppa}(as, as_1))$ becomes $Y(\mathrm{dneppa}(\mathrm{snoc}(as, a_2), as_2))$ which also follows immediately from the assumption.

4.3 Fan theorem

The result we present here is a type-theoretic formulation of a special case of the fan theorem. Given a set *A* and a predicate *U* over List(*A*) such that *U* is a monotone bar, then as a consequence of the fan theorem the following holds. For any finitary branching tree whose nodes are labeled with elements of *A*, there exists a natural number *n* such that for all paths of the tree the initial segment of length *n* satisfies *U*. This holds in particular for any tree obtained from an infinite sequence $as_0, as_1, \ldots$ of lists of elements of *A* in the following way. For every natural number *i*, every node of the tree of depth *i* has as many children as elements are in as_i, and the labels of the children are precisely the elements in as_i. This is a particular kind of finitary branching tree in which the children of a node only depend on the node's depth. That is, all the nodes of the same depth have identical children. For any path of such a tree, the initial segment of length *n* consists of one element from each of the lists $as_0, \ldots, as_{n-1}$. The collection of the initial segments of length *n* is similar to a Cartesian product of those lists. The statement we prove in type theory is that all such segments satisfy *U*.

We define the function cartSnoc which when applied to a list of lists computes the list of all such segments. First we define the binary Cartesian product binCartWith parametrized with a function *f*. Then, the finitary Cartesian product cartWith also parametrized. And finally we instantiate it with snoc to obtain the list of segments.

binCartWith ∈ (*f* ∈ (*A*; *B*) *C*; *as* ∈ List(*A*); *bs* ∈ List(*B*)) List(*C*)
  binCartWith ≡ [*f*, *as*, *bs*]fold([], [*cs*, *a*]append(*cs*, map(*f*(*a*), *bs*)), *as*)
cartWith ∈ (*b* ∈ *B*; *f* ∈ (*B*; *A*) *B*; *ass* ∈ List(List(*A*))) List(*B*)
  cartWith ≡ [*b*, *f*]fold(snoc([], *b*), binCartWith(*f*))
cartSnoc ∈ (*ass* ∈ List(List(*A*))) List(List(*A*))
  cartSnoc ≡ cartWith([], snoc)

We can formulate a particular version of the fan theorem whose proof we omit. Given a set *A* and a predicate *U* over List(*A*), then [*ass*]All(*U*, cartSnoc(*ass*)) is a predicate over List(List(*A*)).

Theorem 16 (Fan theorem). *Given a set A and a monotone predicate U over* List(*A*)*, then if U is an inductive bar, so is the predicate* [*ass*]All(*U*, cartSnoc(*ass*)).

4.4 Ramsey theorem

Consider given two sets *A* and *B*, a relation *R* over *A* and a relation *S* over *B*. We define the set C and the relation T over C.

C ∈ **Set**
  C ≡ And(*A*, *B*)

T ∈ (c_1, c_2 ∈ C) **Set**
  T ≡ [c_1, c_2]And(*R*(fst(c_1), fst(c_2)), *S*(snd(c_1), snd(c_2)))

As explained in [Fri93] the intuitionistic Ramsey theorem [VB93] can be formulated in type theory as follows.

Theorem 17 (Ramsey theorem). *If R and S have the fbp, so does* T.

To prove it we define the family of sets Ψ

```
Ψ ∈ (as ∈ List(A); bs ∈ List(B); cs ∈ List(C)) Set
  Ψ ≡
    [as, bs, cs]
      Or5(Good(R, as),
          Some([c]Some([a]R(a, fst(c)), as), cs),
          Good(S, bs),
          Some([c]Some([b]S(b, snd(c)), bs), cs),
          Good(T, cs))
```

and prove the following lemma.

Lemma 18. *If R and S have the fbp, then given as in* List(*A*) *and bs in* List(*B*) *the following hold:*

1. Ψ(*as*,*bs*) *is monotone*
2. (Bar(Ψ([],[]), []))fbp(T)
3. (Bar(Good(*R*), *as*); Bar(Good(*S*), *bs*)) Bar(Ψ(*as*,*bs*), [])

The monotonicity of Ψ(*as*,*bs*) is trivial. Property *2* is more involved than it seems. One would expect it to follow from the fact that Ψ([],[]) is included in Good(T), but contrary to the intuition this is not derivable, since its interpretation in the proof-irrelevant model is false. Property *2* follows instead from the fact that for all *c* in C, Bar(Ψ([],[]), snoc([], *c*)) implies Bar(Good(T), snoc([], *c*)). It is surprising that to prove this, we can use now that Ψ([],[]) is included in Good(T) since now C is assumed inhabited, and then, not only the inclusion becomes interpreted as true but it even becomes provable. The proof requires manipulation of impossible cases, namely, those corresponding to the first four disjuncts in the definition of Ψ. All those cases are solved appealing to the reflexivity of T, which follows from that of *R* and *S*, and which guarantees Good(T, snoc(snoc([], *c*), *c*)), which in turn, in the presence of an impossible situation, implies Good(T, *cs*) for any *cs* in List(*C*). Property *3* is proved by two applications of bar induction. The base cases are trivial, since Good(*R*, *as*) makes Ψ(*as*,*bs*) true and so does Good(*S*, *bs*). The remaining case follows from the following lemma.

Lemma 19. *If R and S have the fbp, then for all as in* List(*A*), *bs in* List(*B*) *and c in* C, *if* Bar(Ψ(snoc(*as*, fst(*c*)),*bs*), []) *and* Bar(Ψ(*as*,snoc(*bs*, snd(*c*))), []) *hold, so does* Bar(Ψ(*as*,*bs*), snoc([], *c*)).

To prove this we show that for all *cs*, (Bar(Ψ(*as*,snoc(*bs*, snd(*c*))), *cs*))Ω(*cs*), where

```
Ω ∈ (cs ∈ List(C)) Set
  Ω ≡ [cs]Imply(All([c1]R(fst(c), fst(c1)), cs), ∀(List(List(C)), [css]Bar(Ψ(as, bs), μ1)))
```

and $\mu_1 \equiv$ intercalate(append(snoc([], c), cs), css). The precise definition of intercalate does not need to concern us here. In vague terms, it takes a list as and a list ass of lists and returns a list, which is obtained from as by inserting, between every two elements, all the elements of the corresponding list in ass. Therefore, the elements of as are in the result in the same order, thus, if as is good, so is the result. Similarly, if there is an element in as satisfying a property, it will still be in the result.

Notice that intercalate(append(snoc([], c), []), []) $\equiv$ snoc([], c), which explains that Ω([]) implies Bar(Ψ(as,bs), snoc([], c)). Since by Lemma 18, Ψ(as,snoc(bs, snd(c))) is monotone, in the proof that (Bar(Ψ(as,snoc(bs, snd(c))), cs)) Ω(cs) we can apply bar induction. In the base case, we take any cs in List(C), assume Ψ(as,snoc(bs, snd(c)),cs) and All([c_1]R(fst(c),fst(c_1)), cs), and prove that for any css in List(List(C)), Ψ(as,bs,μ_1). This is done by analyzing the five cases of Ψ(as,snoc(bs, snd(c)),cs), the first assumption. The only case in which Ψ(as,bs,μ_1) does not follow immediately is when Some([c_1]S(snd(c),snd(c_1)), cs). But then, we can derive Some([c_1]T(c,c_1), cs) from the second assumption, and so, Good(T, μ_1).

For the inductive case consider any cs in List(C), such that the induction hypothesis holds, that is, such that for all c_2 in C, Ω(snoc(cs, c_2)). To prove Ω(cs), we assume All([c_1]R(fst(c),fst(c_1)), cs) and prove that for any css in List(List(C)), Bar(Ψ(as,bs), μ_1). We use the hypothesis Bar(Ψ(snoc(as, fst(c)),bs), []) of the lemma. We prove that for any cs_1 in List(C), if Bar(Ψ(snoc(as, fst(c)),bs), cs_1) holds, then so does Bar(Ψ(as,bs), append(μ_1, cs_1)), using bar induction. Now the inductive case is trivial, and the base case is an analysis of the five cases of Ψ(snoc(as, fst(c)),bs,cs_1). The only case in which Bar(Ψ(as,bs), append(μ_1, cs_1)) is not immediate is when Some([c_1]R(fst(c),fst(c_1)), cs_1), but then it follows from the induction hypothesis and the assumption All([c_1]R(fst(c),fst(c_1)), cs).

4.5 Higman's lemma

We prove Higman's lemma as in Theorem 6, which with formal notation becomes

Theorem 20 (Higman's lemma). ($A \in$ **Set**; $S \in$ (A;A)**Set**; fbp(S)) fbp(Star(S)).

Since Ctxt(S, []) is included in S and Star and Bar preserve inclusion, it is enough to prove that fbp(S) implies fbp(Star(Ctxt(S, []))), which is an instance of the statement that for all as in List(A), if Bar(Good(S), as), then fbp(S^*(as)), where

$A^* \in$ **Set**	$S^* \in$ ($as \in$ List(A); $w_1, w_2 \in A^*$) **Set**
$A^* \equiv$ List(A)	$S^* \equiv$ [as]Star(Ctxt(S, as))

That statement can be proved by bar induction, showing that

Lemma 21. *If S has the fbp, then for any as in* List(A), *the following hold:*

1. (Good(S, as))fbp(S^*(as))
2. (($a \in A$)fbp(S^*(snoc(as, a))))fbp(S^*(as))

When Good(S, as) holds, the relation Ctxt(S, as) is always true, and then, to be Ctxt(S, as)-embeddable in becomes to be not longer than. Property *1* consists in showing that this relation has the fbp.

For property *2* we assume the induction hypothesis $(a \in A)$fbp(S^*(snoc(as, a))) and prove that for any word w in A^*, Bar(Good($S^*(as)$), snoc([], w)), by induction on w. The base case is trivial, since the empty word is always embeddable in any other word.

The inductive case amounts to prove that for any w in A^*, for any a in A, if Bar(Good($S^*(as)$), snoc([], w)) then Bar(Good($S^*(as)$), snoc([], snoc(w, a))). The following lemma will allows us to apply Ramsey theorem.

Lemma 22. *If the following relations*

$$\text{Ctxt}(S^*(as), \text{snoc}([], w)) \qquad \text{Ctxt}(S, as) \qquad S^*(\text{snoc}(as, a))$$

have the fbp, then Bar(Good($S^*(as)$), snoc([], snoc(w, a))) *holds.*

The hypotheses of the lemma hold, since the fbp of the first relation follows by Proposition 13 from the assumption Bar(Good($S^*(as)$), snoc([], w)), the fbp of the second relation, from the hypothesis of Higman's lemma fbp(S), and the fbp of the third relation, from the induction hypothesis mentioned above, again by Proposition 13.

The proof of the lemma consists in proving first, from the fbp of the three relations, that the relation S_T has the fbp, where S_T is the following relation on triples of type T.

```
T ∈ Set                         S_T ∈ (t1, t2 ∈ T) Set
   T ≡ And3(A*, A, A*)             S_T ≡
                                      [t1, t2]
                                         And3(Ctxt(S*(as), snoc([], w), fst3(t1), fst3(t2)),
                                              Ctxt(S, as, snd3(t1), snd3(t2)),
                                              S*(snoc(as, a), trd3(t1), trd3(t2)))
```

And second, that the fbp of S_T implies Bar(Good($S^*(as)$), snoc([], snoc(w, a))).

Intuitively, a triple t in T represents the three parts of a word with respect to one of its middle elements: the left subword, the middle element itself and the right subword.

The fbp of S_T follows from the fbp of the three relations in Lemma 22 by two applications of Ramsey theorem. Then, by the fan theorem we get that the predicate [tss]All(Good(S_T), cartSnoc(tss)) over List(List(T)) is an inductive bar. We define the predicate U_{A^*} over List(A^*).

$$U_{A^*} = [ws]\text{All}(\text{Good}(S_T), \text{cartSnoc}(\text{map}(\text{LmR}, ws))),$$

where LmR is a function which when applied to a word computes all the possible decompositions of the word in triples. Therefore, if $U_{A^*}(ws)$ holds for some list ws of words, then no matter how each word of ws is decomposed in a triple, the list ts consisting of a triple for each word satisfies Good(S_T). From Proposition 14 it follows that U_{A^*} is an inductive bar.

To prove that Bar(Good($S^*(as)$), snoc([], snoc(w, a))) holds, we use bar induction and prove that for all lists of words ws

$$(\text{Bar}(U_{A^*}, ws))\text{All}(J, \text{cartSnoc}(\text{map}(\text{LmR}, ws)))$$

where

J ∈ (ts ∈ List(T)) **Set**
J ≡ [ts]Imply(All([t]Ctxt(S, as, a, $snd_3(t)$), ts), ∀(List(List(A^*)), [wss]Bar(Good($S^*(as)$), μ))

and μ ≡ intercalate(append(snoc([], snoc(w, a)), map(flat,ts)), wss). The function flat combines the three components of a triple in the proper order into a word. We will get Bar(Good($S^*(as)$), snoc([], snoc(w, a))) as a corollary, by applying that proof to the fact that U_{A^*} is an inductive bar.

The proof consists in showing

1. U_{A^*} is monotone,
2. for all ws, if $U_{A^*}(ws)$ then All(J, cartSnoc(map(LmR, ws))), and
3. for all ws, if for all w_1 in A^* All(J, cartSnoc(map(LmR, snoc(ws, w_1)))) holds, then All(J, cartSnoc(map(LmR, ws))) holds as well.

The first item follows from the monotonicity of Good(S_T).

To prove the third item we take any list of triples ts, assume that for any triple t_1 if Ctxt(S, as, a, $snd_3(t_1)$) then for all lists wss of lists of words Good($S^*(as)$) bars μ_1, where

$$\mu_1 \equiv \text{intercalate}(\text{append}(\text{snoc}([], \text{snoc}(w, a)), \text{map}(\text{flat}, \text{snoc}(ts, t_1))), wss)$$

and prove that for all lists wss of lists of words, Good($S^*(as)$) bars μ. This can be proved using that the relation S^*(snoc(as, a)) has the fbp. We prove that for all lists ws of words, if Good(S^*(snoc(as, a))) bars ws then Good($S^*(as)$) bars append(μ, ws) by bar induction. The inductive case is trivial. The base case follows from the fact that if Good(S^*(snoc(as, a)), ws) then either Good($S^*(as)$, ws) or some word w of those in ws can be decomposed in a triple t_1 such that Ctxt(S, as, a, $snd_3(t_1)$) holds. In the first case Good($S^*(as)$) bars append(μ, ws) because Good($S^*(as)$, ws) holds. In the second, because append(μ, ws) is the same as μ_1 for a suitable wss.

The proof of the second item is the only part of the proof presented in this paper in which we did not find a way to avoid equality, which we use to define the notion of being a decomposition. To prove the second item it is enough to prove that given a list ws such that $U_{A^*}(ws)$ holds, then for all possible decompositions in triples ts of the words in ws, if All([t]Ctxt(S, as, a, $snd_3(t)$), ts) holds then Good($S^*(as)$, μ_2) holds too, where μ_2 is the list append(snoc([], snoc(w, a)), map(flat, ts)). From $U_{A^*}(ws)$ we know that for any such ts, Good(S_T, ts) holds. We let ts be of the form $t_0, \ldots, t_{n-1}$. Then, it is possible to find $i < j$ such that the following hold.

1. $\text{Ctxt}(S^*(as), \text{snoc}([], w), \text{fst}_3(t_i), \text{fst}_3(t_j))$, and therefore, Proposition 11 implies that either $S^*(as, w, \text{fst}_3(t_i))$ or $S^*(as, \text{fst}_3(t_i), \text{fst}_3(t_j))$.
2. $\text{Ctxt}(S, as, \text{snd}_3(t_i), \text{snd}_3(t_j))$.
3. $S^*(\text{snoc}(as, a), \text{trd}_3(t_i), \text{trd}_3(t_j))$. By Proposition 12 either $S^*(as, \text{snoc}([], a), \text{trd}_3(t_i))$, or $S^*(as, \text{trd}_3(t_i), \text{trd}_3(t_j))$.

If $S^*(as, \text{fst}_3(t_i), \text{fst}_3(t_j))$ and $S^*(as, \text{trd}_3(t_i), \text{trd}_3(t_j))$ hold then, $S^*(as, \text{flat}(t_i), \text{flat}(t_j))$ also holds, and then so does $\text{Good}(S^*(as), \mu_2)$. Otherwise, if $S^*(as, w, \text{fst}_3(t_i))$ holds, then we get $S^*(as, \text{snoc}(w, a), \text{flat}(t_i))$, because we assumed $\text{Ctxt}(S, as, a, \text{snd}_3(t_i))$. Thus, $\text{Good}(S^*(as), \mu_2)$ holds also in this case. Finally, the third possible case is when $S^*(as, \text{snoc}([], a), \text{trd}_3(t_i))$. Here we cannot conclude that $\text{Good}(S^*(as), \mu_2)$ holds. But we know that it must exist a letter a_1 in $\text{trd}_3(t_i)$ such that $\text{Ctxt}(S, as, a, a_1)$. Then, we can take the triple s_i such that $\text{flat}(s_i)$ is equal to $\text{flat}(t_i)$, the third component of s_i is shorter than the third component of t_i, and the second component of s_i is a_1. We take ts_1 to be the same as ts except in the i-th position, in which instead of t_i it is s_i. Then, we are back at the beginning, that is, both $\text{Good}(S_T, ts_1)$ and $\text{All}([t]\text{Ctxt}(S, as, a, \text{snd}_3(t)), ts_1)$ hold and we still have to prove the same thing, namely, that $\text{Good}(S^*(as), \mu_2)$ holds, since $\text{map}(\text{flat}, ts_1)$ is equal to $\text{map}(\text{flat}, ts)$. But some progress have been done since the third component of the i-th member is shorter now. The iteration of this argument either produces a proof of $\text{Good}(S^*(as), \mu_2)$ or gives lists of triples each of them equal to the previous one except in one position in which the third component is shorter. This procedure necessarily terminates and therefore, it produces a proof of $\text{Good}(S^*(as), \mu_2)$. This intuitive argument is formalized with an inductive argument on a well-founded relation defined on triples.

Concluding remarks

We have given an account of the history of Higman's lemma and proved a version of it in Martin-Löf's type theory, which consisted in formalizing Veldman's intuitionistic proof. The main difference with previous type-theoretic proofs of the lemma is that relations are not required to be decidable. This is a significant difference. Notice that given an infinite sequence of words, the problem of finding two words in it such that one of them is embedded in the other may seem unsolvable when the relation in question is not decidable since one cannot even test whether two given letters are related or not. Any solution to the problem relies on the constructive content of the notion of fbp.

The proof is also an experiment in formalizing a considerable proof in a limited version of Martin-Löf's type theory. This paper illustrates how to cope with the limitations of this formal system. Finally, the paper explains the notion of inductive bar and presents a type-theoretic formulation of the fan theorem.

Acknowledgements

I am grateful to Thierry Coquand for his many suggestions and ideas and to Wim Veldman for sharing with me his proof, which is indispensable for this paper. Marc Bezem, Henrik Persson, Monika Seisenberger, Jan Smith and an anonymous referee made valuable comments on earlier versions of this paper.

References

[ACJT96] P. Abdulla, K. Cerans, B. Jonsson, and Y.-K. Tsay. General decidability theorems for infinite-state systems. In *11th Annual IEEE Symposium on Logic in Computer Science. Proceedings*, 1996.

[AJ93] P. Abdulla and B. Jonsson. Verifying programs with unreliable channels. In *8th Annual IEEE Symposium on Logic in Computer Science. Proceedings*, pages 160–170, 1993.

[Bro54] L. Brouwer. Points and spaces. *Canadian Journal of Mathematics*, 6:1–17, 1954.

[CF58] H. Curry and R. Feys. *Combinatory Logic*, volume I. North-Holland, 1958.

[CFH93] T. Coquand, D. Fridlender, and H. Herbelin. A proof of higman's lemma by structural induction. Unpublished manuscript, 1993.

[Con86] R. Constable et al. *Implementing Mathematics with the NuPRL Proof Development System.* Prentice-Hall, Englewood Cliffs, NJ, 1986.

[Coq92] T. Coquand. Pattern matching with dependent types. In *Proceeding from the logical framework workshop at Båstad*, June 1992.

[Dic13] L. Dickson. Finiteness of the odd perfect and primitive abundant numbers with n distinct prime factors. *American Journal of Mathematics*, 35:413–426, 1913.

[DJ90] N. Dershowitz and J.-P. Jouannaud. Rewrite systems. In J. Van Leeuwen, editor, *Handbook of Theoretical Computer Science*, volume B, chapter 6, page 273. Elsevier, 1990.

[Dum77] M. Dummett. *Elements of intuitionism.* Clarendon Press, Oxford, 1977.

[Dyb94] P. Dybjer. Inductive families. *Formal Aspects of Computing*, 6:440–465, 1994.

[ER52] P. Erdös and R. Rado. Sets having a divisor property. *American Mathematical Monthly*, 59:255–257, 1952.

[Erd49] P. Erdös. Problem 4358. *American Mathematical Monthly*, 56:480, 1949.

[Fri78] H. Friedman. Classically and intuitionistically provably recursive functions. In D. Scott and G. Muller, editors, *Higher Set Theory*, volume 669 of *Lecture Notes in Mathematics*, pages 21–28. Springer-Verlag, 1978.

[Fri93] D. Fridlender. Ramsey's theorem in type theory. Licentiate Thesis, Chalmers University of Technology and University of Göteborg, Sweden, October 1993.

[Göd33] K. Gödel. Zur intuitionistischen arithmetik und zahlentheorie. *Ergebnisse eines mathematischen Kolloquiums*, 4:34–38, 1933. English: [Göd65].

[Göd65] K. Gödel. On intuitionistic arithmetic and number theory. In M. Davis, editor, *The Undecidable*, pages 75–81. Raven Press, 1965.

[Hai69] L. Haines. On free monoids partially ordered by embedding. *Journal of Combinatorial Theory*, 6:94–98, 1969.

[Hig52] G. Higman. Ordering by divisibility in abstract algebras. *Proceedings of the London Mathematical Society*, (3) 2:326–336, 1952.

[How80] W. Howard. The formulae-as-types notion of construction. In J. Seldin and J. Hindley, editors, *To H.B. Curry: Essays on Combinatory Logic, Lambda Calculus and Formalism*, pages 479–490. Academic Press, London, 1980.

[JP77] D. de Jongh and R. Parikh. Well-partial orderings and hierarchies. *Indagationes Mathematicae*, 39:195–207, 1977.

[Jul68] P. Jullien. Sur un théorème d'extension dans la théorie des mots. *Comptes Rendus de la Academie de Sciences de Paris*, (A) 266:851–854, 1968.

[Kru60] J. Kruskal. Well-Quasi-Ordering, the tree theorem, and Vazsonyi's conjecture. *Transactions of the American Mathematical Society*, 95:210–225, 1960.

[Kru72] J. Kruskal. The Theory of Well-Quasi-Ordering: A Frequently Discovered Concept. *Journal of Combinatorial Theory (A)*, 13:297–305, 1972.

[Mag94] L. Magnusson. *The Implementation of ALF - a Proof Editor based on Martin-Löf's Monomorphic Type Theory with Explicit Substitution*. PhD thesis, Department of Computing Science, Chalmers University of Technology and University of Göteborg, 1994.

[Mar68] P. Martin-Löf. *Notes on Constructive Mathematics*. Almqvist & Wiksell, 1968.

[Mar75] P. Martin-Löf. An Intuitionistic Theory of Types: Predicative Part. In H. E. Rose and J. C. Shepherdson, editors, *Logic Colloquium 1973*, pages 73–118, Amsterdam, 1975. North-Holland Publishing Company.

[Mar84] P. Martin-Löf. *Intuitionistic Type Theory*. Bibliopolis, Napoli, 1984.

[MG79] E. Martino and P. Giaretta. Brouwer, dummett and the bar theorem. In *Atti del Convengo Nazionale di Logica*. Bibliopolis, 1979.

[MR90] C. Murthy and J. Russell. A constructive proof of higman's lemma. In *Fifth annual IEEE Symposium on Logic in Computer Science*, pages 257–267, 1990.

[Mur90] C. Murthy. *Extracting Constructive Content from Classical Proofs*. PhD thesis, Cornell University, 1990.

[Nas63] C. Nash-Williams. On well-quasi-ordering finite trees. *Proceedings of the Cambridge Philosophical Society*, 59:833–835, 1963.

[Neu49] B. Neumann. On ordered division rings. *Transaction of the American Mathematical Society*, 66:202–252, 1949.

[NPS90] B. Nordström, K. Petersson, and J. Smith. *Programming in Martin-Löf's Type Theory. An Introduction*. Oxford University Press, 1990.

[RS93] F. Richman and G. Stolzenberg. Well Quasi-Ordered Sets. *Advances in Mathematics*, 97:145–153, 1993.

[Sch79] D. Schmidt. Well-Partial-Orderings and Their Maximal Order Types. Habilitationsschrift, 1979.

[Sim88] S. Simpson. Ordinal numbers and the hilbert basis theorem. *The Journal of Symbolic Logic*, 53:961–974, 1988.

[Smi88] J. Smith. The Independence of Peano's Fourth Axiom from Martin-Löf's Type Theory without Universes. *Journal of Symbolic Logic*, 53:840–845, 1988.

[SS85] K. Schütte and S. Simpson. Ein in der reinen zahlentheorie unberweisbarer satz über endliche folgen von natürlichen zahlen. *Archiv für Mathematische Logik und Grundlagenfroschung*, 25:75–89, 1985.

[Tas97] A. Tasistro. *Substitution, record types and subtyping in type theory, with applications to the theory of programming*. PhD thesis, Department of Computing Science at Chalmers University of Technology and University of Göteborg, 1997.

[VB93] W. Veldman and M. Bezem. Ramsey's theorem and the pigeonhole principle in intuitionistic mathematics. *Journal of the London Mathematical Society*, (2)47:193–211, 1993.

[Vel94] W. Veldman. Intuitionistic proof of the general non-decidable case of higman's lemma. Personal communication, 1994.

A Proof of Weak Termination of Typed $\lambda\sigma$-Calculi

Jean Goubault-Larrecq

G.I.E. Dyade et projet Coq, I.N.R.I.A.

Abstract. We show that reducing any simply-typed $\lambda\sigma$-term (resp. $\lambda\sigma_{\Uparrow}$) by applying the rules in σ (resp. $\sigma_{\Uparrow}$) eagerly always terminates, by a translation to the simply-typed λ-calculus. This holds even with term and substitution meta-variables. In fact, every reduction terminates provided that (β)-redexes are only contracted under so-called safe contexts; and in σ, resp. $\sigma_{\Uparrow}$-normal forms, all contexts around terms of sort T are safe. The result is then extended to $\lambda\tau$ and a simple second-order type system.

1 Introduction

The simply-typed $\lambda\sigma$-calculus does not terminate strongly [10, 11], but it terminates in the weak sense: every typed term has a normal form. We present a proof of this; in fact, we prove the widely believed claim that every reduction where σ steps are applied eagerly is finite, as a consequence of a more general theorem stating that every reduction where (β)-contraction only occurs under so-called *safe contexts* terminates. For the sake of generality, we show this even in the presence of term and substitution metavariables, and for a calculus that encompasses both the original $\lambda\sigma$-calculus [1] and the $\lambda\sigma_{\Uparrow}$-calculus, a.k.a. $\lambda\mathcal{E}$ [6].

Related works on this subject include [14] (Theorem 7), which proves the analogue of σ-eager termination for a left-linear cousin of $\lambda\sigma$ named λ_{ϕ}, using reducibility techniques —the same technique applies to $\lambda\sigma$ as well— and [3] which shows that several related calculi, among which the simply-typed $\lambda\zeta$ and $\lambda\upsilon$-calculi [12, 9], are strongly normalizing in the simply-typed case (see also [2], Theorem 3, p. 11 for $\lambda\upsilon$). The latter calculi were already known to preserve strong normalization [12, 9], i.e., if u is a $\lambda\zeta$ or a $\lambda\upsilon$-term that is the translation of a strongly normalizing λ-term, then u is itself strongly normalizing. This is different from (strong) normalization of typed $\lambda\zeta$ or $\lambda\upsilon$-terms, at least because on the one hand not all strongly normalizing terms have simple typings, and on the other hand not all $\lambda\zeta$ or $\lambda\upsilon$-terms are translations of λ-terms.

The plan is as follows: We recapitulate some basic definitions in Section 2 and give the idea of our proof in Section 3. We prove our main theorem in Section 4: every reduction where (β)-contraction occurs only under so-called *safe* contexts always terminates. This result is applied in Section 5 to show that all normalization strategies that apply σ (resp. $\sigma_{\Uparrow}$) eagerly in the $\lambda\sigma$-calculus (resp. in $\lambda\sigma_{\Uparrow}$) terminate. The method is easily carried over to other calculi, and we take the examples of Ríos' $\lambda\tau$-calculus in Section 6, and of a simple second-order type system in Section 7.

2 Definitions

Consider the language $\lambda\sigma_{\Uparrow}$ defined as $T \cup S$, where the sublanguage T and that of *explicit substitutions* or *stacks* S are given by:

$$T ::= \mathcal{V}_T \mid \lambda T \mid TT \mid T[S] \mid 1$$
$$S ::= \mathcal{V}_S \mid S \circ S \mid id \mid T \cdot S \mid\uparrow\mid\Uparrow S$$

where $\mathcal{V}_T$ and $\mathcal{V}_S$ are disjoint infinite sets of *term variables* x, y, z, ..., and *stack variables* X, Y, Z, etc. The $\lambda\sigma$-terms are those $\lambda\sigma_{\Uparrow}$-terms where $\Uparrow$ does not occur.

We call (untyped) $\lambda\sigma$-calculus the rewrite system of Figure 1; σ denotes the subsystem without (β). It is a slight generalization, in the sense that it can simulate every reduction, of both the $\lambda\sigma$-calculus of [1] and of the $\lambda\sigma_{\Uparrow}$-calculus (the $\lambda\mathcal{E}$-calculus of [6]). Notice that, because of rule $(\eta \Uparrow)$, all the other rules with $\Uparrow$ in their names are superfluous. The $\lambda\sigma_{\Uparrow}$-calculus is $\lambda\sigma$ minus the three rules with an η in their names; and $\sigma_{\Uparrow}$ denotes $\lambda\sigma_{\Uparrow}$ minus (β).

(β)	$(\lambda u)v \to u[v \cdot id]$	$(\eta \Uparrow)$	$\Uparrow w \to 1 \cdot (w \circ \uparrow)$
$([id])$	$u[id] \to u$	$(\eta \cdot)$	$1 \cdot \uparrow \to id$
$(\circ id)$	$u \circ id \to u$	$(\eta \cdot \circ)$	$(1[u]) \cdot (\uparrow \circ u) \to u$
$(id \circ)$	$id \circ u \to u$	$(1 \Uparrow)$	$1[\Uparrow u] \to 1$
$([])$	$(u[v])[w] \to u[v \circ w]$	$(1 \Uparrow \circ)$	$1[\Uparrow u \circ v] \to 1[v]$
$(\circ)$	$(u \circ v) \circ w \to u \circ (v \circ w)$	$(\uparrow\Uparrow)$	$\uparrow \circ \Uparrow u \to u \circ \uparrow$
(1)	$1[u \cdot v] \to u$	$(\uparrow\Uparrow \circ)$	$\uparrow \circ (\Uparrow u \circ v) \to u \circ (\uparrow \circ v)$
$(\uparrow)$	$\uparrow \circ (u \cdot v) \to v$	$(\Uparrow\Uparrow)$	$\Uparrow u \circ \Uparrow v \to \Uparrow (u \circ v)$
$(\cdot)$	$(u \cdot v) \circ w \to (u[w]) \cdot (v \circ w)$	$(\Uparrow\Uparrow \circ)$	$\Uparrow u \circ (\Uparrow v \circ w) \to \Uparrow (u \circ v) \circ w$
(λ)	$(\lambda u)[w] \to \lambda(u[\Uparrow w])$	$(\Uparrow \cdot)$	$\Uparrow u \circ (v \cdot w) \to v \cdot (u \circ w)$
(app)	$(uv)[w] \to (u[w])(v[w])$	$(\Uparrow id)$	$\Uparrow id \to id$

Fig. 1. The $\lambda\sigma_{\Uparrow}$-calculus

The purpose of this paper is in particular to show that the simply-typed $\lambda\sigma$-calculus terminates, when restricted to *σ-eager rewrites*, i.e. rewrite sequences where (β)-redexes are only contracted inside σ-normal terms. In particular, because σ terminates (see Appendix A), all σ-eager rewrites are of the form:

$$u \xrightarrow{\sigma}{}^{*} u_1 \xrightarrow{(\beta)} u_1' \xrightarrow{\sigma}{}^{*} u_2 \xrightarrow{(\beta)} u_2' \xrightarrow{\sigma}{}^{*} \ldots \xrightarrow{\sigma}{}^{*} u_k \xrightarrow{(\beta)} u_k' \xrightarrow{\sigma}{}^{*} \ldots$$

where $u_1, u_2, \ldots, u_k, \ldots$ are σ-normal. We shall also show that the simply-typed $\lambda\sigma_{\Uparrow}$-calculus terminates, when rewrites are restricted to be $\sigma_{\Uparrow}$-eager rewrites, defined similarly.

The typing rules are given in Figure 2. Types are either *term types* or *stack types*. Term types are *sequents* $\Gamma \vdash \tau$, where τ is a formula and Γ is a finite list of formulas $\tau_1, \ldots, \tau_n, \cdot$, where we use $\cdot$ to mark the end of the list; formulas τ are either atoms α, β, ..., or implications (arrow types) $\tau_1 \to \tau_2$; in this, we follow [4] in spirit. Stack types are sequents $\Gamma \vdash \Delta$, with Δ a finite list of formulas as well. For simplicity, we shall assume that the calculus is given in Church style: variables $x_{\Gamma \vdash \tau}$ are annotated with their type $\Gamma \vdash \tau$; we write them x when no confusion arises. (Writing terms in Church style will allow us to translate $\lambda\sigma$-terms to λ-terms in Section 4; otherwise, we would need to translate typing derivations, which is not that different, but is much less readable.)

$$\frac{}{X_{\Gamma \vdash \Delta} : \Gamma \vdash \Delta}\,(Var_S) \qquad \frac{}{x_{\Gamma \vdash \tau} : \Gamma \vdash \tau}\,(Var_T) \qquad \frac{}{id : \Gamma \vdash \Gamma}\,(I)$$

$$\frac{u : \Gamma \vdash \tau \quad v : \Gamma \vdash \Delta}{u \cdot v : \Gamma \vdash \tau, \Delta}\,(,I) \qquad \frac{}{1 : \tau, \Gamma \vdash \tau}\,(,E_1) \qquad \frac{}{\uparrow : \tau, \Gamma \vdash \Gamma}\,(,E_2)$$

$$\frac{u : \tau_1, \Gamma \vdash \tau_2}{\lambda u : \Gamma \vdash \tau_1 \to \tau_2}\,(\to I) \qquad \frac{u : \Gamma \vdash \tau_1 \to \tau_2 \quad v : \Gamma \vdash \tau_1}{uv : \Gamma \vdash \tau_2}\,(\to E) \qquad \frac{u : \Gamma \vdash \Delta}{\Uparrow u : \tau, \Gamma \vdash \tau, \Delta}\,(\Uparrow)$$

$$\frac{u : \Xi \vdash \Delta \quad v : \Gamma \vdash \Xi}{u \circ v : \Gamma \vdash \Delta}\,(Cut_S) \qquad \frac{u : \Xi \vdash \tau \quad v : \Gamma \vdash \Xi}{u[v] : \Gamma \vdash \tau}\,(Cut_T)$$

Fig. 2. Typing rules

To get a calculus in Church style, we also need to annotate the terms 1, $\uparrow$, *id* and $\Uparrow u$ with types agreeing with the rules of Figure 2. We shall usually write these terms without their type annotations when context permits, however.

Then, every typed term has a unique type. There is a unique way of lifting the rules of Figure 1 to the typed case so that the resulting typed calculus has the subject reduction property: see Figure 3.

3 Basic Ideas

Because $\lambda\sigma$ is so close to the λ-calculus, it is tempting to translate back typed $\lambda\sigma$-terms to typed λ-terms, and use the fact that the latter are strongly normalizing [7]. Let's see informally how, what goes wrong and how we can repair it.

Since we are still at an informal stage, imagine that we have an unspecified language of values, say, integers, booleans, functions from integers to booleans, and so on. (In the sequel, these so-called values will be arbitrary typed λ-terms.) Each typed $\lambda\sigma$-term, say of sequent type $\tau_1, \ldots, \tau_n, \cdot \vdash \tau$, is a piece of program which, when evaluated in a stack of n values s_1 of type τ_1, ..., s_n of type τ_n (in fact, *at least* n values, but let's not be pesky at this point), will return a value of type τ. This is particularly clear for the $\lambda\sigma$-constant 1, which we read as the program that picks the first element s_1 of the stack, and returns it, therefore vindicating its (sequent) type $\tau_1, \ldots, \tau_n, \cdot \vdash \tau_1$.

(β)	$(\lambda u)v \to u[v \cdot id_{\Gamma \vdash \Gamma}]$ where $v : \Gamma \vdash \tau$	$(\eta \Uparrow)$	$(\Uparrow w)_{\tau,\Gamma\vdash\tau,\Delta} \to 1_{\tau,\Gamma\vdash\tau} \cdot (w \circ \uparrow_{\tau,\Gamma\vdash\Gamma})$
		$(\eta\cdot)$	$1_{\tau,\Gamma\vdash\tau} \cdot \uparrow_{\tau,\Gamma\vdash\Gamma} \to id_{\tau,\Gamma\vdash\tau,\Gamma}$
$([id])$	$u[id_{\Gamma\vdash\Gamma}] \to u$	$(\eta \cdot \circ)$	$(1_{\tau,\Gamma\vdash\tau}[u]) \cdot (\uparrow_{\tau,\Gamma\vdash\Gamma} \circ u) \to u$
$(\circ id)$	$u \circ id_{\Gamma\vdash\Gamma} \to u$	$(1 \Uparrow)$	$1_{\tau,\Delta\vdash\tau}[(\Uparrow u)_{\tau,\Gamma\vdash\tau,\Delta}] \to 1_{\tau,\Gamma\vdash\tau}$
$(id\circ)$	$id_{\Gamma\vdash\Gamma} \circ u \to u$	$(1 \Uparrow \circ)$	$1_{\tau,\Delta\vdash\tau}[(\Uparrow u)_{\tau,\Gamma\vdash\tau,\Delta} \circ v] \to 1_{\tau,\Gamma\vdash\tau}[v]$
$([])$	$(u[v])[w] \to u[v \circ w]$	$(\uparrow\Uparrow)$	$\uparrow_{\tau,\Delta\vdash\Delta} \circ (\Uparrow u)_{\tau,\Gamma\vdash\tau,\Delta} \to u \circ \uparrow_{\tau,\Gamma\vdash\Gamma}$
$(\circ)$	$(u \circ v) \circ w \to u \circ (v \circ w)$	$(\uparrow\Uparrow \circ)$	$\uparrow_{\tau,\Delta\vdash\Delta} \circ ((\Uparrow u)_{\tau,\Gamma\vdash\tau,\Delta} \circ v)$ $\to u \circ (\uparrow_{\tau,\Gamma\vdash\Gamma} \circ v)$
(1)	$1_{\Gamma\vdash\tau}[u \cdot v] \to u$	$(\Uparrow\Uparrow)$	$(\Uparrow u)_{\tau,\Xi\vdash\tau,\Delta} \circ (\Uparrow v)_{\tau,\Gamma\vdash\tau,\Xi}$ $\to (\Uparrow (u \circ v))_{\tau,\Gamma\vdash\tau,\Delta}$
$(\uparrow)$	$\uparrow_{\Gamma\vdash\Delta} \circ (u \cdot v) \to v$		
$(\cdot)$	$(u \cdot v) \circ w \to (u[w]) \cdot (v \circ w)$	$(\Uparrow\Uparrow \circ)$	$(\Uparrow u)_{\tau,\Xi\vdash\tau,\Delta} \circ ((\Uparrow v)_{\tau,\Gamma\vdash\tau,\Xi} \circ w)$ $\to (\Uparrow (u \circ v))_{\tau,\Gamma\vdash\tau,\Delta} \circ w$
(λ)	$(\lambda u)[w] \to \lambda(u[(\Uparrow w)_{\tau,\Gamma\vdash\tau,\Delta}])$ where $w : \Gamma \vdash \Delta,\ u : \tau, \Delta \vdash \tau'$	$(\Uparrow \cdot)$	$(\Uparrow u)_{\tau,\Gamma\vdash\tau,\Delta} \circ (v \cdot w) \to v \cdot (u \circ w)$
(app)	$(uv)[w] \to (u[w])(v[w])$	$(\Uparrow id)$	$(\Uparrow id_{\Gamma\vdash\Gamma})_{\tau,\Gamma\vdash\tau,\Gamma} \to id_{\tau,\Gamma\vdash\tau,\Gamma}$

Fig. 3. The typed reduction rules

The invisible application symbol enjoys a similar interpretation: if $u : \Gamma \vdash \tau \to \tau'$ and $v : \Gamma \vdash \tau$, and $\Gamma = \tau_1, \ldots, \tau_n, \cdot$, then u is a term that evaluates to a functional value, of type $\tau \to \tau'$, under any stack of n elements s_1 of type τ_1, $\ldots$, s_n of type τ_n, and v is a term that evaluates to an argument value of type τ under the same stack. So uv should evaluate to a value of τ_2 under this same stack, for instance to the result of applying the value of u to that of v.

Similarly, λ acts as follows: in a stack as above, the value of $\lambda u : \Gamma \vdash \tau \to \tau'$ is the function that pushes its argument value (of type τ) onto the current stack (which now has type τ, Γ), and evaluates u in this new stack, yielding a result value of type τ'.

$$
\begin{aligned}
\overline{\lambda u} \quad & = \lambda x_1 \cdot \ldots \cdot \lambda x_n \cdot \lambda x \cdot \overline{u} x x_1 \ldots x_n \\
& \quad \text{where } u : \tau, \tau_1, \ldots, \tau_n, \cdot \vdash \tau' \\
\overline{uv} \quad & = \lambda x_1 \cdot \ldots \cdot \lambda x_n \cdot (\overline{u} x_1 \ldots x_n)(\overline{v} x_1 \ldots x_n) \\
& \quad \text{where } u : \tau_1, \ldots, \tau_n, \cdot \vdash \tau \to \tau', v : \tau_1, \ldots, \tau_n, \cdot \vdash \tau \\
\overline{id_{\tau_1,\ldots,\tau_n,\cdot\vdash\tau_1,\ldots,\tau_n,\cdot}} \quad & = (\lambda x_1 \cdot \ldots \cdot \lambda x_n \cdot x_1,\ \ldots,\ \lambda x_1 \cdot \ldots \cdot \lambda x_n \cdot x_n) \\
\overline{u \cdot v} \quad & = (\lambda x_1 \cdot \ldots \cdot \lambda x_n \cdot \overline{u} x_1 \ldots x_n,\ s_1,\ \ldots,\ s_m) \\
& \quad \text{where } \overline{v} = (s_1, \ldots, s_m) \text{ and } u : \tau_1, \ldots, \tau_n, \cdot \vdash \tau \\
\overline{u[v]} \quad & = \lambda x_1 \cdot \ldots \cdot \lambda x_n \cdot \overline{u}(s_1 x_1 \ldots x_n) \ldots (s_m x_1 \ldots x_n) \\
& \quad \text{where } \overline{v} = (s_1, \ldots, s_m) \text{ and } v : \tau_1, \ldots, \tau_n, \cdot \vdash \tau'_1, \ldots, \tau'_m, \cdot
\end{aligned}
$$

Fig. 4. A naive translation to the λ-calculus

Stack operators id, $\uparrow$, $\Uparrow$, $\cdot$, and $\circ$ are interpreted as returning not values, but whole new stacks of values. For instance, $id_{\Gamma\vdash\Gamma}$, where $\Gamma = \tau_1, \ldots, \tau_n, \cdot$, just returns the list $s_1, \ldots, s_n$, of all elements in the current stack. $\uparrow_{\tau,\Gamma\vdash\Gamma}$, returns all elements but the first, namely $s_2, \ldots, s_n$, provided that $n \geq 1$, and so on.

These considerations justify a naive translation $u \mapsto \overline{u}$ to the simply-typed λ-calculus, where programs returning values under n-element stacks are interpreted as λ-terms taking n corresponding arguments, and programs returning stacks are viewed as lists of similar λ-terms. (See Figure 4; we only show the cases that we need in the sequel.)

It is easy to complete the translation so that whenever $u : \tau_1, \ldots, \tau_n, \cdot \vdash \tau$, then $\overline{u} : \tau_1 \to \ldots \to \tau_n \to \tau$, and so that two convertible typed $\lambda\sigma$-terms have convertible translations. What is lost is the *direction* of the conversion. Consider indeed rule (β): $(\lambda u)v \to u[v \cdot id]$, and assume that $u : \tau, \tau_1, \ldots, \tau_n, \cdot \vdash \tau'$ and $v : \tau_1, \ldots, \tau_n, \cdot \vdash \tau$. Then:

$$\begin{aligned}\overline{(\lambda u)v} &= \lambda x_1 \cdot \ldots \cdot \lambda x_n \cdot (\overline{\lambda u} x_1 \ldots x_n)(\overline{v} x_1 \ldots x_n) \\ &= \lambda x_1 \cdot \ldots \cdot \lambda x_n \cdot ((\lambda x_1 \cdot \ldots \cdot \lambda x_n \cdot \lambda x \cdot \overline{u} x x_1 \ldots x_n) x_1 \ldots x_n)(\overline{v} x_1 \ldots x_n) \\ &\longrightarrow^* \lambda x_1 \cdot \ldots \cdot \lambda x_n \cdot (\lambda x \cdot \overline{u} x x_1 \ldots x_n)(\overline{v} x_1 \ldots x_n) \\ &\longrightarrow \lambda x_1 \cdot \ldots \cdot \lambda x_n \cdot \overline{u}(\overline{v} x_1 \ldots x_n) x_1 \ldots x_n \qquad (1)\end{aligned}$$

while:

$$\overline{u[v \cdot id]} = \lambda x_1 \cdot \ldots \cdot \lambda x_n \cdot \overline{u}(s_1 x_1 \ldots x_n)(s_2 x_1 \ldots x_n) \ldots (s_m x_1 \ldots x_n)$$

where $\overline{v \cdot id} = (s_1, s_2, \ldots, s_m)$. Since $\overline{v \cdot id} = (\lambda x_1 \cdot \ldots \cdot \lambda x_n \cdot \overline{v} x_1 \ldots x_n,\ \lambda x_1 \cdot \ldots \cdot \lambda x_n \cdot x_1,\ \ldots,\ \lambda x_1 \cdot \ldots \cdot \lambda x_n \cdot x_n)$, it follows that $m = n + 1$ and:

$$\begin{aligned}\overline{u[v \cdot id]} = \lambda x_1 \cdot \ldots \cdot \lambda x_n \cdot \overline{u}\ &((\lambda x_1 \cdot \ldots \cdot \lambda x_n \cdot \overline{v} x_1 \ldots x_n) x_1 \ldots x_n) \\ &((\lambda x_1 \cdot \ldots \cdot \lambda x_n \cdot x_1) x_1 \ldots x_n) \\ &\ldots \\ &((\lambda x_1 \cdot \ldots \cdot \lambda x_n \cdot x_n) x_1 \ldots x_n) \\ \longrightarrow^* \lambda x_1 \cdot \ldots \cdot \lambda x_n \cdot &\overline{u}(\overline{v} x_1 \ldots x_n) x_1 \ldots x_n \qquad (2)\end{aligned}$$

So, the interpretation preserves conversion, in that $\overline{(\lambda u)v}$ and $\overline{u[v \cdot id]}$ are convertible in the λ-calculus, but in general the first does not reduce to the second. The problem is in (2) above, where the reduction goes the wrong way around. In fact, we would like all the $\lambda x_1 \cdot$, …, $\lambda x_n \cdot$ to be such that $(\lambda x_i \cdot s)t$ really equals $s[t/x_i]$ instead of reducing to it. This way, (2) would become an equality, and we would be saved, at least in this case. We still have to consider the $\lambda x \cdot$ that is involved in the definition of $\overline{\lambda u}$ (Figure 4) as a real λ-abstraction, though, otherwise (1) would not be a contraction any longer.

We shall therefore modify our translation so that it maps $\lambda\sigma$-terms $u : \tau_1, \ldots, \tau_n, \cdot \vdash \tau$ not to λ-terms directly, but to *functions* (in the usual, mathematical sense) taking n λ-terms $x_1, \ldots, x_n$ of respective types $\tau_1, \ldots, \tau_n$ to λ-terms of type τ. For instance, $\overline{\lambda u}$ will be the function mapping $x_1, \ldots, x_n$ to the term $\lambda x \cdot \overline{u}(x, x_1, \ldots, x_n)$. The real translation will differ slightly, for technical reasons that we shall explain in the course of the formal development.

4 Reduction Under Safe Contexts Terminates

We translate each $\lambda\sigma$-term with Church-style typing into a family of λ-terms, typed à la Church as well. Let $\top$ be a given arbitrary type. We assume that we have infinitely many variables of each type.

With each term variable $x_{\tau_1,\ldots,\tau_n,\cdot\vdash\tau}$ of $\lambda\sigma$, we associate a constant[1] $\hat{x}_{\tau_1\to\ldots\to\tau_n\to\top\to\tau}$ of the λ-calculus of the indicated type. Similarly, we map each stack variable $X_{\tau_1,\ldots,\tau_n,\cdot\vdash\tau'_1,\ldots,\tau'_{n'},\cdot}$ to a list $\hat{X}_{1\ \tau_1\to\ldots\to\tau_n\to\top\to\tau'_1} :: \ldots :: \hat{X}_{n'\ \tau_1\to\ldots\to\tau_n\to\top\to\tau'_{n'}} :: \hat{X}_{n'+1\ \tau_1\to\ldots\to\tau_n\to\top\to\top}$ of λ-constants of the indicated types. (The cons operator :: is the standard list forming constructor and does not belong to the λ-calculus; :: is right-associative.)

Our translation maps every $\lambda\sigma$-term u of type $\tau_1,\ldots,\tau_n,\cdot\vdash\tau$ to a function $[\![u]\!]$ taking a list of $n+1$ λ-terms $t_1 :: \ldots :: t_n :: t_{n+1}$ of respective types τ_1, …, τ_n and $\top$, and returns a λ-term $[\![u]\!](t_1 :: \ldots :: t_n :: t_{n+1})$ of type τ. Similarly, our translation maps every $\lambda\sigma$-term u of type $\tau_1,\ldots,\tau_n,\cdot\vdash\tau'_1,\ldots,\tau'_{n'},\cdot$ to a function $[\![u]\!]$ taking a list of $n+1$ λ-terms $t_1 :: \ldots :: t_n :: t_{n+1}$ of respective types τ_1, …, τ_n and $\top$, and returns a list of $n'+1$ λ-terms of respective types τ'_1, …, $\tau'_{n'}$ and $\top$. The translation is given in Figure 5. (The reason for the extra $n+1$st argument of type $\top$ is technical; it will only be used in the proof of Lemma 6 —and we shall explain there why it was needed.)

$$
\begin{array}{ll}
[\![x_{\tau_1,\ldots,\tau_n,\cdot\vdash\tau}]\!](t_1 :: \ldots :: t_n :: t_{n+1}) & = \hat{x}_{\tau_1\to\ldots\to\tau_n\to\top\to\tau}\, t_1 \ldots t_n t_{n+1} \\
[\![X_{\tau_1,\ldots,\tau_n,\cdot\vdash\tau'_1,\ldots,\tau'_{n'},\cdot}]\!](t_1 :: \ldots :: t_n :: t_{n+1}) & = (\hat{X}_{1\ \tau_1\to\ldots\to\tau_n\to\top\to\tau'_1}\, t_1 \ldots t_n t_{n+1}) \\
 & \quad :: \ldots \\
 & \quad :: (\hat{X}_{n'\ \tau_1\to\ldots\to\tau_n\to\top\to\tau'_{n'}}\, t_1 \ldots t_n t_{n+1}) \\
 & \quad :: (\hat{X}_{n'+1\ \tau_1\to\ldots\to\tau_n\to\top\to\top}\, t_1 \ldots t_n t_{n+1}) \\
[\![\lambda u]\!](s) & = \lambda z_\tau \cdot [\![u]\!](z :: s) \quad \text{where } u : \tau, \Gamma \vdash \tau' \\
[\![uv]\!](s) & = ([\![u]\!](s))([\![v]\!](s)) \\
[\![u[v]]\!](s) & = [\![u]\!]([\![v]\!](s)) \\
[\![1_{\tau,\Gamma\vdash\tau}]\!](t :: s) & = t \\
[\![u \circ v]\!](s) & = [\![u]\!]([\![v]\!](s)) \\
[\![id_{\Gamma\vdash\Gamma}]\!](s) & = s \\
[\![u \cdot v]\!](s) & = [\![u]\!](s) :: [\![v]\!](s) \\
[\![\uparrow_{\tau,\Gamma\vdash\Gamma}]\!](t :: s) & = s \\
[\![\Uparrow u]\!](t :: s) & = t :: [\![u]\!](s)
\end{array}
$$

Fig. 5. Translation to the simply-typed λ-calculus

The β rule $(\lambda x \cdot t)t' \to t[t'/x]$ (where the latter denotes t with t' substituted for x, avoiding variable captures) defines a rewrite relation on λ-terms that we again write $\longrightarrow$. Recall that the simply-typed λ-calculus terminates [7]. We write $\longrightarrow^+$,

[1] We follow a suggestion of César Muñoz here in using constants instead of variables.

resp. $\longrightarrow^*$, its (resp. reflexive) transitive closure. These notions are extended to lists: $t_1 :: \ldots :: t_n :: t_{n+1} \longrightarrow^* t'_1 :: \ldots :: t'_n :: t'_{n+1}$ if and only if $t_i \longrightarrow^* t'_i$ for every i, $1 \leq i \leq n+1$; and $t_1 :: \ldots :: t_n :: t_{n+1} \longrightarrow^+ t'_1 :: \ldots :: t'_n :: t'_{n+1}$ if in addition $t_i \longrightarrow^+ t'_i$ for some i, $1 \leq i \leq n+1$.

We define the quasi-ordering $\succeq$ and the strict ordering $\succ$ on typed $\lambda\sigma$-terms by: $u \succeq v$ if and only if u and v have the same type and $[\![u]\!](s) \longrightarrow^* [\![v]\!](s)$ for every list s of λ-terms of the right types. Similarly, $u \succ v$ if and only if u and v have the same type and $[\![u]\!](s) \longrightarrow^+ [\![v]\!](s)$ for every list s of λ-terms of the right types. (Note that $\succ$ is in particular irreflexive because $\longrightarrow^+$ is a strict ordering *and* there are λ-terms of any given type, namely variables.) We also let $u \approx v$ if and only if $[\![u]\!](s) = [\![v]\!](s)$ for every list s of λ-terms of the right types.

The interpretation is monotonic in the following sense:

Lemma 1. *If* $s \longrightarrow^* s'$, *then* $[\![u]\!](s) \longrightarrow^* [\![u]\!](s')$.

Proof: Follows from the next Lemma. □

Lemma 2. *For any terms* $t_1, \ldots, t_n, t_{n+1}$ *of the right types, for any fresh variables* $x_1, \ldots, x_n, x_{n+1}$ *of the right types:*

$$\begin{aligned}&[\![u]\!](t_1 :: \ldots :: t_n :: t_{n+1})\\ &= ([\![u]\!](x_1 :: \ldots :: x_n :: x_{n+1}))[t_1/x_1, \ldots, t_n/x_n, t_{n+1}/x_{n+1}]\end{aligned}$$

where substitution is extended componentwise when u is a stack.

Proof: By structural induction on u.

If $u = v[w]$, then $[\![u]\!](t_1 :: \ldots :: t_n :: t_{n+1}) = [\![v]\!](t'_1 :: \ldots :: t'_{n'} :: t'_{n'+1})$, where $t'_1 :: \ldots :: t'_{n'} :: t'_{n'+1} = [\![w]\!](t_1 :: \ldots :: t_n :: t_{n+1})$. By induction hypothesis, $t'_1 :: \ldots :: t'_{n'} :: t'_{n'+1} = [\![w]\!](x_1 :: \ldots :: x_n :: x_{n+1})[t_1/x_1, \ldots, t_n/x_n, t_{n+1}/x_{n+1}]$. Let: (1) $t''_1 :: \ldots :: t''_{n'} :: t''_{n'+1}$ be $[\![w]\!](x_1 :: \ldots :: x_n :: x_{n+1})$, then for each i', $1 \leq i' \leq n'+1$: (2) $t'_{i'} = t''_{i'}[t_1/x_1, \ldots, t_n/x_n]$. Then:

$$\begin{aligned}&[\![u]\!](t_1 :: \ldots :: t_n :: t_{n+1})\\
&= [\![v]\!](t'_1 :: \ldots :: t'_{n'} :: t'_{n'+1})\\
&= [\![v]\!](x'_1 :: \ldots :: x'_{n'} :: x'_{n'+1})[t'_1/x'_1, \ldots, t'_{n'}/x'_{n'}, t'_{n'+1}/x'_{n'+1}]\\
&\quad \text{(by induction hypothesis again)}\\
&= [\![v]\!](x'_1 :: \ldots :: x'_{n'} :: x'_{n'+1})\\
&\quad [t''_1[t_1/x_1, \ldots, t_n/x_n, t_{n+1}/x_{n+1}]/x'_1, \ldots,\\
&\quad t''_{n'+1}[t_1/x_1, \ldots, t_n/x_n, t_{n+1}/x_{n+1}]/x'_{n'}] \quad \text{(by (2))}\\
&= [\![v]\!](x'_1 :: \ldots :: x'_{n'} :: x'_{n'+1})[t''_1/x'_1, \ldots, t''_{n'+1}/x'_{n'+1}]\\
&\quad [t_1/x_1, \ldots, t_n/x_n, t_{n+1}/x_{n+1}]\\
&= [\![v]\!](t''_1 :: \ldots :: t''_{n'} :: t''_{n'+1})[t_1/x_1, \ldots, t_n/x_n, t_{n+1}/x_{n+1}]\\
&\quad \text{(by induction hypothesis again)}\\
&= [\![u]\!](x_1 :: \ldots :: x_n :: x_{n+1})[t_1/x_1, \ldots, t_n/x_n, t_{n+1}/x_{n+1}] \quad \text{(by (1))}\end{aligned}$$

If $u = v \circ w$, then the argument is identical; all other cases are trivial. □

Recall that a *context* C is any term with a distinguished occurrence $\_$, which we call the *hole*. For any term t, $C\{t\}$ denotes C with the hole replaced by t. (We use braces {} instead of the more conventional brackets [] to distinguish them from the $\_[\_]$ operator.) Similarly if t is itself a context, in which case we get a new context.

The interpretation is then also monotonic in the following sense:

Lemma 3. *If $u \succeq v$, then $\mathcal{C}\{u\} \succeq \mathcal{C}\{v\}$ for any context $\mathcal{C}$. If $u \approx v$, then $\mathcal{C}\{u\} \approx \mathcal{C}\{v\}$ for any context $\mathcal{C}$.*

Proof: The case of $\approx$ is trivial, because our definition of $[\![\_]\!]$ is compositional. That is, for any context $\mathcal{C}$, there is a functional $[\![\mathcal{C}]\!]$ such that, for every u, $[\![\mathcal{C}\{u\}]\!] = [\![\mathcal{C}]\!]([\![u]\!])$: this is an easy structural induction on $\mathcal{C}$.

We prove the first claim by structural induction on the context $\mathcal{C}$ as well. The base case, when $\mathcal{C}$ is the empty context $\_$, is clear. Otherwise, the induction case reduces to the elementary cases that whenever $u \succeq v$, then $f(\ldots, u, \ldots) \succeq f(\ldots, v, \ldots)$ for each function symbol f in the language of $\lambda\sigma$ and each argument position.

For example, if $f = \lambda$: $[\![\lambda u]\!](s) = \lambda z \cdot [\![u]\!](z :: s) \longrightarrow^* \lambda z \cdot [\![v]\!](z :: s)$ (since $u \succeq v$) $= [\![\lambda v]\!](s)$. Since s is arbitrary, $\lambda u \succeq \lambda v$.

The cases when f is the application symbol or the $\cdot$ pair operator (whatever the argument position), or the $\Uparrow$ lift operator are equally easy.

When f is the $\_[\_]$ operator, we have two cases. At argument position 1, we must show that $u \succeq v$ entails $u[w] \succeq v[w]$: indeed, $[\![u[w]]\!](s) = [\![u]\!]([\![w]\!](s)) \longrightarrow^* [\![v]\!]([\![w]\!](s))$ (by assumption) $= [\![v[w]]\!](s)$. At argument position 2, we must show that $u \succeq v$ entails $w[u] \succeq w[v]$; and indeed $[\![w[u]]\!](s) = [\![w]\!]([\![u]\!](s)) \longrightarrow^* [\![w]\!]([\![v]\!](s))$ (since $u \succeq v$ and by Lemma 1) $= [\![w[v]]\!](s)$. Similarly when f is $\circ$. □

The interpretation is not *strictly* monotonic, in that $u \succ v$ does not imply $\mathcal{C}\{u\} \succ \mathcal{C}\{v\}$, only $\mathcal{C}\{u\} \succeq \mathcal{C}\{v\}$: consider e.g. the context $\mathcal{C} = \uparrow \circ (\_ \cdot w)$ for any w. This is the only thing that prevents our technique from proving that the simply-typed $\lambda\sigma$-calculus normalizes strongly; such a difficulty was bound to happen, since it actually does *not* terminate [10, 11]. But we can still conclude when reduction is constrained to occur under those contexts $\mathcal{C}$ such that $u \succ v$ implies $\mathcal{C}\{u\} \succ \mathcal{C}\{v\}$:

Definition 1 *A context $\mathcal{C}$ is called* safe *if and only if $u \succ v$ implies $\mathcal{C}\{u\} \succ \mathcal{C}\{v\}$ for every terms u and v of the same type such that $\mathcal{C}\{u\}$ and $\mathcal{C}\{v\}$ are typable.*

We shall see in Section 5 that there are enough safe contexts for all typed $\lambda\sigma$-terms to be reduced to normal form, using reductions under safe contexts only. It will follow that all these terms are weakly normalizing.

Lemma 4. *For each rule $l \to r$ except (β) in Figure 3, $l \approx r$. For rule (β), $l \succ r$.*

Proof: We omit all type information for clarity, unless strictly necessary.

Rule (β):

$$[\![l]\!](s) = ([\![\lambda u]\!](s))([\![v]\!](s)) = (\lambda z \cdot [\![u]\!](z :: s))([\![v]\!](s))$$
$$\longrightarrow ([\![u]\!](z :: s))[[\![v]\!](s)/z] = [\![u]\!]([\![v]\!](s) :: s)$$

by Lemma 2, while $[\![r]\!](s) = [\![u]\!]([\![v \cdot id]\!](s)) = [\![u]\!]([\![v]\!](s) :: s)$.

The cases of rules $([id])$, $(\circ id)$ and $(id\circ)$ are obvious: $[\![l]\!](s) = [\![r]\!](s) = [\![u]\!](s)$ in all three cases.

Rule $([])$: $[\![l]\!](s) = [\![u[v]]\!]([\![w]\!](s)) = [\![u]\!]([\![v]\!]([\![w]\!](s))) = [\![u]\!]([\![v \circ w]\!](s)) = [\![u[v \circ w]]\!](s)$, and similarly for rule $(\circ)$.

Rule (1): $[\![l]\!](s) = [\![1]\!]([\![u \cdot v]\!](s)) = [\![1]\!]([\![u]\!](s) :: [\![v]\!](s)) = [\![u]\!](s) = [\![r]\!](s)$.

Rule $(\uparrow)$: $[\![l]\!](s) = [\![\uparrow]\!]([\![u \cdot v]\!](s)) = [\![\uparrow]\!]([\![u]\!](s) :: [\![v]\!](s)) = [\![v]\!](s) = [\![r]\!](s)$.

Rule $(\cdot)$: $[\![l]\!](s) = [\![u \cdot v]\!]([\![w]\!](s)) = [\![u]\!]([\![w]\!](s)) :: [\![v]\!]([\![w]\!](s)) = [\![u[w]]\!](s) :: [\![v \circ w]\!](s) = [\![(u[w]) \cdot (v \circ w)]\!](s) = [\![r]\!](s)$.

Rule (λ): $[\![l]\!](s) = [\![\lambda u]\!]([\![w]\!](s)) = \lambda z_\tau \cdot [\![u]\!](z :: [\![w]\!](s))$, while $[\![r]\!](s) = \lambda z_\tau \cdot [\![u[\Uparrow w]]\!](z :: s) = \lambda z_\tau \cdot [\![u]\!]([\![\Uparrow w]\!](z :: s)) = \lambda z_\tau \cdot [\![u]\!](z :: [\![w]\!](s))$.

Rule (app): similar argument as for rule $(\cdot)$.

Rule $(\eta \Uparrow)$: $[\![l]\!](t :: s) = t :: [\![w]\!](s)$, while $[\![r]\!](t :: s) = [\![1]\!](t :: s) :: [\![w \circ \uparrow]\!](t :: s) = t :: [\![w \circ \uparrow]\!](t :: s) = t :: [\![w]\!]([\![\uparrow]\!](t :: s)) = t :: [\![w]\!](s)$.

Rule $(\eta\cdot)$: $[\![l]\!](t :: s) = [\![1]\!](t :: s) :: [\![\uparrow]\!](t :: s) = t :: s = [\![r]\!](t :: s)$; and $t :: s$ is the most general form of argument to $[\![l]\!]$ by typing, so $l \approx r$.

Rule $(\eta \cdot \circ)$: $l = (1[u]) \cdot (\uparrow \circ u) \approx (1 \cdot \uparrow) \circ u$ (by case $([])$) $\approx id \circ u$ (by case $(\eta\cdot)$) $\approx u = r$ (by case $(id\circ)$). Observe that we have used Lemma 3 (the $\approx$ part) implicitly throughout. All the other rules are dealt with similarly:

Rule $(1 \Uparrow)$: $l = 1[\Uparrow u] \approx 1[1 \cdot (u \circ \uparrow)]$ (by $(\eta \Uparrow)$) $\approx 1 = r$ (by (1)).

Rule $(1 \Uparrow \circ)$: $l = 1[\Uparrow u \circ v] \approx 1[(1 \cdot (u \circ \uparrow)) \circ v]$ (by $(\eta \Uparrow)$) $\approx 1[(1[v]) \cdot ((u \circ \uparrow) \circ v)]$ (by $(\cdot)$) $\approx 1[v] = r$ (by (1)).

Rule $(\uparrow\Uparrow)$: $l = \uparrow \circ \Uparrow u \approx \uparrow \circ (1 \cdot (u \circ \uparrow))$ (by $(\eta \Uparrow)$) $\approx u \circ \uparrow = r$ (by $(\uparrow)$).

Rule $(\uparrow\Uparrow \circ)$: $l = \uparrow \circ (\Uparrow u \circ v) \approx \uparrow \circ ((1 \cdot (u \circ \uparrow)) \circ v)$ (by $(\eta \Uparrow)$) $\approx \uparrow \circ ((1[v]) \cdot ((u \circ \uparrow) \circ v))$ (by $(\cdot)$) $\approx (u \circ \uparrow) \circ v$ (by $(\uparrow)$) $\approx u \circ (\uparrow \circ v) = r$ (by $(\circ)$).

Rule $(\Uparrow\Uparrow)$: $l = \Uparrow u \circ \Uparrow v \approx (1 \cdot (u \circ \uparrow)) \circ \Uparrow v$ (by $(\eta \Uparrow)$) $\approx (1[\Uparrow v]) \cdot ((u \circ \uparrow) \circ \Uparrow v)$ (by $(\cdot)$) $\approx 1 \cdot ((u \circ \uparrow) \circ \Uparrow v)$ (by $(1 \Uparrow)$) $\approx 1 \cdot (u \circ (\uparrow \circ \Uparrow v))$ (by $(\circ)$) $\approx 1 \cdot (u \circ (v \circ \uparrow))$ (by $(\uparrow\Uparrow)$) $\approx 1 \cdot ((u \circ v) \circ \uparrow)$ (by $(\circ)$ used in the opposite direction) $\approx \Uparrow (u \circ v) = r$ (by $(\eta \Uparrow)$ used in the opposite direction).

Rule $(\Uparrow\Uparrow \circ)$: $l = \Uparrow u \circ (\Uparrow v \circ w) \approx (\Uparrow u \circ \Uparrow v) \circ w$ (by $(\circ)$ used in the opposite direction) $\approx \Uparrow (u \circ v) \circ w = r$ (by $(\Uparrow\Uparrow)$).

Rule $(\Uparrow \cdot)$: $l = \Uparrow u \circ (v \cdot w) \approx (1 \cdot (u \circ \uparrow)) \circ (v \cdot w)$ (by $(\eta \Uparrow)$) $\approx (1[v \cdot w]) \cdot ((u \circ \uparrow) \circ (v \cdot w))$ (by $(\cdot)$) $\approx v \cdot ((u \circ \uparrow) \circ (v \cdot w))$ (by (1)) $\approx v \cdot (u \circ (\uparrow \circ (v \cdot w)))$ (by $(\circ)$) $\approx v \cdot (u \circ w) = r$ (by $(\uparrow)$).

Rule $(\Uparrow id)$: $l = \Uparrow id \approx 1 \cdot (id \circ \uparrow)$ (by $(\eta \Uparrow)$) $\approx 1 \cdot \uparrow$ (by $(id\circ)$) $\approx id = r$ (by $(\eta\cdot)$). □

Theorem 1 *Every reduction in the typed $\lambda\sigma$-calculus, where every contracted (β)-redex occurs under a safe context, is finite.*

Proof: Any step in such a reduction is either a (β)-contraction $\mathcal{C}\{(\lambda u)v\} \longrightarrow \mathcal{C}\{u[v \cdot id]\}$, then $\mathcal{C}\{(\lambda u)v\} \succ \mathcal{C}\{u[v \cdot id]\}$ by Lemma 4 and the fact that $\mathcal{C}$ is safe; or a σ-contraction $u \longrightarrow_\sigma v$, where $u \approx v$ by Lemma 4 and Lemma 3. Therefore each rewrite step is strictly decreasing in the lexicographic product of $\succ$ and $\longrightarrow_\sigma^+$, which is well-founded since the typed λ-calculus terminates (for $\succ$) and σ terminates (see Appendix A). □

5 Some Safe Contexts

It remains to produce some non-trivial safe contexts:

Definition 2 *Let the* syntactically safe contexts *be defined as those in* $\mathcal{S}_T \cup \mathcal{S}_S$*, where:*

$$\begin{aligned}
\mathcal{S}_T &::= _ \mid \lambda\mathcal{S}_T \mid \mathcal{S}_T T \mid T\mathcal{S}_T \mid \mathcal{S}_T[S] \mid \mathcal{V}_T[\mathcal{S}_S] \mid 1[\mathcal{S}'_S] \\
\mathcal{S}_S &::= \mathcal{S}'_S \mid \mathcal{S}_T \cdot S \mid T \cdot \mathcal{S}_S \mid \Uparrow \mathcal{S}_S \mid \Uparrow S \circ \mathcal{S}'_S \mid \Uparrow S \circ (\mathcal{S}_T \cdot S) \mid \mathcal{S}_S \circ S \\
\mathcal{S}'_S &::= \mathcal{V}_S \circ \mathcal{S}_S \mid \uparrow \circ \mathcal{S}'_S \mid \mathcal{S}'_S \circ S
\end{aligned}$$

Before we show Lemma 6, we need the following technical lemma. Let tl be defined by $tl(t :: s) = s$, and let tl^n be defined by: $tl^0(s) = s$, $tl^{n+1} = tl \circ tl^n$.

Lemma 5. *For every context C' in $\mathcal{S}'_S$, there is a stack variable X, a proper subcontext C of C' in $\mathcal{S}_S$ and an integer $m \in \mathbb{N}$ such that, for every term u such that $C'\{u\}$ is well-typed, for every s' of the right type, for some s, $[\![C'\{u\}]\!](s') = tl^m([\![X]\!]([\![C\{u\}]\!](s)))$.*

Proof: By structural induction on C'. This is obvious if C' has the form $X \circ C$, with $C \in \mathcal{S}_S$: $m = 0$ and $s = s'$.

If $C' = \uparrow \circ C''$ with $C'' \in \mathcal{S}'_S$, then for every u such that $C'\{u\}$ is well-typed, in particular $C''\{u\}$ is well-typed, so by induction hypothesis $[\![C''\{u\}]\!](s') = tl^m([\![X]\!]([\![C\{u\}]\!](s)))$ for some $m \geq 0$ and some s. Then $[\![C'\{u\}]\!](s') = [\![\uparrow]\!]([\![C''\{u\}]\!](s')) = tl([\![C''\{u\}]\!](s')) = tl^{m+1}([\![X]\!]([\![C\{u\}]\!](s)))$.

If $C' = C'' \circ w$, where $C'' \in \mathcal{S}'_S$, then for every u such that $C'\{u\}$ is well-typed, in particular $C''\{u\}$ is well-typed, so by induction hypothesis, for every s'_1 of the right type, $[\![C''\{u\}]\!](s'_1) = tl^m([\![X]\!]([\![C\{u\}]\!](s_1)))$ for some $m \geq 0$ and some s_1. Then $[\![C'\{u\}]\!](s') = [\![C''\{u\}]\!]([\![w]\!](s'))$; letting s'_1 be $[\![w]\!](s')$, $[\![C'\{u\}]\!](s') = [\![C''\{u\}]\!](s'_1) = tl^m([\![X]\!]([\![C\{u\}]\!](s_1)))$. □

Lemma 6. *Every syntactically safe context is safe.*

Proof: We have to show that if $u \succ v$, then $C\{u\} \succ C\{v\}$ for any syntactically safe context C. This is by structural induction on C, using Definition 2. The base case, when C is the empty context $\_$, is clear. Otherwise:

If $C = \lambda C_1$, where $C_1 \in \mathcal{S}_T$, then $[\![C\{u\}]\!](s) = \lambda z \cdot [\![C_1\{u\}]\!](z :: s) \longrightarrow^+ \lambda z \cdot [\![C_1\{v\}]\!](z :: s) = [\![C\{v\}]\!](s)$ by induction hypothesis. Similarly when $C = C_1 w$ or $C = wC_1$, or $C = C_1 \cdot w$ for some term w and some $C_1 \in \mathcal{S}_T$, or $C = \Uparrow C_1$ or $C = w \cdot C_1$ for some term w and some $C_1 \in \mathcal{S}_S$.

If $C = C_1[w]$ for some $C_1 \in \mathcal{S}_T$ and some stack w, then $[\![C\{u\}]\!](s) = [\![C_1\{u\}]\!]([\![w]\!](s)) \longrightarrow^+ [\![C_1\{v\}]\!]([\![w]\!](s)) = [\![C\{v\}]\!](s)$ by induction hypothesis. Similarly when $C = C_1 \circ w$ for some C_1 in $\mathcal{S}_S$ and some stack w.

If $C = x[C_1]$ where x is a term variable and $C_1 \in \mathcal{S}_S$, then $[\![C\{u\}]\!](s) = \hat{x} t_1 \ldots t_n t_{n+1}$ where $t_1 :: \ldots :: t_n :: t_{n+1} = [\![C_1\{u\}]\!](s) \longrightarrow^+ [\![C_1\{v\}]\!](s)$ by induction hypothesis. Let $(t'_1, \ldots, t'_n, t'_{n+1})$ be $[\![C_1\{v\}]\!](s)$: this means that $t_i \longrightarrow^* t'_i$ for every i, $1 \leq i \leq n+1$, and that $t_i \longrightarrow^+ t'_i$ for some i. So $\hat{x} t_1 \ldots t_n t_{n+1} \longrightarrow^+ \hat{x} t'_1 \ldots t'_n t'_{n+1} = [\![C\{v\}]\!](s)$.

If $C = \Uparrow w_1 \circ (C_1 \cdot w_2)$ with $C_1 \in \mathcal{S}_T$ and where w_1 and w_2 are stacks, then $[\![C\{u\}]\!](s) = [\![\Uparrow w_1]\!]([\![C_1\{u\} \cdot w_2]\!](s)) = [\![\Uparrow w_1]\!]([\![C_1\{u\}]\!](s) :: [\![w_2]\!](s)) = [\![C_1\{u\}]\!](s) :: [\![w_1]\!]([\![w_2]\!](s)) \longrightarrow^+ [\![C_1\{v\}]\!](s) :: [\![w_1]\!]([\![w_2]\!](s))$ (by induction hypothesis) $= [\![C\{v\}]\!](s)$.

It remains to deal with the cases when C is in $\mathcal{S}'_S$, and when C is of the form $1[C']$ or $\Uparrow w \circ C'$ with $C' \in \mathcal{S}'_S$.

Consider first the case where C is some context C' in $\mathcal{S}'_S$. By Lemma 5, there is a stack variable X, a proper subcontext C_1 in $\mathcal{S}_S$ and an integer $m \geq 0$ such that for every u of the right type, for every s' of the right type, there is a λ-term s such that $[\![C'\{u\}]\!](s') = tl^m([\![X]\!]([\![C_1\{u\}]\!](s)))$. Let X be $X_{\Gamma \vdash \tau_1, \ldots, \tau_p}$, where by typing $p \geq m$. Let also $t_1 :: \ldots :: t_n :: t_{n+1}$ denote $[\![C_1\{u\}]\!](s)$, and $t'_1 :: \ldots :: t'_n :: t'_{n+1}$ denote $[\![C_1\{v\}]\!](s)$. Then:

$[\![C'\{u\}]\!](s')$
$= tl^m((\hat{X}_1 t_1 \ldots t_n t_{n+1}) :: \ldots :: (\hat{X}_m t_1 \ldots t_n t_{n+1})$
$\quad :: (\hat{X}_{m+1} t_1 \ldots t_n t_{n+1}) :: \ldots :: (\hat{X}_{p+1} t_1 \ldots t_n t_{n+1}))$
$= (\hat{X}_{m+1} t_1 \ldots t_n t_{n+1}) :: \ldots :: (\hat{X}_{p+1} t_1 \ldots t_n t_{n+1})$
$\longrightarrow^+ (\hat{X}_{m+1} t'_1 \ldots t'_n t'_{n+1}) :: \ldots :: (\hat{X}_{p+1} t'_1 \ldots t'_n t'_{n+1})$ (by induction hypothesis)
(This is where we need the extra $n+1$st argument of type $\top$: otherwise, in the case where $n = 0$, $\hat{X}_{m+1}, \ldots, \hat{X}_{p+1}$ would take no argument and the line above would be an equality, not a reduction.)
$= tl^m((\hat{X}_1 t'_1 \ldots t'_n t'_{n+1}) :: \ldots :: (\hat{X}_m t'_1 \ldots t'_n t'_{n+1})$
$\quad :: (\hat{X}_{m+1} t'_1 \ldots t'_n t'_{n+1}) :: \ldots :: (\hat{X}_{p+1} t'_1 \ldots t'_n t'_{n+1}))$
$= [\![C'\{v\}]\!](s')$; so $C\{u\} \succ C\{v\}$.

If $C = 1[C']$, then taking the same notation as above:

$[\![C\{u\}]\!](s') = \hat{X}_{m+1} t_1 \ldots t_n t_{n+1}$
$\longrightarrow^+ \hat{X}_{m+1} t'_1 \ldots t'_n t'_{n+1}$ (by induction hypothesis; $p > m$ because of typing)
$= [\![C\{v\}]\!](s')$; so again $C\{u\} \succ C\{v\}$

And if $C = \Uparrow w \circ C'$, then:

$[\![C\{u\}]\!](s')$
$= (\hat{X}_{m+1} t_1 \ldots t_n t_{n+1}) :: [\![w]\!](tl([\![C'\{u\}]\!](s')))$
$\longrightarrow^* (\hat{X}_{m+1} t_1 \ldots t_n t_{n+1}) :: [\![w]\!](tl([\![C'\{v\}]\!](s')))$ (by Lemma 3)
$\longrightarrow^+ (\hat{X}_{m+1} t'_1 \ldots t'_n t'_{n+1}) :: [\![w]\!](tl([\![C'\{v\}]\!](s')))$ (by induction hypothesis)
$= [\![C\{v\}]\!](s')$; so $C\{u\} \succ C\{v\}$.

□

Lemma 7. *Let $C\{u\}$ be a σ-normal simply-typed term, where $u \in T$. Then C is a syntactically safe context.*

Proof: Recall that the σ-normal forms ([15], p.76) are all elements of the languages described by the following grammar:

$$\text{In } T\text{: } t ::= 1 \mid \lambda t \mid tt \mid \mathcal{V}_T \mid \mathcal{V}_T[s] \mid 1[s']$$
$$\text{In } S\text{: } s ::= s' \mid id \mid t \cdot s$$
$$s' ::= \uparrow \mid \mathcal{V}_S \mid \mathcal{V}_S \circ s \mid \uparrow \circ s'$$

(Although our σ is different from Ríos', it is easy to see that it has exactly the same normal forms.) Therefore the contexts having a hole accepting terms of T are elements of the languages defined by the grammar:

$$\begin{array}{ll}\text{In } T: & C_t ::= \_ \mid \lambda C_t \mid C_t t \mid t C_t \mid C_t[s] \mid \mathcal{V}_T[C_s] \mid 1[C'_s] \\ \text{In } S: & C_s ::= C'_s \mid C_t \cdot s \mid t \cdot C_s \\ & C'_s ::= \mathcal{V}_S \circ C_s \mid\uparrow \circ C'_s\end{array}$$

which clearly defines sublanguages of $\mathcal{S}_T$, $\mathcal{S}_S$ and $\mathcal{S}'_S$ respectively. □

Notice however that there are many syntactically safe contexts which cannot occur in σ-normal terms, for example $\_[w]$ for any stack w, or $(\_ \cdot w_1) \circ w_2$ for instance. In particular, the following Corollary is really only a special case of the fact that rewrites where we contract only (β)-redexes under syntactically safe redexes terminate (itself a special case of Theorem 1).

Corollary 2 *In the simply-typed $\lambda\sigma$-calculus, every σ-eager rewrite is finite. In particular, the simply-typed $\lambda\sigma$-calculus is weakly normalizing.*

Proof: In every σ-eager rewrite, every (β) is performed under a syntactically safe context by Lemma 7, which is safe by Lemma 6, so Theorem 1 applies. □

We can do the same thing with the $\lambda\sigma_\Uparrow$-calculus and $\sigma_\Uparrow$-eager rewrites:

Lemma 8. *Let $C\{u\}$ be a $\sigma_\Uparrow$-normal simply-typed term, where $u \in T$. Then C is a syntactically safe context.*

Proof: An easy argument, similar to those found in [15], shows that the $\sigma_\Uparrow$-normal forms are all in the languages described by the following grammar:

$$\begin{array}{ll}\text{In } T: & t ::= 1 \mid \lambda t \mid tt \mid \mathcal{V}_T \mid \mathcal{V}_T[s] \mid 1[s'] \\ \text{In } S: & s ::= s' \mid id \mid t \cdot s \mid\Uparrow s \mid\Uparrow s \circ s' \\ & s' ::=\uparrow\mid \mathcal{V}_S \mid \mathcal{V}_S \circ s \mid\uparrow \circ s'\end{array}$$

Indeed, we show by structural induction on the $\sigma_\Uparrow$-normal term u that: (1) if u is in T, then u is in language t, (2) if u is a stack, then u is in language s, (3) if u is a stack and $1[u]$ is $\sigma_\Uparrow$-normal, then u is in language s', (4) if u is a stack and $\uparrow \circ u$ is $\sigma_\Uparrow$-normal, then u is in language s', and (5) if u is a stack and $\Uparrow v \circ u$ is $\sigma_\Uparrow$-normal, then u is in language s'.

First, observe that (2) implies (3): since $1[u]$ is $\sigma_\Uparrow$-normal, u cannot be id (by rule $([id])$), a cons $v \cdot w$ (rule (1) would be applicable) or a lift $\Uparrow v$ (rule $(1 \Uparrow)$ would be applicable), or of the form $\Uparrow v \circ w$ (rule $(1 \Uparrow \circ)$ would be applicable).

Similarly, (2) implies (4), because of rules $(\circ id)$, $(\uparrow)$, $(\uparrow\uparrow)$ and $(\uparrow\Uparrow \circ)$. And (2) implies (5) because of rules $(\circ id)$, $(\Uparrow \cdot)$, $(\Uparrow\Uparrow)$ and $(\Uparrow\Uparrow \circ)$.

We now show (2). Let u be a $\sigma_\Uparrow$-normal stack. If u is in $\mathcal{V}_S$ or is $\uparrow$, then u is clearly in s', hence in s. If $u = id$ or if u is a cons $v \cdot w$ or a lift $\Uparrow v$, then u is also in s. Finally, if u is a composition $v \circ w$, then in particular v is in s; but v cannot be id (rule $(id\circ)$ would apply), or a cons $v_1 \cdot v_2$ (rule $(\cdot)$ would apply), or a composition $v_1 \circ v_2$ (rule $(\circ)$ would apply); so v must be of the form $\Uparrow v_1$ (then

u has the form $\Uparrow v_1 \circ w$ with $v_1 \in s$ and $w \in s$ by induction hypothesis; since (2) implies (5), w is actually in s', so u is in s), or $v = \uparrow$ (then $u = \uparrow \circ w$, where $w \in s$ by induction hypothesis; since (2) implies (4), w is actually in s', so u is in s', hence in s), or v is a variable X in $\mathcal{V}_S$ (then $u = X \circ w$ with $w \in s$ by induction hypothesis, so u is in s', hence in s).

We now show (1). Let u be a $\sigma_{\Uparrow}$-normal term in T. If u is a variable in $\mathcal{V}_T$, an abstraction λv, an application vw or 1, then u is in t. Finally, if u is of the form $v[w]$, then v must be a variable in $\mathcal{V}_T$ or be equal to 1: the other cases would be reducible by rules (λ), (*app*) or ([]). Moreover, by induction hypothesis w is in s. If v is a variable x in $\mathcal{V}_T$, then $u = x[w]$ is in t. If $v = 1$, then $u = 1[w]$ where w is in s, and since (2) implies (3), w is actually in s'; so u is in t again.

It follows that the contexts having a hole accepting terms in T are in the languages defined by the grammar:

$$\begin{array}{ll} \text{In } T\text{:} & C_t ::= \_ \mid \lambda C_t \mid C_t t \mid t C_t \mid C_t[s] \mid \mathcal{V}_T[C_s] \mid 1[C'_s] \\ \text{In } S\text{:} & C_s ::= C'_s \mid C_t \cdot s \mid t \cdot C_s \mid \Uparrow C_s \mid \Uparrow C_s \circ s' \mid \Uparrow s \circ C'_s \\ & C'_s ::= \mathcal{V}_S \circ C_s \mid \uparrow \circ C'_s \end{array}$$

and C_t, C_s, C'_s are clearly sublanguages of $\mathcal{S}_T$, $\mathcal{S}_S$ and $\mathcal{S}'_S$ respectively. □

Corollary 3 *In the simply-typed $\lambda\sigma_{\Uparrow}$-calculus, every $\sigma_{\Uparrow}$-eager rewrite is finite. In particular, the simply-typed $\lambda\sigma_{\Uparrow}$-calculus is weakly normalizing.*

Proof: In every $\sigma_{\Uparrow}$-eager rewrite, every (β) is performed under a syntactically safe context by Lemma 8, which is safe by Lemma 6, so Theorem 1 applies. □

6 The $\lambda\tau$-Calculus

Our technique adapts to other λ-calculi with explicit substitutions, for instance to Ríos' *$\lambda\tau$-calculus* [15], a left-linear alternative to $\lambda\sigma$. Its language (extended with term and stack variables) is the same as for $\lambda\sigma$, except that the binary operator $\cdot$ is replaced by a postfix unary operator /:

$$\begin{array}{l} T ::= \mathcal{V}_T \mid \lambda T \mid TT \mid T[S] \mid 1 \\ S ::= \mathcal{V}_S \mid S \circ S \mid id \mid T/ \mid \uparrow \mid \Uparrow S \end{array}$$

Intuitively, $u/$ denotes $u \cdot id$. The (untyped) reduction rules are given in Figure 6. We call τ the set of all rules in $\lambda\tau$ except (β_τ).

The typing rules are as for the $\lambda\sigma$-calculus of Section 2, except that rule $(, I)$ is replaced by:

$$\frac{u : \Gamma \vdash \tau}{u/ : \Gamma \vdash \tau, \Gamma}\,(, I/)$$

Notice that the rules of the $\lambda\tau$-calculus form essentially a subset of those of the $\lambda\sigma$-calculus, except for three minor modifications (rules (β_τ), (1/) and ($\uparrow$ /) instead of (β), (1) and ($\uparrow$)) and a major one (rule (/), which cannot be simulated by any rule in σ). Again, we can get a calculus in Church style by annotating 1,

(β_τ)	$(\lambda u)v \to u[v/]$		
$([id])$	$u[id] \to u$		
$(\circ id)$	$u \circ id \to u$		
$(id\circ)$	$id \circ u \to u$	$(1\Uparrow)$	$1[\Uparrow u] \to 1$
$([])$	$(u[v])[w] \to u[v \circ w]$	$(1\Uparrow\circ)$	$1[\Uparrow u \circ v] \to 1[v]$
$(\circ)$	$(u \circ v) \circ w \to u \circ (v \circ w)$	$(\uparrow\Uparrow)$	$\uparrow \circ \Uparrow u \to u \circ \uparrow$
$(1/)$	$1[u/] \to u$	$(\uparrow\Uparrow\circ)$	$\uparrow \circ (\Uparrow u \circ v) \to u \circ (\uparrow \circ v)$
$(\uparrow/)$	$\uparrow \circ u/ \to id$	$(\Uparrow\Uparrow)$	$\Uparrow u \circ \Uparrow v \to \Uparrow (u \circ v)$
$(/)$	$u/ \circ w \to \Uparrow w \circ (u[w])/$	$(\Uparrow\Uparrow\circ)$	$\Uparrow u \circ (\Uparrow v \circ w) \to \Uparrow (u \circ v) \circ w$
(λ)	$(\lambda u)[w] \to \lambda(u[\Uparrow w])$		
(app)	$(uv)[w] \to (u[w])(v[w])$	$(\Uparrow id)$	$\Uparrow id \to id$

Fig. 6. The reduction rules of the $\lambda\tau$-calculus

$\uparrow$, id and $\Uparrow u$ with types agreeing with the typing rules. We then need to adapt the rules of Figure 3 by letting:

$(\beta_\tau)\ (\lambda u)v \to u[v/]$	$(1/)\ 1[u/] \to u$
$(/)\ \ u/ \circ w \to (\Uparrow w)_{\tau,\Gamma\vdash\tau,\Delta} \circ (u[w])/$	$(\uparrow /)\ \uparrow [u/] \to id_{\Gamma\vdash\Gamma}$
where $u : \Delta \vdash \tau,\ w : \Gamma \vdash \Delta$	where $u : \Gamma \vdash \tau$

Contrarily to σ, τ does not terminate, even in the typed case [8] (see Appendix B). On the other hand, τ normalizes weakly, since leftmost-innermost reductions terminate [15]. So consider *weak-τ-eager rewrites*, defined as:

$$u \xrightarrow{\tau}{}^{*} u_1 \xrightarrow{(\beta)} u_1' \xrightarrow{\tau}{}^{*} u_2 \xrightarrow{(\beta)} u_2' \xrightarrow{\tau}{}^{*} \ldots \xrightarrow{\tau}{}^{*} u_k \xrightarrow{(\beta)} u_k' \xrightarrow{\tau}{}^{*} \ldots$$

where u_1, u_2, ..., u_k, ... are τ-normal. (We cannot guarantee that τ-eager rewrites have this form, unless we restrict ourselves to, say, leftmost-innermost τ-rewrites.)

Extend the interpretation of Figure 5 by: $[\![u/]\!](s) = [\![u]\!](s) :: s$. The new interpretation is monotonic just as the old was (see Lemma 1, Lemma 2, Lemma 3), and Lemma 4 still holds:

Lemma 9. *For each rule $l \to r$ except (β) in the simply-typed $\lambda\tau$-calculus, $l \approx r$. For rule (β), $l \succ r$.*

Proof: We only examine the new rules, and do as though $\cdot$ was still in the language. Notice that $[\![u/]\!](s) = [\![u \cdot id]\!](s)$, so the case of all old rules, plus (β_τ), $(1/)$, $(\uparrow /)$, is immediate. It remains to examine rule $(/)$, for which $l = u/ \circ w$ and $r = \Uparrow w \circ (u \circ w)/$. But then $[\![l]\!](s) = [\![u/]\!]([\![w]\!](s)) = [\![u]\!]([\![w]\!](s)) :: [\![w]\!](s)$, and $[\![r]\!](s) = [\![\Uparrow w \circ (u \circ w)/]\!](s) = [\![\Uparrow w]\!]([\![(u \circ w)/]\!](s)) = [\![\Uparrow w]\!]([\![u \circ w]\!](s) :: s) = [\![u \circ w]\!](s) :: [\![w]\!](s) = [\![u]\!]([\![w]\!](s)) :: [\![w]\!](s)$, and those two terms are equal. □

Because $u/$ works essentially like an abbreviation of $u \cdot id$, as far as $[\![\_]\!]$ is concerned, it is easy to see that we can redefine the syntactically safe contexts in $\lambda\tau$

as those in $\mathcal{S}_T \cup \mathcal{S}_S$, where:

$$\begin{aligned}
\mathcal{S}_T &::= _ \mid \lambda\mathcal{S}_T \mid \mathcal{S}_T T \mid T\mathcal{S}_T \mid \mathcal{S}_T[S] \mid \mathcal{V}_T[\mathcal{S}_S] \mid 1[\mathcal{S}'_S] \\
\mathcal{S}_S &::= \mathcal{S}'_S \mid \mathcal{S}_T/ \mid \Uparrow \mathcal{S}_S \mid \Uparrow S \circ \mathcal{S}'_S \mid \Uparrow S \circ \mathcal{C}_T/ \mid \mathcal{S}_S \circ S \\
\mathcal{S}'_S &::= \mathcal{V}_S \circ \mathcal{S}_S \mid \uparrow \circ \mathcal{S}'_S \mid \mathcal{S}'_S \circ S
\end{aligned}$$

and we immediately get the analogue of Lemma 6: every syntactically safe context is safe. Moreover, the τ-normal forms are described by the grammar:

$$\begin{aligned}
\text{In } T\text{:}\quad t &::= 1 \mid \lambda t \mid tt \mid \mathcal{V}_T \mid \mathcal{V}_T[s] \mid 1[s'] \\
\text{In } S\text{:}\quad s &::= s'' \mid id \mid \Uparrow s \mid \Uparrow s \circ s'' \\
s' &::= \uparrow \mid \mathcal{V}_S \mid \mathcal{V}_S \circ s \mid \uparrow \circ s' \\
s'' &::= s' \mid t/
\end{aligned}$$

As in Lemma 8, indeed, s' is the class of τ-normal stacks w such that $1[w]$ is τ-normal, or equivalently such that $\uparrow \circ w$ is τ-normal, and s'' is that of τ-normal stacks w such that $\Uparrow u \circ w$ is τ-normal for some u. Every context around a term of sort T is then of the form:

$$\begin{aligned}
\text{In } T\text{:}\quad C_t &::= _ \mid \lambda C_t \mid C_t t \mid t C_t \mid C_t[s] \mid \mathcal{V}_T[C_s] \mid 1[C'_s] \\
\text{In } S\text{:}\quad C_s &::= C''_s \mid \Uparrow C_s \mid \Uparrow C_s \circ s'' \mid \Uparrow s \circ C''_s \\
C'_s &::= \mathcal{V}_S \circ C_s \mid \uparrow \circ C'_s \\
C''_s &::= C'_s \mid C_t/
\end{aligned}$$

and C_t, C_s, C'_s are clearly sublanguages of $\mathcal{S}_T$, $\mathcal{S}_S$, $\mathcal{S}_{S'}$ respectively. It follows:

Corollary 4 *In the simply-typed $\lambda\tau$-calculus, every weak-τ-eager rewrite is finite. In particular, the simply-typed $\lambda\tau$-calculus is weakly normalizing.*

7 Second-Order Types

Our translation technique is not limited to simple type systems either. We offer an illustration —but not full proofs, due to space considerations— on a variant of Girard's system F_2 (see [5]). System F presents a problem in that the non-left-linear rule $(\eta \cdot \circ)$ breaks subject reduction, and similarly in dependent type systems [13], so we use a variant $\lambda\sigma^\forall$ of F_2 simply to illustrate the technique in a setting where no such problem arises. Be aware that we *don't* use the more complicated second-order system of [1].

Formulas of $\lambda\sigma^\forall$ are now either atoms α, β, ..., (and there are infinitely many of them) or implications $\tau_1 \to \tau_2$, or universal quantifications $\forall\alpha \cdot \tau$. Term and stack types are then augmented accordingly. Correspondingly, we add new terms $\Lambda\alpha \cdot u$ (type abstraction) and $u\tau$ (type application), so that:

$$\begin{aligned}
T^\forall &::= \mathcal{V}_T \mid \lambda T^\forall \mid T^\forall T^\forall \mid T^\forall[S^\forall] \mid 1 \mid \Lambda\alpha \cdot T^\forall \mid T^\forall \tau \\
S^\forall &::= \mathcal{V}_S \mid S^\forall \circ S^\forall \mid id \mid T^\forall \cdot S^\forall \mid \uparrow \mid \Uparrow S^\forall
\end{aligned}$$

We consider two α-equivalent terms as equal, where α-equivalence is the smallest congruence such that $\Lambda\alpha\cdot u = \Lambda\beta\cdot(u[\beta/\alpha])$, where $s[\tau'/\alpha]$ denotes the substitution of τ' for α in s. We then add the following typing rules to those of Figure 2:

$$\frac{u : \Gamma \vdash \tau \qquad \alpha \text{ not free in } \Gamma}{\Lambda\alpha \cdot u : \Gamma \vdash \forall\alpha \cdot \tau}(\forall I) \qquad \frac{u : \Gamma \vdash \forall\alpha \cdot \tau}{u\tau' : \Gamma \vdash \tau[\tau'/\alpha]}(\forall E)$$

And we add the following reduction rules to those of Figure 3:

(B) $(\Lambda\alpha \cdot u)\tau \to u[\tau/\alpha]$	
(Λ) $(\Lambda\alpha \cdot u)[v] \to \Lambda\alpha \cdot u[v]$ provided that α is not free in v	(App) $(u\tau)[v] \to (u[v])\tau$

These extra rules obey subject reduction; the only non-trivial case is for rule (Λ), where the derivation for the left-hand side is:

$$\dfrac{\dfrac{\dfrac{\vdots\,\pi_1}{u : \Gamma \vdash \tau}}{\Lambda\alpha \cdot u : \Gamma \vdash \forall\alpha \cdot \tau}(\forall I) \qquad v : \Delta \vdash \Gamma}{(\Lambda\alpha \cdot u)[v] : \Delta \vdash \forall\alpha \cdot \tau}(Cut_T)$$

A tedious but easy structural induction on derivations shows that, if $u : \Gamma \vdash \tau$, then $u\sigma : \Gamma\sigma \vdash \tau\sigma$ for any substitution σ of formulas for atoms (this uses α-conversion in the case of (Λ)). So there is a derivation π_1' of $u[\beta/\alpha] : \Gamma \vdash \tau[\beta/\alpha]$ for any atom β; choose β not free in Δ, and produce:

$$\dfrac{\dfrac{\dfrac{\vdots\,\pi_1'}{u[\beta/\alpha] : \Gamma \vdash \tau[\beta/\alpha]} \quad v : \Delta \vdash \Gamma}{u[\beta/\alpha][v] : \Delta \vdash \tau[\beta/\alpha]}(Cut_T)}{\Lambda\beta \cdot u[\beta/\alpha][v] : \Delta \vdash \forall\alpha \cdot \tau}(\forall I)$$

But this is really a derivation of the right-hand side $\Lambda\alpha\cdot u[v]$ since $\Lambda\beta\cdot u[\beta/\alpha][v] = \Lambda\beta \cdot u[v][\beta/\alpha]$ (because α is not free in v) $= \Lambda\alpha \cdot u[v]$ (by α-renaming).

Let $\sigma^\forall$ denote σ plus the rules (Λ) and (App), and let $\sigma^\forall_\Uparrow$ be $\sigma_\Uparrow$ plus (Λ) and (App). The argument of Appendix A extends to this case, so that $\sigma^\forall$ terminates (even in the untyped case): we just need to extend the interpretations to deal with the added rules, e.g. $[u\tau]_1 = [\Lambda\alpha \cdot u]_1 = [u]_1$, $[u\tau]_2 = [\Lambda\alpha \cdot u]_2 = [u]_2$, $[u\tau]_3 = [\Lambda\alpha \cdot u]_3 = [u]_3 + 1$.

We extend the translation of Figure 5 so that it now maps second-order $\lambda\sigma$-terms to λ-terms typed in Girard's F_2 (i.e., to $\lambda^\forall$-terms [5]). Recall that $\lambda^\forall$-terms are variables x_τ, constants c_τ, applications uv, abstractions $\lambda x_\tau \cdot u$, type applications $u\tau$ or type abstractions $\Lambda\alpha \cdot u$, where u, v are $\lambda^\forall$-terms and τ is any type. The $\lambda^\forall$-notion of reduction is defined by the two rules:

$$(\lambda x \cdot u)v \to u[v/x]$$
$$(\Lambda\alpha \cdot u)\tau \to u[\tau/\alpha]$$

and its typing rules are:

$$\frac{}{\Xi, x_\tau : \tau \vdash x : \tau} \qquad \frac{}{\Xi \vdash c_\tau : \tau}$$

$$\frac{\Xi, x_\tau : \tau \vdash u : \tau'}{\Xi \vdash \lambda x_\tau \cdot u : \tau \to \tau'} \qquad \frac{\Xi \vdash u : \tau \to \tau' \qquad \Xi \vdash v : \tau}{\Xi \vdash uv : \tau'}$$

$$\frac{\Xi \vdash u : \tau \qquad \alpha \text{ not free in } \Xi}{\Xi \vdash \Lambda\alpha \cdot u : \forall\alpha \cdot \tau} \qquad \frac{\Xi \vdash u : \forall\alpha \cdot \tau}{\Xi \vdash u\tau' : \tau[\tau'/\alpha]}$$

The typed $\lambda^\forall$-calculus then normalizes strongly (by standard reducibility arguments, see e.g. [5, 7]).

Our translation extends trivially to $\lambda\sigma^\forall$ by:

$$\begin{aligned} [\![\Lambda\alpha \cdot u]\!](s) &= \Lambda\alpha \cdot ([\![u]\!](s)) \\ [\![u\tau]\!](s) &= ([\![u]\!](s))\tau \end{aligned}$$

We then need to check:

Lemma 10. *If $u : \Gamma \vdash \tau$ is derivable in $\lambda\sigma^\forall$, where $\Gamma = \tau_1, \ldots, \tau_n, \cdot$ and $\Xi \vdash t_1 : \tau_1, \ldots, \Xi \vdash t_n : \tau_n, \Xi \vdash t_{n+1} : \top$ are derivable in $\lambda^\forall$, then $\Xi \vdash [\![u]\!](t_1 :: \ldots :: t_n :: t_{n+1}) : \tau$ is derivable in $\lambda^\forall$.*

Proof: By structural induction on u, we show this and simultaneously the similar result that if $u : \Gamma \vdash \tau'_1, \ldots, \tau'_{n'}, \cdot$, then $[\![u]\!](s)$, where $s = (t_1 :: \ldots :: t_n :: t_{n+1})$, is of the form $t'_1 :: \ldots :: t'_{n'} :: t'_{n'+1}$ with $\Xi \vdash t'_j : \tau'_j$ for every j, $1 \leq j \leq n+1$. The only non-trivial case is when u is of the form $\Lambda\alpha \cdot v$, where by α-renaming (of u) we may assume that α is not free in Ξ. Since $u : \Gamma \vdash \tau$ holds, we must have $\tau = \forall\alpha \cdot \tau'$ with $v : \Gamma \vdash \tau'$, so by induction hypothesis $\Xi \vdash [\![v]\!](s) : \tau'$, and because α is not free in Ξ, we can derive $\Xi \vdash [\![u]\!](s) : \forall\alpha \cdot \tau'$. This works because the translation maps α-equivalent terms in $\lambda\sigma^\forall$ to α-equivalent terms in $\lambda^\forall$, which is established by an easy structural induction on $\lambda\sigma^\forall$-terms. □

It is then easy to check that monotonicity still holds (Lemmas 1 and 3), and that the analogue of Lemma 4 still holds, i.e. for every rule $l \to r$ of $\lambda\sigma^\forall$, $l \approx r$ if this rule is neither (β) nor (B), and $l \succ r$ for (β) and (B), where $\succ$ and $\approx$ are defined from the notion of reduction of $\lambda^\forall$ as it was defined in terms of the simply-typed notion of reduction in Section 4. It follows:

Theorem 5 *Every reduction in the typed $\lambda\sigma^\forall$-calculus, where every contracted (β)-redex or (B)-redex occurs under a safe context, is finite.*

Now extend the syntactically safe contexts by: $\mathcal{S}_T ::= \ldots \mid \Lambda\alpha \cdot \mathcal{S}_T \mid \mathcal{S}_T\tau$. Every syntactically safe context in the extended sense is still safe, and $\sigma^\forall$-normal and $\sigma^\forall_\Uparrow$-normal typed terms of the form $C\{u\}$ with $u \in T$ are such that C is syntactically safe. (The normal forms in T are defined exactly as in Lemma 7, resp. Lemma 8, with two new alternatives: $\ldots \mid \Lambda\alpha \cdot t \mid t\tau$.) Then:

Corollary 6 *In the typed $\lambda\sigma^{\forall}$, resp. $\lambda\sigma^{\forall}_{\Uparrow}$-calculus, every $\sigma^{\forall}$-eager, resp.$\sigma^{\forall}_{\Uparrow}$-eager rewrite is finite. Therefore these calculi normalize weakly.*

Notice finally that the technique applies to all type systems such that (1) the corresponding fragment of $\lambda\sigma$ obeys subject reduction, (2) typed $\lambda\sigma$-terms translate to typed λ-terms in a corresponding type system, and (3) in the latter, typed λ-terms terminate. Although types of terms are unique in $\lambda\sigma$ and in $\lambda\sigma^{\forall}$, this is not in general needed for our method to work: just define an interpretation $[\![u]\!]_t$ indexed by the possible types t of its argument u. This is in particular necessary for variants of system F; we expect the method to work without effort —but (1) needs to be obeyed, which is not the case for $\lambda\sigma$.

Finally, the technique applies to other λ-calculi with explicit substitutions, although it seems too elementary to show that the typed $\lambda\zeta$ [12] and $\lambda\upsilon$ [9] calculi are *strongly* normalizing [3]. In particular, our technique, as it stands, always enforces that $u[v][w]$ and $u[v \circ w]$ have the same interpretation, and this prevents us from carrying the technique over to these calculi. We conjecture that this could be achieved by adapting the technique, and in particular the translation of terms of the form $u[v]$.

A Termination of σ

We use Zantema's distribution elimination technique [16] to show that σ terminates. (Refer to this paper for notations and concepts; our σ is slightly more complicated than the σ that Zantema considers, but the argument is similar.) We actually show that σ is totally terminating, i.e. that the reduction relation for σ is included in the strict part of a *total* well-founded strictly monotonic quasi-ordering on terms. Total termination implies *simple* termination, namely that σ plus all rules of the form $f(\ldots, u, \ldots) \to u$, for every function symbol f, terminates.

Now consider the following rewrite system σ', which is obtained from σ by replacing $u[v]$ by $u \circ v$, uv by $u \cdot v$, id by $1 \cdot \uparrow$, merging duplicate rules, eliminating rule $(\eta\cdot)$ and adding rule $(d \Uparrow)$:

$(d \Uparrow)$	$\Uparrow u \circ (v \cdot w) \to (\Uparrow u \circ v) \cdot (\Uparrow u \circ w)$	$(\eta \Uparrow)$	$\Uparrow w \to 1 \cdot (w \circ \uparrow)$
$(\circ id)$	$u \circ (1 \cdot \uparrow) \to u$	$(\eta \cdot \circ)$	$(1 \circ u) \cdot (\uparrow \circ u) \to u$
$(id \circ)$	$(1 \cdot \uparrow) \circ u \to u$	$(1 \Uparrow)$	$1 \circ \Uparrow u \to 1$
		$(1 \Uparrow \circ)$	$1 \circ (\Uparrow u \circ v) \to 1 \circ v$
$(\circ)$	$(u \circ v) \circ w \to u \circ (v \circ w)$	$(\uparrow\Uparrow)$	$\uparrow \circ \Uparrow u \to u \circ \uparrow$
(1)	$1 \circ (u \cdot v) \to u$	$(\uparrow\Uparrow \circ)$	$\uparrow \circ (\Uparrow u \circ v) \to u \circ (\uparrow \circ v)$
$(\uparrow)$	$\uparrow \circ (u \cdot v) \to v$	$(\Uparrow\Uparrow)$	$\Uparrow u \circ \Uparrow v \to \Uparrow (u \circ v)$
$(\cdot)$	$(u \cdot v) \circ w \to (u \circ w) \cdot (v \circ w)$	$(\Uparrow\Uparrow \circ)$	$\Uparrow u \circ (\Uparrow v \circ w) \to \Uparrow (u \circ v) \circ w$
(λ)	$(\lambda u) \circ w \to \lambda(u \circ \Uparrow w)$	$(\Uparrow \cdot)$	$\Uparrow u \circ (v \cdot w) \to v \cdot (u \circ w)$
		$(\Uparrow id)$	$\Uparrow (1 \cdot \uparrow) \to (1 \cdot \uparrow)$

If σ' is totally terminating, then σ is totally terminating as well. Let indeed $\geq$ be any total well-founded strictly monotonic quasi-ordering whose strict part extends the rewrite relation of σ'. This lifts to a total well-founded strictly monotonic quasi-ordering on $\lambda\sigma$-terms whose strict part extends all the rules in σ except $(\eta\cdot)$ (for which both sides are equal). Let $\geq'$ be such that $u \geq' v$ if and only if u has at least as many occurrences of $\cdot$ than v: the lexicographic product of $\geq$ and $\geq'$ is a total well-founded strictly monotonic quasi-ordering whose strict part extends the rewrite relation of σ.

Now call a rule *embedding* if and only if its right-hand side is homeomorphically embedded in its left-hand side (i.e., it can be simulated by a sequence of rewrite steps of the form $f(\ldots, u, \ldots) \to u$). The rules $(\circ id)$, $(id\circ)$, (1), $(\uparrow)$, $(\eta\cdot\circ)$, $(1\Uparrow)$, $(1\Uparrow\circ)$, $(\Uparrow id)$ are embedding. Since total termination implies simple termination, σ' is totally terminating if and only if σ' minus these rules is. Moreover, $(\Uparrow\cdot)$ can be simulated by $(d\Uparrow)$ plus embedding, so we can ignore the former for purposes of total termination. To sum up, σ' is totally terminating if and only if the following system σ'' is totally terminating:

$$
\begin{array}{llll}
(d\Uparrow) & \Uparrow u\circ(v\cdot w)\to(\Uparrow u\circ v)\cdot(\Uparrow u\circ w) & (\eta\Uparrow) & \Uparrow w\to 1\cdot(w\circ\uparrow) \\
(\circ) & (u\circ v)\circ w\to u\circ(v\circ w) & (\uparrow\Uparrow) & \uparrow\circ\Uparrow u\to u\circ\uparrow \\
 & & (\uparrow\Uparrow\circ) & \uparrow\circ(\Uparrow u\circ v)\to u\circ(\uparrow\circ v) \\
 & & (\Uparrow\Uparrow) & \Uparrow u\circ\Uparrow v\to\Uparrow(u\circ v) \\
(\cdot) & (u\cdot v)\circ w\to(u\circ w)\cdot(v\circ w) & (\Uparrow\Uparrow\circ) & \Uparrow u\circ(\Uparrow v\circ w)\to\Uparrow(u\circ v)\circ w \\
(\lambda) & (\lambda u)\circ w\to\lambda(u\circ\Uparrow w) & &
\end{array}
$$

Now, in σ'' the rules $(d\Uparrow)$ and $(\cdot)$ are *distribution rules* for $\cdot$, and no other rule features $\cdot$ on the left-hand side. Zantema's theorem [16] then states that the rewrite system σ''' obtained from σ'' by dropping these distribution rules and replacing each rule with some subterm $u\cdot v$ on the right-hand side by two rules, one with $u\cdot v$ replaced by u, the other with $u\cdot v$ replaced by v, is totally terminating if and only if σ'' is. Here is σ''':

$$
\begin{array}{llll}
(\eta\Uparrow_1) & \Uparrow w\to 1 & (\eta\Uparrow_2) & \Uparrow w\to w\circ\uparrow \\
(\circ) & (u\circ v)\circ w\to u\circ(v\circ w) & (\uparrow\Uparrow) & \uparrow\circ\Uparrow u\to u\circ\uparrow \\
(\uparrow\Uparrow\circ) & \uparrow\circ(\Uparrow u\circ v)\to u\circ(\uparrow\circ v) & (\Uparrow\Uparrow) & \Uparrow u\circ\Uparrow v\to\Uparrow(u\circ v) \\
(\Uparrow\Uparrow\circ) & \Uparrow u\circ(\Uparrow v\circ w)\to\Uparrow(u\circ v)\circ w & (\lambda) & (\lambda u)\circ w\to\lambda(u\circ\Uparrow w)
\end{array}
$$

We then use the following interpretations, essentially taken from [16, 6]:

$$
\begin{array}{lll}
[u\circ v]_1=[u]_1+[v]_1 & [u\circ v]_2=[u]_1([v]_1+1) & [u\circ v]_3=[u]_3([v]_3+1) \\
 & \qquad +[u]_2+[v]_2 & \\
[\Uparrow u]_1=[u]_1 & [\Uparrow u]_2=[u]_1+[u]_2 & [\Uparrow u]_3=3[u]_3 \\
[1]_1=[\uparrow]_1=0 & [1]_2=[\uparrow]_2=0 & [1]_3=[\uparrow]_3=1 \\
[\lambda u]_1=[u]_1+1 & [\lambda u]_2=[u]_2 & [\lambda u]_3=[u]_3
\end{array}
$$

Calculation then shows that for every rule $l\to r$ above but (λ), $[l]_2\geq[r]_2$ (equality in fact holds for all these rules but $(\eta\Uparrow_1)$, $(\circ)$, $(\uparrow\Uparrow\circ)$), and $[l]_3>[r]_3$ while for (λ) $[l]_2>[r]_2$. The lexicographic ordering on $u\mapsto([u]_2,[u]_3)$ is then a total well-founded strictly monotonic ordering, so σ is totally terminating.

B τ Does Not Terminate

Since [8] is not easily reached, here is a counterexample to the termination of τ, found independently: let u and v be any terms of respective types $\tau', \Gamma \vdash \tau$ and $\Gamma \vdash \tau'$, and let $v_0 = v$, $v_1 = u[v/]$ (of respective types $\Gamma \vdash \tau'$ and $\Gamma \vdash \tau$), and for every $n \geq 0$, $v_{n+2} = v_n[\uparrow \circ v_{n+1}/]$ (of type $\Gamma \vdash \tau'$ if n is even, $\Gamma \vdash \tau$ if n is odd). Then $\uparrow \circ(v_n/\circ(\uparrow \circ v_{n+1}/))$ (of type $\Gamma \vdash \Gamma$ for every n) rewrites in 4 steps to $\uparrow \circ(v_{n+1}/\circ(\uparrow \circ v_{n+2}/))$, leading to an infinite reduction. Indeed:

$$\begin{array}{rll}\uparrow \circ(v_n/\circ(\uparrow \circ v_{n+1}/)) & \longrightarrow \uparrow \circ(\Uparrow(\uparrow \circ v_{n+1}/)\circ v_n[\uparrow \circ v_{n+1}/]/) & \text{by } (/) \\ & \longrightarrow (\uparrow \circ v_{n+1}/)\circ(\uparrow \circ v_n[\uparrow \circ v_{n+1}/]/) & \text{by } (\uparrow\Uparrow\circ) \\ & \longrightarrow \uparrow \circ(v_{n+1}/\circ(\uparrow \circ v_n[\uparrow \circ v_{n+1}/]/)) & \text{by } (\circ) \\ & = \ \uparrow \circ(v_{n+1}/\circ(\uparrow \circ v_{n+2}/)) & \end{array}$$

References

1. M. Abadi, L. Cardelli, P.-L. Curien, and J.-J. Lévy. Explicit substitutions. In *17th PoPL*, pages 31–46, 1990.
2. D. Briaud. Higher-order unification as a typed narrowing. Technical Report 96-R-112, CRIN, 1996.
3. R. Di Cosmo and D. Kesner. Strong normalization of explicit substitutions via cut elimination in proof nets (extended abstract). In *12th LICS*, 1997.
4. G. Dowek, T. Hardin, and C. Kirchner. Higher-order unification via explicit substitutions (extended abstract). In *10th LICS*, pages 366–374, 1995.
5. J. H. Gallier. On Girard's "candidats de réductibilité". In P. Odifreddi, editor, *Logic and Computer Science*, volume 31 of *APIC Series*, pages 123–203. Academic Press, 1990.
6. T. Hardin and J.-J. Lévy. A confluent calculus of substitutions. In *France-Japan Artificial Intelligence and Computer Science Symposium*, 1989.
7. J.-L. Krivine. *Lambda-calcul, types et modèles.* Masson, 1992.
8. P. Lescanne. τ does not terminate. Working group of the PRC Math-Info "Mélanges de systèmes de réécriture algébrique et de systèmes logiques", 1996.
9. P. Lescanne and J. Rouyer-Degli. From $\lambda\sigma$ to λv: a journey through calculi of explicit substitutions. In *21st PoPL*, 1994.
10. P.-A. Melliès. Typed lambda-calculi with explicit substitutions may not terminate. In *CONFER workshop*, 1994.
11. P.-A. Melliès. Typed lambda-calculi with explicit substitutions may not terminate. In *2nd TLCA*, pages 328–334. Springer Verlag LNCS 902, 1995.
12. C. A. Muñoz Hurtado. Confluence and preservation of strong normalization in an explicit substitutions calculus. In *11th LICS*, 1996.
13. C. A. Muñoz Hurtado. Dependent types with explicit substitutions: A meta-theoretical development. In *TYPES'96*, 1997. This volume.
14. C. A. Muñoz Hurtado. Meta-theoretical properties of λ_ϕ: A left-linear variant of λ_σ. Technical Report RR-3107, Inria, 1997.
15. A. Ríos. *Contributions à l'étude des lambda-calculs avec substitutions explicites.* PhD thesis, École Normale Supérieure, 1993.
16. H. Zantema. Termination of term rewriting: Interpretation and type elimination. *J. Symbolic Computation*, 17:23–50, 1994.

Proof Style

John Harrison

University of Cambridge Computer Laboratory
New Museums Site, Pembroke Street
Cambridge CB2 3QG, England

Abstract. We are concerned with how computer theorem provers should expect users to communicate proofs to them. There are many stylistic choices that still allow the machine to generate a completely formal proof object. The most obvious choice is the amount of guidance required from the user, or from the machine perspective, the degree of automation provided. But another important consideration, which we consider particularly significant, is the bias towards a 'procedural' or 'declarative' proof style. We will explore this choice in depth, and discuss the strengths and weaknesses of declarative and procedural styles for proofs in pure mathematics and for verification applications. We conclude with a brief summary of our own experiments in trying to combine both approaches.

1 What is a proof?

The word 'proof' is used in several different ways, and it is worth making clear from the outset the way in which we employ the word. With mechanized reasoning in mind, a proof may be:

1. What is found in a mathematical textbook, typically a sketch given in a mixture of formal symbols and natural language, taking for granted certain knowledge on the part of the reader (Trybulec and Święczkowska 1992).
2. A script to be presented to a machine for checking. This might also be a sketch in some sense, but is itself written in a formal (or at least non-natural) language. It may even be a program telling the machine how to construct a formal proof (Constable, Knoblock, and Bates 1985).
3. A proof object in a particular formal system, e.g. one of the standard axiomatizations of first order set theory or intuitionistic type theory.
4. A 'canonical proof' used as a theoretical idea in the explication of the intuitionistic meaning of the logical connectives.

We will normally use 'proof' in the second sense, i.e. a proof is a formal script to be presented to a machine for checking. Our title should be understood in this sense: we will focus on the style of such a proof. A reasonable goal in choosing a style is that our 'type 2' proofs should be almost as easy to read and write as proofs of type 1, while allowing the machine to construct a proof of type 3 from them. The former objective is likely to be necessary if we are ever to entice a large body of pure mathematicians to use our proof assistants. The latter lends our proofs the reliability that a real programme of formalization demands.

While we want to make the gap between 1 and 2 small, it is not essential that it be made completely negligible. The success of TeX and LaTeX shows that mathematicians are prepared to learn to use tricky computer-based systems if they can see clear benefits, and perhaps, get a certain aesthetic or creative satisfaction. TeX and LaTeX turn out, after a modest investment of effort, to be cheaper and more efficient than the traditional reliance on specially skilled secretaries. It's doubtful whether mechanized reasoning will become, in the near future, the most efficient way to produce a proof, but it may turn out to be the most efficient way to produce a *correct* proof.

2 Classification of proof styles

We can classify proof styles according to several criteria.

1. The level of automation the style admits. Provers differ greatly in how much they can prove, and how much they will try to prove, without user intervention.
2. The degree of user control afforded. A high level of automation is often felt to be in conflict with controllability, but there is no reason why this should be so. The SAM project (Guard, Oglesby, Bennett, and Settle 1969) was one of the earliest attempts to combine automation and interaction judiciously.
3. The potential for extensibility, i.e. whether and to what extent ordinary users can modify the proof style to suite their particular needs.
4. The emphasis on a declarative style, where the user merely states the facts to be proved and some general information about the method of solution, or on a procedural style where the user instructs the machine more or less explicitly.
5. Proof direction. Some systems insist that proofs must proceed forward from premisses to conclusion. Others insist that on the contrary they must proceed by refinement, from the conclusion to the premisses. Still others allow the two styles to be intermixed, or even allow a proof to be attacked from different places in a more or less arbitrary order, while retaining a clear idea about when all the extant proof obligations have been satisfied.
6. Whether proofs are processed interactively or via a script submitted to a batch process. The pioneering proof checking systems such as AUTOMATH (de Bruijn 1970) and Mizar (Trybulec 1978) were all batch-oriented, whereas most recent systems support an interactive style of working. Partly this is a matter of general fashion in computing, but we believe there are a few objective qualities of batch mode that deserve consideration.

The divide between 'declarative' and 'procedural' in computer science is a traditional and long-established one, arguably traceable back to the contrast between Gödel's and Turing's approaches to computability (Robinson 1994). However it is also notoriously hard to make sharp. We will not attempt to do so in our context, but we think the division is useful and thought-provoking, even if understood in a fairly weak and impressionistic way. Prolog, for example, is usually considered a declarative language, but it does nevertheless give full control information. The only real difference is that the control information is implicit, or perhaps more honestly, less obvious to a human reader. By the way, TeX and LaTeX illustrate the distinction, with the latter being avowedly more declarative and less procedural.

In programming languages, there is a strong association between the phrases 'declarative' and 'high level'. Indeed, one might argue that a declarative style of proof, if it is to be successful, should feature a high level of automation. On this view, rather than the level of automation and the proof style being independent properties, automation is an essential 'enabling technology' for a good declarative style.

3 Some existing systems

Various positions on the automatic-manual and procedural-declarative axes are exemplified by some existing systems.

AUTOMATH (low automation, procedural)

AUTOMATH (de Bruijn 1970), perhaps the earliest 'proof checker', was used in some pioneering experiments by van Bentham Jutting (1977) in the formalization of mathematics. It provides low automation and the style of proof is procedural. The user does not have to provide a completely explicit formal proof, though the proof commands provided have limited power, and require the user to be fairly thorough.

Mizar (low automation, declarative)

Mizar (Trybulec 1978), of all present-day systems, has been used for the greatest amount of formalized mathematics. It provides a rather low degree of automation, and no user extensibility, but the automation has been chosen judiciously and supports a declarative proof style rather well. Proofs are structured according to a 'skeleton' which lays out the basic patterns of natural deduction steps. The intermediate parts are written in a linear sequence, indicating at all times from which hypotheses the current line follows, but giving no information about *how* it follows. Mizar is, in a sense, the only system supporting a proof style that is declarative and that really provides user control over the proof.

PVS (high automation, procedural)

PVS (Owre, Rushby, and Shankar 1992) is designed to provide cost-effective support for proofs in computer system verification. It is distinguished from its predecessor EHDM particularly in providing a high level of interactive control of the proof. At the same time, it provides a powerful suite of decision procedures, e.g. for linear arithmetic, which can make it easy to perform proofs in certain theories. The proof style is highly procedural, based on fairly high-level tactics for performing backward proof in sequent calculus.

NQTHM (high automation, declarative)

The NQTHM prover (Boyer and Moore 1979) represents an interesting extreme in two respects. First, it offers a high degree of automation, including powerful rewriting and linear arithmetic procedures together with the automation of induction proofs. It includes very few interactive features to guide the proof (the PC-NQTHM extension tries to remedy this problem). Many traditional provers for first order logic show similar characteristics in their respective domain.

However, the state of the art in automation falls well short (and will probably do so for the foreseeable future) of being able to prove many theorems of real mathematical substance without a great deal of help. As already stated, NQTHM offers no interactive features to provide user control. However it is possible to expand the knowledge base available to the prover by proving useful lemmas. In practice, then, one approaches a difficult theorem step by step via a series of carefully graded lemmas, each of which can be proved automatically given the previous lemmas.

Therefore NQTHM's proof style is almost exclusively declarative: one states what one wants proved, and the only procedural information about how to prove it consists in the series of hints given by the choice of previous lemmas, as well as some associated tags indicating how each one is to be used (e.g. as a rewrite, or an induction lemma). All the same, this proof style is only concerned with 'proof' in a fairly weak sense. Such a series of lemmas is unlike a conventional proof; perhaps it could be said to correspond to a textbook consisting largely of a series of graded exercises. (This would fit naturally with certain pedagogical approaches such as the Socratic or 'Moore' method, which emphasize student participation.)

LP (the middle way?)

The Larch Prover (Garland and Guttag 1991) occupies an interesting intermediate position. The level of automation provided is high in the area of equational reasoning (the system is descended from Reve, a pure term rewriting system), but low elsewhere. The proof style is mainly procedural, but in comparison with say HOL or PVS, contains some nods towards a declarative style. Proofs often proceed by explicitly quoting the current 'proof state' (i.e. the facts that have been established and any corresponding context), though these are usually interspersed with explicit proof methods. In fact it is possible for the proof method in a `prove` command to be omitted; Larch will then use one of the currently selected proof methods. However none of these methods are really as general as in Mizar; the only really powerful ones are concerned with equational reasoning, while, as with Mizar, there are no facilities for adding others.

4 Declarative and procedural proofs

To illustrate the distinction between declarative and procedural proofs, here are a couple of examples. Both are from HOL, but the first is done in a 'Mizar style' that we discuss later, and the second in a traditional procedural style using HOL tactics. The first proof is of the Knaster-Tarski fixpoint theorem that every monotone function on the complete lattice of subsets has a fixed point. The details of the syntax are not important for our present purposes, but let us note that /\ represents conjunction ('and') and ==> implication ('if ... then ...'), while ! is the universal quantifier ('for all') and ? the existential ('there exists').

```
!f. (!x y. x <= y /\ y <= x ==> (x = y)) /\
    (!x y z. x <= y /\ y <= z ==> x <= z) /\
    (!x y. x <= y ==> f x <= f y) /\
    (!X. ?s:A. (!x. x IN X ==> s <= x) /\
               (!s'. (!x. x IN X ==> s' <= x) ==> s' <= s))
    ==> ?x. f x = x
proof
  let f be A->A;
  assume antisymmetry: (!x y. x <= y /\ y <= x ==> (x = y)) by L;
    and transitivity: (!x y z. x <= y /\ y <= z ==> x <= z) by L;
    and monotonicity: (!x y. x <= y ==> f x <= f y) by L;
    and greatest_lower_bound:
      (!X. ?s:A. (!x. x IN X ==> s <= x) /\
                 (!s'. (!x. x IN X ==> s' <= x) ==> s' <= s));
  set Y_def: Y = {b | f b <= b};
  Y_thm: !b. b IN Y = f b <= b by Y_def,IN_ELIM_THM,BETA_THM;
  consider a such that
      glb: (!x. x IN Y ==> a <= x) /\
           (!a'. (!x. x IN Y ==> a' <= x) ==> a' <= a)
      by greatest_lower_bound;
  take a;
  now let b be A;
      assume b_in_Y: b IN Y;
      then L0: f b <= b by Y_thm;
      a <= b by b_in_Y, glb;
      so f a <= f b by monotonicity;
      hence f a <= b by L0, transitivity;
      end;
  so Part1: f(a) <= a by glb;
  so f(f(a)) <= f(a) by monotonicity;
  so f(a) IN Y by Y_thm;
  so a <= f(a) by glb;
  hence thesis by Part1, antisymmetry;
end
```

Observe that the proof is structured to look like a textbook proof. Even though certain lines do have a procedural reading (e.g. '`let f be A->A`' as 'introduce a universal quantifier'), this is nicely kept implicit. Moreover each of the main assertions is not tagged with any proof method, merely with the other assertions from which it is deemed to follow (e.g. 'by monotonicity'). Contrast the following proof, from the HOL real analysis library, that the composition of continuous functions is continuous:

```
let CONT_COMPOSE = prove
 ('!f g x. f contl x /\ g contl (f x) ==> (\x. g(f x)) contl x',
  REPEAT GEN_TAC THEN REWRITE_TAC[contl; LIM; REAL_SUB_RZERO] THEN
  BETA_TAC THEN DISCH_TAC THEN X_GEN_TAC 'e:real' THEN DISCH_TAC THEN
  FIRST_ASSUM(UNDISCH_TAC o assert is_conj o concl) THEN
  DISCH_THEN(CONJUNCTS_THEN MP_TAC) THEN
  DISCH_THEN(fun th -> FIRST_ASSUM(MP_TAC o MATCH_MP th)) THEN
  DISCH_THEN(X_CHOOSE_THEN 'd:real' STRIP_ASSUME_TAC) THEN
  DISCH_THEN(MP_TAC o SPEC 'd:real') THEN ASM_REWRITE_TAC[] THEN
  DISCH_THEN(X_CHOOSE_THEN 'c:real' STRIP_ASSUME_TAC) THEN
  EXISTS_TAC 'c:real' THEN ASM_REWRITE_TAC[] THEN
  X_GEN_TAC 'h:real' THEN DISCH_THEN(ANTE_RES_THEN MP_TAC) THEN
  ASM_CASES_TAC '&0 < abs(f(x + h) - f(x))' THENL
   [UNDISCH_TAC '&0 < abs(f(x + h) - f(x))' THEN
    DISCH_THEN(fun th -> DISCH_THEN(MP_TAC o CONJ th)) THEN
    DISCH_THEN(ANTE_RES_THEN MP_TAC) THEN REWRITE_TAC[REAL_SUB_ADD2];
    UNDISCH_TAC '~(&0 < abs(f(x + h) - f(x)))' THEN
    REWRITE_TAC[GSYM ABS_NZ; REAL_SUB_0] THEN DISCH_THEN SUBST1_TAC THEN
    ASM_REWRITE_TAC[REAL_SUB_REFL; ABS_0]]);;
```

Here almost all the steps are direct instructions to HOL as to how to proceed: repeatedly strip off universal quantifiers, rewrite with the following theorems, perform beta reduction, and so on. There is little declarative content.

5 Extensibility and full programmability

Present-day systems descended from LCF (Gordon, Milner, and Wadsworth 1979) attain an extreme of extensibility, in that a full Turing-complete programming language is available to write special proof procedures. The lack of such a language is felt to be a significant defect by many users of PVS, for example. Even this level of power is felt by some to be insufficient. Pollack (1995) has suggested using, instead of a conventional programming language like ML, a dependently typed metalanguage of total functions. This allows one to ensure that tactics always terminate and, in some sense, produce a correct result, merely by virtue of their type.

The use of a full programming language brings the 'Java problem'[1] — one wants programming power without allowing the user to do anything dangerous, in this case produce false 'theorems'. The LCF approach (Gordon, Milner, and

[1] Many standard browsers for the World Wide Web allow programs written in Java to be downloaded automatically and executed on the user's machine, e.g. to perform sophisticated animation.

Wadsworth 1979) solves this difficulty by the use of an abstract datatype of theorems. However it brings other problems. The availability of a Turing-complete language requires, in the context of proof, many activities normally associated with programming. For example, designing an interface to a prover is harder, as it needs, *in extremis*, to support arbitrary programming. Finding errors in proof scripts may require the use of a full debugger.

Given that there are, therefore, disadvantages as well as advantages in having a full programming language, let us consider just what the uses of LCF-style programmability are.

1. First it is used to make substantial, difficult enhancements to the proof system. These are written only once and with a considerable expenditure of time and effort, but then become available to other users.
2. It is also used to write small nonce programs to automate currently tiresome problems. These tend to be ad hoc programs, thrown together quickly and seldom re-used even by their author.

Since the programs of the first kind are so widely used, they can be considered almost as a standard extension of the proof system. As such, they are not in such sharp conflict with the idea of a declarative proof style, especially when some of the most useful proof procedures allow one to replace an explicit proof with a casual indication such as 'by arithmetic'. However the second kind of program is more problematical. We speculate that the need for such programs results partly from a bad choice of existing primitives. (For example in HOL there are poor facilities for manipulating assumptions.) Were such problems remedied, we imagine there would be much less use of small ad hoc programs. They may be useful, though, in some verification proofs, e.g. performing what is effectively symbolic execution by proof.

The Coq system is a good illustration of an intermediate position consistent with the above remarks. It provides a fixed proof language for everyday use, whereas many LCF-style systems present the user with ML, the actual implementation language. Coq does however permit new proof commands to be written in ML à la LCF, and linked to names for new proof commands. Since the procedure is not completely trivial, this tends to discourage the development of small nonce programs, which as we have said, may be a good thing. However more experience is necessary to find out whether this is still the case for verification proofs. We are not sure whether most of those unhappy with PVS's primitive proof language are concerned about large extensions or small nonce programs.

6 Assessment of proof styles

How are we to assess the strengths and weaknesses of different proof styles? We will discuss several important considerations.

Writability

How easy is it to make a machine accept a valid proof? A typical problem with machine-checkable proofs is that they are long compared with their informal counterparts. de Bruijn (1970) suggests that the ratio tends to be more or less constant, but this was based on work translating a single, highly meticulous textbook (Landau 1930) into AUTOMATH. More recently Paulson and Grąbczewski (1996) report much more variable results, even within a single textbook. Significant though proof size is, it is not a direct indicator of how difficult a proof is to construct. Probably at least as important is how the structure of the proof script compares with (or aptly formalizes) that of an informal proof.

Since there often occur in proofs repeated patterns and 'clichés', it seems that extensibility is an important issue for writability (Pollack 1995). Just how important this is depends on the domain of application.

Readability

Actually, once a proof has been accepted by a machine, then there is a tendency, unless the proof has a particular wit or charm, rare in verification applications, to accept the theorem as true and forget about the proof. (At least if the proof checker is accepted as trustworthy.) Similarly, when a program appears to work, one is apt to treat it as a black box and forget its internal structure. But these tendencies are dangerous, for the same reason, and we shall discuss this in the next section.

Whatever the form of the proof, it is perfectly possible for the machine to produce a transcript of it in some form considered more suitable for human consumption. NQTHM includes facilities for producing a readable summary of the proof it finds. An early investigation of providing a readable form of HOL proofs is given by Cohn (1990); a prototype system for producing text from Coq proofs is described by Coscoy, Kahn, and Théry (1995), while the PVS prover is capable of generating summaries of important parts of its proofs.

Alternatively, users can intersperse formal proofs with a series of informal comments designed for humans, just as programmers can for their programs. One of the standard systems for 'literate programming' can be used to separate out the threads in a single document. However there are obvious attractions in making the formal proof submitted to the machine reasonably pleasant for people to read. Then the same document can serve as input to the computer and as a record of the proof for people; that is, we have 'self documenting' proofs. This document-centred view of computing is standard in, for example, WYSIWYG word processing. It also provides a link to the low-tech analogue of writing a proof with pen and paper.

What makes a proof pleasant to read is of course highly subjective. An obvious target is to make the proofs look similar to those found in mathematics texts. However this may not be suitable for all applications, e.g. in verification proofs involving special proof algorithms and very large terms. It is sometimes claimed that proofs are better presented using new techniques such as hierarchical structuring (Lamport 1993) or structured calculational proof (Back, Grundy, and von Wright 1996).[2] Moreover, restricting ourselves to a traditional textual display might be considered anachronistic, with new possibilities opened up by hypertext (Grundy 1996). We will not enter into these questions here, but content ourselves with noting that there are differences in readability on which all can agree.

Maintainability

Writing a machine-checkable proof is generally a lot of work, and one wants to be able to re-use as much as possible of this work in a related situation. For example, in verification work, the system specification or implementation may change slightly — how easy is it to modify the proof for the new situation? This has been considered by Curzon (1995). Again, suppose the infrastructure of the prover is enhanced, or that the foundational system supported is changed; similar questions arise. These problems are quite similar to those that come up when modifying existing software for a different situation, and give rise to many of the same pitfalls.

Readability is always helpful for maintainability, if only in providing orientation when a proof does break. Moreover, note that in verification, maintainability can be an essential component even of writing the proof in the first place. Commonly, one finds errors in one's intended specification or implementation, or at least in some lemmas or invariants, necessitating a rewrite of significant parts of the proof. This means that improvements in maintainability often have consequential benefits for writability. This might apply to proofs in pure mathematics too if the theorem prover were being used as an aid to proof discovery. However that is seldom the case at present; one usually starts with a clear and correct informal proof.

Efficiency of processing

We have focused on the difficulty of reading and writing the proof for humans. But what of the difficulty for the machine in checking a proof script? This can also cause inconvenience for people. One measure is the computational demand made, which translates into user waiting time. Another is implementation difficulty.

In the final analysis, this factor is decisive, since if a proof cannot feasibly be processed in a reasonable time, or a proof checker cannot reasonably be written, the whole business of mechanized reasoning grinds to a halt. However within reason, one can always accept a certain inefficiency, given that computers are still getting faster all the time. A moderate emphasis on human considerations is likely to be vindicated by technological progress.

[2] Actually, Lamport even suggests that hierarchical structuring gives a better way to write proofs in the first place.

Other factors

There are other properties that certain people may consider important. For example, it is often desirable to support the basic theorem prover with a suite of additional tools, including a convenient interface. The Mizar system has tools to find unnecessary assumptions and unused proof steps. The style of proof can have a significant impact on how easy it is to provide such tools.

For constructivists interested in extracting programs or answers from proofs, the level of user control afforded over the formal proof object eventually produced (or implicitly produced) may be highly significant. We will have little to say about this, since our own experience is in classical logic. However we should note that typically it is only a tiny part of a proof that is really interesting, even to a constructivist. For example, it has often been pointed out, e.g. by Kreisel (1985), that there is normally little point in constructivizing the proofs of universal lemmas at all, let alone in optimizing the proof structure.

7 Procedural versus declarative

What can we conclude about the merits of a procedural or declarative style from the experience of present-day systems? First let us say that, since our experience is necessarily limited, much of the following is anecdotal. In particular, we have more experience with procedural proof styles than with declarative ones, which gives us a sharpened awareness of the potential and the defects of the procedural. Moreover, it's worth noting that other factors can influence the suitability of a particular proof style — in particular the logical system supported. For example, type theory is often felt to be easier to mechanize than set theory, in that many proof obligations are automatable. However it may be that in a declarative style, or with a higher level of automation, this difference is much less significant. For example, Paulson (1990) was fairly negative about the suitability of set theory for mechanization, but in recent publications he is much more positive — perhaps the change can be attributed to the superior automation now available in the Isabelle system.

Writability

Tastes differ on what is easier to write, and once one has got used to a particular style, the taste tends to stick. We can at least say that declarative styles are easier for the beginner, simply because they tend to require a smaller 'vocabulary'. Even in highly automated theorem provers such as PVS, one needs to master a fairly large number of proof commands in order to avoid getting stuck. In HOL, with a panoply of low-level proof procedures together with a full (and probably unfamiliar) programming language, the situation is worse. In a declarative system, things are much easier; one just needs a little background knowledge about the general format of proofs, and thereafter merely has to make the proof script simple enough to be understood by the machine.

In the case of NQTHM, one can imagine that it is very easy to get started, since one just needs to type in the theorems to be proved. Of course, one needs to develop strong intuitions about the power of the prover in order to make effective use of the 'series of graded lemmas' approach. Sometimes it will be frustrating that there are no ways to direct the proof procedurally, and additions to NQTHM have been developed to meet these problems. Nevertheless it seems that with such highly declarative systems the learning curve is not as steep at the very beginning as it is with, say, HOL. At worst, one can proceed in such tiny steps that the automated prover is certain to plug the gaps.

We believe that in general, declarative proofs are closer to those found in mathematics texts. These normally have very little procedural content, and the reader is expected to plug 'obvious' gaps. (Most readers will have had the experience of finding certain gaps, thought by the author to be obvious, difficult or even impossible to fill.) A notable exception is the realm of classical geometry, where proofs often proceed via a series of constructions (drop a perpendicular, produce this line, ...).

For verification proofs, a procedural style is often more appealing. In particular one can develop customized proof commands to deal with various situations, such as the symbolic execution of the system being modelled. These can also be directly parametrized, e.g. by the size of a machine word, whereas in a declarative style, this is difficult, usually necessitating manual editing.

Readability

We claim as the most striking advantage of declarative proofs their greater readability. In order to construct the proof state partway through a procedural script, one needs in general to *execute* all the previous steps. This is analogous to replaying a chess game in one's head given just the series of moves. Few enough people can even do that — how much more difficult to anticipate the result of running what are, in the final analysis, arbitrary programs on a fast computer. Certainly, each step is deterministic, and many of them are fairly straightforward. However proof commands often make apparently arbitrary choices, e.g. over the order in which to execute non-confluent rewrites, or which conditional expression to case-split over. (HOL's `RES_TAC` which performs undirected forward chaining, and PVS's `inst?` which instantiates quantified variables by finding a match in the rest of the sequent, are well known examples in the respective user communities.) And in general they can do so much computation that it is impossible in practice to visualize the result without actually running the proof script.

One possibility is to annotate the proof with intermediate steps, just as, to continue our analogy, one typically includes a few diagrams in the text of a chess game. However this gives a rather artificial separation between the parts of the proof intended for human consumption and those parts for the machine. Really, this is just a form of commenting, and we have already discussed this in general terms.

The above assessment was biased towards 'clean' proofs with a fairly abstract structure, e.g. those typically found in pure mathematics. The assessment may need to be reversed, however, for many verification proofs, where the terms involved are very large. Quoting such terms explicitly may be out of the question, and spotting the modest differences between nearby terms may be quite impractical, whereas a procedural style might help to focus the mind on which parts are being manipulated.

Even if one still wants a separate document giving a (more) palatable transcript of the proof, it seems that a declarative base document is a better starting point. One simple idea is simply to have the machine fill in some of the gaps that it can justify as 'obvious', merely making the user's proof outline more explicit while preserving its overall structure.

Maintainability

This is a thorny problem, and we are not yet in a position to make a clear assessment of whether procedural or declarative proofs are more maintainable, though anecdotal evidence tends to support declarative proofs. There are two aspects to maintainability: how likely proofs are to break (under various perturbations of the system and/or the problem) and how easy they are to fix once broken. For the latter, it seems clear that declarative proofs are better, because of the better readability we have already drawn attention to.

We believe that declarative proofs are certainly stabler under changes to the prover. In the extreme case of full automation, then provided the prover's power increases monotonically, proofs will never break. By contrast, in procedural scripts, quite small changes to a single proof command can be very troublesome, since these changes can propagate to the proof state following each instance of it, causing the rest of the script to become inappropriate. Fixing this then becomes a tedious debugging exercise.

For stability under changes to the problem, the situation is not quite so clear cut. In some sense, declarative proofs are more robust, since very often the proof is insensitive to small changes, such as reversing the order of disjuncts in a theorem. By contrast, this may dramatically alter the procedural script required. Against that, declarative proofs rely more heavily on explicit quotation of terms, and so can require alteration if the underlying terms change. However the fact that this information is explicit rather than (in the case of procedural proofs) implicit is arguably a strength rather than a weakness, since the changes can be effected by standard editing operations on the text. Most existing experience (Chen 1992; Gonthier 1996) supports the declarative style as yielding proofs that are easier to maintain.

Efficiency of processing

Here procedural proofs are definitely better. They instruct the computer precisely how to construct the proof, and cut out most search. Of course the basic procedural components may themselves indulge in a substantial amount of search, but at least they do not have to construct the basic structure of the given proof. By contract, search procedures often come to the fore in a declarative style.

One possibility to improve the efficiency of automatic proof procedures, whatever the proof style, is to process the proof into some intermediate form (perhaps not human-readable) containing more explicit information about the proof. This can then cut out a large part of the search when the proof is re-run. Of course it needs to be 'recompiled' if the original proof changes, but nevertheless it seems quite promising. Such an idea has been tried in PVS.

Tool support

Many of the properties making declarative proofs more readable also make them more suitable for support with other tools. For example, one often wants an interface to allow one to navigate about the proof freely. This requires the establishment of context at any given point in the script. Though not quite as difficult for the computer as for the user, this is still in general tedious and time-consuming, since it requires the intermediate proof steps to be executed. Moreover this has some negative consequences for modularity, because these support tools then become tied to the prover itself as an indispensable subroutine. Similar problems would apply if one tried to implement in a procedural system some of the supporting tools provided with Mizar. For example, to detect redundant hypotheses, one would need to re-execute steps in a variety of slightly modified situations. With a declarative style, one can even support computer-aided proof construction, where the computer makes explicit some of its automatic reasoning, or helps to lay out the proof like an advanced structure editor (Syme 1997a).

Style of working

Declarative proof scripts give a wider choice over how work is processed, again because of the relative ease of establishing context. It becomes a real possibility to process small parts of a large proof independently, just as one typically compiles small parts of a large program separately. This is more difficult in a procedural system, which therefore tends to impose a rather rigid structure on the order in which proofs are tackled. For example, to get round this problem in HOL, one often temporarily asserts lemmas using the loophole `mk_thm` in order to tackle the interesting parts first. Inevitably, mistakes creep in and may only be detected in a final 'sanity check'. With declarative proof scripts, the work can be dealt with in any order in a freer fashion.

Declarative styles also make a batch style of working more convenient (and this is the style supported by Mizar). Error recovery is easier, since even if a given proof step fails, the proof context can be recovered and useful errors given for the remainder of the script. Though interactive proof development is often attractive, particularly when feeling one's way towards a proof in an exploratory fashion, it is sometimes more convenient to write a proof sketch, submit it for checking, then refine it according to the error messages received. In particular, this is the standard model for programming language compilation, as well as TEX-style word processing, and so has a certain familiarity for many people. This could serve to reduce the 'culture shock' felt by many people when tackling mechanized reasoning systems for the first time.

What about automation?

It could be argued that the level of automation itself has as much importance as a declarative style for each of the above factors. For example, a high level of automation often has direct benefits for maintainability. This is true at least when the automated steps actually *solve* goals, but perhaps not when the highly automated parts are intermediate steps. Certainly, anecdotal evidence from users of Isabelle and PVS supports the view that, as users rely more heavily on powerful automation, their proofs become more robust. Moreover, proofs certainly become easier to write. However they can become hard to read if the prover is capable of making jumps of baffling complexity. For example, a tendency to insert extra rewrites into the background automatically may have considerable benefits for those writing a proof, at great detriment to its eventual readability. A balance needs to be struck between too much power and too little, the difficulty being that the notion of 'obviousness' differs fundamentally for people and for machines (Rudnicki 1987).

Conclusions

We have pointed out many advantages of a declarative style of working. Indeed, we believe this idea has been unduly neglected by the main stream of research in mechanized reasoning. (We exclude NQTHM, which belongs solidly to this main stream, because it hardly considers *proofs* in the conventional sense.) At the same time, the declarative style is not without its disadvantages. Intuitively one feels that many large verification proofs would be much easier in PVS or HOL than in a more declarative system such as Mizar. Roughly speaking, a declarative proof style is good for pure, abstract proofs, whereas a procedural one is good for big, ugly, concrete proofs. Occasionally this assessment may need reversing. For example Gonthier (1996) presents Larch proofs of a distributed garbage collection algorithm, and the proof scripts have a strongly declarative flavour. More recently, Syme (1997b) has proved type soundness for a subset of Java using a declarative system called DECLARE (Syme 1997a). On the other side of the coin, nowadays a number of mathematical results are established with the aid of computer checking (Lam 1990); it seems that a procedural proof style offers more possibilities of absorbing these results into mechanized reasoning.

8 The best of both worlds?

Since the merits of the two styles are not clear cut, the ideal is perhaps to have a free choice of both. We have experimented with supporting Mizar-style proofs in the HOL system (Harrison 1996). The objective is to combine the strengths of HOL (reliability, extensibility and interactivity) with those of Mizar (readability and declarative style).

True to our remarks on the subjectivity of the declarative/procedural divide, the method is to find a procedural reading for each Mizar construct within the HOL tactic mechanism. To bridge the 'obvious' gaps, the user can install arbitrary automated provers; a default prover is provided which is capable of basic first order reasoning and a few other limited functions. At the same time, a degree of procedural content can be injected into the Mizar/HOL proof scripts by explicitly indicating a particular automated prover, e.g. '`by rewriting with X`' or '`by arithmetic with Y`'. At the same time, conventional HOL tactics can be interspersed arbitrarily with Mizar constructs, even within a single proof.

This mixture of styles seems especially suitable for our own current research interest of verifying floating point algorithms, mainly for the transcendental functions. Such proofs often involve a mix of abstract pure mathematics and specialized procedures used to extract verification conditions, e.g. proving that loop invariants are maintained. To arrive at the right proof style, more experience of real proofs in a range of areas is the most valuable guide, together with a real willingness for system designers to learn from each other.

Related work

Chen (1992) contrasts a declarative and procedural style of proof (exemplified for him by Ontic and Nuprl respectively) and the desirability of combining the best features of each. Prasetya (1993) points out how the standard HOL proof styles differ from those in textbooks and discusses a prototype system to improve matters.

Acknowledgements

The importance of the declarative style of proof was brought home to me by Andrzej Trybulec and the success of his Mizar system. Many of the issues discussed in this paper were inspired by conversations with Donald Syme. In particular I owe to him many observations about the difficulty of establishing context in procedural proof scripts, and the issues connected with having a full programming language available. I'm also grateful to David Basin and Paul Jackson for some pointers to relevant literature. Richard Boulton, Mike Gordon, Michael Norrish and Mark Staples offered some valuable comments on this work, and in particular on the slippery distinction between procedural and declarative, while Konrad Slind's comments on the paper have improved several key parts, as have the comments of anonymous referees. Thanks also to Natarajan Shankar who pointed out that I originally wrote 'least upper bound' where I meant 'greatest lower bound' in the Mizar example. Many of those present at the TYPES'96 workshop provided valuable suggestions and advice; thanks to Christine Paulin-Mohring and the other organizers for giving me the opportunity to present these ideas. The work described was funded by the European Commission under the HCM scheme, and by the UK Engineering and Physical Sciences Research Council.

Glossary of systems

Here we will give some starting points for finding out more about the theorem proving systems mentioned in the text.

AUTOMATH The system is no longer used, but there is an extensive collection of papers (Nederpelt, Geuvers, and de Vrijer 1994) describing the system, its applications, and the underlying philosophy.

Coq The Coq system and its documentation can be found via the Web page `http://pauillac.inria.fr/coq/systeme_coq-eng.html`.

HOL HOL is described in a book by Gordon and Melham (1993), and the two versions of the system, as well as documentation and numerous papers, are available from `http://www.cl.cam.ac.uk/Research/HVG/HOL/index.html`. Of particular note is an extensive bibliography of HOL-related papers available as `http://www.dcs.glasgow.ac.uk/~tfm/hol-bib.html`.

Isabelle Isabelle is described in a book by Paulson (1994), and there is a Web page for the system: `http://www.cl.cam.ac.uk/Research/HVG/Isabelle/`.

Larch The Larch Prover is described by Garland and Guttag (1991), and the page `http://larch-www.lcs.mit.edu:8001/larch/LP/overview.html` has additional information.

LCF The original Edinburgh LCF project is described in a book by Gordon, Milner, and Wadsworth (1979), and the later Cambridge version by Paulson (1987). As far as we know, the system is no longer used, but Coq, HOL, Isabelle and Nuprl are all descended from it and follow the same general approach to proof.

Mizar A good overview of Mizar is given by Rudnicki (1992). There are some older papers describing the system by Trybulec (1978) and by Trybulec and Blair (1985). The system manuals are a good guide, but are mostly out of print. However the entire set of the *Journal of Formalized Mathematics* is devoted to Mizar formalizations, and this is now online at `http://mizar.uw.bialystok.pl/JFM/`. The Web page `http://web.cs.ualberta.ca:80/~piotr/Mizar/` is a good starting point.

Nuprl An older version of Nuprl is described in a book (Constable 1986); the current version and supporting documentation and bibliographic information is online at `http://www.cs.cornell.edu/Info/Projects/NuPrl/nuprl.html`.

Ontic Ontic seems not to be widely used now, but is described by McAllester (1989).

NQTHM NQTHM is described in the classic book by Boyer and Moore (1979); `http://www.cs.utexas.edu/users/moore/best-ideas/nqthm/index.html` is a short description of the system's history including a link to the FTP distribution. A newer prover called ACL2 supersedes NQTHM in most important respects, and `http://www.cs.utexas.edu/users/moore/acl2/index.html` includes the system, documentation and examples.

PVS PVS is described by Owre, Rushby, and Shankar (1992). The system and associated documentation and bibliographic data is available via the Web page `http://www.csl.sri.com/pvs.html`.

References

Back, R., Grundy, J., and von Wright, J. (1996) Structured calculational proof. Technical Report 65, Turku Centre for Computer Science (TUCS), Lemminkäisenkatu 14 A, FIN-20520 Turku, Finland. Also available as Technical Report TR-CS-96-09 from the Australian National University.

Boyer, R. S. and Moore, J S. (1979) *A Computational Logic.* ACM Monograph Series. Academic Press.

de Bruijn, N. G. (1970) The mathematical language AUTOMATH, its usage and some of its extensions. In Laudet, M., Lacombe, D., Nolin, L., and Schützenberger, M. (eds.), *Symposium on Automatic Demonstration*, Volume 125 of *Lecture Notes in Mathematics*, pp. 29–61. Springer-Verlag.

Chen, W. (1992) Tactic-based theorem proving and knowledge-based forward chaining. See Kapur (1992), pp. 552–566.

Cohn, A. (1990) Proof accounts in HOL (incomplete draft). Available on the Web as `http://www.cl.cam.ac.uk/users/mjcg/AccountsPaper.ps.gz`.

Constable, R. (1986) *Implementing Mathematics with The Nuprl Proof Development System.* Prentice-Hall.

Constable, R. L., Knoblock, T. B., and Bates, J. L. (1985) Writing programs that construct proofs. *Journal of Automated Reasoning*, **1**, 285–326.

Coscoy, Y., Kahn, G., and Théry, L. (1995) Extracting text from proofs. In Dezani-Ciancaglini, M. and Plotkin, G. (eds.), *Second International Conference on Typed Lambda Calculi and Applications, TLCA'95*, Volume 902 of *Lecture Notes in Computer Science*, Edinburgh, pp. 109–123. Springer-Verlag.

Curzon, P. (1995) Tracking design changes with formal machine-checked proof. *The Computer Journal*, **38**, 91–100.

Garland, S. J. and Guttag, J. V. (1991) A guide to LP, the Larch Prover. Technical report, MIT Laboratory for Computer Science.

Gonthier, G. (1996) Verifying the safety of a practical concurrent garbage collector. In Alur, R. and Henzinger, T. A. (eds.), *Proceedings of the 8th international conference on computer aided verification (CAV'96)*, Volume 1102 of *Lecture Notes in Computer Science*, New Brunswick, NJ, pp. 462–465. Springer-Verlag.

Gordon, M. J. C. and Melham, T. F. (1993) *Introduction to HOL: a theorem proving environment for higher order logic*. Cambridge University Press.

Gordon, M. J. C., Milner, R., and Wadsworth, C. P. (1979) *Edinburgh LCF: A Mechanised Logic of Computation*, Volume 78 of *Lecture Notes in Computer Science*. Springer-Verlag.

Grundy, J. (1996) A browsable format for proof presentation. In Gefwert, C., Orponen, P., and Seppänen, J. (eds.), *Proceedings of the Finnish Artificial Intelligence Society Symposium: Logic, Mathematics and the Computer*, Volume 14 of *Suomen Tekoälyseuran julkaisuja*, pp. 171–178. Finnish Artificial Intelligence Society.

Guard, J. R., Oglesby, F. C., Bennett, J. H., and Settle, L. G. (1969) Semi-automated mathematics. *Journal of the ACM*, **16**, 49–62.

Harrison, J. (1996) A Mizar mode for HOL. In von Wright, J., Grundy, J., and Harrison, J. (eds.), *Theorem Proving in Higher Order Logics: 9th International Conference, TPHOLs'96*, Volume 1125 of *Lecture Notes in Computer Science*, Turku, Finland, pp. 203–220. Springer-Verlag.

van Bentham Jutting, L. S. (1977) *Checking Landau's "Grundlagen" in the AUTOMATH System*. Ph. D. thesis, Eindhoven University of Technology. Useful summary in Nederpelt, Geuvers, and de Vrijer (1994), pp. 701–732.

Kapur, D. (ed.) (1992) *11th International Conference on Automated Deduction*, Volume 607 of *Lecture Notes in Computer Science*, Saratoga, NY. Springer-Verlag.

Kreisel, G. (1985) Proof theory and the synthesis of programs: Potential and limitations. In Buchberger, B. (ed.), *EUROCAL '85: European Conference on Computer Algebra*, Volume 203 of *Lecture Notes in Computer Science*, pp. 136–150. Springer-Verlag.

Lam, C. W. H. (1990) How reliable is a computer-based proof? *The Mathematical Intelligencer*, **12**, 8–12.

Lamport, L. (1993) How to write a proof. Research Report 94, DEC Systems Research Center, 130 Lytton Avenue, Palo Alto, California 94301, USA.

Landau, E. (1930) *Grundlagen der Analysis*. Leipzig. English translation by F. Steinhardt: 'Foundations of analysis: the arithmetic of whole, rational, irrational, and complex numbers. A supplement to textbooks on the differential and integral calculus', published by Chelsea; 3rd edition 1966.

McAllester, D. A. (1989) *ONTIC: A Knowledge Representation System for Mathematics*. MIT Press.

Nederpelt, R. P., Geuvers, J. H., and de Vrijer, R. C. (eds.) (1994) *Selected Papers on Automath*, Volume 133 of *Studies in Logic and the Foundations of Mathematics*. North-Holland.

Owre, S., Rushby, J. M., and Shankar, N. (1992) PVS: A prototype verification system. See Kapur (1992), pp. 748–752.

Paulson, L. C. (1987) *Logic and computation: interactive proof with Cambridge LCF*, Volume 2 of *Cambridge Tracts in Theoretical Computer Science*. Cambridge University Press.

Paulson, L. C. (1990) Isabelle: The next 700 theorem provers. In Odifreddi, P. G. (ed.), *Logic and Computer Science*, Volume 31 of *APIC Studies in Data Processing*, pp. 361–386. Academic Press.

Paulson, L. C. (1994) *Isabelle: a generic theorem prover*, Volume 828 of *Lecture Notes in Computer Science*. Springer-Verlag. With contributions by Tobias Nipkow.

Paulson, L. C. and Grąbczewski, K. (1996) Mechanizing set theory: Cardinal arithmetic and the axiom of choice. *Journal of Automated Reasoning*, **17**, 291–323.

Pollack, R. (1995) On extensibility of proof checkers. In Dybjer, P., Nordström, B., and Smith, J. (eds.), *Types for Proofs and Programs: selected papers from TYPES'94*, Volume 996 of *Lecture Notes in Computer Science*, Båstad, pp. 140–161. Springer-Verlag.

Prasetya, I. S. W. B. (1993) On the style of mechanical proving. In Joyce, J. J. and Seger, C. (eds.), *Proceedings of the 1993 International Workshop on the HOL theorem proving system and its applications*, Volume 780 of *Lecture Notes in Computer Science*, UBC, Vancouver, Canada, pp. 475–488. Springer-Verlag.

Robinson, J. A. (1994) Logic, computers, Turing and von Neumann. In Furukawa, K., Michie, D., and Muggleton, S. (eds.), *Machine Intelligence 13*, pp. 1–35. Clarendon Press.

Rudnicki, P. (1987) Obvious inferences. *Journal of Automated Reasoning*, **3**, 383–393.

Rudnicki, P. (1992) An overview of the MIZAR project. Available by anonymous FTP from `menaik.cs.ualberta.ca` as `pub/Mizar/Mizar_Over.tar.Z`.

Syme, D. (1997a) DECLARE: A prototype declarative proof system for higher order logic. Technical Report 416, University of Cambridge Computer Laboratory, New Museums Site, Pembroke Street, Cambridge, CB2 3QG, UK.

Syme, D. (1997b) Proving Java type soundness. Technical Report 427, University of Cambridge Computer Laboratory, New Museums Site, Pembroke Street, Cambridge, CB2 3QG, UK.

Trybulec, A. (1978) The Mizar-QC/6000 logic information language. *ALLC Bulletin (Association for Literary and Linguistic Computing)*, **6**, 136–140.

Trybulec, A. and Blair, H. A. (1985) Computer aided reasoning. In Parikh, R. (ed.), *Logics of Programs*, Volume 193 of *Lecture Notes in Computer Science*, Brooklyn, pp. 406–412. Springer-Verlag.

Trybulec, Z. and Święczkowska, H. (1991-1992) The language of mathematical texts. *Studies in Logic, Grammar and Rhetoric, Białystok*, **10/11**, 103–124.

Some Algorithmic and Proof-Theoretical Aspects of Coercive Subtyping

Alex Jones, Zhaohui Luo and Sergei Soloviev
Computer Science Department, Durham University
South Road, Durham DH1 3LE, U.K.
E-mail: A.P.Jones, Zhaohui.Luo, Sergei.Soloviev @durham.ac.uk

Abstract. Coercive subtyping offers a conceptually simple but powerful framework to understand subtyping and subset relationships in type theory. In this paper we study some of its proof-theoretic and computational properties.

1 Introduction

Coercive subtyping, as first introduced in [Luo96], offers a conceptually simple but powerful framework to understand subtyping and subset relationships in type theories with sophisticated type structures such as dependent types, inductive types, and type universes. A basic idea behind coercive subtyping is that subtyping provides a powerful mechanism for notational abbreviation in type theory. If A is a subtype of B given by a specified coercion function, an object of type A can be regarded as an object of type B, that is, its image via the coercion function, and hence objects of a subtype can be used as abbreviations for objects of a supertype.

With coercive subtyping, this abbreviational mechanism is formally treated at the level of the logical framework – the meta-level language used to specify type theories. Given two kinds (meta-level types) K and K', where K is a (proper) subkind of K' and a functional operation f whose source kind is K', one can apply f to any object a of kind K as well as those of kind K'. The meaning of such an application is that $f(a)$ is definitionally equal to $f(c(a))$, where c is the coercion between K and K'.

This simple extension of the logical framework (and hence of the specified type theories such as Martin-Löf's type theory [NPS90] and the type theory UTT [Luo94,Gog94]), provides a surprisingly powerful mechanism that facilitates useful ways of reasoning about subsets of objects, helps proof reuse and modularisation, and gives a proper treatment of the subtyping relation between type universes (see [Luo96] for details). These provide the basis for more efficient subset and substructure reasoning and proof reuse (cf. [Jon95,Bai93]). For instance, if we define the type of groups as a subset of the type of monoids, then any proof to do with monoids can then be automatically applied to groups. Such a mechanism has been implemented by Bailey in LEGO [Bai96] and Saibi in Coq [Sai97] to support proof reuse and notational abbreviation. Similar mechanisms can be used for development of program specification and verification proofs (c.f., [Luo93]).

In this paper, we study some of the basic proof-theoretic and computational properties of coercive subtyping. The formal system we consider, as presented in Section 2, is essentially the same as that in [Luo96] except for one major change: we use subkinding judgements with explicitly associated coercion terms, of the form $K <_c K'$. We also restrict the basic coercions to be closed terms between closed types (as considered in [Luo96]). The presentation of a more general framework of coercive subtyping can be found in [Luo97], which uses subkinding judgements with explicit coercion terms and also allows more general basic subtyping rules such as those for parameterised inductive types.

In section 3 we prove several important meta-theoretic results, including substitution elimination, uniqueness of coercions, presupposition theorems, transitivity elimination, and some results about the relationship between the original type theory and its extension with coercive subtyping. There are at least two important aspects of this meta-theoretic development that deserve attention. One is that we study the meta-theory of the resulting type system with judgemental equality *directly*, without considering a meta-level notion of conversion.[1] Actually, as discussed in the paper, to prove various elimination results requires a careful treatment of the rules in LF by first considering elimination results of their weaker versions.

Another meta-theoretic development reported here is to show that, for the system considered in this paper, the extension with coercive subtyping is conservative over the original type theory. This can be seen as a justification of the claim that coercive subtyping is essentially an abbreviational mechanism [Luo96]. Furthermore, we expect that further development along this line will allow us to transfer the meta-theoretic results for the original type theory to its extension with coercive subtyping.

In section 4 we present a type-checking algorithm for coercive subtyping and prove its soundness using some of the meta-theoretic results of section 3. This is a part of our ongoing effort to study the computational behaviour of type theory with coercive subtyping and different computational strategies for efficient implementation.

Discussions on future research topics can be found in the Conclusion.

2 Coercive subtyping: the formal system

The basic system on which the formal systems considered here are based is the logical framework LF, a typed version of Martin-Löf's logical framework [NPS90]. The formulation of LF and a detailed discussion on how to use LF in

[1] The work by Healfdene Goguen on typed operational semantics (TOS) [Gog94] may be regarded as an indirect development of the meta-theory of LF and UTT, where for example, substitution elimination results are obtained by proving the soundness of TOS wrt the system with substitution rules and the completeness of TOS wrt the system without substitution rules.

specifying type theories (with formal definitions and examples) can be found in Chapter 9 of [Luo94]. Here it is enough to say, that a judgement in a type theory T, specified in LF is derivable if it is derivable in the extension of LF by the constants and computation rules specifying the type theory.

The extension of any type theory T (specified in LF) with coercive subtyping is defined with respect to a set $\mathcal{C}$ of triples (a subtype, a supertype and a coercion term, representing an embedding of a subtype into its supertype). One of our main goals is to investigate the general meta-theoretic properties of this subtyping extension (we shall denote it by T[$\mathcal{C}$]) and its relationship with the original type theory T, since many of them can be studied independently from the underlying type theory[2]. Let us notice that the systems we are going to consider are ordered by inclusion as follows: $LF \subseteq T \subseteq T[\mathcal{C}]$.

2.1 Judgement forms

Besides context validity, we have the following basic judgements forms in the language:

- K:**kind** asserts that K is a *kind*.
- $k{:}K$ asserts that K is the *principal kind* of k.
- $K = K'$ asserts that K and K' are equal kinds.
- $k = k'{:}K$ asserts that k and k' are equal objects with principal kind K.
- $A <_c B$:**Type** asserts that A is a *proper subtype of* B *with coercion* c.
- $K <_c K'$ asserts that K is a *proper subkind of* K' *with coercion* c.

The above are the judgement forms included in our formal presentation. With these judgement forms we can define other judgement forms, for example:

- $K < K'$ (K is a proper subkind of K') stands for '$K <_c K'$ for some c'.
- $K \leq K'$ (K is a subkind of K') stands for '$K = K'$ or $K <_c K'$ for some c'.
- $k :: K$ (k is of kind K) stands for '$k{:}K$ or $k{:}K_0$ for some K_0 such that $K_0 <_c K$ for some c'.
- $k = k' :: K$ (k and k' are equal objects of kind K) stands for '$k = k'{:}K$ or $k = k'{:}K_0$ for some K_0 such that $K_0 <_c K$ for some c'.

2.2 The logical framework LF

The logical framework LF is presented as in [Luo94]. We shall denote by $\equiv$ syntactic equality (up to α-conversion, i.e., renaming of bound variables.) Here, we only list the inference rules of LF.

Contexts and assumptions

$$(1.1)\ \frac{}{<>\vdash \textbf{valid}} \qquad (1.2)\ \frac{\Gamma \vdash K{:}\textbf{kind}\quad x \notin FV(\Gamma)}{\Gamma, x{:}K \vdash \textbf{valid}} \qquad (1.3)\ \frac{\Gamma, x{:}K, \Gamma' \vdash \textbf{valid}}{\Gamma, x{:}K, \Gamma' \vdash x{:}K}$$

[2] Types on meta-level are called *kinds*, and one may say that in this paper we are mostly studying properties of *subkinding*.

General equality rules

$$(2.1)\ \frac{\Gamma \vdash K{:}\mathbf{kind}}{\Gamma \vdash K = K} \qquad (2.2)\ \frac{\Gamma \vdash K = K'}{\Gamma \vdash K' = K} \qquad (2.3)\ \frac{\Gamma \vdash K = K' \quad \Gamma \vdash K' = K''}{\Gamma \vdash K = K''}$$

$$(2.4)\ \frac{\Gamma \vdash k{:}K}{\Gamma \vdash k = k{:}K} \qquad (2.5)\ \frac{\Gamma \vdash k = k'{:}K}{\Gamma \vdash k' = k{:}K} \qquad (2.6)\frac{\Gamma \vdash k = k'{:}K \quad \Gamma \vdash k' = k''{:}K}{\Gamma \vdash k = k''{:}K}$$

Equality typing rules

$$(3.1)\frac{\Gamma \vdash k{:}K \quad \Gamma \vdash K = K'}{\Gamma \vdash k{:}K'} \qquad (3.2)\frac{\Gamma \vdash k = k'{:}K \quad \Gamma \vdash K = K'}{\Gamma \vdash k = k'{:}K'}$$

The kind Type

$$(4.1)\frac{\Gamma \vdash \mathbf{valid}}{\Gamma \vdash \mathbf{Type}{:}\mathbf{kind}} \qquad (4.2)\frac{\Gamma \vdash A{:}\mathbf{Type}}{\Gamma \vdash El(A){:}\mathbf{kind}} \qquad (4.3)\frac{\Gamma \vdash A = B{:}\mathbf{Type}}{\Gamma \vdash El(A) = El(B)}$$

Rules for dependent product kinds and $\beta\eta$-equalities

$$(5.1)\frac{\Gamma, x{:}K \vdash K'{:}\mathbf{kind}}{\Gamma \vdash (x{:}K)K'{:}\mathbf{kind}} \qquad (5.2)\frac{\Gamma \vdash K_1 = K_2 \quad \Gamma, x{:}K_1 \vdash K_1' = K_2'}{\Gamma \vdash (x{:}K_1)K_1' = (x{:}K_2)K_2'}$$

$$(5.3)\frac{\Gamma, x{:}K \vdash k{:}K'}{\Gamma \vdash [x{:}K]k{:}(x{:}K)K'} \qquad (5.4)\frac{\Gamma \vdash K_1 = K_2 \quad \Gamma, x{:}K_1 \vdash k_1 = k_2{:}K}{\Gamma \vdash [x{:}K_1]k_1 = [x{:}K_2]k_2{:}(x{:}K_1)K}$$

$$(5.5)\frac{\Gamma \vdash f{:}(x{:}K)K' \quad \Gamma \vdash k{:}K}{\Gamma \vdash f(k){:}[k/x]K'} \qquad (5.6)\frac{\Gamma \vdash f = f'{:}(x{:}K)K' \quad \Gamma \vdash k_1 = k_2{:}K}{\Gamma \vdash f(k_1) = f'(k_2){:}[k_1/x]K'}$$

$$(5.7)\frac{\Gamma, x{:}K \vdash k'{:}K' \quad \Gamma \vdash k{:}K}{\Gamma \vdash ([x{:}K]k')k = [k/x]k'{:}[k/x]K'} \qquad (5.8)\frac{\Gamma \vdash f{:}(x{:}K)K' \quad x \notin FV(\Gamma)}{\Gamma \vdash [x{:}K]f(x) = f{:}(x{:}K)K'}$$

We shall call EL-kinds the kinds of the form $El(A)$, and product-kinds the kinds of the form $(x{:}K)K'$. A standard notational convention is that if in the kind $(x{:}K)K'$ the variable x does not occur freely in K', we may write $(K)K'$.

The substitution rules below are separated into two groups, since their formal behaviours are quite different (see section 3).

Simple substitutions

$$(6.1)\frac{\Gamma, x{:}K, \Gamma' \vdash \mathbf{valid} \quad \Gamma \vdash k{:}K}{\Gamma, [k/x]\Gamma' \vdash \mathbf{valid}} \qquad (6.2)\frac{\Gamma, x{:}K, \Gamma' \vdash K'{:}\mathbf{kind} \quad \Gamma \vdash k{:}K}{\Gamma, [k/x]\Gamma' \vdash [k/x]K'{:}\mathbf{kind}}$$

$$(6.3)\frac{\Gamma, x{:}K, \Gamma' \vdash k'{:}K' \quad \Gamma \vdash k{:}K}{\Gamma, [k/x]\Gamma' \vdash [k/x]k'{:}[k/x]K'} \qquad (6.4)\ \frac{\Gamma, x{:}K, \Gamma' \vdash K' = K'' \quad \Gamma \vdash k{:}K}{\Gamma, [k/x]\Gamma' \vdash [k/x]K' = [k/x]K''}$$

$$(6.5)\frac{\Gamma, x{:}K, \Gamma' \vdash k' = k''{:}K' \quad \Gamma \vdash k{:}K}{\Gamma, [k/x]\Gamma' \vdash [k/x]k' = [k/x]k''{:}K'}$$

Equality substitutions

$$(6.6)\ \frac{\Gamma, x{:}K, \Gamma' \vdash K'{:}\mathbf{kind} \quad \Gamma \vdash k_1 = k_2{:}K}{\Gamma, [k_1/x]\Gamma' \vdash [k_1/x]K' = [k_2/x]K'}$$

$$(6.7)\ \frac{\Gamma, x{:}K, \Gamma' \vdash k'{:}K' \quad \Gamma \vdash k_1 = k_2{:}K}{\Gamma, [k/x]\Gamma' \vdash [k_1/x]k' = [k_1/x]k'{:}[k/x]K'}$$

2.3 Coercive subtyping and subkinding

Let T be any type theory specified in LF (without subtyping and subkinding), as described in [Luo94]. We consider two new judgement forms:

- $\Gamma \vdash A <_c B{:}\mathbf{Type}$ asserts that A is a proper subtype of B with coercion c.
- $\Gamma \vdash K <_c K'$ asserts that K is a proper subkind of K' with coercion c.

The label c will be called a coercion term. It will be *proved* that, for any derivable judgement $\Gamma \vdash K <_c K'$, $\Gamma \vdash c{:}(K)K'$ is derivable.

Subtyping We first consider an intermediate system $T[\mathcal{C}]_0$, which spells out how subtyping relations are set up. $T[\mathcal{C}]_0$ is obtained from T by adding the subtyping judgement form $\Gamma \vdash A <_c B{:}\mathbf{Type}$ and the following rules:

- Basic subtyping rules.
- Transitivity rules for subtyping.
- Substitution rule for subtyping.

In this paper, the basic subtyping rules correspond to a set $\mathcal{C}$ of basic coercions:

$$(ST.1)\frac{\Gamma \vdash A{:}\mathbf{Type} \quad \Gamma \vdash B{:}\mathbf{Type} \quad \Gamma \vdash c{:}(El(A))El(B) \quad (A, c, B) \in \mathcal{C}}{\Gamma \vdash A <_c B{:}\mathbf{Type}},$$

where A, c, and B do not contain free variables. For a more general framework allowing more general basic subtyping rules, see [Luo97].

Transitivity rules

$$(ST.2)\frac{\Gamma \vdash A <_c B{:}\mathbf{Type} \quad \Gamma \vdash A = A'{:}\mathbf{Type}}{\Gamma \vdash A' <_c B{:}\mathbf{Type}}$$

$$(ST.3)\frac{\Gamma \vdash A <_c B{:}\mathbf{Type} \quad \Gamma \vdash B = B'{:}\mathbf{Type}}{\Gamma \vdash A <_c B'{:}\mathbf{Type}}$$

$$(ST.4)\frac{\Gamma \vdash A <_{c_1} B{:}\mathbf{Type} \quad \Gamma \vdash B <_{c_2} C{:}\mathbf{Type}}{\Gamma \vdash A <_{[x:El(A)]c_2(c_1(x))} C{:}\mathbf{Type}}$$

Substitution rule for subtyping

$$(ST.5)\frac{\Gamma, x{:}K, \Gamma' \vdash A <_c B{:}\mathbf{Type} \quad \Gamma \vdash k{:}K}{\Gamma, [k/x']\Gamma' \vdash [k/x]A <_{[k/x]c} [k/x]B{:}\mathbf{Type}}$$

Coherence conditions The following lemma is obvious, because the extension above has no means to obtain a judgement which is not of subtyping form from a subtyping judgement.

Lemma 1. *$T[\mathcal{C}]_0$ is a conservative extension of T. That is, if J is not of the form $A <_c B$:***Type***, then $\Gamma \vdash J$ is derivable in T if and only if $\Gamma \vdash J$ is derivable in $T[\mathcal{C}]_0$.*

Definition 2. (coherence conditions) We say that $\mathcal{C}$ is coherent if $T[\mathcal{C}]_0$ has the following properties:

1. $\Gamma \not\vdash A <_c A{:}\mathbf{Type}$ for any Γ, A and c.
2. If $\Gamma \vdash A <_c B{:}\mathbf{Type}$ and $\Gamma \vdash A <_{c'} B{:}\mathbf{Type}$, then $\Gamma \vdash c = c'{:}(El(A))El(B)$.

In this paper, we assume that $\mathcal{C}$ is coherent.

Subkinding A further intermediate system $T[\mathcal{C}]_{0K}$ is obtained by adding the new subkinding judgement form $\Gamma \vdash K <_c K'$, and the following inference rules $(SK.1-8)$.

The basic subkinding rule

$$(SK.1)\frac{\Gamma \vdash A <_c B{:}\mathbf{Type}}{\Gamma \vdash El(A) <_c El(B)},$$

Subkinding for dependent products kinds

$$(SK.2)\frac{\Gamma \vdash K_1' <_{c_1} K_1 \quad \Gamma, x'{:}K_1' \vdash [c_1(x')/x]K_2 = K_2' \quad \Gamma, x{:}K_1 \vdash K_2 \ \mathbf{:kind}}{\Gamma \vdash (x{:}K_1)K_2 <_c (x'{:}K_1')K_2'},$$

where $c = [f{:}(x{:}K_1)K_2][x'{:}K_1']f(c_1(x'))$;

$$(SK.3)\frac{\Gamma \vdash K_1' = K_1 \quad \Gamma, x{:}K_1' \vdash K_2 <_{c_2} K_2' \quad \Gamma, x{:}K_1 \vdash K_2 \ \mathbf{:kind}}{\Gamma \vdash (x{:}K_1)K_2 <_c (x{:}K_1')K_2'},$$

where $c = [f{:}(x{:}K_1)K_2][x{:}K_1']c_2(f(x))$;

$$(SK.4)\frac{\Gamma \vdash K_1' <_{c_1} K_1 \quad \Gamma, x'{:}K_1' \vdash [c_1(x')/x]K_2 <_{c_2} K_2' \quad \Gamma, x{:}K_1 \vdash K_2 \ \mathbf{:kind}}{\Gamma \vdash (x{:}K_1)K_2 <_c (x'{:}K_1')K_2'},$$

where $c = [f{:}(x{:}K_1)K_2][x'{:}K_1']c_2(f(c_1(x')))$.

Transitivity rules for subkinding

$$(SK.5)\frac{\Gamma \vdash K_1 <_c K_2 \quad \Gamma \vdash K_2 = K_2'}{\Gamma \vdash K_1' <_{c'} K_2'} \quad (SK.6)\frac{\Gamma \vdash K_1 <_c K_2 \quad \Gamma \vdash K_1 = K_1'}{\Gamma \vdash K_1' <_{c'} K_2'}$$

$$(SK.7)\frac{\Gamma \vdash K <_{c_1} K' \quad \Gamma \vdash K' <_{c_2} K''}{\Gamma \vdash K <_{[x:K]c_2(c_1(x))} K''}$$

Substitution rule for subkinding

$$(SK.8)\frac{\Gamma, x{:}K, \Gamma' \vdash K_1 <_c K_2 \quad \Gamma \vdash k{:}K}{\Gamma, [k/x]\Gamma' \vdash [k/x]K_1 <_{[k/x]c} [k/x]K_2}$$

Lemma 3. *$T[\mathcal{C}]_{0K}$ is a conservative extension of T and $T[\mathcal{C}]_0$.*

Because $T[\mathcal{C}]_{0K}$ is conservative extension of $T[\mathcal{C}]_0$, coherence conditions hold also in $T[\mathcal{C}]_{0K}$.

Coercive rules The extension of T with coercive subtyping, the system $T[\mathcal{C}]$, is obtained from $T[\mathcal{C}]_{0K}$ by adding the following rules, which establish the essential connection between the original system T and its subtyping/subkinding extension.

New rules for application

$$(CA.1)\frac{\Gamma \vdash f{:}(x{:}K)K' \quad \Gamma \vdash k{:}K_0 \quad \Gamma \vdash K_0 <_c K}{\Gamma \vdash f(k){:}[c(k)/x]K'}$$

$$(CA.2)\frac{\Gamma \vdash f = f'{:}(x{:}K)K' \quad \Gamma \vdash k_1 = k_2{:}K_0 \quad \Gamma \vdash K_0 <_c K}{\Gamma \vdash f(k_1) = f'(k_2){:}[c(k_1)/x]K'}$$

Coercive definition rule

$$(CD)\frac{\Gamma \vdash f{:}(x{:}K)K' \quad \Gamma \vdash k_0{:}K_0 \quad \Gamma \vdash K_0 <_c K}{\Gamma \vdash f(k_0) = f(c(k_0)){:}[c(k_0)/x]K'}$$

Note that, unlike $T[\mathcal{C}]_0$, it is not at all obvious that $T[\mathcal{C}]$ is a conservative extension of T, because now there are means to derive judgements of other forms using subtyping/subkinding judgements. See subsection 3.5 for further discussions.

3 Basic Meta-Theoretical Properties

A relatively large calculus, like our T[$\mathcal{C}$], contains many groups of rules, interacting in a complex and not always obvious way. To make it a really efficient instrument for the development of the meta-theory, it is necessary to investigate first its basic properties. This includes several results which may be considered as forms of (partial) cut-elimination. Take, for example, elimination of the substitution rules and the transitivity rules for subkinding. Such results will be very helpful in the part, corresponding to the typechecking algorithm.

Another important question is that of "presupposed" judgements and their derivations (one of the characteristic features of dependent type theories). For example, the derivability of a judgement

$$x_1{:}Q_1,...,x_n{:}Q_n \vdash K_1 = K_2$$

presupposes conceptually the derivability of judgements

$$x_1{:}Q_1,...,x_{i-1}{:}Q_{i-1} \vdash Q_i{:}\mathbf{kind} \quad x_1{:}Q_1,...,x_i{:}Q_i \vdash \mathbf{valid}(i \leq n)$$

and $x_1{:}Q_1,...,x_n{:}Q_n \vdash K_j{:}\mathbf{kind}(j = 1,2)$. If instead of $K_1 = K_2$ we take $k_1 = k_2{:}K$, presupposed judgements will include $x_1{:}Q_1,...,x_n{:}Q_n \vdash K{:}\mathbf{kind}$ and $x_1{:}Q_1,...,x_n{:}Q_n \vdash k_j{:}K(j = 1,2)$. Subkinding $K_1 <_c K_2$ presupposes in addition the derivability of $x_1{:}Q_1,...,x_n{:}Q_n \vdash c{:}(K_1)K_2$ etc. But how may a complex judgement be "split", how do the derivations of the "presupposed" judgements correspond to the main derivation?

Neither the elimination problem nor the "splitting" of complex judgements admit straightforward solutions.

As an illustration of the possible difficulties, let us consider several examples. They will also give us a better understanding of the order in which the lemmas leading to the main results are organised.

Let us try, for example, to eliminate equality substitutions using some sort of induction on derivations. Consider the inference

$$(6.7)\frac{(3.2)\dfrac{\Gamma, x{:}K, \Gamma' \vdash k{:}K'' \quad \Gamma, x{:}K, \Gamma' \vdash K'' = K'}{\Gamma, x{:}K, \Gamma' \vdash k{:}K'} \qquad \overline{\Gamma \vdash k_1 = k_2{:}K}}{\Gamma, [k_1/x]\Gamma' \vdash [k_1/x]k = [k_2/x]k{:}[k_1/x]K'}$$

It seems natural to apply substitution and the inductive hypothesis to the left premise of 3.2. The result is $\Gamma, [k_1/x]\Gamma' \vdash [k_1/x]k = [k_2/x]k{:}[k_1/x]K'$.

To replace the kind $[k_1/x]K''$ by $[k_1/x]K'$ one may derive the judgement $\Gamma, [k_1/x]\Gamma' \vdash [k_1/x]K'' = [k_1/x]K'$ by simple substitution from $\Gamma' \vdash K'' = K'$. But to obtain the premise $\Gamma \vdash k_1{:}K$ for this substitution we need to "split" $\Gamma \vdash k_1 = k_2{:}K$.

Meanwhile, "splitting" itself poses problems. To prove it, again by some induction on derivations, new substitutions could be necessary, as in case of a derivation, ending by

$$(5.6)\frac{\Gamma \vdash f = f'{:}(x{:}K)K' \quad \Gamma \vdash k_1 = k_2{:}K}{\Gamma \vdash f(k_1) = f'(k_2){:}[k_1/x]K'}$$

(By "splitting" premises and using application without equality 5.5 one obtains for the right part only $\Gamma \vdash f'(k_2){:}[k_2/x]K$ whereas the kind should be $[k_1/x]K$.) In other cases one may even need a rule which is not included in the formulation of the system.

Consider, for example, a derivation ending with

$$\frac{\Gamma, x{:}K_1 \vdash K_1' = K_2' \quad \Gamma \vdash K_1 = K_2}{\Gamma \vdash (x{:}K_1)K_1' = (x{:}K_2)K_2'}(5.2)$$

By the inductive hypothesis applied to the left premise, one obtains $\Gamma, x{:}K_1 \vdash K_1'$ and $\Gamma, x{:}K_1 \vdash K_2'$. From the first judgement one has, by 5.1, $\Gamma \vdash (x{:}K_1)K_1'$, as required. But 5.1 applied to the second will give $\Gamma \vdash (x{:}K_1)K_2'$. The kind K_1 should be changed to K_2 first. To save the situation, one apparently needs the rule

$$\frac{\Gamma, x{:}K, \Gamma' \vdash J \quad \Gamma \vdash K_1 = K_2}{\Gamma, x{:}K', \Gamma' \vdash J}.$$

We solve these problems by considering first some weaker, less problematic rules, proving, with their help, a variant of the "split-theorem" and only then passing to the rules that present the main difficulties.

3.1 Some basic lemmas

The next three lemmas hold for T[$\mathcal{C}$] and any of its subsystems and are proved by straightforward induction on the length of derivation.

Lemma 4. *(a) If a judgement of the form $\Gamma \vdash K{:}$**kind** is derivable, then K is either an El-kind, product-kind or the kind* **Type**. *(b) If $\Gamma \vdash K = K'$ is derivable, then both K, K' are either El-kinds or product-kinds or else the kind* **Type**. *(c)If $\Gamma \vdash K <_c K'$ is derivable, then both K, K' are either El-kinds or product-kinds.*

Lemma 5. *If $\Gamma \vdash J$, then $FV(J) \subseteq FV(\Gamma)$*

Lemma 6. *If $\Gamma, x{:}A \vdash$* **valid**, *then $x \notin FV(\Gamma)$.*

3.2 Elimination results

Let T[$\mathcal{C}$]$^-$($T[\mathcal{C}]_0^-, T[\mathcal{C}]_{0K}^-$) be the system obtained from T[$\mathcal{C}$]($T[\mathcal{C}]_0, T[\mathcal{C}]_{0K}$ respectively) by removing

- the substitution rules in LF(rules 6.1-6.7);
- the substitution rules for subtyping and subkinding (rules ST.5, SK.8).

We shall show, that every derivation in T[$\mathcal{C}$]may be transformed into a T[$\mathcal{C}$]$^-$-derivation of the same judgement.

Temporarily we need a system with even more restricted rules, where some subtyping and subkinding rules have more premises than usual. We take

$$(ST.2')\frac{\Gamma \vdash A <_c B{:}\mathbf{Type} \quad \Gamma \vdash A = A'{:}\mathbf{Type} \quad \Gamma \vdash A'{:}\mathbf{Type}}{\Gamma \vdash A' <_c B{:}\mathbf{Type}}(= -right)$$

instead of ST.2. We add in a similar way the premise $\Gamma \vdash B'$:**Type** to ST.3, the premise $\Gamma, x':K_1' \vdash K_2'$:**kind** to SK.2-4 (product-introductions for subkinding), the premises $\Gamma \vdash K_2'$:**kind**, $\Gamma \vdash K_1'$:**kind** and $\Gamma \vdash c':(K)K'$ to $SK.5(= -right)$ and $SK.6(= -left)$.

Let us call this system $T[\mathcal{C}]^=$. The following lemma holds for $T[\mathcal{C}]^-$ as well as $T[\mathcal{C}]^=$ and is proved by straightforward induction on the size (number of rules) of the derivation.

Lemma 7. *a)Every derivation of $\Gamma_1, \Gamma_2 \vdash J$ contains a sub-derivation of $\Gamma_1 \vdash$* **valid** *in the same system. b)Every derivation of $\Gamma_1, x:K, \Gamma_2 \vdash J$ contains a sub-derivation of $\Gamma_1 \vdash K$:**kind** in the same system. c) Every derivation of $\Gamma \vdash (x:K_1)K_2$ contains a sub-derivation of $\Gamma, x:K_1 \vdash K_2$.*

Lemma 8. *There are algorithms that transform every derivation of a judgement of the form $\Gamma \vdash A <_c B$:**Type** (of the form $\Gamma \vdash K <_c K'$) in $T[\mathcal{C}]^=$ into derivations of $\Gamma \vdash A$:**Type**, $\Gamma \vdash B$:**Type**, $\Gamma \vdash c:(El(A))El(B)$ (respectively derivations of $\Gamma \vdash K$:**kind**, $\Gamma \vdash K'$:**kind**, $\Gamma \vdash c:(K)K'$) in the same calculus.*

Proof. Straightforward induction (the presence of the extra premise is essential for it). □

Lemma 9. *(weakening) There is an algorithm that transforms every derivation in $T[\mathcal{C}]^=$ extended by the following weakening rule:*

$$\frac{\Gamma_1, \Gamma_2 \vdash J \quad \Gamma_1, \Gamma_3 \vdash \textbf{valid}}{\Gamma_1, \Gamma_3, \Gamma_2 \vdash J}(wkn)$$

(where $FV(\Gamma_2) \cap FV(\Gamma_3) = \emptyset$) into a $T[\mathcal{C}]^=$-derivation of the same judgement.

Proof. First we consider the case of a derivation containing exactly one wkn at the end, and prove the lemma by induction on the size of the derivation of its left premise. Then the proof is completed by trivial induction on the number of wkn rules (topmost are eliminated first). □

Lemma 10. *(Elimination of simple substitutions.) There is an algorithm that transforms every derivation in $T[\mathcal{C}]^= \cup \{6.1 - 6.5\}$ into a derivation in $T[\mathcal{C}]^=$.*

Proof is essentially similar to the proof of lemma 9, though contains more cases. □

Lemma 11. *(Elimination of retypings.) There is an algorithm that transforms every derivation in $T[\mathcal{C}]^=$ extended by the following rule*

$$\frac{\Gamma, x:K, \Gamma' \vdash J \quad \Gamma \vdash K = K' \quad \Gamma \vdash K':\textbf{kind}}{\Gamma, x:K', \Gamma' \vdash J}$$

(J stands for any form of judgement) into a derivation in $T[\mathcal{C}]^=$.

Proof as above. □

In the following lemma we consider "weak" equality substitutions:

$$(6.6')\ \frac{\Gamma, x{:}K, \Gamma' \vdash K'{:}\mathbf{kind}\quad \Gamma \vdash k_1 = k_2{:}K\quad \Gamma \vdash k_1{:}K\quad \Gamma \vdash k_2{:}K}{\Gamma, [k_1/x]\Gamma' \vdash [k_1/x]K' = [k_2/x]K'}$$

$$(6.7')\ \frac{\Gamma, x{:}K, \Gamma' \vdash k'{:}K'\quad \Gamma \vdash k_1 = k_2{:}K\quad \Gamma \vdash k_1{:}K\quad \Gamma \vdash k_2{:}K}{\Gamma, [k/x]\Gamma' \vdash [k_1/x]k' = [k_1/x]k'{:}[k/x]K'}$$

Lemma 12. *There is an algorithm that transforms every derivation in* $T[\mathcal{C}]^= \cup \{6.6', 6.7'\}$ *into a derivation in* $T[\mathcal{C}]^=$

Proof as above; in each case when "splitting" would be necessary for ordinary 6.6., 6.7 the extra premises are used. □

3.3 The "Split-theorem" and its consequences

Theorem 13. *(Split-theorem) In* $T[\mathcal{C}]^=$ *there are algorithms that transform every derivation of*

1. $\Gamma \vdash K_1 = K_2$ *into a derivation of* $\Gamma \vdash K_1{:}\mathbf{kind}$ *and of* $\Gamma \vdash K_2{:}\mathbf{kind}$;
2. $\Gamma \vdash k_1 = k_2{:}K$ *into a derivation of* $\Gamma \vdash k_1{:}K$ *and* $\Gamma \vdash k_2{:}K$;
3. $\Gamma \vdash \Sigma{:}K$ *into a derivation of* $\Gamma \vdash K{:}\mathbf{kind}$ *(Σ denotes here term or term equality);*

Proof By simultaneous induction on the size of the main derivation, using elimination lemmas 9, 10, 11, 12 and lemma 8. To illustrate why only weak formulations of the rules are enough, let's consider statement 1). Assume that the derivation ends with

$$\frac{\Gamma, x{:}K_1 \vdash K_1' = K_2'\quad \Gamma \vdash K_1 = K_2}{\Gamma \vdash (x{:}K_1)K_1' = (x{:}K_2)K_2'}(5.2)$$

By applying the inductive hypothesis to the left premise we obtain $\Gamma, x{:}K_1 \vdash K_1'$ and $\Gamma, x{:}K_1 \vdash K_2'$. From the first judgement we have by 5.1 $\Gamma \vdash (x{:}K_1)K_1'$, as required. We apply the inductive hypothesis to the second premise of 5.2 and obtain a derivation of $\Gamma \vdash K_2$ (this is why only "retyping" with three premises is needed.) Now

$$(5.1)\frac{\dfrac{\Gamma, x{:}K_1 \vdash K_2'\quad \Gamma \vdash K_1 = K_2\quad \Gamma \vdash K_2}{\Gamma, x{:}K_2 \vdash K_2'}}{\Gamma \vdash (x{:}K_2)K_2'}$$

The weak "retyping" may be eliminated by lemma 11. In other cases weakenings, substitutions and equality substitutions may appear, but the inductive hypothesis always allows us to derive extra premises and use appropriate lemmas. □.

Remark 14. The following rule

$$\frac{\Gamma, x{:}K, \Gamma' \vdash J \quad \Gamma \vdash K = K'}{\Gamma, x{:}K', \Gamma' \vdash J}$$

is admissible. We shall call it "context-retyping".

The following lemma clarifies the relationship between $T[\mathcal{C}]^-$and $T[\mathcal{C}]^=$.

Lemma 15. *There is an algorithm that transforms every derivation in $T[\mathcal{C}]^-$ into a derivation of the same judgement in $T[\mathcal{C}]^=$, and an inverse algorithm from $T[\mathcal{C}]^=$-derivations to $T[\mathcal{C}]^-$-derivation.*

Proof. Theorem 13 is used to obtain the extra premises with their derivations in the algorithm that transforms $T[\mathcal{C}]^-$-derivations into $T[\mathcal{C}]^=$-derivations. The inverse algorithm cuts off the extra premises. □

Theorem 16. *There are algorithms that transform every derivation in $T[\mathcal{C}]$into a derivation of the same judgement in $T[\mathcal{C}]^=$ and $T[\mathcal{C}]^-$.*

Proof is similar to the proof of the previous lemma, using in addition to the "split-theorem" (which provides extra premises) the elimination lemmas. It also uses previous lemma. □

Note, that the reduction above does not change coercion terms at all. Thus, lemma 4 holds for the whole $T[\mathcal{C}]$.

The following lemmas are easy consequences of results above. They hold in $T[\mathcal{C}]$and its subsystems $T[\mathcal{C}]^-$ and $T[\mathcal{C}]^=$.

Lemma 17. *(a)If $\Gamma \vdash (x_1{:}K_1)Q$, then $\Gamma \vdash K_1{:}\mathbf{kind}$ and $\Gamma, x_1{:}K_1 \vdash Q{:}\mathbf{kind}$.*
(b)If $\Gamma \vdash (x_1{:}K_1)Q = (x_1{:}K_1')Q'$ then $\Gamma \vdash K_1 = K_1'$ $\Gamma, x_1{:}K_1 \vdash Q = Q'$.

Lemma 18. *If $\Gamma \vdash [x{:}A]k{:}(x{:}A')K$, then $\Gamma, x{:}A \vdash k{:}K$ and $\Gamma \vdash A = A'{:}\mathbf{kind}$.*

Lemma 19. *The coercion terms are unique up to equality in $T[\mathcal{C}]$. If $\Gamma \vdash K <_{c_1} K'$, $\Gamma \vdash K <_{c_2} K'$ derivable in $T[\mathcal{C}]$, then $\Gamma \vdash c_1 = c_2{:}(K)K'$.*

Proof. We may assume that the derivations belong to $T[\mathcal{C}]^-$. By lemma 8, $\Gamma \vdash K$, $\Gamma \vdash K'$. The two judgements are used to derive $\Gamma, x{:}K \vdash$ **valid**, $\Gamma, x{:}K \vdash x{:}K$ and $\Gamma \vdash [y{:}K']y{:}(K')K'$ (we assume x, y fresh). Now we add $x{:}K$ to Γ in $\Gamma \vdash K <_{c_i} K'$, $\Gamma \vdash [y{:}K']y{:}(K')K'$ by *wkn* and apply the coercive definition rule CD to obtain $\Gamma, x{:}K \vdash [y{:}K']y(c_i(x)) = ([y{:}K']y)x{:}K'$. Using the β-rule we derive $\Gamma, x{:}K \vdash c_i(x) = ([y{:}K']y)x{:}K'$, and, by the symmetry and transitivity of $=$, $\Gamma, x{:}K \vdash c_1(x) = c_2(x){:}K'$. From this, $\Gamma \vdash [x{:}K]c_1(x) = [x{:}K]c_2(x){:}(K)K'$. With help of the η-rule we obtain $\Gamma \vdash c_1 = c_2{:}(K)K'$. □

Theorem 20. *If $\Gamma \vdash k{:}K$ and $\Gamma \vdash k{:}K'$ are derivable in $T[\mathcal{C}]$, then $\Gamma \vdash K = K'{:}\mathbf{kind}$ in $T[\mathcal{C}]$.*

Proof. We may assume that both derivations belong to T[$\mathcal{C}$]$^-$. The proof is by induction on the sum of sizes of derivations using the previous lemma. □

Remark 21. The proofs of all lemmas and theorems above (except lemma 19) go through without essential changes if we replace T[$\mathcal{C}$]and T[$\mathcal{C}$]$^-$by $T[\mathcal{C}]_0$ and $T[\mathcal{C}]_0^-$, $T[\mathcal{C}]_{0K}$ and $T[\mathcal{C}]_{0K}^-$ respectively. (We have only to drop some cases.)

Lemma 19 will still be true (with T-equality instead of T[$\mathcal{C}$]-equality), but its proof has to be changed (see below).

The proof of lemma 19 shows the power of the coercive rules more so than anything about the nature of T[$\mathcal{C}$]-equality and its relationship to the equality in T. This provides additional motivation to consider the conservativity issue.

3.4 Elimination of transitivity of subkinding

To prove the following lemmas, we introduce a *rank* of kinds in such a way, that $rank(El(k)) = 0$, $rank((x{:}K_1)K_2) = max(rank(K_1), rank(K_2)) + 1$, and $rank([k/x]K) = rank(k)$ (the last property holds, because substitution into kinds will always fall in scope of some *El*). The lemmas are proved by induction on rank.

Lemma 22. *There is an algorithm that transforms every derivation d of a subkinding judgement* $\Gamma \vdash K <_c K'$ *in T[C](*$T[\mathcal{C}]_{0K}$*), where d has exactly one application of one of =-left (SK.5), =-right (SK.6) into a derivation d′ of the same judgement in T[C](*$T[\mathcal{C}]_{0K}$*) which does not contain transitivity rules at all.*

Lemma 23. *There is an algorithm that transforms every derivation d of a subkinding judgement* $\Gamma \vdash K <_c K'$ *in T[C](*$T[\mathcal{C}]_{0K}$*), where d has exactly one application of SK.7 at the end, into a derivation d′ of the judgement* $\Gamma \vdash K <_{c'} K'$*, and* $\Gamma \vdash c = c'{:}(K)K'$ *in T[C](in T).*

Theorem 24. *(Elimination of transitivity for subkinding in* $T[\mathcal{C}]_{0K}$*.) a)There is an algorithm that transforms every derivation of the judgement* $\Gamma \vdash K <_c K'$ *in* $T[\mathcal{C}]_{0K}$ *into a derivation of the judgement* $\Gamma \vdash K <_{c'} K'$ *in the same calculus, not containing the rules* $SK.5 - 7$*, and such that* $\Gamma \vdash c' = c{:}(K)K'$ *in T.*

b)If $\Gamma \vdash K <_c K'$ *and* $\Gamma \vdash K <_{c'} K'$ *in* $T[\mathcal{C}]_{0K}$*, then* $\Gamma \vdash c' = c{:}(u{:}K)K'$ *in T.*

*Proof.*a) It is enough to consider the derivations in $T[\mathcal{C}]_{0K}^-$. We use induction on the number of transitivity rules, using previous lemmas.

b) If $\Gamma \vdash K <_c K'$ and $\Gamma \vdash K <_{c'} K'$ are derived without transitivity, the statement follows (by induction on derivations) from coherence conditions. But every coercion term , by a), is T-equal to the term corresponding to some derivation without transitivity. □

The situation in T[$\mathcal{C}$]is complicated by the presence of coercive application and definition rules. Note, that uniqueness of coercion terms (up to $T[\mathcal{C}]$-equality) is already proved (lemma 19).

Theorem 25. *(Elimination of transitivity for subkinding in T[C].) There is an algorithm that transforms every T[C]-derivation of the judgement $\Gamma \vdash J$, where J does not have subkinding form, into a derivation of the same judgement, and also every derivation of $\Gamma \vdash K <_c K'$ into a derivation of the judgement $\Gamma \vdash K <_{c'} K'$, not containing the rules $SK.5-7$, and such that $\Gamma \vdash c' = c{:}(K)K'$ in T[C].*

Proof. We may consider derivations in $\mathrm{T}[\mathcal{C}]^-$. The proof proceeds by induction on the number of judgements in the derivation, whose sub-derivation contains at least one application of transitivity rules $SK.5-7$. We consider the last rule in the derivation and apply inductive hypothesis to its premises. If this last rule was itself transitivity, we use afterwards lemma 22 or 23. Of the rest, only the coercive rules CA.1, CA.2, CD present some difficulties. The inductive hypothesis guarantees only that the premise $\Gamma \vdash K <_c K'$ will be replaced by $\Gamma \vdash K <_{c'} K'$ with $\Gamma \vdash c' = c{:}(K)K'$. To have in the conclusion a judgement which is identical to the original one, we derive appropriate equality between kinds and use 3.1. In case of CD we have to derive also equality between terms and use 2.6. □

3.5 Results about coercion completion

The safety of coercions as an abbreviational mechanism relies strongly on the possibility to insert in some uniform way all the coercions which were omitted (when CA.1, CA.2 and CD were applied). Presumably, a derivation in the underlying type theory T should be obtained.

Consider an inference of, say, coercive application rule $CA.1$.

$$\frac{\Gamma \vdash f{:}(x{:}K)K' \quad \Gamma \vdash k{:}K_0 \quad \Gamma \vdash K_0 <_c K}{\Gamma \vdash f(k){:}[c(k)/x]K'}$$

Assume that there exist some T-derivations of the premises $\Gamma \vdash f{:}(x{:}K)K'$ and $\Gamma \vdash k{:}K_0$, and a $T[\mathcal{C}]_{0K}$-derivation of $\Gamma \vdash K_0 <_c K$. From the $T[\mathcal{C}]_{0K}$-derivation of $\Gamma \vdash K_0 <_c K$ we obtain by lemma 4 a T-derivation of $\Gamma \vdash c{:}(K_0)K$. Now we obtain a T-derivation of the judgement $\Gamma \vdash f(c(k)){:}[c(k)/x]K'$ (using the LF-rules) as follows:

$$\frac{\overline{\Gamma \vdash f{:}(x{:}K)K'} \quad \dfrac{\Gamma \vdash c{:}(K_0)K \quad \Gamma \vdash k{:}K_0}{\Gamma \vdash c(k){:}K}(5.1)}{\Gamma \vdash f(c(k)){:}[c(k)/x]K'}(5.1).$$

The coercive equality application rule and coercive definition rule may be modified in the same way.

This construction suggests an idea of how to define a transformation Θ on the whole derivation. We should begin at the top, and move to the bottom replacing subkinding judgements in the premises of the coercive rules CA.1, CA.2 and CD by the derivations of their coercion terms, and modifying the rules accordingly. The intended result is a T-derivation of the judgement forms which are present in

T, and a derivation in its conservative extensions $T[\mathcal{C}]_0$ or $T[\mathcal{C}]_{0K}$ for subtyping and subkinding judgements respectively.

This idea will work correctly only if we can guarantee that the premises of all rules will be matching (at least, up to equality in T). Note, that even the identical kinds or terms may be modified in different ways in different derivations, since different coercion terms may be inserted.

For example, if we consider the ordinary application rule

$$\frac{\Gamma \vdash f{:}(x{:}K_1)K_2 \quad \Gamma \vdash k{:}K_1}{\Gamma \vdash f(k){:}[k/x]K_2},$$

and assume that some T[$\mathcal{C}$]-derivations of its premises, say, d_1, d_2 became the derivations $\Theta(d_1), \Theta(d_2)$ in T of $\Gamma' \vdash f'{:}(x{:}K_1')K_2'$ and $\Gamma'' \vdash k''{:}K_1''$ respectively, then the corresponding kinds in Γ' and Γ'' should be equal in T, and the same for K_1' and K_1''. If they are T-equal, we insert the appropriate instances of the equality rules 3.1, 3.2, of the admissible rule 3.3, and then use the same rule as in the main derivation.

We say that the transformation Θ is defined for a derivation d if the construction outlined above can be performed on the whole of d. In order to use technical results, obtained above, we define it on the class of derivations, including substitutions, the rules *wkn*, *context − retyping* and the rules with extra premises (they may be eliminated later from the resulting derivation). If a derivation does not contain coercive rules then Θ is the identity and the derivation is not changed. In principle, how a judgement is modified depends on its derivation and if we have two derivations of the same judgement, then applying Θ we may obtain two T-derivations of two different judgements.

We have a proof-sketch of the following results. (The technical details still have yet to be checked.)

Lemma 26. *Let d be a derivation. Assume that one of the lemmas 9, 10, 11, 12 or 8 holds. Let d' be obtained from d by the algorithm described in that lemma. If Θ is defined for d then it is defined for d' and the final judgements of $\Theta(d)$ and $\Theta(d')$ are equal in T component-wise (i.e., they have the same form, their contexts have equal length, the kinds of corresponding variables are T-equal and so on).*

Lemma 27. *Let d be a derivation of some judgement of the form $\Gamma \vdash J$. Let $\Gamma \vdash J'$ be one of its presupposed judgements as described in theorem 13, and d' be its derivation, obtained by the corresponding algorithm. If Θ is defined for d then it is defined for d'. If $\Theta_d(\Gamma \vdash J)$ is the final judgement of $\Theta(d)$, then the final judgement of $\Theta(d')$ is T-equal component-wise to the corresponding presupposed judgement of $\Theta_d(\Gamma \vdash J)$.*

Lemma 28. *Let d be a derivation. Assume that theorem 16 holds. Let d' be obtained from d by the algorithm described in that theorem. If Θ is defined for d then it is defined for d' and the final judgements of $\Theta(d)$ and $\Theta(d')$ are equal in T component-wise.*

Theorem 29. *The transformation Θ is defined for all derivations in T[C]and if d, d' are derivations of the same judgement $\Gamma \vdash J$, then the judgements $\Theta_d(\Gamma \vdash J)$ and $\Theta'_d(\Gamma \vdash J)$ are T-equal.*

Corollary 30. *If $\Gamma \vdash K = K'$ in T[C], and $\Gamma \vdash K$:**kind**, $\Gamma \vdash K'$:**kind** in T, then $\Gamma \vdash K = K'$:**kind** is derivable in T.*

Proof. Applying Θ to the derivation d of $\Gamma \vdash K = K'$:**kind** in T[C]and to the corresponding derivations d', d'' of the presupposed judgements $\Gamma \vdash K$:**kind** and $\Gamma \vdash K'$:**kind**, we obtain the T-derivations of $\Theta_d(\Gamma \vdash K = K'$:**kind**), $\Theta'_d(\Gamma \vdash K$:**kind**) and $\Theta''_d(\Gamma \vdash K')$. By lemma 27, the corresponding parts of these judgements are T-equal. Let d_0, d'_0 be some derivations of $\Gamma \vdash K$:**kind**, $\Gamma \vdash K'$:**kind**.

$$\Theta_{d_0}(\Gamma \vdash K{:}\mathbf{kind}) \equiv \Gamma \vdash K{:}\mathbf{kind}, \Theta_{d'_0}(\Gamma \vdash K'{:}\mathbf{kind}) \equiv \Gamma \vdash K'{:}\mathbf{kind}$$

Applying theorem 29 to d', d_0, d'', d'_0 respectively, and putting together all T-equalities, we see, that $\Gamma \vdash K = K'$ in T. □

4 A type-checking algorithm and its soundness proof

In this section, we present a type-checking algorithm, which is based on Coquand's algorithm described in [Coq91] but uses the notion of *typed reduction*, and prove its soundness using the meta-results in section 3.

4.1 The notion of typed reduction

The intended notion of computation for the extended type theory T[C] is the notion of *typed reduction*, which is is the reflexive and transitive closure generated from the following rules and the computation rules for the original type theory T.

$$\frac{\Gamma \vdash K_1 \rhd K_2 \quad \Gamma, x{:}K_1 \vdash K'_1 \rhd K'_2}{\Gamma \vdash (x{:}K_1)K'_1 \rhd (x{:}K_2)K'_2} \qquad (\rhd_\xi) \quad \frac{\Gamma \vdash K_1 \rhd K_2 \quad \Gamma, x{:}K_1 \vdash k_1 \rhd k_2 : K}{\Gamma \vdash [x{:}K_1]k_1 \rhd [x{:}K_2]k_2 : (x{:}K_1)K}$$

$$(\rhd_\beta) \quad \frac{\Gamma, x{:}K \vdash k' : K' \quad \Gamma \vdash k : K}{\Gamma \vdash ([x{:}K]k')(k) \rhd [k/x]k' : [k/x]K'} \qquad (\rhd_\eta) \quad \frac{\Gamma \vdash f : (x{:}K)K' \quad x \notin FV(f)}{\Gamma \vdash [x{:}K]f(x) \rhd f : (x{:}K)K'}$$

$$\frac{\Gamma \vdash f \rhd f'{:}(x{:}K)K' \quad \Gamma \vdash k_1 \rhd k_2{:}K_0 \quad \Gamma \vdash K_0 <_c K}{\Gamma \vdash f(k_1) \rhd f'(k_2){:}[c(k_1)/x]K'}$$

$$\frac{\Gamma \vdash f{:}(x{:}K)K' \quad \Gamma \vdash k_0{:}K_0 \quad \Gamma \vdash K_0 <_c K}{\Gamma \vdash f(k_0) \rhd f(c(k_0)){:}[c(k_0)/x]K'} (\rhd_c)$$

Note that typed reduction is restricted by principal kinding requirements, in contrast to the usual untyped reduction. For instance, if $\Gamma \vdash K_1 <_c K_2$, then with untyped reduction, we have

$$[x{:}K_1]([y{:}K_2]y)(x) \rhd_\beta [x{:}K_1]x$$
$$[x{:}K_1]([y{:}K_2]y)(x) \rhd_\eta [y{:}K_2]y$$

Hence, there are two different normal forms. With a typed reduction strategy, neither of the above reductions can be made. For the first, x would have to have kind K_2 and for the second the target of $[y{:}K_2]y$ would have to be K_1. In fact, with the typed reduction strategy the above reduction steps would not be admissible, but what we can do is the following:

$$\begin{aligned}[x{:}K_1]([y{:}K_2]y)(x) &\rhd_c [x{:}K_1]([y{:}K_2]y)(c(x)) \\ &\rhd_\beta [x{:}K_1]c(x) \\ &\rhd_\eta c\end{aligned}$$

4.2 Type-checking

In type-checkers such as LEGO ([LP92]) and Coq ([H+96]) type-checking is based upon the methods described in [Hue89]. The main thrust here is placed on a conversion algorithm as it is the most tricky part of type-checking. Conversion in these systems is tested by reducing both terms to a head normal form and then by recursively checking the structure of both head normal forms. It is important to note here that this method gives us a reduction strategy (outward reductions are performed first) and that both reduction and conversion are untyped. This then gives us a rather efficient method of type-checking.

Our algorithm is based on Coquand's algorithm described in [Coq91] which deals with $\beta\eta$-conversion. The method of checking whether two terms are convertible here is to reduce both to an unkinded β-weak head-normal form (whnf). The structures of the whnfs are then compared and if the terms are of the form $\lambda x.M$ and N, then M and $N.x$ are tested, thus checking for η-conversion.

In the presence of coercive subtyping, an unkinded algorithm leads away from uniqueness of normal forms as demonstrated in the example above and thus our algorithm is partially kinded. Kinding information is always checked before an attempt at either β, η or c-conversion and also when we want to return a weak head-normal form (whnf) of an arbitrary term. Kinds are not checked when we are dealing with the conversion of two terms and recursively checking their syntactic structure. Any less kinding makes the proof of soundness very difficult and any more kinding makes the proof of completeness more difficult. The proof of completeness is still an open problem

The structure of the algorithm The algorithm is divided mainly into the nine separate functions listed below, given that C is the graph of coercions and Γ is the current context:

- $\mathtt{valid}^C(\Gamma)$ is the predicate that checks to see if Γ is a valid context,
- $\mathtt{whnf}^C_\Gamma(k)$ computes the β, c-weak head-normal form of k,
- $\mathtt{conv}^C_\Gamma(k_1, k_2)$ checks whether k_1 and k_2 are equal objects of some kind K or of **kind** itself.
- $\mathtt{kcheck}^C_\Gamma(k, K)$ checks whether k is an object of kind K in Γ.
- $\mathtt{kinfer}^C_\Gamma(k)$ computes a kind of k,

- $\mathtt{iskind}^C_\Gamma(K)$ returns true iff $\mathtt{kinfer}^C_\Gamma(K) \equiv \mathbf{kind}$.
- $\mathtt{subkind}^C_\Gamma(K, K')$ checks to see if K is a proper subkind of K' with some coercion c.
- $\mathtt{coercion}^C_\Gamma(K, K')$ computes the coercion above coercion c if the subkinding predicate holds. Its behaviour is undefined otherwise.

In the rest of this section we give more detailed description of the main functions used in the algorithm. It is to be understood that for each part of the algorithm the cases are to be tried sequentially until a suitable case is found. If no such case is found, then the algorithm returns either false or failure.

Substitution Substitution is taken as a syntactic operation on terms.

Adding new free variables

1. $$\frac{}{\mathtt{valid}^C(\langle\rangle)}$$
2. $$\frac{\mathtt{valid}^C(\Gamma)\ \ \mathtt{iskind}^C_\Gamma(A)\ \ x \notin FV(\Gamma)}{\mathtt{valid}^C(\Gamma, x{:}A)}$$

Note that in everything to follow it is assumed that all contexts are valid.

Weak Head-Normal Form

1. $$\frac{\begin{array}{ll}\mathtt{whnf}^C_\Gamma(f) \equiv [x{:}A]f' & \mathtt{kinfer}^C_\Gamma(f) \equiv (x{:}A)B \\ \mathtt{kinfer}^C_\Gamma(k) \equiv K & \mathtt{conv}^C_\Gamma(A, K) \\ \mathtt{whnf}^C_{\Gamma,x:A}([k/x]f') \equiv k' & \end{array}}{\mathtt{whnf}^C_\Gamma(f(k)) \equiv k'}$$
2. $$\frac{\begin{array}{ll}\mathtt{kinfer}^C_\Gamma(f) \equiv (x{:}A)B & \mathtt{kinfer}^C_\Gamma(k) \equiv K \\ \mathtt{subkind}^C_\Gamma(K, A) & \mathtt{coercion}^C_\Gamma(K, A) \equiv c \\ \mathtt{whnf}^C_\Gamma(f(c(k))) \equiv k' & \end{array}}{\mathtt{whnf}^C_\Gamma(f(k)) \equiv k'}$$
3. $$\frac{\mathtt{kinfer}^C_\Gamma(k) \equiv K}{\mathtt{whnf}^C_\Gamma(k) \equiv k}$$

Note that the above case is only tried if the first two fail. This means that it covers every other possible case such as product kinds and the constant type. The premise of the above case means that only well-typed terms have a whnf. Thus, in particular, **kind** does not have a whnf.

Conversion Note that the conversion relation is defined so that it is obviously symmetric.

1. $$\frac{\mathtt{whnf}^C_\Gamma(m) \equiv \mathbf{Type}\ \ \mathtt{whnf}^C_\Gamma(n) \equiv \mathbf{Type}}{\mathtt{conv}^C_\Gamma(m, n)}$$

2. $$\frac{\mathtt{whnf}_\Gamma^C(m) \equiv x \ \mathtt{whnf}_\Gamma^C(n) \equiv x}{\mathtt{conv}_\Gamma^C(m,n)}$$

3. $$\frac{\begin{array}{l}\mathtt{whnf}_\Gamma^C(m) \equiv El(A) \ \mathtt{whnf}_\Gamma^C(n) \equiv El(B) \\ \mathtt{conv}_\Gamma^C(A,B)\end{array}}{\mathtt{conv}_\Gamma^C(m,n)}$$

4. $$\frac{\begin{array}{ll}\mathtt{whnf}_\Gamma^C(m) \equiv (x{:}A)B \ \mathtt{whnf}_\Gamma^C(n) \equiv (x{:}A')B' & \\ \mathtt{conv}_{\Gamma,x:A}^C(B,B') & \mathtt{conv}_{\Gamma,x:A'}^C(B,B') \\ \mathtt{conv}_\Gamma^C(A,A') & \end{array}}{\mathtt{conv}_\Gamma^C(m,n)}$$

5. $$\frac{\begin{array}{ll}\mathtt{whnf}_\Gamma^C(m) \equiv [x{:}A]k \ \mathtt{whnf}_\Gamma^C(n) \equiv [x{:}A']k' & \\ \mathtt{conv}_{\Gamma,x:A}^C(k,k') & \mathtt{conv}_{\Gamma,x:A'}^C(k,k') \\ \mathtt{conv}_\Gamma^C(A,A') & \end{array}}{\mathtt{conv}_\Gamma^C(m,n)}$$

6. $$\frac{\begin{array}{ll}\mathtt{whnf}_\Gamma^C(m) \equiv f(k) & \mathtt{whnf}_\Gamma^C(n) \equiv f'(k') \\ \mathtt{kinfer}_\Gamma^C(f) \equiv (x{:}A)B & \mathtt{kcheck}_\Gamma^C(f',(x{:}A)B) \\ \mathtt{kcheck}_\Gamma^C(k,A) & \mathtt{kcheck}_\Gamma^C(k',A) \\ \mathtt{conv}_\Gamma^C(f,f') & \mathtt{conv}_\Gamma^C(k,k')\end{array}}{\mathtt{conv}_\Gamma^C(m,n)}$$

7. $$\frac{\begin{array}{ll}\mathtt{whnf}_\Gamma^C(m) \equiv [x{:}A]k & \mathtt{whnf}_\Gamma^C(n) \equiv n' \\ \mathtt{kinfer}_\Gamma^C(m) \equiv (x{:}A)K & \mathtt{kcheck}_\Gamma^C(n,(x{:}A)K) \\ \mathtt{conv}_{\Gamma,x:A}^C(k,n'(x)) & \end{array}}{\mathtt{conv}_\Gamma^C(m,n)}$$

8. $$\frac{\begin{array}{ll}\mathtt{whnf}_\Gamma^C(m) \equiv m' & \mathtt{whnf}_\Gamma^C(n) \equiv [x{:}A]k \\ \mathtt{kinfer}_\Gamma^C(n) \equiv (x{:}A)K & \mathtt{kcheck}_\Gamma^C(m,(x{:}A)K) \\ \mathtt{conv}_{\Gamma,x:A}^C(k,m'(x)) & \end{array}}{\mathtt{conv}_\Gamma^C(m,n)}$$

Kind checking

1. $$\frac{\begin{array}{l}\mathtt{kinfer}_\Gamma^C(k) \equiv K' \ \mathtt{iskind}_\Gamma^C(K) \\ \mathtt{conv}_\Gamma^C(K,K')\end{array}}{\mathtt{kcheck}_\Gamma^C(k,K)} \text{ if } K \not\equiv \mathbf{kind},$$

2. $$\frac{\mathtt{iskind}_\Gamma^C(K)}{\mathtt{kcheck}_\Gamma^C(K,\mathbf{kind})}$$

Kind Inference

1. $$\frac{\mathtt{valid}^C(\Gamma)}{\mathtt{kinfer}_\Gamma^C(x) \equiv \Gamma(x)}$$

2. $$\frac{\mathtt{kinfer}_{\Gamma,x:A}^C(k) \equiv B}{\mathtt{kinfer}_\Gamma^C([x{:}A]k) \equiv (x{:}A)B}$$

3. $$\frac{\mathtt{iskind}_{\Gamma,x:A}^C(B)}{\mathtt{kinfer}_\Gamma^C((x{:}A)B) \equiv \mathbf{kind}}$$

4. $$\frac{\mathtt{kinfer}^{C}_{\Gamma}(f) \equiv (x{:}A)B \;\; \mathtt{kinfer}^{C}_{\Gamma}(k) \equiv K \quad \mathtt{conv}^{C}_{\Gamma}(K, A)}{\mathtt{kinfer}^{C}_{\Gamma}(f(k)) \equiv [k/x]B}$$

5. $$\frac{\mathtt{kinfer}^{C}_{\Gamma}(f) \equiv (x{:}A)B \quad \mathtt{kinfer}^{C}_{\Gamma}(k) \equiv K \quad \mathtt{subkind}^{C}_{\Gamma}(K, A) \quad \mathtt{coercion}^{C}_{\Gamma}(K, A) \equiv c}{\mathtt{kinfer}^{C}_{\Gamma}(f(k)) \equiv [c(k)/x]B}$$

6. $\mathtt{kinfer}^{C}_{\Gamma}(\mathbf{Type}) \equiv \mathbf{kind}$

7. $$\frac{\mathtt{kinfer}^{C}_{\Gamma}(A) \equiv \mathbf{Type}}{\mathtt{kinfer}^{C}_{\Gamma}(El(A)) \equiv \mathbf{kind}}$$

Checking for Kinds

1. $$\frac{\mathtt{kinfer}^{C}_{\Gamma}(K) \equiv \mathbf{kind}}{\mathtt{iskind}^{C}_{\Gamma}(K)}$$

The subkinding relation

1. $$\frac{\mathtt{kcheck}^{C}_{\Gamma}(A, \mathbf{Type}) \quad \mathtt{kcheck}^{C}_{\Gamma}(B, \mathbf{Type}) \quad \mathtt{kcheck}^{C}_{\Gamma}(c, (x{:}El(A))El(B)) \quad (A, c, B) \in C^*}{\mathtt{subkind}^{C}_{\Gamma}(El(A), El(B)) \quad \mathtt{coercion}^{C}_{\Gamma}(El(A), El(B)) \equiv c}$$

2. $$\frac{\mathtt{iskind}^{C}_{\Gamma,x:K_1}(K_2) \quad \mathtt{subkind}^{C}_{\Gamma}(K'_1, K_1) \quad \mathtt{subkind}^{C}_{\Gamma,x:K_1}([x/K_2], K'_2) \quad \mathtt{coercion}^{C}_{\Gamma}(K'_1, K_1) \equiv c_1 \quad \mathtt{coercion}^{C}_{\Gamma,x:K_1}(K_2, K'_2) \equiv c_2}{\mathtt{subkind}^{C}_{\Gamma}((x{:}K_1)K_2, (x{:}K'_1)K'_2) \quad \mathtt{coercion}^{C}_{\Gamma}((x{:}K_1)K_2, (x{:}K'_1)K'_2) \equiv [f{:}(x{:}K_1)K_2][x{:}K'_1]c_2(f(c_1(x)))}$$

3. $$\frac{\mathtt{iskind}^{C}_{\Gamma,x:K_1}(K_2) \quad \mathtt{subkind}^{C}_{\Gamma}(K'_1, K_1) \quad \mathtt{conv}^{C}_{\Gamma,x:K_1}([x/K_2], K'_2) \;\; \mathtt{coercion}^{C}_{\Gamma}(K'_1, K_1) \equiv c_1}{\mathtt{subkind}^{C}_{\Gamma}((x{:}K_1)K_2, (x{:}K'_1)K'_2) \quad \mathtt{coercion}^{C}_{\Gamma}((x{:}K_1)K_2, (x{:}K'_1)K'_2) \equiv [f{:}(x{:}K_1)K_2][x{:}K'_1]f(c_1(x))}$$

4. $$\frac{\mathtt{iskind}^{C}_{\Gamma}(K_2) \quad \mathtt{conv}^{C}_{\Gamma}(K'_1, K_1) \quad \mathtt{subkind}^{C}_{\Gamma,x:K_1}(K_2, K'_2) \;\; \mathtt{coercion}^{C}_{\Gamma,x:K_1}(K_2, K'_2) \equiv c_2}{\mathtt{subkind}^{C}_{\Gamma}((x{:}K_1)K_2, (x{:}K'_1)K'_2) \quad \mathtt{coercion}^{C}_{\Gamma}((x{:}K_1)K_2, (x{:}K'_1)K'_2) \equiv [f{:}(x{:}K_1)K_2][x{:}K'_1]c_2(f(x))}$$

4.3 Soundness of the algorithm

The algorithm presented above is sound.

Theorem 31. *The following hold:*

1. *If* $\mathtt{valid}^{C}(\Gamma)$, *then* $\Gamma \vdash \mathbf{valid}$,
2. *If* $\Gamma \vdash k{:}K$ *and* $\mathtt{whnf}^{C}_{\Gamma}(k) \equiv k'$, *then* $\Gamma \vdash k = k'{:}K$,
3. *If* $\Gamma \vdash k{:}K$, $\Gamma \vdash k'{:}K$ *and* $\mathtt{conv}^{C}_{\Gamma}(k, k')$, *then* $\Gamma \vdash k = k'{:}K$,

4. *If* $\mathit{kcheck}_\Gamma^C(k, K)$*, then* $\Gamma \vdash k{:}K$,
5. *If* $\mathit{kinfer}_\Gamma^C(k) \equiv K$*, then* $\Gamma \vdash k{:}K$,
6. *If* $\mathit{iskind}_\Gamma^C(K)$*, then* $\Gamma \vdash K{:}\mathbf{kind}$,
7. *If* $\mathit{subkind}_\Gamma^C(K, K')$ *and* $\mathit{coercion}_\Gamma^C(K, K') \equiv c$*, then* $\Gamma \vdash K <_c K'$.

Proof: The proof is by induction on derivations of the algorithm. Only the more complex cases are described below.

(whnf.1) Assume $\Gamma \vdash f(k){:}K^*$. Also assume:

$$\begin{array}{ll} \mathbf{whnf}_\Gamma^C(f) \equiv [x{:}A]f' & \mathbf{kinfer}_\Gamma^C(f) \equiv (x{:}A)B \\ \mathbf{kinfer}_\Gamma^C(k) \equiv K & \mathbf{conv}_\Gamma^C(A, K) \\ \mathbf{whnf}_\Gamma^C([k/x]f') \equiv k' & \end{array}$$

By the I.H. we get both $\Gamma \vdash k{:}K$ and $\Gamma \vdash f{:}(x{:}A)B$ and so, by Theorem 13, $\Gamma \vdash (x{:}A)B{:}\mathbf{kind}$ and then, by Lemma 17, $\Gamma \vdash A{:}\mathbf{kind}$. Therefore, we can use the I.H. to get:

$$\Gamma \vdash f = f{:}[x{:}A']f'{:}(x{:}A)B \;\; \Gamma \vdash A = K{:}\mathbf{kind}$$

We can then use the Split Lemma to show $\Gamma \vdash [x{:}A]f'{:}(x{:}A)B$ and so Lemma 18 gives us $\Gamma, x{:}A \vdash f'{:}B$. Then the I.H. gives us:

$$\Gamma, x{:}A \vdash [k/x]f' = k'{:}[k/x]B$$

and the result soon follows using the (β)-rule.

(conv.5) This result follows if we use the admissible rule $\dfrac{\Gamma \vdash K = K'{:}\mathbf{kind} \;\; \Gamma, x{:}K \vdash \mathbf{J}}{\Gamma, x{:}K' \vdash \mathbf{J}}$

(conv.7) This rule follows similarly, using the I.H, the (η)-rule and Theorem 20.

Corollary 32. *The following are also true.*

1. *If* $\mathit{kcheck}_\Gamma^C(k, K)$ *and* $\mathit{whnf}_\Gamma^C(k) \equiv k'$*, then* $\Gamma \vdash k = k'{:}K$,
2. *If* $\mathit{kcheck}_\Gamma^C(k, K)$*,* $\mathit{kcheck}_\Gamma^C(k', K)$ *and* $\mathit{conv}_\Gamma^C(k, k')$*, then* $\Gamma \vdash k = k'{:}K$,

Proof: Immediate, using Theorem 31.

5 Conclusion and related work

Reported here is the development of some basic but important meta-theoretic properties of the framework with coercive subtyping and a sound type-checking algorithm for coercive subtyping. The presentation of the framework in this paper also allows us to show more clearly what sort of connection there is between subtyping and coherence problems. Such a connection for subtyping in the second order lambda-calculus (system F) was investigated in [LMS95,LMS], where the importance of cut-elimination (ie, elimination of transitivity) is shown to be of particular importance. This is also the case in our work reported here.

Traditional meta-theoretic studies on dependent type theories have mostly been considered for type systems with an underlying conversion relation (e.g., the presentation of Pure Type Systems) rather than those with equality judgements (e.g., the presentation of Martin-Löf's type theory and that used for coercive subtyping in this paper). The relationship between these two kinds of presentations of type theories has been a subtle and difficult problem. Coquand in [Coq91] deals with this problem and Goguen in his PhD thesis [Gog94] has developed a theory of typed operational semantics for the meta-theory of type theory. The approach in this paper is to develop the meta-theory of coercive subtyping by studying the system with judgemental equality directly and try, as far as we can, to separate the meta-theory of the LF with subtyping (at the kind level) from that of the underlying type theory. This is reflected in our treatment and presentation of the meta-theoretic results in this paper. For example, the existence of the coercion insertion map (Theorem 29) is an important factor that allows important computational properties of the extended system to be studied independently from the underlying type theory. In other words, many results can take the form that 'if the underlying type theory T has properties that ..., then T[$\mathcal{C}$] has the property that ...'. The results in this paper has laid down a basis for such a development.

The type-checking algorithm presented here uses the notion of typed reduction, rather than the untyped reduction. We have explained why this is the case by considering an example in Section 4.1. However, this example also suggests that there is a possibility to study more efficient reduction strategies for coercive subtyping. Notice that the following three judgements can be derived:

$$\Gamma \vdash [x{:}K_1]([y{:}K_2]y)(x){:}(K_1)K_2$$
$$\Gamma \vdash [x{:}K_1]x{:}(K_1)K_1$$
$$\Gamma \vdash [y{:}K_2]y{:}(K_2)K_2$$

Now $\Gamma \vdash (K_1)K_1 <_{c^A} (K_1)K_2$ and $\Gamma \vdash (K_2)K_2 <_{c^B} (K_1)K_2$ where

$$c^A \equiv [f{:}(x{:}K_1)A][x{:}K_1]c(f(x))$$
$$c^B \equiv [f{:}(x{:}K_2)B][x{:}K_1]f(c(x)).$$

It can then be shown that $c^A([x{:}K_1]x)$ and $c^B([y{:}K_2]y)$ are convertible. We hope that some generalisation of this example will lead to a strategy that requires a lot less typing. The consideration of the fully typed algorithm in this paper is a necessary step towards further study of, for example, more efficient reduction strategies.

A lot of work has been presented already on subtyping. People such as Cardelli ([Car88,Car89]) and Aspinall and Compagnoni ([AC96]) present systems with subtyping that do not use coercions. Bailey [Bai96] and Saibi [Sai97] have already implemented coercive subtyping into current proof assistant programs as notational abbreviations. Our approach should lead to better understanding of such implementations and possibly better implementation of type-checking algorithms.

References

[AC96] D. Aspinall and A. Compagnoni. Subtyping dependent types. *Proc. of LICS96*, 1996.

[Bai93] Anthony Bailey. Representing algebra in LEGO. Master's thesis, Department of Computer Science, University of Edinburgh, 1993.

[Bai96] A. Bailey. Lego with implicit coercions. 1996. Draft.

[Car88] L. Cardelli. Type-checking dependent types and subtypes. *Lecture Notes in Computer Science*, 306, 1988.

[Car89] L. Cardelli. Typeful programming. Lecture notes for the IFIP State of the Art Seminar on Formal Description of Programming Concepts, Rio de Janeiro, Brazil, 1989.

[Coq91] Th. Coquand. An algorithm for testing conversion in Type Theory. In G. Huet and G. Plotkin, editors, *Logical Frameworks*. Cambridge University Press, 1991.

[Gog94] H. Goguen. *A Typed Operational Semantics for Type Theory*. PhD thesis, University of Edinburgh, 1994.

[H+96] G. Huet et al. *The Coq Proof Assistant Reference Manual*. INRIA-Rocquencourt, February 1996.

[Hue89] Gérard Huet. The constructive engine. In R. Narasimhan, editor, *A Perspective in Theoretical Computer Science*. World Scientific Publishing, 1989. Commemorative Volume for Gift Siromoney.

[Jon95] Alex Jones. The formalization of linear algebra in LEGO: The decidable dependency theorem. Master's thesis, Department of Mathematics, University of Manchester, 1995.

[LMS] Giuseppe Longo, Kathleen Milsted, and Sergei Soloviev. Coherence and transitivity of subtyping as entailment. *To appear in Journal of Logic and Computation*.

[LMS95] G. Longo, K. Milsted, and S. Soloviev. A logic of subtyping. In *Proc. of LICS'95*, 1995.

[LP92] Zhaohui Luo and Robert Pollack. LEGO proof development system: User's manual. Technical Report LFCS Report ECS-LFCS-92-211, Department of Computer Science, University of Edinburgh, 1992.

[Luo93] Z. Luo. Program specification and data refinement in type theory. *Mathematical Structures in Computer Science*, 3(3), 1993.

[Luo94] Z. Luo. *Computation and Reasoning: A Type Theory for Computer Science*. Oxford University Press, 1994.

[Luo96] Z. Luo. Coercive subtyping in type theory. *Proc. of CSL'96, the 1996 Annual Conference of the European Association for Computer Science Logic, Utrecht. LNCS 1258*, 1996.

[Luo97] Z Luo. Coercive suptyping. Draft submitted for publication, 1997.

[NPS90] B. Nordström, K. Petersson, and J. Smith. *Programming in Martin-Löf's Type Theory: An Introduction*. Oxford University Press, 1990.

[Sai97] A. Saibi. Typing algorithm in type theory with inheritance. *Proc of POPL'97*, 1997.

Semantical BNF

Petri Mäenpää

University of Helsinki

Abstract. BNF (Backus Naur Formalism) grammar is extended by semantic structures. This yields a grammatical formalism that describes semantics uniformly with syntax, semantical BNF. It is formulated in type theoretical grammar, which is a categorial grammar designed for natural languages and formulated in constructive type theory. Semantical BNF applies type theoretical grammar to formal languages, in particular programming languages.

From the point of view of BNF, semantical BNF extends its productions by semantic structures. They allow the grammarian to write rules that generate only semantically as well as syntactically well-formed expressions. This stands in contrast to approaches to grammar in terms of BNF such as attribute grammar. They first generate expressions by BNF productions. Then a separate phase of type checking discards those expressions which are syntactically well-formed but meaningless, i.e. semantically ill-formed. Furthermore, this type checking phase typically does not relate to the syntactic phase of generation in a theoretically rigorous way. Semantical BNF integrates these two phases in terms of a uniform syntactic-semantic grammatical formalism.

From the point of view of constructive type theory, semantical BNF can be seen as its extension with syntactic categories. This allows making syntactic distinctions that are otherwise unavailable in constructive type theory. They are necessary for describing the abstract syntax of a language, and can also be used to vary concrete syntax. A mathematical interpretation function maps the extension back into constructive type theory.

To show how a formal language with variables is described grammatically, Knuth's binary number grammar is interpreted as a semantical BNF grammar, and extended into a small, functional language with typed lambda terms. Semantical BNF is also related to standard contemporary grammars of programming languages that use denotational semantics and to the theory of higher-order abstract syntax.

1 Introduction

BNF is the standard grammatical formalism for describing the syntax of programming languages, but it applies to formal languages in general. It can be seen as a variant notation for context-free phrase structure grammar, which is one of the standard syntactic formalisms for natural languages.

BNF does not have enough power to describe formal languages semantically. Therefore BNF grammars alone are not suitable for compiling (=translating) or interpreting formal languages, in particular programming languages. To this end, the BNF grammarian typically uses attribute grammar, introduced by Knuth (1968). One widespread application of attribute grammar is YACC. An attribute grammar consists of BNF productions with associated semantic rules.

Syntactic description by BNF quite evidently lies on a more solid theoretical foundation than semantic description by attribute grammar (see Aho, Sethi, and Ullman 1986). This calls for alternatives to attribute grammar. The present paper proposes a type-theoretical one: a new grammatical formalism for describing the syntax and semantics of programming languages and of formal languages in general, semantical BNF.

Although attribute grammar lacks theoretical rigour compared to other semantic formalisms, it is used extensively due to its considerable intuitive appeal. Our aim is to preserve the intuitive appeal of attribute grammar by extending its syntactic component BNF in a new, natural way, with semantic structures that are theoretically rigorous. We shall motivate this extension by carefully relating attribute grammar to semantical BNF, and describe how an attribute grammar is interpreted as a semantical BNF grammar.

Attribute grammar controls overgeneration by means of semantic rules associated with BNF productions. Semantical BNF, in contrast, incorporates the required semantic information directly into BNF rules. In particular, the semantic information contains type information that enforces type checking of expressions upon formation. This guarantees that semantical BNF generates only well-formed expressions in the semantic as well as the syntactic sense. All generated expressions admit interpretation.

Attribute grammar separates type checking from generation. It generates expressions by BNF productions, which are syntactic. These syntactically well-formed expressions may be semantically ill-formed, that is meaningless. In that case they are discarded at the stage of type checking. For example, the BNF grammar

$$
\begin{array}{l}
\mathrm{E} \rightarrow \mathrm{E} + \mathrm{E} \\
\mathrm{E} \rightarrow \mathrm{B} \mid \mathrm{Bool} \\
\mathrm{B} \rightarrow 0 \mid 1 \\
\mathrm{Bool} \rightarrow \textsf{true} \mid \textsf{false}
\end{array}
$$

generates the meaningless expression 1+**true** from the nonterminal E. Type checking would then discard this expression in attribute grammar, as Section 4 shows. A truth value cannot be added to a number. Semantical BNF allows the grammarian to write these rules in a way that rules out such overgeneration. This is achieved by adding semantic information.

Knuth (1971, p. 227) ascribes the success of context-free grammar, such as BNF, as a syntactic formalism, "to its intuitive appeal (since the syntactic tree structures form a first approximation to the semantic structures)". Semantical BNF incorporates semantic structures as additional structures of BNF syntax trees. This formalizes Knuth's intuitive notion of syntactic structure approximating semantic structure in a natural and theoretically rigorous way.

Semantical BNF is formulated in type theoretical grammar, introduced by Ranta (1994), and itself formulated in constructive type theory (Martin-Löf

1984). Type theoretical grammar generalizes Montague grammar by replacing the type structure of simple type theory with the dependent type structure of constructive type theory. Montague grammar is a logical formalization of phrase structure grammar for natural language, with associated semantics.

Our generalization and interpretation of BNF into semantical BNF is modeled upon Ranta's (1995a, 1995b, 1996, 1997) analogous generalization and interpretation of phrase structure grammar of natural language into type theoretical grammar with syntactic categories. The present work's contribution is to extend the domain of application of type theoretical grammar from natural languages to formal languages. Our interpretation of attribute grammar in semantical BNF does not seem to correspond to anything carried out in natural language semantics.

To our knowledge, no previous work explores the systematic utilization of dependent types in programming language grammar. The formalism of higher-order abstract syntax (see e.g. Despeyroux et al. 1995) makes use of the higher-order structures and inductively defined types of constructive type theory, but it seems to us that dependent types are not made essential grammatical use of there. A predicate is defined to distinguish semantically well-formed from 'exotic' expressions. This is analogous to type checking in attribute grammar.

This paper is organized as follows. The generalization of BNF into semantical BNF is presented by way of an example, Knuth's grammar for binary numbers (Section 2).

Four new kinds of formal structure incorporate semantic information into BNF. First, BNF nonterminal symbols are interpreted as syntactic categories of categorial grammar, that is, as categories of expressions. The expressions are then made explicit in the formalism. Attribute grammar is also given a type-theoretical interpretation in terms of categorial grammar (Section 3).

Second, semantical BNF extends BNF with semantic categories and their objects. Third, categories are allowed to depend on one another. In particular, letting syntactic categories depend on semantic ones gives the grammarian means of preventing overgeneration. He can impose semantic restrictions on the expressions generated. Constructive type theory provides the dependent type structure required for dependencies between grammatical categories (Section 4).

Fourth, syntactic categories are allowed to depend on contexts. Contexts are used for describing variable binding, and for checking that the use of a variable agrees with its declaration, given by a context (Section 5).

Finally, the example semantical BNF grammar for binary numbers is extended into one for a small functional language with simply typed lambda terms. This allows for comparison with higher-order abstract syntax. Grammatical rules are formulated for a simple type system (Section 6), and for variable abstraction and function application (Section 7).

2 An attribute grammar for binary numbers

Knuth introduced attribute grammar in terms of the following grammar for binary numbers. (In fact, his grammatical formalism has been named attribute grammar only later on—he did not use any proper name for it.) It consists of two components: BNF productions describe the syntax, and semantic rules tell how to assign meaning to a string generated by the syntax.

Syntactic rules	*Semantic rules*
$B \to 0$	$v(B) = 0$
$B \to 1$	$v(B) = 2^{s(B)}$
$L \to B$	$v(L) = v(B),\ s(B) = s(L),\ l(L) = 1$
$L_1 \to L_2\ B$	$v(L_1) = v(L_2) + v(B),\ s(B) = s(L_1),$ $s(L_2) = s(L_1) + 1,\ l(L_1) = l(L_2) + 1$
$N \to L$	$v(N) = v(L),\ s(L) = 0$
$N \to L_1 . L_2$	$v(N) = v(L_1) + v(L_2),\ s(L_1) = 0$ $s(L_2) = -l(L_2)$

The syntactic rules generate binary numerals. These numerals denote real numbers, although the grammar leaves this implicit. Knuth's definition of binary numbers entails, to take his example, that the meaning of the string 1101.01 is 13.25. This consequence depends on a certain evaluation order of the *attributes* v (value), s (scale), and l (length). The following syntax tree, annotated with attribute values, illustrates the evaluation.

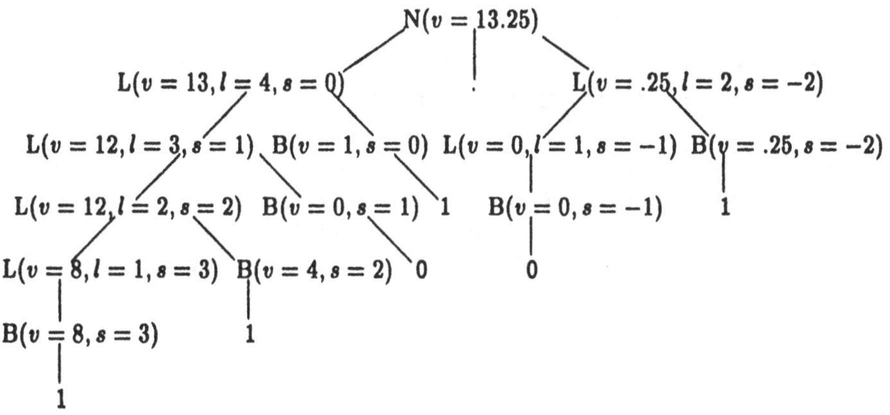

A *synthesized* attribute, like v and l in the present grammar, is evaluated bottom-up in the syntax tree, that is, from constituent expressions to their compounds. An *inherited* attribute, like s here, is evaluated top-down, that is, from compounds to their constituents. This is because a synthesized attribute is defined in terms of the attributes of the descendants of the nonterminal in a syntax tree, and an inherited attribute in a dual manner in terms of the attributes of the ancestors (Knuth 1968, p. 130).

Intuitively, inherited attributes represent the contribution of the context of an expression to its meaning, while synthesized attributes represent the contribution of its constituents. Attribute grammar represents this idea mathematically so that the semantic rules attached to a syntactic rule define the synthesized attributes of the nonterminal on the left hand side and the inherited attributes of the nonterminals on the right hand side.

Not just any order of evaluating the attributes yields a value. Evaluation order must respect the dependencies defined in the semantic rules. This grammar has two such dependencies to consider. The semantic rule for the production $B \rightarrow 1$ defines the value of the synthesized attribute v in terms of that of the inherited attribute s, and the last semantic rule for the production $N \rightarrow L_1 . L_2$ defines the value of s in terms of that of the inherited attribute l. (A systematic explanation of the subscripts in semantic rules is given in Section 3.)

To evaluate the attributes, one must therefore first traverse the syntax tree bottom-up to evaluate l. This yields the length of every string generated by a production for a list of bits (L). Then s is evaluated top-down, to determine the scale of each bit (B) and list of bits. In the present grammar, scale means position relative to radix point (or to rightmost bit if there is no radix point). Finally, the attribute v is evaluated bottom-up. This yields the numeric value of the whole binary numeral (N) in terms of the values of its constituents.

Besides evaluation order, the attribute grammarian must check that the dependencies established by the definitions of attributes are not circular. Attribute grammar employs general recursive functions to define attributes, which allows nonterminating definitional chains. Knuth (1968) gives an algorithm for detecting potentially circular definitions.

3 Generalization of BNF into semantical BNF. Interpretation of attribute grammar

We are now ready to generalize BNF into semantical BNF. Let us proceed by first constructing the semantical BNF interpretation of Knuth's example attribute grammar. This example will then illustrate the generalization.

BNF productions appear to the left, and the corresponding semantical BNF rules to the right.

$B \rightarrow 0$

$$\begin{aligned} &\mathbf{0} : \mathrm{B} \\ &\mathbf{0}^{\star}(s) = 0 \\ &\mathbf{0}^{\circ} = 0 \end{aligned}$$

$B \rightarrow 1$

$$\begin{aligned} &\mathbf{1} : \mathrm{B} \\ &\mathbf{1}^{\star}(s) = 2^{s} \\ &\mathbf{1}^{\circ} = 1 \end{aligned}$$

$L \rightarrow B$

$$\frac{b : \mathrm{B}}{\begin{array}{l}\mathrm{OneBit}(b) \; : \; \mathrm{L} \\ \mathrm{OneBit}(b)^{\star}(s) \; = \; b^{\star}(s) \\ \mathrm{OneBit}(b)^{\circ} \; = \; b^{\circ}\end{array}}$$

$$l(\mathrm{OneBit}(b)) = 1$$

L → L B

$$\frac{a : \mathrm{L} \quad b : \mathrm{B}}{\begin{array}{l}\mathrm{BitList}(a, b) \; : \; \mathrm{L} \\ \mathrm{BitList}(a, b)^{\star}(s) \; = \; a^{\star}(s+1) + b^{\star}(s) \\ \mathrm{BitList}(a, b)^{\circ} \; = \; a^{\circ}\, b^{\circ}\end{array}}$$

$$l(\mathrm{BitList}(a, b)) = l(a) + 1$$

N → L

$$\frac{a : \mathrm{L}}{\begin{array}{l}\mathrm{Num}(a) \; : \; \mathrm{N} \\ \mathrm{Num}(a)^{\star} \; = \; a^{\star}(0) \\ \mathrm{Num}(a)^{\circ} \; = \; a^{\circ}\end{array}}$$

N → L . L

$$\frac{a : \mathrm{L} \quad b : \mathrm{L}}{\begin{array}{l}\mathrm{RadixNum}(a, b) \; : \; \mathrm{N} \\ \mathrm{RadixNum}(a, b)^{\star} \; = \; a^{\star}(0) + b^{\star}(-l(b)) \\ \mathrm{RadixNum}(a, b)^{\circ} \; = \; a^{\circ} \,.\, b^{\circ}\end{array}}$$

Semantical BNF rules are triples: a rule for *forming*, *interpreting* (*), and *linearizing* ($^{\circ}$) a syntax tree. For example, the syntax tree **0** of type B interprets into the number 0, and linearizes into the the string 0. That is, $\mathbf{0}^{\star} = 0$ and $\mathbf{0}^{\circ} = \mathtt{0}$.

Given a BNF production, the corresponding semantical BNF syntax tree is formed by interpreting BNF nonterminals as syntactic categories, that is as categories (=types) of expressions. In contrast to BNF, the expressions are made explicit, as syntax trees. The interpretation rule defines what mathematical object an expression denotes. This is a kind of *denotational semantics.* Finally, the linearization rules yield the linear string form of an expression in tree form. (The term 'linearization' is introduced in Ranta 1997 and replaces 'sugaring', which was used previously in type theoretical grammar).

The type-theoretical basis of this extension of BNF is using the form of judgement

$$a : A$$

to represent the typing of a syntax tree,

expression a belongs to the syntactic category A.

To take a slightly more complicated example, the BNF production

$$\mathrm{L} \to \mathrm{L}\ \mathrm{B}$$

combines an expression of category L with an expression of category B into an expression of category L. These expressions can be made explicit by augmenting the production into the rule

$$\frac{a : \mathrm{L} \quad b : \mathrm{B}}{\mathrm{BitList}(a, b) \ : \ \mathrm{L}}.$$

Thus the combination of expressions is formalized as functional composition.

This rule allows forming for instance the expression $\mathrm{BitList}(\mathrm{OneBit}(\mathbf{1}), \mathbf{0}) \ : \ \mathrm{L}$, which linearizes into the string 10 and interprets into the number 2. In BNF, this string can be obtained by the derivation

$$\mathrm{L} \to \mathrm{L}\ \mathrm{B} \to \mathrm{B}\ \mathrm{B} \to 1\ \mathrm{B} \to 10$$

as the BNF formalism does not contain syntax trees. Hence it has no concept of linearization either. Rather, strings are generated directly by applying productions repeatedly.

Each nonterminal of the right hand side of a BNF production is interpreted as a premiss of the corresponding semantical BNF rule, and the nonterminal on the left hand side as the conclusion. Terminals are produced by the linearization rules.

The rules for forming syntax trees in semantical BNF are introduction rules of type theory. BNF productions are thus generalized into introduction rules for syntactic categories. The operators that form syntax trees, like **0**, **1**, and BitList, are thus constructors.

This interpretation is quite natural, because the rules of BNF in fact combine expressions, not nonterminals. These expressions belong to certain categories in semantical BNF, namely the nonterminals.

The fully explicit form of the linearization rule $\mathrm{BitList}(a, b)^\circ \ = \ a^\circ\ b^\circ$ is

$$\mathrm{linL}(\mathrm{BitList}(a, b)) \ = \ \mathrm{linL}(a) \ \_\ \mathrm{linB}(b) \ : \ \mathrm{Bin}$$

because each syntactic category is assigned its proper linearization function, for example the category L the function linL. Bin is the the set of strings generated by the grammar.

The abbreviated form of linearization rules will be used in the following, with the result type suppressed and the operator $^\circ$ overloaded, instead of explicitly using a separate linearization function for each syntactic category. Concatenation is indicated by juxtaposition instead of the explicit operator _ , uniformly with BNF notation.

Consider Knuth's example of a string generated by his grammar, 1101.01. In semantical BNF, it is the linearized form of the syntax tree

$$\begin{aligned}\mathrm{RadixNum}(\, & \mathrm{BitList}(\mathrm{BitList}(\mathrm{BitList}(\mathrm{OneBit}(\mathbf{1}), \mathbf{1}), \mathbf{0}), \mathbf{1}), \\ & \mathrm{BitList}(\mathrm{OneBit}(\mathbf{0}), \mathbf{1})),\end{aligned}$$

whose interpretation is 13.25. The string 1101.01 results from taking the leaves of the syntax tree from left to right. This illustrates linearization at its simplest.

In general, linearization may be more complicated, as the rules in the following sections will illustrate. However, the essential principle of *compositionality* is adhered to in type theoretical grammar, just like for interpretation: the linearization of a syntax tree must be a function of the linearizations of its immediate constituents (Ranta 1996).

Besides a linearization rule, type theoretical grammar assigns an interpretation rule to each type of syntax trees. For example, the interpretation rule for a bit list generated by the production L $\rightarrow$ L B is

$$\text{intL}(\text{BitList}(a, b)) = \text{intL}(a) + \text{intB}(b) : \text{Real},$$

disregarding, for now, the contribution of inherited attributes. This interpretation rule corresponds to Knuth's valuation rule, for the synthesized attribute v. As in linearization rules, the value type will be omitted in rules of interpretation, and the overloaded interpretation operator * will be used instead of explicitly using separate functions, such as intB, intL, and intN, for each category. The above rule of interpretation thus abbreviates to

$$\text{BitList}(a, b)^\star = a^\star + b^\star.$$

Now consider the meaning contribution of Knuth's inherited scale attribute s to bit lists. The interpretation function for category B has an argument place for the scale of a bit, and the function for L an argument place for the scale of a list of bits. This argument place of * interprets the attribute s in the semantical BNF grammar. For example, the interpretation rule $\text{BitList}(a, b)^\star = a^\star + b^\star$ extends to

$$\text{BitList}(a, b)^\star(s) = a^\star(s + 1) + b^\star(s).$$

A synthesized attribute is interpreted in semantical BNF as a primitive recursive function on syntax trees. There is a distinct function for each nonterminal that the attribute operates on. The syntax trees are defined inductively, and the functions on syntax trees by primitive recursion along the inductive definition.

This interpretation is illustrated at its simplest in the case of Knuth's synthesized attribute l. The semantical BNF function l is defined only on syntax trees of type L, because the attribute l operates only on the nonterminal L. The primitive recursive definition consists of two equations, one for each of the constructors OneBit and BitList of L.

Knuth's other synthesized attribute v is interpreted as * in the same way. As v operates on several distinct nonterminals in the attribute grammar, a distinct function is defined correspondingly in semantical BNF for each type of syntax tree it operates on. Now v is defined on all three nonterminals, so its interpretation consists of an interpretation function for each of them, intB, intL, and intN. They are all abbreviated in the present rule notation to the one overloaded function *.

The interpretation function $\star$ also has an argument place that Knuth's attribute v lacks, the one for scale. This brings us back to the interpretation of inherited attributes in semantical BNF.

If a synthesized attribute is defined in terms of an inherited attribute, then the inherited attribute is interpreted as an argument of the function that interprets the synthesized attribute. Thus in the present case s is interpreted as an argument of $\star$. The value of the inherited attribute, as given in a semantic rule of attribute grammar, becomes the value of the argument in the semantical BNF rule.

Semantical BNF omits the arguments of inherited attributes, because they are not needed. They just identify, in the present interpretation, the argument place to which the value of the inherited attribute is assigned.

At its simplest, the value of an inherited attribute is interpreted just as a variable that occupies an argument place of a function in semantical BNF. A case in point is the interpretation rule $\mathbf{1}^\star(s) = 2^s$ assigned to the syntax tree $\mathbf{1} : \mathrm{B}$, which corresponds to the BNF production $\mathrm{B} \rightarrow 1$. The argument B of the inherited attribute s in Knuth's semantic rule $v(\mathrm{B}) = 2^{s(\mathrm{B})}$ is omitted, and s becomes an argument of $\star$. In type-theoretical terms, the argument s is given by the context of $\star$. The full form of the interpretation rule is $\mathrm{intB}(\mathbf{1}, s) = 2^s : \mathrm{Real} \quad (s : \mathrm{Int})$, where Int is the set of integers.

This interpretation of inherited attributes in semantical BNF agrees thus perfectly with the original intuition that inherited attributes represent the contribution of the context of an expression to its meaning.

The values of inherited attributes are slightly more complicated in the semantic rules for the production $\mathrm{L}_1 \rightarrow \mathrm{L}_2\ \mathrm{B}$. Now the inherited attribute s is defined by the rules $s(\mathrm{B}) = s(\mathrm{L}_1)$ and $s(\mathrm{L}_2) = s(\mathrm{L}_1) + 1$. These values are incorporated in the interpretation rule $\mathrm{BitList}(a, b)^\star(s) = a^\star(s+1) + b^\star(s)$ as arguments.

Yet another variation appears in the semantic rule $s(\mathrm{L}) = 0$ associated with the BNF production $\mathrm{N} \rightarrow \mathrm{L}$. Now the inherited attribute has a constant value 0, so the argument in the interpretation rule $\mathrm{RadixNum}(a)^\star = a^\star(0)$ is just 0, with no appearance of the variable s of the previous interpretation rules. The left hand side of this equation has no scale argument, because the scale attribute only operates on the nonterminals B and L, not N.

The present interpretation of attribute grammar also explains systematically the role of the numerical subscripts of nonterminals in attribute grammar. They serve to distinguish, in the semantic rules, between the occurrences of a nonterminal in a BNF production. For instance, the semantic rule $v(\mathrm{L}_1) = v(\mathrm{L}_2) + v(\mathrm{B})$ associated with the production $\mathrm{L}_1 \rightarrow \mathrm{L}_2\ \mathrm{B}$ refers to the two occurrences of the nonterminal L in the production by means of the subscripts. As there really is just one nonterminal, not two, this device is not quite satisfactory theoretically. In fact, the semantic rule makes reference to two different expressions that belong to the category L, not to the two occurrences of L itself. By making these expressions explicit in the formalism, semantical BNF distinguishes them in a natural way. The numerical subscripts then become obsolete.

Judging from the appearance of an attribute grammar, attributes seem to operate on nonterminals. To understand the numerical subscripts of nonterminals, attributes must however be understood as operating on the expressions that are objects of the nonterminals, interpreted as categories. This could be spelled out informally in the explanation of the grammatical formalism, but it seems theoretically more satisfactory to incorporate this idea into the grammatical formalism itself.

Semantical BNF uses just the primitive recursive functions of higher type of constructive type theory, instead of general recursive functions of ground type like attribute grammar. Using primitive recursive functions of higher type is characteristic of constructive type theory. This rules out nonterminating definitional chains, so that potential circularity need not be checked, and allows dropping the restrictions on the evaluation order of attributes. Semantics is assigned to a syntax tree compositionally along its inductively defined structure. However, giving a denotation by higher-order primitive recursive functions may sometimes be difficult.

Standard contemporary grammars of programming languages do not incorporate syntax trees into the grammatical formalism (see e.g. Schmidt 1994, Tennent 1991). An interpretation function is defined apparently on strings, but in fact on their derivations in terms of syntax trees. In contrast, semantical BNF incorporates syntax trees directly into the grammatical formalism. This allows a rigorous definition of interpretation and linearization. Also concrete syntax can then be defined rigorously, by linearization, not just abstract syntax.

To sum up the interpretation, let us return to the question of intuitive appeal, and compare semantical BNF in this respect to attribute grammar. The intuitive purpose of inherited attributes is to pass context-dependent semantic information. It is therefore natural to formalize them as function arguments, whose values are given in context. Also the present interpretation of synthesized attributes is natural, because their intuitive purpose is to define the meaning of an expression in terms of the meanings of its constituent expressions. This idea is given formal precision by introducing the expressions into the grammatical formalism as inductively defined syntax trees on which synthesized attributes are defined by primitive recursion. Combining these interpretations of inherited and synthesized attributes gives, furthermore, a theoretically rigourous way of describing the semantics of languages that are defined syntactically by BNF productions. This also rules out circular semantic definitions.

4 Relativization of BNF nonterminals to semantic categories

Semantical BNF builds type checking into the rules for forming syntax trees. This is achieved by relativizing BNF nonterminals, interpreted as syntactic categories, to semantic categories. The semantic categories used in this relativization are domains of individuals in the sense of logic, so the outcome is a system of *domain-relative* syntactic categories. In type theory, any set can be regarded as a domain of individuals. The relativization follows that of Ranta (1995a) for phrase structure grammar of natural language.

Knuth's grammar for binary numbers is about one domain of individuals only, the reals. To illustrate type checking, the grammar must be augmented with more domains. Let us employ the two basic domains of integers (Int) and reals (Real). The domains of the object language must be distinguished from the sets of the type-theoretical metalanguage, because we don't want to use all sets as domains in a particular grammar. A universe dom : set is set up for this purpose. Intuitively, dom can be considered as a subset of set.

Domains can also be composed by means of operators. Our example grammar uses the operator → for forming function domains. This paper uses an informal notation that does not distinguish domains as codes in the universe dom from domains as sets. Making the codes and decoding operators explicit would make the notation unnecessarily heavy.

To add the domain of reals to Knuth's grammar, let us replace the nonterminal N by the two nonterminals N_Z and N_R. Now the grammar defines binary integers (N_Z) in addition to binary reals (N_R). (This subscripting should not be confused with that of Knuth, because N_Z and N_R are different nonterminals, whereas L_1 is the same nonterminal as L_2.)

$\mathrm{N}_Z \rightarrow \mathrm{L}$

$$\frac{a : \mathrm{L}}{\begin{array}{l}\mathrm{IntNum}(a) : \mathrm{N}_Z \\ \mathrm{IntNum}(a)^\star = a^\star(0) \\ \mathrm{IntNum}(a)^\circ = a^\circ\end{array}}$$

$\mathrm{N}_R \rightarrow \mathrm{L} \,.\, \mathrm{L}$

$$\frac{a : \mathrm{L} \quad b : \mathrm{L}}{\begin{array}{l}\mathrm{RealNum}(a,b) : \mathrm{N}_R \\ \mathrm{RealNum}(a,b)^\star = a^\star(0) + b^\star(-l(b)) \\ \mathrm{RealNum}(a,b)^\circ = a^\circ \,.\, b^\circ\end{array}}$$

For example, 1 is a binary integer numeral, an 1.0 a binary real numeral.

We now introduce a new syntactic category E for binary expressions. They can be numerals, variables, or operators combined with their operands. The dependent type structure of constructive type theory allows E to be *split semantically*, in the sense introduced by Ranta (1995a). This yields the categories E(Int) of integer expressions, E(Real) of real expressions, E(Int → Real) of expressions of functions from integers to reals, and so on. There is a category for each domain. This is achieved by relativizing the nonterminal E to domains. E is categorized as a family of sets indexed by semantic categories, E : (dom)set, instead of as a set, like the nonterminals B, L, N_Z, and N_R employed so far. Syntax trees of type E(Int) and N_Z are interpreted as integers, and those of type E(Real), B, L, and N_R as reals.

One way of forming an expression of E is from a binary numeral, either integer or real.

$\mathrm{E} \rightarrow \mathrm{N}_Z \mid \mathrm{N}_R$

$$\frac{n : \mathrm{N}_Z}{\begin{array}{l}\mathrm{IntNumExpr}(n) : \mathrm{E}(\mathrm{Int}) \\ \mathrm{IntNumExpr}(n)^\star = n^\star \\ \mathrm{IntNumExpr}(n)^\circ = n^\circ\end{array}} \qquad \frac{n : \mathrm{N}_R}{\begin{array}{l}\mathrm{RealNumExpr}(n) : \mathrm{E}(\mathrm{Real}) \\ \mathrm{RealNumExpr}(n)^\star = n^\star \\ \mathrm{RealNumExpr}(n)^\circ = n^\circ\end{array}}$$

Another way is by means of an infix operator (Inop) and two expressions of appropriate types as operands.

$\mathrm{E} \rightarrow (\ \mathrm{E}\ \mathrm{Inop}\ \mathrm{E}\ )$

$$\frac{A, B, C : \mathrm{dom} \quad d : \mathrm{E}(A) \quad f : \mathrm{Inop}(A, B, C) \quad e : \mathrm{E}(B)}{\begin{array}{l}\mathrm{InopExpr}(A, B, C, d, f, e) : \mathrm{E}(C) \\ \mathrm{InopExpr}(A, B, C, d, f, e)^\star = f^\star(d^\star, e^\star) \\ \mathrm{InopExpr}(A, B, C, d, f, e)^\circ = (\ d^\circ\ f^\circ\ e^\circ\ )\end{array}}$$

Such an infix expression is type checked upon formation, because the rule incorporates the domains A and B of the operands and the domain C of the value. Semantical BNF thus allows the categorization of operators to incorporate their operand and value types. An example of infix operators with argument and value types is

$\mathrm{Inop} \rightarrow +$

$$\begin{array}{ll}\mathrm{AddZ} : \mathrm{Inop}(\mathrm{Int}, \mathrm{Int}, \mathrm{Int}) & \mathrm{AddR} : \mathrm{Inop}(\mathrm{Real}, \mathrm{Real}, \mathrm{Real}) \\ \mathrm{AddZ}^\star = +_Z & \mathrm{AddR}^\star = +_R \\ \mathrm{AddZ}^\circ = + & \mathrm{AddR}^\circ = +\end{array}$$

These rules show how semantical BNF treats *overloading*, an important kind of ambiguity. The operator + is overloaded, because it is a linearization of two different syntax trees. One of them interprets into integer addition $+_Z$ and the other into real addition $+_R$. A syntax tree of type $\mathrm{Inop}(A, B, C)$ is interpreted as an object of type (A)(B)C.

An example of an infix expression is

$$\begin{array}{l}\mathrm{InopExpr}(\mathrm{Int}, \mathrm{Int}, \mathrm{Int}, \mathrm{IntNumExpr}(\mathrm{IntNum}(\mathrm{OneBit}(\mathbf{0}))), \\ \qquad \mathrm{AddZ}, \\ \qquad \mathrm{IntNumExpr}(\mathrm{IntNum}(\mathrm{OneBit}(\mathbf{1})))),\end{array}$$

which interprets into the integer $+_Z(0, 1)$, i.e. 1, and linearizes into (0+1).

To show how concrete syntax can be varied, let us formulate a rule for prefix expressions corresponding to the one for infix expressions.

$\mathrm{E} \rightarrow (\ \mathrm{Preop}\ \mathrm{E}\ \mathrm{E}\ )$

$$\frac{A, B, C : \mathrm{dom} \quad f : \mathrm{Preop}(A, B, C) \quad d : \mathrm{E}(A) \quad e : \mathrm{E}(B)}{\begin{array}{l}\mathrm{PreopExpr}(A, B, C, f, d, e) : \mathrm{E}(C) \\ \mathrm{PreopExpr}(A, B, C, f, d, e)^\star = f^\star(d^\star, e^\star) \\ \mathrm{PreopExpr}(A, B, C, f, d, e)^\circ = (\ f^\circ\ d^\circ\ e^\circ\ )\end{array}}$$

Now one may express a sum of integers or reals in infix as well as prefix syntax, provided that a prefix addition operator is defined in the same way as the infix addition operator above.

The attribute grammarian would use the BNF production

$$\mathrm{E}_1 \rightarrow (\ \mathrm{Preop}\ \mathrm{E}_2\ \mathrm{E}_3\ )$$

with numeric subscripts instead. This production allows generating the syntactically well-formed but semantically ill-formed string (+ 1 true), given the rules for booleans of Section 1. The meaningless string would then be ruled out in the separate phase of type checking, typically by means of a procedural rule such as

$$\begin{array}{l} \textbf{if } \mathit{type}(\mathrm{E}_2) = \mathit{type}(\mathrm{E}_3) \\ \textbf{then } \mathit{type}(\mathrm{E}_1) := \mathit{type}(\mathrm{E}_2) \\ \textbf{else } \mathrm{type\_error} \end{array}$$

where *type* is a synthesized attribute.

Semantical BNF, in contrast, employs declarative, purely logical semantics for the same purpose, with no such low-level procedural descriptions. The attribute *type* is interpreted in semantical BNF differently from the other synthesized attributes. It is not interpreted as a function on syntax trees, but by types of type theory, namely the domains. This is illustrated by the rule for forming infix expressions. The reason for this exceptional interpretation is of course that types in the sense of type theory directly capture the intuitive notion of type that attribute grammar represents as an attribute. Judgements of constructive type theory can be type checked mechanically, which is why it suits the grammatical purpose of type checking perfectly.

Some contemporary accounts of programming language grammar, such as Schmidt (1994), use 'typing attributes'. They are a variant of the type attributes of attribute grammar and serve the purpose of domain-relative syntactic categories. Schmidt uses the typing notation $a : A$ to express that the derivation of string a has typing attribute A. His derivations of strings are trees of such typings, not linear sequences of BNF production applications. They are thus a special kind of syntax trees. The same string of a 'syntax domain' (=syntactic category) may in general be assigned different typing attributes, so that *unicity of typing* does not necessarily hold. In contrast, semantical BNF enforces unicity of typing of expressions in the sense of syntax trees, because it is an inherent property of the underlying formalism of constructive type theory. From the point of view of semantical BNF, Schmidt's syntax domains are semantically split into typing attributes, but his grammatical formalism does not reflect this by making typing attributes parametrized syntax domains.

Tennent (1991) also derives strings by trees of typings. His typings come much closer to those of semantical BNF than Schmidt's. An example is 0 : exp[int], which means that the (derivation of) string 0 is an integer expression. Here exp is a 'phrase type' (=syntactic category) and int is a 'data type' (=domain). The bracket notation corresponds to the domain-relativity of our syntactic categories, which constructive type theory represents naturally by dependent types.

Indeed, semantical BNF can be seen as a type-theoretical analogue of the kind of grammar that Tennent describes, with syntax trees incorporated as inductively defined objects of his 'phrase types'.

5 Relativization of BNF nonterminals to contexts

An important further way of forming an expression (E) is from a variable. To achieve this, the nonterminals of BNF are relativized to contexts. A context is understood here in the sense of constructive type theory, that is, as a progressive list of variable declarations. Ranta introduced *context-relative* syntactic categories into type theoretical grammar in his (1996).

This relativization generalizes the type checking by means of semantic categories presented in the previous section. It allows checking the semantic well-formedness of a use of a variable directly upon its formation. Type theoretical grammar achieves this by determining whether the use agrees with the declaration of the variable given by the context.

A variable declaration is semantic information that attribute grammar typically describes by means of inherited attributes—they serve to pass context-dependent semantic information. However, instead of the type-theoretical structure of context, attribute grammar employs theoretically much less rigourous devices, typically symbol tables. From the point of view of attribute grammar, one could therefore see syntactic categories relativized to contexts as BNF nonterminals with associated symbol tables.

A context, in the present grammatical sense, is formed inductively by the following pair of rules.

$$() : \text{cont} \qquad \frac{\Gamma : \text{cont} \quad A : \text{dom}/\Gamma \quad t : \text{symb}}{(\Gamma,\ x_t : A) : \text{cont}}$$

The first rule forms the empty context, and the second rule extends a given context Γ with the declaration of a new variable x of type A that linearizes into the symbol t. As t is given by a premiss, the grammarian has full control over the names of variables in the expressions he forms. Here A may depend on variables declared in Γ. Futhermore, x has to be a fresh variable and t a fresh symbol with respect to Γ.

This notion of contexts was introduced by Ranta (1996). It uses the notation of Martin-Löf's substitution calculus formulation of type theory, whose presentation in a slightly different notation can be found in Tasistro (1993). This notation is used because in type theoretical grammar judgements in context J/Γ are intended to be understood like the ones of substitution calculus.

However, the present contexts are not real contexts of type theory. Real contexts don't allow variables to carry linearization names. The present contexts are in fact encoded in a universe of contexts. Intuitively, this universe is a subset of the Σ sets of type theory. The present paper does not make this encoding explicit in order not to make the notation unnecessarily heavy.

Now that the context mechanism has been introduced, we are ready to add a rule for forming an expression (E) from a variable (Var).

E → Var

$$\frac{\Gamma : \text{cont} \quad A : \text{dom}/\Gamma \qquad v : \text{Var}(\Gamma, A)}{\begin{array}{rcl} \text{VarExpr}(\Gamma, A, v) & : & \text{E}(\Gamma, A) \\ \text{VarExpr}(\Gamma, A, v)^\star & = & v^\star \\ \text{VarExpr}(\Gamma, A, v)^\circ & = & v^\circ \end{array}}$$

The last premiss gives a variable of type A in context Γ, from which the rule forms an expression of type A in context Γ. Now the syntactic category E is relativized to contexts in addition to domains. Furthermore, the domain A is relativized to the context Γ. This gives the generalized categorization E : $(\Gamma : \text{cont})(\text{dom}/\Gamma)\text{set}$.

The new syntactic category Var is context- and domain-relative in the same way as E. These two categories *syntactically split* the domain A they are relative to, in the sense that syntax trees of type Var(Γ, A) and E(Γ, A) are both interpreted as objects $a : A/\Gamma$, that is, as elements of the set A that may depend on the context Γ.

Type theory has to be extended by syntactic categories in order to make syntactic distinctions in the grammatical description of formal languages. From the semantic point of view, the categories Var(Γ, A) and E(Γ, A) are the same. In defining the syntax of a formal language, however, this distinction is vital. For example, it does not make syntactic sense to use just any expression as a formal parameter. It must be a variable.

The rules for forming infix and postfix expressions given in the previous section generalize straightforwardly to the context-relative form introduced in this section. For example, the infix expression rule becomes

E → (E Inop E)

$$\frac{\Gamma : \text{cont} \quad A, B, C : \text{dom} \quad d : \text{E}(\Gamma, A) \quad f : \text{Inop}(A, B, C) \quad e : \text{E}(\Gamma, B)}{\begin{array}{rcl} \text{InopExpr}(\Gamma, A, B, C, d, f, e) & : & \text{E}(\Gamma, C) \\ \text{InopExpr}(\Gamma, A, B, C, d, f, e)^\star & = & f^\star(d^\star, e^\star) \\ \text{InopExpr}(\Gamma, A, B, C, d, f, e)^\circ & = & (\ d^\circ\ f^\circ\ e^\circ\ ) \end{array}}$$

The notion of syntactically splitting a semantic category was introduced by Montague (1974) and generalized to the setting of domain- (1995a) and context-relative (1996) syntactic categories by Ranta. Ranta's decisive innovation with respect to Montague grammar is the dual notion of splitting syntactic categories semantically by the two kinds of relativizations. This notion applies usefully here also to the grammar of formal languages, and not only to that of natural languages, for which Ranta introduced it.

Next, the example grammar needs rules for forming variable expressions (Var). These rules were introduced by Ranta (1996) for the informal language of mathematics. The present formulation is adapted from his (1997).

To form a variable expression, any variable of appropriate type and given in context will do. There are two ways in which a variable declaration can occur in the context: either as the newest declaration or deeper. Therefore, type theoretical grammar employs two rules for forming variable expressions. The first rule forms a variable expression from the newest variable declared in the context.

Var $\rightarrow$ symb

$$\frac{\Gamma : \text{cont} \quad A : \text{dom}/\Gamma \quad t : \text{symb}}{\begin{array}{l}\text{NewVar}(\Gamma, A, t) : \text{Var}((\Gamma,\ x_t : A), A) \\ \text{NewVar}(\Gamma, A, t)^\star = x \\ \text{NewVar}(\Gamma, A, t)^\circ = t\end{array}}$$

The second way of forming a variable expression is from a variable declared deeper in the context.

Var $\rightarrow$ Var

$$\frac{\Gamma : \text{cont} \quad A : \text{dom}/\Gamma \quad B : \text{dom}/\Gamma \quad t : \text{symb} \quad v : \text{Var}(\Gamma, A)}{\begin{array}{l}\text{OldVar}(\Gamma, A, B, t, v) : \text{Var}((\Gamma,\ x_t : B), A) \\ \text{OldVar}(\Gamma, A, B, t, v)^\star = v^\star \\ \text{OldVar}(\Gamma, A, B, t, v)^\circ = v^\circ\end{array}}$$

Given a variable of type A in context Γ, this rule forms a variable of type A in the context Γ extended with a variable of any given type B. The variable is formed by referring one declaration deeper than the newest one. The last premiss guarantees that there is a variable of type A in the context Γ. It can be referred to for forming a variable by applying this rule, repeatedly if needed. Each application increases the *reference depth* by one. The notion of the reference depth of a variable was introduced by de Bruijn (1972), and generalized in type theoretical grammar by Ranta (1996).

The rules for Var generalize de Bruijn's *index* representation of variables in the setting of categorial grammar by relativizing it to contexts and domains, with compositional interpretation and linearization. Ranta (1997) defines these indices in type theoretical grammar as $0(t) = \text{NewVar}(t)$, $1(t) = \text{OldVar}(\text{NewVar}(t))$, $2(t) = \text{OldVar}(\text{OldVar}(\text{NewVar}(t)))$, etc. Context and domain arguments of syntax trees are suppressed in this definition.

For example, $1(t)$ and $0(u)$ refer respectively to the variables of the context $(x_t : \text{Int}, f_u : \text{Int} \rightarrow \text{Real})$.

Using the rules of this section, we can introduce some variation into our previous example of a syntax tree for the string (0+1). Let us replace the constant 0 by a variable n given in context. The ensuing syntax tree

$$\begin{array}{ll}\text{InopExpr}((x_n : \text{Int}), \text{Int}, \text{Int}, \text{Int}, & \text{VarExpr}((x_n : \text{Int}), \text{Int}, \text{NewVar}((), \text{Int}, n)), \\ & \text{AddZ}, \\ & \text{IntNumExpr}((x_n : \text{Int}), \text{IntNum}(\text{OneBit}(\mathbf{1}))))\end{array}$$

of type $\text{E}((x_n : \text{Int}), \text{Int})$ interprets into the integer $+_Z(x, 1)$ and linearizes into the string $(n+1)$.

6 Simple types for a functional language

A grammar for a small simply typed functional language requires rules for describing the syntax and semantics of variable abstraction and function application. We shall formulate a system of simply typed lambda terms, with the difference to the type-theoretical metalanguage that abstracted variables are typed. To abstract a variable in a typed language, a type mechanism must first be set up, because there are no bare variables but only variables of a certain type.

Our example grammar has three type formation rules, for the syntactic category Type. Although the type structure described in this paper is simple, we make the category Type context-relative. This allows for describing a system of dependent types in semantical BNF, and is coherent with the context-relativity of domains. The basic types are formed as follows:

Type $\rightarrow$ int | real

$$\frac{\Gamma : \text{cont}}{\begin{array}{l}\text{IntType}(\Gamma) : \text{Type}(\Gamma)\\ \text{IntType}(\Gamma)^{\star} = \text{Int}\\ \text{IntType}(\Gamma)^{\circ} = \texttt{int}\end{array}} \qquad \frac{\Gamma : \text{cont}}{\begin{array}{l}\text{RealType}(\Gamma) : \text{Type}(\Gamma)\\ \text{RealType}(\Gamma)^{\star} = \text{Real}\\ \text{RealType}(\Gamma)^{\circ} = \texttt{real}\end{array}}$$

Then the language needs a rule for forming a function type $A \longrightarrow B$.

Type $\rightarrow$ (Type $\longrightarrow$ Type)

$$\frac{\Gamma : \text{cont} \quad A : \text{Type}(\Gamma) \quad B : \text{Type}(\Gamma)}{\begin{array}{l}\text{FunType}(\Gamma, A, B) : \text{Type}(\Gamma)\\ \text{FunType}(\Gamma, A, B)^{\star} = A^{\star} \rightarrow B^{\star}\\ \text{FunType}(\Gamma, A, B)^{\circ} = (\ A^{\circ} \longrightarrow B^{\circ}\ )\end{array}}$$

This rule contains an arrow symbol in three different senses. The first arrow $\rightarrow$ in the BNF production is the usual rewriting symbol. This same symbol appears in the interpretation rule and denotes the function space former of the metalanguage. Finally, the longer arrow $\longrightarrow$ is a nonterminal of the BNF grammar and thus appears also in the linearization rule.

A syntax tree of category Type(Γ) is interpreted as an object $A : \text{dom}/\Gamma$, so the objects of Type(Γ) correspond to semantic categories on the syntactic level. The metalanguage has sets, some of which are distinguished as domains of the object language by encoding them in dom, and some as types of the object language by defining the respective type expressions. As objects of dom decode into sets, so type expressions interpret into domains. However, not all sets are conversely encoded in dom, or expressible in the object language as types.

7 Variable abstraction and function application

Now that a type structure has been set up, a rule for typed variable abstraction can be formulated.

E $\rightarrow$ (λ symb : Type) E

$$\frac{\Gamma : \text{cont} \quad A : \text{Type}(\Gamma) \quad B : \text{dom}/\Gamma \quad t : \text{symb} \quad e : \text{E}((\Gamma,\ x_t : A^{\star}), B)}{\begin{array}{l}\text{AbsExpr}(\Gamma, A, B, t, e) : \text{E}(\Gamma, A^{\star} \rightarrow B)\\ \text{AbsExpr}(\Gamma, A, B, t, e)^{\star} = \text{lambda}((x)e^{\star})\\ \text{AbsExpr}(\Gamma, A, B, t, e)^{\circ} = (\ \lambda\, t : A^{\circ}\ )\ e^{\circ}\end{array}}$$

Given a type expression A and an expression e of type B that may depend on a variable of type $A^\star$, the rule forms a typed lambda abstract of e. The linearization name t of this variable is given as a symbol. The expression formed belongs to the semantic category $A^\star \rightarrow B$, because it is a function abstract. Its interpretation is therefore the lambda abstract of the interpretation of e. To avoid ambiguities, we use AbsExpr for the operator that forms a lambda abstract syntax tree, lambda for the metalanguage lambda operator of Π type, and λ for the object language lambda operator.

Note how type information is represented by means of semantic as well as syntactic categories. The type B is given as a semantic category, whereas the type A is given as a syntactic category. This is because semantical BNF follows the principle of type theoretical grammar (Ranta 1995a) that linearization deletes all and only semantic information. Linearizing a syntax tree into a string deletes those and only those arguments of the syntax tree that are semantic, that is the context and semantic domain arguments, like Γ and B in the present rule. The argument A is an object of the syntactic category Type, so it is preserved. Also the argument e belongs to a syntactic category (E), so linearization preserves it. The symbol t is of course a syntactic argument as well.

The type of e must contain an occurrence of $A^\star$ instead of just A, because the occurrence is in a context. According to the rules of context formation given in Section 5, a context is extended by a variable of a domain type, not of a syntax tree type. Interpreting the type expression A yields the domain $A^\star$, as required. The type of the conclusion of this rule must also have an occurrence of $A^\star$ instead of A, because the occurrence is in a domain. Domains cannot be formed from type expressions.

Let us now introduce more syntactic structure into our previous example of a syntax tree for the string $(n+1)$. Instead of referring to the variable n declared in the context, let us abstract the expression over it. Using the abbreviation s for the previous syntax tree, the new syntax tree

$$\mathrm{AbsExpr}((), \mathrm{IntType}(()), \mathrm{Int}, n, s)$$

of type $\mathrm{E}((), \mathrm{Int} \rightarrow \mathrm{Int})$ interprets into the function $\mathrm{lambda}((x) +_Z (x, 1))$ from integers to integers, and linearizes into the string $(\lambda n{:}\mathsf{int})(n+1)$.

Higher-order abstract syntax (Despeyroux et al. 1995) defines lambda abstraction, function application and forming an expression from a variable by the typings

$$\begin{aligned} \mathrm{lam} &: ((\mathrm{Var})\mathrm{L})\mathrm{L} \\ \mathrm{app} &: (\mathrm{L})(\mathrm{L})\mathrm{L} \\ \mathrm{var} &: (\mathrm{Var})\mathrm{L} \end{aligned}$$

They correspond to our rules for AbsExpr above, AppExpr below and VarExpr in section 5. Here L is an inductively defined type of lambda expressions that corresponds to our E, and lam, app and var are constructors of L.

Semantical BNF uses the context-relativity of E to carry out lambda abstraction: the abstracted variable x_t is declared in the context of the expression e that is abstracted. This is not possible in higher order abstract syntax, because its syntactic categories are simple types. Therefore it uses the function type (Var)L instead of a context-relative category L in the typing of lam.

The essential difference of semantical BNF to higher-order abstract syntax is thus the relativization of syntactic categories to context and domain, which allows only semantically well-formed variable abstracts and expressions in general to be formed. Higher-order abstract syntax must distinguish them from meaningless ones by means of a Valid predicate. Another difference is that semantical BNF allows describing also concrete syntax.

Finally, our functional language needs a rule of function application.

$$\mathrm{E} \rightarrow (\ \mathrm{E}\ \mathrm{E}\ )$$

$$\frac{\Gamma : \mathrm{cont} \quad A : \mathrm{dom}/\Gamma \quad B : \mathrm{dom}/\Gamma \quad d : \mathrm{E}(\Gamma, A \rightarrow B) \quad e : \mathrm{E}(\Gamma, A)}{\begin{array}{l}\mathrm{AppExpr}(\Gamma, A, B, d, e) : \mathrm{E}(\Gamma, B)\\ \mathrm{AppExpr}(\Gamma, A, B, d, e)^{\star} = \mathrm{app}(d^{\star}, e^{\star})\\ \mathrm{AppExpr}(\Gamma, A, B, d, e)^{\circ} = (\ d^{\circ}\ e^{\circ}\ )\end{array}}$$

Here app is the metalanguage application operator for functions of Π type. Given a function expression d from type A to type B and an expression e of type A, the rule applies d to e and yields an expression of type B.

As an example, let us form an application of the abstraction syntax tree above. Using the abbreviation r for it, the resulting syntax tree

$$\mathrm{AppExpr}((), \mathrm{Int}, \mathrm{Int}, r, \mathrm{IntNumExpr}(\mathrm{IntNum}(\mathrm{OneBit}(0))))$$

of type $\mathrm{E}((), \mathrm{Int})$ interprets into the integer $\mathrm{app}(\mathrm{lambda}((x) +_Z (x, 1)), 0)$, i.e. 1, and linearizes into the string ($(\lambda n$:int$)(n$+1) 0).

8 Conclusion

We have described a grammar for formal languages that describes syntax and semantics in a uniform type-theoretical setting. Thus the syntax tree formation rules of the previous section combine syntactic and semantic information in a way that is not present in other grammatical formalisms for programming languages. Syntax trees of semantical BNF are a hybrid form of representation that contain the semantic information needed for interpretation as well as the syntactic information needed for linearization. As linearization deletes semantic information, so interpretation correspondingly deletes syntactic information. The purpose of interpretation is indeed to do away with syntactic distinctions. The interpretation of a syntax tree is a purely semantic object, that is an object of constructive type theory. Its linearization, on the other hand, is a purely syntactic object, a string.

If one thinks of the grammatical description of a language as purely syntactic, then the semantic information in semantical BNF rules belongs to the metalanguage. This semantic information consists of semantic categories and contexts. In this sense, the object language depends on the metalanguage. Metamathematics, however, typically operates in informal metalanguage. Here the metamathematical level must also be formal. Otherwise the grammatical rules would not be formal, as they contain semantic information.

One may view a syntax tree of semantical BNF as representing abstract syntax, and the string that it linearizes into as the corresponding concrete syntax. Abstract syntax in this sense is really an admixture of syntax and semantics. Concrete syntax may be varied by using alternative syntax trees that have the same interpretation, for example the ones for infix and prefix expressions.

References

Alfred V. Aho, Ravi Sethi, and Jeffrey D. Ullman. *Compilers. Principles, Techniques, and Tools.* Addison-Wesley, Reading, Massachusetts, 1986.

N. G. de Bruijn. Lambda calculus notation with nameless dummies, a tool for automatic formula manipulation, with application to the Church-Rosser theorem. *Indagationes Mathematicae*, 34:381–392, 1972. Reprinted in R. Nederpelt et al., editors, *Selected Papers on Automath*, pages 865–935. North-Holland, Amsterdam, 1994.

Joëlle Despeyroux, Amy Felty, and André Hirschowitz. Higher-order abstract syntax in Coq. In M. Dezani and G. Plotkin, editors, Proceedings of the International Conference on Typed Lambda Calculi and Applications, pages 124–138. *Lecture Notes in Computer Science* 902, Springer-Verlag, Heidelberg, 1995.

Donald E. Knuth. Semantics of context-free languages. *Mathematical Systems Theory*, 2:127–145, 1968. Errata 5:95–96, 1971.

Donald E. Knuth. Examples of formal semantics. In E. Engeler, editor, Symposium on Semantics of Algorithmic Languages, pages 212–235. *Lecture Notes in Mathematics* 188, Springer-Verlag, Heidelberg, 1971.

Per Martin-Löf. *Intuitionistic Type Theory.* Bibliopolis, Naples, 1984.

Richard Montague. *Formal Philosophy.* Collected papers edited by Richmond Thomason. Yale University Press, New Haven, 1974.

Aarne Ranta. *Type Theoretical Grammar.* Oxford University Press, Oxford, 1994.

Aarne Ranta. Type-theoretical interpretation and generalization of phrase structure grammar. *Bulletin of the IGPL*, 3:319–342, 1995a.

Aarne Ranta. Syntactic categories in the language of mathematics. In P. Dybjer, B. Nordström, and J. Smith, editors, Types for Proofs and Programs, pages 162–182. *Lecture Notes in Computer Science* 996, Springer-Verlag, Heidelberg, 1995b.

Aarne Ranta. Context-dependent syntactic categories and the formalization of mathematical text. In S. Berardi and M. Coppo, editors, Types for Proofs and Programs, pages 162–182. *Lecture Notes in Computer Science* 1158, Springer-Verlag, Heidelberg, 1996.

Aarne Ranta. Structures grammaticales dans le français mathématique. To appear in *Mathématiques, Informatique, Sciences humaines*, 1997.

David A. Schmidt. *The Structure of Typed Programming Languages.* MIT Press, Massachusetts, 1994.

Alvaro Tasistro. Formulation of Martin-Löf's theory of types with explicit substitutions. Licentiate's thesis, Chalmers University of Technology and University of Göteborg, 1993.

R. D. Tennent. *Semantics of Programming Languages.* Prentice Hall, New York, 1991.

The Internal Type Theory of a Heyting Pretopos

Maria Emilia Maietti

Dipartimento di Matematica Pura ed Applicata, Università di Padova,
via G. Belzoni n.7, I-35131 Padova, Italy
e-mail: maietti@math.unipd.it

Abstract. We present the internal type theory of a Heyting pretopos with a natural numbers object. The resulting theory is based on dependent types and proof-terms. We prove that there is a sort of equivalence between such type theories and the category of Heyting pretoposes. By using the type theory we also build the free Heyting pretopos generated by a category.

Introduction

An elementary topos can be viewed as a generalized universe of sets to develop mathematics. From a logical point of view, topos theory corresponds to an intuitionistic higher order logic with typed variables [LS86]. Suitable toposes provide models of restricted Zermelo set theory [MM92]. Recently, Joyal and Moerdijk built a model of the whole intuitionistic set theory by using the notion of small map and by taking a Heyting pretopos with a natural numbers object as the categorical universe [JM95]. The main difference w.r.t. a topos is that a Heyting pretopos (H-pretopos, for short) correspond to a first order logical framework, precisely to a first order dependent type theory with quotients, called the HP typed calculus in [Mai97]. This calculus is valid and complete w.r.t. the class of H-pretoposes. It consists of the following dependent types: the terminal type, the falsum type, the indexed sum type, the extensional equality type, the disjoint sum type with the disjointness axiom, the natural numbers type, as in the extensional version of Martin-Löf's type theory [Mar84], the forall type, i.e. the product type restricted to types with at most one proof, and finally a particular quotient type satisfying an effectiveness axiom.

This type theory may be of interest to computer scientists expecially for the proposal of effective quotient types based only on proof-irrelevance equivalence relations. These particular quotient types are different from the extensional quotient types of Nuprl, where effectiveness is not always available (it holds certainly for decidable equivalence relations).

In this paper, we show that the internal type theory of a given H-pretopos is a particular HP type theory plus specific dependent types and terms. To this purpose, we prove that there is a sort of equivalence between such type theories and H-pretoposes. The type theory of a given H-pretopos $\mathcal{P}$

is described by a categorical semantics: it combines together the notion of model given by display maps [HP89], [See84] with the tools provided by contextual categories to interpret substitution correctly [Car86]. We shall emphasise context formation. Indeed, the judgement $B\ [\Gamma]$, asserting that B is a dependent type under the context Γ, is interpreted as a suitable sequence of morphisms of $\mathcal{P}$ to the terminal object. Moreover, the judgement $b \in B[\Gamma]$, asserting that b is a term of type B under the context Γ, is interpreted as a section of the last morphism of the sequence representing the dependent type B. Since we want to express substitution by means of pullback, which is determined up to isomorphisms, we use fibred functors, as in [Hof94] to interpret substitution correctly. But in our semantics, a type judgement corresponds to a sequence of fibred functors, which represents the type under a context with all its possible substitutions, and a term judgement corresponds to a natural transformation, which also represents the term under a context with all its possible substitutions. The specific dependent types of $\mathcal{P}$ correspond to sequences of fibred functors obtained by pullback from a sequence of morphisms of $\mathcal{P}$.

By means of the type theory, we can build the free H-pretopos generated by a category: it is sufficient to consider the objects of the category as closed types and its morphisms as dependent terms. This is the free construction for categories corresponding to dependent typed lambda calculi. For example, in the same way, one can build both the free category with finite limits - corresponding to the type theory with the terminal type, the extensional equality type, the indexed sum type- and the free locally cartesian closed category with finite coproducts and a natural numbers object -corresponding to Martin-Löf's type theory with extensional equality but without universes and well founded sets [Mar84].

The type theory of a H-pretopos constitutes a new tool to analyze, from a type theoretical point of view, the notion of small map used in [JM95] to provide a model of intuitionistic set theory. Moreover, it seems interesting to investigate how much of the type theory of H-pretoposes can be formalized within Martin-Löf's type theory.

The paper is divided as follows: in section 1 we describe the categorical preliminaries to interpret the HP dependent typed calculus in a H-pretopos; in section 2 we show the HP type theory arising from a given H-pretopos, in section 3 we prove a sort of equivalence between the HP type theories and the category of H-pretoposes, in section 4 we build the free H-pretopos and finally we draw the conclusions.

1 Preliminaries

First of all we recall the categorical definition of Heyting pretopos [JM95]. The notion of pretopos was introduced by Grothendieck [MR77].

Definition 1. A *pretopos* is a category equipped with finite limits, stable finite disjoint coproducts and stable effective quotients of equivalence relations. A *Heyting pretopos* is a pretopos where pullback functors on subobjects have right adjoints.

In the following, by H-pretopos we shall mean a Heyting pretopos also with a natural numbers object. Since we intend to describe syntactically categorical properties, we shall assume that, with a H-pretopos, a given choice of categorical constructors is made, i.e. fixed choices of finite limits, initial object, coproducts, quotients of equivalence relations and right adjoints on subobjects.

An essential feature for the interpretation of a dependent typed calculus is the local property of a H-pretopos: for every object A of the H-pretopos $\mathcal{P}$, the comma category $\mathcal{P}/A$ is a H-pretopos. Indeed, constructing a type, which depends on a context Γ, from other types corresponds to a categorical property of $\mathcal{P}/A$, where A is determined by Γ. Moreover, since substitution corresponds to pullback, the various categorical properties must be stable under pullback. By the way, in a H-pretopos also Beck-Chevalley conditions for right adjoints are satisfied.

Given a H-pretopos $\mathcal{P}$ we want to describe its internal dependent type theory $T(\mathcal{P})$. The type theory is based on the HP typed calculus for H-pretoposes (see the appendix), augmented with the specific type and term judgements of $\mathcal{P}$. As in [Mai97], the idea is to consider a dependent type as a sequence of morphisms of $\mathcal{P}$, ending with the terminal object 1, whereas the terms are sections of the last morphism of the type to which they belong. Thus, we consider the algebraic development of the fibration *cod* of $\mathcal{P}$: it is the category $Pgr(\mathcal{P})$.

Definition 2. The objects of the category $\boldsymbol{Pgr(\mathcal{P})}$ are finite sequences $a_1, a_2, ..., a_n$ of morphisms of $\mathcal{P}$

$$A_n \xrightarrow{a_n} \cdots\cdots A_2 \xrightarrow{a_2} A_1 \xrightarrow{a_1} 1$$

and a morphism from $a_1, a_2, ..., a_n$ to $b_1, b_2, ..., b_m$ is a morphism b of $\mathcal{P}$ such that $b_n \cdot b = a_n$

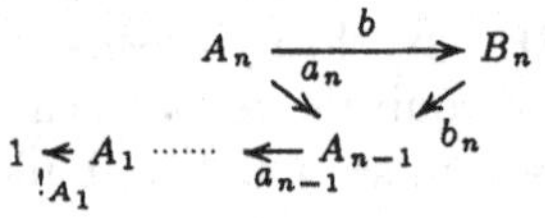

provided $m = n$ and $a_i = b_i$ for $i = 1, ..., n-1$.

Remark 3. We would like to interpret substitution by means of pullback, using the indexed pseudofunctor $F : \mathcal{P}^{OP} \longrightarrow Cat$ defined as follows: F associates to every $A \in Ob\mathcal{P}$ the category $\mathcal{P}/A$ and to every morphism $f : B \to A$ of $\mathcal{P}$ the pullback pseudofunctor $f^* : \mathcal{P}/A \to \mathcal{P}/B$. But, in general, for an arbitrary choice of pullbacks, F would not be a functor: for instance, even $F(id)$ may not be an identity. Therefore, if substitution were interpreted by F then it would not be well defined. The solution is to replace F by an equivalent pseudofunctor $S : \mathcal{P}^{OP} \longrightarrow Cat$ [Ben85], [Jac91]. S is defined as follows. For every object A in $\mathcal{P}$, $S(A) \equiv Fib(\mathcal{P}/A, \mathcal{P}^{\rightarrow})$, where $Fib(\mathcal{P}/A, \mathcal{P}^{\rightarrow})$ is the class of functors $\sigma : \mathcal{P}/A \rightarrow \mathcal{P}^{\rightarrow}$, fibred from dom_A to cod_A (they send cartesian morphisms of dom_A to cartesian morphisms of cod_A). A fibred functor $\sigma : \mathcal{P}/A \rightarrow \mathcal{P}^{\rightarrow}$ associates to every triangle $\begin{array}{ccc} C & \xrightarrow{t} & B \\ & {\scriptstyle b'}\searrow \quad \swarrow{\scriptstyle b} & \\ & A & \end{array}$ a pullback diagram $\begin{array}{ccc} C' & \xrightarrow{q(t,\sigma(b))} & B' \\ {\scriptstyle \sigma(b\cdot t)}\downarrow & & \downarrow{\scriptstyle \sigma(b)} \\ C & \xrightarrow[t]{} & B \end{array}$. Moreover, for a morphism $f : B \rightarrow A$ of $\mathcal{P}$, the functor $S(f) : Fib(\mathcal{P}/A, \mathcal{P}^{\rightarrow}) \rightarrow Fib(\mathcal{P}/B, \mathcal{P}^{\rightarrow})$ associates to every fibred functor σ a fibred functor $\sigma[f]$. $\sigma[f]$ is defined as follows: for every $t : C \rightarrow B$, $\sigma[f](t) \equiv \sigma(f \cdot t)$. Besides, for every natural transformation ρ, $S(f)(\rho) \equiv \rho[f]$, where $\rho[f](t) \equiv \rho(f \cdot t)$ for every $t : C \rightarrow B$. Note that the pseudofunctor $F : \mathcal{P}^{OP} \longrightarrow Cat$ is equivalent to the functor S in the appropriate 2-category of pseudofunctors. The functors establishing such an equivalence can be described as follows. To define the functor from $\mathcal{P}/A$ to $Fib(\mathcal{P}/A, \mathcal{P}^{\rightarrow})$, first we choose pullbacks, then we associate to every object $b : B \rightarrow A$ the fibred functor $\widehat{b}$, defined as $\widehat{b}(t) \equiv t^*(b)$ in the pullback[1] $\begin{array}{ccc} B_\Sigma & \xrightarrow{b^*(t)} & B \\ {\scriptstyle t^*(b)}\downarrow & & \downarrow{\scriptstyle b} \\ D & \xrightarrow[t]{} & A \end{array}$ and extended to morphisms by the universal property of pullback. In order to define a functor from $Fib(\mathcal{P}/A, \mathcal{P}^{\rightarrow})$ to $\mathcal{P}/A$, we associate to every fibred functor its evaluation on the identity of the object A.

We use fibred functors to interpret the dependent types with all its possible substitutions, as in [Hof94]. Moreover, we use natural transformations to represent terms with all its possible substitutions. We call preinterpretation an assignment of fibred functors to type judgements and of natural transformations to term judgements. To this purpose, we consider the category $Pgf(\mathcal{P})$, where the judgements of the typed calculus for H-pretoposes are preinterpreted. We put $I(\sigma) = A$ if $\sigma \in [\mathcal{P}/A, \mathcal{P}^{\rightarrow}]$.

Definition 4. The objects of the category $\boldsymbol{Pgf(\mathcal{P})}$ are finite sequences $\sigma_1, \sigma_2, ..., \sigma_n$ of fibred functors such that $\sigma_1(id_{A_1}), \sigma_2(id_{A_2}), ..., \sigma_n(id_{A_n})$ is an object of $Pgr(\mathcal{P})$, where $A_i = I(\sigma_i)$ for $i = 1, ..., n$. The morphisms of $Pgf(\mathcal{P})$ from $\sigma_1, \sigma_2, ..., \sigma_m$ to $\tau_1, \tau_2, ..., \tau_n$ are defined only if $m = n$ and $\sigma_i = \tau_i$ for $i = 1, ..., n-1$, and they are natural transformations from the functor σ_n to τ_n such that, if $A_n = I(\sigma_n) = I(\tau_n)$, then for every $b : B \rightarrow A_n$

[1] We call the second projection $b^*(t)$, since the notation $q(t, b)$ is reserved for projections of functorial choices and not any choice of pullback is functorial.

the second member of $\rho(b)$ is the identity (recall that $\rho(b)$ is a morphism of $\mathcal{P}^{\rightarrow}$), that is the triangle

$$\begin{array}{ccc} \sigma_n(b) & \xrightarrow{\rho_1(b)} & \tau_n(b) \\ & \searrow \quad \swarrow & \\ & B & \end{array}$$

commutes.

In the following, since the second member of $\rho(b)$ is always the identity, we confuse $\rho(b)$ with the first member $\rho_1(b)$.

Besides, notice that by naturality any component $\rho(b)$ of a morphism ρ of $Pgf(\mathcal{P})$ is determined by the properties of pullback from $\rho(id_{A_n})$. Indeed, if we consider

$$\begin{array}{ccc} B & \xrightarrow{b} & A_n \\ & {\scriptstyle b}\searrow \quad \swarrow{\scriptstyle id} & \\ & A_n & \end{array}$$

, we get that $\rho(b)$ is equal to $b^*(\rho(id_{A_n}))$, that is the unique morphism from $\sigma_n(b)$ to $\tau_n(b)$, which are obtained respectively by the pullbacks of b and $\sigma_n(id)$ and of b and $\tau_n(id)$.

Finally, for every $A \in Ob\mathcal{P}$, we define the fibred functor $i_A : \mathcal{P}/A \rightarrow \mathcal{P}^{\rightarrow}$ which associates to every triangle

$$\begin{array}{ccc} C & \xrightarrow{t} & B \\ & {\scriptstyle b'}\searrow \quad \swarrow{\scriptstyle b} & \\ & A & \end{array}$$

the following pullback diagram

$$\begin{array}{ccc} C & \xrightarrow{t} & B \\ {\scriptstyle id}\downarrow & & \downarrow{\scriptstyle id} \\ C & \xrightarrow[t]{} & B \end{array}.$$

2 The type theory of $\mathcal{P}$

The type theory $T(\mathcal{P})$ of a H-pretopos $\mathcal{P}$, with a fixed choice of its categorical structure, is a particular HP calculus plus type judgements and term judgements that are specific to $\mathcal{P}$. It is formulated in the style of Martin-Löf's type theory with four kinds of judgements [NPS90]. There are the type judgements and the judgements about equality between types, which are given by formation rules, the term judgements given by introduction and elimination rules, and the judgements about equality between terms of the same type given by conversion rules. Since the types are allowed to depend on variables of other types, the contexts are telescopic [dB91]. We assume all the inference rules about the formation of contexts, declarations of typed variables, about reflexivity, symmetry and transitivity of the equality between types and terms and finally, the substitution rules for all the four kinds of judgements [NPS90]. The dependent types are introduced under a context. A type judgement arises from a object of $Pgf(\mathcal{P})$, which represents a dependent type with all its possible substitutions. More precisely, a type judgement corresponds to the evaluation of a finite sequence of fibred functors on the identity. Indeed, for a sequence of fibred functors $\alpha_1, \alpha_2, ..., \alpha_n, \beta$ of $Pgf(\mathcal{P})$, we define

$$\beta^{-1}(x_1, ..., x_n)[x_1 \in \alpha_1^{-1}, ..., x_n \in \alpha_n^{-1}(x_1, ..., x_{n-1})]$$

as the type judgement corresponding to

$$B \xrightarrow{\beta(id)} A_n \xrightarrow{\alpha_n(id)} \cdots\cdots A_1 \xrightarrow{\alpha_1(id)} 1$$

by thinking of the fibers of the morphism $\beta(id)$. This notation turns out to be very clear when we look at the category of paths built on any syntactic H-pretopos. The equality between types corresponds to the equality between objects of $Pgf(\mathcal{P})$, which implies the equality between objects of $Pgr(\mathcal{P})$. For short, we use the abbreviation $\Gamma_n \equiv x_1 \in \alpha_1^{-1}, ..., x_n \in \alpha_n^{-1}(x_1, ..., x_{n-1})$ in the contexts. On the other hand, a term judgement arises from a morphism of $Pgf(\mathcal{P})$, which is a natural transformation representing a term with all its possible substitutions. The evaluation of a natural transformation on the identical substitution is a term judgement. Indeed, for a suitable morphism b of $Pgf(\mathcal{P})$ from $\alpha_1, \alpha_1, ..., \alpha_n, i_{A_n}$ to $\alpha_1, \alpha_2, ..., \alpha_n, \beta$, the term judgement

$$b \in \beta^{-1}(x_1, ..., x_n)[\Gamma_n]$$

corresponds to a section of $\beta(id)$ 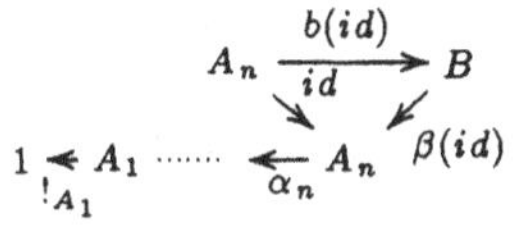 by choosing the identity as the terminal object in $\mathcal{P}/A_n$.

The equality between terms corresponds to the equality between morphisms of $Pgf(\mathcal{P})$. The contexts are generated from the following formation rules:

$$1C)\ \ \emptyset\ \ cont \qquad 2C)\ \ \frac{\Gamma\ \ cont \qquad A\ type\ [\Gamma]}{\Gamma, x \in A\ \ cont}\ \ (x \in A \notin \Gamma)$$

In the following, to make formulas more readable in type judgements, we will write $\beta[\Gamma_n]$ instead of $\beta^{-1}[\Gamma_n]$. In the diagrams we will often write σ_i instead of $\sigma_i(id_{A_i})$ for fibred functors and b instead of $b(id)$ for natural transformations.

The rules for *substitution* of variables in a type and in a term and for *weakening* of a variable w.r.t type and term judgements are the usual ones. We only show how they work in these particular cases:

$$sT\ \ \frac{\gamma[\Gamma_n, y \in \beta] \quad b \in \beta[\Gamma_n]}{\gamma[b(id)][\Gamma_n]}$$ is

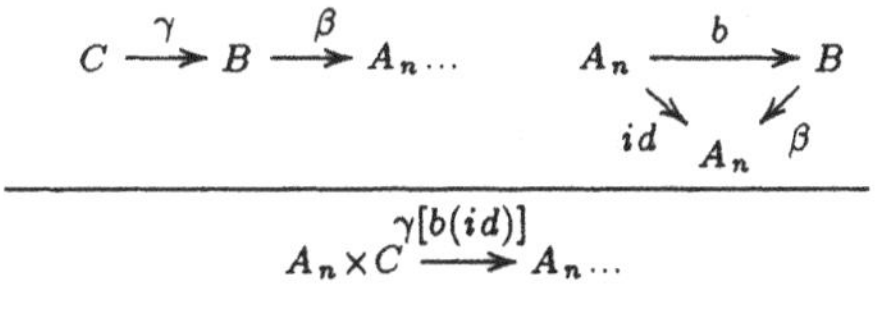

where we put $\gamma[b(id)](id) \equiv \gamma(b(id))$

$$st\ \ \frac{c \in \gamma[\Gamma_n, y \in \beta] \quad b \in \beta[\Gamma_n]}{c[b(id)] \in \gamma[b(id)][\Gamma_n]}$$ is

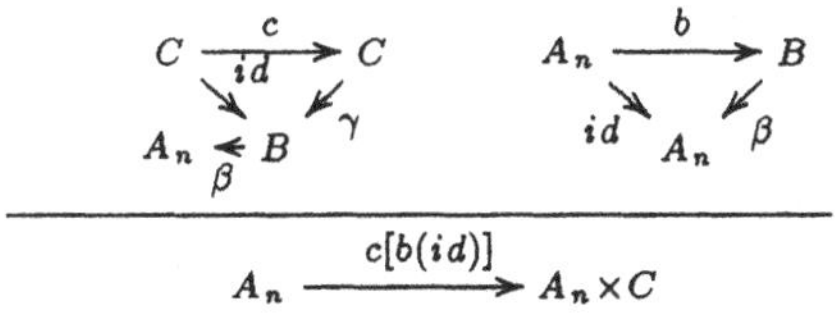

where we put $c[b(id)](id) \equiv c(b(id))$

$$wT\ \frac{\beta[\Gamma_n] \quad \delta[\Gamma_n]}{\beta[\Gamma_n, y \in \delta]} \qquad \text{is}$$

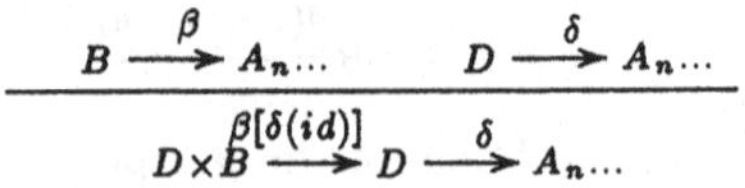
B → A_n ... (β)
D → A_n ... (δ)
D×B → D → A_n ... (β[δ(id)], δ)

where we put $\beta[\delta(id)](id) \equiv \beta(\delta(id))$

$$wt\ \frac{b \in \beta[\Gamma_n] \quad \xi[\Gamma_n]}{b \in \beta[\Gamma_n, w \in \xi]} \qquad \text{is}$$

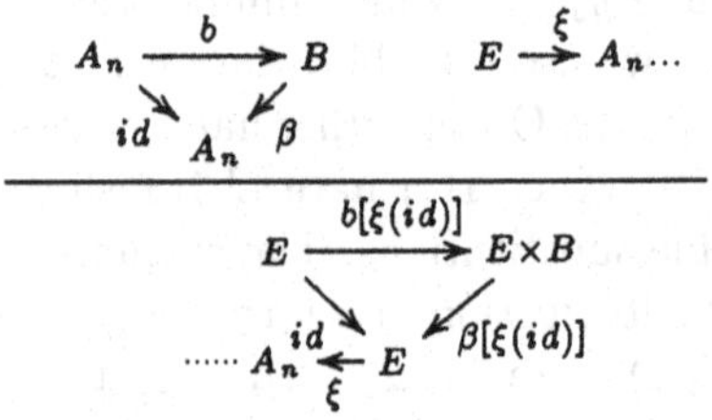

where we put $b[\xi(id)](id) \equiv (\xi(id))^*(b(id))$, that is the unique morphism of $\mathcal{P}/E$ from $i_{A_n}(\xi(id))$ to $\beta(\xi(id))$, obtained from $b(id)$ by the properties of pullback.

The rule expressing the *assumption of variable* is the following:

$$var\ \frac{\beta\ [\Gamma_n]}{x \in \beta[\Gamma_n, x \in \beta]} \qquad \text{is}$$

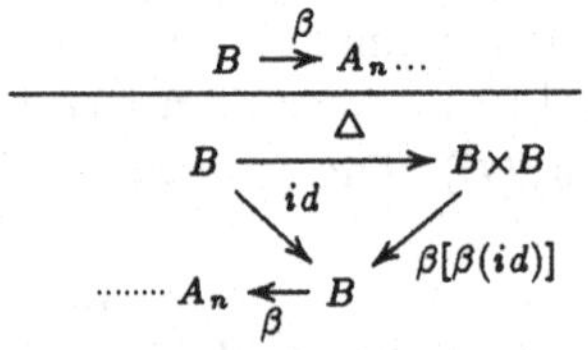

where $x(id) \equiv \Delta_B \equiv \langle id_B, id_B \rangle$.

Now, we show the formation rules for types and then the introduction, elimination and conversion rules for their terms.

The *proper types* and *terms* of $T(\mathcal{P})$ are described as follows. Proper type judgements arise from objects of $Pgr(\mathcal{P})$ and proper term judgements arise from morphisms of $Pgr(\mathcal{P})$. For every object of $Pgr(\mathcal{P})$ $\boldsymbol{a_1, a_2, ..., a_n, t}$ we consider the sequence obtained by making the pullback of a_1 along the identity, then by making the pullback of a_2 along the second projection p_1 of the previous pullback, and so on, that is we obtain the following sequence of pullbacks:

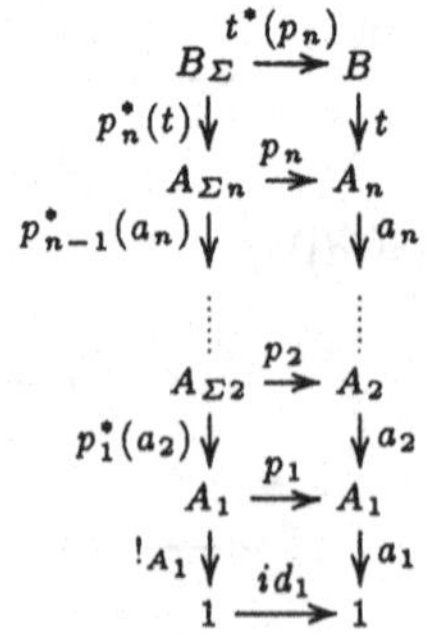

where p_i is the second projection of the pullback of a_i and p_{i-1}, for $i = 1, \ldots, n$. Finally, we consider the associate sequence of fibred functors

$$\widehat{A_1},\ \widehat{a_2}[p_1],\ \widehat{a_3}[p_2],\ \ldots, \widehat{a_n}[p_{n-1}],\ \widehat{t}[p_n]$$

where $\widehat{A_1} \equiv \widehat{a_1}$, hence we introduce a new dependent type t^{-1} and finally we state that

$$t^{-1}[x_1 \in A_1, \ldots, x_n \in a_n^{-1}] \text{ is } \quad B_\Sigma \xrightarrow{\widehat{t}[p_n]} A_{\Sigma n} \xrightarrow{\widehat{a_n}[p_{n-1}]} \cdots\cdots A_{\Sigma 1} \xrightarrow{\widehat{A_1}} 1$$

where the Σ subscript is used for the interpretation of the series of judgements of proper types introduced by an object of $Pgr(\mathcal{P})$.

Moreover, given a sequence of fibred functors $\alpha_1, \alpha_2, \ldots, \alpha_n, \beta$ of $Pgf(\mathcal{P})$, for every morphism c of $Pgr(\mathcal{P})$ A_n \xrightarrow{\ c\ } B 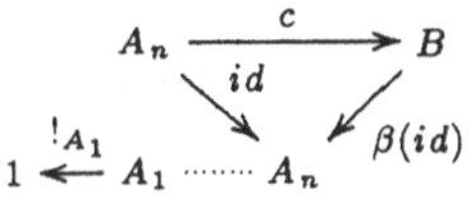 we introduce a new term c and we state that

$$c \in \beta(id)[x_1 \in A_1, \ldots, x_n \in \alpha_n] \quad \text{is}$$

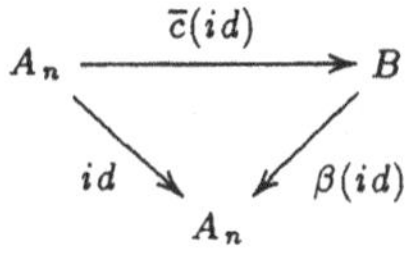

where $\overline{c}(id) \equiv c$.

Finally, we add all the types and terms of the HP typed calculus (see the appendix for the inference rules). This calculus is valid and complete with respect to the class of H-pretoposes and is described as follows [2]. Given a H-pretopos the terminal type corresponds to the terminal object, the extensional equality types to the equalizers, the indexed sum types to pullbacks, the falsum type to the initial object, the disjoint sum types with the axiom of disjointness to disjoint coproducts, the natural numbers type to the natural numbers object and all these types are already presented in the extensional version of Martin-Löf's type theory [Mar84]. The key point in finding the typed calculus of H-pretoposes is to have noticed that a monomorphism turns out to be the interpretation of a type with at most one proof, also called proof-irrelevant in the literature, but here called *mono type*. Therefore, the novelty of this calculus lies in the presence of the forall type, that is the product type restricted to mono types, and also in the presence of the quotient types based only on mono equivalence relations such that the effectiveness holds. Here, we describe in details the forall type, the quotient type and the natural numbers type and we refer to [Mai97] and [Hof94] for details on the other types. Note that we define the fibred functors only on objects of the various slice categories $\mathcal{P}/A$, since on morphisms they turn out to be defined by

[2] Our definition of internal language of a category follows [LS86], for instance, and it is different from that in [Tay97].

the universal property of pullback. Moreover, they turn out to be fibred by stability or Beck-Chevalley conditions of the categorical property involved.

The *Forall type* corresponds to the right adjoint of pullback functor on subobjects:

$$\forall)\ \frac{\gamma(y)[\Gamma_n, y \in \beta] \quad d \in Eq(\gamma, w, z)[\Gamma_n, y \in \beta, w \in \gamma(y), z \in \gamma(y)]}{\forall_{y \in \beta}\gamma(y)\ [\Gamma_n]}$$

$$\text{is} \qquad \frac{C \stackrel{\gamma}{\rightarrowtail} B \stackrel{\beta}{\longrightarrow} A_n \ldots}{\forall_\beta C \stackrel{\forall_\beta \gamma}{\rightarrowtail} A_n \ldots}$$

where $\forall_\beta\gamma : \mathcal{P}/A_n \to \mathcal{P}^{\to}$ is the functor defined in the following manner: for every $t : D \to A_n$, we put $\forall_\beta\gamma(t) \equiv \forall_{\beta(t)}\gamma(q(t, \beta(id)))$. Note that $\gamma(id)$ turns out to be a monomorphism, because the interpretation of $z \in \gamma[\Gamma_n, y \in \beta, w \in \gamma(y), z \in \gamma(y)]$ and $w \in \gamma[\Gamma_n, y \in \beta, w \in \gamma(y), z \in \gamma(y)]$, which are isomorphic with the same isomorphism respectively to the first and second projections of the product $\gamma(id) \times \gamma(id)$, are equal by hypothesis and by the validity of the extensional elimination rule for the equality type.

$$\text{I-}\forall)\ \frac{c \in \gamma(y)[\Gamma_n, y \in \beta]}{\lambda y.c \in \forall_{y \in \beta}\gamma(y)[\Gamma_n]} \qquad \text{is} \qquad \frac{B \stackrel{c}{\longrightarrow} C}{A_n \stackrel{(\lambda y.c)}{\longrightarrow} \forall_{y \in \beta} C}$$

$$\text{E-}\forall)\ \frac{b \in \beta[\Gamma_n] \quad f \in \forall_{y \in \beta}\gamma(y)[\Gamma_n, y \in \beta]}{Ap(f, b) \in \gamma(b)[\Gamma_n]} \quad \text{is} \quad \frac{A_n \stackrel{b}{\longrightarrow} B \qquad A_n \stackrel{f}{\longrightarrow} \forall_\beta C}{A_n \stackrel{Ap(f,b)}{\longrightarrow} A_n \times C}$$

with $(\lambda y.c)(id) \equiv \psi(c(id))$ and $Ap(f, b)(id) \equiv b(id)^*(\psi^{-1}(f(id)))$, where

$$\psi : Sub(B)(\beta(id)^*(id_{A_n}), \gamma(id)) \to Sub(A_n)(id_{A_n}, \forall_{\beta(id)}(\gamma(id)))$$

is the bijection of the adjunction $\beta(id)^* \dashv \forall_\beta$, by putting $\beta(id)^*(t) \equiv q(t, \beta(id))$ for every $t : B \to A_n$, that is we are considering the choice of pullback given by the split fibration. The conversion rules, that are the usual β and η conversion rules as in the extensional version of Martin-Löf's type theory [Mar84], are also valid.

The *Quotient type* corresponds to the effective quotients of equivalence relations (in the premisses we omit to add the generic context Γ_n):

$$\text{Q)}\ \frac{\begin{array}{l}\rho(x,y)\ type\ [x \in \alpha, y \in \alpha],\ d \in Eq(\rho, z, w)[x \in \alpha, y \in \alpha, z \in \rho, w \in \rho],\\ c_1 \in \rho(x,x)[x \in \alpha], \qquad c_2 \in \rho(y,x)[x \in \alpha, y \in \alpha, z \in \rho(x,y)],\\ c_3 \in \rho(x,z)[x \in \alpha, y \in \alpha, z \in \alpha, w \in \rho(x,y), w' \in \rho(y,z)]\end{array}}{\alpha/\rho\ [\Gamma_n]}$$

corresponds to

$$\frac{R \stackrel{\rho(id)}{\rightarrowtail} A \times A \stackrel{\alpha(id)\cdot\pi_1}{\longrightarrow} A_n \ldots}{A/R \stackrel{Q(\alpha)(id)}{\longrightarrow} A_n \ldots}$$

where $\pi_1 \equiv \alpha(\alpha(id))$, $\pi_2 \equiv q(\alpha(id), \alpha(id))$ and $Q(\alpha)(id)$ is defined as follows. In the case of the forall type, we have already noticed that a mono type corresponds to a monomorphism. Here, we can prove that $\rho(id)$ turns out to be also an equivalence relation in $\mathcal{P}/A_n$. Therefore, there exists the coequalizer $c : A \to A/R$ of $\pi_1 \cdot \rho(id)$ and $\pi_2 \cdot \rho(id)$. Moreover, as $\alpha(id) \cdot (\pi_1 \cdot \rho(id)) = \alpha(id) \cdot (\pi_2 \cdot \rho(id))$, we get $Q(\alpha(id))$ such that the following triangle diagram commutes

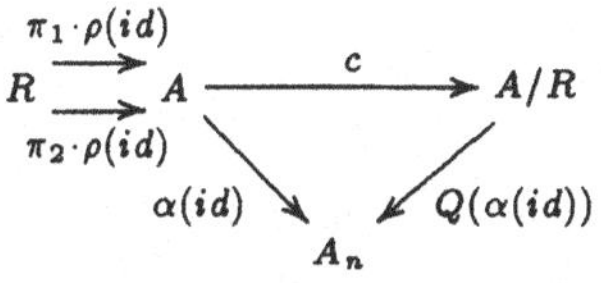

Therefore we define $Q(\alpha) : \mathcal{P}/A_n \to \mathcal{P}^{\to}$ in the following manner: for every $t : D \to A_n$ we put $Q(\alpha)(t) \equiv Q(\alpha(t))$, where $Q(\alpha(t))$ is the unique morphism such that $\alpha(t) = Q(\alpha(t)) \cdot c(t)$ and $c(t)$ is the coequalizer of the equivalence relation $\rho(t)$. The *introduction* rule for the quotient type is the next one:

$$\text{I-Q)}\ \frac{a \in \alpha\ [\Gamma_n]}{[a] \in \alpha/\rho\ [\Gamma_n]} \quad \text{is} \quad \frac{A_n \xrightarrow{a(id)} A}{A_n \xrightarrow{c \cdot (a(id))} A/R}$$

and the following *equality rule* is valid

$$\text{eq)}\ \frac{a \in \alpha[\Gamma_n] \quad b \in \alpha[\Gamma_n] \quad d \in \rho(a,b)[\Gamma_n]}{[a] = [b] \in \alpha/\rho\ [\Gamma_n]}$$

By using the indexed sum type, the *elimination* and *conversion* rules of the quotient type for dependent types (see the appendix) are equivalent to the following weaker elimination and conversion rules of the quotient type for types not depending on α or α/ρ, which are also derivable in $T(\mathcal{P})$

$$\text{E}_s\text{-Q)}\ \frac{m(x) \in \mu\ [x \in \alpha] \quad m(x) = m(y) \in \mu\ [x \in \alpha, y \in \alpha, d \in \rho(x,y)]}{Q_s(m, z) \in \mu\ [z \in \alpha/\rho]}$$

$$\text{C}_{1s}\text{-Q)}\ \frac{a \in \alpha \quad m(x) \in \mu\ [x \in \alpha] \quad m(x) = m(y) \in \mu\ [x \in \alpha, y \in \alpha, d \in \rho(x,y)]}{Q_s(m, [a]) = m(a) \in \mu}$$

$$\text{C}_{2s}\text{-Q)}\ \frac{t(z) \in \mu\ [z \in A/R]}{Q_s((x)t([x]), z) = t(z) \in \mu\ [z \in \alpha/\rho]}$$

where $M \xrightarrow{\mu(id)} A_n$ and $A \xrightarrow{\alpha(id)} A_n$. In the weaker elimination rule E_s-Q

$$Q_s(m, z) \in \mu\ [\Gamma_n, z \in \alpha/\rho] \quad \text{is} \quad A/R \xrightarrow{\langle id, u \rangle} A/R \times M$$

where u is the morphism in $\mathcal{P}/A_n$ such that $u \cdot c = q(\alpha(id), \mu(id)) \cdot m(id)$, which exists because by hypothesis $m(id) \cdot (\pi_1 \cdot \rho(id)) = m(id) \cdot (\pi_2 \cdot \rho(id))$, and

c is the coequalizer of $\pi_1 \cdot \rho(id)$ and $\pi_2 \cdot \rho(id)$. Moreover, since by hypothesis $\mu(id) \cdot (q(\alpha(id), \mu(id)) \cdot m(id)) = \alpha(id)$ we also have that by uniqueness $\mu(id) \cdot u = Q(\alpha(id))$. The C_{1_s} and C_{2_s} conversion rules are valid. Besides, the axiom of *Effectiveness* also holds:

$$\frac{a \in \alpha \quad b \in \alpha \quad [a] = [b] \in \alpha/\rho}{f(a,b) \in \rho(a,b)} \quad \text{is} \quad \frac{A_n \xrightarrow{a(id)} A \qquad A_n \xrightarrow{b(id)} A}{A_n \xrightarrow{\langle id,t\rangle} R}$$

where $\langle id, t\rangle$ is defined as follows. Since by hypothesis $c \cdot a(id) = c \cdot b(id)$ and since the quotient is effective in $\mathcal{P}/A_n$, then there exists a morphism $t : A_n \to R$ such that $(\pi_1 \cdot \rho(id)) \cdot t = a(id)$ and $(\pi_2 \cdot \rho(id)) \cdot t = b(id)$.

The *Natural Numbers type* corresponds to the natural numbers object:

$$\text{nat)} \quad N[\,] \quad \text{is} \quad \mathcal{N}_\Sigma \xrightarrow{\widehat{\mathcal{N}}(id)} 1$$

where $\widehat{\mathcal{N}} : \mathcal{P}/1 \to \mathcal{P}^{\to}$ is the functor defined in the following manner: for every $!_D : D \to 1$ we put $\widehat{\mathcal{N}}(!_D) \equiv (!_D)^*(!_{\mathcal{N}})$ and $\mathcal{N}$ is a natural numbers object of $\mathcal{P}$.

Now, we show the *introduction* rules.

$$\text{I}_1\text{-nat)} \quad 0 \in N[\Gamma_n] \quad \text{is} \quad A_n \xrightarrow{\langle id, o\cdot !_{A_n}\rangle} A_n \times \mathcal{N}$$

where $o : 1 \to \mathcal{N}$ is the zero map in the H-pretopos $\mathcal{P}$. From now on, we call $\pi_1 \equiv \widehat{\mathcal{N}}(!_{A_n})$ and $\pi_2 \equiv q(!_{A_n}, \widehat{\mathcal{N}}(id))$.

$$\text{I}_2\text{-nat)} \quad s(n) \in N[\Gamma_n, n \in N] \quad \text{is} \quad A_n \times \mathcal{N} \xrightarrow{\langle id, \bar{s}\cdot\pi_2\rangle} A_n \times \mathcal{N} \times \mathcal{N}$$

where $s : \mathcal{N} \to \mathcal{N}$ is the successor map in the H-pretopos $\mathcal{P}$, $\bar{s} \equiv id_1^*(s)$ and $\langle id, \bar{s} \cdot \pi_2\rangle$ is the unique morphism towards the pullback of $!_{A_n \times \mathcal{N}}$ and $\widehat{\mathcal{N}}(!_1)$. By using the indexed sum type, the *elimination* and *conversion* rules of the natural numbers type for dependent types, as in the extensional version of Martin-Löf's type theory [NPS90], are equivalent to the following weaker elimination and conversion rules of the natural numbers type for types not depending on $\mathcal{N}$, which are also derivable in $T(\mathcal{P})$

$$\text{E}_s\text{-nat)} \quad \frac{a \in L \quad l(y) \in L\ [y \in L]}{Rec_s(a,l,n) \in L\ [n \in N]}$$

$$\text{C}_1\text{-nat)} \quad \frac{a \in L \quad l(y) \in L\ [y \in L]}{Rec_s(a,l,0) = a \in L}$$

$$\text{C}_2\text{-nat)} \quad \frac{a \in L \quad l(y) \in L\ [y \in L]}{Rec_s(a,l,s(n)) = l(Rec_s(a,l,n)) \in L\ [n \in N]}$$

$$\text{C}_3\text{-nat)}\quad \frac{\begin{array}{ccc} a \in L & l(y) \in L\ [y \in L] & f(n) \in L\ [n \in N] \\ f(0) = a \in L\ f(s(n)) = l(f(n)) \in L & & \end{array}}{Rec_s(a,l,n) = f(n) \in L\ [n \in N]}$$

In the weaker elimination rule E$_s$-nat

$$Rec_s(a,l,n) \quad \text{is} \quad A_n \times \mathcal{N} \xrightarrow{\langle id, r\rangle} (A_n \times \mathcal{N}) \times L$$

where r is the unique morphism that makes the diagram below commute, by the property of natural numbers object in $\mathcal{P}/A_n$ with $\pi_2^L \equiv q(\xi(id), \xi(id))$

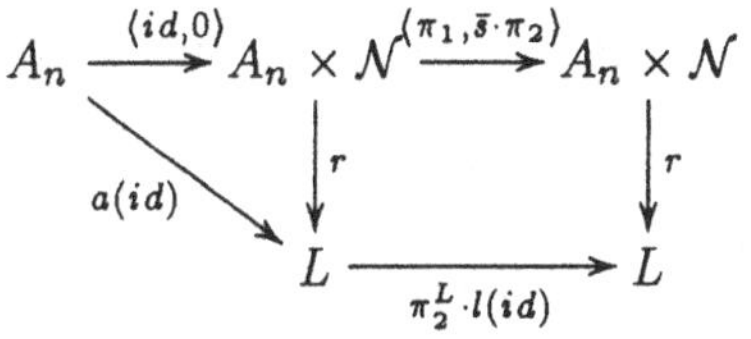

The conversion rules for the natural numbers type are also valid.

3 The relation between the type theories and the H-pretoposes

There is a sort of equivalence between the type theories described in the previous section and the category of H-pretoposes. So we can state that the type theory $T(\mathcal{P})$ is the internal language of the H-pretopos $\mathcal{P}$. First of all, we define the following categories:

1. *Lang* whose objects are the type theories of H-pretoposes and whose morphisms are translations: they send types to types so as to preserve the type and term constructors, closed terms to closed terms and variables to variables; we call *Lang** the category whose objects are those of *Lang*, but whose morphisms are translations preserving type and term constructors up to isomorphisms;
2. $HPretop_o$ whose objects are H-pretoposes with a fixed choice of H-pretopos structure and whose morphisms are strict logical functors, that is functors preserving the H-pretopos structure w.r.t. the fixed choices; we call $HPretop$ the category whose objects are those of $HPretop_o$, but whose morphisms are functors preserving the H-pretopos structure up to isomorphisms.

Now, we define a functor from H-pretoposes to type theories

$$T : HPretop_o \longrightarrow Lang$$

that associates to every H-pretopos $\mathcal{P}$ the internal type theory $T(\mathcal{P})$ described in the previous section. The functor T associates to every morphism $F : \mathcal{P} \rightarrow$

$\mathcal{D}$ of $HPretop_o$ the translation $T(F) : T(\mathcal{P}) \to T(\mathcal{D})$ defined as follows. Given a fibred functor $\sigma : \mathcal{P}/A \to \mathcal{P}^{\to}$, corresponding to a type judgement, and a natural transformation c, corresponding to a term judgement, we define $T(F)(\sigma)$ and $T(F)(c)$ by induction on the signature of $T(\mathcal{P})$. Indeed, if $\sigma = \widehat{b}$ for any $b : B \to A$ of $\mathcal{P}$, then we put $F(\sigma) = \widehat{F(b)}$, since the chosen pullbacks of $\mathcal{P}$ are sent into the chosen pullbacks of $\mathcal{D}$ by F. If σ is obtained by an inference rule, then we simply define $F(\sigma)$ such that $F(\sigma)(id) = F(\sigma(id))$, in order to make $T(F)$ be a translation. For example, we put $F(\Sigma_\beta(\gamma)) \equiv \Sigma_{F(\beta)}(F(\gamma))$. This definition of $T(F)$ is good, since the functor F preserves the H-pretopos structure w.r.t. the fixed choices used in the internal type theories of $\mathcal{P}$ and $\mathcal{D}$.

Moreover, we define a functor from type theories to H-pretoposes

$$P : Lang \longrightarrow HPretop_o$$

that associates to every type theory $\mathcal{T}$ the category $P(\mathcal{T})$, whose objects are closed types $A, B, C, \ldots$ and whose morphisms are the expressions $(x)b(x)$ corresponding to $b(x) \in B[x \in A]$, where the type B does not depend on A. We can prove that $P(\mathcal{T})$ is a H-pretopos by fixing a choice of its structure[3] (see [Mai97]). The functor P associates to every morphism of $Lang$ $L : \mathcal{T} \to \mathcal{T}'$ the functor $P(L) : P(\mathcal{T}) \to P(\mathcal{T}')$ defined as follows. For every closed type A, we put $P(L)(A) \equiv L(A)$, which is well defined since a translation sends closed types to closed types. For every morphism $b(x) \in B[x \in A]$ of $P(\mathcal{T})$ we put

$$P(L)(b(x) \in B[x \in A]) \equiv L(b(x)) \in L(B)[x \in L(A)]$$

Since L is a translation, then $P(L)$ is a functor preserving the H-pretopos structure. In order to describe the relation between type theories and H-pretoposes, we have to consider a type theory $\mathcal{T}$ as a category. We think of $\mathcal{T}$ as the category whose objects are the same as $Pgr(P(\mathcal{T}))$, but whose morphisms are sequences of morphisms by which we built a series of commutative squares. More precisely, the objects of $\mathcal{T}$ are the dependent types under a context $B(x_1, \ldots, x_n)[x_1 \in A_1, \ldots, x_n \in A_n]$. The morphisms of $\mathcal{T}$ exist only from $B[x_1 \in A_1, \ldots, x_n \in A_n]$ to $B'[x'_1 \in A'_1, \ldots, x'_n \in A'_n]$ and they are[4]

$$b' \in B'(a'_1, \ldots, a'_n)[x_1 \in A_1, \ldots, x_n \in A_n, y \in B(x_1, \ldots, x_n)]$$

such that $a_1 \in A'_1[x_1 \in A_1]$ and $a'_i \in A'_i(a'_1, \ldots, a'_{i-1})[x_1 \in A_1, \ldots, x_i \in A_i]$ for $i = 1, \ldots, n$. The composition is the substitution and the identity is $y \in B(x_1, \ldots, x_n)[x_1 \in A_1, \ldots, x_n \in A_n, y \in B]$. Therefore, we can consider equivalences of type theories. In the following we mean with ID the identity functor.

---

[3] For the choices of finite limits and right adjoints see [See84], for coproducts use disjoint sum types and for quotients use quotient types with indexed sum types.

[4] One could also consider the usual morphisms of contexts.

Proposition 5. *Let $T : HPretop_o \to Lang$ and $P : Lang \to HPretop_o$ be the functors defined above. There are two natural transformations: η from ID to $T \cdot P$, thought as functors from Lang to Lang*, and ϵ from $P \cdot T$ to ID, thought as functors from $HPretop_o$ to $HPretop$, such that for every type theory $\mathcal{T}$ and for every H-pretopos $\mathcal{P}$, $\eta_\mathcal{T} : \mathcal{T} \to T(P(\mathcal{T}))$ and $\epsilon_\mathcal{P} : P(T(\mathcal{P})) \to \mathcal{P}$ are equivalences.*

Proof. In order to obtain the natural transformation η, for every type theory $\mathcal{T}$ we define

$$\eta_\mathcal{T} : \mathcal{T} \to T(P(\mathcal{T}))$$

as follows. For any closed type $\eta_\mathcal{T}(A[\,]) \equiv \widehat{A}(id) : A_\Sigma \to 1$. For dependent type judgements, $\eta_\mathcal{T}(C(x,y)[x \in A, y \in B(x)])$ is the type judgement of $T(P(\mathcal{T}))$ corresponding to the sequence

$$\Sigma_{z \in \tilde{B}} C(z)_\Sigma \xrightarrow{q_3(id)} \Sigma_{x \in A} B(x)_\Sigma \xrightarrow{q_2(id)} A_\Sigma \xrightarrow{\widehat{A}(id)} 1$$

where $\tilde{B} \equiv \Sigma_{x \in A} B(x)$ and $q_i \equiv \widehat{\pi_1}[p_{i-1}]$ for $i = 2, 3$. This is the dependent type judgement arising from the following sequence

$$\Sigma_{z \in \Sigma_{x \in A} B(x)} C(z) \xrightarrow{\pi_1} \Sigma_{x \in A} B(x) \xrightarrow{\pi_1} A \xrightarrow{*} 1$$

in the internal type theory $T(P(\mathcal{T}))$, as it is described in the previous section. For term judgements, $\eta_\mathcal{T}(c \in C(x,y)[x \in A, y \in B(x)])$ is

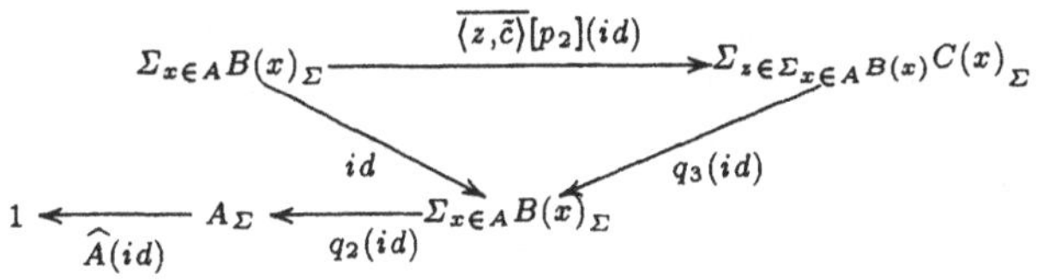

where $\tilde{c} \equiv c[x/\pi_1(z), y/\pi_2(z)][z \in \Sigma_{x \in A} B(x)]$. This is the term judgement arising from $\langle z, \tilde{c} \rangle$ in the internal type theory $T(P(\mathcal{T}))$, as it is described in the previous section. We can obviously imagine how $\eta_\mathcal{T}$ is defined in the case of having a generic context of n types. We can see that η is a natural transformation, since translations preserve indexed sum types and projections. $\eta_\mathcal{T}$ is a translation up to isomorphisms and it is an equivalence of categories since the functor is faithfull, full and essentially surjective. Indeed, we can define a natural transformation η^{-1} such that, given a type theory $\mathcal{T}$, the component $\eta_\mathcal{T}^{-1} : T(P(\mathcal{T})) \to \mathcal{T}$ is defined as follows. Given a type judgement $B \xrightarrow{\beta(id)} A \xrightarrow{\alpha(id)} 1$ of $T(P(\mathcal{T}))$ we define

$$\eta_\mathcal{T}^{-1}(\alpha(id), \beta(id)) \equiv \beta(id)^{-1}(x)[x \in A]$$

where $\beta(id)^{-1}(x) \equiv \Sigma_{z\in B} Eq(A, \beta(id)(z), x)$, that is the fibers of $\beta(id)$. Given the term judgement

$$\begin{array}{ccc} A & \xrightarrow{c(id)} & B \\ & {\scriptstyle id}\searrow \quad \swarrow{\scriptstyle \beta(id)} & \\ 1 \xleftarrow{\alpha(id)} & A & \end{array}$$

of $T(P(\mathcal{T}))$, provided that $c(id)$ is $c(x) \in B[x \in A]$, $\eta_{\mathcal{T}}^{-1}$ associates to it the term judgement of $\mathcal{T}$

$$\langle c(x), eq\rangle \in \Sigma_{z\in B} Eq(A, \beta(id)(z), x)[x \in A]$$

We can see that η^{-1} is a natural transformation, since translations preserve indexed sum types, projections and equality types. We can prove that, for every type theory $\mathcal{T}$, $\eta_{\mathcal{T}}$ and $\eta_{\mathcal{T}}^{-1}$ give rise to an equivalence of categories (also see [See84]).

Moreover, we define a natural transformation ϵ such that for every H-pretopos $\mathcal{P}$ the component

$$\epsilon_{\mathcal{P}} : P(T(\mathcal{P})) \to \mathcal{P}$$

is defined as follows. $\epsilon_{\mathcal{P}}$ associates to every object $A \xrightarrow{\sigma(id)} 1$ of $P(T(\mathcal{P}))$ the object A and it associates to the morphism

$$\begin{array}{ccc} A & \xrightarrow{b(id)} & A\times B \\ & {\scriptstyle id}\searrow \quad \swarrow{\scriptstyle \beta(!_A)} & \\ 1 \xleftarrow{\sigma(id)} & A & \end{array}$$

the morphism $q(!_A, \beta(id))\cdot b(id) : A \to B$. We can easily prove that $\epsilon_{\mathcal{P}}$ is a functor preserving the H-pretopos structure up to isomorphisms[5]. We have that $\epsilon_{\mathcal{P}}$ gives rise to a natural transformation, since the functors preserve the H-pretopos structure w.r.t. the fixed choices. Moreover, $\epsilon_{\mathcal{P}}$ is an equivalence of categories, since it is faithfull by uniqueness of morphisms towards pullbacks, full because every section of a fibred functor has got a name in the language, and essentially surjective. Indeed, we can define a natural transformation ϵ^{-1} such that for every H-pretopos $\mathcal{P}$ the component $\epsilon_{\mathcal{P}}^{-1} : \mathcal{P} \to P(T(\mathcal{P}))$ is defined as follows. For every object A of $\mathcal{P}$, $\epsilon_{\mathcal{P}}^{-1}(A)$ is the closed type corresponding to $A_\Sigma \xrightarrow{\widehat{A}(id)} 1$. For every morphism $b : A \to B$ of $\mathcal{P}$, $\epsilon_{\mathcal{P}}^{-1}(b)$ is the term corresponding to

$$\begin{array}{ccc} A_\Sigma & \xrightarrow{\overline{\langle id, b'\rangle}(id)} & A_\Sigma\times B_\Sigma \\ & {\scriptstyle id}\searrow \quad \swarrow{\scriptstyle \widehat{B}(!_{A_\Sigma})} & \\ 1 \xleftarrow{\widehat{A}(id)} & A_\Sigma & \end{array}$$

where $b' = \pi_B^{-1} \cdot b \cdot \pi_A$ and where π_B and π_A are the second projections of the pullbacks of $!_A$ and $!_B$ along the identity. We conclude that for every H-pretopos $\mathcal{P}$, $\epsilon_{\mathcal{P}}$ and $\epsilon_{\mathcal{P}}^{-1}$ give rise to an equivalence of categories.

---

[5] This is due to the choices of split fibration: see, for instance, the terminal object.

4 The free H-pretopos

The main idea is to generate a H-pretopos from a given category $\mathcal{C}$ by considering its objects as closed types and its morphisms as terms with a free variable. We can prove the universal property by the construction of the category of paths, which represents the dependent types in a categorical way.

Given a category $\mathcal{C}$, we consider the dependent type theory $T(\mathcal{C})$ generated by the inference rules as follows:

1. For every object $\boldsymbol{A}$ of $Ob\mathcal{C}$ we introduce a new type A and we state the closed type judgement $A\ [\,]$.
   Given $A \in Ob\mathcal{C}$ and $B \in Ob\mathcal{C}$ we state $A = B\ [\,]$, if they are the same object in $Ob\mathcal{C}$.
2. For every morphism $\boldsymbol{b} : \boldsymbol{A} \to \boldsymbol{B}$ in $\mathcal{C}$, we introduce a new term $b(x)$ and we state $b(x) \in B\ [x \in A]$, where A and B are closed types.
   Given $b : A \to B$ and $d : A \to B$ in $\mathcal{C}$, we state $b(x) = d(x) \in B\ [x \in A]$, provided that b and d are the same morphism in $\mathcal{C}$.
   Given $b : A \to B$ and $a : D \to A$ in $\mathcal{C}$, we state about composition $b(x)[x := a(y)] = (b \cdot a)(y) \in B\ [y \in D]$.
3. There are all the inference rules of the typed calculus for H-pretoposes as in the appendix.

Therefore $T(\mathcal{C})$ is a type theory of H-pretoposes.

Now, we can prove:

Proposition 6. *Let $P : Lang \longrightarrow HPretop_o$ be the functor described in section 3. The category $P(T(\mathcal{C}))$ is the free H-pretopos generated by the category $\mathcal{C}$.*

Proof. We know that $P(T(\mathcal{C}))$ is a H-pretopos from the definition of P. Given a functor $G : \mathcal{C} \to \mathcal{P}$, from the category $\mathcal{C}$ to the H-pretopos $\mathcal{P}$, we claim that there exists a unique functor $\tilde{G} : P(T(\mathcal{C})) \to \mathcal{P}$ in $HPretop_o$ such that the diagram

$$\begin{array}{ccc} \mathcal{C} & \xrightarrow{I} & P(T(\mathcal{C})) \\ & {\scriptstyle G}\searrow \quad \swarrow{\scriptstyle \tilde{G}} & \\ & \mathcal{P} & \end{array}$$

commutes, where $I : \mathcal{C} \to P(T(\mathcal{C}))$ is the following functor: for every object $A \in Ob\mathcal{C}$ we put $I(A) \equiv A\ [\,]$ and for every morphism $b : A \to B$ we put $I(b) \equiv b(x) \in B[x \in A]$.

In order to define $\tilde{G}$ on $P(T(\mathcal{C}))$, we define an interpretation $\mathcal{J} : T(\mathcal{C}) \to Pgr(\mathcal{P})$, by passing to $Pgf(\mathcal{P})$, with the warning that we have to normalize the evaluation. This is done by adding the value of every fibred functor $\sigma \in Fib(\mathcal{P}/1, \mathcal{P}^{\to})$ on the empty, by induction on the signature, such that a type judgement will be interpreted by a sequence of $Pgr(\mathcal{P})$ like

$$\alpha_1(\emptyset), \alpha_2(id_{A_1}), ..., \alpha_n(id_{A_{n-1}})$$

The interpretation is the same as for the internal type theory, except for closed types and terms, which are interpreted in fibred functors evaluated on $\emptyset$. The reason is that we want to put $\tilde{G}(A[\,]) \equiv \mathrm{dom}\mathcal{J}(A[\,])$ and $\tilde{G}(b \in B[x \in A]) \equiv q(\mathcal{J}(A[\,]), \mathcal{J}(B[\,])) \cdot \mathcal{J}(b \in B[x \in A])$, but if we adopt for $\mathcal{J}$ the semantics defined in section 2, then $\tilde{G}$ would commute with G up to isomorphisms. So, for every object A of $Ob\mathcal{P}$, we extend the functor $\widehat{A}$ by adding $\widehat{A}(\emptyset) \equiv !_A$ and for every object B, $q(!_B, \widehat{A}(\emptyset))$ is the second projection of the pullback of $!_B$ and $\widehat{A}(\emptyset)$. For example, for the natural numbers $\mathcal{J}(N[\,]) \equiv \widehat{\mathcal{N}}(\emptyset) = !_{\mathcal{N}}$, instead of being interpreted as $!_{1\times\mathcal{N}}$ like in the semantics defined in section 2. Moreover, $\mathcal{J}(0 \in N[\,])$ is $1 \xrightarrow{\widehat{o}(\emptyset)} \mathcal{N}$ (with $id_1 : 1 \to 1$ and $\widehat{\mathcal{N}}(\emptyset) : \mathcal{N} \to 1$) where $\widehat{o}(\emptyset) \equiv o$ and $o : 1 \to \mathcal{N}$ is the zero map in $\mathcal{P}$. Finally, given a proper type arising from an object $A \in Ob\mathcal{C}$, we put $\mathcal{J}(A[\,]) \equiv \widehat{G(A)}(\emptyset)$ and given a proper term arising from a morphism $b : A \to B$ of $\mathcal{C}$, we put $\mathcal{J}(b \in B[x \in A]) \equiv \langle id_{G(A)}, G(b)\rangle$ section of $\widehat{G(B)}(\widehat{G(A)}(\emptyset)) : G(A) \times G(B) \to G(A)$. By definition $\tilde{G}$ preserves the H-pretopos structure and we get $\tilde{G} \cdot I = G$. Moreover, $\tilde{G}$ is obviously unique for fixed choices of the H-pretopos structure, which are required to interpret the type theory $T(\mathcal{C})$ into $Pgr(\mathcal{P})$.

The free structure gives rise to a monad. It would be interesting to investigate if the category $HPretop_o$ is monadic on *Cat* and *Graph*. Or at least, if we prove that $HPretop_o$ is essentially algebraic, as for the categorical models of *ITT* in[Obt89], we would get a representation theorem of $HPretop_o$ into a category of presheaves [AR94].

5 Some other free structures: the *Lex* and *ITT* categories

A similar correspondence to that one between type theories and H-pretoposes can be established for the category *Lex* and *ITT*. The category *Lex*, whose objects are the categories with finite limits and whose morphisms are functors strictly preserving finite limits, provides a valid and complete semantics for the typed calculus with terminal type, extensional equality types and indexed sum types. In the same way, the *ITT* category, whose objects are the locally cartesian closed categories with finite coproducts and a natural numbers object and whose morphisms are functors strictly preserving the *ITT* structure, provides a valid and complete semantics for the fragment of Martin-Löf's type theory with extensional equality and without universes and well-orders [Mar84]. These validity and completeness theorems can be proved in a similar way to that for H-pretoposes. We can easily notice that these dependent typed calculi allow us to build the free structure for *Lex* and *ITT* over *Cat*, in the same way we proved for the category $HPretop_o$. The free structures give a presentation of two monads, whose algebras correspond respectively to *Lex* and *ITT*, since *Lex* and *ITT* are monadic over *Graph* [Bur81] and admit an equational presentation.

Acknowledgements. I would like to thank Pino Rosolini and Silvio Valentini for helpful discussions, and Ieke Moerdijk for making my visit at Utrecht extremely useful. Finally, I want to thank the referees for their comments on the preliminary version of this paper.

6 Appendix: the HP typed calculus

Terminal type

$$\text{Tr)}\ \top\ type \qquad \text{I-Tr)}\ \star \in \top \qquad \text{C-Tr)}\ \frac{t \in \top}{t = \star \in \top}$$

False type

$$\text{Fs)}\ \bot\ type \qquad \text{E-Fs)}\ \frac{a \in \bot \quad A\ type}{r_o(a) \in A}$$

Indexed Sum type

$$\Sigma)\ \frac{C(x)\ type\ \ [x \in B]}{\Sigma_{x \in B} C(x)\ type} \qquad \text{I-}\Sigma)\ \frac{b \in B \quad c \in C(b)}{\langle b, c\rangle \in \Sigma_{x \in B} C(x)}$$

$$\text{E-}\Sigma)\ \frac{d \in \Sigma_{x \in B} C(x) \quad m(x,y) \in M(\langle x, y\rangle)\ [x \in B, y \in C(x)]}{s(d, m) \in M(d)}$$

$$\text{C-}\Sigma)\ \frac{b \in B \quad c \in C(b) \quad m(x,y) \in M(\langle x, y\rangle)\ [x \in B, y \in C(x)]}{s(\langle b, c\rangle, m) = m(b, c) \in M(\langle b, c\rangle)}$$

Equality type

$$\text{Eq)}\ \frac{C\ type \quad c \in C \quad d \in C}{Eq(C, c, d)\ type} \qquad \text{I-Eq)}\ \frac{c = d \in C}{eq_C \in Eq(C, c, d)}$$

$$\text{E-Eq)}\ \frac{p \in Eq(C, c, d)}{c = d \in C} \qquad \text{C-Eq)}\ \frac{p \in Eq(C, c, d)}{p = eq_C \in Eq(C, c, d)}$$

Disjoint Sum type

$$\oplus)\ \frac{C\ type \quad D\ type}{C \oplus D\ type} \qquad \text{I}_1\text{-}\oplus)\ \frac{c \in C}{\epsilon_1(c) \in C \oplus D} \qquad \text{I}_2\text{-}\oplus)\ \frac{d \in D}{\epsilon_2(d) \in C \oplus D}$$

$$\text{E-}\oplus)\ \frac{w \in C \oplus D \quad a_C(x) \in A(\epsilon_1(x))[x \in C] \quad a_D(y) \in A(\epsilon_2(y))[y \in D]}{D(w, a_C, a_D) \in A(w)}$$

$$\text{C}_1\text{-}\oplus)\ \frac{c \in C \quad a_C(x) \in A(\epsilon_1(x))[x \in C] \quad a_D(y) \in A(\epsilon_2(y))[y \in D]}{D(\epsilon_1(c), a_C, a_D) = a_C(c) \in A(\epsilon_1(c))}$$

$$\text{C}_2\text{-}\oplus)\ \frac{d \in D \quad a_C(x) \in A(\epsilon_1(x))[x \in C] \quad a_D(y) \in A(\epsilon_2(y))[y \in D]}{D(\epsilon_2(d), a_C, a_D) = a_D(d) \in A(\epsilon_2(d))}$$

Disjointness

$$\frac{c \in C \quad d \in D \quad \epsilon_1(c) = \epsilon_2(d) \in C \oplus D}{m(c, d) \in \bot}$$

Forall type

$$\forall)\quad \frac{C(x)\ type[x \in B] \quad d \in Eq(C(x), y, z)[x \in B, y \in C(x), z \in C(x)]}{\forall_{x \in B} C(x)\ type}$$

$$\text{I-}\forall)\quad \frac{c \in C(x)[x \in B] \quad d \in Eq(C(x), y, z)[x \in B, y \in C(x), z \in C(x)]}{\lambda x^B.c \in \forall_{x \in B} C(x)}$$

$$\text{E-}\forall)\quad \frac{b \in B \quad f \in \forall_{x \in B} C(x)}{Ap(f, b) \in C(b)}$$

$$\beta\text{C-}\forall)\quad \frac{b \in B \quad c \in C(x)[x \in B] \quad d \in Eq(C(x), y, z)[x \in B, y \in C(x), z \in C(x)]}{Ap(\lambda x^B.c, b) = c(b) \in C(b)}$$

$$\eta\text{C-}\forall)\quad \frac{f \in \forall_{x \in B} C(x)}{\lambda x^B.Ap(f, x) = f \in \forall_{x \in B} C(x)}$$

Quotient type

$$\text{Q)}\quad \frac{\begin{array}{l} R(x,y)\ type\ [x \in A, y \in A], d \in Eq(R(x,y), z, w)[x \in A, y \in A, z \in R(x,y), w \in R(x,y)] \\ c_1 \in R(x,x)[x \in A], \qquad c_2 \in R(y,x)[x \in A, y \in A, z \in R(x,y)] \\ c_3 \in R(x,z)[x \in A, y \in A, z \in A, w \in R(x,y), w' \in R(y,z)] \end{array}}{A/R\ type}$$

$$\text{I-Q)}\quad \frac{a \in A}{[a] \in A/R} \qquad \text{eq-}Q)\quad \frac{a \in A \quad b \in A \quad d \in R(a,b)}{[a] = [b] \in A/R}$$

$$\text{E-Q)}\quad \frac{s \in A/R \quad l(x) \in L([x])[x \in A] \quad l(x) = l(y) \in L([x])[x \in A, y \in A, d \in R(x,y)]}{Q(l, s) \in L(s)}$$

$$\text{C-Q)}\quad \frac{a \in A \quad l(x) \in L([x])[x \in A] \quad l(x) = l(y) \in L([x])[x \in A, y \in A, d \in R(x,y)]}{Q(l, [a]) = l(a) \in L([a])}$$

Effectiveness

$$\frac{a \in A \quad b \in A \quad [a] = [b] \in A/R}{f(a,b) \in R(a,b)}$$

Natural Numbers type

$$\text{nat)}\ N\ type \qquad \text{I}_1\text{-nat)}\ 0 \in N \qquad \text{I}_2\text{-nat)}\quad \frac{n \in N}{s(n) \in N}$$

$$\text{E-nat)}\quad \frac{n \in N \quad a \in L(0) \quad l(x,y) \in L(s(x))[x \in N, y \in L(x)]}{Rec(a, l, n) \in L(n)}$$

$$\text{C}_1\text{-nat)}\quad \frac{a \in L(0) \quad l(x,y) \in L(s(x))[x \in N, y \in L(x)]}{Rec(a, l, 0) = a \in L(0)}$$

$$\text{C}_2\text{-nat)}\quad \frac{n \in N \quad a \in L(0) \quad l(x,y) \in L(s(x))[x \in N, y \in L(x)]}{Rec(a, l, s(n)) = l(n, Rec(a, l, n)) \in L(s(n))}$$

References

[AR94] J. Adamek and J. Rosicky. *Locally presentable and accessible categories.*, volume 189 of *Lecture Notes Series*. Cambridge University Press, 1994.

[Ben85] J. Benabou. Fibred categories and the foundations of naive category theory. *Journal of Symbolic Logic*, 50:10–37, 1985.

[Bur81] A. Burroni. Algebres graphiques. *Cahiers de topologie et geometrie differentielle*, 12:249–265, 1981.

[Car86] J. Cartmell. Generalised algebraic theories and contextual categories. *Annals of Pure and Applied Logic*, 32:209–243, 1986.

[Con86] R. Constable et al. *Implementing mathematics with the Nuprl Development System*. Prentice Hall, 1986.

[dB91] N.G. de Bruijn. Telescopic mapping in typed lambda calculus. *Information and Computation*, 91:189–204, 1991.

[DK83] E.J. Dubuc and G. M. Kelly. A presentation of topoi as algebraic relative to categories and graphs. *Journal of Algebra*, 81:420–433, 1983.

[Hof94] M. Hofmann. On the interpretation of type theory in locally cartesian closed categories. In Proceedings of CSL'94, September 1994.

[Hof95] M. Hofmann. *Extensional concept in intensional type theory.* PhD thesis, University of Edinburgh, July 1995.

[HP89] J.M.E. Hyland and A. M. Pitts. The theory of constructions: Categorical semantics and topos theoretic models. In J. W. Gray and A. Scedrov, editors, *Categories in Computer Science and Logic*, volume 92 of *Contemporary Mathematics*, pages 137–199, 1989.

[Jac91] B. Jacobs. *Categorical type theory.* PhD thesis, University of Nijmegen, 1991.

[JM95] A. Joyal and I. Moerdijk. *Algebraic set theory.*, volume 220 of *Lecture Note Series*. Cambridge University Press, 1995.

[LS86] J. Lambek and P. J. Scott. *An introduction to higher order categorical logic.*, volume 7 of *Studies in Advanced Mathematics*. Cambridge University Press, 1986.

[Mai97] M.E. Maietti. The typed theory of Heyting Pretopoi. *Preprint-University of Padova*, January 1997.

[Mar84] P. Martin-Löf. *Intuitionistic Type Theory, notes by G. Sambin of a series of lectures given in Padua.* Bibliopolis, Naples, 1984.

[MM92] S. MacLane and I. Moerdijk. *Sheaves in Geometry and Logic. A first introduction to Topos Theory.* Springer Verlag, 1992.

[MR77] M. Makkai and G. Reyes. *First order categorical logic.*, volume 611 of *Lecture Notes in Mathematics*. Springer Verlag, 1977.

[NPS90] B. Nordström, K. Peterson, and J. Smith. *Programming in Martin Löf's Type Theory.* Clarendon Press, Oxford, 1990.

[Obt89] A. Obtulowicz. Categorical and algebraic aspects of Martin Löf's type theory. *Studia Logica*, 3:299–317, 1989.

[See84] R. Seely. Locally cartesian closed categories and type theory. *Math. Proc. Cambr. Phyl. Soc.*, 95:33–48, 1984.

[Tay97] P. Taylor. *Practical Foundations of Mathematics*, volume 99 of *Cambridge studies in advanced mathematics.* Cambridge University Press, 1997.

Inverting Inductively Defined Relations in LEGO

Conor McBride

Department of Computer Science
University of Edinburgh

1 Introduction

Inverting an inductively defined relation essentially consists of observing that any of its inhabitants must be derivable by at least one of its inference rules.

For example, let us define $\leq$ inductively by the rules

$$\frac{}{\mathbf{zero} \leq n} \leq_z \qquad \frac{m \leq n}{\mathbf{suc}\, m \leq \mathbf{suc}\, n} \leq_s$$

Now suppose we have the hypothesis, $x \leq zero$. Inverting, we see that, since **zero** cannot equal **suc** n, only rule $\leq_z$ could have yielded this conclusion, thus we deduce that $x = \mathbf{zero}$. Likewise, if we have $\mathbf{suc}\, x \leq y$, inversion shows that only rule $\leq_s$ could have applied, hence $y = \mathbf{suc}\, z$ for some z and, moreover $x \leq z$.

In essence, inverting a hypothesis gives us its 'predecessor' premises with respect to each rule, constrained by equations which reflect the validity of the rule instance.

The notion of 'inversion' has a history in logic [Pra65]. It is analogous to Clark's notion of the 'completion' of a logic program, used to give a semantics of 'negation as failure' [Cla78], and also bears considerable resemblance to the idea of 'definitional reflection' given by Hallnäs in [Hal91]. Given a hypothesis, we may gain useful information by asking how it can have come to be true—it is this natural mode of reasoning which inversion captures.

An inversion principle corresponds to case analysis on a derivation, rather than the full recursion inherent in an induction principle. Although it reduces a known inhabitant of the relation to the premises from which it follows, it provides no inductive hypotheses for those premises. However, as Burstall observes in [Bur96], an inversion is often all that is necessary to complete a proof by induction over a related structure. Indeed, rule induction for $\leq$ can be derived from its inversion principle by induction over the natural numbers.

The impetus behind our work is the inversion facility in the Coq system [Coq], originally implemented by Murthy, with subsequent elaboration by Cornes and

Terrasse [CT95]. Our approach differs from theirs in that it is centred on unification. For a given hypothesis to follow from a particular rule, it must unify with that rule's conclusion, and the premises, instantiated by the unifier, must hold.

Where the Coq package proves particular inversion lemmas for particular hypotheses, we prove a generic lemma for each inductively defined relation, internalising the unification problems as systems of equations. We then supply a tactic which solves a certain class of first-order unification problems—this can be applied uniformly to the subgoals generated by an inversion.

We believe that this approach yields a clearer presentation of inversion which is relatively simple to implement. We shall also see that it solves a larger class of problems.

2 Generic Inversion Lemmas

In general, an inductively defined relation $R\,\vec{t}$, where $\vec{t}$ is a sequence of parameters, may be given by a set of inference rules like so:

$$\frac{\vec{P}_1[\vec{x}_1]}{R\,\vec{t}_1[\vec{x}_1]}\,rule_1 \qquad \cdots \qquad \frac{\vec{P}_n[\vec{x}_n]}{R\,\vec{t}_n[\vec{x}_n]}\,rule_n$$

where $\vec{P}_i$ is a sequence of premises (perhaps involving R) and the $\vec{x}_i$ are the schematic variables for $rule_i$.

LEGO's `Inductive` command [Pol94] allows such relations to be represented as Dybjer-style inductive families of types [Dyb91], provided they fall within the positivity restrictions given by Luo in [Luo94]. The induction principle and reductions corresponding to the rules are then generated in accordance with Luo's characterisation and added as assumptions to the local context.

The generic inversion lemma which we shall use is as follows:

$$\frac{R\,\vec{s} \qquad \begin{array}{c} \forall \vec{x}_1 .\, \vec{s} = \vec{t}_1[\vec{x}_1] \rightarrow \vec{P}_1[\vec{x}_1] \rightarrow \Phi \\ \vdots \\ \forall \vec{x}_n .\, \vec{s} = \vec{t}_n[\vec{x}_n] \rightarrow \vec{P}_n[\vec{x}_n] \rightarrow \Phi \end{array}}{\Phi} \qquad (\dagger)$$

This should be recognisable, via currying of the higher order definition of disjunction, as the Clark-style completion lemma:

$$\forall \vec{s}.\, R\,\vec{s} \rightarrow \bigvee_{i=1}^{n} \exists \vec{x}_i .\, (\vec{s} = \vec{t}_i \wedge \vec{P}_i[\vec{x}_i])$$

Provided the equations are well-typed, we can generate this lemma as a type in LEGO and prove it by an easy induction on the derivation of $R\,\vec{s}$. The inductive case for $rule_i$ instantiates $\vec{s}$ to $\vec{t}_i[\vec{x}_i]$ and supplies the $\vec{P}_i[\vec{x}_i]$ as hypotheses, so the corresponding premise of the inversion lemma can be applied to prove Φ.

Observe that the effect of applying this lemma to an instance $R\,\vec{s}$ of the family R is to replace a goal Φ by a bunch of subgoals, one for each $rule_i$, like so:

$$\forall \vec{x}_i.\, \vec{s} = \vec{t}_i[\vec{x}_i] \to \vec{P}_i[\vec{x}_i] \to \Phi$$

The $\vec{s} = \vec{t}_i[\vec{x}_i]$ conditions capture the requirement that our hypothesis unifies with the conclusion of $rule_i$, while the $\vec{P}_i[\vec{x}_i]$ conditions force the rule's premises to hold. If there is no unifier, then the subgoal is vacuous. If we can establish a most general unifier, σ, then the subgoal reduces to

$$\sigma\vec{P}_i[\vec{x}_i] \to \sigma\Phi$$

In this light, our inversion lemma bears a strong resemblance to Tamaki and Sato's unfold transformations for logic programs [TS84] and Eriksson's proposed rule of definitional reflection [Eri91]:

$$\frac{\{\sigma\Gamma, \sigma C \vdash \sigma A \;:\; \sigma = \mathrm{mgu}(a, b) \text{ for definition } b \Leftarrow C\}}{\Gamma, a \vdash A}$$

The crucial distinction is that the unification in our treatment is at the object level. In systems such as ALF [Mag95], where the type theory is strengthened by pattern matching, inversion comes for free.

The inversion facility added to LEGO establishes the generic lemma (†) for each R once and for all at the time R is defined. Reducing the subgoals generated for specific R-hypotheses then depends on our ability to solve the unification problems they contain.

The current implementation is limited by the requirement that the equations representing the unification problems be well-typed. This can fail to be the case when there is type dependency between parameters of the relation. For example, a relation $R : \Pi t : \mathtt{SET}.\, (\mathtt{list}\, t) \to \mathtt{Prop}$ would give rise to equations

$$s = t \to ls = lt \to \ldots$$

where ls has type $(\mathtt{list}\, s)$ but lt has type $(\mathtt{list}\, t)$. Inversion principles are not automatically generated in these cases. Similar problems can arise in expressing the injectivity of datatype constructors (see section 4.4).

3 First-Order Unification for Constructor Forms

In their survey of rule-based unification, [JK91], Jouannaud and Kirchner give a first-order unification algorithm, 'Tree-Unify', which is complete for what they call 'constructor forms'. We have adapted it for inductive datatypes in LEGO. A partial implementation of Tree-Unify is the basis of a tactic specifically intended to simplify the subgoals generated by inversion.

Given variables X, we define the constructor forms T of an inductive datatype with constructors C recursively as follows:

$$T ::= X \mid C\, T_1 \ldots T_n$$

Now, motivated by the structure of subgoals left by inversion, let us represent a unification problem by a sequence of equational premises in a goal:

$$s_1 = t_{i1} \rightarrow \ldots \rightarrow s_j = t_{ij} \rightarrow \Phi$$

We present the algorithm Tree-Unify in a refinement style. The backwards-directed transition rules in figure 1 are applied repeatedly until either the goal is proved or no equations remain. The leading equation, $s = t$ determines which rule is appropriate at each step in a syntax-directed way. Figure 2 tabulates this choice according to the form of s (ranging vertically) and t (ranging horizontally).

For example, if we have the equation $x = y$ for distinct variables x and y, then **coalescence** is chosen, removing the superfluous variable; if the two sides have distinct outermost constructors c and c', then **conflict** applies, proving the goal.

It is easily shown that each transition preserves the constructor form property of these unification problems.

$$\textbf{deletion}\quad \frac{\Phi}{x = x \to \Phi}$$

$$\textbf{coalescence}\quad \frac{[y \mapsto x]\Phi}{y = x \to \Phi}\ x, y \text{ distinct}$$

$$\textbf{conflict}\quad \frac{}{c\,\vec{s} = c'\,\vec{t} \to \Phi}\ c \neq c'$$

$$\textbf{injectivity}\quad \frac{\vec{s} = \vec{t} \to \Phi}{c\,\vec{s} = c\,\vec{t} \to \Phi}$$

$$\textbf{checking}\quad \frac{}{c\,\vec{s} = x \to \Phi}\ x \in \mathrm{FV}(\vec{s})$$

$$\textbf{elimination}\quad \frac{[x \mapsto c\,\vec{s}]\Phi}{c\,\vec{s} = x \to \Phi}\ x \notin \mathrm{FV}(\vec{s})$$

Fig. 1. Transition rules for Tree-Unify

$s = t$	t is x $(x \neq y)$	t is $c\,\vec{t}$	t is $c'\,\vec{t}$
s is x	**deletion**	apply symmetry	
s is y	**coalescence**		
s is $c\,\vec{s}$ $(c \neq c')$	if $x \in \mathrm{FV}(\vec{s})$ then **checking** else **elimination**	**injectivity**	**conflict**

Fig. 2. Tree-Unify is syntax directed by leading equation $s = t$

Theorem 1. *Tree-Unify terminates.*

Proof. Examining the behaviour of the transitions, we find that **conflict** and **checking** cause termination directly.

Further, the side-condition on **elimination** ensures that both it and **coalescence** strictly reduce the number of distinct variables remaining in the problem.

The **deletion** and **injectivity** rules each reduce the total size of the terms in the problem, where the size of a term is simply the total number of variable references and constructor applications therein. Neither rule introduces new variables.

Hence termination follows by a lexicographic induction on the number of distinct variables in the problem, then the total size of the problem. □

The soundness of any implementation of Tree-Unify is ultimately guaranteed by the requirement that the synthesised proofs should typecheck. Nonetheless, it seems appropriate to make an informal argument for the soundness of the algorithm. We postpone discussion of the implementation difficulties until the next section.

Theorem 2. *Tree-Unify is sound.*

Proof. We examine each transition rule.

deletion is trivial. **coalescence** and **elimination** follow from the substitutivity of equality.

conflict holds because the equation $c\vec{s} = c'\vec{t}$ fails to have the Leibnitz property—by case analysis, we can check that $c\,\vec{s}$ has c as its head, while $c'\,\vec{t}$ does not.

injectivity is essentially the observation that equality is preserved by the application of the 'predecessor' functions which map $c\,\vec{t}$ to each t_i. (There is a practical problem constructing these 'predecessor' functions in the presence of dependently-typed arguments, as we shall see in section 4.4.)

This leaves **checking**. For any inductive datatype, we can define the strict subterm ordering $<$ and show by induction that $s < t \rightarrow s \neq t$. If $x \in FV(\vec{s})$ then x is a strict subterm of $c\,\vec{s}$, hence the hypothesis $c\,\vec{s} = x$ is absurd. □

We turn now to the question of completeness.

Theorem 3. *Given goal,*

$$s_1 = t_1 \rightarrow \ldots \rightarrow s_j = t_j \rightarrow \Phi$$

with s_i, t_i in constructor form, Tree-Unify will either prove the goal or reduce it to $\sigma\Phi$ where σ is a most general unifier for the initial j equations.

Proof. We have seen that if the head equation is in constructor form, there is always exactly one transition rule applicable, and that the transition rules preserve the constructor form property of the problem. Since Tree-Unify always terminates, it must either prove the goal or remove the leading j equations, applying a sequence of substitutions σ to the remainder of the goal. It remains, therefore, to show that this σ is a most general unifier for those equations. We shall make an argument by induction over the sequence of transition rules applied.

If Tree-Unify applies no transition rules, then there must be no constructor form equations—the identity substitution is trivially a most general unifier for the empty problem.

Now we must check that each transition rule preserves this completeness property. For **conflict** and **checking** there is nothing to prove, whilst for **deletion** and **injectivity**, the requirement is trivial.

Both **coalescence** and **elimination** may be treated as instances of

$$\frac{[x \mapsto s]\Phi}{s = x \to \Phi}\; x \notin FV(s)$$

Suppose, inductively, that the substitution sequence σ generated for $[x \mapsto s]\Phi$ is a most general unifier for that problem.

We must show that $\sigma \circ [x \mapsto s]$ is a most general unifier for $s = x \to \Phi$.

By hypothesis, σ unifies $[x \mapsto s]\Phi$, so $\sigma \circ [x \mapsto s]$ certainly unifies Φ. Clearly, it also unifies x with s. Hence $\sigma \circ [x \mapsto s]$ is certainly a unifier for $s = x \to \Phi$.

Now suppose some ρ unifies $s = x \to \Phi$. Necessarily, $\rho = \rho \circ [x \mapsto s]$. Hence, ρ unifies $[x \mapsto s]\Phi$.

Again, our inductive hypothesis tells us that, since σ is a most general unifier for $[x \mapsto s]\Phi$, $\rho = \tau \circ \sigma$ for some τ.

Hence $\rho = \rho \circ [x \mapsto s] = \tau \circ \sigma \circ [x \mapsto s]$.

Hence $\sigma \circ [x \mapsto s]$ is a most general unifier for $s = x \to \Phi$ as required. □

4 `Qnify`: A Partial Implementation of Tree-Unify

The previous section exhibited the unification algorithm Tree-Unify and some of its properties. In this section, we examine its implementation as the new LEGO tactic, **`Qnify`**[1], and point out some of the pragmatic issues and difficulties which arose in this task.

The representation of a unification problem as a goal with equational premises enables a very simple implementation which makes considerable use of existing data structures and tactics (see [LEGO]). The state of the problem is just the goal itself, viewed as a stack of equations. The transition rules correspond to refinement tactics executed according to a simple syntactic analysis of the head equation. The current implementation performs no reduction on terms and hence fails to detect expressions which convert to constructor applications, although the user can force this computation explicitly beforehand—the possibility of introducing some weak head normalisation into the mechanism is under investigation.

[1] pronounced '*kunify*' to emphasise it is a unification tactic, and named after the substitution tactic `Qrepl`, on which it heavily relies

Qnify handles equations not susceptible to any of the transition rules by introducing them into the context and proceeding with the remainder of the problem. **Qnify** will introduce non-equational premises in the same way, in order to gain access to an equation further down the goal.

4.1 Deletion

We remove the initial $x = x$ from the goal, simply by introducing it into the context.

4.2 Coalescence

Given an initial $y = x$ premise, we introduce it to the context and use the existing **Qrepl** tactic to substitute one variable for the other in the remainder of the goal.

This begs the pragmatic question of which way round to make the substitution. A generic inversion lemma will often introduce variables which are not required for some applications, and our tactic is geared to eliminate them. We achieve this by choosing to substitute for the variable which has smaller scope. The remaining variable, being 'more global', tends to be more useful.

4.3 Conflict

In their treatment of inversion [CT95], Cornes and Terrasse show us how to prove equations $c\,\vec{s} = c'\,\vec{t}$ absurd using the computational power of the calculus and the substitutive property of equality.

For each constructor c of each inductive type T, we construct a discriminator function $T\texttt{\_is\_}c : T \rightarrow \texttt{Prop}$ which returns $\top$ for any $c\,\vec{s}$ and $\bot$ otherwise.

If c' is any other constructor, we then have

$$\dfrac{\dfrac{c\,\vec{s} = c'\,\vec{t} \qquad \dfrac{\dfrac{}{\top}}{T\texttt{\_is\_}c\,(c\,\vec{s})}\,equiv}{T\texttt{\_is\_}c\,(c'\,\vec{t})}\,=_{subst}}{\bot}\,equiv$$

If requested, LEGO will generate the discriminator functions at declaration time for any simple inductive datatype. **Qnify** will then deploy them in **conflict** proofs.

4.4 Injectivity

Again, our attempts to prove constructors injective follow the same pattern as those of Cornes and Terrasse, and have the same successes and failures.

If we can define a batch of suitable predecessor functions $c\_\mathtt{pred}_i$ which return t_i given $c\vec{t}$ and a suitably typed dummy value otherwise, then the corresponding injectivity proof is given by

$$\dfrac{\dfrac{c\,\vec{s} = c\,\vec{t} \qquad \dfrac{\dfrac{}{s_i = s_i}=_{refl}}{s_i = c\_\mathtt{pred}_i\,(c\,\vec{s})}\,equiv}{s_i = c\_\mathtt{pred}_i\,(c\,\vec{t})}=_{subst}}{s_i = t_i}\,equiv$$

However, the choice of dummy value is not always straightforward. For simple inductive datatypes, any element will do. If we construct the predecessor functions locally to the injectivity theorem, we can simply use the hypothetical s_i itself. For inductive families, the dummy values required may vary in type, and are frequently far from obvious. Hence injectivity theorems are only generated for simple inductive datatypes.

As with inversion principles, type dependency between the arguments of a constructor may prevent injected equalities from typechecking. For example, if constructor c has type $\Pi n : \mathtt{nat}.\,(\mathtt{vect}\; n) \to T$, then $c\,m\,u = c\,n\,v$ gives rise to the ill-typed injected equality $u = v$. At present, our implementation detects this problem and does not attempt to prove injectivity for such constructors, issuing a warning, but allowing the rest of the definition to go through.

4.5 Checking

Given an equation $x = t$, substituting $[x \mapsto t]$ without checking that $x \notin \mathrm{FV}(t)$ runs the risk of infinite regress. However, automating the proof of the **checking** rule is far from easy. `Qnify` responds to such cases by warning the user, making no substitution and deleting the offending equation from the problem.

The strict subterm ordering argument presented in the previous section would require the automatic generation of much extra equipment for each inductive datatype. Such facilities would be of benefit to users in a wide variety of applications, but the task is large and has not been done.

In the mean time, a more specific technique for automating the disproof of $c\,\vec{s}[x] = x$ (arising from conversations with Andrew Adams) is to select one occurrence of x within $\bar{s}[x]$ and construct the recursive function **f** (given here in ML style):

$$\begin{array}{lll} \texttt{fun f } c\,\bar{s}[x] & = & \texttt{suc (f } x\texttt{)} \\ \quad\texttt{| f } \quad \_ & = & \texttt{zero} \end{array}$$

Applying **f** to both sides of the offending equation, we get

$$\texttt{suc (f } x\texttt{)} = \texttt{f } x$$

We need merely have proved in advance that $\forall n.\,\texttt{suc}\,n \neq n$ and the result follows at once.

This technique should be implementable easily in Coq, where pattern-matching definition and fixpoint recursion are both supported [Cor96, Gim94], allowing the function to be represented directly at the object level, whatever its depth of recursion. LEGO provides only one-step elimination rules for its inductive datatypes, requiring **f** to be 'compiled' into primitive recursive form. An experimental implementation of this procedure is in progress at time of writing.

4.6 Elimination

Given an equation $x = t$, and having checked that $x \notin \mathrm{FV}(t)$, `Qnify` uses `Qrepl` to substitute $[x \mapsto t]$.

`Qnify` does not check that t is in constructor form. However, the occurrence check is sufficient to guarantee termination.

5 Examples and Comparative Study

In this section, we consider three example inversion proofs which show the power of our treatment and also help to justify some of the pragmatic choices made in the implementation. We will also examine similar facilities in other theorem-proving systems.

Our presentation follows the convention of labelling assumptions in the context with identifiers and outstanding proof obligations with ? symbols.

5.1 Induction and Inversion for $\leq$

This simple example shows a proof by natural number induction and $\leq$ inversion, where perhaps one might have expected rule induction. We shall prove

$$? : \forall x.\, \mathtt{suc}\, x \leq x \longrightarrow \bot$$

As we have already remarked, rule induction on the $\leq$ premise is not required. Induction on x and inversion of $\leq$ is sufficient.

For the case $x = \mathtt{zero}$, inverting the hypothesis $\mathtt{suc}\,\mathtt{zero} \leq \mathtt{zero}$ yields subgoals which zero with a successor. **Qnify** proves both of these:

$$? : \forall n.\, \mathtt{suc}\,\mathtt{zero} = \mathtt{zero} \longrightarrow \mathtt{zero} = n \longrightarrow \bot$$
$$? : \forall m.\, \mathtt{suc}\,\mathtt{zero} = \mathtt{suc}\, m \longrightarrow \forall n.\, \mathtt{zero} = \mathtt{suc}\, n \longrightarrow m \leq n \longrightarrow \bot$$

Observe how the implementation has placed the equations as far left as their dependencies permits. LEGO does not distinguish between 'schematic variables' like m and n here, and 'premises' like $m \leq n$. They are merely arguments to a dependently typed constructor function. It seems desirable to position the equations so that **Qnify** applies its substitutions as widely as possible, as we shall see when establishing the inductive step:

$$x\_ih : \mathtt{suc}\, x \leq x \longrightarrow \bot$$
$$? : \mathtt{suc}\,(\mathtt{suc}\, x) \leq \mathtt{suc}\, x \longrightarrow \bot$$

The interesting case of the inversion is then

$$? : \forall m.\, \mathtt{suc}\,(\mathtt{suc}\, x) = \mathtt{suc}\, m \longrightarrow \forall n.\, \mathtt{suc}\, x = \mathtt{suc}\, n \longrightarrow m \leq n \longrightarrow \bot$$

Qnify applies injectivity and substitutes $[m \mapsto \mathtt{suc}\, x]$ and $[n \mapsto x]$. Note that the positioning of the equations ensures that these apply to the $m \leq n$ premise, and that it is better to keep x, which occurs in the inductive hypothesis, than n which is local to the inversion. The simplified subgoal follows immediately:

$$? : \mathtt{suc}\, x \leq x \longrightarrow \bot$$

5.2 The Advantage of Unification

Coq's inversion facilities (see [CT95]) prove specific inversion lemmas for specific hypotheses. Where our generic lemma has a case for each inference rule, Coq will simplify and possibly eliminate these cases from a given lemma by applying constructor conflict and injectivity results. However, by performing substitution steps within the equational problem, we capitalise on the power of unification where Coq does not.

Consider the datatype of unlabelled binary trees:

$$\frac{}{\texttt{leaf} : \texttt{tree}} \qquad \frac{s, t : \texttt{tree}}{\texttt{node}\, s\, t : \texttt{tree}}$$

The reflexive relation, **refl**, on this datatype can be represented as an inductively defined relation with inference rule:

$$\frac{}{\texttt{refl}\, t\, t}$$

The corresponding inversion principle encapsulates the idea that the two arguments of any inhabitant of this relation must unify. Our approach addresses this question where mere appeals to constructor conflict and injectivity do not. Similarly, repeated instances of the same schematic variable must correspond to terms which unify.

The proof of the following goal shows how our facility addresses both of these issues:

$$? : \forall x.\, \texttt{refl}\,(\texttt{node}\, x\, \texttt{leaf})\,(\texttt{node}\,(\texttt{node}\,\texttt{leaf}\,\texttt{leaf})\, x) \longrightarrow \bot$$

Inverting the **refl** premise gives us

$$? : \forall t.\, (\texttt{node}\, x\, \texttt{leaf}) = t \longrightarrow (\texttt{node}\,(\texttt{node}\,\texttt{leaf}\,\texttt{leaf})\, x) = t \longrightarrow \bot$$

Qnify applies **elimination**

$$(\texttt{node}\,(\texttt{node}\,\texttt{leaf}\,\texttt{leaf})\, x) = (\texttt{node}\, x\, \texttt{leaf}) \longrightarrow \bot$$

then **injectivity**,

$$(\texttt{node}\,\texttt{leaf}\,\texttt{leaf}) = x \longrightarrow x = \texttt{leaf} \longrightarrow \bot$$

then **elimination**,

$$(\texttt{node}\,\texttt{leaf}\,\texttt{leaf}) = \texttt{leaf} \longrightarrow \bot$$

and finally proves the goal by **conflict**.

At present, the '**Inversion**' tactic in Coq does not attempt to unify the two instantiations of x, and hence stops short of proving this goal. The extra steps could easily be done by hand or by a user-supplied tactic. It should not be difficult to adapt Coq's inversion package to the same range of problems addressed by **Qnify**.

5.3 Proving an Operational Semantics Deterministic

In this example, we sketch the proof that the operational semantics for a simple 'while' language is deterministic. This example is partly motivated by the similar example given by Camilleri and Melham for their inductive relation package in the HOL system [HOL, CM92].

A command C executed in state s yields state t (denoted $s < C > t$) according to the inductive definition given in figure 3

$$\frac{}{s < \mathtt{skip} > s}$$

$$\frac{}{s < V := E > ([V := E]s)}$$

$$\frac{s < C > t \qquad t < C' > u}{s < C ; C' > u}$$

$$\frac{s < C' > t}{s < \mathtt{if}\ B\ \mathbf{then}\ C\ \mathtt{else}\ C' > t}\ B\ s = \mathtt{false}$$

$$\frac{s < C > t}{s < \mathtt{if}\ B\ \mathbf{then}\ C\ \mathtt{else}\ C' > t}\ B\ s = \mathtt{true}$$

$$\frac{}{s < \mathtt{while}\ B\ \mathbf{do}\ C > t}\ B\ s = \mathtt{false}$$

$$\frac{s < C > t \qquad t < \mathtt{while}\ B\ \mathbf{do}\ C > u}{s < \mathtt{while}\ B\ \mathbf{do}\ C > u}\ B\ s = \mathtt{true}$$

Fig. 3. Evaluation Relation for a Simple Imperative Language

Our goal is to show this semantics deterministic, ie:

$$? : \forall C. \forall s, t. \forall H : s < C > t. \forall u. \forall H' : s < C > u. t = u$$

The proof proceeds by induction on H and inversion of H'. We may use the new features of LEGO to express this plan as a composite tactic, also adding hints to dispose of the trivial cases:

```
Lego> Induction H Then intros Then Invert H' Then Qnify
        Then (Refine Eq_refl Else Immed);
```

Qnify eliminates the bulk of the uninteresting cases by **conflict**—those where H and H' take different values of C. Reflexivity of equality is enough for both **skip** and **:=**, whilst the **Immed** catches the trivial inductions—again, the pragmatic positioning of equalities in the inversion lemma and the substitution of older variables for newer ones reduces a number of cases directly to their inductive hypotheses.

The only cases which require user intervention are:

- sequential composition and **while** with $B\,s =$ **true**

  These both have two inductive hypotheses, corresponding to two phases of execution. Using the first inductive hypothesis, the intermediate states resulting from the two executions of C are shown to be the same. Having made this substitution explicitly, the second inductive hypothesis then completes the result.

- **if** and **while** with $B\,s =$ **true** $=$ **false**

  $B s$ cannot be **true** in H and **false** in H' or vice versa. However, $B s$ is not in constructor form, so the user must assist in these four cases. A substitution gives **true** $=$ **false**, and **Qnify** finishes the **conflict** proof.

Camilleri and Melham give the full HOL90 source for their treatment of this operational semantics at

`http://www.dcs.glasgow.ac.uk/ tfm/ftp2.html`

Their package, as detailed in [CM92], enables the definition of the evaluation and the automatic derivation of theorems corresponding to the induction and inversion principles generated by LEGO. Other tactics automatically prove conflict and injectivity properties for the constructors of the language syntax.

However, they provide nothing akin to **Qnify** which simplifies inversion subgoals by attacking the unification problems they contain. Progress from the inversion is largely ad hoc, although HOL users have at their disposal a large library of rewriting tactics and the full power of ML for programming with them.

The proof of determinacy is built from the bottom up. Firstly, the inversion principle '**ecases**', the conflict theorems '**distinct**' and the injectivity theorems '**const11**' are combined into a tactic similar to the unification-free inversion tactic in Coq.

```
val SIMPLIFY = REWRITE_RULE (distinct :: const11);

val CASE_TAC = DISCH_THEN
                (STRIP_ASSUME_TAC o
                 SIMPLIFY o
                 ONCE_REWRITE_RULE[ecases]);
```

Next, CASE_TAC is used to build a specific inversion lemma for each inference rule of the evaluation relation. Here is the derivation for **skip**:

```
val SKIP_THM = store_thm("SKIP_THM",
     (--`!s1 s2. EVAL skip s1 s2 = (s1 = s2)`--),
     REPEAT GEN_TAC THEN EQ_TAC THENL
     [CASE_TAC THEN ASM_REWRITE_TAC [],
      DISCH_THEN SUBST1_TAC THEN MAP_FIRST RULE_TAC rules]);
```

Finally, these lemmas are used in the induction itself:

```
val DETERMINISTIC = store_thm ("DETERMINISTIC",
(--`!C st1 st2. EVAL C st1 st2 ==>
         !st3. EVAL C st1 st3 ==> (st2 = st3)`--),
     RULE_INDUCT_TAC THEN REPEAT GEN_TAC THENL
     [REWRITE_TAC [SKIP_THM],
      REWRITE_TAC [ASSIGN_THM],
      PURE_ONCE_REWRITE_TAC [SEQ_THM] THEN STRIP_TAC THEN
        FIRST_ASSUM MATCH_MP_TAC THEN
        RES_TAC THEN ASM_REWRITE_TAC [],
      IMP_RES_TAC IF_T_THM THEN ASM_REWRITE_TAC [],
      IMP_RES_TAC IF_F_THM THEN ASM_REWRITE_TAC [],
      IMP_RES_TAC WHILE_F_THM THEN ASM_REWRITE_TAC [],
      IMP_RES_THEN
        (fn th =>  PURE_ONCE_REWRITE_TAC [th]) WHILE_T_THM THEN
        STRIP_TAC THEN FIRST_ASSUM MATCH_MP_TAC THEN
        RES_TAC THEN ASM_REWRITE_TAC []]);
```

Although it is perhaps a little unfair to compare the raw ML of HOL with the cleaner interfaces of LEGO or Coq, it seems clear from this example that the unification and rewriting preformed by the single LEGO tactic `Qnify` captures a wide variety of cases which must be addressed individually and by hand in HOL.

6 Conclusions and Further Work

This work owes a considerable debt to that of Cornes and Terrasse in Coq ([CT95]). Our formulation and proof of generic inversion principles follow theirs, as do our constructor conflict and injectivity results.

However, the insight

'inversion = predecessor premises + equational constraints'

has led us to a treatment which is intuitive, easy to implement and highly effective in practice. We analyse the equational information separately via the unification algorithm described in this paper. Its specification is clear, it is sound and complete with respect to constructor forms and the tactic `Qnify`, to which it gives rise, has proved independently useful.

For example, recent work extends the inversion facility to cover full induction on the derivation of a relation. A goal of form

$$? : \forall \vec{x}.\, R\,\vec{t}[\vec{x}] \longrightarrow \Phi$$

is first rewritten

$$? : \forall \vec{y}.\, R\,\vec{y} \longrightarrow \forall \vec{x}.\, \vec{y} = \vec{t}[\vec{x}] \longrightarrow \Phi$$

so that the induction principle generated for R is applicable. The equations introduced are ripe for simplification with `Qnify`.

This new `Induction` tactic deals with the problem of type dependency within parameters yielding ill-typed equations by packaging the related parameters in tuples which share the same Σ-type. A similar repair could be made to both inversion and injectivity theorems, extending the class of definition for which they can be generated.

It would seem both worthwhile and tractable to extend all of these new facilities to encompass mutual inductive definitions. This work may be carried out in the near future.

At present, work is in progress implementing **checking** proofs. The compilation of the necessary functions does appear both systematic and tractable, without recourse to fixpoints.

All the new facilities described in this paper, together with documentation describing their usage is available on the web at

http://www.dcs.ed.ac.uk/home/lego/html/alpha/

Acknowledgements The author would like to thank Cristina Cornes for providing the model for this work and much useful advice. Much gratitude is due also to Rod Burstall, James McKinna and Alan Smaill for their patience, guidance and support.

References

[Bur96] R. M. Burstall. Inductively Defined Relations: A Brief Tutorial. Extended Abstract. In Haveraan, M., and Owe, O., and Dahl, O.-J., editors, Recent Trends in Data Types Specification. Springer LNCS 1130, pp14–17. 1996.

[CM92] J. Camilleri and T. Melham. Reasoning with Inductively Defined Relations in the HOL Theorem Prover. Technical Report No. 265 University of Cambridge Computer Laboratory. 1992.

[Cla78] K. Clark. Negation as Failure. pp293-322 of Logic and Data Bases, edited by H. Gallaire and J. Minker. Plenum Press. 1978.

[Coq] C. Cornes, J. Courant, J.F. Fillaître, G. Huet, C. Murthy, C. Parent, C. Paulin, B. Werner. The Coq Proof Assistant Reference Manual, Version 5.10. Projet Coq, Inria-Rocquencourt and CNRS-ENS Lyon, France.

[Cor96] C. Cornes Compilation du Filtrage avec Types Dépendants dans le Système Coq. Actes de la réunion du pôle Spécification et Preuves du GDR Programmation. Orleans, Novembre 1996.

[CT95] C. Cornes, D. Terrasse. Automating Inversion of Inductive Predicates in Coq. In BRA Workshop on Types for Proofs and Programs, Turin, June 1995. To appear in LNCS series.

[Eri91] L.-H. Eriksson. A finitary version of the calculus of partial inductive definitions. In: L.-H. Eriksson, L. Hallnäs & P. Schroeder-Heister (editors), Extensions of Logic Programming. Second International Workshop, ELP-91, Stockholm. Springer LNCS 596, pp89–134. 1992.

[Dyb91] P. Dybjer. Inductive Sets and Families in Martin-Löf's Type Theory. pp280–306 of Logical Frameworks, edited by G. Huet and G. Plotkin. CUP 1991.

[Gim94] E. Giminez. Codifying guarded definitions with recursive schemes. Proceedings of Types 94, pp39–59.

[Hal91] L. Hallnäs. Partial Inductive Definitions. Theoretical Computer Science. Vol. 87. pp115–142. 1991.

[HOL] Introduction to HOL; A theorem proving environment for higher order logic. Edited by M.J.C. Gordon and T.F. Melham. CUP 1993.

[JK91] Jean-Pierre Jouannaud and Claude Kirchner. Solving Equations in Abstract Algebras: A Rule-Based Survey of Unification. pp257–321 of Computational Logic: Essays in Honor of Alan Robinson, edited by Jean-Louis Lassez and Gordon Plotkin, MIT Press, 1991.

[Luo94] Zhaohui Luo. Computation and Reasoning: A Type Theory for Computer Science. OUP 1994.

[LEGO] Zhaohui Luo, Randy Pollack. LEGO Proof Development System: User Manual. Technical Note, 1992.

[Mag95] Lena Magnusson. The Implementation of ALF. PhD Thesis. Chalmers University of Technology and University of Göteborg, Sweden. January 1995.

[Pau87] L. Paulson. Logic and Computation: Interactive Proof with Cambridge LCF. Cambridge Tracts in Theoretical Computer Science 2. CUP 1987.

[Pol94] Randy Pollack. Incremental Changes in LEGO: Technical Note, 1994.

[Pra65] Prawitz, D. Natural Deduction: A Proof-Theoretical Study. Almqvist & Wiksell. Stockholm, 1965.

[TS84] H. Tamaki, T. Sato. Unfold/Fold Transformation of Logic Programs. Proceedings of Second International Logic Programming Conference. pp127–138. Uppsala, 1984.

A Generic Normalisation Proof for Pure Type Systems

Paul-André Melliès and Benjamin Werner

[1] University of Edinburgh, Department of Computer Science, James Clerk Maxwell Building , Edinburgh EH9 3JZ, Scotland
[2] INRIA–Rocquencourt, BP 105, F-78 153 LECHESNAY cedex, FRANCE

Abstract. We prove the strong normalisation for any PTS, provided the existence of a certain Λ-set $\mathfrak{A}^{\Uparrow}(s)$ for every sort s of the system. The properties verified by the $\mathfrak{A}^{\Uparrow}(s)$'s depend of the axiom and rules of the type system.

1 Introduction

1.1 Brief History

This work is an attempt to deal with the structure of complex Type Theories. Historically, once Girard had transposed the Burali-Forti paradox to type theory, Martin-Löf replied by suppressing the guilty Type : Type rule and remediated to the resulting loss of expressiveness by introducing a new concept of stratified *universes* [10]. Today this notion can be found, in different forms and variants, in most Type Theories, especially the ones with foundational ambitions. For example, it appears in the theories used in actually implemented proof-checkers (NuPRL, Coq, Lego...).

The main idea is that all types are no longer equal. Each one inhabits a certain *universe* (Martin-Löf) or *sort* (Pure Type Systems). In general, universes are embedded in each other following a monotone hierarchy. The key point is that quantification inside a given type is restricted to types of the same (or smaller) univers(es)[1].

Since, this episode has often been presented as part of a long-going predicative vs. non-predicative debate. It however had another consequence for type theories viewed as practical and actually usable logical formalisms: The fact that all types are no longer equal puzzles the newcomer and makes it more difficult to grasp the underlying intuitions of the formalisms. This may become particularly acute when types are used as propositions: for some formalisms, depending upon in which universe it is done, proving "there exists an element x of type A" will not have the same meaning, i.e. we may or may not exhibit a constructive witness.

More generally, lots of very technical choices have to be made; in particular:

- Concerning the theory itself: as mentioned above, and would it be only for pragmatic reasons, most up-to-date type theories are build on top of a more or less complex structure defining the interactions between the different kinds of types. The corresponding rules are however almost always, if slightly, different from one theory to another. No current mathematical tools deal with the study of these structures and are thus likely to provide objective comparison criterions.

[1] With the exception of the impredicative universe when there is one; but even then, elimination has to be restricted for the existential quantifier.

- When formalizing a piece of mathematics in such a theory, one has to decide at which level the objects, respectively the propositions, of the work to be formalized have to be put. There is, for now, no canonical way of deciding this, and this choice will depend upon the way the objects are going to be used. Schematizing, we might say that if every piece of known mathematics seems to be, more or less, formalizable in a powerful type theory, there is no uniform and canonical way of doing so since it requires non-trivial choices to be made concerning the status of its objects. From the outsider's point of view, these choices often have to be made by a Type Theory wizard.

For these reasons, the world of Type Theories might, at first glance, bear some similitude with the late Ptolemeic astronomy. We hope to demonstrate that what seems to be chaotic actually yields some order and structure[2].

1.2 Why Pure Type systems ?

In the process of studying the structure of type theories, a first clarification attempt has been the introduction of *Pure Type Systems* (PTSs). The concept is due to Terlouw and Berardi and largely owes its fame to Barendregt.

We refer to the bibliography [2] and to the definitions below for more details. The formalism of PTSs allows to describe a wide range of λ-calculi like simple types, F, F_ω, the Calculus of Constructions, but also non-normalizable systems, especially Girard's system U or Martin-Lof's Type:Type. Until now, with the notable exception of Terlouw's work [12], the only properties proved on large classes of PTSs were of combinatorial nature (confluence, subject reduction) and did not deal with normalization and its counterpart, logical consistency.

The techniques presented in the present work do apply to extensions of Pure Type Systems (inductive types...). Since our main aim was to confront with complex structures, a generic study of PTSs was the natural first step.

1.3 About this paper

Technically, the main difficulty, when trying to build up a generic normalization proof for PTSs, is that syntactically similar operations (abstraction, application) have to be interpreted in different ways, depending upon the sort in which they are performed: whereas basic types are always treated like in Girard's original work [6] (that is, as sets of terms), functions from types to types (object of type $* \rightarrow *$ in F_ω) have to be seen as extensional functions mapping sets of terms to sets of terms. Thus the homogeneity of the syntax is lost.

An answer was proposed by Altenkirch [1] with the introduction of Λ-sets. These are ω-sets [8] modified for normalization proofs. The advantage is that if types are interpreted by Λ-sets, function types can be treated in a fully generic way.

What is done in the present work is therefore merely the next step: we axiomatize, for every PTS, the properties of a structure of Λ-sets (sect. 4), which allows the carrying through of a generic normalization proof (sect. 5). The existence of such a structure is therefore a sufficient condition for strong normalization. We construct such structures for well-known PTSs like F, CC, ECC (sect. 6). In other words, we specify a particular

[2] This was originally *not* suposed to be a quotation of Jean-Yves Girard.

model of type systems, whose existence is sufficient for strong normalization. A difference with [12] is that the specification of the model directly reflects the structure (i.e. sorts, axioms and rules) of the PTS.

For matters of space, this paper had to be shortened for these proceedings. Some proofs are therefore ommited. A full version of this paper is available as INRIA research report.

2 Definition

In the whole paper, we will consider a single pure type system, described by a *set of sorts* $\mathcal{S}$, a set of *axioms* $\mathcal{A} \subset \mathcal{S} \times \mathcal{S}$ and a set of *rules* $\mathcal{R} \subset \mathcal{S} \times \mathcal{S} \times \mathcal{S}$.

We give ourselves a countable set $\mathcal{V}$ of variables (generally denoted by $x, y, \ldots$).

In the meta-theoretic study hereafter, we will consider a variant of the usual presentation of Pure Type Systems: the terms will carry more type information than usual in the cases of λ-abstraction and application. This approach can be seen as related to the labeled terms used in [4]. However, here, we will use these labels to restrict the usual formulation of β-reduction, see [1,3]. In section 7, we will verify that, provided the strong normalization property holds, our definition of PTS's is equivalent to the usual ones, and hence strong normalization itself is inherited by the "unlabeled" PTS.

Definition 1. A term is described by

$$M \ := \ x \mid s \mid \mathrm{app}_{x:M.M}(M, M) \mid \lambda_{x:M.M} x.M \mid (x : M)M.$$

The set of terms is written $\mathcal{T}$. A context (Γ) is a list of pairs $(x : A) \in \mathcal{V} \times \mathcal{T}$, $[]$ being the empty context.

The letters $M, N, A, B, C, T, U, V, t, u, v$, etc will be used to denote terms, greek capitals Γ, Δ for contexts and a, b, c, x, y, z for variables.

Term conversion will here be taken care of by the following reduction, due to Torsten Altenkirch:

Definition 2 (tight reduction). We define $\triangleright_\beta$ as the contextual closure of:

$$\mathrm{app}_{y:A.B}((\lambda_{y:A.B} x.M), N) \triangleright_\beta M[x \setminus N]$$

As usual, we will write $\triangleright^+_\beta$ (respectively $\triangleright^*_\beta$, $=_\beta$) for the transitive (respectively transitive-reflexive, symmetric-transitive-reflexive) closure of $\triangleright_\beta$.

Remark 3. The tight-reduction does *not* enjoy the Church-Rosser property on non well-typed terms. We do not give the proof, but it is quite easy to adapt the counter examples for confluence for λ-calculi with surjective pairing. See [7] for details. Of course, Church-Rosser will hold for terms well-typed in a strongly normalizing PTS.

Definition 4 (Strong Normalization). A term t is said to be strongly normalizing if and only if there is no infinite sequence of reductions starting from t.

The typing rules We use two kind of judgements: $\vdash\ \Gamma\ \ wf$ expresses that the context Γ is well-formed, $\Gamma\ \vdash\ t : T$ that the term t is of type T in the context Γ. The set of *derivable judgements* is inductively defined by the following inference rules:

$$(\textsc{Start}) \qquad \vdash\ []\ \ wf$$

$$(\textsc{Axiom}) \qquad \frac{\vdash\ \Gamma\ \ wf}{\Gamma\ \vdash\ s_1 : s_2} \qquad \text{if } (s_1, s_2) \in \mathcal{A}$$

$$(\textsc{Weak}) \qquad \frac{\Gamma\ \vdash\ A : s}{\vdash\ \Gamma, x : A\ \ wf}$$

$$(\textsc{Var}) \qquad \frac{\vdash\ \Gamma, x : A, \Gamma'\ \ wf}{\Gamma, x : A, \Gamma'\ \vdash\ x : A} \qquad \text{if } \mathsf{binder}(\Gamma') \cap \mathsf{free}(A) = \emptyset$$

$$(\textsc{Prod}) \qquad \frac{\Gamma\ \vdash\ A : s_1 \qquad \Gamma, x : A\ \vdash\ B : s_2}{\Gamma\ \vdash\ (x : A)B : s_3} \qquad \text{if } (s_1, s_2, s_3) \in \mathcal{R}$$

$$(\textsc{Lambda}) \qquad \frac{\Gamma, x : A\ \vdash\ M : B \qquad \Gamma\ \vdash\ (x : A)B : s}{\Gamma\ \vdash\ \lambda_{x:A.B}x.M : (x : A)B}$$

$$(\textsc{App}) \qquad \frac{\Gamma\ \vdash\ M : (x : A)B \qquad \Gamma\ \vdash\ N : A}{\Gamma\ \vdash\ \mathsf{app}_{x:A.B}(M, N) : B[x \setminus N]}$$

$$(\textsc{Conv}) \qquad \frac{\Gamma\ \vdash\ M : A \qquad \Gamma\ \vdash\ B : s \qquad A \rhd^*_\beta B \text{ or } B \rhd^*_\beta A}{\Gamma\ \vdash\ M : B}$$

Remark 5. We consider that each judgement represents an α-conversion class: for instance, $x : s\ \vdash\ x : s$ and $y : s\ \vdash\ y : s$ should be considered as two α-equivalent judgements. The judgement $\Gamma\ \vdash\ \lambda_{x:A.B}x.M : (x : A)B$ obtained with the rule (Lambda) is also equivalent to $\Gamma\ \vdash\ \lambda_{x:A.B}x.M : (y : A)B'$ or $\Gamma\ \vdash\ \lambda_{y:A.B'}x.M : (x : A)B$ where $B' = B[x \setminus y]$ and y is not free in B.

We can now state some elementary syntactic results. The proofs are quite similar to their counter-parts for usual PTSs and are often simplified by the presence of labels. We therefore do not detail the proofs; actually, all the following lemmas are proved by induction over the structure of the corresponding derivation. For matters of space, we also only state the results which will be necessary in the rest of the paper.

Lemma 6 (Free Variables). *Given any derivable judgement $\Gamma \vdash t : T$, every free variable of t or T is bound in Γ.*

Lemma 7 (Subterms). *Any subterm of any derivable judgement is well-formed.*

Lemma 8 (Substitution). *Given the two following derivable judgements:*

$$\Gamma, x : A, \Delta\ \vdash\ t : T \qquad \textit{and} \qquad \Gamma\ \vdash\ u : A$$

there exists a derivation of:

$$\Gamma, \Delta[x \setminus u]\ \vdash\ t[x \setminus u] : T[x \setminus u].$$

Provided, of course there is no other binding occurrence of x in Δ; in this case, we have:

$$\Gamma, \Delta[x \setminus u] \vdash t : T.$$

Lemma 9 (Weakening). *Given the two following derivable judgements $\Gamma, \Delta \vdash t : T$ and $\Gamma \vdash A : s$, there exists a derivation of $\Gamma, x : A, \Delta \vdash t : T$ for any variable x which is not free in Δ, t and T.*

Lemma 10 (Subject Reduction). *Let $\Gamma \vdash t : T$ be a derivable judgement. If $t \triangleright_\beta t'$ and $\Gamma \triangleright_\beta \Gamma'$, then the two following judgements are derivable:*

$$\Gamma \vdash t' : T \quad \text{and} \quad \Gamma' \vdash t : T.$$

3 Structures for the interpretation

3.1 Λ-sets

As mentioned before, one of the main steps of this work will be to interpret each type of the system by a Λ-set. This section is devoted to the definition of this notion, and is therefore largely inspired by the work of Altenkirch [1].

Definition 11 (Atomic terms). A term is said to be atomic if it is of the form

$$\mathrm{app}_{x_n:A_n.B_n}(\ldots(\mathrm{app}_{x_1:A_1.B_1}(P, Q_1), \ldots, Q_n)$$

with P of one of the following forms: s, x, $(x : A)B$. We write $\mathcal{AT}$ for the set of atomic terms.

The following is essentially Tait's (and Krivine's and other's) [11,5] version of reducibility candidates [6].

Definition 12 (Saturated sets). A set $\mathcal{C}$ of terms is said to be saturated, if and only if

1. $\mathcal{C} \subset \mathcal{SN}$
2. $(\mathcal{SN} \cap \mathcal{AT}) \subset \mathcal{C}$
3. if $(A, B, P) \in \mathcal{SN}^3$ and

$$\mathrm{app}_{x_n:A_n.B_n}(\ldots(\mathrm{app}_{x_1:A_1.B_1}(M[x \setminus P], Q_1), \ldots, Q_n) \in \mathcal{C}$$

then

$$\mathrm{app}_{x_n:A_n.B_n}(\ldots(\mathrm{app}_{x_1:A_1.B_1}(\mathrm{app}_{x:A.B}(\lambda_{x:A.B}x.M, P), Q_1), \ldots, Q_n) \in \mathcal{C}$$

Definition 13 (Λ-set). A Λ-set is a couple $(X_0, \models)$, where

- X_0 is some set,
- and $\models$ a relation between X_0 and the set of terms: $\models \subset X_0 \times \mathcal{T}$.

The elements of X_0 are called the *carriers* of X and X_0 is the *carrier-set*. The terms M such that $M \models_X \alpha$ for some $\alpha \in X_0$ are called the *realizers* of α (or more generally the realizers of X).

Alternativly, one may view a Λ-set as a family of sets of terms indexed over X_0.

Notation If X is a Λ-set, we write X_0 for its first component and $\models_X$ for the second.

Definition 14 (saturated Λ-set). A Λ-set X is said to be *saturated* if and only if:

1. Every realizer is strongly normalizable.
2. There is one element of X_0 which is realized by any atomic strongly normalizable term.
3. For every $\alpha \in X_0$, the set of realizers of α is closed by reverse head β-expansion, i.e. verifies the condition 3 of definition 12:
$\forall (A, B, P) \in \mathcal{SN} \,.\, \mathrm{app}_{x_n:A_n.B_n}(\cdots(\mathrm{app}_{x_1:A_1.B_1}(M[x \setminus P], Q_1), \ldots, Q_n) \models_X \alpha \Longrightarrow$
$\mathrm{app}_{x_n:A_n.B_n}(\cdots(\mathrm{app}_{x_1:A_1.B_1}(\mathrm{app}_{x:A.B}(\lambda_{x:A.B}x.M, P), Q_1), \ldots, Q_n) \models_X \alpha.$

Remark 15. If a Λ-set is saturated, the set of its realizers is a saturated set.

This means we can also see a saturated Λ-set as a saturated set of terms with some additional information given by the carriers.
Notation Let X be a Λ-set. We write $x \sqsubset X$ for $x \in X_0$.

Definition 16 (Λ-morphism). Let X and Y be two Λ-sets. A morphism p from X to Y is a function $p : X_0 \to Y_0$ such that $M \models_X f \Longrightarrow M \models_Y p(f)$.

Definition 17 (Λ-isos). Let X and Y be two Λ-sets. An Λ-iso p from X to Y is a one-to-one function $p : X_0 \to Y_0$ such that $M \models_X f \iff M \models_Y p(f)$.

3.2 $\mathfrak{C}$-sets

A usual difficulty when building a model of a typed λ-calculus is to restrict the size of the function spaces, in order not to "get lost in a sea of set-theoretic functions" (Girard). One radical possibility is to assume the existence of inaccessible cardinals; here, we prefer to avoid this by defining a finer structure on our Λ-sets using adapted equivalence relations. The underlying idea should appear more clearly in the next sections. For a first reading, it is possible to forget about the details of these relations.

Hereafter we give ourselves a fixed set $\mathfrak{C}$ which will index the equivalence relations.

Definition 18 ($\mathfrak{C}$-set). An $\mathfrak{C}$-set $\mathfrak{A}$ is a set of Λ-sets which, for every $i \in \mathfrak{C}$, is enriched with:

1. an equivalence relation $\left\|\begin{smallmatrix} i \\ \mathfrak{A} \end{smallmatrix}\right\|$ over $\mathfrak{A}$,
2. an equivalence relation $\left|\begin{smallmatrix} i \\ \mathfrak{A} \end{smallmatrix}\right|$ over $\bigcup_{X \in \mathfrak{A}} X_0$ (i.e. a relation between the carriers α of elements of $\mathfrak{A}$).

Definition 19 (product). Let $\mathfrak{A}_1$ and $\mathfrak{A}_2$ be two $\mathfrak{C}$-sets. Let X be a Λ-set element of $\mathfrak{A}_1$, and $Y \equiv (Y_\alpha)_{\alpha \in X_0}$ a family of Λ-sets elements of $\mathfrak{A}_2$ (and indexed over X_0). We define the Λ-set $\Pi(X, Y)$ by:

$$\Pi(X,Y)_0 \quad \equiv \quad \{f \in \Pi_{\alpha \in X_0}(Y_\alpha)_0 \mid \forall \alpha, \alpha' \in X_0, \forall i \in \mathfrak{C}, \alpha \left|\begin{smallmatrix} i \\ \mathfrak{A}_1 \end{smallmatrix}\right| \alpha' \Longrightarrow f(\alpha) \left|\begin{smallmatrix} i \\ \mathfrak{A}_2 \end{smallmatrix}\right| f(\alpha')\}$$

$$M \models_{\Pi(X,Y)} f \iff \forall \alpha \in X_0,\ \forall N \models_X \alpha \,.\, \forall A, B \in \mathcal{SN} \,.\, \forall x \in \mathcal{V} \,.\, \mathrm{app}_{x:A.B}(M, N) \models_{Y_\alpha} f(\alpha)$$

Lemma 20. *If X and every Y_x are saturated, then so is $\Pi(X,Y)$.*

Proof We separate the proofs of the three conditions:

1. If $M \models_{\Pi(X,Y)} f$, we know there exists $\alpha \sqsubset X$ such that (for example) $x \models_X \alpha$. Thus $\mathsf{app}_{x:x.x}(M,x) \models_{Y_\alpha} f(\alpha)$ which implies that M is strongly normalizable.
2. For any $\alpha \sqsubset X$, we know there exists a carrier $\underline{Y_\alpha}$ of Y_α which is realized by any atomic strongly normalizable term. We define f as the function which to any $\alpha \sqsubset X$ associates $\underline{Y_\alpha}$. Since $\left|\overset{i}{\mathfrak{A}_1}\right|$ and $\left|\overset{i}{\mathfrak{A}_2}\right|$ are equivalence relations, it is easy to check that $f \sqsubset \Pi(X,Y)$. Now let M be a strongly normalizable atomic term; we have
$$\forall\alpha \sqsubset X \,.\, \forall N \models_X \alpha \,.\, \forall A,B \in \mathcal{SN} \,.\, \mathsf{app}_{x:A.B}(M,N) \in \mathcal{SN} \cap \mathcal{AT}$$
and hence
$$\mathsf{app}_{x:A.B}(M,N) \models_{Y_\alpha} \underline{Y_\alpha}.$$
Which is sufficient for $M \models_{\Pi(X,Y)} f$.
3. The proof is easy and simillar to its counterpart for saturated sets. See [1,5] for example.

■

Definition 21 ($\mathfrak{C}$-relation product). Let $\mathfrak{A}_1$ and $\mathfrak{A}_2$ be two $\mathfrak{C}$-set. Let there be elements X and X' of $\mathfrak{A}_1$, and two families $(Y_\alpha)_{\alpha\in X_0}$ and $(Y'_{\alpha'})_{\alpha'\in X'_0}$ of Λ-sets elements of $\mathfrak{A}_2$ indexed over X_0 and X'_0. The following definitions extend the $\left\|\overset{i}{\mathfrak{A}}\right\|$ and $\left|\overset{i}{\mathfrak{A}}\right|$ to $\Pi(X,Y)$ and $\Pi(X',Y')$, for $i \in \mathfrak{C}$:

1. $$\Pi(X,Y)\left\|\overset{i}{\Pi(\mathfrak{A}_1,\mathfrak{A}_2)}\right\|\Pi(X',Y') \Leftrightarrow \begin{cases} X\left\|\overset{i}{\mathfrak{A}_1}\right\|X' \text{ and} \\ \forall\alpha \sqsubset X, \forall\alpha' \sqsubset X', \alpha\left|\overset{i}{\mathfrak{A}_1}\right|\alpha' \Rightarrow Y_\alpha\left\|\overset{i}{\mathfrak{A}_2}\right\|Y'_{\alpha} \end{cases}$$
2. when $\Pi(X,Y)\left\|\overset{i}{\Pi(\mathfrak{A}_1,\mathfrak{A}_2)}\right\|\Pi(X',Y')$, the relation $\left|\overset{i}{\Pi(\mathfrak{A}_1,\mathfrak{A}_2)}\right|$ can be defined as:
$$f\left|\overset{i}{\Pi(\mathfrak{A}_1,\mathfrak{A}_2)}\right|g \Leftrightarrow (\forall\alpha \sqsubset X, \forall\alpha' \sqsubset X', \alpha\left|\overset{i}{\mathfrak{A}_1}\right|\alpha' \Rightarrow f(\alpha)\left|\overset{i}{\mathfrak{A}_2}\right|g(\alpha'))$$

Note that the relations $\left\|\overset{i}{\Pi(\mathfrak{A}_1,\mathfrak{A}_2)}\right\|$ and $\left|\overset{i}{\Pi(\mathfrak{A}_1,\mathfrak{A}_2)}\right|$ are not expected to live in any $\mathfrak{C}$-set $\Pi(\mathfrak{A}_1,\mathfrak{A}_2)$.

4 The universes of the interpretations

This is the key of the proof. We suppose that for every sort s, there exists an $\mathfrak{C}$-set $\mathfrak{A}^{\Uparrow}(s)$ and a saturated Λ-set $\mathfrak{A}_{\Downarrow}(s)$. We shall construct in $\mathfrak{A}^{\Uparrow}(s)$ the interpretation of types A of sort s ; and in $\mathfrak{A}_{\Downarrow}(s)$ the interpretation of terms M of type s. One notable difficulty is that a type A of sort s is at the same time a term A of type s (and vice-versa). Thus, for every sort s we suppose the existence of two one-to-one mappings $\Downarrow_s : \mathfrak{A}^{\Uparrow}(s) \to \mathfrak{A}_{\Downarrow}(s)_0$ and $\Uparrow_s : \mathfrak{A}_{\Downarrow}(s)_0 \to \mathfrak{A}^{\Uparrow}(s)$ such that:

$$\Uparrow_s \circ \Downarrow_s = Id_{\mathfrak{A}^{\Uparrow}(s)} \qquad \Downarrow_s \circ \Uparrow_s = Id_{\mathfrak{A}_{\Downarrow}(s)_0}$$

In fact, if α is the "type" interpretation of $\Gamma \vdash A$ in $\mathfrak{A}^{\Uparrow}(s)$ then $\Downarrow_s \langle\alpha\rangle$ is its "term" interpretation in $\mathfrak{A}_{\Downarrow}(s)$. In the other direction, the "term" interpretation μ of $\Gamma \vdash M$ in $\mathfrak{A}_{\Downarrow}(s)$ can be lifted to its "type" interpretation $\Uparrow_s \langle\mu\rangle$ in $\mathfrak{A}^{\Uparrow}(s)$. The two equations above imply that the lift and unlift operations are revertible:

$$\Uparrow_s \langle \Downarrow_s \langle\alpha\rangle\rangle = \alpha \text{ and } \Downarrow_s \langle \Uparrow_s \langle\mu\rangle\rangle = \mu$$

In all the literature, the two denotational universes $\mathfrak{A}^{\Uparrow}(s)$ and $\mathfrak{A}_{\Downarrow}(s)$ are identified to a unique $\mathfrak{A}(s)$, with $\Downarrow_s = \Uparrow_s = Id_{\mathfrak{A}(s)}$. Our forthcoming interpretation of derivations shows that the distinction we introduce is natural — moreover it shall play an important role in circular Pure Type Systems.

The structure of the PTS is reflected in the fact that $\mathfrak{A}^{\Uparrow}(s)$, $\mathfrak{A}_{\Downarrow}(s)$, $\Downarrow_s$ and $\Uparrow_s$ shall verify the conditions described below.

Condition 1 (hierarchy of universe). We require that for any sort s, $\mathfrak{A}^{\Uparrow}(s)$ and $\mathfrak{A}_{\Downarrow}(s)$ verify the following conditions:

1. The elements of $\mathfrak{A}^{\Uparrow}(s)$ are *saturated* Λ-sets; every carrier of $\mathfrak{A}_{\Downarrow}(s)$ is realized by any strongly normalizing term.
2. If $(s_1, s_2) \in \mathcal{A}$, then
$$\mathfrak{A}_{\Downarrow}(s_1) \in \mathfrak{A}^{\Uparrow}(s_2).$$
3. If $(s_1, s_2, s_3) \in \mathcal{R}$, then let there be $X \in \mathfrak{A}^{\Uparrow}(s_1)$ and a family $(Y_\alpha)_{\alpha \in X_0}$ with $Y_\alpha \in \mathfrak{A}^{\Uparrow}(s_2)$ such that:
$$\forall(\alpha, \alpha') \in X_0^2 . \forall i \in \mathfrak{E} . \alpha \left| \overset{i}{\mathfrak{A}^{\Uparrow}(s_1)} \right| \alpha' \Longrightarrow Y_\alpha \left\| \overset{i}{\mathfrak{A}^{\Uparrow}(s_2)} \right\| Y_{\alpha'}$$
there exists a Λ-iso $\downarrow_{\Pi(X,Y)}$ from $\Pi(X, Y)$ to an element $\Pi_\downarrow(X, Y) \in \mathfrak{A}^{\Uparrow}(s_3)$:
$$\downarrow_{\Pi(X,Y)} : \Pi(X, Y) \to \Pi_\downarrow(X, Y) \in \mathfrak{A}^{\Uparrow}(s_3).$$

We ask here that $\Pi_\downarrow(X, Y)$ and $\downarrow_{\Pi(X,Y)}$ do not depend on (s_1, s_2, s_3). However a quick look at the definition 19 of products shows that the construction $\Pi(X, Y)$ depends on the equivalence relations $\left| \overset{i}{\mathfrak{A}^{\Uparrow}(s_1)} \right|$ and $\left| \overset{i}{\mathfrak{A}^{\Uparrow}(s_2)} \right|$. In order to ensure that the construction of $\Pi(X, Y)$ itself does not depend on the universes $\mathfrak{A}^{\Uparrow}(s_1)$ and $\mathfrak{A}^{\Uparrow}(s_2)$ we impose the following uniformity condition:

Condition 2 (uniformity of equivalence relations).

1. if $X, X' \in \mathfrak{A}^{\Uparrow}(s_1)$ and $\mathfrak{A}_{\Downarrow}(s_1) \in \mathfrak{A}^{\Uparrow}(s_2)$ then
$$\forall i \in \mathfrak{E}, \quad X \left\| \overset{i}{\mathfrak{A}^{\Uparrow}(s_1)} \right\| X' \Leftrightarrow \Downarrow_{s_1} \langle X \rangle \left| \overset{i}{\mathfrak{A}^{\Uparrow}(s_2)} \right| \Downarrow_{s_1} \langle X' \rangle$$

2. if $\alpha \sqsubset X_1 \in \mathfrak{A}^{\Uparrow}(s_1)$, $\alpha' \sqsubset X_1' \in \mathfrak{A}^{\Uparrow}(s_1)$ and $\alpha \sqsubset X_2 \in \mathfrak{A}^{\Uparrow}(s_2)$, $\alpha' \sqsubset X_2' \in \mathfrak{A}^{\Uparrow}(s_2)$ then

$$\forall i \in \mathfrak{C}: \quad \alpha \left| \overset{i}{\mathfrak{A}^{\Uparrow}(s_1)} \right| \alpha' \Longleftrightarrow \alpha \left| \overset{i}{\mathfrak{A}^{\Uparrow}(s_2)} \right| \alpha'.$$

The required properties on the equivalence relations $\left\| \overset{i}{\mathfrak{A}^{\Uparrow}(s_3)} \right\|$ and $\left| \overset{i}{\mathfrak{A}^{\Uparrow}(s_3)} \right|$ in the case of a (collapsed) product construction are expressed by the following condition.

Condition 3 (collapsed products).
if $i \in \mathfrak{C}$ and $(s_1, s_2, s_3) \in \mathcal{R}$, then given any elements $X, X' \in \mathfrak{A}^{\Uparrow}(s_1)$ and $Y_\alpha, Y_{\alpha'} \in \mathfrak{A}^{\Uparrow}(s_2)$ respectively indexed by $\alpha \sqsubset X$ and $\alpha' \sqsubset X'$:

1. $$\Pi(X,Y) \left\| \overset{i}{\Pi(\mathfrak{A}^{\Uparrow}(s_1), \mathfrak{A}^{\Uparrow}(s_2))} \right\| \Pi(X',Y') \Longrightarrow \Pi_{\downarrow}(X,Y) \left\| \overset{i}{\mathfrak{A}^{\Uparrow}(s_3)} \right\| \Pi_{\downarrow}(X',Y')$$

2. if $\Pi(X,Y) \left\| \overset{i}{\Pi(\mathfrak{A}^{\Uparrow}(s_1), \mathfrak{A}^{\Uparrow}(s_2))} \right\| \Pi(X',Y')$ then $f \sqsubset \Pi(X,Y)$ and $g \sqsubset \Pi(X',Y')$ imply that:

$$f \left| \overset{i}{\Pi(\mathfrak{A}^{\Uparrow}(s_1), \mathfrak{A}^{\Uparrow}(s_2))} \right| g \Longleftrightarrow \downarrow_{\Pi(X,Y)} \langle f \rangle \left| \overset{i}{\mathfrak{A}^{\Uparrow}(s_3)} \right| \downarrow_{\Pi(X',Y')} \langle g \rangle$$

The last condition tells that the lift and unlift procedures should not depend on the universe they proceed in.

Condition 4 (uniformity of lift/unlift procedures).
We require that the $\Downarrow_s$ and the $\Uparrow_s$ verify the following conditions:

1. if $\alpha \in \mathfrak{A}^{\Uparrow}(s)$ and $\alpha \in \mathfrak{A}^{\Uparrow}(s')$ then $\Downarrow_s \langle \alpha \rangle = \Downarrow_{s'} \langle \alpha \rangle$
2. if $\alpha \sqsubset \mathfrak{A}_{\Downarrow}(s)$ and $\alpha \sqsubset \mathfrak{A}_{\Downarrow}(s')$ then $\Uparrow_s \langle \alpha \rangle = \Uparrow_{s'} \langle \alpha \rangle$

Remark 22. This means that instead of considering a the family of $\Uparrow_s$ isos (resp. $\Downarrow_s$), we might assume the existence of a single $\Uparrow \equiv \bigcup_{s \in S} \Uparrow_s$ respectively $\Downarrow \equiv \bigcup_{s \in S} \Downarrow_s$. In other words, the sort in $\Uparrow_s$, respectively $\Downarrow_s$, may simply be seen as an annotation.

We define for any Λ-iso $\downarrow_{\Pi(X,Y)}$ the inverse Λ-iso $\uparrow_{\Pi(X,Y)}$ such that $\uparrow_{\Pi(X,Y)} \circ \downarrow_{\Pi(X,Y)} = Id_{\Pi(X,Y)}$ and $\downarrow_{\Pi(X,Y)} \circ \uparrow_{\Pi(X,Y)} = Id_{\Pi_{\downarrow}(X,Y)}$.

5 The Interpretation

This section follows the usual pattern of reducibility proofs. For any derivable judgement, we will define an interpretation. Like in [1], the interpretation of a type will be a Λ-set and the interpretations of its terms will be carriers of this Λ-set. Strong normalization being assured by the fact that every well-typed term realizes its interpretation.

5.1 Definition

We will associate two interpretations $[\Gamma \vdash M]$ and $\llbracket \Gamma \vdash M \rrbracket$ to any judgement $\Gamma \vdash M : A$. We also associate an interpretation $\llbracket \Gamma \rrbracket$ to any well formed context Γ.

The construction is by structural induction on Γ and M:

Definition 23.

$$\llbracket [] \rrbracket \equiv \{\emptyset\} \tag{1}$$

$$\llbracket \Gamma, x : A \rrbracket \equiv \{(\gamma, \alpha), \gamma \in \llbracket \Gamma \rrbracket \wedge \alpha \sqsubset \llbracket \Gamma \vdash A \rrbracket(\gamma)\} \tag{2}$$

$$\llbracket \Gamma \vdash s \rrbracket(\gamma) \equiv \mathfrak{A}_{\Downarrow}(s) \tag{3}$$

$$\llbracket \Gamma \vdash (x : A)B \rrbracket(\gamma) \equiv \Pi_{\downarrow}(\llbracket \Gamma \vdash A \rrbracket(\gamma), \llbracket \Gamma, x : A \vdash B \rrbracket(\gamma, \_)) \tag{4}$$

$$[\Gamma \vdash x_i](\gamma) \equiv \gamma_i \tag{5}$$

$$[\Gamma \vdash \lambda_{x:A.B} x.M](\gamma) \equiv \downarrow_{\Pi(\llbracket \Gamma \vdash A \rrbracket(\gamma), \llbracket \Gamma, x:A \vdash B \rrbracket(\gamma,\_))} \langle [\Gamma, x : A \vdash M](\gamma, \_) \rangle \tag{6}$$

$$[\Gamma \vdash \mathsf{app}_{x:A.B}(M, N)](\gamma) \equiv \uparrow_{\Pi(\llbracket \Gamma \vdash A \rrbracket(\gamma), \llbracket \Gamma, x:A \vdash B \rrbracket(\gamma,\_))} \langle [\Gamma \vdash M](\gamma) \rangle \, ([\Gamma \vdash N](\gamma)) \tag{7}$$

and for all the other cases:

$$\llbracket \Gamma \vdash A \rrbracket(\gamma) \equiv \Uparrow_s \langle [\Gamma \vdash A](\gamma) \rangle \tag{8}$$

$$[\Gamma \vdash A](\gamma) \equiv \Downarrow_s \langle \llbracket \Gamma \vdash A \rrbracket(\gamma) \rangle \tag{9}$$

In the above, and the rest of the paper, $\llbracket \Gamma, x : A \vdash B \rrbracket(\gamma, \_)$, respectively $[\Gamma, x : A \vdash M](\gamma, \_)$ is a short-cut for the function

$$\alpha \sqsubset \llbracket \Gamma \vdash A \rrbracket(\gamma) \mapsto \llbracket \Gamma, x : A \vdash B \rrbracket(\gamma, \alpha)$$

respectively

$$\alpha \sqsubset \llbracket \Gamma \vdash A \rrbracket(\gamma) \mapsto [\Gamma, x : A \vdash M](\gamma, \alpha).$$

The definition is not total. We explicit the sufficient properties for each interpretation step:

- for all cases but (1) we require that $\llbracket \Gamma \rrbracket$ is defined.

(2) both $\llbracket \Gamma \rrbracket$ and $\llbracket \Gamma \vdash A \rrbracket$ are defined and $\llbracket \Gamma \vdash A \rrbracket(\gamma)$ there exists a sort s such that $\llbracket \Gamma \vdash A \rrbracket(\gamma) \in \mathfrak{A}^{\Uparrow}(s)$ for any $\gamma \in \llbracket \Gamma \rrbracket$.

(4,6 and 7) there exist $(s_1, s_2, s_3) \in \mathcal{R}$ such that for any $\gamma \in \llbracket \Gamma \rrbracket$:

- $\llbracket \Gamma \vdash A \rrbracket(\gamma) \sqsubset \mathfrak{A}^{\Uparrow}(s_1)$
- $\forall \alpha \sqsubset \llbracket \Gamma \vdash A \rrbracket(\gamma) \,.\, \llbracket \Gamma, x : A \vdash B \rrbracket(\gamma, \alpha) \sqsubset \mathfrak{A}^{\Uparrow}(s_2)$
- $\forall i \in \mathfrak{C} \,.\, \forall (\alpha, \alpha') \in \llbracket \Gamma \vdash A \rrbracket(\gamma)^2 \,.\, \alpha \left| \overset{i}{\mathfrak{A}^{\Uparrow}(s_1)} \right| \alpha' \Longrightarrow$

$$\llbracket \Gamma, x : A \vdash B \rrbracket(\gamma, \alpha) \left\| \overset{i}{\mathfrak{A}^{\Uparrow}(s_2)} \right\| \llbracket \Gamma, x : A \vdash B \rrbracket(\gamma, \alpha')$$

(6) for any $\gamma \in \llbracket \Gamma \rrbracket$, for any $\alpha \sqsubset \llbracket \Gamma \vdash A \rrbracket(\gamma)$, $[\Gamma, x : A \vdash M](\gamma, \alpha)$ is defined, and:

$$(\alpha \sqsubset \llbracket \Gamma \vdash A \rrbracket(\gamma) \mapsto [\Gamma, x : A \vdash M](\gamma, \alpha)) \sqsubset \Pi(\llbracket \Gamma \vdash A \rrbracket(\gamma), \llbracket \Gamma, x : A \vdash B \rrbracket(\gamma, \_))$$

(7) $[\Gamma \vdash M](\gamma) \sqsubset \llbracket \Gamma \vdash (x : A)B \rrbracket(\gamma)$ and $[\Gamma \vdash N](\gamma) \sqsubset \llbracket \Gamma \vdash A \rrbracket(\gamma)$ for any $\gamma \in \llbracket \Gamma \rrbracket$

(8) $[\Gamma \vdash A](\gamma) \sqsubset \mathfrak{A}_{\Downarrow}(s)$ for any $\gamma \in \llbracket \Gamma \rrbracket$

(9) $\llbracket \Gamma \vdash A \rrbracket(\gamma) \in \mathfrak{A}^{\Uparrow}(s)$ for any $\gamma \in \llbracket \Gamma \rrbracket$.

From now on, the main work will be to state and prove the soundness of our interpretation. The strong normalization will follow quite easily, as it is usual in reducibility proofs.

5.2 Subject reduction properties

Lemma 24 (Subject reduction A).

$$[\Gamma \vdash \mathsf{app}_{x:A.B}((\lambda_{x:A.B}x.M), N)](\gamma) = [\Gamma, x : A \vdash M](\gamma, [\Gamma \vdash N](\gamma))$$

Proof using that

$$\uparrow_{\Pi([\![\Gamma \vdash A]\!](\gamma), [\![\Gamma, x:A \vdash B]\!](\gamma, \_))} \circ \downarrow_{\Pi([\![\Gamma \vdash A]\!](\gamma), [\![\Gamma, x:A \vdash B]\!](\gamma, \_))} = \mathrm{id}_{\Pi([\![\Gamma \vdash A]\!](\gamma), [\![\Gamma, x:A \vdash B]\!](\gamma, \_))}$$ ■

Lemma 25 (Weakening for the interpretation, A). *Suppose that $[\![\Gamma \vdash C]\!](\gamma) \in \mathfrak{A}^{\Uparrow}(s)$. We prove three results in one:*

1) if $[\![\Gamma, \Delta]\!]$ is defined and z is not free in Δ then $[\![\Gamma, z : C, \Delta]\!]$ is defined and

$$[\![\Gamma, z : C, \Delta]\!] = \{(\gamma, \zeta, \delta) \mid (\gamma, \delta) \in [\![\Gamma, \Delta]\!] \text{ and } \zeta \in [\![\Gamma \vdash C]\!](\gamma)\}$$

2) if $[\Gamma, \Delta \vdash M](\gamma, \delta)$ is defined and z is not free in Δ or in M then $[\Gamma, z : C, \Delta \vdash M](\gamma, \zeta, \delta)$ is defined and furthermore

$$[\Gamma, z : C, \Delta \vdash M](\gamma, \zeta, \delta) = [\Gamma, \Delta \vdash M](\gamma, \delta).$$

3) if $[\![\Gamma, \Delta \vdash M]\!](\gamma, \delta)$ is defined and z is not free in Δ or in M then $[\![\Gamma, z : C, \Delta \vdash M]\!](\gamma, \zeta, \delta)$ is also defined and:

$$[\![\Gamma, z : C, \Delta \vdash M]\!](\gamma, \zeta, \delta) = [\![\Gamma, \Delta \vdash M]\!](\gamma, \delta).$$

Proof By induction over the constructions of $[\![\Gamma, \Delta]\!]$, $[\Gamma, \Delta \vdash M](\gamma, \delta)$, $[\![\Gamma, \Delta \vdash M]\!](\gamma, \delta)$. For matters of space, we cannot give details here and refer to the full version for details. ■

Lemma 26 (Weakening for the interpretation, B). *If $[\Gamma \vdash M](\gamma)$ and $[\![\Gamma, \Delta]\!]$ are defined and all the variables bound by Δ do not occur free in M then $[\Gamma, \Delta \vdash M](\gamma, \delta)$ is defined and furthermore*

$$[\Gamma, \Delta \vdash M](\gamma, \delta) = [\Gamma \vdash M](\gamma).$$

And similarly for $[\![\Gamma \vdash M]\!](\gamma)$.

Proof using the lemma 25 as many times there are variables in Δ. ■

Lemma 27 (Substitution for the interpretation). *If $\Gamma, x : A, \Delta \vdash M : B$ and $\Gamma \vdash P : A$ are derivable, $\gamma \in [\![\Gamma]\!]$, $\pi \equiv [\Gamma \vdash P](\gamma)$ is defined, $(\gamma, \pi, \delta) \in [\![\Gamma, x : A, \Delta]\!]$ and $[\Gamma, x : A, \Delta \vdash M](\gamma, \pi, \delta)$ is defined, then $[\Gamma, \Delta[x \setminus P] \vdash M[x \setminus P]](\gamma, \delta)$ is defined, and*

$$[\Gamma, \Delta[x \setminus P] \vdash M[x \setminus P]](\gamma, \delta) = [\Gamma, x : A, \Delta \vdash M](\gamma, \pi, \delta).$$

Similarly, if $[\![\Gamma, x : A, \Delta \vdash M]\!](\gamma, \pi, \delta)$ is defined:

$$[\![\Gamma, \Delta[x \setminus P] \vdash M[x \setminus P]]\!](\gamma, \delta) = [\![\Gamma, x : A, \Delta \vdash M]\!](\gamma, \pi, \delta).$$

Proof By induction over the structure of M. The key case is $M = x$ which is treated by the previous lemma. We also detail the case of λ-abstraction; if $M = \lambda_{x:A.B}x.N$ . . ■

Lemma 28 (Subject Reduction for the interpretation). *If $\Gamma \vdash M : A$, $M \rhd_\beta M'$ and $[\Gamma \vdash M](\gamma)$ is defined then so is $[\Gamma \vdash M'](\gamma)$ and*

$$[\Gamma \vdash M](\gamma) = [\Gamma \vdash M'](\gamma).$$

And similarly for $[\![\Gamma \vdash M]\!](\gamma)$ and $[\![\Gamma \vdash M']\!](\gamma)$.

Proof By induction over the structure of M, or more precisely over the proof that $M \rhd_\beta M'$. The key case is of course the one where M is itself the reduced redex. It is treated by the previous lemma. ■

5.3 Soundness

Definition 29. Let $i \in \mathfrak{E}$ and $[\![\Gamma]\!]$ be well-defined. The relation $\Big|\overset{i}{\mathfrak{E}}\Big|$ between the sequences γ of $[\![\Gamma]\!]$ is constructed by structural induction on Γ:

- $\forall \alpha, \alpha' \in [\![x : A]\!]$:

$$\alpha \Big|\overset{i}{\mathfrak{E}}\Big| \alpha' \Leftrightarrow \exists s \in \mathcal{S}, \alpha \Big|\overset{i}{\mathfrak{A}^{\Uparrow}(s)}\Big| \alpha'$$

- $\forall (\gamma, \alpha), (\gamma', \alpha') \in [\![\Gamma, x : A]\!]$:

$$(\gamma, \alpha) \Big|\overset{i}{\mathfrak{E}}\Big| (\gamma', \alpha') \Leftrightarrow \gamma \Big|\overset{i}{\mathfrak{E}}\Big| \gamma' \text{ and } \exists s \in \mathcal{S}, \alpha \Big|\overset{i}{\mathfrak{A}^{\Uparrow}(s)}\Big| \alpha'$$

Theorem 30 (Well-formedness and soundness of the interpretation). *If Γ wf is derivable, then $[\![\Gamma]\!]$ is defined. If the judgement $\Gamma \vdash M : A$ is derivable, then for any $\gamma \in [\![\Gamma]\!]$ the following holds:*

1. *$[\Gamma \vdash M](\gamma)$ and $[\![\Gamma \vdash A]\!](\gamma)$ are defined with*

$$[\Gamma \vdash M](\gamma) \sqsubset [\![\Gamma \vdash A]\!](\gamma).$$

Moreover, if there exists a sort s such that $[\![\Gamma \vdash A]\!](\gamma) \in \mathfrak{A}^{\Uparrow}(s)$, then:

$$\forall i \in \mathfrak{E} \,.\, \gamma \Big|\overset{i}{\mathfrak{E}}\Big| \gamma' \Rightarrow [\Gamma \vdash M](\gamma) \Big|\overset{i}{\mathfrak{A}^{\Uparrow}(s)}\Big| [\Gamma \vdash M](\gamma')$$

2. *if $A = s$ then $[\![\Gamma \vdash M]\!](\gamma)$ is defined, and $[\![\Gamma \vdash M]\!](\gamma) \in \mathfrak{A}^{\Uparrow}(s)$. Moreover:*

$$\forall i \in \mathfrak{E} \,.\, \gamma \Big|\overset{i}{\mathfrak{E}}\Big| \gamma' \Rightarrow [\![\Gamma \vdash M]\!](\gamma) \Big\|\overset{i}{\mathfrak{A}^{\Uparrow}(s)}\Big\| [\![\Gamma \vdash M]\!](\gamma')$$

Remark 31. We remark that clause 2 is equivalent to clause 1, provided $A = s_1$ and the Λ-set $\mathfrak{A}_{\Downarrow}(s_1)$ is element of an $\mathfrak{E}$-set $\mathfrak{A}^{\Uparrow}(s_2)$. This is typically the case when $A = s_1$ and $(s_1, s_2) \in \mathcal{A}$.

Proof

2 ⇒ 1 Suppose that clause 2 applies and that $A = s_1$. Then $[\Gamma \vdash M](\gamma)$ is defined either directly or as $\Downarrow_{s_1} \langle [\![\Gamma \vdash M]\!](\gamma)\rangle$. In both cases, by $\Downarrow_{s_1} \circ \Uparrow_{s_1} = Id_{\mathfrak{A}_{\Downarrow}(s_1)_0}$, we have:

$$[\Gamma \vdash M](\gamma) = \Downarrow_{s_1} \langle [\![\Gamma \vdash M]\!](\gamma)\rangle$$

and therefore:

$$[\Gamma \vdash M](\gamma) \sqsubset \mathfrak{A}_{\Downarrow}(s_1) = [\![\Gamma \vdash A]\!](\gamma)$$

Suppose now that $\mathfrak{A}_{\Downarrow}(s_1)$ is element of $\mathfrak{A}^{\Uparrow}(s)$ for some sort s. The condition 2(1) infers from

$$[\![\Gamma \vdash M]\!](\gamma) \left\| \begin{smallmatrix} i \\ \mathfrak{A}^{\Uparrow}(s_1) \end{smallmatrix} \right\| [\![\Gamma \vdash M]\!](\gamma')$$

that:

$$[\Gamma \vdash M](\gamma) \left| \begin{smallmatrix} i \\ \mathfrak{A}^{\Uparrow}(s) \end{smallmatrix} \right| [\Gamma \vdash M](\gamma')$$

when $\gamma \left| \begin{smallmatrix} i \\ \mathfrak{C} \end{smallmatrix} \right| \gamma'$; we conclude clause 1.

1 ⇒ 2 conversely, suppose that clause 1 applies and that $A = s_1$ with $\mathfrak{A}_{\Downarrow}(s_1) \in \mathfrak{A}^{\Uparrow}(s_2)$. Then for every $\gamma \in [\![\Gamma]\!], [\![\Gamma \vdash M]\!](\gamma)$ is defined either directly or as $\Uparrow_{s_1} \langle [\Gamma \vdash M](\gamma)\rangle$. In both cases, by $\Uparrow_{s_1} \circ \Downarrow_{s_1} = Id_{\mathfrak{A}^{\Uparrow}(s_1)}$, we have $[\![\Gamma \vdash M]\!](\gamma) = \Uparrow_{s_1} \langle [\Gamma \vdash M](\gamma)\rangle$, hence

$$[\![\Gamma \vdash M]\!](\gamma) \in \mathfrak{A}^{\Uparrow}(s_1)$$

Moreover, by clause 1 and $\mathfrak{A}_{\Downarrow}(s_1) \in \mathfrak{A}^{\Uparrow}(s_2)$ we have:

$$\forall i \in \mathfrak{C}.\quad \gamma \left| \begin{smallmatrix} i \\ \mathfrak{C} \end{smallmatrix} \right| \gamma' \Rightarrow [\Gamma \vdash M](\gamma) \left| \begin{smallmatrix} i \\ \mathfrak{A}^{\Uparrow}(s_2) \end{smallmatrix} \right| [\Gamma \vdash M](\gamma')$$

therefore by condition 2(1) we deduce:

$$\forall i \in \mathfrak{C}.\quad \gamma \left| \begin{smallmatrix} i \\ \mathfrak{C} \end{smallmatrix} \right| \gamma' \Rightarrow [\![\Gamma \vdash M]\!](\gamma) \left\| \begin{smallmatrix} i \\ \mathfrak{A}^{\Uparrow}(s_1) \end{smallmatrix} \right\| [\![\Gamma \vdash M]\!](\gamma')$$

■

Proof **(theorem 30)** Not surprisingly, the proof proceeds by induction over the structure of the derivation. Again, we refer to the full version of this work for details. ■

5.4 Strong Normalisation

Definition 32. Let $(\gamma_1, ..., \gamma_n) \in [\![\Gamma]\!]$. We define $(P_1, ..., P_n) \models (\gamma_1, ..., \gamma_n)$ by induction on n:

- **if $\Gamma, x_{n+1} : A_{n+1}$ is well formed and $\gamma_1, ..., \gamma_{n+1} \in [\![\Gamma, x_{n+1} : A_{n+1}]\!]$ then $(P_1, ..., P_{n+1}) \models (\gamma_1, ..., \gamma_{n+1})$ iff $(P_1, ..., P_n) \models (\gamma_1, ..., \gamma_n)$ and $P_{n+1} \models [\![\Gamma \vdash A]\!](\gamma_1, ..., \gamma_{n+1})$.**

If $(\gamma_1, ..., \gamma_n) \in [\![x_1 : A_1, ..., x_n : A_n]\!]$ and $(P_1, ..., P_n) \models (\gamma_1, ..., \gamma_n)$ then $\{\{M\}\}(P_1, ..., P_n)$ is defined as $M[x_n \setminus P_n, \ldots, x_1 \setminus P_1]$.

Lemma 33. *Let $\Gamma \vdash M : A$ be derivable. If $(\gamma_1, ..., \gamma_n) \in [\![\Gamma]\!]$ and $(P_1, ..., P_n) \models \gamma$ then*

$$\{\{M\}\}(P_1, ..., P_n) \models_{[\![\Gamma \vdash A]\!](\gamma)} [\Gamma \vdash M](\gamma)$$

Proof By induction over the structure of the derivation. We only detail two cases:

LAMBDA We have to check that

$$\{\{\lambda_{x:A.B}x.M\}\}(P_1,...,P_n) \models_{[\Gamma\vdash(X:A)B](\gamma)} [\Gamma \vdash \lambda_{x:A.B}x.M](\gamma)$$

because $\downarrow_{\Pi([\Gamma\vdash A](\gamma),[\vdash\Gamma,x:A\vdash B](\gamma,\_))}$ is a Λ-iso, and unfolding the definitions, we see this is equivalent to

$$\{\{\lambda_{x:A.B}x.M\}\}(P_1,...,P_n,N) \models_{\Pi([\Gamma\vdash A](\gamma),[\Gamma,x:A\vdash B](\gamma,\_)} [\Gamma, x : A \vdash M](\gamma, \_)$$

or equivalently,
$\forall\alpha \sqsubset [\![\Gamma \vdash A]\!](\gamma)\ .\ \forall N \models_{[\Gamma\vdash A](\gamma)} \alpha\ .\ \forall A', B' \in \mathcal{SN}\ .$
$\{\{\mathsf{app}_{x:A'.B'}(\lambda_{x:A.B}x.M\}\}(P_1,...,P_n), N) \models_{[\Gamma,x:A\vdash B](\gamma,\alpha)} [\Gamma, x : A \vdash M](\gamma, \alpha)$.
Now, the induction hypothesis ensures that

$$\{\{M\}\}(P_1,\ldots,P_n,N) \models_{[\Gamma,x:A\vdash B](\gamma,\alpha)} [\Gamma, x : A \vdash M](\gamma, \alpha)$$

which, since $[\![\Gamma, x : A \vdash B]\!](\gamma, \alpha)$ is a saturated Λ-set, is equivalent to the previous proposition.

PROD We simply have to check (condition 1(1)), that $\{\{(x : A)B\}\}(p_1,\ldots,P_n)$ is strongly normalizing. It is an immediate consequence of the induction hypothesis, which states that $\{\{A\}\}(p_1,\ldots,P_n)$ and $\{\{B\}\}(P_1,\ldots,P_n,x)$ are both strongly normalizing.

■

Theorem 34. *If $\Gamma \vdash M : A$ is derivable, then M is strongly normalizable.*

Proof Let $\Gamma = [x_1 : A_1;\ldots;x_n : A_n]$. We know that $[\![x_a : A_1]\!]$ is a saturated Λ-set; thus the second clause of definition 14 ensures there exists $\gamma_1 \sqsubset [\![x_1 : A_1]\!]$ such that γ_1 is realized by any strongly normalizing atomic term. Iterating this construction we obtain $\gamma \equiv (\gamma_1,\ldots,\gamma_n)$ such that $\gamma \in [\![\Gamma]\!]$ and $(x_1,\ldots,x_n) \models (\gamma_1,\ldots,\gamma_n)$. The previous lemma then ensures that $M[x_n \setminus P_n,\ldots,x_1 \setminus P_1] \models_{[\Gamma\vdash A](\gamma)}$ and hence M is strongly normalizing. ■

6 Universe Constructions for Different Type Systems

Definition 35 (degenerated Λ-sets). A Λ-set X is said to be degenerated if X_0 is a singleton $\{\mathcal{C}\}$ where $\mathcal{C}$ is a saturated set of terms and

$$M \models_X \mathcal{C} \iff M \in \mathcal{C}.$$

There is of course a trivial one-to-one correspondence between saturated degenerated Λ-sets and saturated sets of terms.

Remark 36. The family of degenerated Λ-sets is a set.

Any non-empty set X can be viewed as a Λ-set $J(X)$ whose indexes are the elements of X and such that

$$\forall x \in J(X)\ .\ \forall M \in \Lambda\ .\ M \models_{\mathfrak{U}(*)} \mathcal{C} \iff M \in \mathcal{SN}.$$

Hereafter we usually identify the set X and the (saturated) Λ-set $J(X)$.

6.1 System F

Girard's system F, also called second order polymorphic λ-calculus is defined as a PTS by:

$$\mathcal{S} \equiv \{*, \square\} \qquad \mathcal{A} \equiv \{(*, \square)\} \qquad \mathcal{R} \equiv \{(*, *, *), (\square, *, *)\}$$

Here, the set $\mathfrak{E}$ is empty, which means that we do not care about the relations. For every sort s we take $\mathfrak{A}^{\Uparrow}(s) = \mathfrak{A}_{\Downarrow}(s) = \mathfrak{A}(s)$ and thus $\Uparrow_s = \Downarrow_s = Id_{\mathfrak{A}^{\Uparrow}(s)}$. We define $\mathfrak{A}(*)$ as the set of saturated degenerated Λ-sets ; the set $\mathfrak{A}(\square)_0$ is the singleton $\{\mathfrak{A}(*)\}$.

Conditions 2, 3 and 4 are trivial because $\mathfrak{E}$ is empty. The first two points in condition 1 are easy:

1. all elements of $\mathfrak{A}(\star)$ and $\mathfrak{A}(\square)$ are saturated Λ-sets
2. $\mathfrak{A}(\star)$ is (the only) element of $\mathfrak{A}(\square)$.

Let us prove the point 3. Suppose that X is a Λ-set either element of $\mathfrak{A}(*)$ or $\mathfrak{A}(\square)$, and $(Y_\alpha)_{\alpha \in X_0}$ is a family of saturated degenerated Λ-sets $Y_\alpha \in \mathfrak{A}*$. Since all the Y_α have exactly one carrier y_α, the saturated Λ-set $\Pi_\downarrow(X, Y)$ is naturally defined as the degenerated Λ-set corresponding to the following saturated set:

$$\{M, \forall (A, B, N) \in \mathcal{SN}^3 . \forall \alpha \sqsubset X . \forall N \models_X \alpha . \text{app}_{x:A.B}(M, N) \models_{Y_\alpha} y_\alpha\}.$$

The element of this set are exactly the realisers of the only index of $\pi \sqsubset \Pi(X, Y)$. Thus we have defined a Λ-iso

$$\downarrow_{\Pi(X,Y)} \colon \Pi(X, Y) \to \Pi_\downarrow(X, Y) \in \mathfrak{A}^{\Uparrow}(*).$$

which associates π to $\emptyset$. This proves criterion 1.

6.2 CC

The Calculus of Construction which extends system F is defined as a PTS by:

$$\mathcal{S} \equiv \{*, \square\} \qquad \mathcal{A} \equiv \{(*, \square)\} \qquad \mathcal{R} \equiv \{(*, *, *), (\square, *, *), (*, \square, \square), (\square, \square, \square)\}$$

Our model extends the model of system F. We use a singleton set $\mathfrak{E} = \{1\}$ to treat the rule $(\square, \square, \square)$ inside set theory. For every sort s we take $\mathfrak{A}^{\Uparrow}(s) = \mathfrak{A}_{\Downarrow}(s) = \mathfrak{A}(s)$ and thus $\Uparrow_s = \Downarrow_s = Id_{\mathfrak{A}^{\Uparrow}(s)}$. $\mathfrak{A}(*)$ is the set of saturated degenerated Λ-sets. $\mathfrak{A}(\square)$ is constructed as the union of all level_n for $n \in \omega^+$, where ω^+ is the set of strictly positive natural numbers.

1. level_1 is the singleton $\{\mathfrak{A}(*)\}$,
2. $\text{level}_{\leq n}$ is defined as the union of all level_k for $1 \leq k \leq n$,
3.
$$\begin{aligned} \text{level}_{n+1} = \quad & \{\Pi(X, Y), X \in \mathfrak{A}(*), Y_\alpha \in \text{level}_n\} \\ \cup \; & \{\Pi(X, Y), X \in \text{level}_n, Y_\alpha \in \text{level}_{\leq n}\} \\ \cup \; & \{\Pi(X, Y), X \in \text{level}_{\leq n}, Y_\alpha \in \text{level}_n\} \end{aligned}$$

We check easily that the level_n are disjoint sets. Let us introduce the equivalence relations:

1. $\left\| \begin{matrix} 1 \\ \mathfrak{A}(*) \end{matrix} \right\|$ relates every two elements of $\mathfrak{A}(*)$, and $\left| \begin{matrix} 1 \\ \mathfrak{A}(*) \end{matrix} \right|$ relates every two indexes $\emptyset$ of saturated degenerated Λ-set $X, X' \in \mathfrak{A}(*)$,

2. two elements of $\mathfrak{A}^{\Uparrow}(\Box)$ are related by $\left\| \frac{1}{\mathfrak{A}(\Box)} \right\|$ if and only if they are in the same set level_n,
3. every two indexes α and α' of X and X' in $\mathfrak{A}^{\Uparrow}(\Box)$ are related by $\left| \frac{1}{\mathfrak{A}(\Box)} \right|$.

The isos

$$\downarrow_{\Pi(X,Y)} : \Pi(X,Y) \to \Pi_{\downarrow}(X,Y)$$

are defined:

1. as in system F for the rules $(*,*,*)$ and $(\Box,*,*)$
2. as the identity $\Pi(X,Y) = \Pi_{\downarrow}(X,Y)$ for the rules $(*,\Box,\Box)$ and $(\Box,\Box,\Box)$.

Remark that the Λ-iso $\downarrow_{\Pi(X,Y)}$ does not depend on the rules because $\mathfrak{A}^{\Uparrow}(*)$ and $\mathfrak{A}^{\Uparrow}(\Box)$ are disjoint sets.

In this short version, we ommit the proof that this construction fullfills the required conditions.

6.3 ECC

The Extended Calculus of Construction is defined as a PTS by:

$$\mathcal{S} \equiv \{*, \Box_i \mid i \in \omega^+\} \qquad \mathcal{A} \equiv \{(*, \Box_i), (\Box_i, \Box_{i+1}) \mid i \in \omega^+\}$$

$$\mathcal{R} \equiv \{(*,*,*), (\Box_i,*,*), (*,\Box_i,\Box_i), (\Box_j,\Box_k,\Box_m) \mid i,j,k \in (\omega^+)^3, m = max(j,k)\}$$

The construction of the $\mathfrak{A}(\Box_i)$'s extends the construction of $\mathfrak{A}(\Box)$ in the case of ECC. Here, $\mathfrak{C}$ is the set ω^+. For every sort s we take $\mathfrak{A}^{\Uparrow}(s) = \mathfrak{A}_{\Downarrow}(s) = \mathfrak{A}(s)$ and thus $\Uparrow_s = \Downarrow_s = Id_{\mathfrak{A}^{\Uparrow}(s)}$. Again, the set $\mathfrak{A}(*)$ is the set of saturated degenerated Λ-sets. The sets $\mathfrak{A}(\Box_i)$'s are defined as the union of all $\mathsf{level}_{(i,n)}$ for $n < \omega$:

1. $\mathsf{level}_{(1,0)}$ is the singleton $\{\mathfrak{A}(*)\}$,
2. $\mathsf{level}_{\leq(i,n)}$ is defined as the union of all $\mathsf{level}_{(j,p)}$ for (j,p) lexicographically[3] less than (i,n),
3. $$\begin{aligned} \mathsf{level}_{(i,n+1)} = \; & \{\Pi(X,Y), X \in \mathfrak{A}(*), Y_\alpha \in \mathsf{level}_{(i,n)}\} \\ & \cup \{\Pi(X,Y), X \in \mathsf{level}_{(i,n)}, Y_\alpha \in \mathsf{level}_{\leq(i,n)}\} \\ & \cup \{\Pi(X,Y), X \in \mathsf{level}_{\leq(i,n)}, Y_\alpha \in \mathsf{level}_{(i,n)}\} \end{aligned}$$
4. $\mathsf{level}_{(i+1,0)}$ is the singleton $\{\mathfrak{A}(\Box_i)\}$.

All sets $\mathsf{level}_{(i,n)}$ are disjoint sets. In the case of CC we were able to give a direct definition of the relations $\left| \frac{1}{\mathfrak{A}^{\Uparrow}(\Box)} \right|$ and $\left\| \frac{1}{\mathfrak{A}^{\Uparrow}(\Box)} \right\|$ in terms of the levels in $\mathfrak{A}(\Box)$. This would be very hard indeed in the case of ECC. As a consequence at some point the definition of $\left| \frac{j}{\mathfrak{A}^{\Uparrow}(s)} \right|$ and $\left\| \frac{j}{\mathfrak{A}^{\Uparrow}(s)} \right\|$ for $j \in \mathfrak{C}$ and $s \in \mathcal{S}$ makes use of an induction argument on the construction steps $\mathsf{level}_{(i,n)}$.

For the universe $\mathfrak{A}(*)$ $\left\| \frac{j}{\mathfrak{A}(*)} \right\|$ relates all elements of $\mathfrak{A}(*)$, and $\left| \frac{j}{\mathfrak{A}(*)} \right|$ relates all indexes $\emptyset$ of saturated degenerated Λ-set $X, X' \in \mathfrak{A}(*)$,

[3] That is $j < i$ or ($j = i$ and $p \leq n$).

For the universe $\mathfrak{A}(\Box_i)$ when $i < j$ $\left\|\overset{j}{\mathfrak{A}(\Box_i)}\right\|$ relates all elements X and X' of $\mathfrak{A}^{\Uparrow}(\Box_i)$ and $\left|\overset{j}{\mathfrak{A}(\Box_i)}\right|$ relates every two indexes $\alpha \sqsubset X$ and $\alpha \sqsubset X'$.

For the universe $\mathfrak{A}(\Box_j)$ Two elements X and X' of $\mathfrak{A}^{\Uparrow}(\Box_j)$ are related by $\left\|\overset{j}{\mathfrak{A}(\Box_j)}\right\|$ if and only they are in the same set $\mathsf{level}_{(j,n)}$. $\left|\overset{j}{\mathfrak{A}(\Box_j)}\right|$ relates every two indexes $\alpha \sqsubset X$ and $\alpha' \sqsubset X'$ in any two Λ-sets X, X' in $\mathfrak{A}(\Box_j)$.

For the universe $\mathfrak{A}(\Box_i)$ when $i > j$ The two relations $\left|\overset{j}{\mathfrak{A}(\Box_i)}\right|$ and $\left\|\overset{j}{\mathfrak{A}(\Box_i)}\right\|$ are defined by induction on the construction steps $\mathsf{level}_{(i,n)}$. The first step in the construction is to impose that

1. two Λ-sets Z and Z' related by $\left\|\overset{j}{\mathfrak{A}(\Box_i)}\right\|$ are at the same level $\mathsf{level}_{(i,n)}$,
2. two indexes $\alpha \sqsubset Z$ and $\alpha' \sqsubset Z'$ related by $\left|\overset{j}{\mathfrak{A}(\Box_i)}\right|$ have their Λ-sets Z and Z' at the same level $\mathsf{level}_{(i,n)}$.

Thus, it is enough to construct $\left\|\overset{j}{\mathfrak{A}(\Box_i)}\right\|$ and $\left|\overset{j}{\mathfrak{A}(\Box_i)}\right|$ at each level $\mathsf{level}_{(i,n)}$. Let there be two elements Z and Z' of $\mathsf{level}_{(i,n)}$:

1. if $n = 0$ then by construction of $\mathfrak{A}(\Box_i)$, Z and Z' are equal to $\mathfrak{A}_{\Downarrow}(\Box_{i-1})$ and thus related by $\left\|\overset{j}{\mathfrak{A}(\Box_i)}\right\|$. Let there be two indexes f and g of $\mathfrak{A}_{\Downarrow}(\Box_{i-1})$. Then

$$f \left|\overset{j}{\mathfrak{A}(\Box_i)}\right| g \quad \text{if and only if} \quad f \left\|\overset{j}{\mathfrak{A}(\Box_{i-1})}\right\| g$$

2. if $n = p + 1$ then Z and Z' are of the form:

$$Z = \Pi(X, Y) \quad \text{and} \quad Z' = \Pi(X', Y')$$

where X, X' and $Y_\alpha, Y'_{\alpha'}$ are elements of $\mathsf{level}_{\leq(i,p)}$, for any $\alpha \sqsubset X$ and $\alpha' \sqsubset X'$. We impose that the relation $\left\|\overset{j}{\mathfrak{A}(\Box_i)}\right\|$ only relates the Λ-sets Z and Z' when there are two sorts s_1 and s_2 among $\{*, \Box_m \mid m \leq i\}$ such that
   - both Λ-sets X and X' elements of $\mathfrak{A}(s_1)$,
   - for any $\alpha \sqsubset X$ and $\alpha' \sqsubset X'$, both Λ-sets Y_α and $Y_{\alpha'}$ are elements of $\mathfrak{A}(s_2)$.

   The relation $\left\|\overset{j}{\mathfrak{A}^{\Uparrow}(\Box_i)}\right\|$ is defined as follows:

$$\Pi(X, Y) \left\|\overset{j}{\mathfrak{A}^{\Uparrow}(\Box_i)}\right\| \Pi(X', Y')$$

if and only if:

$$X \left\| \overset{j}{\mathfrak{A}^{\Uparrow}(\Box_i)} \right\| X'$$

and for any $\alpha \sqsubset X$ and $\alpha' \sqsubset X'$,

$$\alpha \left| \overset{j}{\mathfrak{A}(s_1)} \right| \alpha' \Longrightarrow Y_\alpha \left\| \overset{j}{\mathfrak{A}(s_2)} \right\| Y'_{\alpha'}$$

3. the relation $\left| \overset{j}{\mathfrak{A}(\Box_i)} \right|$ is defined on any index $f \sqsubset Z$ and $g \sqsubset Z'$ with $Z, Z' \in$ $\mathsf{level}_{(i,n)}$ as follows:

$$f \left| \overset{j}{\mathfrak{A}(\Box_i)} \right| g$$

if and only if

$$Z \left\| \overset{j}{\mathfrak{A}(\Box_i)} \right\| Z' \quad \text{and} \quad f \left| \overset{j}{\Pi(\mathfrak{A}(s_1), \mathfrak{A}(s_2))} \right| g$$

Once having expressed the equivalence relation, we introduce the isos

$$\downarrow_{\Pi(X,Y)} : \Pi(X,Y) \to \Pi_{\downarrow}(X,Y)$$

which are defined like in CC:

1. as in system F for the rules $(*,*,*)$ and $(\Box_i,*,*)$
2. as the identity $\Pi(X,Y) = \Pi_{\downarrow}(X,Y)$ for the rules $(*,\Box_i,\Box_i)$ and $(\Box_j,\Box_k,\Box_m)$ with $m = max(k,m)$.

Again, the Λ-iso $\downarrow_{\Pi(X,Y)}$ does only depend on X and Y since $\mathfrak{A}^{\Uparrow}(*)$ and the $\mathfrak{A}^{\Uparrow}(\Box_i)$'s are all disjoint.

Let us check the conditions on our model. Conditions 1(1), 1(2) and 4 are trivial, condition 2(2) is true because the $\mathfrak{A}^{\Uparrow}(s)$'s are disjoint and condition 2(1) is the consequence of the fact that

1. $\left\| \overset{j}{\mathfrak{A}^{\Uparrow}(*)} \right\|$ and $\left| \overset{1}{\mathfrak{A}_{\Downarrow}(\Box_1)} \right|$ are the same relation on $\mathfrak{A}^{\Uparrow}(*) = \mathfrak{A}_{\Downarrow}(*)$,
2. $\left\| \overset{j}{\mathfrak{A}^{\Uparrow}(\Box_i)} \right\|$ and $\left| \overset{j}{\mathfrak{A}_{\Downarrow}(\Box_i)} \right|$ are the same relation on $\mathfrak{A}^{\Uparrow}(\Box_i) = \mathfrak{A}_{\Downarrow}(\Box_i)$, for $i, j < \omega$.

Condition 1(3) is true:

1. on the rules $(*,*,*)$ and $(\Box_i,*,*)$ because every product $\Pi(X,Y)$ of saturated degenerated Λ-sets Y_α is collapsed by $\downarrow_{\Pi(X,Y)}$ to the saturated degenerated Λ-set $\Pi_{\downarrow}(X,Y)$;
2. on the rules $(\Box_i,\Box_j,\Box_j)$ when $i \leq j$ because the equivalence relation $\left| \overset{j}{\mathfrak{A}(\Box_i)} \right|$ is designed so as to relate every two indexes α and α' in a Λ-set X element of $\Box_i$. As a consequence, if $(Y_\alpha)_{\alpha \in X_0}$ is a family of elements in $\mathfrak{A}(\Box)$ such that

$$\forall (\alpha,\alpha') \in X_0^2 . \alpha \left| \overset{1}{\mathfrak{A}^{\Uparrow}(s_1)} \right| \alpha' \Longrightarrow Y_\alpha \left\| \overset{1}{\mathfrak{A}^{\Uparrow}(\Box)} \right\| Y_{\alpha'}$$

then all Y_α's are in the same level level_n. It follows that $\Pi(X,Y)$ is an element of level_{n+1} and as such, an element of $\mathfrak{A}(\Box)$.
3. on the rules $(\Box_j,\Box_i,\Box_j)$ for $i \leq j$ because all products $\Pi(X,Y)$ where X is element of $\mathsf{level}_{(j,n)}$ and $(Y_\alpha)_{\alpha \sqsubset X}$ is a family of elements of $\mathfrak{A}(\Box_i)$ indexed by indexes of X, are in $\mathsf{level}_{(j,n+1)}$, and hence in $\mathfrak{A}(\Box_j)$.

Let us check condition 3 on the relations $\left| \overset{j}{\mathfrak{A}(s)} \right|$ and $\left\| \overset{j}{\mathfrak{A}(s)} \right\|$ for a given element j of $\mathfrak{C}$:

For the rules (s_1, s_2, s_3) where $s_2 = s_3 = *$ or $s_3 = \Box_i$ with $i < j$ The conditions 3(1) and 3(2) are true here for the same reasons as in CC:

- $\left\| \overset{j}{\mathfrak{A}(s_2)} \right\|$ and $\left\| \overset{j}{\mathfrak{A}(s_3)} \right\|$ relate all elements of $\mathfrak{A}(s_2)$ and $\mathfrak{A}(s_3)$,
- $\left| \overset{j}{\mathfrak{A}(s_2)} \right|$ and $\left| \overset{j}{\mathfrak{A}(s_3)} \right|$ relate all indexes of elements of $\mathfrak{A}(s_2)$ and $\mathfrak{A}(s_3)$.

For the rules $(s_1, s_2, \Box_j)$ The proof of conditions 3(1) follows the same line as in the case of CC: A product $\Pi(X,Y)$ is in $\mathsf{level}_{(j,p)}$ if and only if there are (i_1, n_1) and (i_2, n_2) such that

1. $X \in \mathsf{level}_{(i_1,n_1)}$ and $Y_\alpha \in \mathsf{level}_{(i_2,n_2)}$ for any $\alpha \sqsubset X$, and (j,p) is the (lexicographical) maximum of (i_1, n_1) and (i_2, n_2),
2. or $X \in \mathfrak{A}^{\Uparrow}(*)$ and $Y_\alpha \in \mathsf{level}_{(j,p-1)}$ for any $\alpha \sqsubset X$.

The reasons for condition 3(2) are the same as in the previous case since all indexes of elements of $\mathfrak{A}(\Box_j)$ are related by $\left| \overset{j}{\mathfrak{A}(\Box_j)} \right|$.

For the rules $(s_1, s_2, \Box_i)$ for $i > j$ The inductive definition of $\left\| \overset{j}{\mathfrak{A}(\Box_i)} \right\|$ and $\left| \overset{j}{\mathfrak{A}(\Box_i)} \right|$ for $i > j$ follows explicitly the requirements of conditions 2(1) and 3. For this reason both conditions are fulfilled.

6.4 System U^-

It is well-known that Girard's system U^- yields non-normalizable terms, and thus we cannot find a collection of $\mathfrak{A}^{\Uparrow}(s)$ fitting its rules. However, it is reassuring to check that the rules do *not* allow the usual model construction.

As a PTS, system U^- is defined with three sorts $\mathcal{R} \equiv \{*, \Box, \triangle\}$ and the following axioms and rules:
$\mathcal{A} = \{(*, \Box), (\Box, \triangle)\}$ and $\mathcal{R} = \{(*,*,*), (\Box,*,*), (\Box,\Box,\Box), (\triangle,\Box,\Box)\}$.

The three first rules are exactly the rules of system F_ω. The last one however is obviously problematic:

- because of the second axiom, we need to have completed the construction of $\mathfrak{A}(\Box)$ in order to define $\mathfrak{A}(\triangle)$,
- on the other hand, because of the last rule, we need to quantify over all elements of $\mathfrak{A}(\triangle)$ while constructing $\mathfrak{A}(\Box)$.

It is obviously not possible to break this vicious circle. In other words, we see how polymorphism cannot be authorized for higher sorts.

6.5 Cyclic F

The following PTS does not seem more expressive than system F. It might however be worth noting that it fits easily in our pattern. $\mathcal{A} = \{(*, \Box), (\Box, *)\}$ and $\mathcal{R} = \{(*,*,*), (\Box,*,*)\}$

$\mathfrak{A}(*)$ is the Λ-set of degenerated Λ-sets. $\mathfrak{A}^{\Uparrow}(\Box)$ is the singleton $\mathfrak{A}(*)$. $\mathfrak{A}_{\Downarrow}(\Box)$ is a degenerated Λ-set. It is easy to finish the proof.

7 The Church-Rosser Property

We now focus on the relation between the labeled PTSs considered in this paper and the usual presentation. The first step is to verify the Church-Rosser property for the first one.

¿From now on, we suppose given a PTS (i.e. the sets $\mathcal{S}$, $\mathcal{A}$ and $\mathcal{R}$) and we assume it verifies the strong normalization property. We will make another assumption (uniqueness of type) just before lemma 43.

Definition 37 (loose reduction). Loose reduction (written $\triangleright_l$) is the contextual closure of

$$\mathrm{app}_{x:A.B}(\lambda_{x:A'.B'}x.M, N) \triangleright_l M[x \setminus N].$$

Again, we write $\triangleright_l^*$ (respectively $=_l$) for the reflexive-transitive (respectively reflexive transitive and symmetric) closure of $\triangleright_l$.

Lemma 38. *The $\triangleright_l$ property enjoys the Church-Rosser property on pseudo-terms:*

$$\forall t, t' \;.\; t =_l t' \Longrightarrow \exists t'' \;.\; t \triangleright_l^* t'' \wedge t' \triangleright_l^* t''.$$

Proof The usual Tait–Martin-Lof style proofs apply. ∎

Lemma 39. *Let* $\mathrm{app}_{x:A.B}(\lambda_{x:A'.B'}x.M, N)$ *be a well-typed term in some context* Γ. *We have* $A =_l A'$ *and* $B =_l B'$.

Proof Looking at the derivation, it is clear that $(x : A)B =_\Gamma (x : A')B'$, and thus we also have $(x : A)B =_l (x : A')B'$. The previous lemma ensures that there exists a $(x : A'')B''$ which is a common (loose) reduct of $(x : A)B$ and $(x : A')B'$. Hence, $A \triangleright_l^* A''$, $A' \triangleright_l^* A''$ $B \triangleright_l^* B''$ $B \triangleright_l^* B''$. ∎

Theorem 40 (Church-Rosser). *Let there be two derivable judgements* $\Gamma \vdash t : T$ *and* $\Gamma \vdash t' : T'$, *such that* $t =_l t'$ *and* t *and* t' *are in normal form (for* $\triangleright_\beta$*). Then* $t = t'$.

Proof We proceed by mutual induction over the size of t and t'. We start by proving that t (respectively t') is in normal form for $\triangleright_l$: suppose t yields a loose redex, i.e. contains a subterm of the form

$$\mathrm{app}_{x:A.B}(\lambda_{x:A'.B'}x.M, N)$$

by the previous lemma, we have $A =_l A'$ and $B =_l B'$ and by induction hypothesis $A = A'$ and $B = B'$. But then we have exhibited and tight redex, and this is impossible since t is in normal form.

Now lemma 38 states there exists t'' such that $t \triangleright_l^* t''$ and $t' \triangleright_l^* t''$. But since t and t' are normal with respect to $\triangleright_l$, we have $t = t'' = t'$. ∎

Corollary 41. *Let* t *and* t' *be two well-formed terms in a same context* Γ. *If* $t =_l t'$, *then* t *and* t' *have a common unique normal form.*

What now follows is a little boring and straightforward, but necessary to extend the previous results to usual PTSs.

We can now define the usual PTSs and state our equivalence theorem. The *unlabeled terms* are defined by the following grammar:

$$M \quad := \quad x \mid s \mid (M\ M) \mid \lambda x : M.M \mid (x : M)M.$$

We overload the symbol $\triangleright_l$ (respectively $\triangleright_l^*$, etc) by defining reduction on unlabeled terms:

$$(\lambda x : A.M\ N) \triangleright_l M[x \setminus N].$$

The rules for unlabeled judgements $\Gamma \vdash_l M : T$ are then defined as usual (see [2] for example). The main point is of course that the conversion rule now goes:

$$(\text{CONV})\ \frac{\Gamma \vdash_l M : A \qquad \Gamma \vdash_l B : s \qquad A =_l B}{\Gamma \vdash_l M : B}$$

Definition 42 (Unstripped term). We define the map $||\_||$ from terms to the usual, naked terms of PTS's:

$$||x|| \equiv x$$
$$||s|| \equiv s$$
$$||\mathsf{app}_{A.B}(M,N)|| \equiv (||M||\ ||N||)$$
$$||\lambda_{x:A.B}x.M|| \equiv \lambda x : ||A||.||t||$$

It is straightforward to extend this map to contexts.

The following results are quite immediate:

- $t =_\beta t' \Longrightarrow ||t|| =_l ||t'||$
- $t =_l t' \Longrightarrow ||t|| =_l ||t'||$
- $\Gamma \vdash t : T \Longrightarrow ||\Gamma|| \vdash_l ||t|| : ||T||$.

But we are mainly interested in the reverse assertion, i.e. theorem 44. Since we do not want to get lost in technical details without much interest, we make the following assumption.

Assumption *If the judgements $\Gamma \vdash_l t : T$ and $\Gamma \vdash_l t : T'$ are derivable, then $T =_l T'$.*

The first thing to check is:

Lemma 43. *Let $\Gamma \vdash t : T$ and $\Gamma \vdash t' : T'$ be two derivable (tight) judgements. If $||t|| =_l ||t'||$, then $t =_\beta t'$.*

Proof Thanks to strong normalization, we might restrict ourselves to the case were t and t' are both normal. Thanks to previous results, this implies that $||t|| = ||t'||$. We may then proceed by mutual structural induction over t and t'. The only non-trivial cases are:

- $t = \lambda_{x:A.B}x.M$ and $t' = \lambda_{x:A'.B'}x.M'$. Since both terms are normal and $=_l$-convertible, we have $A =_l A'$, $B =_l B'$ and $M =_l M'$. The induction thus implies that $A = A'$ and also $B = B'$ (respectively $M = M'$), since B and B' (respectively M and M') are well-typed in $\Gamma, x : A$.

- $t = \mathrm{app}_{x_1:A_1.B_1}(\mathrm{app}_{x_2:A_2.B_2}(\dots \mathrm{app}_{x_n:A_n.B_n}(y, M_n)\dots, M_2), M_1)$
  and
  $t' = \mathrm{app}_{x'_1:A'_1.B'_1}(\mathrm{app}_{x'_2:A'_2.B'_2}(\dots \mathrm{app}_{x'_n:A'_n.B'_n}(y, M'_n)\dots, M'_2), M'_1)$.
  We know that $(x_n : A_n)B_n$ and $(x'_n : A'_n)B'_n$ are both correct types for y in $||\Gamma||$. They are therefore convertible and the induction hypothesis applies. We also know that $||M_n|| = ||M'_n||$ and may apply the induction hypothesis. We iterate these two steps n times to conclude $t = t'$.

■

Theorem 44. *Given a derivable judgement $\Gamma \vdash_l t : T$, there exists a derivable judgement $\Delta \vdash u : V$ such that $||\Delta|| = \Gamma$, $||u|| = t$ and $||V|| = T$.*

Proof By induction over the derivation. All steps are straightforward but the conversion rule, which is taken care by the previous lemma. ■

Corollary 45. *If $\Gamma \vdash_l t : T$ is derivable, then t and T are strongly normalizing with respect to $\rhd_l$.*

8 Conclusion

We hope that this work might shed some new light on the interaction between model construction and strong normalization, which is the syntactical approach to logical consistency. We realize that the definition of the interpretation, as well as the construction of the universes for particular systems is complicated by the presence of the equivalence relations in the $\mathfrak{A}^{\Uparrow}(s)$. This seems the price to pay for avoiding the use of inaccessible cardinals. We however conjecture that inaccessible cardinals are necessary to prove normalization for more powerful theories, for instance when adding full inductive types to ECC. This leads to possible directions for future work:

- Give a clean categorical setting to this work, since most of the constructions seem to be of categorical nature.
- Extend this approach to other theories, especially to inductive types.
- Understand to what extent these construction might be used for more traditional applications of models, like consistency for additional axioms (excluded middle, choice) or new reductions.

Acknowledgements

We would like to thank Thorsten Altenkirch, Martin Hofmann, Ralph Loader and Thomas Streicher for useful comments and suggestions on earlier versions of this work.

References

1. T. Altenkirch. *Constructions, Inductive Types and Strong Normalization.* Ph.D. Thesis, University of Edinburgh, 1993.
2. H. Barendregt. Lambda Calculi with Types. In *Handbook of Logic in Computer Science*, Vol II, Elsevier, 1992
3. G. Barthe, P.-A. Melliès. On the Subject Reduction property for algebraic type systems. In *Proceedings CSL'96*, LNCS 1258, Springer Verlag, 1996.

4. G. Dowek, G. Huet and B. Werner. On the Definition of the η-long Normal Form in Type Systems of the Cube. Submitted to publication. See also `http://pauillac.inria.fr/~werner/`, 1996.
5. H. Geuvers et M.-J. Nederhof. A modular proof of strong normalization for the Calculus of Constructions. *Journal of Functional Programming*, 1 (2):155–189, 1991.
6. J.-Y. Girard. *Interprétation fonctionnelle et élimination des coupures de l'arithmétique d'ordre supérieur*, Thèse d'Etat, Université Paris 7, 1972.
7. J. W. Klop, *Combinatory Reduction Systems*. Ph.D. Thesis, Utrecht University, 1980.
8. G. Longo and E. Moggi. Constructive Natural Deduction and its ω-set Interpretation.
9. Z. Luo. *An Extended Calculus of Constructions*. Ph.D. Thesis, University of Edinburgh, 1990.
10. P. Martin-Löf. *Intuitionistic Type Theory*. Studies in Proof Theory, Bibliopolis, 1984.
11. W. W. Tait. A realizability interpretation of the theory of species. In *Logic Colloquium*, R. Parikh Ed. LNM 453, Springer-Verlag, 1975.
12. J. Terlouw. Strong Normalization in Type Systems: a model theoretical approach. In *Dirk van Dalen Festschrift*, Henk Barendregt, Marc Bezem and Jan Willem Klop Eds. Dept. of Philosophy, Utrecht University, 1993.

Proving a Real Time Algorithm for ATM in Coq

Jean-François Monin

France Télécom - CNET, DTL/MSV
2, av. P. Marzin
22307 Lannion Cedex
monin@lannion.cnet.fr

Abstract. This paper presents the techniques used for proving, in the framework of type theory, the correctness of an algorithm recently standardized at ITU-T that handles time explicitly. The structure of the proof and its formalization in Coq are described, as well as the main tools which have been developed: an abstract model of "real-time" that makes no assumption on the nature of time and a way to actually find proofs employing transitivity, using only logical definitions and an existing tactic.

1 Context and Motivation

1.1 Conformance Control in ATM

In an ATM (Asynchronous Transfer Mode) network, data cells sent by a user must not exceed a rate depending on the state of the network. Several modes for using an ATM network, called "ATM transfer capabilities" (ATC) have been defined. Each ATC may be seen as a generic contract between the user and the network, saying that the network must guarantee a number of characteristics of the connection (transfer delay and so on) provided the user sends only compliant data cells—their rate must be bounded by a value defined by the current contract. Actually, in the most interesting, recent and complicated ATC, this allowed cell rate (ACR) may vary during the same session, depending on the current state of the network. Such ATC are designed for irregular sources, that need high cell rates from time to time, but that may wait when the network is busy. A servo-mechanism is then proposed in order to let the user know whether he can send data or not. This mechanism has to be well defined, in order to have a clear contract. The key is a public algorithm for checking conformance of cells. Each ATC comes with its own conformance control algorithm.

In fact, a new ATC cannot be accepted (as an international standard) without an efficient conformance control algorithm, and some evidence that this algorithm has the intended behavior.

1.2 The Case of ABR

In the case of the ATC called ABR (available bit rate), a simple but very inefficient algorithm had been proposed in a first stage, and reasonably efficient algorithms proposed later turned out to be fairly complicated. This situation has been settled when one of them has been proved correct in relation to the simple one [9]: this algorithm is now part of the I.373.1 standard. The corresponding proof was hand written, lengthy (15 pages) and somewhat tricky in places, hence we decided to formalize it in type theory in order to get a proof automatically checked by COQ.

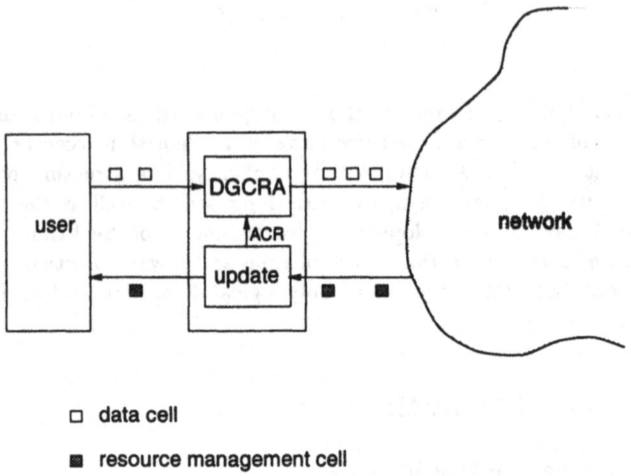

Fig. 1. conformance control

The conformance control algorithm for ABR has two parts (see fig. 1). The first one is called DGCRA (dynamic generic control of cell rate algorithm). It just checks that the rate of data cells emitted by the user is not higher than a value which is approximately Acr, the allowed cell rate. Excess cells may be discarded by DGCRA. Note that, in the case of ABR, Acr depends on time: its value has to be known each time a new data cell comes from the user. This part is quite simple and has no interest here. The hard side, called "update" in fig. 1, is the computation of $\mathsf{Acr}(t)$, which depends on the sequence of values (ER_n) carried by resource management cells coming from the network. For the sake of simplicity, the cell carrying ER_n will be called itself ER_n.

Of course, $\mathsf{Acr}(t)$ depends only on cells ER_n whose arrival time t_n is such that $t_n < t$ (we order resource management cells so that $t_n < t_{n+1}$ for any n). In fact, $\mathsf{Acr}(t)$ depends only on cells ER_i such that either $t - \tau_2 < t_i \leq t - \tau_3$, or $t_i \leq t - \tau_2 < t_{i+1}$, where τ_2 and τ_3 are fixed parameters such that $\tau_3 < \tau_2$: $\mathsf{Acr}(t)$ is just the maximum of these values[1].

[1] In the protocol ABR, a resource management cell carries a value of Acr, that should be reached as soon as possible. However, because of electric propagation time, the user is aware of this expected value only after a while. Everything included, the

1.3 Effective Computation of Acr

A direct computation of $\mathsf{Acr}(t)$ would be very inefficient. However, it is not difficult to see that $\mathsf{Acr}(t)$ is constant on any interval that contains no value among $\{t_n + \tau \mid \tau = \tau_2 \vee \tau = \tau_3\}$. In other words, $\mathsf{Acr}(t)$ is determined by a sequence of values. It then becomes possible to use a scheduler handling future changes of $\mathsf{Acr}(t)$. This scheduler is updated when a new cell ER_n is received. Roughly, if s is the current time, ER_n will be taken into account at time $s + \tau_3$, while ER_{n-1} will not be taken into account after $s + \tau_2$.

The control conformance algorithm considered here exploits this idea, with the further constraint that only a small amount of memory is allocated to the scheduler. This means that information is lost. *We then just expect that the actual value of $\mathsf{Acr}(t)$ is greater or equal to its theoretical value, as defined above.*

1.4 On the Use of Coq in this Application

Coq follows the LCF approach. The user states definitions and theorems, then he (she) proves the latters by the means of *scripts* made of *tactics* and *tacticals*. Tactics are either primitive (e.g. Intro or Apply), or higher level, like Auto. Tacticals allow you to build complex tactics from simpler ones, for instance Try... Then.... However scripts *are not* proofs. Scripts *produce* actual proofs, which are data (terms) to be checked by the kernel of the proof assistant. The kernel (i.e. the type checker in the case of Coq) is only a small part of the whole code and is programmed with special care. Hence, even if scripts are difficult to read or if subtle tactics involving big programs are used (e.g. EAuto, see below), the user can be very confident in theorems proved in such a tool. This is particularly important in the application discussed here, because the manual proof seemed somewhat suspect.

Thanks to the LCF application, the user can safely program himself ad-hoc tactics. However, in this case study, existing general tactics of Coq turned out to fit our needs. In particular, we will show how EAuto (see 2.2) can be used in an efficient way. Let us explain here the difference between the tactics Auto and EAuto.

Roughly, Auto is able to prove subgoals using a sequence of introductions and of applications of already proved lemmas. For instance, Auto easily finds a proof of mortal(Socrate) from

$(\forall x : \mathsf{being})\ \mathsf{human}(x) \Rightarrow \mathsf{mortal}(x)$,
human(Socrate).

However the same goal cannot be discharged by Auto from

$(\forall x : \mathsf{being})\ (\forall y : \mathsf{beverage})\ \mathsf{human}(x) \Rightarrow \mathsf{drinks}(x, y) \Rightarrow \mathsf{mortal}(x)$,
human(Socrate),
drinks(Socrate, hemlock),

reaction delay of the user is bounded by τ_3 and τ_2. The last resource management cell before $t - \tau_2$ is also needed: consider for instance the case where the set $\{i \mid t - \tau_2 < t_i \leq t - \tau_3\}$ is empty.

because Auto is not able to guess a witness like hemlock. Finding witnesses involves more expensive proof search. On the other hand, the recently implemented tactic EAuto makes this possible thanks to a Prolog-like strategy.

1.5 Structure of this Paper

It should be clear from the informal definition of the control conformance algorithm given in 1.2 and 1.3, that the ability to reason about real time is essential here. The point is that the algorithm itself handles time by the means of a scheduler, which is a data structure containing dates. Comparisons between dates, additions of dates and delays play a central rôle in the algorithm as well as in proofs.

This paper presents the overall structure of correctness proof of the standardized algorithm for ABR conformance, its formalization in Coq and the main tools which have been developed to this aim: an abstract model of "real-time" that makes no assumption on the nature of time; and a way to actually find proofs employing transitivity, using only logical definitions and EAuto. It is organized as follows. We discuss in section 2 the axioms about time used in the development and proof search using them. Section 3 provides an axiomatic specification of the desired algorithm. A useful purely functional program is also given there. Section 4 describes a representation in Coq of the standardized algorithm and sketches some correctness proofs. Finally, the behaviors of a complete system made of the algorithm immersed in its environment are considered in section 5. The algorithm of I.371 for ABR conformance is given in appendix A.

2 Reasonning about Real Time

In our context, time is a linearly ordered structure equipped with an addition and a subtraction. One may ask whether time should be given a discrete or a continuous—or, at least, dense[2]—representation. On the one hand, "real" time is continuous. On the other, we deal with digital systems, which are discrete in essence. But we will introduce a notion of observer, which may well be able to observe (at least a stable part of) the state at an arbitrary instant.

We decided not to choose: we introduce a type parameter DD (for dates and durations) and operations on DD with a small number of axioms. These axioms do not say anything about the discrete or dense nature of time. A special attention has been paid for designing them, in order that:

- they are consistent (we formally proved that they are satisfied on nat);
- they have other models than N, for instance rational numbers;
- they are strong enough for our needs.

[2] We need a decidable equality, which is available on rational numbers.

2.1 A Small Theory of Dates and Durations

We consider that dates and duration share a common type, DD. Distinguishing two types (respectively Da and Du) would have been more accurate. For instance, we could introduce an addition of type Du $\rightarrow$ Du $\rightarrow$ Du and another of type Da $\rightarrow$ Du $\rightarrow$ Da, but no of type Da $\rightarrow$ Da $\rightarrow$ Da, because adding two dates makes no sense. Moreover, addition of type Du $\rightarrow$ Du $\rightarrow$ Du can be considered as commutative, while commutativity has no meaning on an addition of type Da $\rightarrow$ Du $\rightarrow$ Da. However this distinction would lead us to duplicate most operations, axioms and lemmas, whereas the mathematical structures we have in mind (various kind of numbers) are almost the same. In practice, they are exactly the same, because special properties like commutativity of + on Du are not needed in this case study. Hence we considered that Da = Du = DD would be more convenient here. Note that, in the axioms and lemmas below, it is quite easy to recognize whether a variable represents a date or a duration. This disciplin was strictly followed in the whole development.

In order to check that the axioms given below are consistent, we can interpret DD by a concrete inductive type, abstract operations by operations defined on this type, and we prove the formulae obtained by interpreting the axioms. The simplest model for DD is certainly the type of natural numbers. However it does not satisfy properties like $(\forall t, x)\ x - t + t = x$. The following is true on N: $(\forall t, x)\ t \leq x \rightarrow x - t + t = x$, but it is inadequate because we have to consider cases where x is a date and t is a duration: then comparing t with x does not make sense. For instance, we do not want to exclude models with negative values, where x may be negative and t may be positive; but the premise $t \leq x$ would then not be provable. A suitable axiom is given below (A.7). We can then prove $(\forall t, x, z)\ z + t \leq x \rightarrow x - t + t = x$ and other lemmas with similar premises. Those premises do not harm, because we only have to consider dates taking place after an origin, which is roughly the starting date of the algorithm.

Formally, we work in the following context.

DD : Set.

leD : DD $\rightarrow$ DD $\rightarrow$ Prop. *(* notation: $x \leq y$ *)*

ltD(x, y), noted $x < y$, is defined by $x \leq y \wedge \neg(x = y)$. The axioms saying that $\leq$ is a total linear order and that equality is decidable are obvious. A zero in DD is not necessary. When we need to say that a duration τ is positive, we just write $(\forall x)\ x \leq x + \tau$. We give the axioms relating + and − with $\leq$ and =. No further axioms are needed.

$$(\forall t, x, y : \mathsf{DD})\quad x \leq y \rightarrow x + t \leq y + t. \tag{A.1}$$

$$(\forall x, t, s : \mathsf{DD})\quad t \leq s \rightarrow x + t \leq x + s. \tag{A.2}$$

$$(\forall t, x : \mathsf{DD})\quad (x + t) - t = x. \tag{A.3}$$

$$(\forall t, x : \mathsf{DD})\quad x \leq (x - t) + t. \tag{A.4}$$

$$(\forall t, x, y : \mathsf{DD})\quad x \leq y \rightarrow x - t \leq y - t. \tag{A.5}$$

$$(\forall t, s, x : \mathsf{DD})\quad s \leq t \rightarrow x - t \leq x - s. \tag{A.6}$$

$$(\forall x, y, z, t : \mathsf{DD}) \quad z + t \leq y \to x \leq y - t \to x + t \leq y. \tag{A.7}$$

Then we get a number of lemmas. Some of them are:

$$(\forall t, x, z : \mathsf{DD}) \quad z + t \leq x \to (x - t) + t = x. \tag{L.1}$$
$$(\forall t, x, y : \mathsf{DD}) \quad (x + t) = (y + t) \to x = y. \tag{L.2}$$
$$(\forall t, x, y : \mathsf{DD}) \quad x + t \leq y + t \to x \leq y. \tag{L.3}$$
$$(\forall x, y, z, t : \mathsf{DD}) \quad z + t \leq x \to x < y + t \to x - t < y. \tag{L.4}$$

We think that it would be difficult to find a smaller system of (still understable) axioms. Here are some comments. (A.2) could be avoided in the presence of (A.1), if $+$ was commutative. See at the beginning of this subsection why we reject commutativity. (A.5) and (A.6) would be consequences of (A.2) and (A.1) if we provided a notion of opposite. But we cannot hope to get such a notion if we want N to be a model of our axioms. This requirement is explicit in (A.4).

Formulae (A.7) and (L.1) are equivalent in presence of other axioms, hence choosing one or the other as an axiom is a matter of taste. More precisely, (L.1) is proved from (A.7) using antisymmetry of $\leq$ and (A.4), while (A.7) is proved from (L.1) using (A.1).

2.2 Proof Search

Typical proof obligations have the form $\Gamma \vdash a < d$ where Γ contains hypotheses $a \leq b$, $c < d$, $b + \tau < u$ and $u \leq c + \tau$, among others. Several tens of similar formulae have to be proved in the case of ABR algorithm. They can be proved directly with the lemmas mentioned above, but this is quite tedious.

We also see that automatic proof search has to find witnesses, because of the heavy use of transitivity. The tactic EAuto makes this possible in Coq. However, it must be used very carefully: four versions of transitivity are available (each of the premises may or not be a strict inequality), and it turns out that the four versions are needed. Reflexivity is also needed. Even a single transitivity rule may be used in two different ways for proving $a < d$ from $a < b$, $b < c$ and $c < d$. Altogether, naive automatic proof search faces a combinatorial explosion.

Following a suggestion of C. Paulin, it is better to work with a better formulation of the lemmas (NB: in this subsection axioms are also considered as lemmas). Intuitively, the set of lemmas used by EAuto can be seen as a Prolog program, and we want this program to be as efficient as possible. Roughly, in our case, hypotheses like $a \leq b$ should be considered as basic facts `arc(a,b)`, and instead of lemmas corresponding to clauses like:

```
le(X,Y) :- arc(X,Y).
le(X,Z) :- le(X,Y) le(Y,Z).
```

with a dangerous left recursion on the second clause, we prefer lemmas corresponding to clauses like:

```
le(X,Y) :- arc(X,Y).
le(X,Z) :- arc(X,Y)  le(Y,Z).
```

Things are a bit more complicated because the conclusion of lemmas like $x + t < y + t \rightarrow x < y$ must also be considered as a "fact", while $x + t < y + t$ should itself be proved by transitivity. This happens in the example given at the beginning of this subsection: the proof cannot be $a \leq b < u - \tau \leq c < d$, using $b + \tau < u \rightarrow b < u - \tau$ and similarly for u and c, but only $a \leq b < c < d$, where $b \leq c$ comes from $b + \tau \leq u \leq c + \tau$. This is so because we banish the use of subtraction as soon as possible, in order to avoid the cycles easily obtained from a combination of lemmas like $x - t \leq y \rightarrow x \leq y + t$ and $x \leq y + t \rightarrow x - t \leq y$.

Before entering into more details, let us remark that a brute change of the relations to be used may have an impact on the formulation of the specification. But it is important to keep the latter as simple and natural as possible, if we want to be convinced that we prove the right properties on the right application. Similarly, we want to keep our lemmas as their are stated in the official presentation of the theory, because they give evidence that our axioms are right. Conversely, artificial definitions and lemmas should remain hidden.

Renaming and merging $\leq$ and $<$. In order to stop the use of transitivity in proof search, we introduce a new relation arc such that

$$\mathsf{arc}(\mathsf{true}) = \mathsf{ltD} \quad \text{and} \quad \mathsf{arc}(\mathsf{false}) = \mathsf{leD}. \tag{1}$$

The basic idea is that that goals $x \leq y$ and $x < y$ are proved only by transitivity, while goals $\mathsf{arc}(b, x, y)$ are proved using assumptions, basic lemmas, or anything but transitivity rules. In the sequel, $\mathsf{arc}(\mathsf{true}, x, y)$ and $\mathsf{arc}(\mathsf{false}, x, y)$ are more conveniently noted $x \leq' y$ and $x < y'$.

Let T be (the type of) a theorem to be proved. Let T' be the formula obtained by replacing $\leq$ by $\leq'$ and $<$ by $<'$ in the premises of T. Admittedly, T' is just a harmless (from the point of view of simplicity) rephrasing of T. On the semantical side, any proof of T *is* a proof of T', because T and T' are β-convertible.

However, during the proof process, premises have now the form $\mathsf{arc}(\mathsf{true}, x, y)$ or $\mathsf{arc}(\mathsf{false}, x, y)$. The crucial point is that the proof assistant bases its proof search on the actual shape of the premises and of the goal, not on their normal form. Basic lemmas of section 2.1 are also rephrased, for instance:

$$(\forall t, x, y : \mathsf{DD}) \quad x + t \leq y + t \rightarrow x \leq' y. \tag{L.3'}$$

Changing transitivity and reflexivity rules. As $x \leq' y$ and $x < y$ are considered as "elementary facts", we first just build the transitive closure of their union. Here arc is used with an arbitrary b as first parameter: we want to conclude $a \leq d$ from $a <' b \leq' c$ without taking care of the strictness of elementary inequalities; nrtle stands for "non reflexive transitive closure of arc for less or equal".

Inductive nrtle : DD → DD → Prop :=
 arc_nrtle : $(\forall b : \mathsf{bool})(x, y : \mathsf{DD})\ \mathsf{arc}(b, x, y) \rightarrow \mathsf{nrtle}(x, y)$ |
 tra_nrtle : $(\forall b : \mathsf{bool})(x, y, z : \mathsf{DD})\ \mathsf{arc}(b, z, y) \rightarrow \mathsf{nrtle}(x, z) \rightarrow \mathsf{nrtle}(x, y)$.

Reflexivity needs to be considered only once on a path.

Inductive tle : DD → DD → Prop :=
  eq_tle : $(\forall x : \mathsf{DD})\ \mathsf{tle}(x, x)$ |
  tle_plus : $(\forall x, y : \mathsf{DD})\ \mathsf{nrtle}(x, y) \rightarrow \mathsf{tle}(x, y)$.

Now, we have the following theorem:

$$(\forall x, y : \mathsf{DD})\ \mathsf{tle}(x, y) \rightarrow x \leq y. \tag{T.1}$$

The proof uses the fact that $\leq$ is transitive and weaker than $<$. Thanks to this theorem, proving any subgoal $x \leq y$ by transitivity amounts to prove $\mathsf{tle}(x, y)$, by the means of eq_tle, tle_plus and then, recursively, arc_nrtle and tra_nrtle. This corresponds to the following algorithm:

- check if $x = y$; if true, we are done;
- if not, try to prove $\mathsf{nrtle}(x, y)$; to his effect,
  - first try to find an arc $\mathsf{arc}(b, x, y)$ (that is, an assumption saying $x < y$ or $x \leq y$, or a lemma like (L.3') whose conclusion matches the desired values for x and y); if such an arc exists, we are done;
  - if not, try to find an arc $\mathsf{arc}(b, z, y)$ for some z (y is fixed but not z);
    - if a suitable z is found, restart the nrtle search procedure using z instead of y;
    - if a suitable z cannot be found, the search fails.

We cope with strict inequalities by following the same lines. Instead of nrtle above, we use tl (transitive transitive closure of arc for less). Here we have to check that a strict inequality occurs at least once on a chain of inequalities.

Mutual Inductive tl : DD → DD → Prop :=
  lt_tl : $(\forall x, y : \mathsf{DD})\ x <' y \rightarrow \mathsf{tl}(x, y)$ |
  tra_tl : $(\forall b : \mathsf{bool})(x, y, z : \mathsf{DD})\ \mathsf{arc}(b, z, y) \rightarrow \mathsf{tl\_aux}(b, x, z) \rightarrow \mathsf{tl}(x, y)$
with
  tl_aux : bool→ DD → DD →Prop :=
    tl_aux_true : $(\forall x, y : \mathsf{DD})\ \mathsf{nrtle}(x, y) \rightarrow \mathsf{tl\_aux}(\mathsf{true}, x, y)$ |
    tl_aux_false : $(\forall x, y : \mathsf{DD})\ \mathsf{tl}(x, y) \rightarrow \mathsf{tl\_aux}(\mathsf{false}, x, y)$.

The clause tra_tl reads: if there is b and z such that $\mathsf{arc}(b, z, y)$, try to prove $\mathsf{tl\_aux}(b, x, z)$. Then we have two cases. If $z <' y$ ($b = \mathsf{true}$), it is enough to prove $x \leq y$, that is $\mathsf{nrtle}(x, y)$, hence the clause tl_aux_true. If $z \leq' y$ ($b = \mathsf{false}$), we have to prove to prove $x < y$, that is $\mathsf{nt}(x, y)$, hence the clause tl_aux_false.

In order to start the corresponding proof search procedure we use the following theorem:

$$(\forall x, y : \mathsf{DD})\ \mathsf{tl}(x, y) \rightarrow x < y. \tag{T.2}$$

Efficiency. Using automatic search proof for inequalities makes scripts much shorter than without this facility. In the case of ABR conformance control, the script for the core of the correctness proof is now half the size of the manual proof given in [9]—which was fairly detailed for reasons given below (6.1).

However, performances must be good enough. They have dramatically increased with the method explained above. Just to give an example, proving $a < d$ from $a \leq b$, $c < d$, $b+t < u$ and $u \leq c+t$ takes 4s with the new procedure on a PC 486 (33 MHz) under linux, against 83s with the old one. Proving $b < d$ from the same hypotheses takes 1s instead of 12s. This is enough for our needs in this case study (less than 4 minutes for the script of the core).

3 Specifications of the Intended Function

First we state an axiomatic characterization of the intended function Acr, which is formalized in 3.1. Then we aim at giving, in 3.3, a much more convenient (for proofs of I.371 algorithm) computational definition of this function: it is the limit of a sequence of functions (Approx_n), where Approx_n depends on Approx_{n-1} and on $\mathsf{ER}(n)$. To this end we give in 3.2 an axiomatic characterization of (Approx_n). The interesting consequence of theorem (T.3) is that $\mathsf{Acr}(t)$ is equal to $\mathsf{Approx}_n(t)$, where n is the number of the last RM cell seen at date t. Loosely speaking, Approx_n is up to date.

Given the sequence of RM cells (ER_i) whose arrival date are respectively (t_i), the desired allowed cell rate at time t is defined by :

$$\mathsf{Acr}(t) = \max\{\mathsf{ER}_i \mid i \in I(t)\}, \tag{2}$$

where I is the interval defined by :

$$i \in I(t) \quad \text{iff} \quad (t - \tau_2 < t_i \leq t - \tau_3) \vee (t_i \leq t - \tau_2 < t_{i+1})\,. \tag{3}$$

The t_i are taken in increasing order : $t_1 < t_2 < \ldots t_n < \ldots$
The following equivalent characterization of $I(t)$ is easier to handle:

$$i \in I(t) \quad \text{iff} \quad t_i + \tau_3 \leq t < t_{i+1} + \tau_2 \tag{4}$$

The initial (inefficient) ABR conformance control algorithm was a direct computation of Acr according to (2).

3.1 Formalization in Type Theory

Intervals are represented by predicates on nat. We need to characterize the maximum of $\{f(n) \mid P(n)\}$. Such a maximum might not exist, but we still have the uniqueness property. We use an inductive predicate.

Inductive is_max $[f : \mathsf{nat} \to \mathsf{nat}; P : \mathsf{nat} \to \mathsf{Prop}] : \mathsf{nat} \to \mathsf{Prop} :=$
is_max_intro :
$(\forall i : \mathsf{nat})\ P(i) \to$
$((\forall j : \mathsf{nat})\ P(j) \to f(j) \leq f(i)) \to$
$\mathsf{is\_max}(f, P, f(i))$.

The formal specification of the expected value is defined by:

$$\mathsf{In}(t,i) = (t_i + \tau_3 \leq t) \wedge (t < t_{i+1} + \tau_2).$$
$$\mathsf{is\_ACR}(a) = \mathsf{is\_max}(\mathsf{ER}, \mathsf{In}, a).$$

The definition of In corresponds to (4) above, but of course we also proved that the formal definition corresponding to (3) is equivalent.

3.2 Approximations of the Ideal Value of Acr

The incremental computation of Acr (t) is intuitively based on the knowledge we have at instant s about t_i and ER(i). Therefore we consider the nth approximation of In(t), defined by:

Inductive I_a $[n : \text{nat}; t : \text{DD}; i : \text{nat}] : \text{Prop} :=$
  like_In : $i < n \to \text{In}(t,i) \to \text{I\_a}(n,t,i)$ |
  last_Ia : $i = n \to t_i + \tau_3 \leq t \to \text{I\_a}(n,t,i)$.

and we check that this approximation agrees with In for the current time s (in fact for any t less than $s + \tau_3$). We represent the fact that n is the number of the last RM cell received until s by current_last(s, n).

$$\text{current\_last}(s : \text{DD}, n : \text{nat}) = (t_n \leq s) \wedge (s < t_{n+1}).$$

In an environment containing the hypothesis current_last(s, ns), we have the theorem:

$$t \leq s + \tau_3 \to \text{In}(t,i) \leftrightarrow \text{I\_a}(ns,t,i).$$

We can then work with is_Approxn instead of is_ACR:

$$\text{is\_Approxn}(n : \text{nat}, t : \text{DD}) = \text{is\_max}(\text{ER}, \text{I\_a}(n,t)).$$

Theorem:

$$(\forall a : \text{nat})\ \text{is\_ACR}(t,a) \leftrightarrow \text{is\_Approxn}(ns,t,a). \qquad \text{(T.3)}$$

We now give a computational definition of is_Approxn(n).

3.3 Purely Functional Realization

Computing the $n+1^{\text{th}}$ approximation of ACR from the nth turns out quite simple in the functional setting. First we need the maximum of two natural numbers. It is defined in a symmetrical way.

Definition tot_le : $(\forall n, m : \text{nat})\{n \leq m\} + \{m \leq n\}$:= ...
Definition maxb(n, m) := **Case** tot_le(n, m) **of** [_]m [_]n **end**.

Then we define, in an environment where the date t is of type DD:

Fixpoint Approx [n:nat] : nat :=
  if $n = 0$ **then** ER(0)
  else **if** $t < t_n + \tau_3$ **then** Approx($n - 1$)

else

  if $t < t_n + \tau_2$ **then** maxb(Approx $(n-1)$, ER(n))

  else ER(n)

Using Ocaml, for instance, we could propose the following implementation for ABR conformance control:

```
(* initially *)
let ACR = ref fun t ->(ER 0)

(* when a new RM cell (ER n) is received, at (t n) *)
ACR:= let oldA= !ACR in fun t ->
        if t < t n + tau3 then oldA t
        else if t < t n + tau2 then max (oldA t) (ER n)
        else ER n
```

This definition of ACR is not a realistic implementation for obvious reasons, but Approx is a basic tool in the sequel. We check that Approx has the expected behavior (s_0 represents the starting time of the algorithm):

Theorem:

$$s_0 \leq t \rightarrow (\forall n : nat)\ \mathsf{is\_Approxn}(n, t, \mathsf{Approx}(n)). \tag{T.4}$$

And then, using theorem (T.3):

Main theorem:

$$s_0 \leq t \rightarrow (\forall n : nat)\ \mathsf{current\_last}(t, n) \rightarrow \mathsf{is\_ACR}(t, \mathsf{Approx}(n)). \tag{T.5}$$

The proof of (T.4) uses a lemma stating that the nth approximation is a decreasing function for dates greater than $t_n + \tau_3$.

Theorem Approxn_decrease :

$$(\forall n : \mathsf{nat})(t, t' : \mathsf{DD})\ t_{ns} + \tau_3 \leq t\ \rightarrow\ t \leq t'\ \rightarrow$$
$$(\forall a : \mathsf{nat})\ \mathsf{is\_Approxn}(ns, t, a)\ \rightarrow\ (\forall a' : \mathsf{nat})\ \mathsf{is\_Approxn}(ns, t', a')\ \rightarrow\ a' \leq a.$$

Incremental computations of maxima using the binary version are based on the following theorem.

$$(\forall P : \mathsf{nat} \rightarrow \mathsf{Prop})(\forall n : \mathsf{nat})(\forall m : \mathsf{nat})$$
$$\mathsf{is\_max}(P(m)) \rightarrow \mathsf{is\_max}(\lambda.j : nat\ (P(j) \vee (j = n))\mathsf{maxb}(m, f(n))).$$

4 States and Transitions

The device to be represented (called update in Fig. 1) is an automaton whose states are made of a few variables. One of them, ACR, is instantaneously delivered to DGCRA upon request. It is not difficult to see that if an arbitrarily large number of RM cells may be received during an interval of length $\tau_2 - \tau_3$, the theoretical value of ACR cannot be computed with a bounded amount of memory. Hence it is only asked that the actual value of ACR is an upper bound of the theoretical value given above. In order to formalize a system made of the device and of an external clock delivering the current time s (the current number of the last RM cell, n, is also needed), and which is able to deliver a suitable value for ACR, we consider a dependent type including having the shape akin to:

```
Record state : Set := mkstate {
  s : DD;
  n : nat ;
  I_n_s : current_last(s, n) ;
  ACR : nat ; ... (* other fields for a scheduler *)
  I_wanted : Approx(s, n) ≤ ACR ;
}.
```

In fact it is a bit more convenient to consider the state at time s, where s is a parameter, and to split I_n_s (see below the next definition of state). The device reacts to two kinds of events.

- External events: a new RM cell is received; then the scheduler is updated.
- Scheduled events (also called internal events); then the field ACR is updated (and the scheduler too).

In each case the device evolves according to the algorithm given in the standard I.371. Such transitions are formalized here by a function from **state**(s) to **state**(s'), where the new current time is either the arrival date of a RM cell, or a date programmed in the scheduler. This ensures that the invariant of the system is preserved during its evolution.

4.1 Type of States

The algorithm under study uses a two places scheduler. The first scheduled event is "at tfi (fi stands for first), the value of ACR will be Efi", the last scheduled event (tla, Ela) is similar. Ela happens to contain the value of the last ER cell received. As an optimization trick, Emx contains the maximum of Efi and Ela. The wanted invariant is replaced by I_tfs and I_Ub1 (I_wanted is a consequence of I_tfs and I_Ub1, because we have either tfi $\leq s$ or $s <$ tfi; in the first case, apply I_tfs; in the second case, apply I_Ub1 with $t := s$).

```
Record state [s:DD ] : Set := mkstate {
  n : nat ;
  I_ns : t_n ≤ s;
  I_sn : s ≤ t_{n+1};
  ACR, Efi, Ela, Emx : nat ;
  tfi, tla : DD;
  I_max : Emx = maxb(Efi, Ela);
  I_Ela : Ela = ER(n);
```

I_fla : tfi $\leq$ tla;
I_lan : tla $\leq tb_n + \tau_2$;
I_tfs : tfi $\leq s \rightarrow (\forall t : \mathsf{DD}) s \leq t \rightarrow$ Approx$(t, n) \leq$ ACR;
I_Et1 : ACR $<$ Efi $\rightarrow$ tfi $\leq t_n + \tau_3$;
I_Et2 : Efi $<$ Ela $\rightarrow$ tla $\leq t_n + \tau_3$;
I_ttE : tfi = tla $\rightarrow$ Efi = Ela;
I_Ub1 : $(\forall t : \mathsf{DD}) s \leq t \rightarrow t <$ tfi $\rightarrow$ Approx$(t, n) \leq$ ACR;
I_Ub2 : $(\forall t : \mathsf{DD})$tfi $\leq t \rightarrow t <$ tla $\rightarrow$ Approx$(t, n) \leq$ Efi;
I_Ub3 : $(\forall t : \mathsf{DD})$tla $\leq t \rightarrow$ Approx$(t, n) \leq$ Ela
}.

4.2 Updating the State

Let e be the state of the system at date s , n the number of the last RM cell, and let s' be a new date. The algorithm under study computes from e a new value of type state(s'), when s' is either t_{n+1} or tfi(s, e). Formally, we just state and prove a goal of the form state(s'). Then we give the witnesses for ACR(s'), Efi(s'), etc., according to I.371 (see appendix A), and we prove the subgoals corresponding to the preservation of invariants.

For instance, let us sketch the treatment of internal events. The number k is defined as the successor of n. We assume two preconditions, stating that tfi(s, e) is greater or equal to the current time (i.e. the scheduler is not empty) and that the next external event will occur after tfi(s, e). Identifiers XXX_ are an abbreviation for XXX(s, e).

Hypothesis Gi1 : $s_- \leq'$ tfi_.
Hypothesis Gi2 : tfi_ $\leq' t_k$.

Definition subsi : (state tfi_).
(n   ACR   Efi   Ela   Emx   tfi   tla   *)*
Exists n_   Efi_   Ela_   Ela_   Ela_   tla_   tla_ ;
(Discharging various proof obligations *)*
Defined.

The treatment of external events is more complicated, because a number of comparisons are done, for instance between ER(k) and ACR, Efi and Ela; but the principle remains the same.

5 Putting Things Together

A trajectory of the system is an inhabitant of $(\forall s : \mathsf{DD}) s_0 \leq s \rightarrow$ **state**(s). We cannot construct such a function in a direct way: we have no inductive definition for DD. But we only need to formalize the ability to observe the state of the system at an arbitrary date t.

To this end we iterate updating steps, and we consider a last transition that do not change the state (only time progresses) from the date s of the last external or scheduled event occuring before t, to t.

Transitions dates have one of the forms t_n, $t_n + \tau_3$ and $t_n + \tau_2$, where t_n is the arrival date of a RM cell. Hence it is clear that if n RM cells arrive before s (the observation dates we consider are bounded by dates of RM cells; we could as well suppose that (t_n) is divergent, that is, for any date u, there is a k such that $u < t_k$; then we take $u := s$), the number of transitions before s is bounded by $3n + 1$.

In order to build the desired trajectory we put together

- the transition function $\mathcal{T}$ described in sec 4.2, which computes, for s' a new date, the state at s' from the old state at s,
- a function $\mathcal{E}$ representing the environment of the system, more precisely the progress of time: given the sequence (t_n), the current date s, the date of the next scheduled event if any, taken from the state of the system at s, and may be an observation date, $\mathcal{E}$ returns a new date s' compatible with these constraints. This ensures that the preconditions of $\mathcal{T}$ are satisfied at s'.

The evolution of the whole is then given by a sequence of alternating $\mathcal{E}$ and $\mathcal{T}$ applied to the initial state.

Finally, we define the state of the system at a date s using at most $3n + 1$ iterations of $\mathcal{T} \circ \mathcal{E}$ (n defined as above), and we get the value a of ACR delivered by the system at t. Thanks to conservation of the invariant and to theorem (T.5), we check that a is greater or equal to the theoretical value of ACR, as desired.

6 Concluding Remarks

6.1 Relation between the Manual and the Formal Proof

Recall that the formalized proof follows the lines of the manual proof. We remarked by the end of section 2.2 that the script for the core of the correctness proof is half the size of the original proof given in [9]. Of course, the same proof in standard mathematical style would be even shorter. But [9] is definitely *not* a standard piece of mathematics: the proof given there was intended to be readable with as little effort as possible by experts in ATM, hence almost nothing was left implicit excepted arithmetic laws.

Let us compare both approaches—manual or using a automated proof assistant. In the former, the reader has to check a semi-formal specification (based on the three formulae at the beginning of section 3 and on the components ACR, Efi, Ela, tfi and tla of the state similar to the ones given in 4.1) the reasonning based on the purely functional realization presented in 3.3 and a bunch of 80 more or less boring semi-formal proofs.

In the latter he (she) has only to check the specification (3.1), the definition of the state given in 4.1, including the invariants, the definition of transitions and the statement of the theorem saying that I_tfs and I_Ub1 implies I_wanted). On the other hand, a completely formal notation makes formulae slightly harder to read. The way of representing a transition corresponding to an assignment may be considerd unnatural. This objection is attenuated if the external reader believes that the Coq user worked on a fair translation of its problem. Moreover, he can check that two Coq users agree on the meaning of the main sentences.

Another advantage of the automatized approach is that studying a new variant of the algorithm can reuse the already developed framework, and even the specification. Finally, recall that the we can be much more confident in the proof checked by a proof tool (especially when the latter is based on the LCF approach) than in a manual proof. As a matter of fact, one of the last 80 proofs of [9] was false! It did not harm so much, because the statement was still provable, but my opinion is now that manual proofs of complicated algorithms should be systematically considered as suspect.

Alltogether, this experience seems to show that using a proof assistant is the most convincing approach.

6.2 Related Work and Future Directions

The general problem we deal with can be stated as follows. Let (e_n) be a sequence of values arriving respectively at the dates (t_n), and let $a(t)$ be a function whose value depends only on $e_0 \dots e_i$, with $t_0 < \dots < t_i \leq t$. In real-time applications, we want $a(t)$ to be provided very quickly. An efficient strategy is to compute a new approximation of the future values of a each time a new e_i arrives, and to schedule these values. The problem is then to verify that such an algorithm conforms to the theoretical value of $a(t)$.

The author is not aware of other experiments using formal methods in such situations, though much work has already be done for proving temporal properties of algorithms. Some of the most popular techniques are model checking [3], TLA [8] and Unity [2]. Unfortunately the notion of time used there is logical, not quantitative. In contrast, the algorithm considered here handles time in an explicit way by the means of a scheduler. Further work has been done for specifying distributed algorithms having real-time properties like "such event actually occurs before such date", since the early 1990's [1,6]. Certain classes of such systems can be dealt with model checking techniques (see [7] for instance). The notion of temporized automaton on a dense time considered in [7] inflenced our specification.

We saw in 2.2 that automatizing proofs employing transitivity requires some work. An interesting possibility would have been to consider DD = nat in order to take profit of a general tactic like Omega[3], which is able to discharge formulae in Presburger arithmetic. Omega is certainly much more efficient and easy to use than EAuto in our context. But then we would loose the benefits of abstraction mentionned in 2. Let us also remark that it is sometimes useful to understand a proof found by the tool. The written form of the proof terms produced by our technique is exploitable, but is hardly helpful for proofs found by Omega.

The algorithm I.371 has been proposed to other researchers in order to test other formal methods (e.g. temporized automata). This work is going on[4]. On

[3] Omega has been implemented by P. Crégut [4].

[4] This work is supported by action FORMA (MENRT, CNRS, DGA). The work presented in this paper has also been partly done in this framework.

the other hand, we are currently investigating the application of the framework presented here to an algorithm due to Francis Klay, that computes a better approximation of Acr than I.371.

Acknowledgement

The problem has been submitted by Christophe Rabadan, who is the main author of the algorithm. This work has benefited of fruitful discussions with him, Annie Gravey and Francis Klay. Many improvements are due to the comments of anonymous referees.

References

1. R. Alur C. Courcoubetis and D. Dill. Model-Checking for Real-Time Systems. In *5th Symp. on Logic in Compouter Science.* IEEE, 1990.
2. K. M. Chandy and J. Misra. *Parallel Program Design.* Austin, Texas, Addison-Wesley, 1989.
3. D. Clark, E. M. Emerson eand A. P. Sistla. Automatic verification of finite state concurrent systems using temporal logic specifications: a practical approach. *Proc. 10th ACM Symp. on Principles of Programming Languages.* 1983.
4. B. Barras, S. Boutin, C. Cornes, J. Courant, J-C. Filliâtre, E. Giménez, H. Herbelin, G. Huet, P. Manoury, C. Muñoz, C. Murthy, C. Parent, C. Paulin-Mohring, A. Saïbi and B. Werner, The Coq Proof Assistant User's Guide, version 6.1 (INRIA-Rocquencourt et CNRS-ENS Lyon, November 1996)
5. ITU-T Recommendation I.371.1 Traffic control and congestion control in B-ISDN, February 1997
6. E. Harel O. Lichtenstein and A. Pnueli. Explicit clock temporal logic. In *5th Symp. on Logic in Compouter Science.* IEEE, 1990.
7. Thomas A. Henzinger, Xavier Nicollin, Joseph Sifakis, and Sergio Yovine. Symbolic Model Checking for Real-Time Systems, *Information and Computation,* **111** (1994) 193–244
8. L. Lamport. The temporal logic of actions. ACM Transactions on Programming Languages and Systems, **16-3** (1994), 872–923.
9. Jean-François Monin and Francis Klay Formal specification and correction of I.371.1 algorithm for ABR conformance, internal report NT DTL/MSV/003, CNET, 1997

A Algorithm I.371 for ABR conformance

When real time reaches t_k :

```
if tk < tfi then
  if Emx ≤ ERk then                                  (* Emx = max(Efi,Ela) *)
    if tfi < tk+τ3 then
      if tk+τ3 < tla ∨ tfi = tla then
        Emx := ERk || Ela := ERk || tla := tk+τ3      (* simultaneous *)
      else                                            (* assignment   *)
        Emx := ERk || Ela := ERk
    else
      if ACR ≤ ERk then
        Emx := ERk || Efi := ERk || Ela := ERk || tfi := tk+τ3 || tla := tk+τ3
      else
        Emx := ERk || Efi := ERk || Ela := ERk || tla := tfi
  else
    if ERk < Ela then
      Efi := Emx || Ela := ERk || tla := tk+τ2
    else
      Efi := Emx || Ela := ERk
else
  if ACR ≤ ERk then
    Efi := ERk || Ela := ERk || Emx := ERk || tfi := tk+τ3 || tla := tk+τ3
  else
    Efi := ERk || Ela := ERk || Emx := ERk || tfi := tk+τ2 || tla := tk+τ2
```

When real time reaches tfi:

ACR := Efi || tfi := tla || Efi := Ela || Emx := Ela

If tfi $= t_k$, we run the algorithm for tfi, then the algorithm for t_k.

Dependent Types with Explicit Substitutions: A Meta-theoretical development

César Muñoz

INRIA Rocquencourt
B.P. 105
78153 Le Chesnay Cedex, France
E-mail: Cesar.Munoz@inria.fr
Tel: (33) 1 39 63 51 57, Fax: (33) 1 39 63 56 84

Abstract. We present a theory of dependent types with explicit substitutions. We follow a meta-theoretical approach where open expressions —expressions with meta-variables— are first-class objects. The system enjoys properties like type uniqueness, subject reduction, soundness, confluence and weak normalization.

1 Introduction

The Dependent Type theory, namely $\lambda\Pi$, is introduced in [12]. Although full polymorphism or inductive definitions are not considered, the difficulties due to the mutual dependence between terms and types arise already in this theory.

In contrast to the simply-typed case, terms and types in $\lambda\Pi$ are in the same syntactical category. However, terms are stratified in several typing levels called *sorts*. The constants of terms *Type* and *Kind*[1] are used to represent sorts. The stratification of terms by means of sorts is necessary to avoid circular typing judgments as "*Type* : *Type*", which leads to the Girard's paradox. In the $\lambda\Pi$-system, the term *Kind* is used as the valid type of the term *Type*.

The arrow type of the simply-typed theory is generalized by a new binding structure called *product*. It has the following introduction and elimination rules:

$$\frac{\Gamma, x{:}B \vdash M : A}{\Gamma \vdash \lambda x{:}B.M : \Pi x{:}B.A}\ (\text{Pi}) \qquad \frac{\Gamma \vdash M : \Pi x{:}B.A \quad \Gamma \vdash N : B}{\Gamma \vdash (M\ N) : A\{x := N\}}\ (\text{ApplPi})$$

where $A\{x := N\}$ is a notation for the substitution of the free occurrences of x in A by N. Hence, the type $A \to B$ is just a notation for the product $\Pi x{:}A.B$ where x does not appear free in B.

The relation $\xrightarrow{\beta}$ is defined as the contextual closure of the rule β: $(\lambda x{:}A.M\ N) \longrightarrow M\{x := N\}$. The equivalence relation $=_\beta$ is defined as the transitive and reflexive closure of $\xrightarrow{\beta}$. The following typing rule allows to identify terms via the relation $=_\beta$:

[1] These names are not standard, other couples of names used in the literature are: $(Set, Type)$, $(Prop, Type)$ and $(*, \Box)$.

$$\frac{\Gamma \vdash M : A \qquad \Gamma \vdash B : s \quad A =_\beta B}{\Gamma \vdash M : B} \text{(Conv)}$$

where $s \in \{Kind, Type\}$.

Recently, λ-calculi of explicit substitutions have been proposed as a framework for higher-order unification [6, 7, 17] and for representation of incomplete proofs [20, 22]. In these approaches, meta-variables[2] represent unification variables or place-holders in λ-terms.

The $\lambda\sigma$-calculus, proposed in [1], is one of the most popular explicit substitution calculus. It is a first-order rewrite system with two sorts of expressions: terms and substitutions. In this calculus, free and bound variables are represented by de Bruijn's indices and their renaming mechanism is handled by the substitution calculus. The $\lambda\sigma$-calculus is confluent on *semi-open expressions* (expressions with meta-variables of terms but without meta-variables of substitutions) [26], and the simply-typed version of $\lambda\sigma$ is weakly normalizing [1]. Weak normalization even holds on open expressions [11, 23].

As it is pointed out in [1], extensions to the simply-typed version of $\lambda\sigma$ lead to unexpected problems. First, the simply-typed $\lambda\sigma$-calculus does not enjoy the same properties as the simply-typed λ-calculus. For instance, it is well known that $\lambda\sigma$ does not preserve strong normalization [21]. Furthermore, in dependent type theories the notions of well-typed expressions with meta-variables and well-typed substitutions are not simple due to mutual dependences between types and terms.

In a λ-calculus *à la de Bruijn* a context of free-variables is just a list of types where the i-th element is the type of the i-th free variable, and a substitution is a list of terms where the i-th variable is substituted by the i-th term of the substitution. So, it seems natural to type explicit substitutions in $\lambda\sigma$ by contexts. A typing judgment of a substitution in $\lambda\sigma$ has the form: $\Gamma \vdash S \rhd \Delta$, and it can be read as "the substitution S has as type the context Δ in Γ".

Notation: Contrary to the $\lambda\sigma$-tradition, —but just like in usual mathematic notations— we denote the application of a substitution S to a term M by $[S]M$ (and not $M[S]$), the composition of substitutions S and T by $T \circ S$ (and not $S \circ T$), and the simultaneous substitutions by $S.M$ (and not $M.S$). In a similar way, we use reversed lists to represents contexts. An advantage of this notation is that, just as in programming languages, a variable can be used just after its declaration.

Let us take the typing rule for simultaneous substitutions —the (Cons) rule— in a simply-typed $\lambda\sigma$-calculus [1]:

$$\frac{\Gamma \vdash S \rhd \Delta \quad \Gamma \vdash M : A}{\Gamma \vdash S \cdot M \rhd \Delta.A} \text{(Cons)}$$

[2] We use the word "meta-variable" in order to avoid confusion with the variables of λ-calculus.

A dependent-typed version of this rules has the form:

$$\frac{\Gamma \vdash S \triangleright \Delta \quad \Gamma \vdash M : \boxed{[S]A} \quad \Delta \vdash A : \mathit{Type}}{\Gamma \vdash S \cdot M \triangleright \Delta.A} \; (\Pi\text{-Cons})$$

The box in the typing rule emphasizes the fact that the type A depends on S.

Note that when we use the above rule (Π-Cons) in a bottom-up manner, e.g. in type inference algorithms, the type that is given to M, by the inductive application of the procedure, is $[S]A$ (up to conversion). To find $\Delta.A$, which is the type of $S \cdot M$, it is necessary to use a higher-order unification procedure!

Another drawback of (Π-Cons) is that it is not sound with respect to the usual typing properties. In particular, a substitution can be typed with two contexts that are not convertible, i.e. types are not unique modulo conversion. For example consider the context[3]:

$$\Gamma = \mathit{nil}.\ \mathit{nat}{:}\mathit{Type}.\ T{:}\mathit{nat} \rightarrow \mathit{Type}.\ l{:}(\Pi n{:}\mathit{nat}.(T\ n)).\ 0{:}\mathit{nat}$$

and the valid typing judgment

$$\Gamma \vdash (l\ 0) : [n := 0](T\ n) \tag{1}$$

Since $[n := 0](T\ n)$ is convertible to $[n := 0](T\ 0)$, we also have:

$$\Gamma \vdash (l\ 0) : [n := 0](T\ 0) \tag{2}$$

Using (Π-Cons) with $\Gamma \vdash [n := 0] \triangleright \Gamma.\ n{:}\mathit{nat}$ and 1, we get:

$$\Gamma \vdash [n := 0 \cdot y := (l\ 0)] \triangleright \Gamma.\ n{:}\mathit{nat}.\ y{:}(T\ 0)$$

and with $\Gamma \vdash [n := 0] \triangleright \Gamma.\ n{:}\mathit{nat}$ and 2:

$$\Gamma \vdash [n := 0 \cdot y := (l\ 0)] \triangleright \Gamma.\ n{:}\mathit{nat}.\ y{:}(T\ n)$$

Clearly, $(T\ 0)$ and $(T\ n)$ are not convertible.

To solve these problems, we use type annotations in substitutions, in a similar way that Church style λ-calculus —as opposed to Curry style— annotates binder variables in abstractions. The final version of (Π-Cons) has the form:

$$\frac{\Gamma \vdash S \triangleright \Delta \quad \Gamma \vdash M : [S]A}{\Gamma \vdash S \cdot M_{:A} \triangleright \Delta.A} \; (\Pi\text{-Cons})$$

Annotations in substitutions act as reminders of types, and they must be introduced and maintained by the calculus of substitutions.

A different way proposed by Bloo in [2] is to introduce substitutions in context, and to give typing rules to deal with these extended contexts. This solution is similar to type systems with definitions [29, 3], where closures are typeable but

[3] For readability, when discussing examples we use named variables and not de Bruijn's indices. Nevertheless, our formal development uses a de Bruijn nameless notation of variables.

substitutions are not considered as typeable objects. We discuss this approach in the last section.

When we consider annotated substitutions, the system $\lambda\sigma$ may lose the subject reduction property in $\lambda\Pi$ due to the non left-linear rule (SCons): $(S \circ \uparrow) \cdot [S]\mathbf{1}_{:A} \xrightarrow{(SCons)} S$. For instance, take the context

$$\Gamma = nil.\ nat{:}Type.\ T{:}nat \rightarrow Type.\ l{:}(\Pi n{:}nat.(T\ n)).\ 0{:}nat.\ m{:}(T\ 0) \rightarrow nat$$

and the substitution $S = (x := 0_{:nat} \cdot y := (l\ 0)_{:(T\ 0)})$.

We verify that the following typing judgments are valid:

$$\Gamma \vdash S \triangleright \Gamma.\ x{:}nat.\ y{:}(T\ 0) \tag{3}$$

$$\Gamma \vdash (S \circ \uparrow) \cdot [S]\mathbf{1}_{:(T\ x)} \triangleright \Gamma.\ x{:}nat.\ y{:}(T\ x) \tag{4}$$

But also, $(S \circ \uparrow) \cdot [S]\mathbf{1}_{:(T\ x)} \xrightarrow{(SCons)} S$. However, since $(T\ 0)$ and $(T\ x)$ are not convertible: $\Gamma \not\vdash S \triangleright \Gamma.\ x{:}nat.\ y{:}(T\ x)$.

The problem here is not with the typing system but with the substitution calculus. Non-left-linear rules —like (SCons)— are not only harmful for typing, but also they are usually responsible of non-confluence problems [18]. Nadathur [24] has remarked that in $\lambda\sigma$ with semi-open terms the (SCons) rule is admissible when the following scheme of rule is maintained: $\uparrow^{n+1} \cdot [\uparrow^n]\mathbf{1} \xrightarrow{(SCons)} \uparrow^n$, where $\uparrow^n$ is a notation for "$\overbrace{\uparrow \circ \ldots \circ \uparrow}^{n\text{-times}}$". Following this idea, we propose in [23] a new variant of $\lambda\sigma$, namely $\lambda_{\mathcal{L}}$. This calculus has the same general features as $\lambda\sigma$, i.e. a simple, finitary and first-order presentation, but it does not contain the (SCons) rule of $\lambda\sigma$.

This paper is structured as follows. In Section 2 we present a dependent-typed version of $\lambda_{\mathcal{L}}$: the $\lambda\Pi_{\mathcal{L}}$-calculus. Just as the λ-calculus extended with the η-rule which is not confluent on *pre-terms* (terms with type annotations, not necessarily well-typed) but it is on well-typed terms, $\lambda\Pi_{\mathcal{L}}$ is not confluent on pre-expressions, due to type annotations on substitutions, but it is on well-typed expressions. Geuvers proposes in [8] a method to prove confluence for $\beta\eta$-reductions on well-typed λ-terms. In Section 3 we show how to adapt Geuvers' technique to the $\lambda\Pi_{\mathcal{L}}$-calculus. In Section 4 we show the elementary typing properties of $\lambda\Pi_{\mathcal{L}}$: sort soundness, type uniqueness, subject reduction and soundness. In Section 5 we prove weak normalization and Church-Rosser property. As corollary we have the decidability of $\lambda\Pi_{\mathcal{L}}$-conversions. Last section summarizes this work and discuss about related works.

2 $\lambda\Pi_{\mathcal{L}}$-Calculus

As usual in explicit substitution calculi, expressions of $\lambda\Pi_{\mathcal{L}}$ are structured in *Terms* and *Substitutions*. Since we use the left-linear variant of $\lambda\sigma$, the $\lambda_{\mathcal{L}}$-calculus, we add the sort of *Naturals*. As we have said, we consider expressions containing only meta-variables of terms, i.e. semi-open expressions. If $\lambda\Pi_{\mathcal{L}}$ is defined as a first-order algebra on a set χ of variables of terms where substitutions and naturals are constants, the meta-variables of $\lambda\Pi_{\mathcal{L}}$ are just the elements of χ.

Formally, the set $\Lambda\Pi_{\mathcal{L}}$ of well-formed pre-expressions is defined by the following grammar:

Naturals	n	$::=$	$0 \mid Succ(n)$
Meta-variables	χ	$::=$	$X \mid Y \mid \ldots$
Terms	M, N	$::=$	$Kind \mid Type \mid \mathbf{1} \mid \Pi_M.N \mid \lambda_M.N \mid (M\ N) \mid [S]M \mid \chi$
Substitutions	S, T	$::=$	$\uparrow^n \mid S \cdot M_{:N} \mid T \circ S$

The equivalence relation $=_{\lambda\Pi_{\mathcal{L}}}$ is defined as the symmetric and transitive closure of the rewrite system in Fig. 1. The system $\Pi_{\mathcal{L}}$ is obtained by dropping the (Beta) rule from $\lambda\Pi_{\mathcal{L}}$. The $\lambda\Pi_{\mathcal{L}}$-calculus does not handle the η-rule.

$(\lambda_{M'}.M\ N)$	$\longrightarrow$	$[\uparrow^0 \cdot N_{:M'}]M$	(Beta)
$[S](\lambda_M.N)$	$\longrightarrow$	$\lambda_{[S]M}.[(\uparrow^{Succ(0)} \circ S) \cdot \mathbf{1}_{:M}]N$	(Lambda)
$[S](\Pi_M.N)$	$\longrightarrow$	$\Pi_{[S]M}.[(\uparrow^{Succ(0)} \circ S) \cdot \mathbf{1}_{:M}]N$	(Pi)
$[S](M\ N)$	$\longrightarrow$	$([S]M\ [S]N)$	(Application)
$[T][S]M$	$\longrightarrow$	$[T \circ S]M$	(Clos)
$[S \cdot M_{:N}]\mathbf{1}$	$\longrightarrow$	M	(VarCons)
$[\uparrow^0]M$	$\longrightarrow$	M	(Id)
$T \circ (S \cdot M_{:N})$	$\longrightarrow$	$(T \circ S) \cdot [T]M_{:N}$	(Map)
$S \circ \uparrow^0$	$\longrightarrow$	S	(IdS)
$(S \cdot M_{:N}) \circ \uparrow^{Succ(n)}$	$\longrightarrow$	$S \circ \uparrow^n$	(ShiftCons)
$\uparrow^m \circ \uparrow^{Succ(n)}$	$\longrightarrow$	$\uparrow^{Succ(m)} \circ \uparrow^n$	(ShiftShift)
$\uparrow^{Succ(0)} \cdot \mathbf{1}_{:M}$	$\longrightarrow$	$\uparrow^0$	(Shift0)
$\uparrow^{Succ(n)} \cdot [\uparrow^n]\mathbf{1}_{:M}$	$\longrightarrow$	$\uparrow^n$	(ShiftS)
$[S]\,Type$	$\longrightarrow$	$Type$	(Type)

Fig. 1. The $\lambda\Pi_{\mathcal{L}}$-rewrite system

Next property has been proved by Hans Zantema [34] using the semantic labelling technique proposed in [33].

Proposition 1. *The $\Pi_{\mathcal{L}}$-calculus is terminating.*

The main operation on meta-variables is *instantiation*. The instantiation of the meta-variable X with a term M in an arbitrary expression e (where e is a term or a substitution), denoted by $e\{X/M\}$, replaces all the occurrences of X in e by M. So, in contrast to the substitution mechanism, instantiation allows capture of free variables. Notice also that instantiation is an atomic and external operation.

We use a context with names, called *signature*, to declare meta-variables. A *meta-variable declaration* has the form $X\colon_{\Gamma} M$, where Γ and M are, respectively, a context and a type associated to the meta-variable X.

Definition 2 Contexts and Signatures. Well formed *contexts* and *signatures* are defined by the following grammar:

$$\begin{array}{lll} \textbf{Contexts} & \Gamma & ::= \; nil \mid \Gamma.M \\ \textbf{Signatures} & \Sigma & ::= \; nil \mid \Sigma.\, X\colon_{\Gamma} M \end{array}$$

We consider typing assertions having one of the following forms:

* $\vdash \Sigma :\cdot \Gamma$, the context Γ is valid in the signature Σ.
* $\Sigma :\cdot \Gamma \vdash M : N$, the term M has type N in $\Sigma :\cdot \Gamma$.
* $\Sigma :\cdot \Gamma \vdash S \rhd \Delta$, the substitution S has as type the context Δ in $\Sigma :\cdot \Gamma$.

In dependent type theories, meta-variables may appear in types and in contexts. Hence, we need scoping rules for meta-variables and variables.

* In the typing assertion $\vdash \Sigma_1.\, X\colon_{\Gamma} M.\, \Sigma_2 :\cdot \Delta$, the context Γ and the term M can use all the meta-variables declared in Σ_1, the indices in M are relative to Γ, and the context Δ can use all the meta-variables declared in the signature $\Sigma_1.\, X\colon_{\Gamma} M.\, \Sigma_2$.
* In the typing assertions $\Sigma :\cdot \Gamma \vdash M : N$ and $\Sigma :\cdot \Gamma \vdash S \rhd \Delta$, the terms M, N, the substitution S and the context Δ can use all the meta-variables declared in Σ, and the indices in M, N and S are relative to Γ.

Notation:

- We use $\vdash \Sigma$, $\vdash \Gamma$, $\Gamma \vdash M : N$, and $\Gamma \vdash S \rhd \Delta$ as notations for $\vdash \Sigma :\cdot nil$, $\vdash nil :\cdot \Gamma$, $nil :\cdot \Gamma \vdash M : N$, and $nil :\cdot \Gamma \vdash S \rhd \Delta$, respectively.
- We use the lowercase letter s to range over the set of sorts $\{Kind, Type\}$.
- The expression "$X \notin \Sigma$" means that the meta-variable X is not declared in Σ, i.e. there is no context Γ and term M such that $X\colon_{\Gamma} M \in \Sigma$.

Typing rules for signatures, contexts, terms and substitutions are all mutually dependent.

Valid Signatures and Contexts

$$\frac{}{\vdash nil :\cdot nil}\ (\text{Empty}) \qquad\qquad \frac{\Sigma :\cdot \Gamma \vdash M : s}{\vdash \Sigma :\cdot \Gamma.M}\ (\text{Var-Decl})$$

$$\frac{\Sigma :\cdot \Gamma \vdash M : s \quad X \notin \Sigma}{\vdash \Sigma.\, X\colon_{\Gamma} M}\ (\text{Metavar-Decl})$$

Valid Terms

$$\frac{\vdash \Sigma :\cdot \Gamma}{\Sigma :\cdot \Gamma \vdash \mathit{Type} : \mathit{Kind}} \text{(Type)}$$

$$\frac{\Sigma :\cdot \Gamma \vdash M : \mathit{Type} \quad \Sigma :\cdot \Gamma.M \vdash N : s}{\Sigma :\cdot \Gamma \vdash \Pi_M.N : s} \text{(Prod)}$$

$$\frac{\Sigma :\cdot \Gamma \vdash S \rhd \Delta \quad \Sigma :\cdot \Delta \vdash M : \mathit{Kind}}{\Sigma :\cdot \Gamma \vdash [S]M : \mathit{Kind}} \text{(Clos-Kind)}$$

$$\frac{\vdash \Sigma :\cdot \Gamma.M}{\Sigma :\cdot \Gamma.M \vdash \mathbf{1} : [\uparrow^{Succ(0)}]M} \text{(Var)}$$

$$\frac{\Sigma :\cdot \Gamma \vdash M : \Pi_{M_1}.M_2 \quad \Sigma :\cdot \Gamma \vdash N : M_1}{\Sigma :\cdot \Gamma \vdash (M\ N) : [\uparrow^0 \cdot N_{:M_1}]M_2} \text{(Appl)}$$

$$\frac{\Sigma :\cdot \Gamma \vdash S \rhd \Delta \quad \Sigma :\cdot \Delta \vdash M : N \quad \Sigma :\cdot \Delta \vdash N : s}{\Sigma :\cdot \Gamma \vdash [S]M : [S]N} \text{(Clos)}$$

$$\frac{\vdash \Sigma :\cdot \Gamma \quad X :_\Delta M \in \Sigma \quad \Delta =_{\lambda \Pi_{\mathcal{L}}} \Gamma}{\Sigma :\cdot \Gamma \vdash X : M} \text{(Metavar)}$$

$$\frac{\Sigma :\cdot \Gamma \vdash M_1 : \mathit{Type} \quad \Sigma :\cdot \Gamma.M_1 \vdash M_2 : N \quad \Sigma :\cdot \Gamma \vdash \Pi_{M_1}.N : s}{\Sigma :\cdot \Gamma \vdash \lambda_{M_1}.M_2 : \Pi_{M_1}.N} \text{(Abs)}$$

$$\frac{\Sigma :\cdot \Gamma \vdash M : M_1 \quad \Sigma :\cdot \Gamma \vdash M_2 : s \quad M_1 =_{\lambda \Pi_{\mathcal{L}}} M_2}{\Sigma :\cdot \Gamma \vdash M : M_2} \text{(Conv)}$$

Valid Substitutions

$$\frac{\vdash \Sigma :\cdot \Gamma}{\Sigma :\cdot \Gamma \vdash \uparrow^0 \rhd \Gamma} \text{(Id)} \qquad \frac{\vdash \Sigma :\cdot \Gamma.M \quad \Sigma :\cdot \Gamma \vdash \uparrow^n \rhd \Delta}{\Sigma :\cdot \Gamma.M \vdash \uparrow^{Succ(n)} \rhd \Delta} \text{(Shift)}$$

$$\frac{\Sigma :\cdot \Gamma \vdash S \rhd \Delta' \quad \Sigma :\cdot \Delta' \vdash T \rhd \Delta}{\Sigma :\cdot \Gamma \vdash S \circ T \rhd \Delta} \text{(Comp)}$$

$$\frac{\Sigma :\cdot \Gamma \vdash S \rhd \Delta \quad \Sigma :\cdot \Gamma \vdash M : [S]N \quad \Sigma :\cdot \Delta \vdash N : \mathit{Type}}{\Sigma :\cdot \Gamma \vdash S \cdot M_{:N} \rhd \Delta.N} \text{(Cons)}$$

$$\frac{\Sigma :\cdot \Gamma \vdash S \rhd \Delta \quad \vdash \Sigma :\cdot \Delta' \quad \Delta =_{\lambda \Pi_{\mathcal{L}}} \Delta'}{\Sigma :\cdot \Gamma \vdash S \rhd \Delta'} \text{(Conv-Subs)}$$

Remark 3. Since there is no typing rules for *Kind*, the term *Kind* does not occur as sub-term of a well-typed expression.

The application of instantiations to contexts and signatures, i.e. $\Gamma\{X/M\}$ and $\Sigma\{X/M\}$, is defined in the obvious way.

Lemma 4 Instantiation Soundness. *Let M be a term such that $\Sigma' :\cdot \Gamma \vdash M : N$, and Σ a signature having the form $\Sigma'.\, X :_{\Gamma} N.\, \Sigma''$,*

1. *if $\vdash \Sigma :\cdot \Delta$, then $\vdash \Sigma'.\, \Sigma''\{X/M\} :\cdot \Delta\{X/M\}$,*
2. *if $\Sigma :\cdot \Delta \vdash M' : N'$, then $\Sigma'.\, \Sigma''\{X/M\} :\cdot \Delta\{X/M\} \vdash M'\{X/M\} : N'\{X/M\}$, and*
3. *if $\Sigma :\cdot \Delta \vdash S \triangleright \Delta'$, then $\Sigma'.\, \Sigma''\{X/M\} :\cdot \Delta\{X/M\} \vdash S\{X/M\} \triangleright \Delta'\{X/M\}$.*

Proof. By induction on typing derivation. □

The use of annotated substitutions in $\lambda\Pi_{\mathcal{L}}$ allows to keep the right type when a substitution goes through an abstraction or a product. However, annotated substitutions raise a technical problem: The $\lambda\Pi_{\mathcal{L}}$-calculus is not confluent on pre-expressions. The problem exists even if we only consider local confluence on ground terms. In fact, the following critical pair is not joinable in the general case, e.g. assume N and N' to be different ground $\lambda\Pi_{\mathcal{L}}$-normal forms:

$$(S \cdot M_{:N'}) \circ (\uparrow^{Succ(0)} \cdot \mathbf{1}_{:N})$$

$$\swarrow \text{(Shift0;IdS)} \qquad \qquad \text{(Map;VarCons;ShiftCons;IdS)} \searrow$$

$$S \cdot M_{:N'} \qquad\qquad\qquad\qquad S \cdot M_{:N}$$

This problem is similar to that pointed out by Nederpelt for the λ-calculus extended with the η-rule. In that case, the confluence property holds on terms without type annotations (λ-calculus in Curry style), but does not on pre-terms (λ-calculus in Church style). Geuvers proposes in [8] a method to prove confluence for $\beta\eta$-reduction on typed λ-terms written in Church style. In the next section we adapt this technique in order to prove the main typing properties of $\lambda\Pi_{\mathcal{L}}$.

3 Geuvers' Lemma

The Geuvers' lemma is a weak form of the Church-Rosser property which suffices to prove the main typing properties in systems where confluence on terms with typing annotations —i.e in Church style— is not available. Geuvers' technique uses a positive reformulation of the counter-example of non-confluence, and the fact that the underlying calculus of terms without typing annotations —i.e. in Curry style— is confluent.

The underlying Curry style of $\lambda\Pi_{\mathcal{L}}$ is called $\lambda\Pi_{\mathcal{L}}^{\square}$. In this calculus substitutions do not have typing annotations (but abstractions keep their type annotations). Thus, we define the set $\Lambda\Pi_{\mathcal{L}}^{\square}$ of well-formed semi-open expressions just like $\Lambda\Pi_{\mathcal{L}}$ but where substitutions have the following grammar:

$$\textbf{Substitutions } S, T \ ::= \ \uparrow^n \mid S \cdot M \mid T \circ S$$

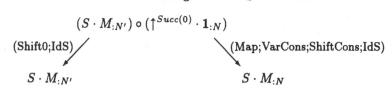

$(\lambda_{M'}.M\ N)$	$\longrightarrow$	$[\uparrow^{0}\cdot N]M$	(Beta)
$[S](\lambda_{M}.N)$	$\longrightarrow$	$\lambda_{[S]M}.[(\uparrow^{Succ(0)}\circ S)\cdot \mathbf{1}]N$	(Lambda)
$[S](\Pi_{M}.N)$	$\longrightarrow$	$\Pi_{[S]M}.[(\uparrow^{Succ(0)}\circ S)\cdot \mathbf{1}]N$	(Pi)
$[S\cdot M]\mathbf{1}$	$\longrightarrow$	M	(VarCons)
$T\circ(S\cdot M)$	$\longrightarrow$	$(T\circ S)\cdot[T]M$	(Map)
$(S\cdot M)\circ\uparrow^{Succ(n)}$	$\longrightarrow$	$S\circ\uparrow^{n}$	(ShiftCons)
$\uparrow^{Succ(0)}\cdot\mathbf{1}$	$\longrightarrow$	$\uparrow^{0}$	(Shift0)
$\uparrow^{Succ(n)}\cdot[\uparrow^{n}]\mathbf{1}$	$\longrightarrow$	$\uparrow^{n}$	(ShiftS)

Fig. 2. Modified rules in the $\lambda\Pi_{\mathcal{L}}^{\Box}$-rewrite system

The rewrite system $\lambda\Pi_{\mathcal{L}}^{\Box}$ is obtained by affecting the reduction system $\lambda\Pi_{\mathcal{L}}$ as shown in Fig. 2.

Termination of the $\Pi_{\mathcal{L}}^{\Box}$-calculus —$\lambda\Pi_{\mathcal{L}}^{\Box}$ without (Beta)— can be derived directly from the termination property of the $\Pi_{\mathcal{L}}$-calculus (Proposition 1).

Proposition 5. *$\Pi_{\mathcal{L}}^{\Box}$ is a terminating rewrite system.*

Lemma 6 Confluence of $\Pi_{\mathcal{L}}^{\Box}$. *The $\Pi_{\mathcal{L}}^{\Box}$-calculus is confluent on $\Lambda\Pi_{\mathcal{L}}^{\Box}$.*

Proof. We check mechanically, for example using the RRL system [16], that $\Pi_{\mathcal{L}}^{\Box}$ has the following critical pairs:

- **(Id-Clos).** $[S]M \xleftarrow{\Pi_{\mathcal{L}}^{\Box+}} [\uparrow^{0}][S]M \xrightarrow{\Pi_{\mathcal{L}}^{\Box+}} [\uparrow^{0}\circ S]M$.
- **(Clos-Clos).** $[T'\circ(T\circ S)]M \xleftarrow{\Pi_{\mathcal{L}}^{\Box+}} [T'][T][S]M \xrightarrow{\Pi_{\mathcal{L}}^{\Box+}} [(T'\circ T)\circ S]M$.
- **(Shift0-Map).** $S \xleftarrow{\Pi_{\mathcal{L}}^{\Box+}} S\circ(\uparrow^{Succ(0)}\cdot\mathbf{1}) \xrightarrow{\Pi_{\mathcal{L}}^{\Box}} (S\circ\uparrow^{Succ(0)})\cdot[S]\mathbf{1}$.
- **(ShiftS-Map).** $S\circ\uparrow^{n} \xleftarrow{\Pi_{\mathcal{L}}^{\Box}} S\circ(\uparrow^{Succ(n)}\cdot[\uparrow^{n}]\mathbf{1}) \xrightarrow{\Pi_{\mathcal{L}}^{\Box+}} (S\circ\uparrow^{Succ(n)}).[S\circ\uparrow^{n}]\mathbf{1}$.
- **(Lambda-Clos).** $\lambda_{[T\circ S]M'}.[(((\uparrow^{Succ(0)}\circ T)\cdot\mathbf{1})\circ(\uparrow^{Succ(0)}\circ S))\cdot\mathbf{1}]M$ $\xleftarrow{\Pi_{\mathcal{L}}^{\Box+}} [T][S](\lambda_{M'}.M) \xrightarrow{\Pi_{\mathcal{L}}^{\Box+}} \lambda_{[T\circ S]M'}.[(\uparrow^{Succ(0)}\circ(T\circ S))\cdot\mathbf{1}]M$.
- **(Pi-Clos).** $\Pi_{[T\circ S]M'}.[(((\uparrow^{Succ(0)}\circ T)\cdot\mathbf{1})\circ(\uparrow^{Succ(0)}\circ S))\cdot\mathbf{1}]N'$ $\xleftarrow{\Pi_{\mathcal{L}}^{\Box+}} [T][S](\Pi_{M'}.N') \xrightarrow{\Pi_{\mathcal{L}}^{\Box+}} \Pi_{[T\circ S]M'}.[(\uparrow^{Succ(0)}\circ(T\circ S))\cdot\mathbf{1}]N'$.

These critical pairs are $\Pi_{\mathcal{L}}^{\Box}$-joinable on $\Lambda\Pi_{\mathcal{L}}^{\Box}$. Using the same arguments that [23] and the extensions to the Critical Pair's Lemma proposed by [15] and [28], we conclude that $\Pi_{\mathcal{L}}^{\Box}$ is locally confluent. Therefore, by Newman's lemma and Proposition 5, $\Pi_{\mathcal{L}}^{\Box}$ is confluent on $\Lambda\Pi_{\mathcal{L}}^{\Box}$. □

Confluence's proof of the $\lambda\Pi_{\mathcal{L}}^{\Box}$-calculus uses a general method coined in [32] to prove confluence of abstract relations: the Yokouchi-Hikita's Lemma. This method avers to be suitable for left-linear calculi of explicit substitutions [5, 25, 23].

Lemma 7 Yokouchi-Hikita's Lemma. *Let R and S be two relations defined on a set X such that: 1. R is confluent and terminating, 2. S is strongly confluent and 3. S and R commute in the following way: for any $x, y, z \in X$, if $x \xrightarrow{R} y$ and $x \xrightarrow{S} z$, then there exists $w \in X$ such that $y \xrightarrow{R^*SR^*} w$ and $z \xrightarrow{R^*} w$. Then the relation R^*SR^* is confluent.*

Proof. See [5]. □

We take the set $\Lambda\Pi_{\mathcal{L}}^{\square}$ as X, $\Pi_{\mathcal{L}}^{\square}$ as R and $B_{\|}$ as S, where $B_{\|}$ is the parallelization of (Beta) defined by:

$$\frac{}{x \longrightarrow x}\ (\text{Refl}_{\|}) \qquad \frac{M \longrightarrow M' \quad N \longrightarrow N'}{\lambda_M.N \longrightarrow \lambda_{M'}.N'}\ (\text{Lambda}_{\|})$$

$$\frac{M \longrightarrow M' \quad N \longrightarrow N'}{\Pi_M.N \longrightarrow \Pi_{M'}.N'}\ (\text{Pi}_{\|}) \qquad \frac{M \longrightarrow N \quad S \longrightarrow T}{[S]M \longrightarrow [T]N}\ (\text{Clos}_{\|})$$

$$\frac{M \longrightarrow M' \quad N \longrightarrow N'}{(M\ N) \longrightarrow (M'\ N')}\ (\text{Application}_{\|}) \qquad \frac{M \longrightarrow N \quad S \longrightarrow T}{S \cdot M \longrightarrow T \cdot N}\ (\text{Cons}_{\|})$$

$$\frac{S \longrightarrow S' \quad T \longrightarrow T'}{T \circ S \longrightarrow T' \circ S'}\ (\text{Comp}_{\|}) \qquad \frac{M \longrightarrow M' \quad N \longrightarrow N'}{(\lambda_{M''}.M\ N) \longrightarrow [\uparrow^0 \cdot N']M'}\ (\text{Beta}_{\|})$$

Lemma 8. *$\Pi_{\mathcal{L}}^{\square}$ commutes over $B_{\|}$, i.e. if x reduces in one $\Pi_{\mathcal{L}}^{\square}$-step to y, and in one $B_{\|}$-step to z, then there exists w such that $y \xrightarrow{\Pi_{\mathcal{L}}^{\square *} B_{\|} \Pi_{\mathcal{L}}^{\square *}} w$ and $z \xrightarrow{\Pi_{\mathcal{L}}^{\square *}} w$.*

Proof. By cases analysis on the redexes. □

Theorem 9 Confluence. *The $\lambda\Pi_{\mathcal{L}}^{\square}$-calculus is confluent on $\Lambda\Pi_{\mathcal{L}}^{\square}$.*

Proof. We verify that $\Pi_{\mathcal{L}}^{\square}$ and $B_{\|}$ satisfy the conditions of the Yokouchi-Hikita's lemma, e.g.

1. $\Pi_{\mathcal{L}}^{\square}$ is terminating and confluent (Proposition 5 and Lemma 6).
2. $B_{\|}$ is strongly confluent, since (Beta) by itself is a left linear system with no critical pairs (c.f. [13]).
3. $\Pi_{\mathcal{L}}^{\square}$ commutes over $B_{\|}$ (Lemma 8).

Therefore, $\Pi_{\mathcal{L}}^{\square *} B_{\|} \Pi_{\mathcal{L}}^{\square *}$ is confluent on $\Lambda\Pi_{\mathcal{L}}^{\square}$.

Note that $\lambda\Pi_{\mathcal{L}}^{\square} \subseteq \Pi_{\mathcal{L}}^{\square *} B_{\|} \Pi_{\mathcal{L}}^{\square *} \subseteq \lambda\Pi_{\mathcal{L}}{}^*$. Let x be a semi-open expressions, if $x \xrightarrow{\lambda\Pi_{\mathcal{L}}{}^*} y$ and $x \xrightarrow{\lambda\Pi_{\mathcal{L}}{}^*} z$, then there exists w such that $y \xrightarrow{(\Pi_{\mathcal{L}}^{\square *} B_{\|} \Pi_{\mathcal{L}}^{\square *})^*} w$ and $z \xrightarrow{(\Pi_{\mathcal{L}}^{\square *} B_{\|} \Pi_{\mathcal{L}}^{\square *})^*} w$. So, $y \xrightarrow{\lambda\Pi_{\mathcal{L}}{}^*} w$ and $z \xrightarrow{\lambda\Pi_{\mathcal{L}}{}^*} w$. □

Definition 10. The erasing map $|.| : \Lambda\Pi_{\mathcal{L}} \to \Lambda\Pi_{\mathcal{L}}^{\square}$ is defined as follows:

$$\begin{array}{lll}
|x| & = x & \text{if } x \in \{\mathbf{1}, \mathit{Type}, \mathit{Kind}\} \text{ or } x \text{ is a meta-variable} \\
|\Pi_M.N| & = \Pi_{|M|}.|N| & \\
|\lambda_M.N| & = \lambda_{|M|}.|N| & \\
|(M\ N)| & = (|M|\ |N|) & \\
|[S]M| & = [|S|]|M| & \\
|\uparrow^n| & = \uparrow^n & \\
|T \circ S| & = |T| \circ |S| & \\
|S \cdot M_{:N}| & = |S| \cdot |M| &
\end{array}$$

Definition 11. Let M be a term in $\Lambda\Pi_{\mathcal{L}}$, the annotation map $(.)^{\underline{M}} : \Lambda\Pi_{\mathcal{L}}^{\square} \to \Lambda\Pi_{\mathcal{L}}$ is defined as follows:

$$\begin{array}{lll}
x^{\underline{M}} & = x & \text{if } x \in \{\mathbf{1}, \mathit{Type}, \mathit{Kind}\} \text{ or } x \text{ is a meta-variable} \\
(\Pi_{M'}.N')^{\underline{M}} & = \Pi_{M'^{\underline{M}}}.N'^{\underline{M}} & \\
(\lambda_{M'}.N')^{\underline{M}} & = \lambda_{M'^{\underline{M}}}.N'^{\underline{M}} & \\
(M'\ N')^{\underline{M}} & = (M'^{\underline{M}}\ N'^{\underline{M}}) & \\
([S]N)^{\underline{M}} & = [S^{\underline{M}}]N^{\underline{M}} & \\
(\uparrow^n)^{\underline{M}} & = \uparrow^n & \\
(T \circ S)^{\underline{M}} & = T^{\underline{M}} \circ S^{\underline{M}} & \\
(S \cdot M')^{\underline{M}} & = S^{\underline{M}} \cdot M'^{\underline{M}}{}_{:M} &
\end{array}$$

Following [8], we use a positive formulation of the counter-example of confluence on pre-expressions.

Lemma 12 Positive Counter-example. *Let x and y be expressions in $\Lambda\Pi_{\mathcal{L}}$, if $|x| = |y|$, then $x =_{\Pi_{\mathcal{L}}} y$, and therefore, $x =_{\lambda\Pi_{\mathcal{L}}} y$.*

Proof. By definition of $|.|$, we have that if $|x| = |y|$, then x and y have the same principal constructor. Now, we proceed by structural induction on x. If $x = \lambda_{M'}.M$, $y = \lambda_{N'}.N$ and $|x| = |y|$, then by definition, $\lambda_{|M'|}.|M| = \lambda_{|N'|}.|N|$ and so, $|M'| = |N'|$ and $|M| = |N|$. By induction hypothesis, $M' =_{\Pi_{\mathcal{L}}} N'$ and $M =_{\Pi_{\mathcal{L}}} N$. The only interesting case is when $x = S \cdot M_{:M'}$ and $y = T \cdot N_{:N'}$. We get by induction hypothesis:

$$M =_{\Pi_{\mathcal{L}}} N \tag{5}$$

$$S =_{\Pi_{\mathcal{L}}} T \tag{6}$$

Note that the function $|.|$ erases typing annotations from substitutions, thus we do not have $M' =_{\Pi_{\mathcal{L}}} N'$. However, using the counter-example, we have

$$S \cdot M_{:N'} \xleftarrow{\Pi_{\mathcal{L}}^*} (S \cdot M_{:N'}) \circ (\uparrow^{Succ(0)} \cdot \mathbf{1}_{:M'}) \xrightarrow{\Pi_{\mathcal{L}}^*} S \cdot M_{:M'}$$

We conclude with equations 5 and 6, that $x = S \cdot M_{:M'} =_{\Pi_{\mathcal{L}}} S \cdot M_{:N'} =_{\Pi_{\mathcal{L}}} T \cdot N_{:N'} = y$. □

Lemma 13. *Let x and y be expressions in $\Lambda\Pi_{\mathcal{L}}$ and w be an expression in $\Lambda\Pi_{\mathcal{L}}^{\square}$, then*

1. *(a) If* $x \xrightarrow{\lambda\Pi_{\mathcal{L}}} y$*, then (* $|x| \xrightarrow{\lambda\Pi^{\square}_{\mathcal{L}}} |y|$ *or* $|x| = |y|$*), and (b) if* $x \xrightarrow{\Pi_{\mathcal{L}}} y$*, then (* $|x| \xrightarrow{\Pi^{\square}_{\mathcal{L}}} |y|$ *or* $|x| = |y|$*).*
2. *(a) If* $|x| \xrightarrow{\lambda\Pi^{\square}_{\mathcal{L}}} w$*, then there exists* w' *in* $\lambda\Pi_{\mathcal{L}}$ *such that* $x \xrightarrow{\lambda\Pi_{\mathcal{L}}} w'$ *and* $|w'| = w$*, and (b) if* $|x| \xrightarrow{\Pi^{\square}_{\mathcal{L}}} w$*, then there exists* w' *in* $\lambda\Pi_{\mathcal{L}}$ *such that* $x \xrightarrow{\Pi_{\mathcal{L}}} w'$ *and* $|w'| = w$*.*

Proof. By structural induction on x. □

Corollary 14. *(a) If* x *is a* $\lambda\Pi_{\mathcal{L}}$*-normal form then* $|x|$ *is a* $\lambda\Pi^{\square}_{\mathcal{L}}$*-normal form, and (b) if* x *is a* $\Pi_{\mathcal{L}}$*-normal form then* $|x|$ *is a* $\Pi^{\square}_{\mathcal{L}}$*-normal form.*

Lemma 15. *Let* x *be an expression in* $\Lambda\Pi_{\mathcal{L}}$ *and* M *be a term in* $\Lambda\Pi_{\mathcal{L}}$*,* $x =_{\lambda\Pi_{\mathcal{L}}} |x|^{\underline{M}}$*.*

Proof. By structural induction on x. □

Lemma 16. *Let* x *and* y *be expressions in* $\Lambda\Pi^{\square}_{\mathcal{L}}$ *and* M *be a term in* $\Lambda\Pi_{\mathcal{L}}$*, if* $x \xrightarrow{\lambda\Pi^{\square}_{\mathcal{L}}} y$*, then* $x^{\underline{M}} =_{\lambda\Pi_{\mathcal{L}}} y^{\underline{M}}$*. Therefore, if* $x \xrightarrow{\lambda\Pi^{\square *}_{\mathcal{L}}} y$*, then* $x^{\underline{M}} =_{\lambda\Pi_{\mathcal{L}}} y^{\underline{M}}$*.*

Proof. By induction on the depth of the $\lambda\Pi^{\square}_{\mathcal{L}}$-redex reduced in x. □

Theorem 17 Geuvers' Lemma. *Let* M_1*,* N_1*,* M_2 *and* N_2 *be in* $\Lambda\Pi_{\mathcal{L}}$*,*

1. *if* $\Pi_{M_1}.N_1 =_{\lambda\Pi_{\mathcal{L}}} \Pi_{M_2}.N_2$*, then* $M_1 =_{\lambda\Pi_{\mathcal{L}}} M_2$ *and* $N_1 =_{\lambda\Pi_{\mathcal{L}}} N_2$*, and*
2. *if* $M_1 =_{\lambda\Pi_{\mathcal{L}}} M_2$*, where* M_2 *is a* $\lambda\Pi_{\mathcal{L}}$*-normal form, then there exists* M' *in* $\lambda\Pi_{\mathcal{L}}$ *such that* $M_1 \xrightarrow{\lambda\Pi_{\mathcal{L}}^*} M'$ *and* $|M'| = |M_2|$*.*

Proof. We show only the first case, since the second is very similar.

By Lemma 13(1) and definition of $|.|$, $\Pi_{|M_1|}.|N_1| =_{\lambda\Pi^{\square}_{\mathcal{L}}} \Pi_{|M_2|}.|N_2|$. Since $\lambda\Pi^{\square}_{\mathcal{L}}$ is confluent on semi-open expressions (Theorem 9), there exists M' in $\lambda\Pi^{\square}_{\mathcal{L}}$ such that $\Pi_{|M_1|}.|N_1| \xrightarrow{\lambda\Pi^{\square *}_{\mathcal{L}}} M'$ and $\Pi_{|M_2|}.|N_2| \xrightarrow{\lambda\Pi^{\square *}_{\mathcal{L}}} M'$. But there are not a $\lambda\Pi^{\square}_{\mathcal{L}}$-redex with the form $\Pi_x.y$, so M' has the form $\Pi_M.N$ where $|M_1| \xrightarrow{\lambda\Pi^{\square *}_{\mathcal{L}}} M$, $|N_1| \xrightarrow{\lambda\Pi^{\square *}_{\mathcal{L}}} N$, $|M_2| \xrightarrow{\lambda\Pi^{\square *}_{\mathcal{L}}} M$ and $|N_2| \xrightarrow{\lambda\Pi^{\square *}_{\mathcal{L}}} N$. By Lemma 15 and Lemma 16, for any $\lambda\Pi_{\mathcal{L}}$-term N', $M_1 =_{\lambda\Pi_{\mathcal{L}}} |M_1|^{\underline{N'}} =_{\lambda\Pi_{\mathcal{L}}} M^{\underline{N'}}$, $N_1 =_{\lambda\Pi_{\mathcal{L}}} |N_1|^{\underline{N'}} =_{\lambda\Pi_{\mathcal{L}}} N^{\underline{N'}}$, $M_2 =_{\lambda\Pi_{\mathcal{L}}} |M_2|^{\underline{N'}} =_{\lambda\Pi_{\mathcal{L}}} M^{\underline{N'}}$ and $N_2 =_{\lambda\Pi_{\mathcal{L}}} |N_2|^{\underline{N'}} =_{\lambda\Pi_{\mathcal{L}}} N^{\underline{N'}}$. Therefore, $M_1 =_{\lambda\Pi_{\mathcal{L}}} M_2$ and $N_1 =_{\lambda\Pi_{\mathcal{L}}} N_2$. □

4 Elementary Typing Properties

Geuvers' Lemma is sufficient to prove the main typing properties of $\lambda\Pi_{\mathcal{L}}$.

Theorem 18 Sort Soundness.

1. *If* $\Sigma :\cdot \Gamma \vdash M : N$*, then* $N = Kind$ *or* $\Sigma :\cdot \Gamma \vdash N : s$*,* $s \in \mathcal{S}$*, and*
2. *if* $\Sigma :\cdot \Gamma \vdash S \triangleright \Delta$ *then* $\Sigma :\cdot \Delta$*.*

Proof. By induction on typing derivation. □

Theorem 19 Type Uniqueness. *Let Γ_1 and Γ_2 be such that $\Gamma_1 =_{\lambda\Pi_{\mathcal{L}}} \Gamma_2$,*

1. *if $\Sigma :\cdot \Gamma_1 \vdash M : N_1$ and $\Sigma :\cdot \Gamma_2 \vdash M : N_2$, then $N_1 =_{\lambda\Pi_{\mathcal{L}}} N_2$, and*
2. *if $\Sigma :\cdot \Gamma_1 \vdash S \triangleright \Delta_1$ and $\Sigma :\cdot \Gamma_2 \vdash S \triangleright \Delta_2$, then $\Delta_1 =_{\lambda\Pi_{\mathcal{L}}} \Delta_2$.*

Proof. By simultaneous structural induction on M and S. □

Theorem 20 Subject Reduction. *$\lambda\Pi_{\mathcal{L}}$ preserves typing, i.e. if $x \xrightarrow{\lambda\Pi_{\mathcal{L}}{}^*} y$, then*

- *if x is a Term and $\Sigma :\cdot \Gamma \vdash x : M$, then $\Sigma :\cdot \Gamma \vdash y : M$, and*
- *if x is a Substitution and $\Sigma :\cdot \Gamma \vdash x \triangleright \Delta$, then $\Sigma :\cdot \Gamma \vdash y \triangleright \Delta$.*

Proof. We show that typing is preserved for one-step reductions (i.e. $\xrightarrow{\lambda\Pi_{\mathcal{L}}}$), and then it is also for the reflexive and transitive closure (i.e. $\xrightarrow{\lambda\Pi_{\mathcal{L}}{}^*}$). Let $x \xrightarrow{\lambda\Pi_{\mathcal{L}}} y$ be a one-step reduction, we proceed by induction on the depth of the redex reduced in x. At the initial case x is reduced at the top level and we show that rules preserve typing. At the induction step we proceed by cases analysis. □

Sometimes the conversion rule (Conv) is expressed in dependent type systems as [10]:

$$\frac{\Gamma \vdash M : N_1 \quad \Gamma \vdash N_2 : s \quad s \in \mathcal{S} \quad (N_1 \longrightarrow N_2 \text{ or } N_2 \longrightarrow N_1)}{\Gamma \vdash M : N_2} \text{(Conv')}$$

The (Conv) rule seems to be more general that the (Conv') rule. In fact, the latter one allows conversions of types only via a path through well-typed terms. Geuvers and Werner [10] define *soundness of a type system* when it holds that convertibility of terms remains in the set of well-typed terms. In sound systems the rules (Conv) and (Conv') are equivalents. Next theorem shows that $\lambda\Pi_{\mathcal{L}}$ is a sound system.

Theorem 21 Soundness. *If $\Sigma :\cdot \Gamma \vdash M : N_1$, $\Sigma :\cdot \Gamma \vdash N : N_2$ and $M =_{\lambda\Pi_{\mathcal{L}}} N$, then there exists a path of well-typed terms to convert M and N.*

Proof. From Lemma 13(1) we have $|M| = |N|$. The confluence property of $\lambda\Pi_{\mathcal{L}}^{\Box}$ says that there exists $x \in \Lambda\Pi_{\mathcal{L}}^{\Box}$ such that $|M| \xrightarrow{\lambda\Pi_{\mathcal{L}}^{\Box}{}^*} x$ and $|N| \xrightarrow{\lambda\Pi_{\mathcal{L}}^{\Box}{}^*} x$. By Lemma 13(2), there exists M' and N' such that $M \xrightarrow{\lambda\Pi_{\mathcal{L}}{}^*} M'$, $N \xrightarrow{\lambda\Pi_{\mathcal{L}}{}^*} N'$ and $|M'| = |N'| = x$. Since $\Pi_{\mathcal{L}}$ is terminating (Proposition 1), there exists M'' and N'' such that $M' \xrightarrow{\Pi_{\mathcal{L}}{}^*} M''$, $N' \xrightarrow{\Pi_{\mathcal{L}}{}^*} N''$ and M'', N'' are $\Pi_{\mathcal{L}}$-normal forms. By the subject reduction property (Theorem 20), $\Sigma :\cdot \Gamma \vdash M'' : N_1$ and $\Sigma :\cdot \Gamma \vdash N'' : N_2$.

Now, from Lemma 13(1), we have that $x \xrightarrow{\Pi_{\mathcal{L}}^{\Box}{}^*} |M''|$ and $x \xrightarrow{\Pi_{\mathcal{L}}^{\Box}{}^*} |N''|$. But M'' and N'' are $\Pi_{\mathcal{L}}$-normal forms, hence, by Corollary 14, $|M''|$ and $|N''|$ are $\Pi_{\mathcal{L}}^{\Box}$-normal forms. Since $\Pi_{\mathcal{L}}^{\Box}$ is confluent, $|M''| = |N''|$. Finally, we reason by structural induction on M'' and N''. □

5 Weak Normalization and Confluence

5.1 Weak Normalization

$\lambda\Pi_{\mathcal{L}}$ does not preserve strong normalization of $\lambda\Pi$. In fact the counterexample shown in [21] for $\lambda\sigma$, may be reproduced in $\lambda\Pi_{\mathcal{L}}$ with some minor modifications.

Nevertheless, we prove that $\lambda\Pi_{\mathcal{L}}$ is weakly normalizing on typed expressions, i.e. there exists a strategy to find $\lambda\Pi_{\mathcal{L}}$-normal forms on typed expressions. In particular, we propose a proof of strong normalization of the strategy that performs one-step of (Beta) reduction followed by a $\Pi_{\mathcal{L}}$-normalization.

We use the standard technique of reducibility, originally due to Tait for the simply-typed λ-calculus, and posteriorly extended by Girard to the system F (the λ-calculus of second-order). From the divers proofs of termination using a reducibility notion, we follow the presentation given in [9] for the calculus of constructions, which is based on saturated sets. We adapt this proof for the $\lambda\Pi_{\mathcal{L}}$-calculus. In order to raise some technical problems due to the non-confluence of the calculus of pre-expressions, we define saturated sets in a different way. However, the structure of the proofs is the same.

We use $(x)\downarrow_{\Pi_{\mathcal{L}}}$ to denote the set of $\Pi_{\mathcal{L}}$-normal forms of x. Since $\lambda\Pi_{\mathcal{L}}$-calculus without annotations of types in substitutions is confluent on semi-open expressions (Lemma 6), we have the following property.

Remark 22. For any $M_1, M_2 \in (M)\downarrow_{\Pi_{\mathcal{L}}}$, $|M_1| = |M_2|$. We write $(M)\downarrow_{\Pi_{\mathcal{L}}^{\Box}}$ to denote the $\Pi_{\mathcal{L}}^{\Box}$-normal form of $|M|$.

We define $\mathcal{NF}_{\mathcal{L}}$ as the set that contains all the $\Pi_{\mathcal{L}}$-normal forms in $\Lambda\Pi_{\mathcal{L}}$.

Definition 23. Let $x, y \in \mathcal{NF}_{\mathcal{L}}$, we say that x *$\beta\Pi_{\mathcal{L}}$-converts* to y, denoted by $x \xrightarrow{\beta\Pi_{\mathcal{L}}} y$, if $x \xrightarrow{\text{(Beta)}} w$ and $y \in (w)\downarrow_{\Pi_{\mathcal{L}}}$.

We denote by $\mathcal{SN}_{\mathcal{L}}$ the set of $\beta\Pi_{\mathcal{L}}$-strongly normalizing expressions of $\mathcal{NF}_{\mathcal{L}}$.

Definition 24. Let M be in $\mathcal{NF}_{\mathcal{L}}$, M is *neutral* if it does not have the form $\lambda_{M_1}.M_2$. The set of neutral terms is denoted by $\mathcal{NT}$.

Definition 25. Let x be in $\mathcal{NF}_{\mathcal{L}}$, the set of *domains* of x, denoted by $\mathrm{D}(x)$, is defined inductively as follows:

$$
\begin{array}{lll}
\mathrm{D}(x) & = \emptyset & \text{if } x \in \{\mathit{Kind}, \mathit{Type}, \mathbf{1}\} \text{ or } x = \uparrow^n \text{ or } x \text{ is a meta-variable} \\
\mathrm{D}(\Pi_{M_1}.M_2) & = \mathrm{D}(M_1) \cup \mathrm{D}(M_2) & \\
\mathrm{D}(\lambda_{M_1}.M_2) & = \mathrm{D}(M_1) \cup \mathrm{D}(M_2) & \\
\mathrm{D}(M\,N) & = \mathrm{D}(M) \cup \mathrm{D}(N) & \\
\mathrm{D}([S]M) & = \mathrm{D}(S) \cup \mathrm{D}(M) & \\
\mathrm{D}(T \circ S) & = \mathrm{D}(T) \cup \mathrm{D}(S) & \\
\mathrm{D}(S \cdot M_{:N}) & = \{N\} \cup \mathrm{D}(S) \cup \mathrm{D}(M) &
\end{array}
$$

Definition 26. A set of terms $\Lambda \subseteq \mathcal{NF}_{\mathcal{L}}$ is *saturated* if

1. $\Lambda \subseteq \mathcal{SN}_{\mathcal{L}}$.
2. If $M \in \Lambda$ and $M \xrightarrow{\beta\Pi_{\mathcal{L}}} M'$, then $M' \in \Lambda$.
3. If $M \in \mathcal{NT}$, and whenever we reduce a $\beta\Pi_{\mathcal{L}}$-redex of M we obtain a term $M' \in \Lambda$, then $M \in \Lambda$.
4. If $M \in \Lambda$, $|M| = |M'|$ and $\mathrm{D}(M') \subseteq \mathcal{SN}_{\mathcal{L}}$, then $M' \in \Lambda$.

The set of saturated sets is denoted by **SAT**.

The following corollary is a particular case of Def. 26(3).

Corollary 27. *Let $M \in \mathcal{NT}$ such that M is a $\beta\Pi_{\mathcal{L}}$-normal form. For any $\Lambda \in \mathbf{SAT}$, $M \in \Lambda$.*

Lemma 28. *For any $\Lambda \in \mathbf{SAT}$, substitution $S \in \mathcal{SN}_{\mathcal{L}}$, and meta-variable X, $([S]X)\downarrow_{\Pi_{\mathcal{L}}} \subseteq \Lambda$.*

Proof. We reason by induction on $\nu(S)$. □

Lemma 29. *For any $\Lambda \in \mathbf{SAT}$, and terms $M, N \in \mathcal{SN}_{\mathcal{L}}$, $\Pi_M.N \in \Lambda$.*

Proof. The term $\Pi_M.N$ is neutral, then by Def. 26(3), it suffices to consider the reductions of $\Pi_M.N$. We reason by induction on $\nu(M) + \nu(N)$. □

Lemma 30. $\mathcal{SN}_{\mathcal{L}} \in \mathbf{SAT}$.

Proof. We verify the conditions of Def. 26. □

Definition 31. If $\Lambda, \Lambda' \in \mathbf{SAT}$, we define the set

$$\Lambda \to \Lambda' = \{M \in \mathcal{NF}_{\mathcal{L}} \mid \forall N \in \Lambda, (M\ N) \in \Lambda'\}$$

Lemma 32. **SAT** *is closed under function spaces, i.e. if $\Lambda, \Lambda' \in \mathbf{SAT}$, then $\Lambda \to \Lambda' \in \mathbf{SAT}$.*

Proof. We verify the conditions of Def. 26. □

Definition 33. The *type interpretation function* of terms in $\Lambda\Pi_{\mathcal{L}}$ is defined inductively as follows:

$$\begin{array}{lcll}
[\![x]\!] & = & \mathcal{SN}_{\mathcal{L}} & \text{if } x \in \{\mathit{Kind}, \mathit{Type}, \mathbf{1}\} \text{ or } x \text{ is a meta-variable} \\
[\![[S]M]\!] & = & [\![M]\!] & \\
[\![(M\ N)]\!] & = & [\![M]\!] & \\
[\![\lambda_M.N]\!] & = & [\![N]\!] & \\
[\![\Pi_M.N]\!] & = & [\![M]\!] \to [\![N]\!] &
\end{array}$$

We have the following corollary of Lemma 32.

Corollary 34. *For any term M, $[\![M]\!] \in \mathbf{SAT}$.*

Definition 35. The *valuations* of Γ, denoted by $[\![\Gamma]\!]$, is a set of substitutions in $\mathcal{NF}_{\mathcal{L}}$ defined inductively on Γ as follows:

$$\begin{aligned} [\![nil]\!] &= \{\uparrow^n \mid \text{for any natural } n\} \\ [\![\Gamma'.N']\!] &= [\![nil]\!] \cup \{S \cdot M_{:N} \in \mathcal{NF}_{\mathcal{L}} \mid S \in [\![\Gamma']\!], M \in [\![N]\!], N \in \mathcal{SN}_{\mathcal{L}}, [\![N]\!] = [\![N']\!]\} \end{aligned}$$

Lemma 36. *For any* Γ, $[\![\Gamma]\!] \subseteq \mathcal{SN}_{\mathcal{L}}$.

Proof. We show by structural induction on S that if $S \in [\![\Gamma]\!]$, then $S \in \mathcal{SN}_{\mathcal{L}}$. □

Definition 37. Let $M, S \in \mathcal{NF}_{\mathcal{L}}$, we define

1. Γ satisfies that M is of type N, denoted by $\Gamma \models M : N$, if and only if $([T]M)\downarrow_{\Pi_{\mathcal{L}}} \subseteq [\![N]\!]$ for any $T \in [\![\Gamma]\!]$.
2. Γ satisfies that S is of type Δ, denoted by $\Gamma \models S \triangleright \Delta$, if and only if $(T \circ S)\downarrow_{\Pi_{\mathcal{L}}} \subseteq [\![\Delta]\!]$ for any $T \in [\![\Gamma]\!]$.

Now we show some technical lemmas.

Lemma 38. *If* $S \in [\![\Gamma]\!]$, $M \in [\![N]\!]$ *and* $N \in \mathcal{SN}_{\mathcal{L}}$, *then* $(S \cdot M_{:N})\downarrow_{\Pi_{\mathcal{L}}} \subseteq [\![\Gamma.N]\!]$.

Proof. Note that $S \cdot M_{:N}$ is not necessarily in $\mathcal{NF}_{\mathcal{L}}$. But there are two cases: $(S \cdot M_{:N})\downarrow_{\Pi_{\mathcal{L}}} = \{S \cdot M_{:N}\}$ or $(S \cdot M_{:N})\downarrow_{\Pi_{\mathcal{L}}} = \{\uparrow^n\}$. In both cases we verify that $(S \cdot M_{:N})\downarrow_{\Pi_{\mathcal{L}}} \subseteq [\![\Gamma.N]\!]$. □

Lemma 39. *If* $\Sigma :\cdot \Gamma \vdash M : N$ *and* $\Sigma :\cdot \Gamma \vdash N : Type$, *then* $[\![M]\!] = \mathcal{SN}_{\mathcal{L}}$.

Proof. By structural induction on M. The proof of this lemma uses the Geuvers' lemma. □

Lemma 40.

1. *If* $\Sigma :\cdot \Gamma \vdash M : N_1$ *and* $\Sigma :\cdot \Gamma \vdash M : N_2$, *then* $[\![N_1]\!] = [\![N_2]\!]$, *and*
2. *if* $\Sigma :\cdot \Gamma \vdash S \triangleright \Delta_1$ *and* $\Sigma :\cdot \Gamma \vdash S \triangleright \Delta_2$, *then* $[\![\Delta_1]\!] = [\![\Delta_2]\!]$.

Proof. We detail the first case. The second one is shown by structural induction on Δ_1. By type uniqueness theorem (Theorem 19), we have that $N_1 =_{\lambda\Pi_{\mathcal{L}}} N_2$, and by sort soundness theorem (Theorem 18), ($N_1 = N_2 = Kind$) or ($\Sigma :\cdot \Gamma \vdash N_1 : s_1$ and $\Sigma :\cdot \Gamma \vdash N_2 : s_2$). The first case is trivial. For the second one, we use typing soundness theorem (Theorem 21) to conclude that N_1 and N_2 are convertible via a path of well typed terms. Hence, it suffices to prove that for any well typed term N if $N \xrightarrow{\beta\Pi_{\mathcal{L}}} N'$, then $[\![N]\!] = [\![N']\!]$. We prove that by induction on the depth of the $\beta\Pi_{\mathcal{L}}$-redex reduced in N. The only interesting case is (VarCons), i.e. $[S \cdot M_{1:M_2}]\mathbf{1} \xrightarrow{\text{(VarCons)}} M_1$. From Def. 33, $[\![[S \cdot M_{1:M_2}]\mathbf{1}]\!] = [\![\mathbf{1}]\!] = \mathcal{SN}_{\mathcal{L}}$. But if $[S \cdot M_{1:M_2}]\mathbf{1}$ is well-typed in $\Sigma :\cdot \Gamma$, then we can conclude that $\Sigma :\cdot \Gamma \vdash M_1 : [S]M_2$ and $\Sigma :\cdot \Gamma \vdash [S]M_2 : Type$. Hence, by Lemma 39, $[\![M_1]\!] = \mathcal{SN}_{\mathcal{L}}$ too. □

Lemma 41. *Let $M \in \mathcal{NF}_{\mathcal{L}}$ and $N_1' \in \mathcal{SN}_{\mathcal{L}}$, if for all $N \in [\![N_1]\!]$, $([\uparrow^0 \cdot N_{:N_1'}]M)\downarrow_{\Pi_{\mathcal{L}}} \subseteq [\![N_2]\!]$, then $\lambda_{N_1'}.M \in [\![N_1]\!] \to [\![N_2]\!]$.*

Proof. Let $N \in [\![N_1]\!]$, we want to show $(\lambda_{N_1'}.M\ N) \in [\![N_2]\!]$. Since $(\lambda_{N_1'}.M\ N) \in \mathcal{NT}$ and $[\![N_2]\!] \subseteq \mathbf{SAT}$, it suffices to prove that if $(\lambda_{N_1'}.M\ N) \xrightarrow{\beta\Pi_{\mathcal{L}}} M''$, then $M'' \in [\![N_2]\!]$. Since for all $N \in [\![N_1]\!]$, $([\uparrow^0 \cdot N_{:N_1'}]M)\downarrow_{\Pi_{\mathcal{L}}} \subseteq [\![N_2]\!] \subseteq \mathcal{SN}_{\mathcal{L}}$, in particular, $([\uparrow^0 \cdot \mathbf{1}_{:N_1'}]M)\downarrow_{\Pi_{\mathcal{L}}} \subseteq \mathcal{SN}_{\mathcal{L}}$, and thus $M \in \mathcal{SN}_{\mathcal{L}}$. But also, $N \in [\![N_1]\!] \subseteq \mathcal{SN}_{\mathcal{L}}$, and $N_1' \in \mathcal{SN}_{\mathcal{L}}$. Thus, we can reason by induction on $\nu(M) + \nu(N) + \nu(N_1')$. In one step $(\lambda_{N_1'}.M\ N)$ $\beta\Pi_{\mathcal{L}}$-reduces to:

- $([\uparrow^0 \cdot N_{:N_1'}]M)\downarrow_{\Pi_{\mathcal{L}}}$. By hypothesis, $([\uparrow^0 \cdot N_{:N_1'}]M)\downarrow_{\Pi_{\mathcal{L}}} \subseteq [\![N_2]\!]$.
- $(\lambda_{N_1'}.M\ N')$, with $N \xrightarrow{\beta\Pi_{\mathcal{L}}} N'$. By Def. 26(2), $N' \in [\![N_1]\!]$, so by hypothesis, $([\uparrow^0 \cdot N'_{:N_1'}]M)\downarrow_{\Pi_{\mathcal{L}}}$
 $\subseteq [\![N_2]\!]$. But also, $\nu(N') < \nu(N)$, so by induction hypothesis, $(\lambda_{N_1'}.M\ N') \in [\![N_2]\!]$.
- $(\lambda_{N_1'}.M\ N)$, with $N_1' \xrightarrow{\beta\Pi_{\mathcal{L}}} N_1''$. Since $N_1' \in \mathcal{SN}_{\mathcal{L}}$, $N_1'' \in \mathcal{SN}_{\mathcal{L}}$ too. By hypothesis, $([\uparrow^0 \cdot N_{:N_1'}]M)\downarrow_{\Pi_{\mathcal{L}}} \subseteq [\![N_2]\!]$, but also
 $([\uparrow^0 \cdot N_{:N_1'}]M)\downarrow_{\Pi_{\mathcal{L}}^{\Box}} = ([\uparrow^0 \cdot N_{:N_1''}]M)\downarrow_{\Pi_{\mathcal{L}}^{\Box}}$. Since $N_1' \in \mathcal{SN}_{\mathcal{L}}$, we have $N_1'' \in \mathcal{SN}_{\mathcal{L}}$, and so, for any $M' \in ([\uparrow^0 \cdot N_{:N_1''}]M)\downarrow_{\Pi_{\mathcal{L}}}$, $\mathrm{D}(M') \subseteq \mathcal{SN}_{\mathcal{L}}$. Therefore, by Def. 26(4), $([\uparrow^0 \cdot N_{:N_1''}]M)\downarrow_{\Pi_{\mathcal{L}}} \subseteq [\![N_2]\!]$.
 Since $([\uparrow^0 \cdot N_{:N_1''}]M)\downarrow_{\Pi_{\mathcal{L}}} \subseteq [\![N_2]\!]$ and $\nu(N_1'') < \nu(N_1')$, we conclude with the induction hypothesis that $(\lambda_{N_1''}.M\ N) \in [\![N_2]\!]$.
- $(\lambda_{N_1'}.M'\ N)$, with $M \xrightarrow{\beta\Pi_{\mathcal{L}}} M'$. Using the properties of $\lambda\Pi_{\mathcal{L}}$ and $\lambda\Pi_{\mathcal{L}}^{\Box}$, we have that if $M_1 \in ([\uparrow^0 \cdot N_{:N_1'}]M)\downarrow_{\Pi_{\mathcal{L}}}$, then $M_1 \xrightarrow{\beta\Pi_{\mathcal{L}}} M_1'$, where $|M_1'| = ([\uparrow^0 \cdot N_{:N_1'}]M')\downarrow_{\Pi_{\mathcal{L}}^{\Box}}$. Since $M_1 \in [\![N_2]\!]$, by Def. 26(2), $M_1 \in [\![N_2]\!]$. But also, for any $M_2 \in ([\uparrow^0 \cdot N_{:N_1'}]M')\downarrow_{\Pi_{\mathcal{L}}}$, $\mathrm{D}(M_2) \subseteq \mathcal{SN}_{\mathcal{L}}$, thus by Def. 26(4), $([\uparrow^0 \cdot N_{:N_1'}]M')\downarrow_{\Pi_{\mathcal{L}}} \subseteq [\![N_2]\!]$.
 Since $([\uparrow^0 \cdot N_{:N_1'}]M')\downarrow_{\Pi_{\mathcal{L}}} \subseteq [\![N_2]\!]$ and $\nu(M') < \nu(M)$, we conclude with the induction hypothesis that $(\lambda_{N_1'}.M'\ N) \in [\![N_2]\!]$.

□

Notation: The expression $\Uparrow_M(T)$ denotes $(\uparrow^{Succ(0)} \circ T) \cdot \mathbf{1}_{:M}$.

Weak normalization proof of $\lambda\Pi_{\mathcal{L}}$ is based on the following proposition.

Proposition 42 Soundness of $\models$.

1. *If $\Sigma :\cdot \Gamma \vdash M : N$, then $\Gamma \models M : N$, and*
2. *if $\Sigma :\cdot \Gamma \vdash S \triangleright \Delta$, then $\Gamma \models S \triangleright \Delta$.*

Proof. By simultaneous structural induction on M and S. We show the main cases.

- $M = X$ (X is a meta-variable). Let $T \in [\![\Gamma]\!]$, there are two cases:

- $T = \uparrow^0$. Therefore, $([T]X)\downarrow_{\Pi_\mathcal{L}} = \{X\}$. But also, X is a neutral $\beta\Pi_\mathcal{L}$-normal form, then by Corollary 27, $X \in [\![N]\!]$.
- $T \neq \uparrow^0$. Therefore, $([T]X)\downarrow_{\Pi_\mathcal{L}} = \{[T]X\}$. By Lemma 36, $T \in \mathcal{SN}_\mathcal{L}$, then by Lemma 28, $[T]X \in [\![N]\!]$.

– $M = \Pi_{M_1}.M_2$. By the typing rules, $\Sigma :\cdot \Gamma \vdash M_1 : \mathit{Type}$ and $\Sigma :\cdot \Gamma.M_1 \vdash M_2 : s$. Let $T \in [\![\Gamma]\!]$. Note that if $M' \in ([T](\Pi_{M_1}.M_2))\downarrow_{\Pi_\mathcal{L}}$, then $M' = \Pi_{N_1}.N_2$ where $N_1 \in ([T]M_1)\downarrow_{\Pi_\mathcal{L}}$ and $N_2 \in ([\Uparrow_{M_1}(T)]M_2)\downarrow_{\Pi_\mathcal{L}}$. By induction hypothesis, $N_1 \in ([T]M_1)\downarrow_{\Pi_\mathcal{L}} \subseteq [\![\mathit{Type}]\!] = \mathcal{SN}_\mathcal{L}$. In particular, if $T = \uparrow^0$, $N_1 \in \mathcal{SN}_\mathcal{L}$ and $([\uparrow^0 \cdot \mathbf{1}_{:M_1}]N_2)\downarrow_{\Pi_\mathcal{L}} \subseteq ([\uparrow^0 \cdot \mathbf{1}_{:M_1}]M_2)\downarrow_{\Pi_\mathcal{L}}$. But also by Def. 35, $\uparrow^0 \cdot \mathbf{1}_{:M_1} \in [\![\Gamma.M_1]\!]$. Thus, by induction hypothesis, $([\uparrow^0 \cdot \mathbf{1}_{:M_1}]N_2)\downarrow_{\Pi_\mathcal{L}} \subseteq ([\uparrow^0 \cdot \mathbf{1}_{:M_1}]M_2)\downarrow_{\Pi_\mathcal{L}} \subseteq [\![s]\!] = \mathcal{SN}_\mathcal{L}$. Therefore, $N_2 \in \mathcal{SN}_\mathcal{L}$, and by Lemma 29, $\Pi_{N_1}.N_2 \in [\![N]\!]$.

– $M = \lambda_{M_1}.M_2$. By the typing rules, $\Sigma :\cdot \Gamma \vdash M_1 : \mathit{Type}$, $\Sigma :\cdot \Gamma.M_1 \vdash M_2 : N'$ and $\Sigma :\cdot \Gamma \vdash \lambda_{M_1}.M_2 : \Pi_{M_1}.N'$. By Lemma 40, $[\![N]\!] = [\![\Pi_{M_1}.N']\!] = [\![M_1]\!] \rightarrow [\![N']\!]$. Let $T \in [\![\Gamma]\!]$, note that if $M' \in ([T](\lambda_{M_1}.M_2))\downarrow_{\Pi_\mathcal{L}}$, then $M' = \lambda_{M_1'}.M_2'$ where $M_1' \in ([T]M_1)\downarrow_{\Pi_\mathcal{L}}$ and $M_2' \in ([\Uparrow_{M_1}(T)]M_2)\downarrow_{\Pi_\mathcal{L}}$. By induction hypothesis, $M_1' \in ([T]M_1)\downarrow_{\Pi_\mathcal{L}} \subseteq [\![\mathit{Type}]\!] = \mathcal{SN}_\mathcal{L}$. In particular, if $T = \uparrow^0$, $M_1' \in \mathcal{SN}_\mathcal{L}$. Now we prove that $\lambda_{M_1'}.M_2' \in [\![M_1]\!] \rightarrow [\![N']\!]$. From Lemma 41, it suffices to prove that for any $M'' \in [\![M_1]\!]$, $([\uparrow^0 \cdot M''_{:M_1'}]M_2')\downarrow_{\Pi_\mathcal{L}} \in [\![N']\!]$. There are two cases:
  - $T = \uparrow^0$. In $\lambda\Pi_\mathcal{L}$ we have $([\uparrow^0 \cdot M''_{:M_1'}]M_2')\downarrow_{\Pi_\mathcal{L}} \subseteq ([\uparrow^0 \cdot M''_{:M_1'}]M_2)\downarrow_{\Pi_\mathcal{L}}$. It is not difficult to see from the typing rules, subject reduction theorem (Theorem 20) and Lemma 40, that $[\![M_1]\!] = [\![M_1']\!]$. Hence, by Def. 35, $\uparrow^0 \cdot M''_{:M_1'} \in [\![\Gamma.M_1]\!]$, and by induction hypothesis, $([\uparrow^0 \cdot M''_{:M_1'}]M_2)\downarrow_{\Pi_\mathcal{L}} \subseteq [\![N']\!]$.
  - $T \neq \uparrow^0$. In $\lambda\Pi_\mathcal{L}$ we have $([\uparrow^0 \cdot M''_{:M_1'}]M_2')\downarrow_{\Pi_\mathcal{L}} \subseteq \bigcup_{S \in (T \cdot M''_{:M_1})\downarrow_{\Pi_\mathcal{L}}} ([S]M_2)\downarrow_{\Pi_\mathcal{L}}$. Remark that $M'' \in [\![M_1]\!]$, $M_1 \in \mathcal{SN}_\mathcal{L}$, and by Def. 26 and Def. 35, $(T)\downarrow_{\Pi_\mathcal{L}} \subseteq [\![\Gamma]\!]$. By Lemma 38, $(T \cdot M''_{:M_1})\downarrow_{\Pi_\mathcal{L}} \subseteq \Gamma.M_1$. Thus, by induction hypothesis, $\bigcup_{S \in (T \cdot M''_{:M_1})\downarrow_{\Pi_\mathcal{L}}} ([S]M_2)\downarrow_{\Pi_\mathcal{L}} \subseteq [\![N']\!]$.

□

Now, we show that $\beta\Pi_\mathcal{L}$ is strongly normalizing.

Lemma 43. *Let M, S be expressions in $\mathcal{NF}_\mathcal{L}$.*

1. *If $\Sigma :\cdot \Gamma \vdash M : N$, then $M \in \mathcal{SN}_\mathcal{L}$, and*
2. *if $\Sigma :\cdot \Gamma \vdash S \triangleright \Delta$, then $S \in \mathcal{SN}_\mathcal{L}$.*

Proof. By Def. 35, $\uparrow^0 \in [\![\Gamma]\!]$. Hence,

1. By Proposition 42, $M \in ([\uparrow^0]M)\downarrow_{\Pi_\mathcal{L}} \subseteq [\![N]\!]$. By Corollary 34 and Def. 26(1), $[\![N]\!] \subseteq \mathcal{SN}_\mathcal{L}$.
2. By Proposition 42, $S \in (\uparrow^0 \circ S)\downarrow_{\Pi_\mathcal{L}} \subseteq [\![\Delta]\!]$, and by Lemma 36, $[\![\Delta]\!] \subseteq \mathcal{SN}_\mathcal{L}$.

□

Finally, we prove weak normalization on typed $\lambda\Pi_\mathcal{L}$-expressions.

Theorem 44 Weak Normalization.

1. *If* $\Sigma :\cdot \Gamma \vdash M : N$, *then* M *is weakly normalizing, and*
2. *if* $\Sigma :\cdot \Gamma \vdash S \rhd \Delta$, *then* S *is weakly normalizing.*

Therefore, M *and* S *have* $\lambda\Pi_{\mathcal{L}}$*-normal forms.*

Proof. By Proposition 1, there exists $M', S' \in \mathcal{NF}_{\mathcal{L}}$ such that $M \xrightarrow{\Pi_{\mathcal{L}}{}^*} M'$ and $S \xrightarrow{\Pi_{\mathcal{L}}{}^*} S'$. The subject reduction theorem (Theorem 20) says that typing is preserved under reductions, hence $\Sigma :\cdot \Gamma \vdash M' : N$ and $\Sigma :\cdot \Gamma \vdash S' \rhd \Delta$. Therefore, by Lemma 43, M' and S' are both in $\mathcal{SN}_{\mathcal{L}}$. Finally, note that $\beta\Pi_{\mathcal{L}}$-normal forms in $\mathcal{NF}_{\mathcal{L}}$ are $\lambda\Pi_{\mathcal{L}}$-normal forms too. □

5.2 Confluence

Church-Rosser property states that if two typed expressions are convertible, then they are joinable. The confluence property says that all the reductions of a typed expression are joinable.

We need the following lemma coined in [31].

Lemma 45. *Let* x *and* y *be* $\lambda\Pi_{\mathcal{L}}$*-normal forms such that* $x =_{\lambda\Pi_{\mathcal{L}}} y$. *Then,* $x = y$ *if*

- x *is a Term,* $\Sigma :\cdot \Gamma_1 \vdash x : N$ *and* $\Sigma :\cdot \Gamma_2 \vdash y : N'$, *or*
- x *is a Substitution,* $\Sigma :\cdot \Gamma_1 \vdash x \rhd \Delta_1$, $\Sigma :\cdot \Gamma_2 \vdash y \rhd \Delta_2$ *and* $\Delta_1 =_{\lambda\Pi_{\mathcal{L}}} \Delta_2$.

Proof. By Corollary 14, $|x|$ and $|y|$ are $\lambda\Pi_{\mathcal{L}}^{\Box}$-normal forms, and by Lemma 13(1), $|x| =_{\lambda\Pi_{\mathcal{L}}^{\Box}} |y|$. Since $\lambda\Pi_{\mathcal{L}}^{\Box}$ is confluent on semi-open expressions (Theorem 9), $|x| = |y|$. Finally we proceed by structural induction on x. □

Theorem 46 Church-Rosser. *Let* x *and* y *be such that* $x =_{\lambda\Pi_{\mathcal{L}}} y$. *Then,* x *and* y *are* $\lambda\Pi_{\mathcal{L}}$*-joinable, i.e. there exists* w *such that* $x \xrightarrow{\lambda\Pi_{\mathcal{L}}{}^*} w$ *and* $y \xrightarrow{\lambda\Pi_{\mathcal{L}}{}^*} w$, *if*

1. x *is a term,* $\Sigma :\cdot \Gamma_1 \vdash x : N_1$ *and* $\Sigma :\cdot \Gamma_2 \vdash y : N_2$, *or*
2. x *is a substitution,* $\Sigma :\cdot \Gamma_1 \vdash x \rhd \Delta_1$, $\Sigma :\cdot \Gamma_2 \vdash y \rhd \Delta_2$ *and* $\Delta_1 =_{\lambda\Pi_{\mathcal{L}}} \Delta_2$.

Proof. By weak normalization theorem (Theorem 44), there exists $\lambda\Pi_{\mathcal{L}}$-normal forms x' and y' such that $x \xrightarrow{\lambda\Pi_{\mathcal{L}}{}^*} x'$ and $y \xrightarrow{\lambda\Pi_{\mathcal{L}}{}^*} y'$. It is sufficient to show that $x' = y'$, which is a consequence of subject reduction theorem (Theorem 20) and Lemma 45. □

The above property is not valid when $\Delta_1 \neq_{\lambda\Pi_{\mathcal{L}}} \Delta_2$. Take the context

$\Gamma = nil.\ nat{:}Type.\ T{:}nat \to Type.\ l{:}(\Pi n{:}nat.(T\ n)).\ 0{:}nat.\ m{:}(T\ 0) \to nat$

and the two substitutions

$$S_1 = x := 0_{:nat} \cdot y := (l\ 0)_{:(T\ x)}$$

and

$$S_2 = x := 0_{:nat} \cdot y := (l\ 0)_{:(T\ 0)}$$

We have, by Lemma 12, $S_1 =_{\lambda\Pi_\mathcal{L}} S_2$. But also,

$$\Gamma \vdash S_1 \triangleright \Gamma.\ x{:}nat.\ y{:}(T\ x)$$

and

$$\Gamma \vdash S_2 \triangleright \Gamma.\ x{:}nat.\ y{:}(T\ 0)$$

However, S_1 and S_2 are not $\lambda\Pi_\mathcal{L}$-joinable.

Confluence of $\lambda\Pi_\mathcal{L}$ is a consequence of Church-Rosser and subject reduction properties.

Corollary 47 Confluence. *Let x be an arbitrary well-typed expression, and y and z be such that $x \xrightarrow{\lambda\Pi_\mathcal{L}^*} y$ and $x \xrightarrow{\lambda\Pi_\mathcal{L}^*} z$, then there exists w such that $y \xrightarrow{\lambda\Pi_\mathcal{L}^*} w$ and $z \xrightarrow{\lambda\Pi_\mathcal{L}^*} w$.*

Since $\lambda\Pi_\mathcal{L}$ enjoys both Church-Rosser and weak normalization, we have that $\lambda\Pi_\mathcal{L}$-normal forms on well-typed terms always exist and they are unique. Thus, the equivalence on well-typed expressions is decidable.

Corollary 48 Decidability. *The equivalence $x =_{\lambda\Pi_\mathcal{L}} y$ is decidable*

- *if x is a term, $\Sigma :\cdot \Gamma_1 \vdash x : N_1$ and $\Sigma :\cdot \Gamma_2 \vdash y : N_2$, or*
- *if x is a substitution, $\Sigma :\cdot \Gamma_1 \vdash x \triangleright \Delta_1$, $\Sigma :\cdot \Gamma_2 \vdash y \triangleright \Delta_2$ and $\Delta_1 =_{\lambda\Pi_\mathcal{L}} \Delta_2$.*

6 Related Works and Conclusions

Some type theories extended with explicit substitutions have been proposed: The Simple Type Theory [1, 19, 6, 14, 4], the Second-Order Type Theory [1], the Martin Löf Type Theory [30], the Calculus of Constructions [27] and Pure Type Systems [2]. Except for the simply-typed version of $\lambda\sigma$ in [6], neither of them consider terms with meta-variables as first-class objects.

Sometimes, explicit substitutions are identified to the `let-in` constructor of functional ML-style programming languages. Both mechanisms allow to have delayed applications of substitutions to terms. For example, `let` $x := 0$ `in` $\lambda y{:}A.x$ will be unfolded in $\lambda y{:}A.0$, in the same way that $[x := 0](\lambda y{:}A.x)$ reduces to $\lambda y{:}A.0$. In their simply-typed versions, explicit substitutions and `let-in` constructors have similar behaviors. However, in dependent type systems the relationship between both mechanisms is not immediate.

To illustrate that, let us take the typing rule for closures —explicit applications of substitutions to terms— in a dependent type system:

$$\frac{\Gamma \vdash S \triangleright \Delta \quad \Delta \vdash M : N}{\Gamma \vdash [S]M : [S]N}\ (\Pi\text{-Clos})$$

Consider the context:

$$\Gamma = nil.\ nat{:}Type.\ T{:}nat \to Type.\ l{:}(\Pi n{:}nat.(T\ n)).\ 0{:}nat.\ m{:}(T\ 0) \to nat$$

Using the above typing rule, the term $[x := 0](m\ (l\ x))$ is ill-typed. This is because the information that the variable x will be substituted by 0 in the term $(m\ (l\ x))$ is not taken into account by the rule (Π-Clos). Therefore, the type of $(l\ x)$ is $(T\ x)$, not $(T\ 0)$ as expected by m. On the other hand, the same term can be written using the `let-in` notation as: `let` $x := 0$ `in` $(m\ (l\ x))$. This term is well-typed because x has the value 0 in $(m\ (l\ x))$, and thus `let` $x := 0$ `in` $(m\ (l\ x))$ is typed as if it was $(m\ (l\ 0))$. However, to unfold definitions before typing is not sufficient when we admit meta-variables in λ-terms since substitutions and meta-variables may appear in normal forms. We cannot escape to have a (Π-Clos)'s like rule.

The approach that we have taken is to consider explicit substitutions different from the `let-in` mechanism. Explicit substitutions is a syntactic feature to allow substitutions to be part of the formal language by means of special constructors and reduction rules. In this way, the term $[x := 0](m\ (l\ x))$ is ill-typed, just as the term $(\lambda x{:}nat.(m\ (l\ x))\ 0)$ is. The `let-in` structure has a more complex behavior. It provides a mechanism for definitions in the language. Formal presentations of type systems with definitions are given in [29, 3].

Our main contribution is the complete meta-theoretical development of a dependent type system with explicit substitutions which handle explicitly open expressions (i.e. expressions with meta-variables). The system enjoys the usual typing properties: type uniqueness, subject reduction, weak normalization and confluence. Application of a such that calculus are representation of incomplete proofs and higher-order unification.

In this paper we have presented the $\lambda\Pi$-theory, but work is in progress to extend this formulation to more complex type theories as for example the Calculus of Inductive Constructions.

Acknowledgments Many thanks to all persons contributing to this work with useful remarks and suggestions, in particular to Gilles Dowek, Delia Kesner, Bruno Barras, Benjamin Werner, and the anonymous referees. The author is very grateful with Thomas Arts and Hans Zantema for their help with Proposition 1, in particular Hans Zantema send to me a complete proof in [34].

References

1. M. Abadi, L. Cardelli, P.-L. Curien, and J.-J. Lévy. Explicit substitution. *Journal of Functional Programming*, 1(4):375–416, 1991.
2. R. Bloo. Manuscript, 1997.
3. R. Bloo, F. Kamareddine, and R. Nederpelt. The Barendregt cube with definitions and generalised reduction. *Information and Computation*, 126(2):123–143, 1 May 1996.
4. R. Di Cosmo and D. Kesner. Strong normalization of explicit substitutions via cut elimination in proof nets. In *To appear in the Proceedings of the 12th Annual IEEE Symposium on Logic in Computer Science (LICS'97) Warsaw, Poland*, July 1997.

5. P.-L. Curien, T. Hardin, and J.-J. Lévy. Confluence properties of weak and strong calculi of explicit substitutions. *Journal of the ACM*, 43(2):362–397, March 1996.
6. G. Dowek, T. Hardin, and C. Kirchner. Higher-order unification via explicit substitutions (extended abstract). In *Proceedings, Tenth Annual IEEE Symposium on Logic in Computer Science*, pages 366–374, San Diego, California, 26–29 June 1995. IEEE Computer Society Press.
7. G. Dowek, T. Hardin, C. Kirchner, and F. Pfenning. Unification via explicit substitutions: The case of higher-order patterns. In M. Maher, editor, *Proceedings of the Joint International Conference and Symposium on Logic Programming*, Bonn, Germany, September 1996. MIT Press. To appear.
8. H. Geuvers. The Church-Rosser property for $\beta\eta$-reduction in typed λ-calculi. In *Proceedings, Seventh Annual IEEE Symposium on Logic in Computer Science*, pages 453–460, Santa Cruz, California, 22–25 June 1992. IEEE Computer Society Press.
9. H. Geuvers. A short and flexible proof of Strong Normalization for the Calculus of Constructions. In P. Dybjer and B. Nordström, editors, *Types for Proofs and Programs, International Workshop TYPES'94*, volume 996 of *LNCS*, pages 14–38, Båstad, Sweden, 1994. Springer.
10. H. Geuvers and B. Werner. On the Church-Rosser property for expressive type systems and its consequences for their metatheoretic study. In *Proceedings, Ninth Annual IEEE Symposium on Logic in Computer Science*, pages 320–329, Paris, France, 4–7 July 1994. IEEE Computer Society Press.
11. J. Goubault-Larrecq. Une preuve de terminaison faible du $\lambda\sigma$-calcul. Technical Report RR-3090, Unité de recherche INRIA-Rocquencourt, Janvier 1997.
12. R. Harper, F. Honsell, and G. Plotkin. A framework for defining logics. *Journal of the Association for Computing Machinery*, 40(1):143–184, 1993.
13. G. Huet. Confluent reductions: Abstract properties and applications to term rewriting systems. *J.A.C.M.*, 27(4), October 1980.
14. F. Kamareddine and A. Ríos. The λ_f-calculus: its typed and its extended versions. manuscript, June 1995.
15. D. Kapur, P. Narendran, and F. Otto. On ground-confluence of term rewriting systems. *Information and Computation*, 86(1):14–31, May 1990.
16. D. Kapur and H. Zhang. RRL: A rewrite rule laboratory-user's manual. Technical Report 89-03, Department of Computer Science, The University of Iowa, 1989.
17. C. Kirchner and C. Ringeissen. Higher order equational unification via explicit substitutions. In *Proceedings International Conference PLILP/ALP/HOA'97*, Southampton (England), September 1997. Lecture Notes in Computer Science. Springer-Verlag.
18. J.-W. Klop. Combinatory reduction systems. *Mathematical Center Tracts*, (27), 1980.
19. P. Lescanne. From $\lambda\sigma$ to $\lambda\upsilon$ a journey through calculi of explicit substitutions. In *Proceedings of the 21st Annual ACM SIGPLAN-SIGACT Symposium on Principles of Programming Languages*, pages 60–69, January 1994.
20. L. Magnusson. *The Implementation of ALF—A Proof Editor Based on Martin-Löf's Monomorphic Type Theory with Explicit Substitution*. PhD thesis, Chalmers University of Technology and Göteborg University, January 1995.
21. P.-A. Melliès. Typed λ-calculi with explicit substitutions may not terminate. In *Typed Lambda Calculi and Applications*, number 902 in LNCS. Second International Conference TLCA'95, Springer-Verlag, 1995.

22. C. Muñoz. Proof representation in type theory: State of the art. In *Proceedings, XXII Latinamerican Conference of Informatics CLEI Panel 96*, Santafé de Bogotá, Colombia, June 1996.
23. C. Muñoz. A left-linear variant of $\lambda\sigma$. In *Proceedings International Conference PLILP/ALP/HOA'97*, Southampton (England), September 1997. Lecture Notes in Computer Science. Springer-Verlag.
24. G. Nadathur. The (SCons) rule. Personal communication, 1996.
25. B. Pagano. Confluent extensions of $\lambda_{\Uparrow}$. Personal communication, 1996.
26. A. Ríos. *Contributions à l'étude de λ-calculs avec des substitutions explicites.* PhD thesis, U. Paris VII, 1993.
27. E. Ritter. Categorical abstract machines for higher-order lambda calculi. *Theoretical Computer Science*, 136(1):125–162, 1994.
28. M. Schmidt-Schauss. *Computational aspects of an order-sorted logic with term declarations*, volume 395 of *Lecture Notes in Computer Science and Lecture Notes in Artificial Intelligence.* Springer-Verlag Inc., New York, NY, USA, 1989.
29. P. Severi. *Normalisation in LAMBDA CALCULUS and its relation to type inference.* PhD thesis, Eindhoven University of Technology, 1996.
30. A. Tasistro. Formulation of Martin-Löf's theory of types with explicit substitutions. Technical report, Chalmers University of Technology, University of Göteborg, Göteborg, Sweden, May 1993.
31. B. Werner. *Une Théorie des Constructions Inductives.* PhD thesis, U. Paris VII, 1994.
32. H. Yokouchi and T. Hikita. A rewriting system for categorical combinators with multiple arguments. *SIAM Journal on Computing*, 19(1):78–97, February 1990.
33. H. Zantema. Termination of term rewriting by semantic labelling. *Fundamenta Informaticae*, 24:89–105, 1995.
34. H. Zantema. Termination of ϕ and Π_ϕ by semantic labelling. Personal communication, 1996.

Type Inference Verified: Algorithm $\mathcal{W}$ in Isabelle/HOL *

Wolfgang Naraschewski and Tobias Nipkow

Technische Universität München**

1 Introduction

Most functional programming languages [14, 11, 2] have a common core: the simply typed λ-calculus enriched with `let`-expressions, i.e. local definitions of polymorphic values. This language is called Mini-ML [3]. The set of well-typed Mini-ML expressions is inductively defined by a set of inference rules. One of the key properties of Mini-ML is that every well-typed expression has a most general type. The computation of the most general type is called *type inference*. It was first studied by Hindley [10] in the context of combinatory logic and later independently by Milner [13] for Mini-ML. Milner's type inference algorithm is known as algorithm $\mathcal{W}$. Damas [4, 5] proved the completeness of $\mathcal{W}$.

This paper presents the first machine-checked proof of correctness and completeness of $\mathcal{W}$. It is an extension of the work by Nazareth and Nipkow [15], who treated the monomorphic case (no `let`-expressions). A partial verification of $\mathcal{W}$ in the proof checker Coq is reported by Dubois and Ménissier-Morain [7]. Our paper provides the definition of (due to lack of space: almost) all concepts, the key lemmas, but almost no proofs. The complete development is accessible via `http://www4.informatik.tu-muenchen.de/~nipkow/isabelle/HOL/MiniML/`.

In the sequel we employ the following terminology: an *informal* proof is one which has been developed on paper in the mathematical tradition, whereas a *formal* proof means a machine-checked one.

2 Isabelle/HOL

Isabelle is an interactive theorem prover which can be instantiated with different object logics. One particularly well-developed instantiation is Isabelle/HOL, which supports Church's formulation of Higher Order Logic and is very close to Gordon's HOL system [8]. In the remainder of the paper HOL is short for Isabelle/HOL. A detailed introduction to Isabelle and HOL can be found elsewhere [19].

Logical expressions are written as usually, except for the fact that we use two different implications ($\Longrightarrow$, $\Rightarrow$) and equalities ($\equiv$, $=$). This distinction stems

* Research supported by Esprit WG TYPES and DFG SPP Deduktion.

** Institut für Informatik, 80290 München, Germany.
`http://www4.informatik.tu-muenchen.de/~{narasche,nipkow}/`
`{narasche,nipkow}@informatik.tu-muenchen.de`

from the object and meta-logic, respectively, and can be ignored while reading this paper. The notation `[| A1; ...; An |]` $\Longrightarrow$ `A` is an abbreviation for the nested implication `A1` $\Longrightarrow \ldots \Longrightarrow$ `An` $\Longrightarrow$ `A`. The predicate $\leq$ is overloaded and applies to natural numbers and to sets.

Types follow the syntax for ML-types, except that the function arrow is $\Rightarrow$ rather than $\rightarrow$. A term `t` is constrained to be of type τ by writing `t ::` τ. Isabelle also provides Haskell-like *type classes* [11], the details of which are explained as we go along. A type variable α is restricted to be of class `c` by writing α `:: c`.

Theories introduce constants with the keyword **consts**, non-recursive definitions with **defs**, and primitive recursive definitions with the keyword **primrec**. For general axioms the keyword **rules** is used. Further constructs are explained as we encounter them.

Although we do not present any of the proofs, we usually indicate their complexity. If we do not state any complexity the proof is almost automatic. That means, it is either solved by rewriting or by the "classical reasoner", `fast_tac` in Isabelle parlance [20]. The latter provides a reasonable degree of automation for predicate calculus proofs. Note, however, that its success depends on the right selection of lemmas supplied as parameters. Furthermore, difficult proofs require manual instantiations of quantifiers.

3 Types, type variables and substitutions

This section describes the language of object-level types of Mini-ML. They should not be confused with Isabelle's built-in meta-level type system described in the previous section. To avoid ambiguities we sometimes call the latter *HOL types*.

This is not a section of exciting theorems but one of basic definitions. Although the corresponding Isabelle theory contains over 90 theorems, only a few are worth mentioning explicitly, many are proved automatically and none are particularly difficult.

3.1 Types and type variables

Types consist only of type variables and the function space constructor. They are immediately formalized as an inductive data type:

```
datatype typ = TVar nat | typ -> typ
```

Type variables are modeled by natural numbers.

In order to express ML-style polymorphism we also need quantified types, so called *type schemes*. They are of the form $\forall\alpha_1,\ldots,\alpha_n.\tau$, where the α_i are type variables and τ is a type. A natural formalization would be a pair of a set or list of type variables and a type. However, anybody familiar with formalizations of terms with bound variables appreciates the advantage of being able to distinguish bound and free variables syntactically (see e.g. [12, 16]). Therefore we decided on the following data type with separate constructors for free and bound variables:

```
datatype type_scheme = FVar nat | BVar nat
                     | type_scheme ↣ type_scheme
```

This is essentially the representation chosen by Dubois and Ménissier-Morain [7].

For example, `BVar i ↣ FVar j` represents the type scheme $\forall\alpha.\alpha \to \beta$. Note that `i` and `j` need not be distinct. In particular, there is no de Bruijn index-like mechanism going on here that requires a particular numbering scheme for bound variables. This is because all quantifiers occur at the same (outermost) level and their order is irrelevant.

Having separated types and type schemes (in contrast to informal treatments, which regard types as a subset of type schemes), we need an embedding:

```
consts  make_scheme :: typ ⇒ type_scheme
primrec typ
  make_scheme (TVar n)   = FVar n
  make_scheme (t1 → t2) = (make_scheme t1) ↣ (make_scheme t2)
```

which is easily proved injective.

There are two functions for collecting the free and the bound variables in a type. In addition we will need to determine the free variables of a type scheme and of a list of type schemes. To avoid cluttering the text with lots of special notation, we use Isabelle's overloading facility which resembles Haskell-style type classes [11]. We introduce a new class `type_struct`

```
classes type_struct < term
```

as a subclass of the predefined class `term` of all HOL types and declare `free_tv` and `bound_tv` for all types of class `type_struct`:

```
consts free_tv, bound_tv :: (α::type_struct) ⇒ nat set
```

There are three instances of class `type_struct`:

```
instance typ ::          type_struct
instance type_scheme :: type_struct
instance list ::         (type_struct)type_struct
```

The final one states that a list over a type of class `type_struct` (for example a context) is again of class `type_struct`. Values of a type of class `type_struct` are called *type structures*. We can now define the corresponding instances of `free_tv`

```
primrec typ
  free_tv (TVar m) = {m}
  free_tv (t1 → t2) = (free_tv t1) ∪ (free_tv t2)

primrec type_scheme
  free_tv (FVar m) = {m}
  free_tv (BVar m) = {}
  free_tv (S1 ↣ S2) = (free_tv S1) ∪ (free_tv S2)
```

```
primrec list
  free_tv [] = {}
  free_tv (x#xs) = (free_tv x) ∪ (free_tv xs)
```

and bound_tv. The latter are omitted because they follow the same pattern.

3.2 Substitutions

The literature usually formalizes substitutions as "finite" functions from variables to types, i.e. functions which are distinct from the identity at finitely many points only. We have chosen to formalize substitutions as ordinary functions:

```
types subst = nat ⇒ typ
```

This is not just in contrast to the informal literature, but also to other formal verifications involving substitutions [18, 7], which use association lists. The two reasons for our choice are:

1. We believe that functions are easier to handle than association lists.
2. We wanted to find out if the restriction to finite functions is essential or not.

The identity substitution is

```
consts id_subst :: subst
defs   id_subst ≡ (λn.TVar n)
```

Strictly speaking there is no need to introduce id_subst because it is identical to TVar by η-contraction. It is only a concession to readability.

Substitutions can be extended to types, type schemes, etc. Thus we introduce an overloaded application operation

```
consts app_subst :: subst ⇒ (α::type_struct) ⇒ α   ("$")
```

which can be applied to arbitrary type structures. The "$" is syntactic sugar for app_subst. Because identifiers in Isabelle may not contain "$" we may write $S instead of $ S. The notation $S emphasizes that we regard "$" as a modifier acting on the substitution S. We define app_subst for types, type schemes and lists:

```
primrec typ
  $S (TVar n) = S n
  $S (t1 → t2) = ($S t1) → ($S t2)

primrec type_scheme
  $S (FVar n) = make_scheme (S n)
  $S (BVar n) = BVar n
  $S (sch1 ↣ sch2) = ($S sch1) ↣ ($S sch2)

defs $S ≡ map ($S)
```

Note that in the last case `$S` on the left has type α `list` $\Rightarrow$ α `list` and on the right type $\alpha \Rightarrow \alpha$, where α`::type_struct`.

The *domain* and *codomain* of a substitution are defined as usual:

```
consts dom, cod :: subst ⇒ nat set
defs   dom S ≡ {n. S n ≠ TVar n}
       cod S ≡ ⋃ m ∈ dom S. free_tv (S m)
```

We call the union of domain and codomain the set of free variables of a substitution. In order to reuse `free_tv` we would need to declare

```
instance subst :: type_struct
```

which is not possible in Isabelle (or Haskell) because `subst` is not an atomic type but abbreviates `nat` $\Rightarrow$ `typ`. Instead, we must state the propagation of class membership for the type constructor $\Rightarrow$. We already met this mechanism when adding the list types to class `type_struct`. In the same way we define a functionality for the type constructor $\Rightarrow$ which is the infix name for `fun`:

```
instance fun :: (term,type_struct)type_struct
```

Because `nat::term` and `typ::type_struct`, this implies `subst::type_struct`. Note, however, that it also implies further types to belong to class `type_struct`, for example `bool` $\Rightarrow$ `typ`. This may seem a bit permissive but does no harm. Now we can define the `subst` instance of `free_tv`:

```
defs free_tv S ≡ (dom S) ∪ (cod S)
```

3.3 New type variables

Algorithm $\mathcal{W}$ needs to generate new type variables. Informal descriptions of the algorithm almost invariably ignore this issue. It is simply assumed that there always exists some type variable never used before. The obvious formalization is to pass the set of already used type variables as an argument to $\mathcal{W}$, add all new variables generated during the execution to this set, and return the enlarged set upon successful termination (see e.g. [17]). Because our type variables are natural numbers and thus ordered linearly, it suffices to pass $\mathcal{W}$ a counter instead of a set of variables and to increment the counter every time a new variable is needed. Predicate `new_tv` formalizes this notion of a new type variable. It takes a type variable and a type structure and determines whether the given variable is greater than any type variable occurring in the structure. Such a type variable is called *new w.r.t. the structure*.

```
consts new_tv :: nat ⇒ (α::type_struct) ⇒ bool
defs   new_tv n ts ≡ ∀m. m ∈ free_tv ts ⟶ m < n
```

This predicate is a necessary precondition for most propositions about algorithm $\mathcal{W}$. A simple consequence is

```
⟦ n ≤ m; new_tv n ts ⟧ ⟹ new_tv m ts
```

which holds for arbitrary type structures ts.

Proofs about $\mathcal{W}$ frequently require that we can choose new variables. This is expressed by the following lemmas

```
∃n. new_tv n (t::typ)
∃n. new_tv n (sch::type_scheme)
∃n. new_tv n (A::type_scheme list)
```

which depend on the finite nature of the type structures involved.

3.4 Unification

Type inference is based on unification of types. Of course the correctness of type inference does not depend on any particular implementation of unification but merely on general properties of unification. Therefore we introduce a function mgu (*most general unifier*), specify its characteristic properties, but provide no implementation. This is the only point in the whole development where we introduce new axioms as opposed to consistency preserving definitions. Of course we know that a function mgu which satisfies the axioms exists. Alternatively, we could have made mgu a parameter of all functions using it and the axioms about mgu preconditions of the theorems about those functions. However, that is overkill because mgu is not intended as a parameter of individual functions but of the whole development. It requires some form of parameterized theories to express this.

Unification may fail. To model the distinction between a successful computation and a failure situation we use the predefined HOL data type

```
datatype α option = None | Some α
```

Unification either terminates normally returning Some(S) for some substitution S, or indicates a failure situation by returning None:

```
consts mgu :: typ ⇒ typ ⇒ subst option
```

A most general unifier should satisfy the following three axioms:

```
rules mgu t1 t2 = Some U ⟹ $U t1 = $U t2
      [ mgu t1 t2 = Some U; $S t1 = $S t2 ] ⟹ ∃R. S = $R o U
      $S t1 = $S t2 ⟹ ∃U. mgu t1 t2 = Some U
```

The first axiom requires the result of mgu to be a unifier of the given types. The second one states that the computed unifier is a most general one. The third one requires mgu to return some result if its arguments are unifyable. This prevents trivial implementations which satisfy the first two axioms by always returning None.

Most general unifiers are only unique up to renaming of variables. Such a renaming may even introduce type variables not occurring in the types to be unified. Because we want to keep track of used variables we need one last axiom:

```
mgu t1 t2 = Some U ⟹ free_tv U ≤ free_tv t1 ∪ free_tv t2        (1)
```

This ensures that the algorithm does not introduce new type variables. We can then show that unification preserves the new type variable property:

$$[\![$$ `mgu t1 t2 = Some U; new_tv n t1; new_tv n t2` $]\!] \Longrightarrow$ `new_tv n U`

4 Well-Typed Expressions

Lambda expressions are written in de Bruijn notation [6] as an inductive data type with constructors for variables, abstraction, application and let:

```
datatype expr = Var nat | Abs expr |
                App expr expr | LET expr expr
```

Note that by `Var` we denote variables of expressions, whereas `TVar` and `FVar` represent type variables. The representation of variables, abstraction and application is quite standard, whereas the representation of the `let`-construct is less familiar. Before illustrating the `let`-constructor, we shortly recapitulate the idea of de Bruijn indices: The index `i` in a subterm `Var i` indicates that, when moving upward, `i` abstractions must be traversed until the corresponding binder is found. If there are no more than `i` surrounding abstractions, the variable is free, e.g. `Var 0` on its own. For example take the expression `Abs (App (Var 0) (Abs (App (Var 0) (Var 1))))` which stands for $\lambda x.(x\ (\lambda y.y\ x))$. This example shows that different occurrences of the same bound variable may be represented by different indices, depending on the depth of abstractions.

Semantically the expression `LET e1 e2` is short for `App (Abs e2) e1`. To see why this representation of `LET` is meaningful, we give the following example. The expression `LET (Abs (Var 0)) (App (Var 0) (Var 0))` is equivalent to `App (Abs (App (Var 0) (Var 0))) (Abs (Var 0))` which in turn stands for the application $(\lambda x.x\ x)\ (\lambda x.x) \xrightarrow{\beta} \lambda x.x\ \lambda x.x$ or in short $let\ f\ =\ \lambda x.x\ in\ f\ f$.

The datatype `expr` represents all lambda-expressions, but we are only interested in *well-typed* expressions, which we identify by a relation. To ensure consistent typing of multiple occurrences of the same variable, we keep track of its type scheme in a context. Since we use de Bruijn notation, the context is simply a list of type schemes, with the type scheme of variable `i` located at the `i`-th position.

```
types ctxt = type_scheme list
```

This is the only place where de Bruijn notation simplifies life for us. Expressions with explicit names require the context to be an association list which complicates lookup a little.

We introduce a relation between contexts, lambda-expressions and types:

```
consts has_type :: (ctxt * expr * typ)set
```

The proposition `(A,e,t)` $\in$ `has_type` should be read as "In context `A` expression `e` has type `t`". This relation allows an expression to have more than one type in a given context. To ease readability, Isabelle permits the more conventional notation `A ⊢ e :: t` instead of `(A,e,t) ∈ has_type`. Note that the delimiter `::` is now used for type annotations both in the logic and in the object level lambda-expressions (`expr`). The latter is easily distinguished by its leading ⊢.

Relation `has_type` is defined inductively, i.e. by a set of inference rules. Proposition `A ⊢ e :: t` holds iff it can be derived from the inference rules. HOL provides a package for defining inductive sets, which defines `has_type` to be the least set closed under the given inference rules.

```
inductive has_type
[ n < length A; t ◁ (nth n A) ] ⟹ A ⊢ Var n :: t
[ (make_scheme t1)#A ⊢ e :: t2 ] ⟹ A ⊢ Abs e :: t1 → t2
[ A ⊢ e1 :: t2 → t1; A ⊢ e2 :: t2 ] ⟹ A ⊢ App e1 e2 :: t1
[ A ⊢ e1 :: t1; (gen A t1)#A ⊢ e2 :: t ] ⟹ A ⊢ LET e1 e2 :: t
```

In the inference rules we encounter some new definitions which we shortly explain before justifying the inference rules themselves.

The function `nth :: nat ⇒ α list ⇒ α` selects the nth element of a list. A tuple `(t,sch)` is related by `◁ :: typ ⇒ type_scheme ⇒ bool` if and only if `t` is generated from `sch` by instantiating types for all bound variables. The function `gen :: ctxt ⇒ typ ⇒ type_scheme` is used to generalize the free variables of a type which do not occur free in the context.

Modulo the fact that we use de Bruijn notation, these are the type inference rules of the system DM' proposed in [3]. We have not based our case study on the original system of Damas [5] since in the equivalent system DM' there is exactly one inference rule for each syntactic construct, which eases the soundness and completeness proof.

Note that the simplicity of the `Abs`-rule is due to de Bruijn notation: the extended context `(make_scheme t1)#A` takes care of the fact that when descending into an abstraction all references to variables bound outside shift by 1. A similar argument holds for the `LET`-rule, except for the fact that `t1` is generalized, which is the only source of polymorphism in the system.

Clearly the properties of ◁ and `gen` play a crucial role in the soundness and completeness proof. Hence we study them in more detail.

4.1 Instances of type schemes

The whole point of type schemes is to represent a set of types, namely all those that can be obtained by instantiating the quantified (i.e. bound) variables. This is formalized by

```
consts bound_typ_inst :: subst ⇒ type_scheme ⇒ typ
primrec type_scheme
  bound_typ_inst S (FVar n) = TVar n
  bound_typ_inst S (BVar n) = S n
  bound_typ_inst S (sch1 ↣ sch2) =
    (bound_typ_inst S sch1) → (bound_typ_inst S sch2)
```

and induces a natural ordering between types and type schemes:

```
consts ◁ :: typ ⇒ type_scheme ⇒ bool (infixr 70)
defs   t ◁ sch ≡ ∃S. t = (bound_typ_inst S sch)
```

This in turn induces an ordering between type schemes:

```
sch' ≤ (sch::type_scheme) ≡ (∀t. t ◁ sch' ⟶ t ◁ sch)
```

Both ◁ and ≤ are pronounced "is a generic instance of". The key property of ≤ is preservation under substitutions:

```
sch' ≤ sch ⟹ $S sch' ≤ $S sch                                        (2)
```

This proposition looks simple enough but its proof eluded us until we consulted Damas [5, Prop. 10, p. 51], where this very lemma is proved. Damas uses an alternative characterization of `sch' ≤ sch`: `sch'` can be obtained by instantiating the quantified variables in `sch` and quantifying once more, subject to certain freeness conditions [5, Prop. 9, p. 50]. In order to formalize this in our framework, we need an operation for replacing bound variables by type schemes:

```
consts bound_scheme_inst ::
         (nat ⇒ type_scheme) ⇒ type_scheme ⇒ type_scheme
primrec type_scheme
  bound_scheme_inst S (FVar n) = FVar n
  bound_scheme_inst S (BVar n) = S n
  bound_scheme_inst S (sch1 ↣ sch2) =
    (bound_scheme_inst S sch1) ↣ (bound_scheme_inst S sch2)
```

Now the analogue of Prop. 9 by Damas simply becomes

```
(sch' ≤ sch) = (∃B. sch' = bound_scheme_inst B sch)                 (3)
```

There are no freeness conditions attached because free and bound variables are syntactically distinct. Using this proposition we can reduce (2) to the goal

```
∃B'. $S (bound_scheme_inst B sch) = bound_scheme_inst B' ($S sch)
```

which becomes trivial when applying the following additional lemma:

```
$S (bound_scheme_inst B sch) = bound_scheme_inst ($S o B) ($S sch)
```

This lemma may look a bit mysterious at first, but it is simply a form of the well known substitution lemma $s[t/x][u/y] = s[u/y][t[u/y]/x]$ provided x is not free in u. The freeness condition again disappears because free and bound variables are kept apart.

It is interesting to note that the proof of (2) required two additional concepts: the function `bound_scheme_inst` and another function (hidden in the proof of (3)) which replaces type variables in types by type schemes. Both functions are purely local to the proof.

4.2 Generalization

As already mentioned, the function **gen** is used to generalize the free variables of a type which do not occur free in the context. Formally this is captured by the following definition:

```
consts gen :: ctxt ⇒ typ ⇒ type_scheme
primrec gen typ
  gen A (TVar n) = if n ∈ (free_tv A) then (FVar n) else (BVar n)
  gen A (t1 → t2) = (gen A t1) ↣ (gen A t2)
```

In the soundness and completeness proof we use some simple propositions about **gen** like

```
free_tv t ≤ free_tv A ⟹ gen A t = make_scheme t
free_tv (gen ($S A) t # $S A) = free_tv ($S A)
gen ($S A) ($S t) ≤ $S (gen A t)                                    (4)
```

which can be proved almost automatically. The only lemma about **gen** that caused substantial problems during the development of the case study is the following:

```
(free_tv S) ∩ (free_tv t - free_tv A) = {}                           (5)
   ⟹ gen ($S A) ($S t) = $S (gen A t)
```

This lemma, which is crucial for the proof that **has_type** is closed under substitution, determines under which circumstances substitutions are compatible with **gen**. To see, why substitutions need not necessarily commute with **gen** consider the following counter-example. The substitution S such that

```
S x = TVar y,   S y = TVar y,   where x ≠ y
```

does not commute with **gen** [FVar y] (TVar x) since

```
gen ($S [FVar y]) ($S (TVar x)) = gen [FVar y] (TVar y) = FVar y
≠ BVar x = $S (BVar x) = $S (gen [FVar y] (TVar x))
```

Though the lemma itself is not difficult to prove, its application in the proofs appeared to be subtle. Each time we intended to use the lemma, its precondition did not hold. In all these cases, though, it was possible to replace the substitution involved by an equivalent one which fulfills the precondition.

4.3 Typing is closed under substitution

The following theorem shows that **has_type** is closed under substitution:

```
A ⊢ e :: t ⟹ ∀S. $S A ⊢ e :: $S t
```

For the monomorphic case it was stated in [15] that the theorem can be proved almost automatically by induction on the derivation of `A ⊢ e :: t`. When dealing with `let`-polymorphism, the induction also includes the `let`-case which is non-trivial and therefore presented in more detail. In this case the goal

```
$S A ⊢ LET e1 e2 :: $S t
```

has to be solved relying on the assumptions

```
∀S. $S A ⊢ e1 :: $S t1
∀S. $S (gen A t1)#A ⊢ e2 :: $S t
```

Applying the LET-rule, the goal splits into the following two subgoals

```
$S A ⊢ e1 :: ?ta                                        (6)
(gen ($S A) ?ta)#($S A) ⊢ e2 :: $S t                    (7)
```

where ?ta is an unknown to be instantiated arbitrarily. For substitutions S which are compatible with gen the subgoals trivially hold, choosing ?ta to be $S t1. Unfortunately the substitution S need not meet the precondition of lemma (5) (see section 4.2). To circumvent this problem, we replace the substitution S in (6) and (7) by the substitution S' = (λx. if x ∈ free_tv A ∪ free_tv t then S x else (TVar x)), which is equivalent in this context. Furthermore, we choose for the unknown ?ta the type $(S' o α) t1 where α is defined as follows:

```
α = λx. if x ∈ free_tv A then x else x + n
```

with n new for A, t, $S A and $S t. The existence of such a variable n is guaranteed by the lemma

```
∃n. new_tv n A ∧ new_tv n t ∧ new_tv n ($S A) ∧ new_tv n ($S t)
```

Note that (after restating) the first subgoal is trivial because by definition of α we have $S A = $(S o α) A. We now can apply the lemma (5) to subgoal (7) since free_tv S' ≤ free_tv A ∪ free_tv t ∪ free_tv $S A ∪ free_tv $S t and free_tv ($(TVar o α) t1) − free_tv A ≤ {x. ∃y. x = n + y}. Subgoal (7) then becomes $S' (gen A ($(TVar o α) t1))#A ⊢ e2 :: $S' t which again is not immediate. To complete the proof, we use the relation ≤ which we explained in Section 4.1. The remaining proof relies on some (non-trivial) lemmas:

```
[ A ⊢ e :: t; A ≤ B ] ⟹ B ⊢ e :: t                     (8)
sch1 ≤ sch2 ⟹ $S sch1 ≤ $S sch2
new n A ⟹ gen A t ≤ gen A ($(TVar o α) t)
```

An alternative formulation of lemma (5) avoids the introduction of the relation ≤ at the price of having to deal with α-conversion explicitely. This includes proving that has_type is invariant under α-conversion. Compared to this solution, the presented solution is more elegant and shorter; in particular since we have to deal with ≤ in the completeness proof anyway.

5 Algorithm $\mathcal{W}$

The aim of the algorithm $\mathcal{W}$ is to compute the most general type of a given λ-term. If $\mathcal{W}$ succeeds, it returns a substitution S together with a type t such that `$S A ⊢ e :: t`. At certain points $\mathcal{W}$ requires fresh type variables. As already explained in Section 3.3, we handle this problem by passing a counter, for which we require an additional result component. Altogether, $\mathcal{W}$ has the following type:

```
consts  W :: expr ⇒ ctxt ⇒ nat ⇒ (subst * typ * nat)option
```

$\mathcal{W}$ is recursively defined on the term structure.

```
primrec W expr
  W (Var i) A n =
      (if i < length A then
         Some(id_subst,
               bound_typ_inst (λb. TVar(b + n)) (nth i A),
               n + (min_new_bound_tv (nth i A)))
         else None)

  W (Abs e) A n = ((S,t,m) := W e ((FVar n)#A) (Suc n);
                   Some(S, (S n) → t, m))

  W (App e1 e2) A n = ((S1,t1,m1) := W e1 A n;
                       (S2,t2,m2) := W e2 ($S1 A) m1;
                       U := mgu ($S2 t1) (t2 → (TVar m2));
                       Some($U o $S2 o S1, U m2, Suc m2))

  W (LET e1 e2) A n =
      ((S1,t1,m1) := W e1 A n;
       (S2,t2,m2) := W e2 ((gen ($S1 A) t1)#($S1 A)) m1;
       Some($S2 o S1, t2, m2))
```

A call `W e A n` fails if `A` contains no entry for some free variable in `e`, or if a call of the unification algorithm `mgu` fails. The failure propagation is invisibly handled by the monadic `option_bind`

```
constdefs
  option_bind :: (α option) ⇒ (α ⇒ (β option)) ⇒ β option
  option_bind m f ≡ case m of None ⇒ None ∨ Some r ⇒ f r
```

for which Isabelle permits the notation `P := E; F` instead of `option_bind E (λP.F)`. Compared with the algorithm in [15], we do not only have to deal with the `let`-case, but also with a slightly modified `var`-case: In the polymorphic algorithm a context comprises type schemes rather than types. To assign a variable `n` its corresponding "type" we have to convert the type scheme `nth n A` into a type by turning bound variables into fresh type variables. This is achieved by the function `bound_typ_inst :: subst ⇒ type_scheme ⇒ typ`. Accordingly, we increase the counter by the smallest bound variable which is new for `nth n`

A. The function `min_new_bound_tv :: type_scheme ⇒ nat` computes this offset. The definition of the `let`-case is a straightforward implementation of the algorithm given in [5].

So far we have ignored the fact that the function **gen** tests whether a variable is an element of a set of variables, which entails the function **gen** to be non-computable. We have chosen this definition of the function **gen** because in the soundness and completeness proofs it is easier to deal with sets of variables than with lists of variables. To ensure the computability of algorithm $\mathcal{W}$ we show that **gen** equals a computable function **gen_ML**:

```
gen A t = gen_ML A t
```

The function **gen_ML** is implemented straightforwardly, relying on an auxiliary function **aux**:

```
consts aux :: nat list ⇒ typ ⇒ type_scheme
primrec aux typ
  aux A (TVar n) = (if (n mem A) then (FVar n) else (BVar n))
  aux A (t1 → t2) = ((aux A t1) ↣ (aux A t2))

consts gen_ML :: ctxt ⇒ typ ⇒ type_scheme
defs gen_ML A t ≡ aux (free_tv_ML A) t
```

The function `free_tv_ML :: type_scheme ⇒ nat list` in this definition is a computable counterpart of the function `free_tv`.

Having introduced the basic definitions and lemmas, we now turn to the main goal of this case study, namely the proof of correctness of algorithm $\mathcal{W}$. Correctness is defined as soundness and completeness w.r.t. the type inference rules.

5.1 Soundness of $\mathcal{W}$

In contrast to the monomorphic case, we use in the soundness of $\mathcal{W}$ already the same lemmas we need for completeness – which was quite surprising to us. Furthermore we have shown soundness only for new counters. This is no real limitation since we can always compute such a new counter (see Section 3.3). Soundness is stated as follows:

```
⟦ new_tv n A; W e A n = Some (S,t,m) ⟧ ⟹ $S A ⊢ e :: t
```

This proposition is shown by induction on the structure of e using some auxiliary lemmas, all of which deal with the problem of new type variables. In mathematical proofs about type inference algorithms (including Damas' own) the problem of new type variables is simply ignored. The first lemma states that the counter for new type variables is never decreased:

```
W e A n = Some (S,t,m) ⟹ n ≤ m
```

It is proved by induction on the structure of e and in turn helps us to prove the following lemma:

$$[\![\texttt{new\_tv n A; W e A n} = \texttt{Some (S,t,m)}]\!] \Longrightarrow \texttt{new\_tv m A} \wedge \texttt{new\_tv m S} \wedge \texttt{new\_tv m t} \tag{9}$$

It expresses that the resulting type variable is new w.r.t. the context, the computed substitution and the computed type term. This fact ensures that we can safely use the returned type variable as new type variable in subsequent computations. Again, we use induction on the structure of `e`. In the `let`-case many explicit instantiations are required whereas further automation seems unlikely.

Now we can prove a proposition that seems to be quite obvious. Roughly speaking, it says that type variables free in either the computed substitution or the computed type term did not materialize out of the blue: they either occur in the given context or were taken from the set of new type variables. Formally, the proposition is expressed as follows:

$$[\![\texttt{W e A n} = \texttt{Some (S,t,m); v} \in \texttt{free\_tv S} \vee \texttt{v} \in \texttt{free\_tv t; v} < \texttt{n}]\!] \Longrightarrow \texttt{v} \in \texttt{free\_tv A}$$

The proof is performed by induction on the structure of term `e`. The complexity of this proof is roughly the same as the complexity of the proof of (9).

5.2 Completeness of $\mathcal{W}$

With the help of these propositions we are able to show completeness of $\mathcal{W}$ w.r.t. the type inference rules: if a closed term `e` has type `t'` then $\mathcal{W}$ terminates successfully and returns a type which is more general than `t'`, i.e. `t'` is an instance of that type.

$$\texttt{[]} \vdash \texttt{e :: t'} \Longrightarrow \exists \texttt{S t. } (\exists \texttt{m. W e [] n} = \texttt{Some(S,t,m)}) \wedge (\exists \texttt{R. t'} = \texttt{\$R t})$$

This proposition needs to be generalized considerably before it is amenable to induction:

$$[\![\texttt{\$S' A} \vdash \texttt{e :: t'; new\_tv n A}]\!] \Longrightarrow \exists \texttt{S t. } (\exists \texttt{m. W e A n} = \texttt{Some (S,t,m)}) \wedge (\exists \texttt{R. \$S' A} = \texttt{\$R (\$S A)} \wedge \texttt{t'} = \texttt{\$R t})$$

The proofs for abstraction and application are quite analogous to the ones in [15]. Proving the `var`-case is more tedious but not really difficult. To show the `let`-case we used the lemmas (4), (8) and (9). Surprisingly, the `let`-case is much more straightforward than application.

6 Conclusion

This verification is more than just another case study. Potentially it is the basis for

1. verified variations of $\mathcal{W}$, of which there exist many. For example, Nipkow and Prehofer [17] give a very detailed but (as we now noticed) still incomplete informal proof of a type inference algorithm for Haskell's type classes.

2. a verified Mini-ML compiler. We are aware of two formal proofs of the back end of a Mini-ML compiler [9, 1], unfortunately conducted in different systems (Elf and Coq). The time is ripe to combine these individual efforts.

How does our proof compare to Damas'?

1. Despite the fact that we consulted his proof only in the few cases where we were stuck, we ended up with an overall proof structure which is remarkably close to his. The same seems to be true for the proof by Dubois and Ménissier-Morain [7]. The latter, however, is harder to judge because they present only a selection of their definitions and their development was not complete at the time.
2. We did not compare the two proofs line by line, but in the cases where we did check, Damas' proof is remarkably detailed and free of flaws. This is certainly a tribute to Damas' thoroughness (which, unfortunately, seems to have failed him in his work on reference types [21, p. 2]).
3. The major complication, which we already encountered in the monomorphic case, is the treatment of new variables, which Damas, as most other authors, simply takes for granted. In the presence of `let` the situation is worse than before, because we now need to think very carefully about new variables already for the soundness proof. Hence our work is more than a mere formalization of Damas' proof.

Concerning the theorem proving process itself, we found that it rarely was the bottleneck. Finding the right formalization of our informal ideas and finding the right lemmas was much more crucial and time consuming than convincing Isabelle that we were right.

Finally, there are two interesting technical points. We have shown that the dogmas of idempotence and finiteness of substitutions can be relaxed quite easily:

1. instead of idempotence, a slightly weaker property (1) of mgus suffices. For details see the discussion in [15].
2. instead of finite functions, substitutions may be arbitrary total functions.

Acknowledgements We sincerely thank Dieter Nazareth for his collaboration in the earlier verification which this paper relies and builds on.

References

1. S. Boutin. Preuve de correction de la compilation de mini-ml en code cam dans le système d'aide à la démonstration coq. Technical Report 2536, INRIA, Apr. 1995.
2. R. Burstall, D. MacQueen, and D. Sannella. Hope: an experimental applicative language. In *Proc. 1980 LISP Conference*, pages 136–143, 1980.
3. D. Clément, J. Despeyroux, T. Despeyroux, and G. Kahn. A simple applicative language: Mini-ML. In *Proc. ACM Conf. Lisp and Functional Programming*, pages 13–27, 1986.

4. L. Damas and R. Milner. Principal type schemes for functional programs. In *Proc. 9th ACM Symp. Principles of Programming Languages*, pages 207–212, 1982.
5. L. M. M. Damas. *Type Assignment in Programming Languages*. PhD thesis, Department of Computer Science, University of Edinburgh, 1985.
6. N. G. de Bruijn. Lambda calculus notation with nameless dummies, a tool for automatic formula manipulation, with application to the Church-Rosser theorem. *Indagationes Mathematicae*, 34:381–392, 1972.
7. C. Dubois and V. Ménissier-Morain. A proved type inference tool for ML: Damas-Milner within Coq (work in progress). In J. von Wright, J. Grundy, and J. Harrison, editors, *Supplementary Proc. 9th Int. Conf. Theorem Proving in Higher Order Logics*, pages 15–30. Turku Centre for Comp. Sci., 1996.
8. M. Gordon and T. Melham. *Introduction to HOL: a theorem-proving environment for higher order logic*. Cambridge University Press, 1993.
9. J. Hannan and F. Pfenning. Compiler verification in LF. In *7th IEEE Symp. Logic in Computer Science*, pages 407–418. IEEE Computer Society Press, 1992.
10. J. R. Hindley. The principal type-scheme of an object in combinatory logic. *Trans. AMS*, 146:29–60, 1969.
11. P. Hudak, S. Peyton Jones, and P. Wadler. Report on the programming language Haskell: A non-strict, purely functional language. *ACM SIGPLAN Notices*, 27(5), May 1992. Version 1.2.
12. J. McKinna and R. Pollack. Pure type systems formalized. In M. Bezem and J. Groote, editors, *Typed Lambda Calculi and Applications*, volume 664 of *Lect. Notes in Comp. Sci.*, pages 289–305. Springer-Verlag, 1993.
13. R. Milner. A theory of type polymorphism in programming. *J. Comp. Sys. Sci.*, 17:348–375, 1978.
14. R. Milner, M. Tofte, and R. Harper. *The Definition of Standard ML*. MIT Press, 1990.
15. D. Nazareth and T. Nipkow. Formal verification of algorithm W: The monomorphic case. In J. von Wright, J. Grundy, and J. Harrison, editors, *Theorem Proving in Higher Order Logics*, volume 1125 of *Lect. Notes in Comp. Sci.*, pages 331–346. Springer-Verlag, 1996.
16. T. Nipkow. Functional unification of higher-order patterns. In *8th IEEE Symp. Logic in Computer Science*, pages 64–74. IEEE Computer Society Press, 1993.
17. T. Nipkow and C. Prehofer. Type reconstruction for type classes. *J. Functional Programming*, 5(2):201–224, 1995.
18. L. C. Paulson. Verifying the unification algorithm in LCF. *Science of Computer Programming*, 5:143–169, 1985.
19. L. C. Paulson. *Isabelle: A Generic Theorem Prover*, volume 828 of *Lect. Notes in Comp. Sci.* Springer-Verlag, 1994.
20. L. C. Paulson. Generic automatic proof tools. Technical Report 396, University of Cambridge, Computer Laboratory, 1996.
21. M. Tofte. Type inference for polymorphic references. *Information and Computation*, 89:1–34, 1990.

Continuous Lattices in Formal Topology

Sara Negri

Department of Philosophy
PL 24, Unioninkatu 40 B
00014 University of Helsinki, Finland
e-mail: negri@helsinki.fi

Abstract. A representation of continuous and prime-continuous lattices via formal topology is found. This representation stems from special examples of formal topologies in constructive analysis that give rise to the definition of the classes of locally Stone and locally Scott formal topologies. As an application, a representation theorem for locally compact spaces is obtained.

1 Introduction

Continuous lattices were first introduced by Dana Scott in [Sc] as models for untyped λ-calculus (cf. [Sc1]). They were later extensively studied (cf. [Comp, BH]) and used as a unifying viewpoint for domain theory (as in [AJ]).

Continuous lattices also arise in formal topology, in applications to constructive analysis, for instance in the definition of formal reals, formal intervals and formal linear functionals (cf. [NS, CN, CCN]).

The purpose of this paper is to make precise the connection between continuous lattices and formal topology, in such a way that these lattices can be seen as lattices of opens of particular formal spaces.

We start with setting down all the basic notions of formal topology needed. Some definitions differ slightly from the ones given for instance in [S], mainly because we avoid using the positivity predicate. We also single out a relation more general than the cover relation, already introduced in [BS] and called there infinitary preorder, that is needed when facing the problem of representing nondistributive structures.

The basic examples of formal topologies recalled in section 3 all have a cover relation with "nice" approximation features that are summarized in the definition of *locally Stone* formal topology. The further example of partial reals, i.e., formal reals allowing imprecise points, is analyzed here, and motivates the definition of *locally Scott* formal topology.

Section 4 is the core of the paper: Here it is shown that these two classes of formal topologies give rise, by considering the corresponding lattices of saturated subsets, to continuous and prime-continuous lattices, respectively, and that every continuous or prime-continuous lattice can be represented in this way via formal topology. The representation for continuous and prime-continuous lattices is part of an equivalence that connects infinitary preorders with sup-lattices and formal topologies with frames.

The idea of representing lattices by means of lattices of opens of a topological space goes back to Stone and was often taken over in the literature for various lattice-theoretic structures. By using poinfree spaces instead of topological spaces, we avoid the use of nonconstructive principles. Moreover, by using formal topology, the main results of the spectral theory of continuous lattices (cf. [HL] and [Comp], ch. V) are obtained in a much simpler and more general way.

In the last section we apply our results to get a representation theorem of sober locally compact spaces via formal topology. The axiom of choice is here needed in order to prove extensionality of locally Stone formal topologies. Apart from this unavoidable use of a nonconstructive principle for matching pointfree and point-set topology, all our results are constructive and the proofs elementary.

All the examples of locally Stone formal topologies given here have been implemented in the type-theoretical proof editor HALF (cf. [JC1, JC2]).

2 Formal Topology

Formal topologies were introduced by Per Martin-Löf and Giovanni Sambin ([S, S1]), as a constructive approach to pointfree topology in the tradition of *locale theory* [I, J, FG], but using Martin-Löf's constructive type theory instead of set theory.

The definition of a formal topology is obtained by abstracting from the definition of a topological space $\langle X, \Omega(X)\rangle$, without mentioning the points. Since a point-set topology can always be presented using one of its bases, the abstract structure that we consider is a commutative monoid $\langle S, \cdot\rangle$ where the set S corresponds to the base of the point-set topology $\Omega(X)$ and the dot corresponds to the operation of intersection between basic subsets.

In a point-set topology any open set is obtained as a union of elements of the base, but union does not make sense if we refuse reference to points; hence we are naturally led to think that an open set may directly correspond to a subset of the set S. For this purpose we introduce a relation $\lhd$, called *cover*, between an element a of S and a subset U of S. In terms of points, when b^* is the set of points of the neighbourhood b, $a \lhd U$ can be interpreted as $a^* \subseteq \bigcup_{b\in U} b^*$. The conditions we require of the cover relation are all justified in such an interpretation in terms of point-set topology.

Definition 1. A *formal topology* over a set S is a structure

$$\mathcal{A} \equiv \langle S, \cdot, \lhd\rangle$$

where $\langle S, \cdot\rangle$ is a commutative monoid, $\lhd$ is a relation, called *cover*, between elements and subsets of S such that, for any $a, b \in S$ and $U, V \subseteq S$, the following conditions hold:

reflexivity $\dfrac{a \in U}{a \lhd U}$

transitivity $\dfrac{a \lhd U \qquad U \lhd V}{a \lhd V}$ where $U \lhd V \equiv (\forall u \in U)\; u \lhd V$

dot - left $\dfrac{a \lhd U}{a \cdot b \lhd U}$

dot - right $\dfrac{a \lhd U \qquad a \lhd V}{a \lhd U \cdot V}$ where $U \cdot V \equiv \{u \cdot v \,|\, u \in U, v \in V\}$

An *infinitary preorder* is a structure $\langle S, \lhd \rangle$, where S is a set and $\lhd$ is a relation between elements and subsets of S satisfying reflexivity and transitivity.

In contrast to the definition of formal topology given in [S], we do not require the base monoid to have a unit, since the role of the unit element can be taken over by the whole monoid S, nor do we have a positivity predicate. The generalization of the definition of formal topology to that of infinitary preorder already appears in [BS] and will be used here for the representation of nondistributive structures.

In the sequel, we shall omit brackets from singleton sets.

The rule of *localization*

$$\frac{a \lhd U}{a \cdot b \lhd U \cdot b}$$

is derivable from the rules for a cover, and is actually equivalent to dot - right if the cover satisfies contraction, i.e., for all $a \in S$, $a \lhd a \cdot a$.

Given an infinitary preorder $\mathcal{A}$, we denote with *Sat*($\mathcal{A}$) the collection of *saturated subsets* of $\mathcal{A}$, that is, of the subsets U of S such that $\mathcal{A}U = U$, where

$$\mathcal{A}U \equiv \{a \in S \mid a \lhd U\}\ .$$

We will write $U =_{\mathcal{A}} V$ for $U \lhd V \,\&\, V \lhd U$.

Sat($\mathcal{A}$) is a complete lattice, with arbitrary joins given by

$$\bigvee_{i \in I} \mathcal{A}U_i \equiv \mathcal{A}(\bigcup_{i \in I} U_i)\ .$$

If $\mathcal{A}$ is a formal topology, the meet in *Sat*($\mathcal{A}$) is given by

$$\mathcal{A}U \wedge \mathcal{A}V \equiv \mathcal{A}U \cap \mathcal{A}V = \mathcal{A}(U \cdot V)$$

and it is easily seen to be distributive over arbitrary joins, thus making *Sat*($\mathcal{A}$) into a frame (cf. [S1, BS]).

In order to connect the pointfree approach to classical point-set topology, a notion of point has to be recovered. Since we reverse the usual conceptual order between points and opens, and take the opens as primitive, points are defined as particular, well behaved, collections of opens. We recall here the definition of formal point of a formal topology:

Definition 2. Let $\mathcal{A} \equiv \langle S, \cdot, \lhd \rangle$ be a formal topology. A subset α of S is said to be a *formal point* if for all $a, b \in S$, $U \subseteq S$ the following conditions hold:

1. $(\exists a \in S)(a \in \alpha)$;
2. $\dfrac{a \in \alpha \quad b \in \alpha}{a \cdot b \in \alpha}$;
3. $\dfrac{a \in \alpha \quad a \lhd U}{(\exists b \in U)(b \in \alpha)}$.

We observe that this definition of formal points reduces to the usual one (as given in [S]) if the formal topology $\mathcal{A}$ is equipped with a unit 1 and a positivity predicate Pos. Indeed, $1 \in \alpha$ follows from condition *1* and $a \lhd 1$ for all a; the rule $\dfrac{a \in \alpha}{Pos(a)}$ follows from the rule of positivity, in the form $a \lhd a^+$, where $U^+ \equiv \{b \in U \mid Pos(b)\}$, and *3*.

In order to maintain the usual intuition on points, we will write $\alpha \Vdash a$ (α forces a, or α is a point in a) in place of $a \in \alpha$.

Formal topologies can be made into a category, **FTop**, whose objects are formal topologies and whose morphisms, corresponding to the inverses of continuous functions between topological spaces, are defined as follows (cf. the appendix of [NV] for a more detailed motivation of this definition):

Definition 3. Let $\mathcal{A} = \langle S, \cdot_{\mathcal{A}}, \lhd_{\mathcal{A}} \rangle$, and $\mathcal{B} = \langle T, \cdot_{\mathcal{B}}, \lhd_{\mathcal{B}} \rangle$ be two formal topologies. A morphism from $\mathcal{A}$ to $\mathcal{B}$ is a map f, from elements of S to subsets of T, such that the following conditions are satisfied:

1. $f(S) =_{\mathcal{B}} T$;
2. $f(a \cdot_{\mathcal{A}} b) =_{\mathcal{B}} f(a) \cdot_{\mathcal{B}} f(b)$;
3. $\dfrac{a \lhd_{\mathcal{A}} U}{f(a) \lhd_{\mathcal{B}} \bigcup_{b \in U} f(b)}$.

Two morphisms f and g from $\mathcal{A}$ to $\mathcal{B}$ are *equal* if, for all $a \in S$, $f(a) =_{\mathcal{B}} g(a)$. If $\mathcal{A}$ and $\mathcal{B}$ are infinitary preorders, a morphism from $\mathcal{A}$ to $\mathcal{B}$ is a map f from S to $\mathcal{P}(T)$ such that the third of the above conditions is satisfied.

In the presence of the unit, the first condition above is equivalent to the usual one,

$$f(1_{\mathcal{A}}) =_{\mathcal{B}} 1_{\mathcal{B}} ,$$

and ensures that the corresponding frame morphism (defined below) preserves finite meets, hence, in particular, the top element, that can be given as the meet of the empty set.

We can extend *Sat* from objects to morphisms as follows: For $U \in Sat(\mathcal{A})$ and f a morphism from $\mathcal{A}$ to $\mathcal{B}$, we put

$$Sat(f)(U) \equiv \mathcal{B}(\bigcup_{b \in U} f(b)) .$$

In this way we obtain a functor that gives an equivalence between the category of infinitary preorders and the category of sup-lattices (cf. [JT] for the latter). Such an equivalence restricts to an equivalence between the category of formal topologies and the category of frames.

We recall that for any formal topology $\mathcal{A}$, the formal space $Pt(\mathcal{A})$ of formal points on $\mathcal{A}$ can be endowed with a topology, called the *extensional topology.* A base of this topology is given by the family $\{ext(a)\}_{a \in S}$ where $a \in S$ and $ext(a)$ is the collection of formal points forcing a.

By the condition of monononicity for formal points, if $a \lhd U$, then for any formal point α such that $\alpha \Vdash a$, we have $\alpha \Vdash U$. The converse does not necessarily hold, and indeed is the defining property of *extensional* formal topologies.

The following result is the counterpart of a well known result for spatial locales; its proof can be easily obtained from the proof of the latter (cf. [J]):

Theorem 4. *The category of extensional formal topologies is equivalent to the category of sober topological spaces with continuous maps.*

In section 5 we will specialize this result to an equivalence between a particular class of formal topologies and locally compact sober topological spaces.

We recall from [S] that a cover $\lhd$ on a base S is called a *Stone* cover if, for all $a \in S$ and $U \subseteq S$, $a \lhd U$ implies $a \lhd U_0$ for some finite subset U_0 of U (written $U_0 \subseteq_\omega U$). We remark that the notion of being Stone can apply not just to a cover, but, with more generality, to any infinitary preorder. In particular, we have:

Proposition 5. *If $\mathcal{A}$ is a Stone infinitary preorder, then $Sat(\mathcal{A})$ is an algebraic lattice, i.e., it has a basis of compact elements.*

Proof: The complete lattice $Sat(\mathcal{A})$ is generated by compact elements since, for any element U we have $U = \bigvee_{a \in U} \mathcal{A}a$, and every element of the base in compact by definition of Stone infinitary preorder. □

We recall from [N] that we also have the related result (seen now as a corollary of the above one just by adding distributivity):

Proposition 6. *If $\mathcal{A}$ is a Stone formal topology, then $Sat(\mathcal{A})$ is a coherent frame.*

We say that a cover $\lhd$ on S is a *Scott cover* (or alternatively, as in [Si], that it has the *Scott property*) if for all $a \in S$ and $U \subseteq S$,

$$a \lhd U \text{ implies } a \lhd b \text{ for some } b \in U \tag{1}$$

We remark that this notion of Scott cover differs from the one given in [S] and used in [SVV], where the condition (1) is only required for positive elements of the base.

As above, this notion of being Scott, can apply as well to an infinitary preorder.

Given two covers $\lhd_1$ and $\lhd_2$ on the same base S, we say that $\lhd_2$ is a *quotient* of $\lhd_1$ (or is *greater* than $\lhd_1$) if for all $a \in S$ and $U \subseteq S$,

$$a \lhd_1 U \Rightarrow a \lhd_2 U \ .$$

The *Stone* (resp. *Scott*) *compactification* of a cover is defined as the greatest Stone (resp. Scott) cover of which the given cover is a quotient. They are defined, respectively, by

$$a \lhd_f U \equiv (\exists U_0 \subseteq_\omega U)(a \lhd U_0)$$

$$a \lhd_s U \equiv (\exists b \in U)(a \lhd b) \ .$$

The Stone and Scott compactifications for infinitary preorders are defined in the same way.

3 Real numbers, intervals and linear functionals

In this section we show examples of formal topologies in which the cover is presented via a Stone or Scott cover. They are all given by means of a *finitary inductive definition* (cf. [A]), where each rule involved has only finitely many premises. We start with the topology of formal reals (cf. [N1], [NS], [CN], [CCN]). This is our motivating example and we therefore recall the presentation in detail.

The following definition, which is the one used in [JC2], was proposed by Thierry Coquand.

Definition 7. The *formal topology of formal reals* is the structure

$$\mathcal{R} \equiv \langle Q \times Q, \cdot, \lhd_{\mathcal{R}} \rangle,$$

where Q is the set of rational numbers and the monoid operation is defined by $(p, q) \cdot (r, s) \equiv (max(p, r), min(q, s))$; the cover $\lhd_{\mathcal{R}}$ is defined by

$$(p, q) \lhd_{\mathcal{R}} U \equiv (\forall p', q')(p < p' < q' < q \rightarrow (p', q') \lhd_{\mathcal{R}_f} U),$$

where the relation $\lhd_{\mathcal{R}_f}$ is inductively defined by

1. $\dfrac{q \leq p}{(p, q) \lhd_{\mathcal{R}_f} U}$;
2. $\dfrac{(p, q) \in U}{(p, q) \lhd_{\mathcal{R}_f} U}$;
3. $\dfrac{(p, s) \lhd_{\mathcal{R}_f} U \quad (r, q) \lhd_{\mathcal{R}_f} U \quad p \leq r < s \leq q}{(p, q) \lhd_{\mathcal{R}_f} U}$;
4. $\dfrac{(p', q') \lhd_{\mathcal{R}_f} U \quad p' \leq p < q \leq q'}{(p, q) \lhd_{\mathcal{R}_f} U}$.

In [CN], it is proved that both $\lhd_{\mathcal{R}}$ and $\lhd_{\mathcal{R}_f}$ are covers, the latter being the Stone compactification of the former.

The proof that $\lhd_{\mathcal{R}}$ is a cover makes essential use of a lemma, that we recall here from [CN] since it will be used elsewhere in this paper and later presented in a more abstract way:

Lemma 8. *Suppose* $(p,q) \lhd_{\mathcal{R}_f} U$, $U \lhd_{\mathcal{R}} V$, *and let* $p < p' < q' < q$. *Then* $(p',q') \lhd_{\mathcal{R}_f} V$.

We can widen the collection of formal reals by allowing also "imprecise" numbers. The presentation of the formal topology having *partial reals* as formal points is obtained by omitting the first and third axiom from the definition we gave for $\lhd_{\mathcal{R}_f}$:

Definition 9. The *formal topology of partial reals* is the structure

$$\mathcal{PR} \equiv \langle Q \times Q, \cdot, \lhd_{\mathcal{PR}} \rangle,$$

with $\lhd_{\mathcal{PR}}$ defined as in definition 7 from a relation $\lhd_{\mathcal{PR}_s}$ fulfilling conditions 2 and 4 of the definition of $\lhd_{\mathcal{R}_f}$.

It is easy to prove the following:

Proposition 10. *1. The relations* $\lhd_{\mathcal{PR}}$ *and* $\lhd_{\mathcal{PR}_s}$ *are covers.*

2. For all $a \in Q \times Q$ *and* $U \subseteq Q \times Q$, $a \lhd_{\mathcal{PR}_s} U$ *implies* $a \lhd_{\mathcal{PR}} U$.

3. For all $a \in Q \times Q$ *and* $U \subseteq Q \times Q$, $a \lhd_{\mathcal{PR}_s} U$ *implies that there exists* $b \in U$ *such that* $a \lhd_{\mathcal{PR}_s} b$.

We will denote with $Pt(\mathcal{PR})$ the formal points of $\mathcal{PR}$.

Formal reals can be described as well-located partial reals. First, we recall the following (cf. [NS]):

Definition 11. For any rational p, $\bar{p}$ is the formal real $\{(r,s) : r < p < s\}$.

Proposition 12. *If* α *and* β *are formal reals, the relations given by*

$\alpha < \beta \equiv (\exists (p,q) \in \alpha)(\exists (r,s) \in \beta)(q < r)$;

$\alpha \leq \beta \equiv \neg(\beta < \alpha)$;

$\alpha \# \beta \equiv \alpha < \beta \vee \beta < \alpha$.

are relations of strict linear order, partial order and apartness, respectively.

Then we can easily characterize those partial reals that are also formal reals:

Proposition 13. *Let* $\alpha \in Pt(\mathcal{PR})$. *Then the following are equivalent:*

1. $\alpha \in Pt(\mathcal{R})$.
2. $(\forall p,q)(p < q \rightarrow \bar{p} < \alpha \vee \alpha < \bar{q})$.
3. $(\forall k \in Q^+)(\exists (p,q))(q - p < k \;\&\; \alpha \Vdash (p,q))$.

A global version of the above characterization is given by the following:

Corollary 14. $Pt(\mathcal{PR}) = Pt(\mathcal{R})$ *iff the relation* $\#$ *is an apartness relation on* $Pt(\mathcal{PR})$.

We now turn to another example of inductively generated formal topology.

Similarly to the definition of formal reals, we can define the formal space $[a, b]$ that corresponds to the closed interval of the real line with rational endpoints a and b (cf. [CN]): The base is the same as the base of the space of formal reals, and the cover relation is defined by

$$(p, q) \lhd_{[a,b]} U \equiv (p, q) \lhd_{\mathcal{R}} U \cup C([a, b])$$

where $C([a, b]) = \{(r, a) \mid r < a\} \cup \{(b, s) \mid b < s\}$. It is then proved that the formal points of this space are exactly the formal reals α with $a \leq \alpha \leq b$.

There is an alternative definition of this space in which an explicit presentation of its Stone compactification is given. This is achieved by adding to the axioms for the finitary cover $\lhd_{\mathcal{R}_f}$ of formal reals two axioms expressing the fact that intervals not overlapping with $[a, b]$ are covered by anything.

Definition 15. Let a, b be rationals with $a < b$. The *formal topology of the closed interval* $[a, b]$ is the structure

$$[a, b] \equiv \langle Q \times Q, \cdot, \lhd' \rangle,$$

with the relation $\lhd'$ defined by

$$(p, q) \lhd' U \equiv (\forall p', q')(p < p' < q' < q \rightarrow (p', q') \lhd'_f U),$$

and the relation $\lhd'_f$ is inductively defined by

1. $\dfrac{(p, q) \lhd_{\mathcal{R}_f} U}{(p, q) \lhd'_f U}$;
2. $\dfrac{q \leq a}{(p, q) \lhd'_f U}$;
3. $\dfrac{b \leq p}{(p, q) \lhd'_f U}$.

Then we have

Proposition 16. *The relation $\lhd'$ is a cover, equivalent to the cover $\lhd_{[a,b]}$, with Stone compactification given by $\lhd'_f$.*

Proof: We start with proving that $\lhd'_f$ is a cover: Since we already know that $\lhd_{\mathcal{R}_f}$ is a cover, to get to the conclusion we only need to prove that transitivity, dot-left and localization hold when $(p, q) \lhd'_f U$ is derived from the new axioms 2 and 3 in definition 15, which is straightforward. In order to prove that $\lhd'$ is a cover, we observe that lemma 8 also holds when $\lhd_{\mathcal{R}}$ and $\lhd_{\mathcal{R}_f}$ are replaced with $\lhd'$ and $\lhd'_f$, respectively: this is seen by the trivial inspection of the cases in which $(p, q) \lhd'_f U$ is obtained by axiom 2 or 3. This directly implies that $\lhd'$ satisfies transitivity. The verification that it satisfies reflexivity, dot-left and dot-right is easy.

We proceed with proving the equivalence between $\lhd'$ and $\lhd_{[a,b]}$. Suppose that $(p, q) \lhd' U$ and let $p < p' < q' < q$. Then by definition we have $(p', q') \lhd'_f U$.

We then prove by induction on the derivation of $(p', q') \lhd'_f U$ that $(p', q') \lhd_{\mathcal{R}_f} U \cup C([a, b])$ follows. If it is obtained by axiom 1 the claim is trivial. If it is derived by 2 or 3, then $(p', q') \lhd_{\mathcal{R}_f} C([a, b])$ and therefore the conclusion follows by reflexivity and transitivity for $\lhd_{\mathcal{R}_f}$. We have thus proved that $(p, q) \lhd_{\mathcal{R}} U \cup C([a, b])$. Conversely, assume that $(p, q) \lhd_{\mathcal{R}} U \cup C([a, b])$, and let $p < p' < q' < q$. Then we have $(p', q') \lhd_{\mathcal{R}_f} U \cup C([a, b])$. We then argue by induction on this derivation in order to prove that $(p', q') \lhd'_f U$. For axiom 1 the claim is trivial. Then suppose that $(p', q') \in U \cup C([a, b])$. If $(p', q') \in U$, the conclusion follows by reflexivity and transitivity for $\lhd'_f$. If $(p', q') \in C([a, b])$, then by axioms 2 and 3 we get $(p', q') \lhd'_f U$. For axioms 3 and 4 we apply the inductive hypotheses to the premises.

The proof that $\lhd'_f$ is a Stone cover is done by induction on the derivation: If $(p, q) \lhd'_f U$ is obtained from $(p, q) \lhd_{\mathcal{R}_f} U$ then the information that $\lhd_{\mathcal{R}_f}$ is a Stone cover provides us with a finite subcover. If it is obtained from $q \leq a$ or $b \leq p$ then the empty set is a finite subcover of (p, q).

The verification that $\lhd'$ is a quotient of $\lhd'_f$ is straightforward.

Finally, we have to prove that if $(p, q) \lhd' U$, with U a finite subset of $Q \times Q$, then $(p, q) \lhd'_f U$. By the above proof of equivalence of the two covers, $(p, q) \lhd' U$ implies $(p, q) \lhd_{[a,b]} U$, that is, $(p, q) \lhd_{\mathcal{R}} U \cup C([a, b])$. By localizing to (p, q) we get $(p, q) \lhd_{\mathcal{R}} U \cup \{(p, a), (b, q)\}$, and therefore, since $\lhd_{\mathcal{R}_f}$ is the Stone compactification of $\lhd_{\mathcal{R}}$, we get $(p, q) \lhd_{\mathcal{R}_f} U \cup \{(p, a), (b, q)\}$. By induction on the derivation of $(p, q) \lhd_{\mathcal{R}_f} U \cup \{(p, a), (b, q)\}$ (the inductive hypothesis being that $(p, q) \lhd_{\mathcal{R}_f} U \cup \{(x, a), (b, y)\}$ implies $(p, q) \lhd'_f U$, for arbitrary x and y), we find that $(p, q) \lhd'_f U$. □

We conclude this section by recalling another example of inductively generated formal topology, the topology of linear and continuous functionals of norm ≤ 1 from a seminormed linear space to the reals (cf. [CCN]).

Seminormed spaces can be defined as in [MP]:

Definition 17. A *seminormed space* A on the rationals Q is a linear space A on Q together with a mapping

$$N : Q^+ \longrightarrow \mathcal{P}(A)$$

from the positive rationals to the subsets of A satisfying the following conditions for $x, x' \in A$, $q, q' \in Q^+$:

$N1.$ $x \in N(q) \rightarrow (\exists q' < q)(x \in N(q'))$;
$N2.$ $(\exists q)(x \in N(q))$;
$N3.$ $x \in N(q)$ & $x' \in N(q') \rightarrow x + x' \in N(q + q')$;
$N4.$ $x \in N(q') \rightarrow qx \in N(qq')$;
$N5.$ $x \in N(q) \rightarrow -x \in N(q)$;
$N6.$ $0 \in N(q)$.

The basic opens of the formal space $\mathcal{L}(A)$ of linear functionals of norm ≤ 1 are finite sets of the form

$$w \equiv \{\langle x_1 \in I_1 \rangle, \ldots, \langle x_n \in I_n \rangle\} ,$$

where $x_1, \ldots, x_n$ are elements of A and $I_1, \ldots, I_n$ are rational intervals. The intuitive reading of a basic open is that of a neighbourhood of functionals in the *weak topology*. We use the notation $\langle x_1 \in I_1, \ldots, x_n \in I_n\rangle$ for $\{\langle x_1 \in I_1\rangle, \ldots, \langle x_n \in I_n\rangle\}$.

We obtain with the operation

$$w_1 w_2 \equiv w_1 \cup w_2$$

a commutative and idempotent monoid with unit given by the empty set. We will denote with $S_{\mathcal{L}(A)}$ such a base of $\mathcal{L}(A)$.

With $I = (p, q)$ and $J = (r, s)$, we write $I < J$ (resp. $I \leq J$) for $r < p < q < s$ (resp. $r \leq p < q \leq s$), and tI for (tp, tq) when $t \geq 0$ and for (tq, tp) when $t < 0$.

Let $w \equiv \langle x_1 \in I_1, \ldots, x_n \in I_n\rangle$, then define

$$w \leq \langle x \in I\rangle \equiv (\exists \langle x_{i_1} \in I_{i_1}\rangle, \ldots, \langle x_{i_p} \in I_{i_p}\rangle \in w)$$
$$(x_{i_1} = \ldots = x_{i_p} = x \ \& \ I_{i_1} \cdot \ldots \cdot I_{i_p} \leq I)$$

and

$$w \leq w' \equiv (\forall \langle x \in I\rangle \in w')(w \leq \langle x \in I\rangle).$$

Then, without assuming decidability of equality in A, $\leq$ is a reflexive and transitive relation.

Equality between basic neighbourhoods is subset equality

$$w = w' \equiv (\forall \langle x \in I\rangle)(\langle x \in I\rangle \in w \Leftrightarrow \langle x \in I\rangle \in w')\ .$$

The relation $\lhd_f$ is inductively defined by:

$$C1 \ \frac{w \in U}{w \lhd_f U}\ ;$$

$$C2 \ \frac{w \leq w' \quad w' \lhd_f U}{w \lhd_f U}\ ;$$

$$C3 \ \frac{V \mathit{finite} \quad I \lhd_{\mathcal{R}_f} V \quad (\forall J \in V)(\langle x \in J\rangle w' \lhd_f U)}{\langle x \in I\rangle w' \lhd_f U}\ ;$$

$$C4 \ \frac{\langle x + y \in I + J\rangle w' \lhd_f U}{\langle x \in I, y \in J\rangle w' \lhd_f U}\ ;$$

$$C5 \ \frac{r \neq 0 \quad \langle rx \in rI\rangle w' \lhd_f U}{\langle x \in I\rangle w' \lhd_f U}\ ;$$

$$C6 \ \frac{x \in N(1) \quad \langle x \in (-1, 1)\rangle w \lhd_f U}{w \lhd_f U}\ .$$

Then $\lhd$ is defined by

$$\langle x_1 \in I_1, \ldots, x_n \in I_n\rangle \lhd U \equiv (\forall J_1 < I_1, \ldots, J_n < I_n)(\langle x_1 \in J_1, \ldots, x_n \in J_n\rangle \lhd_f U).$$

In [CCN] it is then proved that $\lhd$ is a cover and that it is a quotient of the Stone cover $\lhd_f$.

4 Continuous and prime-continuous lattices in formal topology

The examples of the topologies of formal reals, intervals and linear functionals seen in the previous section motivate us to introduce the definition of two particular classes of formal topologies. We will see that these formal topologies permit a representation theorem for continuous and prime-continuous lattices.

Definition 18. A formal topology $\mathcal{A} \equiv \langle S, \cdot, \lhd \rangle$ is called *locally Stone* if there exists a map i from elements to subsets of S such that, for all $a \in S$ and $U \subseteq S$,

$$a \lhd U \Leftrightarrow (\forall b \in i(a))(b \lhd_f U)$$

where $\lhd_f$ is a Stone cover of which $\lhd$ is a quotient.

A formal topology is called *locally Scott* if there exists a map i as above such that, for all $a \in S$ and $U \subseteq S$,

$$a \lhd U \Leftrightarrow (\forall b \in i(a))(b \lhd_s U)$$

where $\lhd_s$ is a Scott cover of which $\lhd$ is a quotient.

It is clear from the results in the previous section that the topology of formal reals and of formal closed intervals are locally Stone and the topology of partial reals is locally Scott. In these examples we have

$$i((p,q)) = \{(p',q') : p < p' < q' < q\} .$$

The topology of linear functionals is locally Stone, and we have

$$i(\langle x_1 \in I_1, \ldots, x_n \in I_n \rangle) = \{\langle x_1 \in J_1, \ldots, x_n \in J_n \rangle \mid J_1 < I_1, \ldots, J_n < I_n\} .$$

The definitions of *locally Stone* and *locally Scott infinitary preorders* are obtained from the above in the obvious way, simply by replacing "formal topology" with "infinitary preorder".

We observe that a Stone (resp. Scott) formal topology $\mathcal{A} \equiv \langle S, \cdot, \lhd \rangle$ is locally Stone (resp. Scott) with $i(a) = \{a\}$ and $\lhd_f$ (resp. $\lhd_s$) the cover $\lhd$ itself. The same holds for infinitary preorders.

We have, with the notation introduced above:

Proposition 19. *If $\mathcal{A}$ is a locally Stone formal topology (or infinitary preorder), then for all a in the base S,*

$$a =_{\mathcal{A}} i(a) .$$

Proof: For all $b \in i(a)$ we have, by reflexivity, $b \lhd_f i(a)$, so by definition of locally Stone cover (or infinitary preorder) we have $a \lhd i(a)$.

Conversely, from $a \lhd a$, we have that for all $b \in i(a)$, $b \lhd_f a$. Since $\lhd$ is a quotient of $\lhd_f$, we also have that for all $b \in i(a)$, $b \lhd a$, i.e., $i(a) \lhd a$. □

We proceed with recalling some definitions and basic facts from domain theory (see [Comp], [AJ]).

Definition 20. Let L be a complete lattice and let $x, y \in L$. We say that x *approximates* y, or x is *way-below* y, and write

$$x \ll y ,$$

if, for all directed subsets A of L, $y \leq \bigvee A$ implies that there exists $a \in A$ such that $x \leq a$.

We say that x *prime-approximates* y, and write

$$x \lll y ,$$

if, for all subsets A of L, $y \leq \bigvee A$ implies that there exists $a \in A$ such that $x \leq a$.

A complete lattice is *continuous* if, for all $x \in L$, $x = \bigvee\{y \mid y \ll x\}$.

A complete lattice is *prime-continuous* if, for all $x \in L$, $x = \bigvee\{y \mid y \lll x\}$.

Definition 21. A subset S of a continuous lattice L is a *base* of L if, for all $a \in L$, the subset $\twoheaddownarrow_S a \equiv \{x \in S \mid x \ll a\}$ is directed with supremum a.

A subset S of a prime-continuous lattice L is a *base* of L if, for all $a \in L$, the subset $\Downarrow_S a \equiv \{x \in S \mid x \lll a\}$ is directed with supremum a.

Proposition 22 (Interpolation property). *In a continuous lattice, if $a \ll b$, there exists c such that $a \ll c \ll b$. In a prime-continuous lattice, if $a \lll b$, there exists c such that $a \lll c \lll b$.*

Proof: Cf. [J], VII 2.4, and [AJ], p. 69. □

We observe that given $a \ll b$ in a continuous lattice with base S, the interpolating c is not necessarily in S, but we can find $c_1, \ldots, c_n$ in S such that $a \ll \bigvee_{i=1}^{n} c_i \ll b$ (for a proof cf. [Si]).

The following two results are instances of theorems 7.1.1 and 7.1.3 in [AJ] (for the equational characterization of the class of continuous lattices, see also theorem I, 2.3 in [Comp]). The proofs of these stronger statements require the axiom of choice, whereas those we need have entirely constructive proofs:

Lemma 23. *A continuous lattice L satisfies the* directed infinite distributive law*: For any $a \in L$ and any directed subset $\{b_i : i \in I\}$ of L,*

$$a \wedge \bigvee_{i \in I} b_i = \bigvee_{i \in I} a \wedge b_i .$$

Proof: The inequality from right to left holds in any lattice, so the claim amounts to proving that $a \wedge \bigvee_{i \in I} b_i \leq \bigvee_{i \in I} a \wedge b_i$. Let $x \ll a \wedge \bigvee_{i \in I} b_i$. Then $x \ll \bigvee_{i \in I} b_i$ and therefore there exists $i \in I$ such that $x \leq b_i$ and indeed such that $x \leq a \wedge b_i$ since $x \leq a$. Thus $x \leq \bigvee_{i \in I} a \wedge b_i$. Since L is continuous this proves the claim. □

Lemma 24. *A distributive continuous lattice L satisfies the* infinite distributive law*: For any $a \in L$ and any subset $\{b_i : i \in I\}$ of L*

$$a \wedge \bigvee_{i \in I} b_i = \bigvee_{i \in I} a \wedge b_i .$$

Proof: Just observe that $\bigvee_{i\in I} b_i = \bigvee_{I_0 \subseteq_\omega I}\{\vee_{i\in I_0} b_i\}$ and that the set of finite subsets of I is directed and so are the suprema indexed on these. □

The above lemma explains why distributive continuous lattices are also called *continuous Heyting algebras.*

Lemma 25. *A prime-continuous lattice L satisfies the infinite distributive law.*

Proof: As 23, using prime-continuity instead of continuity. □

We proceed by showing that examples of continuous and prime-continuous lattices are given by the frames of saturated subsets of locally Stone and locally Scott infinitary preorders.

Theorem 26. *If $\mathcal{A}$ is a locally Stone infinitary preorder, then $Sat(\mathcal{A})$ is a continuous lattice.*

Proof: Let $U \in Sat(\mathcal{A})$. We have to prove that $U = \bigvee\{V \in Sat(\mathcal{A}) : V \ll U\}$, i.e., $U = \mathcal{A}(\bigcup\{V \in Sat(\mathcal{A}) : V \ll U\})$, or equivalently, since $V \ll U$ in $Sat(\mathcal{A})$ implies $V \lhd U$, $U \lhd \bigcup\{V \in Sat(\mathcal{A}) : V \ll U\}$. Observe that $b \in i(a)$ implies $\mathcal{A}b \ll \mathcal{A}a$: If $\mathcal{A}a \leq \bigvee_{i\in I} U_i$ where $\{U_i : i \in I\}$ is a directed subset of $Sat(\mathcal{A})$, then $a \lhd \bigcup_{i\in I} U_i$; since $b \in i(a)$, $b \lhd_f \bigcup_{i\in I} U_i$, and since the family is directed and $\lhd_f$ is a Stone infinitary preorder, there exists $i \in I$ such that $b \lhd_f U_i$, hence such that $b \lhd U_i$, so $\mathcal{A}b \leq \mathcal{A}U_i$. For all $a \in U$ and for all $b \in i(a)$, we have $\mathcal{A}b \ll \mathcal{A}a$, $\mathcal{A}a \leq U$ and therefore $\mathcal{A}b \ll U$, thus, since $U \lhd \bigcup_{a\in U}\{b : b \in i(a)\}$, we have the claim. □

Corollary 27. *If $\mathcal{A}$ is a locally Stone formal topology, then $Sat(\mathcal{A})$ is a distributive continuous lattice.*

We also obtain the converses of the above results, namely:

Theorem 28. *Every continuous lattice is isomorphic to the lattice of saturated subsets of a locally Stone infinitary preorder. If it is distributive it is isomorphic to the lattice of saturated subsets of a locally Stone formal topology.*

Before proving this theorem we need a couple of lemmas:

Lemma 29. *Let L be a continuous lattice. If $b \ll u_1 \vee \ldots \vee u_n$, there exist $b_1 \ll u_1, \ldots, b_n \ll u_n$ such that $b \leq b_1 \vee \ldots \vee b_n$.*

Proof: By continuity we have

$$u_1 \vee \ldots \vee u_n = \bigvee_{b_1 \ll u_1} b_1 \vee \ldots \vee \bigvee_{b_n \ll u_n} b_n$$

and therefore

$$u_1 \vee \ldots \vee u_n = \bigvee_{b_1 \ll u_1, \ldots, b_n \ll u_n} b_1 \vee \ldots \vee b_n$$

where the right-hand side is a directed join. The conclusion follows by definition of the way-below relation. □

The following lemma is an abstract formulation of lemma 8.

Lemma 30. *Let L be a continuous lattice, b, c elements of L and U, V subsets of L. Suppose $b \ll c$, $c \in \mathcal{I}(U)$ (where $\mathcal{I}(U)$ is the ideal generated by U) and for all $u \in U$, $\forall d(d \ll u \to d \in \mathcal{I}(V))$. Then $b \in \mathcal{I}(V)$.*

Proof: If $b \ll c$ and $c \leq u_1 \vee \ldots \vee u_n$, where $u_i \in U$ for $i = 1, \ldots, n$, then $b \ll u_1 \vee \ldots \vee u_n$. By lemma 29, there exist $b_1 \ll u_1, \ldots b_n \ll u_n$ such that $b \leq b_1 \vee \ldots \vee b_n$. By the assumption that for all $u \in U$, $\forall d(d \ll u \to d \in \mathcal{I}(V))$, we have that $b_i \in \mathcal{I}(V)$ for $i = 1, \ldots, n$, and therefore $b \in \mathcal{I}(V)$ as well. □

Proof of theorem 28: Let L be a continuous lattice. Define relations between elements and subsets of L (or of a base S of L which is a meet-semilattice) in the following way:

$$a \lhd U \equiv \forall b(b \ll a \to b \in \mathcal{I}(U)) ,$$

$$a \lhd_f U \equiv a \in \mathcal{I}(U) .$$

It is easy to verify that $\lhd_f$ is an infinitary preorder (satisfying in addition dot-left). As for $\lhd$ we prove the following:

- Reflexivity holds since $b \ll a$ implies $b \leq a$, so if $a \in U$, $b \in \mathcal{I}(U)$.
- Transitivity: Suppose $a \lhd U$ and $U \lhd V$ and let $b \ll a$. By the interpolation property, there exists $c \in L$ such that $b \ll c \ll a$ and therefore $c \in \mathcal{I}(U)$. By lemma 30, $b \in \mathcal{I}(V)$, so $a \lhd V$. In case we are working with a base S of L, the proof requires a closer inspection. By the remark after proposition 22, there exist $c_1, \ldots, c_n$ in S such that $b \ll \bigvee_{i=1}^{n} c_i \ll a$. For all $i \leq n$, $c_i \in \mathcal{I}(U)$, i.e., there exist $u_{i,1}, \ldots, u_{i,n_i}$ in U such that $c \leq u_{i,1} \vee \ldots \vee u_{i,n_i}$ and therefore $b \ll \bigvee_{i \leq n} u_{i,1} \vee \ldots \vee u_{i,n_i}$. By lemma 29, for all $i \leq n$ and for all $j \leq n_i$ there exists $b_{i,j} \ll u_{i,j}$ such that $b \leq \bigvee_{i \leq n} b_{i,1} \vee \ldots \vee b_{i,n_i}$. Since all the $b_{i,j}$'s are in $\mathcal{I}(V)$, so is b.
- Dot-left: If $a \lhd U$ and $b \ll a \wedge c$, then $b \ll a$, so $b \in \mathcal{I}(U)$.

If L is distributive, then $\lhd_f$ also satisfies localization. Localization for $\lhd$ is proved as follows: If $a \lhd U$ and $b \ll a \wedge c$, then $b \ll a$ and therefore $b \in \mathcal{I}(U)$. Since also $b \leq c$ we have, by distributivity, $b \in \mathcal{I}(U \wedge c)$.

Let $\mathcal{A}$ be the infinitary preorder/formal topology thus defined. We are now going to prove that $\lhd_f$ is the Stone compactification of $\lhd$:

- $a \lhd_f U \Rightarrow a \lhd U$ since $b \ll a$ implies $b \leq a$, so if $a \in \mathcal{I}(U)$, also $b \in \mathcal{I}(U)$.
- $a \lhd_f U \Rightarrow (\exists U_0 \subseteq_\omega U)(a \lhd_f U_0)$ holds by definition.
- $a \lhd U \;\&\; U \; finite \Rightarrow a \lhd_f U$: For all $b \ll a$, $b \leq \bigvee U$ and therefore $a \leq \bigvee U$. Since U is finite, $\bigvee U \in \mathcal{I}(U)$, hence $a \in \mathcal{I}(U)$, i.e., $a \lhd_f U$.

Finally, the bijection between L and $Sat(\mathcal{A})$ is given by the two mappings (with $\downarrow a$ replaced by $\downarrow_S a$ if S is a base of L)

$$\begin{array}{ll} Sat(\mathcal{A}) \to L & L \to Sat(\mathcal{A}) \\ U \mapsto \bigvee U & a \mapsto \downarrow a \end{array}$$

which are seen to be lattice/frame homomorphisms and inverses of each other. □

In [HL], a topological representation for distributive continuous lattices is obtained by using the *hull-kernel topology* on the *spectrum* of L. We recall that the spectrum $Spec(L)$ of a lattice L is the set of non-top *prime* elements, i.e. of elements p satisfying

$$a \wedge b \leq p \text{ implies } a \leq p \text{ or } b \leq p \; .$$

The hull-kernel topology is generated by the subsets $Spec(L) - \uparrow a$ with a ranging in L. For complete lattices this is the same as the extensional topology on the space of completely prime filters on L, $Pt(L)$: Every completely prime filter α on L is of the form $L - \downarrow p$ for a prime p (the supremum of the complement of α in L). By mapping p in $L - \downarrow p$ an anti-order isomorphism ϕ is obtained between $Spec(L)$ and $Pt(L)$. Moreover this map induces an isomorphism between the hull-kernel and the extensional topology on these spaces since $\phi(Spec(L) - \uparrow a) = \{\alpha \in Pt(L) \mid a \in \alpha\}$. From this observation it follows that the results concerning the spectral theory of (distributive) continuous lattices are obtained in our setting with dualities replaced by equivalences. In particular, corollary 27 is the poinfree part of the result in [HL] stating that distributive continuous lattices are isomorphic to the lattices of opens of sober locally compact topological spaces. This latter result in turn is obtained in our setting from the extensionality of locally Stone formal topologies (cf. proposition 35 below).

A similar representation theorem holds for prime-continuous lattices:

Theorem 31. *If $\mathcal{A}$ is a locally Scott infinitary preorder, then $Sat(\mathcal{A})$ is a prime-continuous lattice.*

Proof: As in the proof of theorem 26, we obtain $U = \bigvee\{V \in Sat(\mathcal{A}) : V \lll U\}$ since $b \in i(a)$ implies $\mathcal{A}b \lll \mathcal{A}a$ by definition of locally Scott infinitary preorder. □

Theorem 32. *Every prime-continuous lattice is isomorphic to the frame of saturated subsets of a locally Scott formal topology.*

Proof: Given a prime-continuous lattice L, define the following relations between elements and subsets of L (or, as before, of a base S of L which is a meet-semilattice), where $\downarrow U \equiv \bigcup_{u \in u} \downarrow u$:

$$a \lhd U \equiv \forall b(b \lll a \rightarrow b \in \downarrow U) \; ,$$

$$a \lhd_s U \equiv a \in \downarrow U \; .$$

The verification that $\lhd_s$ and $\lhd$ are covers is straightforward. Moreover, it is easy to prove that $\lhd_s$ is the Scott compactification of $\lhd$, since we have:

- $a \lhd_s U \Rightarrow a \lhd U$;
- $a \lhd_s U \Rightarrow (\exists b \in U)(a \lhd_s b)$;
- $a \lhd b \Rightarrow a \lhd_s b$.

The bijection between L and $Sat(\mathcal{A})$ is obtained as before. □

By the representation theorem for continuous lattices via locally Stone infinitary preorders we also obtain an alternative proof of the well known retraction theorem (cf. [Sc]):

Theorem 33. *Every continuous lattice is the retract of an algebraic lattice (via a continuous s-r pair).*

Proof: Let L be a continuous lattice. By theorem 28, there exists a locally Stone infinitary preorder $\mathcal{A}$ such that L is isomorphic to $Sat(\mathcal{A})$.

Let $\mathcal{A}_f$ be the Stone infinitary preorder defining $\mathcal{A}$. We have the following diagram, where s maps an element a of the base into the subset $i(a)$ and r is the identity map

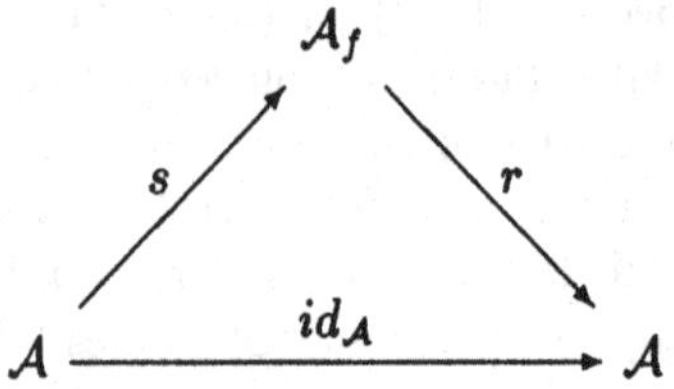

Since $\mathcal{A}$ is locally Stone, by proposition 19 every basic neighbourhood a is equicovered with $i(a)$, and therefore r and s factorize the identity arrow on $\mathcal{A}$ so that the diagram is commutative. By applying the functor *Sat* we obtain another commutative diagram (in the category of sup-lattices)

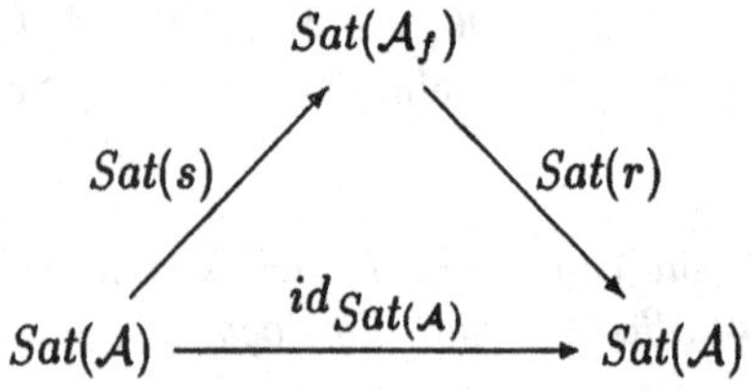

that yields the conclusion since $Sat(\mathcal{A}_f)$ is an algebraic lattice by proposition 5. □

Then, simply by adding distributivity, and using proposition 6, we get:

Corollary 34. *Every distributive continuous lattice is the retract of a coherent frame (via a continuous s-r pair).*

We remark that a different terminology can be found in the literature, where *arithmetic* is sometimes used instead of coherent when properties of the lattice of compact elements are given in terms of properties of the way-below relation. In view of proposition I.4.7 in [Comp], a coherent lattice is the same as an arithmetic lattice.

5 Representation of locally compact spaces

In this section we will see how locally Stone formal topologies can be identified with sober locally compact topological spaces. The identification takes the form of an equivalence of categories.

As usual when an equivalence has to be proved between pointfree and point-set spaces, the axiom of choice is required in the proof of extensionality (cf. the similar proof for locally compact locales in [J]):

Proposition 35. *A locally Stone formal topology $\mathcal{A}$ is extensional.*

Proof: Suppose that a and U are respectively an element and a subset of the base S of $\mathcal{A}$ and that $a \not\lhd U$. Our claim is that there exists a formal point α of $\mathcal{A}$ such that $a \in \alpha$ and $\alpha \cap U = \emptyset$. From the assumption $a \not\lhd U$ and the fact that $\mathcal{A}$ is a locally Stone formal topology, it follows that there exists $c \in i(a)$ such that $c \not\lhd_f U$. In the continuous lattice $Sat(\mathcal{A})$ we have $\mathcal{A}c \ll \mathcal{A}a$, so, by the interpolation property, we can inductively define a sequence $D_0, D_1, \ldots, D_n, D_{n+1}$ in $Sat(\mathcal{A})$ such that

$$\mathcal{A}c \ll D_{n+1} \ll D_n \ll \ldots \ll D_1 \ll D_0 \ll \mathcal{A}a \; .$$

Consider now $F \equiv \bigcup\{\uparrow D_n \,|\, n \geq 0\} = \bigcup\{\Uparrow D_n \,|\, n \geq 0\}$, where $\uparrow D_n = \{U \in Sat(\mathcal{A}) \,|\, D_n \lhd U\}$ and $\Uparrow D_n = \{U \in Sat(\mathcal{A}) \,|\, D_n \ll U\}$. Clearly, F is a filter in $Sat(\mathcal{A})$ and it is Scott open (being a union of basic Scott opens). Moreover, $\mathcal{A}a \in F$ and for all $b \in U$, $\mathcal{A}b \notin F$. By Zorn's lemma, F extends to a Scott open filter G maximal amongst those containing $\mathcal{A}a$ and having empty intersection with $\{\mathcal{A}b \,|\, b \in U\}$. By lemma VII.4.3 in [J], G is prime, and since it is Scott open, it is completely prime. By taking $\alpha \equiv \{b \in S \,|\, \mathcal{A}b \in G\}$ the desired point is obtained. □

We will denote with **LSFTop** the full subcategory of **FTop** given by locally Stone formal topologies. By the above proposition, **LSFTop** is classically a full subcategory of **EFTop**, the category of extensional formal topologies.

We have:

Proposition 36. *If $\mathcal{A}$ is a locally Stone formal topology, the frame of open sets in the extensional topology is a distributive continuous lattice.*

Proof: Since $\mathcal{A}$ is extensional by 35, the frame of opens of $Pt(\mathcal{A})$ with the extensional topology is isomorphic to $Sat(\mathcal{A})$. The conclusion follows by corollary 27. □

Proposition 37. *If $\mathcal{A}$ is a locally Stone formal topology, the formal space $Pt(\mathcal{A})$ with the extensional topology is a sober locally compact topological space.*

Proof: Let α be a point in $Pt(\mathcal{A})$, and let U be a neighbourhood of α in the extensional topology. It is not restrictive to suppose $U = ext(a)$, for some a in the base of $\mathcal{A}$. Since $a \lhd i(a)$ and $a \in \alpha$, by definition of formal points there exists $c \in i(a)$ such that $c \in \alpha$. In $Sat(\mathcal{A})$ we have $\mathcal{A}c \ll \mathcal{A}a$. Let F be the Scott open filter constructed as in the proof of proposition 35. We claim that $ext(F)$ is a compact neighbourhood of α contained in $ext(a)$.

It is clear that $ext(F)$ is a neighbourhood of α contained in $ext(a)$ since $c \lhd F$ implies $ext(c) \subseteq ext(F)$ and $F \lhd a$ implies $ext(F) \subseteq ext(a)$. As for compactness, suppose that $ext(F) \subseteq \bigcup_{i \in I} ext(U_i)$. By extensionality we have $F \lhd \bigcup_{i \in I} U_i$, and in the frame $Sat(\mathcal{A})$,

$$F \leq \bigvee_{U_0 \subseteq_\omega \bigcup_{i \in I} U_i} U_0$$

where the right-hand side is a directed join. Since F is a Scott open filter, there exists $U_0 \subseteq_\omega \bigcup_{i \in I} U_i$ such that $F \leq U_0$. Therefore, there exists $I_0 \subseteq_\omega I$ such that $F \lhd \bigcup_{i \in I_0} U_i$, that is, such that $ext(F) \subseteq \bigcup_{i \in I_0} ext(U_i)$. □

Conversely, we have the following:

Proposition 38. *Let $\langle X, \Omega(X) \rangle$ be a sober locally compact topological space. Then there exists a locally Stone formal topology $\mathcal{A}$ such that $\langle X, \Omega(X) \rangle$ is isomorphic to the formal space $Pt(\mathcal{A})$ with the extensional topology.*

Proof: We already know from the equivalence between formal topologies and sober topological spaces that the basic monoid of the formal topology corresponding to the topological space X consists of the basic opens with monoid operation given by set-theoretic intersection; the cover is defined by

$$a \lhd U \equiv a \subseteq \bigcup U$$

where a is a basic open of X, U is a collection of basic opens, and $\subseteq$ is the usual set-theoretic inclusion. It is straightforward, by the validity of the rules for formal topology in their extensional reading, that this defines a formal topology. In order to prove that this is indeed a locally Stone formal topology, we observe that by local compactness of the space X, the cover can be equivalently defined as follows:

$$a \lhd U \equiv (\forall b \ll a)(b \lhd_f U)$$

with $b \lhd_f U$ iff there exists a finite subset U_0 of U such that $b \subseteq \bigcup U_0$.

For one direction one just uses that $b \ll a$ iff there exists a compact open k with $b \subseteq k \subseteq a$. The converse follows since for any (basic) open set a in a locally compact topological space, $a = \bigcup_{b \ll a} b$. □

Let F be the functor from the category **FTop** to the category **Top** of topological spaces mapping a formal topology $\mathcal{A}$ to the formal space $Pt(\mathcal{A})$ with the extensional topology. It is well known that F gives an equivalence between the category **EFTop** of extensional formal topologies and the category **STop** of sober topological spaces. By a characterization of equivalence of categories (see [MCL]), F is *full*, *faithful* and *dense* (that is, it is bijective on morphisms and surjective, up to isomorphism, on objects). By proposition 37, F restricts to a functor, that we will denote by $\bar{F}$ between the category **LSFTop** and the category **SLCTop** of sober locally compact topological spaces. Since **LSFTop** and **SLCTop** are full subcategories of **EFTop** and **STop**, respectively, $\bar{F}$ is full and faithful. By proposition 38, $\bar{F}$ is dense. Therefore, by restriction of the equivalence between extensional formal topologies and sober topological spaces we have:

Theorem 39. *The category of locally Stone formal topologies is equivalent to the category of sober locally compact topological spaces.*

We observe that we can obtain the equivalence stated above in an alternative indirect way. First, by using the functor *Sat* that to a formal topology associates its frame of saturated subsets, by theorem 26 and theorem 28 we obtain an equivalence between the category of locally Stone formal topologies and the category of distributive continuous lattices. By composing this equivalence with the equivalence between the category of distributive continuous lattices and the category of sober locally compact topological spaces (see e.g. thm. 7.2.16 in [AJ]), we get an equivalence between the category of locally Stone formal topologies and the category of sober locally compact topological spaces.

Concluding remarks and related work

The correspondence between formal spaces and locally compact frames or equivalently, distributive continuous lattices, has been studied in detail in [Si] using neighbourhood systems and generators for cover relations.

An important difference with her work is that here we work constructively, and in addition extend the representation to nondistributive structures using the generalization of the notion of cover relation to that of infinitary preorder.

Another related work is [SiS] where two representations for regular locally compact spaces, one based on domains, another on formal spaces, are compared.

Representations of Scott domains based on formal spaces are given in [Si1, SVV]. In the latter work it is proved that any Scott domain is isomorphic to the partially ordered structure given by the *formal points* of a Scott formal topology, and an essential use of the positivity predicate is made. Here instead we represent continuous lattices via *formal opens* of suitable formal topologies.

A problem left open here is the extension of such a representation to lattices that are complete only with respect to directed joins, namely continuous dcpo's, that generalize both continuous lattices and Scott domains. Lattices of this kind are used in the domain-theoretic approach to integration (cf. [E, EN, EN1]).

Acknowledgement

This research partly originates from my work in the EPSRC project "Foundational Structures in Computer Science" at Imperial College, Department of Computing, that gave me the opportunity to become acquainted with the literature on continuous lattices.

References

[AJ] S. Abramsky, A. Jung. *Domain theory*, in "Handbook of Logic in Computer Science", vol. 3, Clarendon Press, Oxford, pp. 1–168, 1994.

[A] P. Aczel. *An introduction to inductive definitions*, in "Handbook of Mathematical Logic", J. Barwise (ed), North-Holland, pp. 739–782, 1977.

[BH] B. Banaschewski, R.-E. Hoffmann (eds), "Continuous Lattices", Lecture Notes in Mathematics 871, pp. 209–248, Springer, 1981.

[BS] G. Battilotti, G. Sambin. *A uniform presentation of sup-lattices, quantales and frames by means of infinitary preordered sets, pretopologies and formal topologies*, Preprint no. 19, Dept. of Pure and Applied Mathematics, University of Padova, 1993.

[JC] J. Cederquist. *A machine assisted formalization of pointfree topology in type theory*, Chalmers University of Technology and University of Göteborg, Sweden, Licentiate Thesis, 1994.

[JC1] J. Cederquist. *An implementation of the Heine-Borel covering theorem in type theory*, this volume.

[JC2] J. Cederquist. *A machine assisted proof of the Hahn-Banach theorem*, Chalmers University of Technology and University of Göteborg, 1997.

[CCN] J. Cederquist, T. Coquand, S. Negri. *The Hahn-Banach theorem in type theory*, to appear in "Twenty-Five Years of Constructive Type Theory" G. Sambin and J. Smith (eds), Oxford University Press.

[CN] J. Cederquist, S. Negri. *A constructive proof of the Heine-Borel covering theorem for formal reals*, in "Types for Proofs and Programs", S. Berardi and M. Coppo (eds), Lecture Notes in Computer Science 1158, pp. 62–75, Springer, 1996.

[E] A. Edalat. *Domain theory and integration*, Theoretical Computer Science 151, pp. 163–193, 1995.

[EN] A. Edalat, S. Negri. *The generalized Riemann integral on locally compact spaces (extended abstract)*, in "Advances in Theory and Formal Methods of Computing", A. Edalat, S. Jourdan and G. McCusker (eds), World Scientific, Singapore, 1996.

[EN1] A. Edalat, S. Negri. *The generalized Riemann integral on locally compact spaces*, Topology and its Applications (in press).

[FG] M. P. Fourman, R.J. Grayson. *Formal spaces*, in "The L. E. J. Brouwer Centenary Symposium", A. S. Troelstra and D. van Dalen (eds), pp. 107–122, North-Holland, Amsterdam, 1982.

[Comp] G. Gierz, K.H. Hoffmann, K. Keimel, J. D. Lawson, M. Mislove, D. S. Scott. "A Compendium on Continuous Lattices", Springer, 1980.

[HL] K.H. Hoffmann, J.D. Lawson. *The spectral theory of distributive continuous lattices*, Transactions of the American Mathematical Society 246, pp. 285–310, 1978.

[HM] K.H. Hoffmann, M.W. Mislove. *Local compactness and continuous lattices*, in "Continuous Lattices", B. Banaschewski and R.-E. Hoffmann (eds), *op. cit.*.

[I] J.R. Isbell. *Atomless parts of spaces*, Mathematica Scandinavica 31, pp. 5–32, 1972.

[J] P. T. Johnstone. "Stone Spaces", Cambridge University Press, 1982.

[JT] A. Joyal, M. Tierney. *An extension of the Galois theory of Grothendieck*, Memoirs of the American Mathematical Society 51, no. 309, pp. 1–71, 1984.

[MCL] S. MacLane. "Categories for the Working Mathematician", Springer, 1971.

[ML] P. Martin-Löf. "Notes on Constructive Mathematics", Almqvist & Wiksell, Stockholm, 1970.

[ML1] P. Martin-Löf. "Intuitionistic Type Theory", Bibliopolis, Napoli, 1984.

[MP] C.J. Mulvey, J.W. Pelletier. *A globalization of the Hahn-Banach theorem*, Advances in Mathematics 89, pp. 1-60, 1991.

[N] S. Negri. *Stone bases, alias the constructive content of Stone representation*, in "Logic and Algebra", A. Ursini and P. Aglianó (eds), Dekker, New York, pp. 617–636, 1996.

[N1] S. Negri. "Dalla topologia formale all'analisi", Ph. D. thesis, University of Padova, 1996.

[NS] S. Negri, D. Soravia. *The continuum as a formal space*, Archive for Mathematical Logic (in press).

[NV] S. Negri, S. Valentini. *Tychonoff's theorem in the framework of formal topologies*, The Journal of Symbolic Logic (in press).

[NPS] B. Nordström, K. Petersson, J. Smith, "Programming in Martin-Löf's Type Theory", Oxford University Press, 1990.

[S] G. Sambin. *Intuitionistic formal spaces – a first communication*, in "Mathematical Logic and its Applications", D. Skordev (ed), Plenum Press, New York, pp. 187–204, 1987.

[S1] G. Sambin. *Intuitionistic formal spaces and their neighbourhood*, in "Logic Colloquium '88", R. Ferro *et al.*, (eds), pp. 261-285, North-Holland, Amsterdam, 1989.

[SVV] G. Sambin, S. Valentini, P. Virgili. *Constructive domain theory as a branch of intuitionistic pointfree topology*, Theoretical Computer Science 159, pp. 319–341, 1996.

[Sc] D.S. Scott. *Continuous lattices*, in "Toposes, Algebraic Geometry and Logic", F.W. Lawvere (ed), Lecture Notes in Mathematics 274, pp. 97–136, Springer, 1972.

[Sc1] D.S. Scott. *Models for various type-free calculi*, in "Logic, Methodology and Philosophy of Science IV", P. Suppes *et al.* (eds), North-Holland, pp. 157–187, 1973.

[Si] I. Sigstam. "On formal spaces and their effective presentations", Ph. D. thesis, Report 1990:7, Department of Mathematics, University of Uppsala.

[Si1] I. Sigstam. *Formal spaces and their effective presentation*, Archive for Mathematical Logic 34, pp. 211–246, 1995.

[SiS] I. Sigstam, V. Stoltenberg-Hansen. *Representability of locally compact spaces by domains and formal spaces*, Theoretical Computer Science 179, pp. 319–331, 1997.

[SLG] V. Stoltenberg-Hansen, I. Lindström, E.R. Griffor. "Mathematical Theory of Domains", Cambridge University Press, 1994.

[V] S. Vickers. "Topology via Logic", Cambridge University Press, 1989.

Abstract Insertion Sort in an Extension of Type Theory with Record Types and Subtyping

Alvaro Tasistro
Department of Computing Science
Chalmers University of Technology and University of Gothenburg

Current Address:
Instituto de Computación, Facultad de Ingeniería
Universidad de la República
Julio Herrera y Reissig 565, Piso 5
Montevideo, Uruguay.

E-mail:`tato@fing.edu.uy`

Abstract. We describe an extension of Martin-Löf's type theory with dependent record types and subtyping and use it for obtaining a formal definition of a general structure of the algorithms of sorting by insertion. We start by giving a general formulation of the sorting problem according to which the most general sorting algorithms are those that can be used for ordering lists over any set, along any total relation on the set. In particular, the best known members of the family of algorithms of sorting by insertion, namely straight insertion sort and tree sort, are of this kind. The proposed structure of the algorithms of sorting by insertion is based upon a specification of an abstract data type, which we call of *insertion structures.* The general method of sorting by insertion is then written as a program depending on unspecified implementation of insertion structures. We therefore call it *abstract insertion sort.* The concrete algorithms of sorting by insertion correspond to particular implementations of insertion structures. We discuss how it is possible to specify the operations on insertion structures so as to accurately describe the intended family of algorithms. We also derive axioms for the insertion structures so as to obtain a natural decomposition into lemmas of the proofs of correctness of the algorithms of the family.
The whole work serves to illustrate how abstract data types and their implementations can be formally treated in the considered extension of type theory. All the definitions are presented here in ordinary mathematical language using the concepts and some of the notation of the formal theory. They have also been totally formalized and verified using a type checker for the extended theory that has been implemented.

1 Introduction

The purpose of this work is twofold. On the one hand, it is an application of the extension of Martin-Löf's type theory with record types and subtyping that has been formulated in [1]. In particular, we are here interested in the use of type theory as a formal theory of programming. That is, we shall represent specifications of programs as types and interpret the typing judgements $a : \alpha$ as: "a is a program satisfying the specification α". The formal correctness of these judgements can be guaranteed simply by type checking, which is decidable for a class of expressions capable of representing every type and object that can be constructed in accordance to the rules of the theory. As shall be explained later, the motivation of the extension that we consider has been to increase the expressivity of type theory so that types of structures such as algebraic structures and abstract data types can be represented with enough generality. At the same time, the extension preserves the formal character of the theory as described above. That is to say, type checking remains decidable for a class of expressions sufficiently large in practice. A type checker for the extended theory has been implemented and is also described in [1]. A first purpose of the present paper is then to illustrate how abstract data types and their implementations can be formally treated in the extended theory.

On the other hand, we wish to obtain a formal structure of the algorithms of sorting by insertion, as they have been described by Knuth [3]. There, sorting algorithms are classified into several families. Each family corresponds to a general idea of which the various concrete algorithms of the family can be seen as particular cases. Thus there are the algorithms of sorting by enumeration, by insertion, by exchange, by selection, by merging and by distribution. The general methods that define the families are described in a purely informal manner.

In particular, sorting by insertion can be described as follows. The elements of the input are considered one at a time and inserted in proper place into a data structure where the already considered elements are kept sorted. We call this data structure an *insertion structure*. When all the elements have been loaded into the insertion structure, we just list them out, thus producing an ordered permutation of the input.

Our aim is then to obtain a formal account of this idea. For that, we start by investigating a general formulation of the problem of sorting lists. We consider various possible characterizations of the relations between elements of the lists that are used in sorting and conclude that the most general sorting algorithms are those that can be used for ordering lists of elements of any set A along arbitrary total relations on A. In particular, the best known algorithms of sorting by insertion, namely straight insertion sort and tree sort, are of this kind.

We then proceed to specify the notion of insertion structure as an abstract data type. Correspondingly, the general method of sorting by insertion becomes a program depending on an unspecified insertion structure. Therefore we call it *abstract insertion sort*. In developing the specification, care must be taken so that the intended family of algorithms is characterized with precision. We also derive axioms for the insertion structures so as to obtain a natural decomposition into lemmas of the proof of correctness of concrete algorithms of the family. Whether the resulting specification is indeed accurate and natural must by necessity remain a question that can only be answered by intuition or tested with examples. To our view, the result is satisfactory. We give one example of the use of the abstract specification, namely the derivation of the algorithm of straight insertion sort.

Eventually, it turns out that the specification can entirely be expressed in our formal language. As a consequence, we obtain a formulation of the general idea of sorting by insertion as a program in a completely formal notation. This formulation has been type checked using the implementation referred to above. In this paper only a presentation in ordinary mathematical language is provided, which uses the concepts and some of the notation of the formal language.

The rest of the paper proceeds as follows: in the next section we give a review of type theory and of its extension with record types and subtyping. We first discuss in some detail the motivations leading to the extension. Then we show examples of specifications of abstract data types in the extended theory as well as of the expressivity afforded by the use of subtyping. Section 3 contains the discussion on the specification of the problem of sorting lists and the formulation of the abstract insertion sort. Finally, section 4 contains conclusions.

2 Type Theory with Dependent Record Types and Subtyping

Our starting point, to which we refer hereafter as type theory, is the formulation of Martin-Löf's set theory using the theory of types as logical framework [4, 5, 2]. The type structure of type theory is as follows. There are first the ground types: the type of sets, called *Set* and, for each set A, the type of the elements of A. Sets are inductively defined, i.e. they correspond to concrete data types of ordinary functional languages. Also as in functional languages, one can introduce new sets by giving their constructors. In addition to the ground types, there are only the dependent function types. For forming these, one needs the notion of a family of types over a given type. Most commonly, this is explained just as a type expression depending on a variable of the index type. Then the dependent function types are formed as follows. Let α be a type and α' a type depending on variable x of type α; then $(x : \alpha)\alpha'$ is the type of the functions sending objects a of type α to objects of type $\alpha'(x := a)$, where $(x := a)$ denotes the substitution of a for the free occurrences of x in α'. We prefer to denote type families by closed expressions, for reasons that have to do with the formal stipulation of the theory. Thus we employ judgements $\beta : \alpha \rightarrow type$ signifying that β can be applied to objects of type α, which results in a type. Correspondingly, given a type α and $\beta : \alpha \rightarrow type$, we write $\alpha \rightarrow \beta$ for the type of functions that can be applied to objects a of type α thereby returning an object of type βa. Families of types in the latter sense can be formed by abstraction, which we shall write using brackets. Then the ordinary notation for dependent function types can be defined in terms of the one just introduced in an obvious way. In what follows, we shall use the arrow notation also for simple function types, i.e. those whose output type does not depend on objects of the input type.

Propositions are identified with sets. Then, proposition formers, including predicates and relations, can be introduced in the same way as concrete data type formers in ordinary functional languages, i.e. just by giving their introduction rules. We remark that, since it is possible to introduce at any time new primitive set formers, the type of sets is open in the sense that there are no rules for generating all sets. As a consequence, any function defined on *Set* must work uniformly on any set. We shall be interested only in *predicative* extensions of the theory.

Type theory constitutes a basic framework for the formalization of mathematics and programming. Types can be read alternatively as statements of theorems or specifications of programs. Correspondingly, typing judgements $a : \alpha$ can be interpreted as theorems —the object a being the corresponding proof— or read: "a is a program satisfying the specification α". The formal correctness of the judgements can be ensured simply by type checking, which is decidable for a class of expressions capable of representing every type and object that can be constructed in accordance to the rules of the language.

Now, when one considers types of structures such as algebraic structures or abstract data types, it appears that their representation in type theory entails some difficulty. Such structures are naturally represented as tuples. Given the mechanisms of type formation of type theory, we can only introduce tuple types as *sets* of tuples. But then we cannot form a type T of tuples in a way such as to allow *any* arbitrary set to be a component of tuples of type T. For then T, being itself a set, would be allowed to form a part of some of its own objects.

As an example, consider the notion of a set X together with an equivalence relation on it, which has elsewhere been called a *setoid.* If X can indeed be *any* set then the type of setoids itself cannot be a set in a predicative extension of the theory. The example shows a general point: in specifying a type of algebraic structure one should allow any set to be a carrier of a structure of the type in question. Similarly, in specifying abstract data types, one should be able to allow in principle that the objects of the abstract type are represented as elements of any set.

In [1] a detailed discussion of the point is carried out, leading to the conclusion that if the type of sets is to remain open in the sense explained above then the requirements expressed at the end of the preceding paragraph can only be met by introducing a new mechanism of type formation, namely tuple types that are not sets. A similar point was actually already made in [5]. This constitutes the first motivation for the extension of type theory with record types.

Dependent Record Types.

Dependent record types are, like record types of ordinary programming languages, just sequences of *fields* in which *labels* are declared as of certain types:

$$\langle \mathsf{L}_1 : \alpha_1, ..., \mathsf{L}_n : \alpha_n \rangle.$$

But in dependent record types, the type α_i may depend on the preceding labels $\mathsf{L}_1,\ldots,\mathsf{L}_{i-1}$. An example is the type of binary relations on a set:

$$\langle \mathsf{A} : \mathit{Set},\ \mathsf{R} : \mathsf{A} \to \mathsf{A} \to \mathit{Set}\rangle.$$

In the present notation, labels may participate in the formation of types in the same way as ordinary variables or constants do. So, they have to be syntactically distinguished from the latter, in order to avoid ambiguities. We do this here by writing labels in a special font. Let us now name B the type displayed above. Components of objects of a record type are accessed by *selection* of the labels of the record type in question, which is written in the usual dot notation. Then if R is of type B, $R.\mathsf{A}$ is a set and $R.\mathsf{R}$ is a binary relation on $R.\mathsf{A}$.

Record objects are constructed as sequences of fields that are bindings of objects of appropriate types to labels. For instance if N is the set of natural numbers and $\leq$ the usual order relation on N, then the following is an object of type B:

$$\langle \mathsf{A} = N, \mathsf{R} = \leq\rangle.$$

Specifications of abstract data types can be expressed formally as types in this language. The objects of each of these types are the implementations of the abstract data type in question. They are tuples of elements satisfying certain properties, usually called the *axioms* of the abstract data type. Here, for instance, is one formulation of the type of stacks of natural numbers:

$$
\begin{array}{l}
\langle \mathsf{S}{:}\mathit{Set},\\
\quad \mathsf{empty} : \mathsf{S},\\
\quad \mathsf{push} : N \to \mathsf{S} \to \mathsf{S},\\
\quad \mathsf{?empty} : \mathsf{S} \to \mathit{Bool},\\
\quad \mathsf{pop} : (s : \mathsf{S};\ \mathsf{?empty}\ s =_{Bool} \mathit{false})\ \mathsf{S},\\
\quad \mathsf{top} : (s : \mathsf{S};\ \mathsf{?empty}\ s =_{Bool} \mathit{false})\ N,\\
\qquad\quad \mathsf{ax1} : \mathsf{?empty}\ (\mathsf{empty}) =_{Bool} \mathit{true},\\
\qquad\quad \mathsf{ax2} : (n : N;\ s : \mathsf{S})\ \mathsf{?empty}\ (\mathsf{push}\ n\ s) =_{Bool} \mathit{false},\\
\qquad\quad \mathsf{ax3} : (n : N;\ s : \mathsf{S})\ \mathsf{pop}\ (\mathsf{push}\ n\ s)\ (\mathsf{ax2}\ n\ s) =_{\mathsf{S}} s,\\
\qquad\quad \mathsf{ax4} : (n : N;\ s : \mathsf{S})\ \mathsf{top}\ (\mathsf{push}\ n\ s)\ (\mathsf{ax2}\ n\ s) =_N n\\
\rangle.
\end{array}
$$

We use $=_A$ for equality of elements of the set A. The first component is the set of stacks. Each particular implementation will provide a concrete data type corresponding to this component, which will be the particular representation of stacks chosen in the implementation in question. Therefore we usually refer to S above as "the representation" of stacks and similarly in other cases.

Notice that the axioms of the specification have been represented by fields in the corresponding record type. The idea behind this is the following. In type theory, properties of elements become in general function types. And then the way to require that a property is satisfied by some elements is to demand that a proof of this fact is given. In particular, specifications of abstract data types must require proofs that the structures being described satisfy the axioms. Since proofs are objects, we can express this requirement by making the demanded proofs actual components of the structures. Finally, notice too that we have used dependent types for the operations pop and top. They require as second argument a proof that the stack to which they are applied is non-empty.

The specification above can be generalized to stacks over any set, not just natural numbers. For that, we introduce a family of types on *Set*:

$$
\begin{aligned}
&\mathit{Stack} : \mathit{Set}\to \mathit{type}\\
&\mathit{Stack}\ A = \langle \mathsf{S}{:}\mathit{Set},\\
&\qquad \mathsf{empty} : \mathsf{S},\\
&\qquad \mathsf{push} : A \to \mathsf{S} \to \mathsf{S},\\
&\qquad \mathsf{?empty} : \mathsf{S} \to \mathit{Bool},\\
&\qquad \mathsf{pop} : (s : \mathsf{S};\ \mathsf{?empty}\, s =_{\mathit{Bool}} \mathit{false})\ \mathsf{S},\\
&\qquad \mathsf{top} : (s : \mathsf{S};\ \mathsf{?empty}\, s =_{\mathit{Bool}} \mathit{false})\ A,\\
&\qquad\quad \mathsf{ax1} : \mathsf{?empty}\ (\mathsf{empty}) =_{\mathit{Bool}} \mathit{true},\\
&\qquad\quad \mathsf{ax2} : (x : A;\ s : \mathsf{S})\ \mathsf{?empty}\ (\mathsf{push}\ x\ s) =_{\mathit{Bool}} \mathit{false},\\
&\qquad\quad \mathsf{ax3} : (x : A;\ s : \mathsf{S})\ \mathsf{pop}\ (\mathsf{push}\ x\ s)\ (\mathsf{ax2}\ x\ s) =_{\mathsf{S}} s,\\
&\qquad\quad \mathsf{ax4} : (x : A;\ s : \mathsf{S})\ \mathsf{top}\ (\mathsf{push}\ x\ s)\ (\mathsf{ax2}\ x\ s) =_{A} x\\
&\qquad \rangle.
\end{aligned}
$$

The specifications of stacks given above should be compared with those in [5]. In the latter, abstract data types are specified as sets. This restricts the representation of stacks to be chosen among the elements of a universe of sets previously formed.

Subtyping.

So far we have motivated the introduction of record types by showing the necessity of specifying components of tuple types as arbitrary sets. This requirement could, however, be met in a simpler way, namely by introducing types of *dependent pairs*. This type former is the analog at the type level of the disjoint union of a family of sets, usually represented by the letter Σ. Using dependent pairs one can encode types of tuples of arbitrary length.

Now, record types lead naturally to the introduction of yet another useful notion into the language. This is the notion of *subtyping* or *type inclusion*. That α is a subtype of β (in symbols $\alpha \sqsubseteq \beta$) means that every object of α is an object of β and that identical objects of type α are also identical objects of type β. As it is well known from the theory of programming languages, non-trivial cases of subtyping arise between record types, according to the following rule: given two record types ρ and σ, if ρ contains every label of σ (and possibly more) and the types of the common labels are in the inclusion relation then ρ is included in σ. This is justified because then every object of type ρ contains all the components that are required of objects of type σ.

In the present extension of type theory, the rule above is generalized to dependent record types. This requires to formulate rules of type inclusion corresponding to the other type formers of the language. For the dependent function types, we have a generalization of the usual contravariant rule. On the other hand, no proper inclusion is allowed between ground types.

Having type inclusion represents a considerable advantage for the formalization of structures such as algebraic structures or abstract data types. As an example, let us introduce the type of total binary relations on given set. Formally, record types are constructed up from the record type with no fields by iterating the operation of extension of a record type with one more field. This allows us to write:

$T : type$
$T = \langle B,\ \mathsf{totality} : (x, y : \mathsf{A})\ x\mathsf{R}y \vee y\mathsf{R}x\rangle.$

Then T is obviously a subtype of the type of binary relations B. That is to say, every total binary relation is itself a binary relation. This is a principle of reasoning that is used straightforwardly in informal language. However, its formalization is not as obvious. Record types and subtyping constitute a way to directly incorporate it to the formal language of type theory.

The idea underlying the example above carries over to many other cases in the formalization of abstract algebra. By using record types one can represent directly the definitions that introduce a type of structures as the enrichment of a previously given type with further operations or axioms. Then every type thus defined is a subtype of the original one. Further, the rules of subtyping of the extended theory as explained above allow in general a type to be a subtype of several other types, each of which needs not be in the inclusion relation with any of the others. When we use record types to represent systems of algebras, the latter provides a direct formalization of the principle that a system may inherit properties and proofs from several other systems, themselves defined independently of each other. For the detailed stipulation of the rules that constitute the extension and further examples of its use we refer to [1].

In the next section we will use record types for specifying programs and abstract data types. There we will also make use of cases of subtyping, all of them of the simple kind illustrated by the example above. It remains only to say that the present extension of type theory preserves the status of type checking as in the original theory. That is, type checking remains decidable for a class of expressions in which every type and object that can be constructed in the theory can be represented. A type checker for the extended theory has been implemented. It is also described in [1] and has been used for verifying the formalization of the case to be now studied.

3 Abstract Insertion Sort

Sorting.

We consider the problem of sorting lists. We start by discussing what it is for a list to be sorted. A list $[a_1,\ldots,a_n]$ that is sorted along $\preccurlyeq$ satisfies $a_1 \preccurlyeq \cdots \preccurlyeq a_n$. We may take this as the definition of sorted list. It is given inductively by the following three rules:

$$\frac{}{[\,]\ sorted} \qquad\qquad \frac{}{[x]\ sorted}$$

$$\frac{x \preccurlyeq y \quad (y :: ys)\ sorted}{(x :: y :: ys)\ sorted.}$$

Then the problem of sorting lists can be formulated for any set A and binary relation $\preccurlyeq$ on A as that of finding functions sending lists over A to sorted permutations of themselves. Now we can see that solutions for the sorting problem exist only for *total* $\preccurlyeq$, i.e. such that for any pair a, b of elements of A it holds that either $a \preccurlyeq b$ or $b \preccurlyeq a$. Indeed, if there is a sorting algorithm along relation $\preccurlyeq$ it will sort the list $[a, b]$ for any two given elements a, b. The result is either $[a, b]$ and then $a \preccurlyeq b$ or $[b, a]$ in which case $b \preccurlyeq a$. On the other hand, there are several algorithms for sorting lists over any set A along any given total relation on A. Examples are the usual (polymorphic) formulations of straight insertion sort, tree sort, quick sort and merge sort. Let us now consider straight insertion sort. We write $[A]$ for the set of lists over A. We define $\mathcal{L} : [A] \to [A]$ as follows:

$$\begin{aligned} &\mathcal{L}\,[\,] &&= [\,] \\ &\mathcal{L}\,(x :: xs) &&= \mathcal{LI}\ x\ (\mathcal{L}\ xs) \end{aligned}$$

where $\mathcal{LI} : A \to [A] \to [A]$, which we call the algorithm of *list insertion*, is:

$$\begin{aligned} &\mathcal{LI}\ x\,[\,] &&= [x] \\ &\mathcal{LI}\ x\ (y :: ys) &&= \begin{cases} x :: y :: ys & \text{if } x \preccurlyeq y \\ y :: (\mathcal{LI}\ x\ ys) & \text{if } y \preccurlyeq x. \end{cases} \end{aligned}$$

The correctness of $\mathcal{L}$ as a sorting algorithm is proved by induction on lists and reduces eventually to showing that for any element x of A the function $\mathcal{LI}\ x$ produces the same results up to permutation as the constructor $x :: \_$ and that it preserves sortedness. The latter can be shown under the only assumption that $\preccurlyeq$ is total as follows. We use that $\mathcal{LI}\ x\ (y :: ys)$ has either x or y as head, which is evident from the definition of $\mathcal{LI}$. We show that $\mathcal{LI}\ x\ xs$ is sorted by induction on the proofs that xs is sorted. The base case as well as the case in which xs is a singleton are straightforward. Suppose now xs is of the form $y_1 :: y_2 :: ys$ with $y_1 \preccurlyeq y_2$ and $y_2 :: ys$ sorted. If $x \preccurlyeq y_1$ then $\mathcal{LI}\ x\ ys$ is $x :: y_1 :: y_2 :: ys$ and is obviously sorted. If otherwise $y_1 \preccurlyeq x$ then $\mathcal{LI}\ x\ ys$ is $y_1 :: (\mathcal{LI}\ x\ (y_2 :: ys))$. The tail of this list is sorted by induction hypothesis. Moreover, the head h of the tail is either x or y_2. In any case, $y_1 \preccurlyeq h$. Hence the whole list is sorted.

Algorithms like straight insertion sort and the others above mentioned that can be used for sorting lists over any set A along any total relation on A shall be called *generic (sorting algorithms) over total relations.* And similarly for other kinds of binary relations.

Alternatively, we can define a list $[a_1, \ldots, a_n]$ to be sorted along $\preccurlyeq$ when every element of the list is related to all its successors, i.e. when $a_i \preccurlyeq a_j$ for $i < j$. This is given inductively by the rules:

$$\frac{}{[\,]\ sorted} \qquad\qquad \frac{x \,\overline{\preccurlyeq}\, xs \quad xs\ sorted}{(x :: xs)\ sorted.}$$

where $x \,\overline{\preccurlyeq}\, as$ stands for $x \preccurlyeq a$ for every member a of as.

With this definition there are no sorting algorithms generic over total relations. In particular, lists of distinct elements $[a, b, c]$ cannot be sorted in case the elements are related as follows: $a \preccurlyeq b \preccurlyeq c \preccurlyeq a$. The two definitions of sorted list, and hence the corresponding sorting problems, are equivalent in case $\preccurlyeq$ is *total* and *transitive*. Therefore, all the algorithms mentioned above are also generic over total and transitive relations, no matter which definition of sorted list is chosen. Also of this kind are various algorithms of sorting by selection, i.e. by repeated extraction of a minimal (alternatively maximal) element out of the yet unsorted elements.

Now, if sorting is to be considered as instrumental to searching then the cases considered appear to be too general. To begin with, the definition of searching requires an equivalence relation on the set of the elements to be considered. More precisely, searching a in a list xs is the problem of determining whether there exists a member of xs that is equivalent to a. Obviously, if this problem is to have a solution, then the equivalence relation in question must be decidable. The profit afforded by having the given list sorted consists in that the searching methods do not have to inspect the whole list in all cases. This happens when the list is sorted along a (decidable) linear ordering. This notion can be defined in the following way: given a set A and a decidable equivalence relation $\sim$ on A, $\preccurlyeq$ is a decidable linear ordering on A if it is total, transitive and antisymmetric relative to $\sim$, i.e. it satisfies $a \sim b \Leftrightarrow a \preccurlyeq b \;\&\; b \preccurlyeq a$ for any two elements a, b of A. Equivalently, one can consider a set A with an equivalence relation $\sim$ on it and a transitive relation $\prec$ satisfying trichotomy: $a \prec b \oplus a \sim b \oplus b \prec a$ for any two elements a, b, where $\oplus$ stands for exclusive disjunction. Then, when searching a in a list xs sorted along a decidable linear ordering, each possible result of the comparison of a with any member x of xs either leads to success or allows to discard a non-empty part of xs for further searching. Decidable linear orderings is the kind of sorting relations considered in [3]. Sorting by counting the number of predecessors (alt. successors) of each member of the input list is an example of an algorithm that works under the assumption that the sorting relation is of this kind.

We wish here to give the sorting problem as general a formulation as is possible. Let us then now express the corresponding definitions precisely. We will use record types.

We start by introducing lists:

$[\_] : \mathit{Set} \rightarrow \mathit{Set}$
$\quad [\,] : (A : \mathit{Set})\; [A]$
$\quad :: \; : (A : \mathit{Set})\; A \rightarrow [A] \rightarrow [A].$

We maintain the notation so far used for both the list set constructor and individual lists. In particular, then, for each of the constructors [ ] and :: we will omit the argument that corresponds to the set where the elements of the list belong. We also assume the following relation to be properly defined as that which holds between any two lists that are permutations of one another:

$\approx : (A : Set)\ [A] \to [A] \to Set.$

It is not relevant to discuss here particular definitions of $\approx$. When writing the application of this symbol we omit the first argument and use infix notation.

Let us now reintroduce the type of binary relations on given set:

$\mathsf{B} : type$
$\mathsf{B} = \langle \mathsf{A} : Set\, , \preccurlyeq\, : \mathsf{A} \to \mathsf{A} \to Set \rangle.$

We speak of lists over binary relations, meaning of course lists over the corresponding carrier sets. Let us now introduce the notion of sorted list. It is given as a predicate on lists over a binary relation, i.e.:

$sorted : (R : \mathsf{B})\ [R.\mathsf{A}] \to Set.$

The application of *sorted* to a variable $R : \mathsf{B}$ will be written $sorted_{\preccurlyeq}$. And similarly for other predicates defined on binary relations. Now we give the corresponding introduction rules, following the first of the two alternatives discussed above.

$s_0 : (R : \mathsf{B})\ sorted_{\preccurlyeq}\ [\,]$
$s_1 : (R : \mathsf{B};\ x : R.\mathsf{A})\ sorted_{\preccurlyeq}\ [x]$
$s_2 : (R : \mathsf{B};\ x, y : R.\mathsf{A};\ ys : [R.\mathsf{A}])\ x \preccurlyeq y \to sorted_{\preccurlyeq}\ (y :: ys) \to sorted_{\preccurlyeq}\ (x :: y :: ys).$

From now on selections will be left implicit, i.e. we shall write only the corresponding labels. Labels can always be recognized as such and also in every case in which a label is used according to the present convention it will be obvious from which record object it is intended to be selected.

For binary relation R we now introduce a relation $\preccurlyeq\!\sim$ between lists over R. This relation holds when the first list is a sorted permutation of the second one. Formally:

$\preccurlyeq\!\sim\ : (R : \mathsf{B})\ [\mathsf{A}] \to [\mathsf{A}] \to Set$
$xs \preccurlyeq\!\sim ys = xs \approx ys\ \&\ sorted_{\preccurlyeq}\ xs.$

Now we can formulate the problem of sorting lists. A first alternative is to define a predicate on lists over a binary relation that is to be satisfied by the lists that can be sorted. That is, we would have:

$sortable : (R : \mathsf{B})\ [\mathsf{A}] \to Set,$

inductively given by the following rule:

$$\frac{ys \preccurlyeq\!\sim xs}{sortable_{\preccurlyeq}\ xs.}$$

Then the problem of sorting lists over a binary relation R is that of proving that every list over R is sortable; that is to say, of finding functions of type $(xs : [\mathsf{A}])\ sortable_{\preccurlyeq}\ xs$. However, we prefer the following formulation, which allows to consider the sorting algorithm and its verification separately:

$$\mathit{ListSorting} : \mathrm{B} \to \mathit{type}$$
$$\mathit{ListSorting}\ R = \langle \mathsf{p} : [\mathsf{A}] \to [\mathsf{A}],\ \mathsf{v} : (xs : [\mathsf{A}])\ \mathsf{p}\ xs \preccurlyeq\!\!\sim xs \rangle.$$

As already shown, the problem *ListSorting* R has solutions only for total R. The type $(R : \mathrm{B})$ *ListSorting* R is that of the sorting algorithms that are generic over binary relations. It can be proved empty. We aim at eventually obtaining sorting algorithms that are generic over total relations. Total relations are defined as follows:

$$\mathrm{T} : \mathit{type}$$
$$\mathrm{T} = \langle \mathrm{B}\,,\ \mathsf{totality} : (x, y : \mathsf{A})\ x \preccurlyeq y \lor y \preccurlyeq x \rangle.$$

Then, because of the rules of subtyping, the problem of sorting lists over a total relation is also *ListSorting* as defined above and the type of the most general sorting algorithms is $(T : \mathrm{T})$ *ListSorting* T.

Insertion Structures.

Now we turn to consider *sorting by insertion*. The following is a slight rephrasing of Knuth's description of the general idea:

Before examining element x_j*, we assume that the preceding elements* $x_1, \ldots, x_{j-1}$ *have already been sorted; then we insert* x_j *into its proper place among the previously sorted elements.*

Now the most interesting source of variations on this idea is given by the possibility of considering various different data structures for storing the "already sorted" elements. Thus, for instance, straight insertion sort corresponds to choosing this structure to be an ordered list. A tail-recursive formulation of the algorithm makes the list of already-sorted elements explicit:

$$\mathcal{L}'\ xs = \mathcal{L}''\ [\,]\ xs$$

where

$$\mathcal{L}''\ ss\ [\,] = ss$$
$$\mathcal{L}''\ ss\ (x :: xs) = \mathcal{L}''\ (\mathcal{LI}\ x\ ss)\ xs.$$

An alternative is to have the already-sorted elements in a binary search tree. In this case, when all elements of the input list have been stored in the tree we recover them back into the list constituting the output of the algorithm by performing the inorder traversal of the tree. This is the algorithm of *tree sort.*

Further variations on tree sort are possible, choosing search trees different from binary search trees. Also interesting is multiple list insertion, in which the structure of already-sorted elements is composed out of several lists corresponding to different ranges of values. Knuth considers also variations of the insertion procedure on arrays, namely binary insertion and two-way insertion. He also includes Shell's method in the family of sorting by insertion. But there seems to be no other reason for this than the fact that (straight) insertion can be used to perform certain subordinate sorting tasks and not because the method matches the general description of sorting by insertion.

Our aim now is to give a precise formulation of the general idea of sorting by insertion by making it explicit that the method uses an appropriate data structure to store the already-sorted elements. These data structures will hereafter be called *insertion structures.* They will be specified as an abstract data type and, thus, the general method of sorting by insertion will take the form of a function depending on an implementation of insertion structures. To each particular implementation will correspond a concrete member of the family of algorithms of sorting by insertion. When all the constructions that we are about to give are written in a totally formal way, the general method of sorting by insertion becomes a program in the extension of type theory with record types and subtyping.

Now, more precisely, we will specify the type of insertion structures over arbitrary binary relation, i.e. the family of types:

$\mathrm{I} : \mathrm{B} \rightarrow \mathit{type}.$

Correspondingly, we shall be able to define the general method of sorting by insertion as a function:

$\mathrm{A} : (R : \mathrm{B})\ \mathrm{I}\,R \rightarrow \mathit{ListSorting}\ R.$

For each binary relation R the function $\mathrm{A}\,R$ is an abstract sorting algorithm in the sense that it depends on unspecified implementation of the insertion structures over R. Concrete sorting algorithms are obtained as $\mathrm{A}\,R\ i : \mathit{ListSorting}\ R$ for each implementation i of $\mathrm{I}\,R$.

It follows then that we can only expect to find implementations of insertion structures over total relations and that the type $(R : \mathrm{B})\ \mathrm{I}\,R$ of implementations of insertion structures that are generic over binary relations is empty.

On the other hand, we expect to be able to derive generic sorting algorithms over total relations, as are straight insertion sort and tree sort. For deriving such an algorithm $\mathcal{G} : (T : \mathrm{T})\ \mathit{ListSorting}\ T$ from the general abstract method A we need an implementation of insertion structures that is in turn generic over total relations, i.e. $gi : (T : \mathrm{T})\ \mathrm{I}\,T$. Then the generic sorting algorithm $\mathcal{G}$ is defined as follows:

$$\mathcal{G}\ T = \mathrm{A}\ T\ (gi\ T).$$

Notice that, again because of the subtyping rules, I and A are themselves also the insertion structures and the corresponding general abstract method of sorting by insertion over total relations.

Operations on Insertion Structures. The specification of insertion structures will be better understood if we proceed to develop it by succesive refinements. We start from the sorting algorithm depending on unspecified insertion structure. It can be simply described as the sequence of two operations: first the elements of the input list are *loaded* into the insertion structure and then they are *listed* back thereby obtaining a sorted permutation of the original list. Then, for binary relation R, a minimal specification of the insertion structures over R

will require that they carry the two operations l of loading and * of listing, whose composition must be a sorting algorithm. We write * postfixed to its argument:

$$\langle \mathsf{S}: \mathit{Set}, \quad \mathsf{l} : [\mathsf{A}] \to \mathsf{S}, \quad * : \mathsf{S} \to [\mathsf{A}], \quad \mathsf{ax} : (xs : [\mathsf{A}])\ (\mathsf{l}\ xs)* \preccurlyeq^{\sim} xs \rangle.$$

The abstract sort is then defined simply as follows:

$\mathrm{A} : (R : \mathrm{B})\ \mathrm{I}\,R \to \mathit{ListSorting}\ R$

$\mathrm{A}\,R\,i = \langle \mathsf{p} = (\mathsf{l}; *), \mathsf{v} = \mathsf{ax}\rangle.$

Now it turns out that this specification is actually too simple. The resulting algorithm could hardly be called abstract insertion sort, due to its extreme generality. Consider, for instance, implementing insertion structures as lists. Then the operation l could be implemented as the identity function and, correspondingly, * would have to do all the sorting work. In such case, it could be implemented as any sorting algorithm whatsoever. Conversely, one could have * as the identity function and any sorting algorithm as l.

The problem lies in the specification of the insertion structures and consists in that it allows too much generality to both l and *. So we will start the refinement by working on the form and the type of these operations so as to restrict them adequately. We start with the operation of loading.

Going back to the informal description of sorting by insertion we see that the idea should be that elements are considered one at a time and inserted in proper place into the insertion structure. This determines the form of the operation of loading as an iteration on the input list, which should then be defined in terms of more primitive operations on insertion structures. Let us write e for the empty insertion structure and i for the operation that adds a new element to an insertion structure respecting the order therein. The latter will be used in infix form. Then we define the loading operation as:

$$l\,[\,] = \mathsf{e}$$
$$l\,(x :: xs) = x\ \mathsf{i}\ (l\ xs).$$

With this definition, if insertion structures are implemented as (ordered) lists and the operation * as the identity function, then l cannot but constitute some variant of straight insertion sort. That is, e must be implemented as the empty list and i must satisfy the informal specification of the algorithm of list insertion given earlier: the function $x\ \mathsf{i}\ \_$ must produce the same results up to permutation as $x :: \_$ and it must preserve sortedness.

This observation reflects the improvement achieved with respect to the original formulation. But the converse problem remains: the operation i could be defined to be the constructor :: in which case l would behave as the identity function. Then * must do the sorting and it could be implemented as any sorting algorithm whatsoever.

The idea that we have not yet captured in the formulation is that $*$ should not be sensitive to any order in which elements are kept in the insertion structures. That is, the sorting work must be done at the time when the input list is loaded into the insertion structure. After that we use $*$ just to produce a list as output. And in carrying out this operation no comparisons should be performed.

Then the question turns out to be one about the right type of $*$. The first observation is that this operation must not depend on the sorting relation being used. More importantly, given a representation of insertion structures, $*$ must depend only on the form of this representation, and not on the nature of the values stored therein.

If we now specify the type of representations of insertion structures more precisely, we will be able to find the right type for $*$. So far, we have taken the representations of insertion structures to be sets. But a closer look reveals that it is more adequate to say that they are obtained from set formers parameterized on a set. First, it is natural to think of an arbitrary representation of the insertion structures as a framework filled in with components that are the elements being classified. Moreover, if there is going to be an implementation of insertion structures that is generic over total relations, then the corresponding representation of the insertion structures will have to be given as a set former of the kind described above, which can be applied to the carrier of any particular total relation.

Having made this observation, we can be more precise about the type of $*$. Given a representation of insertion structures, i.e. a set former $\mathsf{S} : \mathit{Set} \to \mathit{Set}$, the operation $*$ should work *uniformly* for any set X taking structures of type $\mathsf{S}\,X$ into lists of elements of X. This is guaranteed by specifying $*$ as of type $(X : \mathit{Set})\ \mathsf{S}\,X \to [X]$. The latter is in turn due to the fact already pointed out that, in type theory, the functions that can be defined on Set must work uniformly on any set.

This concludes the refinement of the operations on the insertion structures. It is convenient to define them as a type family:

$$\Sigma_{\mathrm{I}} : \mathrm{B} \to \mathit{type}$$

$$\begin{aligned}\Sigma_{\mathrm{I}}\ R = \langle \mathsf{S}&: \mathit{Set} \to \mathit{Set},\\ \mathsf{e} &: \mathsf{S\,A},\\ \mathsf{i} &: \mathsf{A} \to \mathsf{S\,A} \to \mathsf{S\,A},\\ * &: (X : \mathit{Set})\ \mathsf{S}\,X \to [X]\\ \rangle.\end{aligned}$$

Then the type $\mathrm{I}\,R$ of insertion structures over binary relation R becomes

$$\langle \Sigma_{\mathrm{I}}\ R,\ \mathsf{ax} : (xs : [\mathsf{A}])\ (l\ xs)* \preccurlyeq\!\sim xs\rangle$$

and the abstract insertion sort is:

$$\mathrm{A} : (R : \mathrm{B})\ \mathrm{I}\,R \to \mathit{ListSorting}\ R$$

$$\mathrm{A}\,R\ i = \langle \mathsf{p} = (l; *), \mathsf{v} = \mathsf{ax}\rangle,$$

where $l : [\mathsf{A}] \to \mathsf{S\,A}$ is defined as above.

If we now implement insertion structures as lists, we have that the operation $*$ should copy lists into ordered permutations of themselves, uniformly for whatever type of the elements of the lists. That is, without performing any comparisons. As a consequence, we cannot anymore let i be just :: and, correspondingly, l behave as the identity function. We are actually quite restricted as to the choice in this case, although we still have more than one possibility. The operation $*$ can of course be the identity function which, as already said, determines the entire algorithm to be some variant of straight insertion sort. One, not very interesting, possibility is to have $*$ as the reversing function which would force i to be a reverse ordered insertion. And one could imagine other odd alternatives of this kind. But there seems no be nothing wrong in accepting them as cases of sorting by insertion.

Derivation of Axioms for the Insertion Structures. So far, the only axiom for insertion structures directly expresses the correctness of the abstract sorting algorithm defined as the sequence of loading and listing. For each particular implementation of insertion structures giving rise to a concrete algorithm of sorting by insertion we have to prove that the axiom is satisfied. Now, it turns out that there is some decomposition into lemmas that appears to be a natural one for all these proofs. We will now abstract away those lemmas and formulate them as the axioms governing the operations of the insertion structures. This will be done in a way such that the resulting specification is equivalent to the one just given. Thereby we shall obtain a general form of both the algorithms of sorting by insertion and their correctness proofs.

We start by observing that, given the definition of l, the proofs that the axiom of insertion structures is satisfied by their implementations will in general have to be by induction on the input list. We will now carry out this induction also in an abstract way and thereby decompose the condition of correctness of the abstract sorting algorithm into equivalent conditions that, for each particular implementation of the insertion structures, will have as instances the base case and induction step of an inductive proof of the correctness of the implementation in question. The resulting conditions will then not mention l anymore, but only the primitive operations e, i and $*$. Consider then an inductive proof of $(xs : [\mathsf{A}])\ (l\ xs)* \precsim xs$. In the base case, we must have $(l\ [\,])* \precsim [\,]$. Now $l\ [\,]$ is by definition e. Hence, we must have $\mathsf{e}* \precsim [\,]$ from which we conclude that it must be

$$\mathsf{e}* =_{[\mathsf{A}]} [\,]. \tag{1}$$

As for the inductive step, we have to prove $(l\ (x :: xs))* \precsim (x :: xs)$ from the induction hypothesis $(l\ xs)* \precsim xs$ where $x : \mathsf{A}$ and $xs : [\mathsf{A}]$. Now $l\ (x :: xs)$ is by definition $x\ \mathsf{i}\ (l\ xs)$ and so the desired conclusion becomes $(x\ \mathsf{i}\ (l\ xs))* \precsim (x :: xs)$. Now both this and the induction hypothesis are expressed as properties of $l\ xs$ for arbitrary list xs. Then we can equivalently express them as properties of an individual insertion structure s that is the result of $l\ xs$ for some list xs. We call these structures *loaded*.

More precisely, we define for binary relation R and operations on insertion structures over R:

$loaded : \mathsf{S}\,\mathsf{A} \to Set$

inductively by the two rules:

$$\frac{}{\mathsf{e}\ loaded} \qquad\qquad \frac{s\ loaded}{(x \mathbin{\mathsf{i}} s)\ loaded.}\ (x : \mathsf{A})$$

Then the induction step above can be equivalently rewritten as

$(s : \mathsf{S}\,\mathsf{A};\ s\ loaded;\ xs : [\mathsf{A}];\ x : \mathsf{A})\ s{*} \precsim xs \to (x \mathbin{\mathsf{i}} s){*} \precsim (x{::}\,xs).$

Now the conclusion of this condition is expressed in terms of the relation $\precsim$ which only abbreviates a conjunction. Therefore, natural proofs of the condition will contain in turn proofs of each of the conjuncts arising from the conclusion. We can make this explicit by decomposing the condition into two:

$$(s : \mathsf{S}\,\mathsf{A};\ s\ loaded;\ xs : [\mathsf{A}];\ x : \mathsf{A})\ s{*} \precsim xs \to (x \mathbin{\mathsf{i}} s){*} \approx (x{::}\,xs) \qquad (2)$$

$$(s : \mathsf{S}\,\mathsf{A}; s\ loaded; xs : [\mathsf{A}]; x : \mathsf{A})\ s{*} \precsim xs \to sorted_{\preccurlyeq}\ (x \mathbin{\mathsf{i}} s){*}. \qquad (3)$$

Now from the validity of the three conditions (1), (2) and (3) so far derived it follows that for every loaded structure s there exists a list xs such that $s{*} \precsim xs$. Indeed, since s is loaded we have that s is $l\ xs$ for some list xs. And, since the conditions above are equivalent to the original axiom of correctness of the abstract sorting algorithm, we have that $(l\ xs){*} \precsim xs$. As an immediate consequence of this observation we have that, for every loaded structure s, $s{*}$ is sorted and there exists a list xs such that $s{*} \approx xs$. These conclusions allows us to simplify (2) and (3). In both of these, the assumption $s{*} \precsim xs$ contains the premiss that $s{*}$ is sorted. But this is implied already by the previous assumption that s is loaded. So we can just eliminate the premiss. Then (2) can be rewritten as:

$(s : \mathsf{S}\,\mathsf{A};\ s\ loaded;\ xs : [\mathsf{A}];\ x : \mathsf{A})\ s{*} \approx xs \to (x \mathbin{\mathsf{i}} s){*} \approx (x{::}\,xs)$

or, still equivalently but yet more simply:

$(s : \mathsf{S}\,\mathsf{A};\ s\ loaded;\ x : \mathsf{A})\ (x \mathbin{\mathsf{i}} s){*} \approx x{::}\,(s{*}).$

Doing the same for (3), we obtain

$(s : \mathsf{S}\,\mathsf{A};\ s\ loaded;\ xs : [\mathsf{A}];\ x : \mathsf{A})\ s{*} \approx xs \to sorted_{\preccurlyeq}\ (x \mathbin{\mathsf{i}} s){*}$

which requires that $(x \mathbin{\mathsf{i}} s){*}$ is proved sorted under the assumption that there exists a list xs such that $s{*} \approx xs$. But the latter follows from the previous assumption that s is loaded. So we can write equivalently:

$(s : \mathsf{S}\,\mathsf{A};\ s\ loaded;\ x : \mathsf{A})\ sorted_{\preccurlyeq}\ (x \mathbin{\mathsf{i}} s){*}.$

This seems, however, a little too difficult to satisfy. For particular implementations, this condition will in general be proved as a corollary of the property that $s{*}$ is sorted for every loaded structure s, which in turn will have to be given a separate proof. It is instead more natural to allow also the use of the assumption that $s{*}$ is sorted in the proof that $(x \mathbin{\mathsf{i}} s){*}$ is sorted. Thus we arrive at the definitive version of the specification of insertion structures:

$\mathrm{I} : \mathrm{B} \rightarrow type$

$\mathrm{I}\,R = \langle\ \Sigma_{\mathrm{I}}\ R,\ \mathsf{ax}_0 : \mathsf{e}{*} =_{[\mathsf{A}]} [\,],$
$\quad \mathsf{ax}_1 : (s : \mathsf{S}\,\mathsf{A};\ s\,loaded;\ x : \mathsf{A})\ (x\ \mathsf{i}\ s){*} \approx x :: (s{*}),$
$\quad \mathsf{ax}_2 : (s : \mathsf{S}\,\mathsf{A};\ s\,loaded;\ sorted_{\preccurlyeq}\ s{*};\ x : \mathsf{A})\ sorted_{\preccurlyeq}\ (x\ \mathsf{i}\ s){*}$
$\rangle.$

Correspondingly, the abstract insertion sort will take the form:

$\mathrm{A} : (R : \mathrm{B})\ \mathrm{I}\,R \rightarrow ListSorting\ R$

$\mathrm{A}\,R\,i = \langle \mathsf{p} = (l; *), \mathsf{v} = indproof\rangle.$

where *indproof* is the proof object that represents the inductive proof that we have just sketched.

Straight Insertion Sort Revisited. Now we can look at straight insertion sort as an instance of the general form of algorithms of sorting by insertion that we have just defined. It will arise from an implementation of insertion structures that is generic over total relations. We define:

$ls : (T : \mathrm{T})\ \mathrm{I}\,T$

$ls\ T = \langle\ \mathsf{S} = [\_],$
$\quad \mathsf{e} = [\,],$
$\quad \mathsf{i} = \mathcal{LI},$
$\quad * = id$
$\rangle,$

where $\mathcal{LI}$ is list insertion as defined earlier and *id* is the identity function.

Instantiating accordingly the axioms of insertion structures we obtain the conditions for the correctness of this implementation:

$[\,] =_{[\mathsf{A}]} [\,]$

$(xs : [A];\ xs\,loaded;\ x : \mathsf{A})\ \mathcal{LI}\ x\ xs \approx x :: xs$

$(xs : [A];\ xs\,loaded;\ sorted_{\preccurlyeq}\ xs;\ x : \mathsf{A})\ sorted_{\preccurlyeq}\ (\mathcal{LI}\ x\ xs).$

Except for the assumptions of the form *xs loaded*, the latter two are exactly the lemmas indicated in the direct proof of straight insertion sort sketched at the beginning. There remained to prove the first of these, which follows by an easy induction on *xs*.

The assumptions of the form *xs loaded* are then not necessary in this case. The corresponding instances are not necessary either in proving the correctness of other standard implementations, as tree sort or multiple list insertion. Actually, as it happens, the cases in which assumptions of this form are necessary appear to be quite artificial. One example would be a variant of straight insertion in which the procedure of list insertion checks whether the input list is or not sorted and returns, say, the empty list in case of obtaining a negative result. So it seems to be the case that the stronger specification of insertion structures in which those assumptions are removed is enough for obtaining at least natural implementations.

4 Conclusions

We have presented a general structure of the algorithms of sorting by insertion that formalizes Knuth's general characterization. It is based upon the specification of the abstract data type of insertion structures. The axioms of this data type determine also a natural decomposition into lemmas of the proofs of correctness of the concrete algorithms of the class described.

The specification of the insertion structures can be entirely expressed in the extension of type theory with record types and subtyping. In this way, Knuth's general idea has received a formulation as a program in a completely formal notation. That this has been possible is to be considered a positive result, especially if one takes into account the requirements on expressivity that the problem posed. To begin with, specifying abstract data types by means of record types allows to use set operators for characterizing the representations of the abstract types in question. On the one hand, this provides the minimum of generality that is required by a formal treatment of abstract data types while at the same time preserving the possibility of extending the theory at any time with new primitive set formers. And in particular in our case, it has allowed us to express that the operations of listing of insertion structures must work uniformly for any set from which the elements being classified are taken, which has proved to be essential for obtaining a precise description of the idea of sorting by insertion. In addition to the former, the presence of subtyping has made it possible to use one and the same specification of the problem of sorting lists for different kinds of sorting relations.

That the formalization obtained is indeed natural and adequate cannot but be decided by intuition or by the analysis of examples. Here we have only studied the derivation of straight insertion sort which proceeds quite smoothly. An equally satisfactory treatment is obtained for the case of tree sort. The next most interesting case would be the derivation of multiple list insertion. Then there arises a further use of the rules of subtyping as we shall see now. In a natural formulation of this algorithm one requires to know a partition into ranges of the set of elements to be classified. Moreover, in that case one has to require the sorting relation to be transitive. Therefore, in deriving multiple list insertion we have to consider total binary relations with further properties, which are to be used for constructing the corresponding implementation of insertion structures. However, neither the specification of insertion structures nor the abstract algorithm of sorting by insertion need to suffer any change in order for them to be applicable to this case, due to the fact that the particular relations that have to be considered constitute a subtype of the binary relations.

Finally, a general formulation of the problem of sorting lists has been given.

According to this, it results that several well known algorithms can be used for sorting lists over arbitrary total relation. This is as general as a sorting algorithm can be.

References

1. Betarte G., Tasistro A. *Extension of Martin-Löf's type theory with record types and subtyping.* In Proceedings of the Conference "25 Years of Constructive Type Theory", Oxford University Press, 1997.
2. Coquand, Th., Nordström B., Smith J. M., von Sydow B. *Type theory and programming.* EATCS 52, 1994.
3. Knuth D. *The art of computer programming. Vol. 3: Sorting and searching.* Addison Wesley, 1973.
4. Martin-Löf P. *Philosophical implications of type theory.* Lectures given at the Facoltá de Lettere e Filosofia, Universitá degli Studi di Firenze, Florence, March 15th. - May 15th., 1987. Privately circulated notes.
5. Nordström B., Petersson K., Smith J. M. *Programming in Martin-Löf's type theory. An introduction.* Oxford Science Publications, 1990.

Author Index

Lecture Notes in Computer Science

For information about Vols. 1–1429

please contact your bookseller or Springer-Verlag

Vol. 1430: S. Trigila, A. Mullery, M. Campolargo, H. Vanderstraeten, M. Mampaey (Eds.), Intelligence in Services and Networks: Technology for Ubiquitous Telecom Services. Proceedings, 1998. XII, 550 pages. 1998.

Vol. 1431: H. Imai, Y. Zheng (Eds.), Public Key Cryptography. Proceedings, 1998. XI, 263 pages. 1998.

Vol. 1432: S. Arnborg, L. Ivansson (Eds.), Algorithm Theory – SWAT '98. Proceedings, 1998. IX, 347 pages. 1998.

Vol. 1433: V. Honavar, G. Slutzki (Eds.), Grammatical Inference. Proceedings, 1998. X, 271 pages. 1998. (Subseries LNAI).

Vol. 1434: J.-C. Heudin (Ed.), Virtual Worlds. Proceedings, 1998. XII, 412 pages. 1998. (Subseries LNAI).

Vol. 1435: M. Klusch, G. Weiß (Eds.), Cooperative Information Agents II. Proceedings, 1998. IX, 307 pages. 1998. (Subseries LNAI).

Vol. 1436: D. Wood, S. Yu (Eds.), Automata Implementation. Proceedings, 1997. VIII, 253 pages. 1998.

Vol. 1437: S. Albayrak, F.J. Garijo (Eds.), Intelligent Agents for Telecommunication Applications. Proceedings, 1998. XII, 251 pages. 1998. (Subseries LNAI).

Vol. 1438: C. Boyd, E. Dawson (Eds.), Information Security and Privacy. Proceedings, 1998. XI, 423 pages. 1998.

Vol. 1439: B. Magnusson (Ed.), System Configuration Management. Proceedings, 1998. X, 207 pages. 1998.

Vol. 1440: K.S. McCurley, C.D. Ziegler (Eds.), Advances in Cryptology 1981 – 1997. Proceedings. Approx. XII, 260 pages. 1998.

Vol. 1441: W. Wobcke, M. Pagnucco, C. Zhang (Eds.), Agents and Multi-Agent Systems. Proceedings, 1997. XII, 241 pages. 1998. (Subseries LNAI).

Vol. 1442: A. Fiat. G.J. Woeginger (Eds.), Online Algorithms. XVIII, 436 pages. 1998.

Vol. 1443: K.G. Larsen, S. Skyum, G. Winskel (Eds.), Automata, Languages and Programming. Proceedings, 1998. XVI, 932 pages. 1998.

Vol. 1444: K. Jansen, J. Rolim (Eds.), Approximation Algorithms for Combinatorial Optimization. Proceedings, 1998. VIII, 201 pages. 1998.

Vol. 1445: E. Jul (Ed.), ECOOP'98 – Object-Oriented Programming. Proceedings, 1998. XII, 635 pages. 1998.

Vol. 1446: D. Page (Ed.), Inductive Logic Programming. Proceedings, 1998. VIII, 301 pages. 1998. (Subseries LNAI).

Vol. 1447: V.W. Porto, N. Saravanan, D. Waagen, A.E. Eiben (Eds.), Evolutionary Programming VII. Proceedings, 1998. XVI, 840 pages. 1998.

Vol. 1448: M. Farach-Colton (Ed.), Combinatorial Pattern Matching. Proceedings, 1998. VIII, 251 pages. 1998.

Vol. 1449: W.-L. Hsu, M.-Y. Kao (Eds.), Computing and Combinatorics. Proceedings, 1998. XII, 372 pages. 1998.

Vol. 1450: L. Brim, F. Gruska, J. Zlatuška (Eds.), Mathematical Foundations of Computer Science 1998. Proceedings, 1998. XVII, 846 pages. 1998.

Vol. 1451: A. Amin, D. Dori, P. Pudil, H. Freeman (Eds.), Advances in Pattern Recognition. Proceedings, 1998. XXI, 1048 pages. 1998.

Vol. 1452: B.P. Goettl, H.M. Halff, C.L. Redfield, V.J. Shute (Eds.), Intelligent Tutoring Systems. Proceedings, 1998. XIX, 629 pages. 1998.

Vol. 1453: M.-L. Mugnier, M. Chein (Eds.), Conceptual Structures: Theory, Tools and Applications. Proceedings, 1998. XIII, 439 pages. (Subseries LNAI).

Vol. 1454: I. Smith (Ed.), Artificial Intelligence in Structural Engineering. XI, 497 pages. 1998. (Subseries LNAI).

Vol. 1456: A. Drogoul, M. Tambe, T. Fukuda (Eds.), Collective Robotics. Proceedings, 1998. VII, 161 pages. 1998. (Subseries LNAI).

Vol. 1457: A. Ferreira, J. Rolim, H. Simon, S.-H. Teng (Eds.), Solving Irregularly Structured Problems in Prallel. Proceedings, 1998. X, 408 pages. 1998.

Vol. 1458: V.O. Mittal, H.A. Yanco, J. Aronis, R-. Simpson (Eds.), Assistive Technology in Artificial Intelligence. X, 273 pages. 1998. (Subseries LNAI).

Vol. 1459: D.G. Feitelson, L. Rudolph (Eds.), Job Scheduling Strategies for Parallel Processing. Proceedings, 1998. VII, 257 pages. 1998.

Vol. 1460: G. Quirchmayr, E. Schweighofer, T.J.M. Bench-Capon (Eds.), Database and Expert Systems Applications. Proceedings, 1998. XVI, 905 pages. 1998.

Vol. 1461: G. Bilardi, G.F. Italiano, A. Pietracaprina, G. Pucci (Eds.), Algorithms – ESA'98. Proceedings, 1998. XII, 516 pages. 1998.

Vol. 1462: H. Krawczyk (Ed.), Advances in Cryptology - CRYPTO '98. Proceedings, 1998. XII, 519 pages. 1998.

Vol. 1463: N.E. Fuchs (Ed.), Logic Program Synthesis and Transformation. Proceedings, 1997. X, 343 pages. 1998.

Vol. 1464: H.H.S. Ip, A.W.M. Smeulders (Eds.), Multimedia Information Analysis and Retrieval. Proceedings, 1998. VIII, 264 pages. 1998.

Vol. 1465: R. Hirschfeld (Ed.), Financial Cryptography. Proceedings, 1998. VIII, 311 pages. 1998.

Vol. 1466: D. Sangiorgi, R. de Simone (Eds.), CONCUR'98: Concurrency Theory. Proceedings, 1998. XI, 657 pages. 1998.

Vol. 1467: C. Clack, K. Hammond, T. Davie (Eds.), Implementation of Functional Languages. Proceedings, 1997. X, 375 pages. 1998.

Vol. 1468: P. Husbands, J.-A. Meyer (Eds.), Evolutionary Robotics. Proceedings, 1998. VIII, 247 pages. 1998.

Vol. 1469: R. Puigjaner, N.N. Savino, B. Serra (Eds.), Computer Performance Evaluation. Proceedings, 1998. XIII, 376 pages. 1998.

Vol. 1470: D. Pritchard, J. Reeve (Eds.), Euro-Par'98: Parallel Processing. Proceedings, 1998. XXII, 1157 pages. 1998.

Vol. 1471: J. Dix, L. Moniz Pereira, T.C. Przymusinski (Eds.), Logic Programming and Knowledge Representation. Proceedings, 1997. IX, 246 pages. 1998. (Subseries LNAI).

Vol. 1473: X. Leroy, A. Ohori (Eds.), Types in Compilation. Proceedings, 1998. VIII, 299 pages. 1998.

Vol. 1474: F. Mueller, A. Bestavros (Eds.), Languages, Compilers, and Tools for Embedded Systems. Proceedings, 1998. XIV, 261 pages. 1998.

Vol. 1475: W. Litwin, T. Morzy, G. Vossen (Eds.), Advances in Databases and Information Systems. Proceedings, 1998. XIV, 369 pages. 1998.

Vol. 1476: J. Calmet, J. Plaza (Eds.), Artificial Intelligence and Symbolic Computation. Proceedings, 1998. XI, 309 pages. 1998. (Subseries LNAI).

Vol. 1477: K. Rothermel, F. Hohl (Eds.), Mobile Agents. Proceedings, 1998. VIII, 285 pages. 1998.

Vol. 1478: M. Sipper, D. Mange, A. Pérez-Uribe (Eds.), Evolvable Systems: From Biology to Hardware. Proceedings, 1998. IX, 382 pages. 1998.

Vol. 1479: J. Grundy, M. Newey (Eds.), Theorem Proving in Higher Order Logics. Proceedings, 1998. VIII, 497 pages. 1998.

Vol. 1480: F. Giunchiglia (Ed.), Artificial Intelligence: Methodology, Systems, and Applications. Proceedings, 1998. IX, 502 pages. 1998. (Subseries LNAI).

Vol. 1481: E.V. Munson, C. Nicholas, D. Wood (Eds.), Principles of Digital Document Processing. Proceedings, 1998. VII, 152 pages. 1998.

Vol. 1482: R.W. Hartenstein, A. Keevallik (Eds.), Field-Programmable Logic and Applications. Proceedings, 1998. XI, 533 pages. 1998.

Vol. 1483: T. Plagemann, V. Goebel (Eds.), Interactive Distributed Multimedia Systems and Telecommunication Services. Proceedings, 1998. XV, 326 pages. 1998.

Vol. 1484: H. Coelho (Ed.), Progress in Artificial Intelligence – IBERAMIA 98. Proceedings, 1998. XIII, 421 pages. 1998. (Subseries LNAI).

Vol. 1485: J.-J. Quisquater, Y. Deswarte, C. Meadows, D. Gollmann (Eds.), Computer Security – ESORICS 98. Proceedings, 1998. X, 377 pages. 1998.

Vol. 1486: A.P. Ravn, H. Rischel (Eds.), Formal Techniques in Real-Time and Fault-Tolerant Systems. Proceedings, 1998. VIII, 339 pages. 1998.

Vol. 1487: V. Gruhn (Ed.), Software Process Technology. Proceedings, 1998. VIII, 157 pages. 1998.

Vol. 1488: B. Smyth, P. Cunningham (Eds.), Advances in Case-Based Reasoning. Proceedings, 1998. XI, 482 pages. 1998. (Subseries LNAI).

Vol. 1489: J. Dix, L. Fariñas del Cerro, U. Furbach (Eds.), Logics in Artificial Intelligence. Proceedings, 1998. X, 391 pages. 1998. (Subseries LNAI).

Vol. 1490: C. Palamidessi, H. Glaser, K. Meinke (Eds.), Principles of Declarative Programming. Proceedings, 1998. XI, 497 pages. 1998.

Vol. 1493: J.P. Bowen, A. Fett, M.G. Hinchey (Eds.), ZUM '98: The Z Formal Specification Notation. Proceedings, 1998. XV, 417 pages. 1998.

Vol. 1495: T. Andreasen, H. Christiansen, H.L. Larsen (Eds.), Flexible Query Answering Systems. IX, 393 pages. 1998. (Subseries LNAI).

Vol. 1496: W.M. Wells, A. Colchester, S. Delp (Eds.), Medical Image Computing and Computer-Assisted Intervention – MICCAI'98. Proceedings, 1998. XXII, 1256 pages. 1998.

Vol. 1497: V. Alexandrov, J. Dongarra (Eds.), Recent Advances in Parallel Virtual Machine and Message Passing Interface. Proceedings, 1998. XII, 412 pages. 1998.

Vol. 1498: A.E. Eiben, T. Bäck, M. Schoenauer, H.-P. Schwefel (Eds.), Parallel Problem Solving from Nature – PPSN V. Proceedings, 1998. XXIII, 1041 pages. 1998.

Vol. 1499: S. Kutten (Ed.), Distributed Computing. Proceedings, 1998. XII, 419 pages. 1998.

Vol. 1501: M.M. Richter, C.H. Smith, R. Wiehagen, T. Zeugmann (Eds.), Algorithmic Learning Theory. Proceedings, 1998. XI, 439 pages. 1998. (Subseries LNAI).

Vol. 1502: G. Antoniou, J. Slaney (Eds.), Advanced Topics in Artificial Intelligence. Proceedings, 1998. XI, 333 pages. 1998. (Subseries LNAI).

Vol. 1503: G. Levi (Ed.), Static Analysis. Proceedings, 1998. IX, 383 pages. 1998.

Vol. 1504: O. Herzog, A. Günter (Eds.), KI-98: Advances in Artificial Intelligence. Proceedings, 1998. XI, 355 pages. 1998. (Subseries LNAI).

Vol. 1508: S. Jajodia, M.T. Özsu, A. Dogac (Eds.), Advances in Multimedia Information Systems. Proceedings, 1998. VIII, 207 pages. 1998.

Vol. 1510: J.M. Zytkow, M. Quafafou (Eds.), Principles of Data Mining and Knowledge Discovery. Proceedings, 1998. XI, 482 pages. 1998. (Subseries LNAI).

Vol. 1511: D. O'Hallaron (Ed.), Languages, Compilers, and Run-Time Systems for Scalable Computers. Proceedings, 1998. IX, 412 pages. 1998.

Vol. 1512: E. Giménez, C. Paulin-Mohring (Eds.), Types for Proofs and Programs. Proceedings, 1996. VIII, 373 pages. 1998.

Vol. 1513: C. Nikolaou, C. Stephanidis (Eds.), Research and Advanced Technology for Digital Libraries. Proceedings, 1998. XV, 912 pages. 1998.

Vol. 1514: K. Ohta,, D. Pei (Eds.), Advances in Cryptology – ASIACRYPT'98. Proceedings, 1998. XII, 436 pages. 1998.

Vol. 1516: W. Ehrenberger (Ed.), Computer Safety, Reliability and Security. Proceedings, 1998. XVI, 392 pages. 1998.

Vol. 1518: M. Luby, J. Rolim, M. Serna (Eds.), Randomization and Approximation Techniques in Computer Science. Proceedings, 1998. IX, 385 pages. 1998.